SERENDIPITY
NEW TESTAMENT
FOR
GROUPS

THIRD EDITION
1990

(In this edition the questions are the same as in the Serendipity Bible for Groups.)

NEW INTERNATIONAL VERSION

Tenth Anniversary

1978-1988

Originally published
by Zondervan Publishing House
Grand Rapids, Michigan
under the title
SERENDIPITY BIBLE STUDY BOOK
Copyright ©1986 by Serendipity House

and

Copyright ©1973, 1978, 1984 by International Bible Society.
Used by permission of Zondervan Bible Publishers.

Printed in the United States of America.

90 91 / 10 9 8 7 6 5 4 3 2

SERENDIPITY
NEW TESTAMENT
• FOR •
GROUPS

NEW INTERNATIONAL VERSION

SERENDIPITY HOUSE / Box 1012 / Littleton, CO 80160   TOLL FREE 800-525-9563

GENERAL EDITOR
Lyman Coleman, Littleton, CO

BIBLICAL EDITOR
Richard V. Peace, South Hamilton, MA

EXECUTIVE EDITOR
Dietrich R. Gruen, Madison, WI

ASSOCIATE EDITORS
Gary Christopherson, Tucson, AZ
William F. Cutler, Auburn, ME
Mary H. Naegeli, Moraga, CA
Lance Pierson, London, UK
Denny Rydberg, Seattle, WA

OTHER CONTRIBUTORS
Matthew: Mari R. Anderson, Lancaster, NY; Mary H. Naegeli, Noraga, CA; James M. Singleton, Jr., South Hamilton, MA; **Mark:** Verne Becker, Wheaton, IL; Mary H. Naegeli, Moraga, CA; James M. Singleton, Jr., South Hamilton, MA; **Luke:** Verne Becker, Wheaton, IL; Carol Detoni, Arcadia, CA; **John:** Mari R. Anderson, Lancaster, NY; William F. Cutler, Auburn, ME; **Acts:** William F. Cutler, Auburn, ME; Doug LaBudde, Beverly, MA; **Romans:** Verne Becker, Wheaton, IL; William F. Cutler, Auburn, ME; **1,2 Corinthians:** John T. Anderson, Lancaster, NY; William F. Cutler, Auburn, ME; Mark Horton, Bethel, CT; **Galatians:** John T. Anderson, Lancaster, NY; John Crosby, Glen Ellyn, IL; **Ephesians:** Mari R. Anderson, Lancaster, NY; John and Fay Winson, Beverly, MA; Steve and Betsy Crowe, Wenham, MA; **Philippians:** Mari R. Anderson, Lancaster, NY; John and Fay Winson, Beverly, MA; **Colossians:** Mari R. Anderson, Lancaster, NY; John and Fay Winson, Beverly, MA; **1,2 Thessalonians:** John and Fay Winson, Beverly, MA; **1,2 Timothy:** Mari R. Anderson, Lancaster, NY; Judy Johnson, Madison, WI; **Titus:** Mari R. Anderson, Lancaster, NY; **Philemon:** John and Fay Winson, Beverly, MA; **Hebrews:** James M. Singleton, Jr., South Hamilton, MA; **James:** Mari R. Anderson, Lancaster, NY; **1,2 Peter:** Mark Shepard, Easton, MA; **1,2,3 John:** Bill Tucker, Dubuque, IA; **Jude:** Mari R. Anderson, Lancaster, NY; **Revelation:** Richard Peace, Hamilton, MA; Dietrich Gruen, Madison, WI

ART/DESIGN
Billie Herwig, John Winson, and Doug LaBudde at Frontline Marketing, Beverly, MA; Therese Bortolussi, Cathy Clayton, Erika Tiepel and Sheryl Tongue at Graphics Plus, Littleton, CO.

HOW TO USE THE QUESTIONS IN THE MARGIN FOR EVERY PASSAGE IN THE NEW TESTAMENT

1. OPEN:
Designed to break the ice in the group. Smile. Relax. Get ready for the Bible study. Questions about your childhood that relate to the Bible passage and give you a chance to share your own "story" with the group. Important stuff—like "where did you go fishing" and "what was the biggest fish you caught?" Watch out for laughter. A group is never so vulnerable to the Holy Spirit as when it is laughing!

2. DIG:
Designed to help you scratch, sniff, sift and search for clues in the Scripture passage. Questions are planted like timebombs to go-off just at the right moment in the group—like "what's going on here" or "why do you think . . ." or "what is Jesus really saying?" Always open-ended to give the group a chance to talk about their own point of view—where no one is "right or wrong."

3. REFLECT:
Designed to take personal inventory. Share on a deeper level. Questions like "how would you have reacted in that situation" . . . "what is your own experience of this . . ." or "what is God saying to you in this Scripture passage?" Here's the chance to share your own spiritual journey. Turning points. Struggles. Goals. And where you need the support of the group for the next step in your life.

Mark

1.

OPEN: If John the Baptist tried to do his job in the twentieth century what would he wear? eat? sound like?

DIG: 1. How did the substance of what John preached prepare the people for Jesus? 2. What does it really mean to 'repent'? 3. Why do you think the crowds responded to John as they did?

2.

REFLECT: 1. Who played the role of John the Baptist in your life to prepare you for Jesus? 2. In what areas of your life do you need to hear God's word of forgiveness right now?

3.

OPEN: What is the best thing about a desert? the worst?

DIG: 1. What might have been the significance of the dove and the voice for Jesus? 2. How do you feel about the fact that it was the Spirit who sent Jesus into the desert?

REFLECT: Have you found "deserts" often follow "highs"?

OPEN: Describe the best day that you ever had fishing.

DIG: 1. What do you suppose was this "good news of God" which Jesus was proclaiming? 2. What was the same in Jesus' message as in John's (verse 4)? What was different? 3. Why is it important to both repent and believe? 4. What was Jesus offering in his invitation to the disciples?

REFLECT: 1. What first attracted you to begin following Jesus? 2. What did you have to leave when you followed Him? 3. How did your family respond? 4. What does it mean for you to have the self-identity of a "fisher of men"?

John the Baptist Prepares the Way

1 The beginning of the gospel about Jesus Christ, the Son of God.ᵃ

²It is written in Isaiah the prophet:

"I will send my messenger ahead of you,
who will prepare your way"ᵇ—
³"a voice of one calling in the desert,
'Prepare the way for the Lord,
make straight paths for him.' "ᶜ

⁴And so John came, baptizing in the desert region and preaching a baptism of repentance for the forgiveness of sins. ⁵The whole Judean countryside and all the people of Jerusalem went out to him. Confessing their sins, they were baptized by him in the Jordan River. ⁶John wore clothing made of camel's hair, with a leather belt around his waist, and he ate locusts and wild honey. ⁷And this was his message: "After me will come one more powerful than I, the thongs of whose sandals I am not worthy to stoop down and untie. ⁸I baptize you withᵈ water, but he will baptize you with the Holy Spirit."

The Baptism and Temptation of Jesus

⁹At that time Jesus came from Nazareth in Galilee and was baptized by John in the Jordan. ¹⁰As Jesus was coming up out of the water, he saw heaven being torn open and the Spirit descending on him like a dove. ¹¹And a voice came from heaven: "You are my Son, whom I love; with you I am well pleased."

¹²At once the Spirit sent him out into the desert, ¹³and he was in the desert forty days, being tempted by Satan. He was with the wild animals, and angels attended him.

The Calling of the First Disciples

¹⁴After John was put in prison, Jesus went into Galilee, proclaiming the good news of God. ¹⁵"The time has come," he said. "The kingdom of God is near. Repent and believe the good news!"

¹⁶As Jesus walked beside the Sea of Galilee, he saw Simon and his brother Andrew casting a net into the lake, for they were fishermen. ¹⁷"Come, follow me," Jesus said, "and I will make you fishers of men." ¹⁸At once they left their nets and followed him.

¹⁹When he had gone a little farther, he saw James son of Zebedee and his brother John in a boat, preparing their nets. ²⁰Without delay he called them, and they left their father Zebedee in the boat with the hired men and followed him.

a1 Some manuscripts do not have *the Son of God*.   *b2* Mal 3:1   *c3* Isaiah 40:3
d8 Or *in*

88

Mark 1:-1-8   **JOHN THE BAPTIST PREPARES THE WAY**

LOOKING INTO THE SCRIPTURE/25 Minutes. Read Mark 1:1-8 and discuss. Answer YES, NO or MAYBE to these situations:

1. JOHN THE BAPTIST WAS THE KIND OF GUY THAT I WOULD LIKE TO . . .

Y	N	M	take shopping
Y	N	M	rock me to sleep
Y	N	M	get stuck with in an elevator
Y	N	M	invite to a black tie dinner
Y	N	M	drive with for 500 miles keeping within the speed limit
Y	N	M	send to convert my hard-hearted sister in the hospital
Y	N	M	sit with at an all-you-can-eat buffet

2. Why did the people flock to John the Baptist instead of avoiding him?
   a. he was the first prophet in 300 years
   b. he was more interesting than a circus
   c. anyone will come to see a fire burn
   d. he spoke to the reality of their hearts
   e. he talked about sin and forgiveness

3. In modern words, what was the message of John?
   a. you can have it all
   b. look out for number one
   c. turn or burn
   d. you only go around once, so reach for the gusto
   e. pay me now or pay me later
   f. there's a new day coming

4. Why was the establishment so upset with John?
   a. his popularity
   b. his simple life
   c. his preaching
   d. his attack on sin
   e. his call for change

5. What role did John the Baptist play in the overall plan of God?
   a. shake up the establishment
   b. bridge the Old to New Testament
   c. prepare folks for coming of Jesus
   d. baptize Jesus
   e. alert sinners to the need for a Savior

MY OWN STORY/20 Minutes. Read Mark 1:1-8 again and share your experience.

1. If John the Baptist came to your town with this message, how would he be received?
   a. the media would love it
   b. people would flock to him
   c. church people would be polite
   d. everybody would run for cover
   e. people would ignore him

2. Who played the part of John the Baptist in your life—who "prepared the way" for Jesus?
   a. my parents
   b. a Sunday school teacher
   c. a coach/counselor/teacher
   d. a special friend
   e. a whole lot of people
   f. nobody yet

3. How would you describe your relationship with Jesus right now?
   a. just beginning
   b. nowhere
   c. holding
   d. struggling
   e. roller-coaster
   f. going great

4. What would it take to move you on in your relationship with God?
   a. a little support
   b. a deeper commitment
   c. some spiritual discipline
   d. a big change
   e. a miracle
   f. a strong belief that God loves even me

HOW TO USE THE READY-MADE QUESTIONNAIRES ACROSS FROM THE PASSAGE ON 48 BIBLE STORIES

1. LOOKING INTO THE SCRIPTURE

Questions with multiple-choice options built in. Structured to walk you through the Bible story step by step—pausing along the way to "smell the flowers." Look "between the lines" in the Bible story for the meaning, motives, feelings of the principle characters. The questions flow from easy to not-so-easy, and the options from outrageous to a little revealing. No "easy answers." No "right or wrong." Just a good way to force you to relive the story for yourself. Laugh a little. Think a lot.

2. MY OWN STORY

Now it is your turn. Questions with multiple-choice options built in. Structured to relive your own spiritual journey. Look at the significant turning points. Take inventory. Check out your own feelings, motives, fears, hopes and dreams. Share your "story" with your group and pray for one another. Watch out for the last question in the questionnaire. It can get deep . . . and beautiful. In one short questionnaire, the pendulum swings from the "child" to the "spirit."

HOW TO CHOOSE FROM 10 READY-MADE COURSES FOR SPECIAL INTEREST GROUPS

BUILT INTO THIS NEW TESTAMENT.

No need to buy separate little booklets. Here they are. Ten courses covering ten major areas of interest. All you need to do is pick one of the courses and follow the outlines here.

EACH COURSE HAS SIX SESSIONS.

Just enough to get acquainted with the subject and with one another. If you wish to continue as a group, choose another course and renew your covenant. There are enough courses here to keep you studying for years.

EACH COURSE HAS TWO LEVELS.

If you are a beginning group (don't know each other), use the Gospel Studies in the second column with a questionnaire across from the Bible passage to help you get acquainted. If you are an advanced group (you know each other or have been together for a while), use the Epistle Studies in the third column.

COURSE AND SIX SESSION TOPICS	FOR BEGINNING GROUPS TO GET TO KNOW EACH OTHER	FOR ON-GOING GROUPS TO GO DEEPER IN STUDY

Course One: DISCOVERING MY IDENTITY

SESSION	(A) GOSPEL STUDY	(B) EPISTLE STUDY
1 My Values	Rich Fool/Luke 12:13-21 (167)	1 John 2:15-17 (460)
2 My Strengths	The Talents/Matt 25:14-30 (75)	2 Tim 2:14-26 (408)
3 My Desires	Mary-Martha/Luke 10:38-42 (163)	Phil 3:12-4:1 (379)
4 My Self-image	Sinful Woman/Luke 7:36-50 (153)	Phil 4:10-13 (380)
5 My Faith	Peter's Confession/Matt 16:13-28 (57)	Eph 1:3-14 (368)
6 My Tomorrow	Walk on Water/Matt 14:22-33 (53)	2 Tim 3:10-4:8 (409)

Course Two: WORKING THROUGH MY HANG-UPS

SESSION	(A) GOSPEL STUDY	(B) EPISTLE STUDY
1 Self-worth	Zacchaeus/Luke 19:1-10 (183)	2 Pet 1:3-11 (453)
2 Escapes	Pool Paralytic/John 5:1-15 (213)	Jam 5:13-20 (442)
3 Quitting	Road to Emmaus/Luke 24:13-35 (195)	1 Cor 9:19-27 (333)
4 Rejection	Jesus' Hometown/Luke 4:14-30 (143)	1 Pet 1:3-12 (445)
5 Fear of Failure	Ask, Seek, Knock/Matt 7:7-12 (39)	Heb 11:1-40 (430)
6 Will Power	Gethsemane/Mark 14:32-42 (123)	Phil 2:12-18 (377)

Course Three: DEALING WITH MY PROBLEMS

SESSION	(A) GOSPEL STUDY	(B) EPISTLE STUDY
1 Headaches	Water to Wine/John 2:1-11 (205)	Jam 1:2-18 (438)
2 Hassles	Unforgiving Servant/Matt 18:21-35 (61)	Eph 4:25-32 (371)
3 Stress	The Storm/Mark 4:35-41 (99)	2 Cor 4:1-18 (348)
4 Moral Dilemmas	Jesus before Pilate/Matt 27:11-26 (83)	1 Pet 1:13-2:3 (445)
5 Worry	Do Not Worry/Matt 6:25-34 (37)	Phil 4:4-9 (379)
6 Chronic Illness	Roof Paralytic/Luke 5:17-26 (147)	1 John 1:5-10 (459)

Course Four: LEARNING THE BASICS

SESSION	(A) GOSPEL STUDY	(B) EPISTLE STUDY
1 Jesus	Samaritan Woman/John 4:1-26 (209)	Col 1:15-23 (383)
2 New Birth	Nicodemus/John 3:1-21 (207)	Phil 1:3-11 (376)
3 Temptation	Temptation/Matt 4:1-11 (29)	1 Cor 10:1-13 (334)
4 Prayer	Lord's Prayer/Matt 6:9-13 (35)	1 Tim 2:1-7 (401)
5 The Cross	Jesus' Death/Matt 27:45-56 (85)	Rom 3:21-26 (306)
6 Lordship	Jesus' Call/Matt 16:13-28 (57)	Heb 12:1-13 (432)

Course Five: HANDLING CRISES

SESSION	(A) GOSPEL STUDY	(B) EPISTLE STUDY
1 Failure	Peter Disowns Jesus/Matt 26:69-75 (81)	1 Pet 2:4-12 (446)
2 Grief	Lazarus' Death/John 11:1-44 (227)	2 Cor 1:3-11 (346)
3 Panic	Road to Emmaus/Luke 24:13-35 (195)	Heb 5:11-6:12 (424)
4 Starting Over	Adulterous Woman/John 8:1-11 (220)	1 John 2:28-3:10 (461)
5 Risk Taking	Walk on Water/Matt 14:22-36 (53)	Heb 11:1-40 (430)
6 Despair/Hope	Doubting Thomas/John 20:24-31 (247)	1 Cor 15:1-58 (340)

Course Six: FACING THE ISSUES

SESSION	(A) GOSPEL STUDY	(B) EPISTLE STUDY
1 Money	Expensive Ointment/Mark 14:1-11 (120)	1 Tim 6:3-10 (404)
2 Success	Rich Fool/Luke 12:13-21 (167)	1 Cor 4:8-13 (328)
3 Social Concern	Good Samaritan/Luke 10:25-37 (161)	2 Thes 3:6-15 (396)
4 Corruption/Abuse	Temple Cleansing/Mark 11:12-19 (115)	Rom 13:1-7 (318)
5 Judgmental Eye	Adulterous Woman/John 8:1-11 (220)	Rom 14:1-23 (319)
6 World Vision	Feeding 5000/Mark 6:30-44 (103)	Eph 6:10-20 (373)

USER'S GUIDE

Course Seven: BECOMING A CARING COMMUNITY

SESSION	(A) GOSPEL STUDY	(B) EPISTLE STUDY
1 Getting Acquainted	Jesus' Call/Luke 5:1-11 (145)	1 Thes 1:2-10 (390)
2 Sharing Our Story	Nicodemus/John 3:1-21 (207)	Eph 2:1-10 (369)
3 Being Real	Tax Collector/Luke 18:9-14 (181)	Jam 5:13-16 (442)
4 Caretaking	Roof Paralytic/Luke 5:17-26 (147)	Heb 10:19-39 (429)
5 Accountability	Peter Restored/John 21:15-25 (249)	Gal 6:1-10 (365)
6 Body Ministry	Footwashing/John 13:1-17 (233)	Rom 12:1-21 (317)

Course Eight: RESHAPING MY LIFESTYLE

SESSION	(A) GOSPEL STUDY	(B) EPISTLE STUDY
1 Turnaround	John the Baptist/Mark 1:1-8 (91)	Heb 12:1-11 (432)
2 Mental Attitude	Beatitudes/Matt 5:3-10 (31)	Phil 2:1-11 (377)
3 Moral Issues	Temple Cleansing/Mark 11:12-19 (115)	Col 3:1-17 (385)
4 Priorities	Mary-Martha/Luke 10:38-42 (163)	Rom 13:8-14 (318)
5 Possessions	Do Not Worry/Matt 6:25-34 (37)	1 Tim 6:3-10 (404)
6 Control	Gethsemane/Mark 14:32-42 (123)	Rom 6:15-23 (309)

Course Nine: FAMILY RELATIONSHIPS

SESSION	(A) GOSPEL STUDY	(B) EPISTLE STUDY
1 Roots	First Temple Visit/Luke 2:21-40 (137)	2 Tim 1:3-7 (407)
2 Growing Pains	Second Temple Visit/Luke 2:41-52 (139)	Eph 6:1-4 (373)
3 Parent Expectations	Mother's Request/Matt 20:20-28 (65)	1 Pet 5:1-11 (449)
4 Parents in Pain	Prodigal Son/Luke 15:11-31 (175)	1 Thes 2:7-16 (390)
5 Forgiveness	Unforgiving Servant/Matt 18:21-35 (61)	Phil 2:12-18 (377)
6 Ultimate Love	Footwashing/John 13:1-17 (233)	1 Cor 13:1-13 (337)

Course Ten: DISCOVERING THE DEEPER LIFE

SESSION	(A) GOSPEL STUDY	(B) EPISTLE STUDY
1 Promise	Great Banquet/Luke 14:15-24 (173)	Eph 1:3-14 (368)
2 Yearning	Transfiguration/Mark 9:2-13 (109)	Rom 8:18-39 (312)
3 Abiding	Vine-Branch/John 15:1-17 (237)	Col 1:24-2:5 (384)
4 Asking/Receiving	Ask, Seek, Knock/Matt 7:7-12 (39)	1 John 5:13-21 (463)
5 Fruits	The Sower/Mark 4:1-20 (96)	Gal 5:13-26 (365)
6 Gifts	Loaves and Fish/Mark 6:30-44 (103)	1 Cor 12:1-13:13 (336)

HOW TO CREATE YOUR OWN COURSE FROM THESE READY-MADE QUESTIONNAIRES ON CHRIST'S LIFE

How about a special course for groups during Lent or Pentecost? How about a special course on stewardship or discipleship or spiritual healing? Here's a chance for you to design your own small group course, using the questionnaires across from the Bible passage on the 48 stories in the life of Christ. All you need to do is choose the events in the life of Christ.

USER'S GUIDE

HOW TO OVERCOME THE 8 DEADLY DISEASES OF BIBLE STUDY GROUPS

1. JITTERS AFFLICTION

SYMPTOMS: Palms sweat. Mouth turns to sawdust. Armpits drip blood. Voice sounds like a squeak or nothing at all comes out when "it is your turn."

PROBLEM: Fear of groups, often caused by a "bad experience" in groups.

PRESCRIPTION: Divide the large group into foursomes and ask each foursome to enjoy "table fellowship"— 4 at the dining table, 4 at the kitchen table, etc. Begin every session with an "Open" question, designed to break the ice and get the group talking before moving into Bible study. Food permitted. But no talking with your mouth full.

THE FEARLESS FOURSOME

2. COURTSHIP FAILURE

SYMPTOMS: Communication breakdown. Surface chatter about "football" or "the weather." Group sits like in a poker game with cards held close to chest. Feelings never shared. Or, if somebody does "open up," nobody "hears it." Nobody cares or "gets close."

PROBLEM: No group building. No bonding. No trust.

PRESCRIPTION: Spend the whole first session and the first few minutes of every session getting to know each other. Covenant together (see #8). Share your "God story" with each other. Your spiritual ups and downs. Hopes and dreams. Fears and failures. And where you are struggling right now. The group that plays together stays together. No fair having fun without letting the other guy in on it.

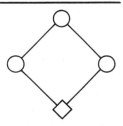

KOINONIA COMMUNITY

3. DEFORMITY

SYMPTOMS: Grotesque, distended group body. One of the parts larger than the rest: either a mammoth brain or heart or tongue that saps all the energy, leaving the rest of the body deformed and deficient. Hideously out of balance. Distorted. Disfunctioning.

PROBLEM: Imbalance of the three necessary ingredients of a healthy group.

PRESCRIPTION: Picture a healthy group with all three "legs" in balance. Have regular "checkups" by a group doctor to see that the group is staying healthy. If not, prescribe some mid-course corrections. If you need a "fourth leg" to stand on, try worship. But don't bring too much joy to God—you might never again need a doctor.

THREE LEGGED STOOL

4. INFANTILE PARALYSIS

SYMPTOMS: Baby talk. Baby diet. Baby concerns... even after years together as a group. Dependent upon an "authority" figure. No signs of growth. No sense of drive, initiative, concern for others or reproduction.

PROBLEM: Stagnation. Growth arrested at infancy.

PRESCRIPTION: Have a clear picture of the stages of group development and expect a group to develop within a year to the completion level. First phase (6-12 weeks) major on group building. Second phase (12-24 weeks) major on Bible study and gift awareness. Third phase (24-36 weeks) major on finding your mission and starting a new group (with the support of the old group).

STAGES OF DEVELOPMENT

5. IN-GROWN SYNDROME

SYMPTOMS: Self-centeredness. Exclusiveness. Deliberate "closing the door" to outsiders because of fear—fear that someone from the outside might ruin the "closeness" or "betray your confidence."

PROBLEM: Clique complex. Anemic mission.

PRESCRIPTION: Envision the church as a place where "sinners" are accepted. Expect your Bible study to energize your vision into reality. Use an empty chair to remind your group that it is always "open" for one more "sinner" in search of God. When you pray, ask God to fill it by the next week. Then pull up more empty chairs.

THE EMPTY CHAIR

6. BURNOUT

SYMPTOMS: Feeling "tired" of the group. Chronic absence. Loss of interest. Feeling guilty because you have lost interest, but don't know how to say "goodbye."

PROBLEM: How to quit gracefully.

PUSH   PUSH   PUSH   OVERDRIVE

ALUMNI SUPPORT GROUP

PRESCRIPTION: Follow the 3-phase lifecycle (see #4) for one year. If the group wants to continue, shift into "overdrive" where you don't consume as much energy. Meet once a month for a pot-luck meal as a reunion group. After the second year, meet occasionally to keep in touch. Here's the principle: the longer the group lasts, the less intensive should be the experience, so that each group member is free to start a new group.

7. DEATH BY OVERDOSE

SYMPTOMS: Feeling worn-out. Burdened. Overworked. Heavy. Used. Put-upon. Stressed-out. killed-off.

PROBLEM: 10% of people in the church are killed off by leadership overdose. 30% are used as helpers. 60% are too "worldly," so never asked.

PILOT GROUP — BECOME LEADERS FOR NEW GROUPS

PILOT GROUP

PRESCRIPTION: Start a pilot group with the 60%ers. (Jesus did.) Look for the "Galilean fringe," not the "Jerusalem establishment." Wanted: Only prodigals; no elder brothers. With their friends mostly outside the church, fringe members are dangerous. Watch out for church growth. And "let the dead bury their dead."

8. FLABBY COMMITMENT

SYMPTOMS: Ill-defined expectations. Unmet goals. No mutual accountability. No basis for evaluating progress.

PROBLEM: Group has yet to "covenant" together.

GROUP COVENANT

PRESCRIPTION: Ask not what the group can do for you . . . Ask what you can do for the group. Verbalize and mobilize your commitment with these sentences:
1. The purpose of our group is. . . .
2. Our specific goals are. . . .
3. We will meet _____ hours, every _____, at _____'s place, for _____ weeks, then we re-evaluate.

We will accept 7 of the following group disciplines:
☐ Regular attendance   ☐ Strict confidentiality
☐ Full participation   ☐ Mutual accountability
☐ Shared leadership   ☐ Scriptural authority
☐ Outreach to _____   ☐ Prayer partner with _____
☐ Homework   ☐ Other _____

"For where two or three
come together
in my name,
there am I with them."

Matthew 18:20 NIV

PREFACE

THE NEW INTERNATIONAL VERSION is a completely new translation of the Holy Bible made by over a hundred scholars working directly from the best available Hebrew, Aramaic and Greek texts. It had its beginning in 1965 when, after several years of exploratory study by committees from the Christian Reformed Church and the National Association of Evangelicals, a group of scholars met at Palos Heights, Illinois, and concurred in the need for a new translation of the Bible in contemporary English. This group, though not made up of official church representatives, was transdenominational. Its conclusion was endorsed by a large number of leaders from many denominations who met in Chicago in 1966.

Responsibility for the new version was delegated by the Palos Heights group to a self-governing body of fifteen, the Committee on Bible Translation, composed for the most part of biblical scholars from colleges, universities and seminaries. In 1967 the New York Bible Society (now the International Bible Society) generously undertook the financial sponsorship of the project—a sponsorship that made it possible to enlist the help of many distinguished scholars. The fact that participants from the United States, Great Britain, Canada, Australia and New Zealand worked together gave the project its international scope. That they were from many denominations—including Anglican, Assemblies of God, Baptist, Brethren, Christian Reformed, Church of Christ, Evangelical Free, Lutheran, Mennonite, Methodist, Nazarene, Presbyterian, Wesleyan and other churches—helped to safeguard the translation from sectarian bias.

How it was made helps to give the New International Version its distinctiveness. The translation of each book was assigned to a team of scholars. Next, one of the Intermediate Editorial Committees revised the initial translation, with constant reference to the Hebrew, Aramaic or Greek. Their work then went to one of the General Editorial Committees, which checked it in detail and made another thorough revision. This revision in turn was carefully reviewed by the Committee on Bible Translation, which made further changes and then released the final version for publication. In this way the entire Bible underwent three revisions, during each of which the translation was examined for its faithfulness to the original languages and for its English style.

All this involved many thousands of hours of research and discussion regarding the meaning of the texts and the precise way of putting them into English. It may well be that no other translation has been made by a more thorough process of review and revision from committee to committee than this one.

From the beginning of the project, the Committee on Bible Translation held to certain goals for the New International Version: that it would be an accurate translation and one that would have clarity and literary quality and so prove suitable for public and private reading, teaching, preaching, memorizing and liturgical use. The Committee also sought to preserve some measure of continuity with the long tradition of translating the Scriptures into English.

In working toward these goals, the translators were united in their commitment to the authority and infallibility of the Bible as God's Word in written form. They believe that it contains the divine answer to the deepest needs of humanity, that it sheds unique light on our path in a dark world, and that it sets forth the way to our eternal well-being.

The first concern of the translators has been the accuracy of the translation and its fidelity to the thought of the biblical writers. They have weighed the significance of the lexical and grammatical details of the Hebrew, Aramaic and Greek texts. At the same time, they have striven for more than a word-for-word translation. Because thought patterns and syntax differ from

Preface

language to language, faithful communication of the meaning of the writers of the Bible demands frequent modifications in sentence structure and constant regard for the contextual meanings of words.

A sensitive feeling for style does not always accompany scholarship. Accordingly the Committee on Bible Translation submitted the developing version to a number of stylistic consultants. Two of them read every book of both Old and New Testaments twice—once before and once after the last major revision—and made invaluable suggestions. Samples of the translation were tested for clarity and ease of reading by various kinds of people—young and old, highly educated and less well educated, ministers and laymen.

Concern for clear and natural English—that the New International Version should be idiomatic but not idiosyncratic, contemporary but not dated—motivated the translators and consultants. At the same time, they tried to reflect the differing styles of the biblical writers. In view of the international use of English, the translators sought to avoid obvious Americanisms on the one hand and obvious Anglicisms on the other. A British edition reflects the comparatively few differences of significant idiom and of spelling.

As for the traditional pronouns "thou," "thee" and "thine" in reference to the Deity, the translators judged that to use these archaisms (along with the old verb forms such as "doest," "wouldest" and "hadst") would violate accuracy in translation. Neither Hebrew, Aramaic nor Greek uses special pronouns for the persons of the Godhead. A present-day translation is not enhanced by forms that in the time of the King James Version were used in everyday speech, whether referring to God or man.

For the Old Testament the standard Hebrew text, the Masoretic Text as published in the latest editions of *Biblia Hebraica,* was used throughout. The Dead Sea Scrolls contain material bearing on an earlier stage of the Hebrew text. They were consulted, as were the Samaritan Pentateuch and the ancient scribal traditions relating to textual changes. Sometimes a variant Hebrew reading in the margin of the Masoretic Text was followed instead of the text itself. Such instances, being variants within the Masoretic tradition, are not specified by footnotes. In rare cases, words in the consonantal text were divided differently from the way they appear in the Masoretic Text. Footnotes indicate this. The translators also consulted the more important early versions—the Septuagint; Aquila, Symmachus and Theodotion; the Vulgate; the Syriac Peshitta; the Targums; and for the Psalms the *Juxta Hebraica* of Jerome. Readings from these versions were occasionally followed where the Masoretic Text seemed doubtful and where accepted principles of textual criticism showed that one or more of these textual witnesses appeared to provide the correct reading. Such instances are footnoted. Sometimes vowel letters and vowel signs did not, in the judgment of the translators, represent the correct vowels for the original consonantal text. Accordingly some words were read with a different set of vowels. These instances are usually not indicated by footnotes.

The Greek text used in translating the New Testament was an eclectic one. No other piece of ancient literature has such an abundance of manuscript witnesses as does the New Testament. Where existing manuscripts differ, the translators made their choice of readings according to accepted principles of New Testament textual criticism. Footnotes call attention to places where there was uncertainty about what the original text was. The best current printed texts of the Greek New Testament were used.

There is a sense in which the work of translation is never wholly finished. This applies to all great literature and uniquely so to the Bible. In 1973 the New Testament in the New International Version was published. Since then, suggestions for corrections and revisions have been received from various sources. The Committee on Bible Translation carefully considered the suggestions and adopted a number of them. These were incorporated in the first printing of the entire Bible in 1978. Additional revisions were made by the Committee on Bible Translation in 1983 and appear in printings after that date.

As in other ancient documents, the precise meaning of the biblical texts is sometimes uncertain. This is more often the case with the Hebrew and Aramaic texts than with the Greek text. Although archaeological and linguistic discoveries in this century aid in understanding difficult passages, some uncertainties remain. The more significant of these have been called to the reader's attention in the footnotes.

In regard to the divine name *YHWH*, commonly referred to as the *Tetragrammaton*, the translators adopted the device used in most English versions of rendering that name as "LORD" in capital letters to distinguish it from *Adonai*, another Hebrew word rendered "Lord," for which small letters are used. Wherever the two names stand together in the Old Testament as a compound name of God, they are rendered "Sovereign LORD."

Because for most readers today the phrases "the LORD of hosts" and "God of hosts" have little meaning, this version renders them "the LORD Almighty" and "God Almighty." These renderings convey the sense of the Hebrew, namely, "he who is sovereign over all the 'hosts' (powers) in heaven and on earth, especially over the 'hosts' (armies) of Israel." For readers unacquainted with Hebrew this does not make clear the distinction between *Sabaoth* ("hosts" or "Almighty") and *Shaddai* (which can also be translated "Almighty"), but the latter occurs infrequently and is always footnoted. When *Adonai* and *YHWH Sabaoth* occur together, they are rendered "the Lord, the LORD Almighty."

As for other proper nouns, the familiar spellings of the King James Version are generally retained. Names traditionally spelled with "ch," except where it is final, are usually spelled in this translation with "k" or "c," since the biblical languages do not have the sound that "ch" frequently indicates in English—for example, in *chant*. For well-known names such as Zechariah, however, the traditional spelling has been retained. Variation in the spelling of names in the original languages has usually not been indicated. Where a person or place has two or more different names in the Hebrew, Aramaic or Greek texts, the more familiar one has generally been used, with footnotes where needed.

To achieve clarity the translators sometimes supplied words not in the original texts but required by the context. If there was uncertainty about such material, it is enclosed in brackets. Also for the sake of clarity or style, nouns, including some proper nouns, are sometimes substituted for pronouns, and vice versa. And though the Hebrew writers often shifted back and forth between first, second and third personal pronouns without change of antecedent, this translation often makes them uniform, in accordance with English style and without the use of footnotes.

Poetical passages are printed as poetry, that is, with indentation of lines and with separate stanzas. These are generally designed to reflect the structure of Hebrew poetry. This poetry is normally characterized by parallelism in balanced lines. Most of the poetry in the Bible is in the Old Testament, and scholars differ regarding the scansion of Hebrew lines. The translators determined the stanza divisions for the most part by analysis of the subject matter. The stanzas therefore serve as poetic paragraphs.

As an aid to the reader, italicized sectional headings are inserted in most of the books. They are not to be regarded as part of the NIV text, are not for oral reading, and are not intended to dictate the interpretation of the sections they head.

The footnotes in this version are of several kinds, most of which need no explanation. Those giving alternative translations begin with "Or" and generally introduce the alternative with the last word preceding it in the text, except when it is a single-word alternative; in poetry quoted in a footnote a slant mark indicates a line division. Footnotes introduced by "Or" do not have uniform significance. In some cases two possible translations were considered to have about equal validity. In other cases, though the translators were convinced that the translation in the text was correct, they judged that another interpretation was possible and of sufficient importance to be represented in a footnote.

In the New Testament, footnotes that refer to uncertainty regarding the original text are introduced by "Some manuscripts" or similar expressions. In the Old Testament, evidence for the reading chosen is given first and evidence for the alternative is added after a semicolon (for

Preface

example: Septuagint; Hebrew *father*). In such notes the term "Hebrew" refers to the Masoretic Text.

It should be noted that minerals, flora and fauna, architectural details, articles of clothing and jewelry, musical instruments and other articles cannot always be identified with precision. Also measures of capacity in the biblical period are particularly uncertain (see the table of weights and measures following the text).

Like all translations of the Bible, made as they are by imperfect man, this one undoubtedly falls short of its goals. Yet we are grateful to God for the extent to which he has enabled us to realize these goals and for the strength he has given us and our colleagues to complete our task. We offer this version of the Bible to him in whose name and for whose glory it has been made. We pray that it will lead many into a better understanding of the Holy Scriptures and a fuller knowledge of Jesus Christ the incarnate Word, of whom the Scriptures so faithfully testify.

The Committee on Bible Translation

June 1978
(Revised August 1983)

Names of the translators and editors may be secured
from the International Bible Society
144 Tices Lane, East Brunswick, New Jersey 08816.

MATTHEW

INTRODUCTION

The Synoptic Gospels

The word "synoptic" means, literally, "able to be seen together." It refers to the first three gospels—Matthew, Mark and Luke—which cover the same events in Jesus' life, often in the same way. A parallel reading of the first three gospels makes it clear that there is some sort of literary connection between them. For example, even the parenthesis in the story of the healing of the paralytic—"He said to the paralytic"—is in the identical place in each account. Compare Matt. 9:6, Mark 2:10, and Luke 5:24.

The nature of this connection is not absolutely certain, but generally it is assumed that Mark was the first gospel, that Matthew and Luke had Mark's text before them when they wrote, and that they included some of Mark's material in their own compositions. One reason scholars conclude this is that of the 105 sections in Mark, all but 4 occur in Matthew or Luke. In fact, Matthew uses 93 of these 105 sections (nearly 90%), including not just the general story but in 51% of the cases Mark's very words.

While it might be argued that Mark merely summarized Matthew and Luke (and so was the *last* synoptic Gospel and not the first), this seems less probable because Matthew and Luke tend to polish up Mark's harsher writing style. Further comparison indicates that Matthew and Luke drew mainly narrative material from Mark—stories about what Jesus did. However, Matthew and Luke also share some two hundred verses not found in Mark, most of which consist of the teachings of Jesus. This discussion material may have come from an early (but now lost) collection of Jesus' teaching.

In any case, it is clear that when the gospel writers put together their accounts, they did so with a clear purpose in mind. Each selected some stories and left out others to produce an account of Jesus' life that would answer the questions and concerns of his particular audience. Mark probably wrote for Christians in Rome who were suffering under Nero's persecution, and so he told about Jesus who was the suffering servant. Luke wrote about the son of Man who came to seek and to save the needy, the lost, the outcasts. Matthew wrote to a Jewish audience and told the story of King Jesus, the Son of David, who came as the long-promised Messiah to claim his throne.

Author

Nowhere is the author named within the first gospel. There is however a long tradition that has assigned it to Matthew, the tax collector who became an apostle. Indeed, Bishop Papias wrote (around A.D. 125) that "Matthew composed the Logia in the Hebrew tongue"—though this reference is not unambiguous or without problematic features.

Little is known about Matthew except that he was a tax gatherer. As such he would have been bitterly hated by the general populace in Israel—with good reason. For one thing, tax collectors worked for Rome, the oppressor, and therefore were seen as traitors to Israel. For another, tax collectors made their living—and many were quite wealthy—by charging above and beyond what Rome required (only the tax collector knew what was owed). Matthew the tax collector stands in contrast to the poor and middle-class fisherman who composed the main body of the disciples.

It has been suggested that it took Matthew's logical accountant's mind to produce a precisely organized gospel such as this one. It is interesting to note that in telling the story of paying tribute, only the gospel of Matthew uses the precise word for the coin involved instead of the more common word (which Mark and Luke used).

Characteristics

Matthew is the most Jewish of all the Gospels. It was written by a Jew to other Jews to convince them that Jesus was, indeed, the Messiah foretold by Old Testament Scripture. Thus the author cites numerous Old Testament prophecies which were fulfilled by Jesus. He uses the phrase "All this took place to fulfill what the Lord had said through the prophets" some sixteen times.

The Jewishness of the gospel is also seen in the fact that Matthew mentions Jewish customs without explanation (e.g., "phylacteries" in 23:5), that he has a very high view of the Law (5:17-20), and that even when recording Jesus' denunciations, he shows more respect for the teachers of the Law and the Pharisees than any other gospel writer (23:2).

Yet one of the most interesting features of Matthew is that although he is so Jewish in his concerns, in his book we discover the universal nature of the gospel—that it is for all the peoples of the world. This emphasis emerges right at the beginning when the Gentile Magi bring gifts to the baby Jesus, and it runs through to the end when Jesus sends His followers out to "make disciples of all nations."

Other features of Matthew include his interest in the church (this is the only gospel to use the word "church") and his concern about the end times—the Second Coming of Jesus, the end of the world, and the final judgment (his is the fullest account).

Structure

It has been said that Matthew is the most orderly in structure of the four gospel accounts. After an introductory section, the material is organized into five blocks of narrative alternated with five blocks of discourse or teaching. We can see that this is not an accidental arrangement, because Matthew ends each teaching section with a similar formula (compare 7:28; 11:1; 13:53 and 26:1).

Overview Study Questions

1. Quickly skim the whole gospel, watching for the divisions noted above. What picture of Jesus emerges from this account?
2. Read about Matthew in the New Testament: Matthew 9:9-13; Mark 2:13-17; Luke 5:27-32; Mark 3:18; Acts 1:13. What picture of this man emerges?

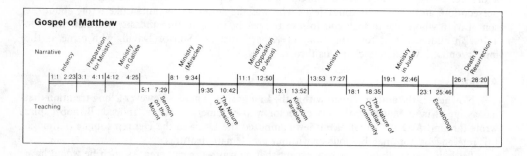

Matthew

The Genealogy of Jesus

1 A record of the genealogy of Jesus Christ the son of David, the son of Abraham:

²Abraham was the father of Isaac,
  Isaac the father of Jacob,
  Jacob the father of Judah and his brothers,
³Judah the father of Perez and Zerah, whose mother was Tamar,
  Perez the father of Hezron,
  Hezron the father of Ram,
⁴Ram the father of Amminadab,
  Amminadab the father of Nahshon,
  Nahshon the father of Salmon,
⁵Salmon the father of Boaz, whose mother was Rahab,
  Boaz the father of Obed, whose mother was Ruth,
  Obed the father of Jesse,
⁶and Jesse the father of King David.

David was the father of Solomon, whose mother had been Uriah's wife,
⁷Solomon the father of Rehoboam,
  Rehoboam the father of Abijah,
  Abijah the father of Asa,
⁸Asa the father of Jehoshaphat,
  Jehoshaphat the father of Jehoram,
  Jehoram the father of Uzziah,
⁹Uzziah the father of Jotham,
  Jotham the father of Ahaz,
  Ahaz the father of Hezekiah,
¹⁰Hezekiah the father of Manasseh,
  Manasseh the father of Amon,
  Amon the father of Josiah,
¹¹and Josiah the father of Jeconiah [a] and his brothers at the time of the exile to Babylon.

¹²After the exile to Babylon:
  Jeconiah was the father of Shealtiel,
  Shealtiel the father of Zerubbabel,
¹³Zerubbabel the father of Abiud,
  Abiud the father of Eliakim,
  Eliakim the father of Azor,
¹⁴Azor the father of Zadok,
  Zadok the father of Akim,
  Akim the father of Eliud,
¹⁵Eliud the father of Eleazar,
  Eleazar the father of Matthan,
  Matthan the father of Jacob,
¹⁶and Jacob the father of Joseph, the husband of Mary, of whom was born Jesus, who is called Christ.

OPEN: 1. When you were a child, what did you like best about your grandparents? What is your most vivid memory of any great-grandparents? **2.** What do you know about your genealogy? What would you like to discover about it? **3.** If you could design a coat of arms for your family, what animal would you choose? Why? What other symbols would you choose?

DIG: 1. What titles does Matthew assign Jesus in verses 1 and 16? What is the meaning of each title? **2.** Which people do you recognize in this genealogy? What do you remember about each of these people? Which people on the list are the most significant in establishing who Jesus is? **3.** Why do you think some women were named when it was not the Jewish custom to include women's names in genealogies? What do you know about these women? **4.** Into what three sections does Matthew divide his genealogical table? What great event climaxes each section? From the promises to Abraham (Ge 12:2-3; 17:6-8), why is it significant that Jesus is Abraham's son (Gal 3:16-18)? From 2 Samuel 7:11-13, why is it significant that he is David's son as well? Of what does that assure us? **5.** If Luke's genealogy (Lk 3:23-38) goes all the way back to *Adam* to emphasize the universality of the gospel, what is Matthew's point in beginning with *Abraham*? What does this account of lineage say to Matthew's Jewish readers?

REFLECT: 1. What does it mean to you that God's promises are trustworthy over the generations? **2.** At what point in your life have you most felt Jesus' presence? **3.** Who are the significant people in your spiritual upbringing? What has been passed on to you spiritually from your forbearers?

---

a11 That is, Jehoiachin; also in verse 12

[17]Thus there were fourteen generations in all from Abraham to David, fourteen from David to the exile to Babylon, and fourteen from the exile to the Christ. [b]

The Birth of Jesus Christ

[18]This is how the birth of Jesus Christ came about: His mother Mary was pledged to be married to Joseph, but before they came together, she was found to be with child through the Holy Spirit. [19]Because Joseph her husband was a righteous man and did not want to expose her to public disgrace, he had in mind to divorce her quietly.

[20]But after he had considered this, an angel of the Lord appeared to him in a dream and said, "Joseph son of David, do not be afraid to take Mary home as your wife, because what is conceived in her is from the Holy Spirit. [21]She will give birth to a son, and you are to give him the name Jesus, [c] because he will save his people from their sins."

[22]All this took place to fulfill what the Lord had said through the prophet: [23]"The virgin will be with child and will give birth to a son, and they will call him Immanuel" [d]—which means, "God with us."

[24]When Joseph woke up, he did what the angel of the Lord had commanded him and took Mary home as his wife. [25]But he had no union with her until she gave birth to a son. And he gave him the name Jesus.

The Visit of the Magi

2 After Jesus was born in Bethlehem in Judea, during the time of King Herod, Magi [e] from the east came to Jerusalem [2]and asked, "Where is the one who has been born king of the Jews? We saw his star in the east [f] and have come to worship him."

[3]When King Herod heard this he was disturbed, and all Jerusalem with him. [4]When he had called together all the people's chief priests and teachers of the law, he asked them where the Christ [g] was to be born. [5]"In Bethlehem in Judea," they replied, "for this is what the prophet has written:

[6]" 'But you, Bethlehem, in the land of Judah,
    are by no means least among the rulers of Judah;
  for out of you will come a ruler
    who will be the shepherd of my people Israel.' [h]"

[7]Then Herod called the Magi secretly and found out from them the exact time the star had appeared. [8]He sent them to Bethlehem and said, "Go and make a careful search for the child. As soon as you find him, report to me, so that I too may go and worship him."

[9]After they had heard the king, they went on their way, and the star they had seen in the east [i] went ahead of them until it stopped over the place where the child was. [10]When they saw

---

---

[b]17 Or Messiah. "The Christ" (Greek) and "the Messiah" (Hebrew) both mean "the Anointed One." [c]21 Jesus is the Greek form of Joshua, which means the LORD saves.
[d]23 Isaiah 7:14 [e]1 Traditionally Wise Men [f]2 Or star when it rose
[g]4 Or Messiah [h]6 Micah 5:2 [i]9 Or seen when it rose

the star, they were overjoyed. [11]On coming to the house, they saw the child with his mother Mary, and they bowed down and worshiped him. Then they opened their treasures and presented him with gifts of gold and of incense and of myrrh. [12]And having been warned in a dream not to go back to Herod, they returned to their country by another route.

The Escape to Egypt

[13]When they had gone, an angel of the Lord appeared to Joseph in a dream. "Get up," he said, "take the child and his mother and escape to Egypt. Stay there until I tell you, for Herod is going to search for the child to kill him."

[14]So he got up, took the child and his mother during the night and left for Egypt, [15]where he stayed until the death of Herod. And so was fulfilled what the Lord had said through the prophet: "Out of Egypt I called my son."[j]

[16]When Herod realized that he had been outwitted by the Magi, he was furious, and he gave orders to kill all the boys in Bethlehem and its vicinity who were two years old and under, in accordance with the time he had learned from the Magi. [17]Then what was said through the prophet Jeremiah was fulfilled:

[18]"A voice is heard in Ramah,
    weeping and great mourning,
Rachel weeping for her children
    and refusing to be comforted,
because they are no more."[k]

The Return to Nazareth

[19]After Herod died, an angel of the Lord appeared in a dream to Joseph in Egypt [20]and said, "Get up, take the child and his mother and go to the land of Israel, for those who were trying to take the child's life are dead."

[21]So he got up, took the child and his mother and went to the land of Israel. [22]But when he heard that Archelaus was reigning in Judea in place of his father Herod, he was afraid to go there. Having been warned in a dream, he withdrew to the district of Galilee, [23]and he went and lived in a town called Nazareth. So was fulfilled what was said through the prophets: "He will be called a Nazarene."

John the Baptist Prepares the Way

3 In those days John the Baptist came, preaching in the Desert of Judea [2]and saying, "Repent, for the kingdom of heaven is near." [3]This is he who was spoken of through the prophet Isaiah:

"A voice of one calling in the desert,
'Prepare the way for the Lord,
    make straight paths for him.' "[l]

[4]John's clothes were made of camel's hair, and he had a leather belt around his waist. His food was locusts and wild

---

OPEN: 1. If you (or your father) were transferred to another country where your company (or your father's) also conducts business, where would you go? What feelings would accompany your special placement (or displacement)? **2.** How far away from where you were born do you now live? Would you ever go back to your birthplace to live now (or retire later)? Why or why not?

DIG: 1. What type of king do you imagine Herod to be? What does his response of fear and anger show about his view of the Messiah? **2.** What is Matthew's point in emphasizing God's watchcare over Jesus? In the fulfillment of Hosea's and Jeremiah's prophecies (vv.17-18, 23)? **3.** What relocation options face Joseph? How did God use prophecy, dreams, faith, and circumstances to guide him?

REFLECT: 1. When, like Herod, have you felt threatened by Jesus' kingship? How do you react at those times? **2.** From Joseph's responsiveness, what do you learn about faith and obedience? How long would it take you to say "yes" if God asked you to move on with him? Why the delay?

OPEN: 1. Who in your group or community would you cast in these roles: (a) Street preacher? (b) Press secretary? (c) Lunatic? (d) Worst dressed? (e) Natural foods freak? (f) Organizational misfit? **2.** When were you baptized, how much water did it take?

DIG: 1. What was John the Baptist like? Why would anyone go out of their way to hear this radical preacher (v.7)? Who did they think he was (see 2Ki 1:8)? **2.** How would you paraphrase John's

---

j15 Hosea 11:1   *k18* Jer. 31:15   *l3* Isaiah 40:3

message (v.2) for people today? What is the "kingdom of heaven"? **3.** What angered John so much about the Pharisees and Sadducees? **4.** What do the images of judgment mean: The coming wrath? The axe? The fire? His winnowing fork? **5.** How do John's and Jesus' ministries compare? **6.** Why did Jesus, who was without sin, come to John to be baptized? What "righteousness" did he fulfill (see Isa 53:12)? **7.** In the context of chapters 3 and 4, what do you think verse 17 meant to Jesus? How does this set the stage for his ministry to begin?

REFLECT: **1.** Who has been a "John the Baptist" in your life? How did he or she prepare you to meet Jesus? **2.** Who are today's "Pharisees and Sadducees"? **3.** How is repentance linked to your experience of salvation: In the past? Now? **4.** How has God affirmed you as his child in Christ?

OPEN: What are you tempted by that is either sinful, expensive or fattening?

DIG: **1.** For each of the three temptations: (a) What is its nature? (b) What potentially might appeal to Jesus? (c) What price would there be were he to yield? (d) How does Jesus respond? **2.** What links these temptations with the baptism of Jesus (vv.1, 3, 6)? **3.** Of these three, which temptation appears most legitimate? Which one is most shrewd? Which one is basic to them all?

REFLECT: **1.** What human need is at the heart of each temptation? How are these needs evident in your life? How does Satan use these to tempt you? **2.** What is your greatest temptation right now? How can others help?

honey. ⁵People went out to him from Jerusalem and all Judea and the whole region of the Jordan. ⁶Confessing their sins, they were baptized by him in the Jordan River.

⁷But when he saw many of the Pharisees and Sadducees coming to where he was baptizing, he said to them: "You brood of vipers! Who warned you to flee from the coming wrath? ⁸Produce fruit in keeping with repentance. ⁹And do not think you can say to yourselves, 'We have Abraham as our father.' I tell you that out of these stones God can raise up children for Abraham. ¹⁰The ax is already at the root of the trees, and every tree that does not produce good fruit will be cut down and thrown into the fire.

¹¹"I baptize you with *m*water for repentance. But after me will come one who is more powerful than I, whose sandals I am not fit to carry. He will baptize you with the Holy Spirit and with fire. ¹²His winnowing fork is in his hand, and he will clear his threshing floor, gathering his wheat into the barn and burning up the chaff with unquenchable fire."

The Baptism of Jesus

¹³Then Jesus came from Galilee to the Jordan to be baptized by John. ¹⁴But John tried to deter him, saying, "I need to be baptized by you, and do you come to me?"

¹⁵Jesus replied, "Let it be so now; it is proper for us to do this to fulfill all righteousness." Then John consented.

¹⁶As soon as Jesus was baptized, he went up out of the water. At that moment heaven was opened, and he saw the Spirit of God descending like a dove and lighting on him. ¹⁷And a voice from heaven said, "This is my Son, whom I love; with him I am well pleased."

The Temptation of Jesus

4 Then Jesus was led by the Spirit into the desert to be tempted by the devil. ²After fasting forty days and forty nights, he was hungry. ³The tempter came to him and said, "If you are the Son of God, tell these stones to become bread."

⁴Jesus answered, "It is written: 'Man does not live on bread alone, but on every word that comes from the mouth of God.'*n*"

⁵Then the devil took him to the holy city and had him stand on the highest point of the temple. ⁶"If you are the Son of God," he said, "throw yourself down. For it is written:

" 'He will command his angels concerning you,
    and they will lift you up in their hands,
so that you will not strike your foot against a stone.'*o*"

⁷Jesus answered him, "It is also written: 'Do not put the Lord your God to the test.'*p*"

⁸Again, the devil took him to a very high mountain and showed him all the kingdoms of the world and their splendor. ⁹"All this I will give you," he said, "if you will bow down and worship me."

*m*11 Or *in*   *n*4 Deut. 8:3   *o*6 Psalm 91:11,12   *p*7 Deut. 6:16

LOOKING INTO THE SCRIPTURE/20 Minutes. Read Matthew 4:1-11 and discuss.

1. What is the longest you have ever gone without food?
   - a. three hours
   - b. one day
   - c. three days
   - d. I've never been hungry

2. What were the circumstances?
   - a. I was on a diet
   - b. I was stranded on a mountaintop
   - c. there was no food in the house
   - d. I decided to fast and pray

3. How did your hunger affect your:
   - a. will power
   - b. emotions
   - c. attitude
   - d. reasoning

4. How would you describe the power struggle going on here?
   - a. this is the classic struggle between good and evil
   - b. Satan is trying to conquer Jesus when he seems weak and powerless
   - c. this power struggle is no different than those we face daily
   - d. Satan is trying to conquer Jesus by tempting him on the physical, intellectual, emotional and spiritual levels

5. What is the devil trying to do with Jesus?
   - a. kill him physically
   - b. play "mind games" with him
   - c. get Jesus to worship him
   - d. enlist Jesus as an ally

6. What tactics does Jesus use to conquer Satan?
   - a. call on angels to help
   - b. quote Scripture to refute claims
   - c. appeal to higher authority
   - d. tell Satan to "beat it"

7. In verse 3, why did the devil challenge Jesus to change stones into bread?
   - a. to see if Jesus could do it
   - b. to exercise control over Jesus
   - c. to mock and dare Jesus
   - d. to attack where Jesus was vulnerable

8. In verse 6, what do you learn about Satan?
   - a. he knows Scripture too
   - b. he can change tactics as circumstances dictate
   - c. he is easily frustrated
   - d. he tempts at the weakest point

MY OWN STORY/25 Minutes.

1. Which of these temptations would be the hardest for you to resist?
   - ☐ Chocolate: All you could eat
   - ☐ Skipping work on a nice day
   - ☐ Sleeping in on Sunday
   - ☐ Taking that long needed vacation
   - ☐ Taking a Porsche for a joy ride
   - ☐ Never passing up a "bargain"
   - ☐ Sneaking into a ball game
   - ☐ Taking a book to bed

2. How would you compare your own temptations with the temptations that Jesus faced?
   - a. different, but just as real
   - b. not quite so big
   - c. not quite so obvious
   - d. I've never been tempted

3. When do you find yourself most vulnerable to the tempter?
   - a. when I'm tired or under stress
   - b. when I'm alone or away from home
   - c. after a spiritual high
   - d. when I'm not expecting it
   - e. when I let my mind dwell on certain things

4. What has helped you to overcome temptation when it comes?
   - a. Scripture (my special passage is . . .)
   - b. telling a friend about it
   - c. prayer
   - d. talking myself out of it
   - e. fleeing/change of scene

5. What has made you feel good about resisting temptation?
   - a. avoiding hurt
   - b. just knowing I did the right thing
   - c. I've gotten stronger as a Christian
   - d. nothing. Given the chance again I'd go for it

[10]Jesus said to him, "Away from me, Satan! For it is written: 'Worship the Lord your God, and serve him only.'*"

[11]Then the devil left him, and angels came and attended him.

Jesus Begins to Preach

[12]When Jesus heard that John had been put in prison, he returned to Galilee. [13]Leaving Nazareth, he went and lived in Capernaum, which was by the lake in the area of Zebulun and Naphtali— [14]to fulfill what was said through the prophet Isaiah:

[15]"Land of Zebulun and land of Naphtali,
　　the way to the sea, along the Jordan,
　　Galilee of the Gentiles—
[16]the people living in darkness
　　have seen a great light;
　on those living in the land of the shadow of death
　　a light has dawned."*

[17]From that time on Jesus began to preach, "Repent, for the kingdom of heaven is near."

The Calling of the First Disciples

[18]As Jesus was walking beside the Sea of Galilee, he saw two brothers, Simon called Peter and his brother Andrew. They were casting a net into the lake, for they were fishermen. [19]"Come, follow me," Jesus said, "and I will make you fishers of men." [20]At once they left their nets and followed him.

[21]Going on from there, he saw two other brothers, James son of Zebedee and his brother John. They were in a boat with their father Zebedee, preparing their nets. Jesus called them, [22]and immediately they left the boat and their father and followed him.

Jesus Heals the Sick

[23]Jesus went throughout Galilee, teaching in their synagogues, preaching the good news of the kingdom, and healing every disease and sickness among the people. [24]News about him spread all over Syria, and people brought to him all who were ill with various diseases, those suffering severe pain, the demon-possessed, those having seizures, and the paralyzed, and he healed them. [25]Large crowds from Galilee, the Decapolis,* Jerusalem, Judea and the region across the Jordan followed him.

The Beatitudes

5 Now when he saw the crowds, he went up on a mountainside and sat down. His disciples came to him, [2]and he began to teach them, saying:

[3]"Blessed are the poor in spirit,
　　for theirs is the kingdom of heaven.
[4]Blessed are those who mourn,
　　for they will be comforted.
[5]Blessed are the meek,
　　for they will inherit the earth.

10 Deut. 6:13　　*16* Isaiah 9:1,2　　*25* That is, the Ten Cities

OPEN: 1. When did you leave home to be "on your own" for the first time? 2. In what part of your life are you experiencing a "sunrise"? A "sunset"?

DIG: 1. How does Jesus react to John's imprisonment? 2. How had they been "living in darkness" (v.16)? What was Jesus' message? What is the relation between repentance, the kingdom of heaven, and the light? 3. What invitations does Jesus give to these fishermen? What seems unusual about their response? What prior knowledge of Jesus do you think they had (vv.13,17)? How might Zebedee have felt (v.22)? 4. From how far away are the crowds coming (vv.23-25; see Bible map)? What needs do they have? What are they seeing about God's kingdom?

REFLECT: 1. How has coming to know Jesus been like moving from darkness to light for you? 2. In what ways does God's kingdom seem "now" for you? In what ways does it seem "not yet"? 3. Spiritually, are you still preparing the nets? Leaving the boat? Following hard after Jesus? Feeling left behind? 4. If you were in the crowds (vv.23-25), what would you ask Jesus to heal for you? Why not pray about that as a group?

OPEN: 1. When you want to get away from people, where do you go and what do you do? 2. What saying or bumper sticker do you keep on your desk or car?

DIG: 1. What is the connection between 4:23-25 and 5:1-2? 2. How do the eight qualities that describe kingdom people relate to the promises that follow them? How do they relate to each other? How would you describe the opposite of each quality? Are the

LOOKING INTO THE SCRIPTURE/25 Minutes. Read Matthew 5:3-10 and measure your-self on these mental attitudes—1 being LOW and 4 being HIGH.

POOR IN SPIRIT: I have come to the place where I feel accepted by God when I feel most unacceptable to myself. I recognize my need for God and know that I do not have to earn His love with wealth, status or spiritual sophistication.

LOW 1 2 3 4 HIGH

MOURN: I have come to the place where I can really feel the empty places in my life. I can let others know when I am hurting and share the grief of others without embarrassment. I can weep like Jesus did.   LOW 1 2 3 4 HIGH

MEEK: I have come to the place where I don't have to be the strong one all the time. I can be tender and gentle with people. I've given the control of my life to God and I don't have to "win" all the time.   LOW 1 2 3 4 HIGH

SPIRITUAL HUNGER: I have come to the place where I want to know God and His will for my life more than anything. I am more excited about God's will for the world than my own financial gain, success in my career, or acceptance by my peers. I long for God's perspective in my decision-making.   LOW 1 2 3 4 HIGH

MERCIFUL: I have come to the place where I can enter into the feelings of someone who is hurting, lonely, or distressed and feel alongside them in their pain. God has given me a sensitivity for the suffering of others.   LOW 1 2 3 4 HIGH

PURE IN HEART: I have come to the place where I can be completely open and honest with God and others—transparent because I have nothing to hide. I don't have to put on "airs," or pretend to be what I'm not.   LOW 1 2 3 4 HIGH

PEACEMAKER: I have come to the place where I really work at keeping the channels of communication open between me and those around me. I deal with anger and dis-agreements immediately and don't allow them to fester. I encourage those around me to work out their differences without hurting one another.   LOW 1 2 3 4 HIGH

PERSECUTION: I have come to the place where I know what I am living for, and for this cause I am not afraid to suffer and, if need be, die. I am willing to "take the heat" and stand alone for what is right. I can take criticism without feeling self-pity or self-righteous.

LOW 1 2 3 4 HIGH

MY OWN STORY/20 Minutes.

1. In what area (beatitude) have you made the most progress in the last year? How have you experienced the "blessing"?

2. In what area do you need to work on something? How could the group help you grow in that area?

3. Below is a list of qualities based on the Beatitudes. In silence, think about the members of your group and jot down their initials next to the beatitude paraphrase where you see each person as strong. (For instance, you might put Bob's initials next to "gentleness".) Then, ask one person to sit in silence while the others explain where they put this person's name. Then, take the next person and do the same until everyone has been affirmed.

☐ SELF-ACCEPTANCE: The ability to accept yourself and your imperfections, and to enable others to be more self-accepting.

☐ EMPATHY: The ability to feel what others feel; to laugh and cry with others.

☐ GENTLENESS: Ability to be tender be-cause you are inwardly strong and to lead without overpowering others.

☐ SPIRITUALITY: Ability to maintain spir-itual priorities and to cause others to seek a deeper walk with Christ.

☐ SENSITIVITY: The ability to pick up on the hurt and pain of others and be "pres-ent" without being pushy or nosey.

☐ TRANSPARENCY: The ability to be your-self without any pretenses and allow the presence of Christ to radiate through you.

☐ PEACEMAKING: The ability to harmonize differences between others without caus-ing either person to "lose."

☐ ENDURANCE: The ability to stand up for what you believe without getting defen-sive or compromising your principles.

promises each separate, or really one? Why? **3.** Is Jesus *describing* who his followers *are*? Or *prescribing* what they must *do*? Why do you think so? **4.** How does this "sermonette" explain the nature of the kingdom? How are these beatitudes related to being "salt" and "light" (vv.13-16)? How are Christians to penetrate society?

REFLECT: **1** . How do these promised blessings compare with what most people in the world prize? Would kingdom people be admired in your society? Why or why not? **2.** Of these eight qualities, which two do you desire most in your life? Why? Who in your group or family do you associate with each? **3.** Based on the beatitudes, is the light of your life shining like a 300-watt bulb? A 100-watt? A night light? Why? How can Jesus enable you to "shine brighter"?

OPEN: As a kid, what family rule did you love to break? Why?

DIG: **1.** Why might Jesus have to explain his position on the Law and Prophets? How does he "fulfill" the Prophets and "accomplish everything" in the Law? **2.** What is Jesus' point about the "least" and the "great"? **3.** How does the righteousness of the Pharisees contrast with that described in verses 3-11? How do we obtain this "surpassing righteousness"?

REFLECT: How can you tell which righteousness is yours?

OPEN: **1.** How did your parents settle disputes between you and your brother/sister? **2.** What's the best advice you have been given for dealing with anger?

DIG: **1.** In this section, how is Jesus like a "new Moses"? How is his law different? **2.** What new standard of right and wrong is Jesus creating (vv.21-26)? How

[6]Blessed are those who hunger and thirst for
  righteousness,
    for they will be filled.
[7]Blessed are the merciful,
    for they will be shown mercy.
[8]Blessed are the pure in heart,
    for they will see God.
[9]Blessed are the peacemakers,
    for they will be called sons of God.
[10]Blessed are those who are persecuted because of
  righteousness,
    for theirs is the kingdom of heaven.

[11]"Blessed are you when people insult you, persecute you and falsely say all kinds of evil against you because of me. [12]Rejoice and be glad, because great is your reward in heaven, for in the same way they persecuted the prophets who were before you.

Salt and Light

[13]"You are the salt of the earth. But if the salt loses its saltiness, how can it be made salty again? It is no longer good for anything, except to be thrown out and trampled by men.

[14]"You are the light of the world. A city on a hill cannot be hidden. [15]Neither do people light a lamp and put it under a bowl. Instead they put it on its stand, and it gives light to everyone in the house. [16]In the same way, let your light shine before men, that they may see your good deeds and praise your Father in heaven.

The Fulfillment of the Law

[17]"Do not think that I have come to abolish the Law or the Prophets; I have not come to abolish them but to fulfill them. [18]I tell you the truth, until heaven and earth disappear, not the smallest letter, not the least stroke of a pen, will by any means disappear from the Law until everything is accomplished. [19]Anyone who breaks one of the least of these commandments and teaches others to do the same will be called least in the kingdom of heaven, but whoever practices and teaches these commands will be called great in the kingdom of heaven. [20]For I tell you that unless your righteousness surpasses that of the Pharisees and the teachers of the law, you will certainly not enter the kingdom of heaven.

Murder

[21]"You have heard that it was said to the people long ago, 'Do not murder,[t] and anyone who murders will be subject to judgment.' [22]But I tell you that anyone who is angry with his brother[u] will be subject to judgment. Again, anyone who says to his brother, 'Raca,[v]' is answerable to the Sanhedrin. But anyone who says, 'You fool!' will be in danger of the fire of hell. [23]"Therefore, if you are offering your gift at the altar and

---

[t]21 Exodus 20:13   [u]22 Some manuscripts *brother without cause*   [v]22 An Aramaic term of contempt

there remember that your brother has something against you, ²⁴leave your gift there in front of the altar. First go and be reconciled to your brother; then come and offer your gift.

²⁵"Settle matters quickly with your adversary who is taking you to court. Do it while you are still with him on the way, or he may hand you over to the judge, and the judge may hand you over to the officer, and you may be thrown into prison. ²⁶I tell you the truth, you will not get out until you have paid the last penny.^w

Adultery

²⁷"You have heard that it was said, 'Do not commit adultery.'^x ²⁸But I tell you that anyone who looks at a woman lustfully has already committed adultery with her in his heart. ²⁹If your right eye causes you to sin, gouge it out and throw it away. It is better for you to lose one part of your body than for your whole body to be thrown into hell. ³⁰And if your right hand causes you to sin, cut it off and throw it away. It is better for you to lose one part of your body than for your whole body to go into hell.

Divorce

³¹"It has been said, 'Anyone who divorces his wife must give her a certificate of divorce.'^y ³²But I tell you that anyone who divorces his wife, except for marital unfaithfulness, causes her to become an adulteress, and anyone who marries the divorced woman commits adultery.

Oaths

³³"Again, you have heard that it was said to the people long ago, 'Do not break your oath, but keep the oaths you have made to the Lord.' ³⁴But I tell you, Do not swear at all: either by heaven, for it is God's throne; ³⁵or by the earth, for it is his footstool; or by Jerusalem, for it is the city of the Great King. ³⁶And do not swear by your head, for you cannot make even one hair white or black. ³⁷Simply let your 'Yes' be 'Yes,' and your 'No,' 'No'; anything beyond this comes from the evil one.

An Eye for an Eye

³⁸"You have heard that it was said, 'Eye for eye, and tooth for tooth.'^z ³⁹But I tell you, Do not resist an evil person. If someone strikes you on the right cheek, turn to him the other also. ⁴⁰And if someone wants to sue you and take your tunic, let him have your cloak as well. ⁴¹If someone forces you to go one mile, go with him two miles. ⁴²Give to the one who asks you, and do not turn away from the one who wants to borrow from you.

does he link anger and murder? Why? What inner attitudes is he stressing by these examples? **3.** How does Jesus apply the principle in verses 21-26 to the commandment about adultery? What is Jesus' point in using such exaggerated language (vv.29-30)? **4.** Some rabbis allowed divorce for nearly any reason a husband wanted it. What was their casual attitude towards divorce promoting? How are they misusing Moses' allowance for divorce (see Dt 24:1-4)? What inner quality is Jesus seeking instead? **5.** How do you imagine the OT teaching about oaths is being misapplied (vv.33-37)? What ought always be true about our speech? **6.** What was the original intent of "eye for eye" and "tooth for tooth" (see Ex 21:24; Lev 24:20)? How is this law being perverted? What qualities ought to replace those desires for revenge? **7.** Only the first part of the quote in verse 43 is from the OT. What does this show about the common use of Scripture at this time? In this context, what does the type of love Jesus calls for involve? **8.** How do the themes in verses 21-48 illustrate what Jesus meant by verses 19-20? How does verse 48 sum it up?

REFLECT: **1.** Since all of us experience something of anger, lust, divorce, duplicity, revenge, selfishness, and hate, what is Jesus saying to us here? Which illustration gets to you the most? **2.** If these standards are like a doctor's thermometer to show us how sick we are, what is the medicine needed to heal us? How does that relate to 5:3? To the rest of the beatitudes? What is the hope for us here? **3.** Although these standards are not a new law that we must attain before God will have mercy on us, what do they suggest about the direction in which God wants us to grow after we have received his mercy? Which of these qualities do you want to cultivate most right now? How would your life be different as God helps you to put this quality into action? **4.** Are these teachings meant to be the basis for social policies (about legal cases, divorce, war, etc.)? Why or why not?

---

^w26 Greek *kodrantes*   ^x27 Exodus 20:14   ^y31 Deut. 24:1
^z38 Exodus 21:24; Lev. 24:20; Deut. 19:21

Love for Enemies

[43]"You have heard that it was said, 'Love your neighbor[a] and hate your enemy.' [44]But I tell you: Love your enemies[b] and pray for those who persecute you, [45]that you may be sons of your Father in heaven. He causes his sun to rise on the evil and the good, and sends rain on the righteous and the unrighteous. [46]If you love those who love you, what reward will you get? Are not even the tax collectors doing that? [47]And if you greet only your brothers, what are you doing more than others? Do not even pagans do that? [48]Be perfect, therefore, as your heavenly Father is perfect.

Giving to the Needy

6 "Be careful not to do your 'acts of righteousness' before men, to be seen by them. If you do, you will have no reward from your Father in heaven.

[2]"So when you give to the needy, do not announce it with trumpets, as the hypocrites do in the synagogues and on the streets, to be honored by men. I tell you the truth, they have received their reward in full. [3]But when you give to the needy, do not let your left hand know what your right hand is doing, [4]so that your giving may be in secret. Then your Father, who sees what is done in secret, will reward you.

Prayer

[5]"And when you pray, do not be like the hypocrites, for they love to pray standing in the synagogues and on the street corners to be seen by men. I tell you the truth, they have received their reward in full. [6]But when you pray, go into your room, close the door and pray to your Father, who is unseen. Then your Father, who sees what is done in secret, will reward you. [7]And when you pray, do not keep on babbling like pagans, for they think they will be heard because of their many words. [8]Do not be like them, for your Father knows what you need before you ask him.

[9]"This, then, is how you should pray:

" 'Our Father in heaven,
hallowed be your name,
[10]your kingdom come,
your will be done
    on earth as it is in heaven.
[11]Give us today our daily bread.
[12]Forgive us our debts,
    as we also have forgiven our debtors.
[13]And lead us not into temptation,
    but deliver us from the evil one.[c]'

[14]For if you forgive men when they sin against you, your heavenly Father will also forgive you. [15]But if you do not forgive men their sins, your Father will not forgive your sins.

OPEN: 1. Did you grow up in an openly "religious" home? Or was religion a private matter, unseen by you until later years? **2.** Were you taught any rote prayers as a child? What was one of the earliest ones you can recall?

DIG: 1. Jesus continues to show what a righteousness surpassing that of the scribes and Pharisees (5:20) looks like by comparing it with three main areas of Jewish piety. How have they corrupted the discipline of giving to the poor? What does their hypocrisy look like? What is its motivation? Its reward? How does it contrast with genuine compassion for the poor? **2.** How does their hypocrisy affect their prayer? How does their reward contrast with that of those who pray sincerely? Why did Jesus warn his followers to avoid wordiness? **3.** In Jesus' model prayer (vv.9-13), what three concerns related to God did he pray about first? What personal concerns follow? What is the relationship between forgiveness and prayer? **4.** If our Father knows what we need before we ask, why pray? **5.** How does the fasting of Jesus' disciples contrast with that of the religious leaders? Why? Why would each group fast?

REFLECT: 1. What "religious disciplines" are valued in your circles? In what way can they be misused as a way to impress others? When have you given in to that temptation? Why? **2.** Do you tend to err on the flashy side, or do you avoid such disciplines as fasting, praying, or giving altogether? What attitudes does it take to practice these religious exercises correctly? How does

---

[a]43 Lev. 19:18   [b]44 Some late manuscripts *enemies, bless those who curse you, do good to those who hate you*   [c]13 Or *from evil*; some late manuscripts *one, / for yours is the kingdom and the power and the glory forever. Amen.*

LOOKING INTO THE SCRIPTURE/20 Minutes. Read Matthew 6:9-13 and evaluate your own prayer life against the model here.

ADORATION OF GOD: *"Our Father in heaven, hallowed be your name."* I spend time praising God for who he is, both holy Lord and compassionate Father.

1. I know God is holy and compassionate by what I see:
   a. in history
   b. in creation
   c. in my relationships
   d. in Jesus Christ

LONGING FOR HIS REIGN: *"Your kingdom come, your will be done on earth as it is in heaven."* I spend time welcoming God's influence into my life and into my world.

2. I would like to know God's will for my life in the following area:
   a. family problems
   b. political issues
   c. life planning
   d. ethical questions

DAILY NEEDS: *"Give us today our daily bread."* I have confidence to ask that today's needs will be provided.

3. How would praying "just for today" change my petitions?
   a. no change
   b. change the quantity of my petitions
   c. change what I ask for
   d. change how often I pray
   e. make me more specific

RELATIONAL HEALING: *"Forgive us our debts, as we also have forgiven our debtors."* In my prayer time, I ask for and experience God's forgiveness. I consciously recall the relationships where I have been hurt or have hurt others and ask for forgiveness.

4. What is my typical method for responding to those who hurt me?
   a. hold a grudge/seek revenge
   b. talk it out
   c. get angry and blow up
   d. forget it

STRENGTH FOR THE SPIRITUAL BATTLE: *"And lead us not into temptation, but deliver us from the evil one."* In my prayer time, I allow God to speak to me about the areas where I am struggling or treading on dangerous ground. I express dependence upon God for the ability to resist temptation.

5. I experience yielding to temptation somewhere on this scale:
THE DEVIL MADE   1   2   3   4   5   6   7   8   9   10   I WALKED INTO IT
ME DO IT   WITH BOTH EYES OPEN

MY OWN LIFE/20 Minutes.

How balanced are you in your prayer life, based on the model in the Lord's prayer of the five elements of prayer? Take the first element (Adoration of God) and ask everyone in your group to respond by using one of the Options below. Then, go around again on the second element (Longing for His Reign), etc., until you have gone through all five elements.

OPTION 1
1. This is *difficult* for me because:
   a. I have trouble believing God cares about this
   b. I feel God is powerless to change this
   c. I struggle with the cooperation I need to give in this prayer
   d. I can't picture the end goal of this
   e. I want to take the credit for success in this area

OPTION 2
2. This prayer element is *easy* for me because:
   a. God's blessing has already been so real in my life
   b. I recognize only God can help me here
   c. I am ready to go where God sends me
   d. I know God has my best good at heart, despite the present circumstances

that relate to the attitudes expressed in 5:3-11? When used properly, what is the value of religious discipline? **3.** What bad habits have you picked up in prayer? What do you want to do to grow out of this habit?

OPEN: 1. When you were a teenager, what did your parents think of your clothes: Weird? Indecent? Tattered? **2.** For each group member, guess where (Saks Fifth Avenue, Sears, garage sale, etc.) he or she buys most of their clothes. Who is the best guesser?

DIG: 1. What alternatives does Jesus propose with respect to treasures (vv.19-21), bodily conditions (vv.22-23) and masters (v.24)? **2.** What is the link between treasure and heart? Heart and eye? Eye and body? Master and money? How does your choice of treasure, master, and sight (vv.19-24) affect your attitude toward life (vv.25-27)? **3.** What does God's care for the birds and lilies teach you? How does the work ethic fit into this passage? How does faith fit in?

REFLECT: 1. Considering this past week, is your "bank" on earth or in heaven? What do you want to do to change accounts? Who has been the boss lately? Why? **2.** Why pray when you can worry? What causes you the most worry? What are the signs that indicate you are worrying too much? **3.** What do you do to counteract anxiety in order to concentrate on the kingdom?

OPEN: 1. Are you more likely to trust until proven wrong, or distrust until a person proves him/herself? **2.** When you're lost, are you more likely to stop and ask directions, or drive around until you find your way?

DIG: 1. This chapter continues to reveal the attitudes and actions

Fasting

[16]"When you fast, do not look somber as the hypocrites do, for they disfigure their faces to show men they are fasting. I tell you the truth, they have received their reward in full. [17]But when you fast, put oil on your head and wash your face, [18]so that it will not be obvious to men that you are fasting, but only to your Father, who is unseen; and your Father, who sees what is done in secret, will reward you.

Treasures in Heaven

[19]"Do not store up for yourselves treasures on earth, where moth and rust destroy, and where thieves break in and steal. [20]But store up for yourselves treasures in heaven, where moth and rust do not destroy, and where thieves do not break in and steal. [21]For where your treasure is, there your heart will be also.

[22]"The eye is the lamp of the body. If your eyes are good, your whole body will be full of light. [23]But if your eyes are bad, your whole body will be full of darkness. If then the light within you is darkness, how great is that darkness!

[24]"No one can serve two masters. Either he will hate the one and love the other, or he will be devoted to the one and despise the other. You cannot serve both God and Money.

Do Not Worry

[25]"Therefore I tell you, do not worry about your life, what you will eat or drink; or about your body, what you will wear. Is not life more important than food, and the body more important than clothes? [26]Look at the birds of the air; they do not sow or reap or store away in barns, and yet your heavenly Father feeds them. Are you not much more valuable than they? [27]Who of you by worrying can add a single hour to his life[d]?

[28]"And why do you worry about clothes? See how the lilies of the field grow. They do not labor or spin. [29]Yet I tell you that not even Solomon in all his splendor was dressed like one of these. [30]If that is how God clothes the grass of the field, which is here today and tomorrow is thrown into the fire, will he not much more clothe you, O you of little faith? [31]So do not worry, saying, 'What shall we eat?' or 'What shall we drink?' or 'What shall we wear?' [32]For the pagans run after all these things, and your heavenly Father knows that you need them. [33]But seek first his kingdom and his righteousness, and all these things will be given to you as well. [34]Therefore do not worry about tomorrow, for tomorrow will worry about itself. Each day has enough trouble of its own.

Judging Others

7 "Do not judge, or you too will be judged. [2]For in the same way you judge others, you will be judged, and with the measure you use, it will be measured to you.

[3]"Why do you look at the speck of sawdust in your brother's eye and pay no attention to the plank in your own eye? [4]How can you say to your brother, 'Let me take the speck out of your

---

[d]27 Or *single cubit to his height*

LOOKING INTO THE SCRIPTURE/15 Minutes.

1. If you could have three wishes, which three would you choose from the list below:
   - ☐ Win the lottery: Never have to work again.
   - ☐ Secure job: Lifetime guarantee with benefits.
   - ☐ Stress-free life: No pain. No struggle. No tension.
   - ☐ Close family: No hassles. Lots of love and support.
   - ☐ Good health: Long life full of vigor and vitality.
   - ☐ One deep abiding friendship: Someone who will stick forever.
   - ☐ Happiness: A life full of joy and surprises.
   - ☐ Success: Fame and recognition in your chosen field.
   - ☐ Direction: To know what you want to do with your life.
   - ☐ Strong, spiritual faith: Deep, satisfying relationship with God.

2. Read Matthew 6:25-34. What does this mean? "Do not worry about your life . . ."
   a. everything will be okay
   b. don't sweat the small stuff
   c. God will bail you out
   d. get out of the fast lane
   e. get your act together

3. "But seek first his kingdom. . . ." What does this mean?
   a. get rid of your Porsche
   b. put God first and keep your Porsche
   c. check it out with God first
   d. Volkswagen buyers are smarter

4. What is Jesus saying here? "Therefore, do not worry about tomorrow. . . ."
   a. don't plan ahead
   b. plan ahead so you don't worry
   c. live for today
   d. take it as it comes
   e. trust God with things you can't control

5. What is the spiritual principle of this passage?
   a. slow down and live longer
   b. if you can't take the heat, get out of the kitchen
   c. Christians never have problems
   d. if it causes worry, check it out
   e. relax. God is in control

MY OWN STORY/25 Minutes.

1. Code the list of concerns below with these symbols in the margin.
   P=My parent's biggest concern
   −5=My biggest concern 5 years ago
   +5=My biggest concern 5 years from now

   X=Something I can do nothing about
   †=Something I can give to God and forget about
   ★=My biggest concern right now

   _____ Children: Doing OK in school

   _____ Parents: Getting old

   _____ Job: Finding or losing it

   _____ Money: Not having enough

   _____ Advancement: Getting ahead

   _____ Older children: Not making it

   _____ Transition: Starting over

   _____ Midlife: Failing my expectations

   _____ Health: Can't work/pay bills

   _____ Retirement: Feeling useless

   _____ Future: Being left alone

   _____ Accidents: Loved one getting hurt

2. If you were to take seriously the Scripture passage, how would it effect your list above?
   a. it would change everything
   b. it would change a few things
   c. it would change the way I view things
   d. it wouldn't change a thing

3. How do you feel after taking this personal inventory?
   a. relieved
   b. angry, because these concerns do not go away
   c. frustrated, because I know I should not be this way
   d. I'll have to think about this

kingdom people are to have. In Jesus' day, who were the "pigs" and "dogs"? What are the "pearls"? What is the difference between the type of judgment Jesus forbids (vv.1-2) and the implied evaluation required (v.6)? **2.** What is Jesus stressing about God in verses 7-11? How is this teaching to encourage his disciples? What is the guiding principle of prayer here? **3.** How does the righteousness described in verse 12 differ from that of the Pharisees? What is the connection between verse 12 and verses 1-5? **4.** What is the point of the two gates, roads, destinies, and crowds? How might verse 12 define what Jesus means by the "narrow gate"? Why is that road less traveled? **5.** How do the warnings in verses 15-20 relate to these gates? What are some of the "good fruits" Jesus is looking for? Is evaluating a person's fruit contradicting the mandate not to judge (v.1)? Why? **6.** What was the fault of those ultimately banished as "evildoers"? If the ability to prophesy, drive out demons, and perform miracles is not what Jesus means by doing the will of the Father, what is it? **7.** How do the similarities and differences between the two house builders reflect the people who heard Jesus? What kind of commitment is Jesus calling for here? What is the alternative? **8.** How would you sum up the attitudes Jesus is encouraging in this chapter? Why are these required for "kingdom people"?

REFLECT: 1. Considering the sermon as a whole, is your foundation on solid rock? Or on sand, but with a nice view? What would you have to tear down in order to shore up that foundation? How do you need others to help you in the process? **2.** At this point in your life, is your pressing need to learn more or to practice what you have already learned? Why? How would you like the group to pray for you to that end? **3.** In light of this section's seriousness, what hope do verses 7-9 give you? How about 5:3? What attribute of "kingdom people" will you ask for?

eye,' when all the time there is a plank in your own eye? ⁵You hypocrite, first take the plank out of your own eye, and then you will see clearly to remove the speck from your brother's eye.

⁶"Do not give dogs what is sacred; do not throw your pearls to pigs. If you do, they may trample them under their feet, and then turn and tear you to pieces.

Ask, Seek, Knock

⁷"Ask and it will be given to you; seek and you will find; knock and the door will be opened to you. ⁸For everyone who asks receives; he who seeks finds; and to him who knocks, the door will be opened.

⁹"Which of you, if his son asks for bread, will give him a stone? ¹⁰Or if he asks for a fish, will give him a snake? ¹¹If you, then, though you are evil, know how to give good gifts to your children, how much more will your Father in heaven give good gifts to those who ask him! ¹²So in everything, do to others what you would have them do to you, for this sums up the Law and the Prophets.

The Narrow and Wide Gates

¹³"Enter through the narrow gate. For wide is the gate and broad is the road that leads to destruction, and many enter through it. ¹⁴But small is the gate and narrow the road that leads to life, and only a few find it.

A Tree and Its Fruit

¹⁵"Watch out for false prophets. They come to you in sheep's clothing, but inwardly they are ferocious wolves. ¹⁶By their fruit you will recognize them. Do people pick grapes from thornbushes, or figs from thistles? ¹⁷Likewise every good tree bears good fruit, but a bad tree bears bad fruit. ¹⁸A good tree cannot bear bad fruit, and a bad tree cannot bear good fruit. ¹⁹Every tree that does not bear good fruit is cut down and thrown into the fire. ²⁰Thus, by their fruit you will recognize them.

²¹"Not everyone who says to me, 'Lord, Lord,' will enter the kingdom of heaven, but only he who does the will of my Father who is in heaven. ²²Many will say to me on that day, 'Lord, Lord, did we not prophesy in your name, and in your name drive out demons and perform many miracles?' ²³Then I will tell them plainly, 'I never knew you. Away from me, you evildoers!'

The Wise and Foolish Builders

²⁴"Therefore everyone who hears these words of mine and puts them into practice is like a wise man who built his house on the rock. ²⁵The rain came down, the streams rose, and the winds blew and beat against that house; yet it did not fall, because it had its foundation on the rock. ²⁶But everyone who hears these words of mine and does not put them into practice is like a foolish man who built his house on sand. ²⁷The rain came down, the streams rose, and the winds blew and beat against that house, and it fell with a great crash."

LOOKING INTO THE SCRIPTURE/20 Minutes. Read Matthew 7:7-12 and discuss.

1. My initial reaction to these promises is:
   a. it's too good to be true
   b. there must be a catch somewhere
   c. God must be crazy to give a blank check
   d. if it's really true, WOW!

2. What does this mean? "Ask and it will be given to you; seek and you will find; knock and the door will be opened to you."
   a. God is waiting for us
   b. you get what you ask for
   c. you have to persevere with God
   d. here's a promise you can't refuse

3. What is the point in the two questions about bread and fish?
   a. God knows best
   b. God has our best interest in mind
   c. God always answers but not always the way we want
   d. God wants to give anything we ask

4. What is God promising to give us?
   a. all the bread and fish we need
   b. whatever we ask in all cases
   c. whatever we need, but he decides
   d. what is best for us

5. What slogan or bumper sticker comes the farthest from the Golden Rule (v. 12)?
   a. I'm easy to get along with as long as you do it my way
   b. If you don't like the way I drive, get off the sidewalk
   c. Treat others like dirt and you'll be the one to get hurt
   d. Who said you can't have it all?
   e. Go ahead. Make my day.
   f. _____

6. What is the Golden Rule really saying?
   a. look out for number 2
   b. never think of yourself
   c. if you love yourself, you will also love others
   d. put yourself in their shoes
   e. be a doormat for God

MY OWN STORY/25 Minutes.

1. If it were my house instead of Dorothy's, my door to the land of Oz would open to reveal:
   a. heaven itself
   b. Oz without the wicked witch
   c. unlimited opportunity for advancement
   d. a yellow brick road with no detours, dead ends, or booby-traps

2. When it comes to prayer, what do you need to do?
   a. find out what I want to pray for
   b. separate my wants from God's desires
   c. separate the "urgent" from the "important"
   d. learn how to pray

3. How do you think of prayer?
   a. enjoying God's presence
   b. getting my marching orders
   c. tapping into God's resources
   d. sitting down for a feast with God
   e. bringing my needs to God

4. When do you get serious about prayer?
   a. when I'm in trouble
   b. when someone I love gets sick
   c. on special occasions
   d. hardly ever
   e. when I am at a crossroads

5. If you were to take God seriously and ask him for one thing now, what would it be?
   a. better relationships at home
   b. to know what he wants me to do
   c. to show me how to cope with where I am
   d. to get me out of this situation
   e. to give me peace of mind

6. What would it take from you for God to answer this prayer?
   a. showing a little patience
   b. taking time off to think through the situation
   c. dealing with a sour relationship
   d. redoubling my efforts
   e. having complete faith that God is at work

7. How would you describe your openness to God right now? Put a dot on the line somewhere between the two extremes.

I AM KNOCKING ON GOD'S
DOOR RIGHT NOW _____

I'M AT GOD'S DOOR BUT I'M
_____ AFRAID TO KNOCK

OPEN: **1.** Would you be more likely to stand in line all night to get tickets to see the Super Bowl, a rock band, or Mother Teresa? **2.** How do you deal with interruptions when you are very busy?

DIG: **1.** What did it mean to be a leper: Physically? Socially? Spiritually? What is significant about Jesus' touch? Why would Jesus want the cleansing to be certified by the priests? What would that imply to the priests about Jesus? **2.** What was the role and citizenship of a centurion? Why is Jesus' offer to go to his house so remarkable? What does it show about Jesus? **3.** What does the centurion's comment (vv.8-9) show about his view of Jesus? Why is this so important to Jesus? **4.** Who are the "many" (vv.11-12)? Who are the subjects of the kingdom? Why is Jesus sharing this with a Jewish audience? **5.** As Peter, what would you think as you watched the scene in verses 14-17? **6.** Given the larger context of Isaiah 53, how do these healings demonstrate what Jesus will do with sin?

REFLECT: **1.** Which character are you most like: The leper—"I hope God will help me, but I'm not sure"? The centurion—"I *know* God can meet my need"? Peter's mother-in-law—"I didn't expect to get well *this* fast"? Why? **2.** What hope do these stories give you as you think of the "disease" of sin in your life? **3.** Both the leper and the centurion were outcasts from the Jews' perspective. Who are the "outcasts" in your community? How do these stories model the way you might relate to them?

²⁸When Jesus had finished saying these things, the crowds were amazed at his teaching, ²⁹because he taught as one who had authority, and not as their teachers of the law.

The Man With Leprosy

8 When he came down from the mountainside, large crowds followed him. ²A man with leprosy*ᵉ* came and knelt before him and said, "Lord, if you are willing, you can make me clean."

³Jesus reached out his hand and touched the man. "I am willing," he said. "Be clean!" Immediately he was cured*ᶠ* of his leprosy. ⁴Then Jesus said to him, "See that you don't tell anyone. But go, show yourself to the priest and offer the gift Moses commanded, as a testimony to them."

The Faith of the Centurion

⁵When Jesus had entered Capernaum, a centurion came to him, asking for help. ⁶"Lord," he said, "my servant lies at home paralyzed and in terrible suffering."

⁷Jesus said to him, "I will go and heal him."

⁸The centurion replied, "Lord, I do not deserve to have you come under my roof. But just say the word, and my servant will be healed. ⁹For I myself am a man under authority, with soldiers under me. I tell this one, 'Go,' and he goes; and that one, 'Come,' and he comes. I say to my servant, 'Do this,' and he does it."

¹⁰When Jesus heard this, he was astonished and said to those following him, "I tell you the truth, I have not found anyone in Israel with such great faith. ¹¹I say to you that many will come from the east and the west, and will take their places at the feast with Abraham, Isaac and Jacob in the kingdom of heaven. ¹²But the subjects of the kingdom will be thrown outside, into the darkness, where there will be weeping and gnashing of teeth."

¹³Then Jesus said to the centurion, "Go! It will be done just as you believed it would." And his servant was healed at that very hour.

Jesus Heals Many

¹⁴When Jesus came into Peter's house, he saw Peter's mother-in-law lying in bed with a fever. ¹⁵He touched her hand and the fever left her, and she got up and began to wait on him.

¹⁶When evening came, many who were demon-possessed were brought to him, and he drove out the spirits with a word and healed all the sick. ¹⁷This was to fulfill what was spoken through the prophet Isaiah:

"He took up our infirmities
and carried our diseases."*ᵍ*

ᵉ2 The Greek word was used for various diseases affecting the skin—not necessarily leprosy.   *ƒ3* Greek *made clean*   *ᵍ17* Isaiah 53:4

The Cost of Following Jesus

¹⁸When Jesus saw the crowd around him, he gave orders to cross to the other side of the lake. ¹⁹Then a teacher of the law came to him and said, "Teacher, I will follow you wherever you go."

²⁰Jesus replied, "Foxes have holes and birds of the air have nests, but the Son of Man has no place to lay his head."

²¹Another disciple said to him, "Lord, first let me go and bury my father."

²²But Jesus told him, "Follow me, and let the dead bury their own dead."

Jesus Calms the Storm

²³Then he got into the boat and his disciples followed him. ²⁴Without warning, a furious storm came up on the lake, so that the waves swept over the boat. But Jesus was sleeping. ²⁵The disciples went and woke him, saying, "Lord, save us! We're going to drown!"

²⁶He replied, "You of little faith, why are you so afraid?" Then he got up and rebuked the winds and the waves, and it was completely calm.

²⁷The men were amazed and asked, "What kind of man is this? Even the winds and the waves obey him!"

The Healing of Two Demon-possessed Men

²⁸When he arrived at the other side in the region of the Gadarenes,ʰ two demon-possessed men coming from the tombs met him. They were so violent that no one could pass that way. ²⁹"What do you want with us, Son of God?" they shouted. "Have you come here to torture us before the appointed time?"

³⁰Some distance from them a large herd of pigs was feeding. ³¹The demons begged Jesus, "If you drive us out, send us into the herd of pigs."

³²He said to them, "Go!" So they came out and went into the pigs, and the whole herd rushed down the steep bank into the lake and died in the water. ³³Those tending the pigs ran off, went into the town and reported all this, including what had happened to the demon-possessed men. ³⁴Then the whole town went out to meet Jesus. And when they saw him, they pleaded with him to leave their region.

Jesus Heals a Paralytic

9 Jesus stepped into a boat, crossed over and came to his own town. ²Some men brought to him a paralytic, lying on a mat. When Jesus saw their faith, he said to the paralytic, "Take heart, son; your sins are forgiven."

³At this, some of the teachers of the law said to themselves, "This fellow is blaspheming!"

⁴Knowing their thoughts, Jesus said, "Why do you entertain evil thoughts in your hearts? ⁵Which is easier: to say, 'Your sins

ʰ28 Some manuscripts *Gergesenes*; others *Gerasenes*

OPEN: What is the best excuse you've heard lately for not getting homework done?

DIG: Why did Jesus respond like this? What do his responses teach about discipleship?

REFLECT: How did you first learn the cost of following Jesus? How is that costing you now?

OPEN: When you were a kid, where did you go or hide in the house when there was a bad storm?

DIG: **1.** What are the disciples feeling as this storm begins? As it whips up? When Jesus silences it? **2.** What was Jesus teaching them by sleeping through the storm? By rebuking it? **3.** How might the disciples feel as they continue across the lake? When they meet these men? **4.** Who's afraid of whom in this story? Why?

REFLECT: **1.** When circumstantial clouds darken your life, do you sense the Son still shining? Or does he seem asleep? Why might it feel that way? **2.** What do you learn about Jesus from these stories? How does that relate to the times you face evil? **3.** What "storms" or "demons" seem too much for you to handle now?

OPEN: Which is more "home" to you: (a) The place you grew up? (b) Where you live now? (c) Other: ____? What makes one place more like "home sweet home"?

DIG: **1.** What did the people expect Jesus to do? Why did Jesus forgive the man's sins instead? **2.** Why would that be considered blasphemy? **3.** How did Jesus demonstrate that he had indeed forgiven the man's sin? How did the people respond? **4.** What is surprising about Jesus' choice of

Matthew? Why? What is the irony in Jesus' response to the Pharisees' criticism? **5.** How does the story of Matthew relate to that of the paralytic?

REFLECT: **1.** If Jesus really does forgive sin, why do many Christians struggle so with their forgiveness? **2.** What would be different about your life if Jesus had come to call "righteous" people instead of "sinners"? **3.** Who are the "Matthews" around you?

___

OPEN: As a kid, did you outgrow your clothes or wear them out?

DIG: **1.** Why don't Jesus' disciples fast at this point? When will they? **2.** How do unshrunk cloth and new wine relate to fasting, the bridegroom, and the kingdom?

REFLECT: Where is the "new wine" in your life? What are the "old wineskins"?

___

OPEN: What type of person are you when you wake up: (a) Rarin' to go when your feet hit the floor? (b) Give me a coffee, a shower, and avoid me? (c) Like Garfield?

DIG: **1.** What feelings prompted the ruler to approach Jesus? How about the woman? If you were the woman, how would you feel just before you reached out to touch Jesus? Just afterward? How was her faith evident? **2.** Compare the ruler and the woman. What does Jesus' response to both show about the kingdom? **3.** What part does faith play in these healings? Why is that stressed now?

REFLECT: The ruler and the woman were desperate. What is the relationship between desperateness and faith? What does this story encourage you to do as you face desperate situations?

are forgiven,' or to say, 'Get up and walk'? [6]But so that you may know that the Son of Man has authority on earth to forgive sins. . . ." Then he said to the paralytic, "Get up, take your mat and go home." [7]And the man got up and went home. [8]When the crowd saw this, they were filled with awe; and they praised God, who had given such authority to men.

The Calling of Matthew

[9]As Jesus went on from there, he saw a man named Matthew sitting at the tax collector's booth. "Follow me," he told him, and Matthew got up and followed him.

[10]While Jesus was having dinner at Matthew's house, many tax collectors and "sinners" came and ate with him and his disciples. [11]When the Pharisees saw this, they asked his disciples, "Why does your teacher eat with tax collectors and 'sinners'?"

[12]On hearing this, Jesus said, "It is not the healthy who need a doctor, but the sick. [13]But go and learn what this means: 'I desire mercy, not sacrifice.'[i] For I have not come to call the righteous, but sinners."

Jesus Questioned About Fasting

[14]Then John's disciples came and asked him, "How is it that we and the Pharisees fast, but your disciples do not fast?"

[15]Jesus answered, "How can the guests of the bridegroom mourn while he is with them? The time will come when the bridegroom will be taken from them; then they will fast.

[16]"No one sews a patch of unshrunk cloth on an old garment, for the patch will pull away from the garment, making the tear worse. [17]Neither do men pour new wine into old wineskins. If they do, the skins will burst, the wine will run out and the wineskins will be ruined. No, they pour new wine into new wineskins, and both are preserved."

A Dead Girl and a Sick Woman

[18]While he was saying this, a ruler came and knelt before him and said, "My daughter has just died. But come and put your hand on her, and she will live." [19]Jesus got up and went with him, and so did his disciples.

[20]Just then a woman who had been subject to bleeding for twelve years came up behind him and touched the edge of his cloak. [21]She said to herself, "If I only touch his cloak, I will be healed."

[22]Jesus turned and saw her. "Take heart, daughter," he said, "your faith has healed you." And the woman was healed from that moment.

[23]When Jesus entered the ruler's house and saw the flute players and the noisy crowd, [24]he said, "Go away. The girl is not dead but asleep." But they laughed at him. [25]After the crowd had been put outside, he went in and took the girl by the hand, and she got up. [26]News of this spread through all that region.

[i]13 Hosea 6:6

Jesus Heals the Blind and Mute

²⁷As Jesus went on from there, two blind men followed him, calling out, "Have mercy on us, Son of David!"

²⁸When he had gone indoors, the blind men came to him, and he asked them, "Do you believe that I am able to do this?"

"Yes, Lord," they replied.

²⁹Then he touched their eyes and said, "According to your faith will it be done to you"; ³⁰and their sight was restored. Jesus warned them sternly, "See that no one knows about this." ³¹But they went out and spread the news about him all over that region.

³²While they were going out, a man who was demon-possessed and could not talk was brought to Jesus. ³³And when the demon was driven out, the man who had been mute spoke. The crowd was amazed and said, "Nothing like this has ever been seen in Israel."

³⁴But the Pharisees said, "It is by the prince of demons that he drives out demons."

The Workers Are Few

³⁵Jesus went through all the towns and villages, teaching in their synagogues, preaching the good news of the kingdom and healing every disease and sickness. ³⁶When he saw the crowds, he had compassion on them, because they were harassed and helpless, like sheep without a shepherd. ³⁷Then he said to his disciples, "The harvest is plentiful but the workers are few. ³⁸Ask the Lord of the harvest, therefore, to send out workers into his harvest field."

Jesus Sends Out the Twelve

10 He called his twelve disciples to him and gave them authority to drive out evil*ʲ* spirits and to heal every disease and sickness.

²These are the names of the twelve apostles: first, Simon (who is called Peter) and his brother Andrew; James son of Zebedee, and his brother John; ³Philip and Bartholomew; Thomas and Matthew the tax collector; James son of Alphaeus, and Thaddaeus; ⁴Simon the Zealot and Judas Iscariot, who betrayed him.

⁵These twelve Jesus sent out with the following instructions: "Do not go among the Gentiles or enter any town of the Samaritans. ⁶Go rather to the lost sheep of Israel. ⁷As you go, preach this message: 'The kingdom of heaven is near.' ⁸Heal the sick, raise the dead, cleanse those who have leprosy,*ᵏ* drive out demons. Freely you have received, freely give. ⁹Do not take along any gold or silver or copper in your belts; ¹⁰take no bag for the journey, or extra tunic, or sandals or a staff; for the worker is worth his keep.

¹¹"Whatever town or village you enter, search for some worthy person there and stay at his house until you leave. ¹²As you enter the home, give it your greeting. ¹³If the home is deserving, let your peace rest on it; if it is not, let your peace

---

ʲ1 Greek unclean   *ᵏ8 The Greek word was used for various diseases affecting the skin—not necessarily leprosy.*

OPEN: Would you describe yourself as gullible or cynical? Why?

DIG: 1. What is the meaning of the title the blind men use for Jesus? How do they show faith? Why does Jesus want them to keep quiet? **2.** How did the crowds react to Jesus' power? How did the Pharisees react? Why the difference? **3.** How do Jesus' actions in verses 35-36 prove the Pharisees wrong? **4.** What does Jesus see in the crowds? In the harvest field? What do the various phrases in verse 38 mean?

REFLECT: 1. In what ways might you still be spiritually "blind" or "dumb"? How can Jesus heal or perfect your sight and speech? **2.** From chapter 9, what have you learned about the kingdom? How do these stories demonstrate what it means to labor in the field where God has placed you?

OPEN: 1. What is the longest you have hiked, or hitch-hiked your way across country? **2.** What kind of person would you want in your expedition party (to complement your weakness) the next time you embark on a "great ad-venture"? **3.** Who was one of the more unusual house guests you or your family ever entertained?

DIG: 1. What did Jesus do before sending out his men? How will the disciples' activities here compare with what Jesus had been doing in chapters 8-9? With what he has just seen (9:36)? With what he has prayed (9:38)? **2.** Which apostles have already been introduced in this book? What do you know about them (relations, hometown, occupations, etc.)? **3.** The "zealots" were guerrilla fighters committed to the freedom of the Jews from Rome. Why would Jesus choose one of them to be on the same team with Matthew, a tax collector who had worked with Rome? What discussions do you imagine they may have had? **4.** What limits did Jesus put on their ministry (v.5)? Why? **5.** What was to be their message? What

43

were they to do? **6.** Why do you think that Jesus told them to take nothing more than the clothes on their backs? **7.** Why do you think their mission excluded Samaritans and Gentiles? Do you think the disciples were disappointed that these groups were excluded? Why? **8.** What was the basic point of Jesus' preparation speech to the disciples? What problems would they (and future disciples) face? How were they to respond to each problem? **9.** What does it mean to be "like sheep among wolves," "shrewd as snakes," "innocent as doves" (v.16)? **10.** Who would persecute them? Why? In times of persecution, what could they expect from God? **11.** How might Christ's truth divide a family? What kind of commitment does Jesus call for in verses 37-39? **12.** How were the disciples to understand their reception (vv.40-42)? What confirming authority does Jesus bestow upon his disciples at the end of his discourse (v.40), as well as at the beginning (v.1)?

REFLECT: 1. If Jesus called you to participate in a ministry, what do you think he would say to you in light of your own personality and needs? **2.** How has Christ's teaching united the members of your family? How has it divided them? **3.** Under what circumstances do you find it most difficult to talk about your faith? **4.** What does the paradox in verse 39 mean to you? How can you lose yourself for Christ this week? **5.** How can you best represent to your neighbors that the kingdom of heaven is near? **6.** What, besides dust on your feet, will stick with you from this passage?

return to you. [14]If anyone will not welcome you or listen to your words, shake the dust off your feet when you leave that home or town. [15]I tell you the truth, it will be more bearable for Sodom and Gomorrah on the day of judgment than for that town. [16]I am sending you out like sheep among wolves. Therefore be as shrewd as snakes and as innocent as doves.

[17]"Be on your guard against men; they will hand you over to the local councils and flog you in their synagogues. [18]On my account you will be brought before governors and kings as witnesses to them and to the Gentiles. [19]But when they arrest you, do not worry about what to say or how to say it. At that time you will be given what to say, [20]for it will not be you speaking, but the Spirit of your Father speaking through you.

[21]"Brother will betray brother to death, and a father his child; children will rebel against their parents and have them put to death. [22]All men will hate you because of me, but he who stands firm to the end will be saved. [23]When you are persecuted in one place, flee to another. I tell you the truth, you will not finish going through the cities of Israel before the Son of Man comes.

[24]"A student is not above his teacher, nor a servant above his master. [25]It is enough for the student to be like his teacher, and the servant like his master. If the head of the house has been called Beelzebub,[l] how much more the members of his household!

[26]"So do not be afraid of them. There is nothing concealed that will not be disclosed, or hidden that will not be made known. [27]What I tell you in the dark, speak in the daylight; what is whispered in your ear, proclaim from the roofs. [28]Do not be afraid of those who kill the body but cannot kill the soul. Rather, be afraid of the One who can destroy both soul and body in hell. [29]Are not two sparrows sold for a penny[m]? Yet not one of them will fall to the ground apart from the will of your Father. [30]And even the very hairs of your head are all numbered. [31]So don't be afraid; you are worth more than many sparrows.

[32]"Whoever acknowledges me before men, I will also acknowledge him before my Father in heaven. [33]But whoever disowns me before men, I will disown him before my Father in heaven.

[34]"Do not suppose that I have come to bring peace to the earth. I did not come to bring peace, but a sword. [35]For I have come to turn

> " 'a man against his father,
> a daughter against her mother,
> a daughter-in-law against her mother-in-law—
> [36] a man's enemies will be the members of his own household.'[n]

[37]"Anyone who loves his father or mother more than me is not worthy of me; anyone who loves his son or daughter more than me is not worthy of me; [38]and anyone who does not take his cross and follow me is not worthy of me. [39]Whoever finds his life will lose it, and whoever loses his life for my sake will find it.

---

[l]25 Greek *Beezeboul* or *Beelzeboul*   [m]29 Greek *an assarion*   [n]36 Micah 7:6

⁴⁰"He who receives you receives me, and he who receives me receives the one who sent me. ⁴¹Anyone who receives a prophet because he is a prophet will receive a prophet's reward, and anyone who receives a righteous man because he is a righteous man will receive a righteous man's reward. ⁴²And if anyone gives even a cup of cold water to one of these little ones because he is my disciple, I tell you the truth, he will certainly not lose his reward."

Jesus and John the Baptist

11 After Jesus had finished instructing his twelve disciples, he went on from there to teach and preach in the towns of Galilee. °

²When John heard in prison what Christ was doing, he sent his disciples ³to ask him, "Are you the one who was to come, or should we expect someone else?"

⁴Jesus replied, "Go back and report to John what you hear and see: ⁵The blind receive sight, the lame walk, those who have leprosy ᵖ are cured, the deaf hear, the dead are raised, and the good news is preached to the poor. ⁶Blessed is the man who does not fall away on account of me."

⁷As John's disciples were leaving, Jesus began to speak to the crowd about John: "What did you go out into the desert to see? A reed swayed by the wind? ⁸If not, what did you go out to see? A man dressed in fine clothes? No, those who wear fine clothes are in kings' palaces. ⁹Then what did you go out to see? A prophet? Yes, I tell you, and more than a prophet. ¹⁰This is the one about whom it is written:

" 'I will send my messenger ahead of you,
who will prepare your way before you.' �q

¹¹I tell you the truth: Among those born of women there has not risen anyone greater than John the Baptist; yet he who is least in the kingdom of heaven is greater than he. ¹²From the days of John the Baptist until now, the kingdom of heaven has been forcefully advancing, and forceful men lay hold of it. ¹³For all the Prophets and the Law prophesied until John. ¹⁴And if you are willing to accept it, he is the Elijah who was to come. ¹⁵He who has ears, let him hear.

¹⁶"To what can I compare this generation? They are like children sitting in the marketplaces and calling out to others:

¹⁷" 'We played the flute for you,
and you did not dance;
we sang a dirge,
and you did not mourn.'

¹⁸For John came neither eating nor drinking, and they say, 'He has a demon.' ¹⁹The Son of Man came eating and drinking, and they say, 'Here is a glutton and a drunkard, a friend of tax collectors and "sinners." ' But wisdom is proved right by her actions."

OPEN: 1. (For the married:) When did you know that the person you married was "the one"? What tipped you off? (For the unmarried:) What is the sign you look for in a potential mate to tell you "this is the one"? **2.** When you "church shop," what three items are on the top of your list for your pastor?

DIG: 1. Having *instructed* his disciples in the nature of ministry (10:1-42), what does Jesus now do that *models* the same? What is significant about that? **2.** Who questions Jesus (v.2)? Where is John? How did he land in prison (see 14:1-5)? **3.** How might prison have raised doubts for John (v.3)? **4.** Does Jesus answer John more with promises or with evidence? Why? How might John, who knew the OT well, have interpreted Jesus' reply (see Isa 35:5-6; 61:1)? What encouragement does Jesus add for John in verse 6? **5.** How was John unlike a weak reed or a well-groomed politician? What does Jesus say about John? **6.** How does John fulfill OT prophecy (see Mal 3:1; 4:5-6)? In what way does he exhibit the faith of the OT? **7.** How is a NT believer greater than John (v.11; see 18:3-4)? **8.** How do the people respond to John? To Jesus? How are they like the children pictured here?

REFLECT: 1. What kinds of "prisons" tend to bring out doubts for you regarding Jesus? **2.** In those periods of discouragement and doubt, what most renews your courage and faith? **3.** In what specific way can you be an encourager to someone in church leadership? In your family? Among your friends?

°1 Greek *in their towns*   ᵖ5 The Greek word was used for various diseases affecting the skin—not necessarily leprosy.   �q10 Mal. 3:1

OPEN: What is your favorite city? Your least favorite? Why?

DIG: 1. What judgment does Jesus pass on each city mentioned? Why will their judgment be worse than that of the pagan cities of the OT? **2.** If the revelation of Jesus and his miracles is rejected, what is the judgment?

REFLECT: What is Jesus' point for you in this warning?

OPEN: What room in your home is the most burdensome to keep up? Which room is the most relaxing for you? Which do you spend more time at — cleaning up or relaxing?

DIG: 1. Why is the gospel hidden from the "wise and learned"? Who truly knows God? **2.** What does Jesus mean by taking up his "yoke"? By the "rest" he promises to those who do? Since a yoke unites two animals in common work, what does this imply about discipleship?

OPEN: As a child, what was Sunday dinner like? What do you like best about Sundays now? Least?

DIG: 1. Regarding the Sabbath, what is the point about David (see 1Sa 21:1-6)? About the priests (see Nu 28:9-10)? **2.** How had the Pharisees neglected the meaning of "I desire mercy, not sacrifice"? **3.** What does Jesus imply by his claim in verse 8? How do the Pharisees react? How is their question in verse 10 a trap for Jesus? **4.** What does Jesus say and do to show that he is the authoritative interpreter of the law? What does the Pharisees' response show?

REFLECT: 1. From this section, how important are your needs to God? How important are other people's needs to you? **2.** When have you fallen into the trap of "offering sacrifice" but "neglecting mercy"? How can you work to reverse that this week?

Woe on Unrepentant Cities

²⁰Then Jesus began to denounce the cities in which most of his miracles had been performed, because they did not repent. ²¹"Woe to you, Korazin! Woe to you, Bethsaida! If the miracles that were performed in you had been performed in Tyre and Sidon, they would have repented long ago in sackcloth and ashes. ²²But I tell you, it will be more bearable for Tyre and Sidon on the day of judgment than for you. ²³And you, Capernaum, will you be lifted up to the skies? No, you will go down to the depths.ʳ If the miracles that were performed in you had been performed in Sodom, it would have remained to this day. ²⁴But I tell you that it will be more bearable for Sodom on the day of judgment than for you."

Rest for the Weary

²⁵At that time Jesus said, "I praise you, Father, Lord of heaven and earth, because you have hidden these things from the wise and learned, and revealed them to little children. ²⁶Yes, Father, for this was your good pleasure.

²⁷"All things have been committed to me by my Father. No one knows the Son except the Father, and no one knows the Father except the Son and those to whom the Son chooses to reveal him.

²⁸"Come to me, all you who are weary and burdened, and I will give you rest. ²⁹Take my yoke upon you and learn from me, for I am gentle and humble in heart, and you will find rest for your souls. ³⁰For my yoke is easy and my burden is light."

Lord of the Sabbath

12 At that time Jesus went through the grainfields on the Sabbath. His disciples were hungry and began to pick some heads of grain and eat them. ²When the Pharisees saw this, they said to him, "Look! Your disciples are doing what is unlawful on the Sabbath."

³He answered, "Haven't you read what David did when he and his companions were hungry? ⁴He entered the house of God, and he and his companions ate the consecrated bread— which was not lawful for them to do, but only for the priests. ⁵Or haven't you read in the Law that on the Sabbath the priests in the temple desecrate the day and yet are innocent? ⁶I tell you that oneˢ greater than the temple is here. ⁷If you had known what these words mean, 'I desire mercy, not sacrifice,'ᵗ you would not have condemned the innocent. ⁸For the Son of Man is Lord of the Sabbath."

⁹Going on from that place, he went into their synagogue, ¹⁰and a man with a shriveled hand was there. Looking for a reason to accuse Jesus, they asked him, "Is it lawful to heal on the Sabbath?"

¹¹He said to them, "If any of you has a sheep and it falls into a pit on the Sabbath, will you not take hold of it and lift it out? ¹²How much more valuable is a man than a sheep! Therefore it is lawful to do good on the Sabbath."

ʳ23 Greek *Hades*   ˢ6 Or *something*; also in verses 41 and 42   ᵗ7 Hosea 6:6

¹³Then he said to the man, "Stretch out your hand." So he stretched it out and it was completely restored, just as sound as the other. ¹⁴But the Pharisees went out and plotted how they might kill Jesus.

God's Chosen Servant

¹⁵Aware of this, Jesus withdrew from that place. Many followed him, and he healed all their sick, ¹⁶warning them not to tell who he was. ¹⁷This was to fulfill what was spoken through the prophet Isaiah:

¹⁸"Here is my servant whom I have chosen,
  the one I love, in whom I delight;
I will put my Spirit on him,
  and he will proclaim justice to the nations.
¹⁹He will not quarrel or cry out;
  no one will hear his voice in the streets.
²⁰A bruised reed he will not break,
  and a smoldering wick he will not snuff out,
  till he leads justice to victory.
²¹ In his name the nations will put their hope." ᵘ

Jesus and Beelzebub

²²Then they brought him a demon-possessed man who was blind and mute, and Jesus healed him, so that he could both talk and see. ²³All the people were astonished and said, "Could this be the Son of David?"

²⁴But when the Pharisees heard this, they said, "It is only by Beelzebub, ᵛ the prince of demons, that this fellow drives out demons."

²⁵Jesus knew their thoughts and said to them, "Every kingdom divided against itself will be ruined, and every city or household divided against itself will not stand. ²⁶If Satan drives out Satan, he is divided against himself. How then can his kingdom stand? ²⁷And if I drive out demons by Beelzebub, by whom do your people drive them out? So then, they will be your judges. ²⁸But if I drive out demons by the Spirit of God, then the kingdom of God has come upon you.

²⁹"Or again, how can anyone enter a strong man's house and carry off his possessions unless he first ties up the strong man? Then he can rob his house.

³⁰"He who is not with me is against me, and he who does not gather with me scatters. ³¹And so I tell you, every sin and blasphemy will be forgiven men, but the blasphemy against the Spirit will not be forgiven. ³²Anyone who speaks a word against the Son of Man will be forgiven, but anyone who speaks against the Holy Spirit will not be forgiven, either in this age or in the age to come.

³³"Make a tree good and its fruit will be good, or make a tree bad and its fruit will be bad, for a tree is recognized by its fruit. ³⁴You brood of vipers, how can you who are evil say anything good? For out of the overflow of the heart the mouth speaks. ³⁵The good man brings good things out of the good stored up

OPEN: Where do you go when life gets too heavy for you? Why?

DIG: 1. In reacting to the Pharisees' hostility (12:14), how does Jesus fulfill prophecy? **2.** What does this say about Jesus' identity? **3.** How does Jesus treat the wounded and weak?

REFLECT: 1. How does Jesus' example encourage your self-restraint when people are hostile to you? **2.** In telling others about Jesus, what use of the OT do you make? **3.** What is one way Jesus has mended your life?

OPEN: In describing your conversational style, are you: (a) Loose lips sink ships? (b) A closed book? (c) Anything goes? (d) Nice and easy? or (e) Apples of gold in settings of silver?

DIG: 1. What were the two main reactions to the healing of the blind and mute man? Who did the people suppose Jesus to be? Who did the Pharisees suspect Jesus to be? Why are Jesus' miracles open to varied interpretations? **2.** What three defenses does Jesus give in answer to the Pharisees' accusations (vv.26,27,29)? By implication, what is Jesus saying about his inauguration of God's kingdom? Is neutrality to Jesus possible? Why or why not? **3.** What is meant by "blasphemy against the Spirit" (vv.31-32)? How have the Pharisees committed this sin? Since forgiveness must be asked for, why is it impossible for this one sin to be forgiven? **4.** What reason does Jesus give for the Pharisees' growing hostility (vv.34-37)?

REFLECT: What real difference does Jesus' power make in your daily struggles against evil? In your freedom to be honest to God? In your daily speech with others?

ᵘ21 Isaiah 42:1-4   ᵛ24 Greek *Beezeboul* or *Beelzeboul*; also in verse 27 in him, and the evil man brings evil things out of the evil stored up in him. ³⁶But I tell you that men will have to give account on the day of judgment for every careless word they have spoken. ³⁷For by your words you will be acquitted, and by your words you will be condemned."

The Sign of Jonah

³⁸Then some of the Pharisees and teachers of the law said to him, "Teacher, we want to see a miraculous sign from you."

³⁹He answered, "A wicked and adulterous generation asks for a miraculous sign! But none will be given it except the sign of the prophet Jonah. ⁴⁰For as Jonah was three days and three nights in the belly of a huge fish, so the Son of Man will be three days and three nights in the heart of the earth. ⁴¹The men of Nineveh will stand up at the judgment with this generation and condemn it; for they repented at the preaching of Jonah, and now one ʷ greater than Jonah is here. ⁴²The Queen of the South will rise at the judgment with this generation and condemn it; for she came from the ends of the earth to listen to Solomon's wisdom, and now one greater than Solomon is here.

⁴³"When an evil ˣ spirit comes out of a man, it goes through arid places seeking rest and does not find it. ⁴⁴Then it says, 'I will return to the house I left.' When it arrives, it finds the house unoccupied, swept clean and put in order. ⁴⁵Then it goes and takes with it seven other spirits more wicked than itself, and they go in and live there. And the final condition of that man is worse than the first. That is how it will be with this wicked generation."

Jesus' Mother and Brothers

⁴⁶While Jesus was still talking to the crowd, his mother and brothers stood outside, wanting to speak to him. ⁴⁷Someone told him, "Your mother and brothers are standing outside, wanting to speak to you." ʸ

⁴⁸He replied to him, "Who is my mother, and who are my brothers?" ⁴⁹Pointing to his disciples, he said, "Here are my mother and my brothers. ⁵⁰For whoever does the will of my Father in heaven is my brother and sister and mother."

The Parable of the Sower

13 That same day Jesus went out of the house and sat by the lake. ²Such large crowds gathered around him that he got into a boat and sat in it, while all the people stood on the shore. ³Then he told them many things in parables, saying: "A farmer went out to sow his seed. ⁴As he was scattering the seed, some fell along the path, and the birds came and ate it up. ⁵Some fell on rocky places, where it did not have much soil. It sprang up quickly, because the soil was shallow. ⁶But when the sun came up, the plants were scorched, and they withered because they had no root. ⁷Other seed fell among thorns, which grew up and choked the plants. ⁸Still other seed fell on good soil, where it

---

OPEN: 1. What bumper sticker or T-shirt design still brings a smile to your face when you think about it? **2.** What is one "pet peeve" that your parents or siblings have against you?

DIG: 1. Why do you think the Pharisees wanted to see a miracle? **2.** How does Jesus feel about "this generation"? Why? **3.** What is the "sign of Jonah"? How is Jesus greater than Jonah? Than Solomon? How might the Pharisees have interpreted this? **4.** How do the Ninevites and the Queen of the South condemn Jesus' generation? **5.** A person who is reformed but neglectful of God's presence is prey to even greater evil. How do Israel's leaders exemplify this principle? **6.** In light of the growing controversy, why might Jesus' mother and brothers be eager to speak with him (see Mk 3:20-21)?

REFLECT: 1. What does Jesus want from you, other than a heart "swept clean and put in order" (v.44)? **2.** From your life this week, would others see you as a "brother or sister" of Jesus, or a distant relative? Why?

OPEN: Regarding house plants, do you: (a) Talk and sing to them like friends? (b) Forget about them till their leaves fall off? (c) Just hope no one gives you one?

DIG: 1. Since both opposition and support for Jesus are growing, what is significant about the timing of these kingdom parables? **2.** What is a parable, anyway? **3.** What four types of soil did Jesus mention? What characterizes each? What happens to the seed in each kind of soil? **4.** What does Jesus' explanation of the parable (vv.18-23) reveal about the seed? About the various soils? The fruit? The farmer? **5.** How might the

---

ʷ41 Or *something*; also in verse 42   ˣ43 Greek *unclean*   ʸ47 Some manuscripts do not have verse 47.

produced a crop—a hundred, sixty or thirty times what was sown. [9]He who has ears, let him hear.''

[10]The disciples came to him and asked, ''Why do you speak to the people in parables?''

[11]He replied, ''The knowledge of the secrets of the kingdom of heaven has been given to you, but not to them. [12]Whoever has will be given more, and he will have an abundance. Whoever does not have, even what he has will be taken from him. [13]This is why I speak to them in parables:

"Though seeing, they do not see;
  though hearing, they do not hear or understand.

[14]In them is fulfilled the prophecy of Isaiah:

" 'You will be ever hearing but never understanding;
  you will be ever seeing but never perceiving.
[15]For this people's heart has become calloused;
  they hardly hear with their ears,
  and they have closed their eyes.
Otherwise they might see with their eyes,
  hear with their ears,
  understand with their hearts
and turn, and I would heal them.' [z]

[16]But blessed are your eyes because they see, and your ears because they hear. [17]For I tell you the truth, many prophets and righteous men longed to see what you see but did not see it, and to hear what you hear but did not hear it.

[18]''Listen then to what the parable of the sower means: [19]When anyone hears the message about the kingdom and does not understand it, the evil one comes and snatches away what was sown in his heart. This is the seed sown along the path. [20]The one who received the seed that fell on rocky places is the man who hears the word and at once receives it with joy. [21]But since he has no root, he lasts only a short time. When trouble or persecution comes because of the word, he quickly falls away. [22]The one who received the seed that fell among the thorns is the man who hears the word, but the worries of this life and the deceitfulness of wealth choke it, making it unfruitful. [23]But the one who received the seed that fell on good soil is the man who hears the word and understands it. He produces a crop, yielding a hundred, sixty or thirty times what was sown.''

The Parable of the Weeds

[24]Jesus told them another parable: ''The kingdom of heaven is like a man who sowed good seed in his field. [25]But while everyone was sleeping, his enemy came and sowed weeds among the wheat, and went away. [26]When the wheat sprouted and formed heads, then the weeds also appeared.

[27]''The owner's servants came to him and said, 'Sir, didn't you sow good seed in your field? Where then did the weeds come from?'

[28]'' 'An enemy did this,' he replied.

[z]*15* Isaiah 6:9,10

parable help the disciples understand what was happening in their ministry? **6.** Why do you think Jesus used parables as his teaching device? What do parables accomplish that simple and direct speech lacks? **7.** How does Jesus' challenge in verse 9 help explain verses 11-12? How does faith open you up to more and more spiritual insight? **8.** How does the quotation from Isaiah (vv.14-15) explain the difficulty of understanding parables (v.13)? **9.** In verses 16-17, Jesus gives a new beatitude. What have these disciples seen and heard that the prophets longed to see and hear? Are we included in this blessing, or was it only for the original disciples? Why do you think so?

REFLECT: 1. Can you see and hear Jesus at work in today's world? If so, how? **2.** How would you explain this parable to a bunch of city kids who don't know anything about sowing a field? What modern analogy would you use? **3.** Why do so many people (not just city kids) misunderstand the gospel? **4.** What deep "roots" help to prevent a believer from falling away? What gives you roots? **5.** What worries have potential to choke your growth in Christ? How can you free your life from these "thorns"? **6.** What "crop" does Jesus want believers to yield? What can you do to increase your "crop productivity"?

OPEN: 1. In your family, who liked to play practical jokes? Any one joke stand out? **2.** What childhood dream has become a reality for you (example—learned to play the piano, became a brain surgeon)? **3.** If you were designing a ride called *Hell* for a major amusement park, how would you make it unbelievably miserable or hellish?

DIG: 1. In this first parable (vv.24-30; also vv.36-43), who is the sower? What does the wheat represent? The weeds? The

49

enemy? The harvest? **2.** How does this parable relate to 7:15-20, which indicates is our responsibility in the church community regarding "wheat" and "weeds"? **3.** Why does this parable so puzzle the disciples? Why is patience and tolerance toward unbelievers difficult for them (and for us)? **4.** What does this passage teach about church purity? Divine patience? Human accountability? **5.** In the second set of parables (vv.31-33), what aspects of Jesus' ministry seem small? What is the promise if the small seed is sown? **6.** How does the kingdom of heaven become evident to others? **7.** What does the summary statement and prophecy here (vv.34-35) reveal about the way (and the reason) Jesus used parables?

REFLECT: 1. In what way can over-zealous judgment of the world and its evils harm our mission as believers? What is the harvest field like where God has placed you? **2.** Where (in your life and in your church) have you seen the "yeast message" or "mustard seed faith" (i.e., something small making a great impact)? **3.** What accountability are you now feeling for yourself? For others? To God? What are you "hearing" God call you to do as a result?

OPEN: 1. What needs sorting out in your garage or basement right now? What is likely to be found in storage: more trivia, trash, or treasure? **2.** With the proceeds from a garage sale or a moving sale, what worthy item would you buy (or have you bought)?

DIG: 1. What do the parables in verses 44-46 teach about the value of the kingdom? With what emotion and energy should it be pursued? **2.** What does the parable of the net teach about the

"The servants asked him, 'Do you want us to go and pull them up?'

²⁹"'No,' he answered, 'because while you are pulling the weeds, you may root up the wheat with them. ³⁰Let both grow together until the harvest. At that time I will tell the harvesters: First collect the weeds and tie them in bundles to be burned; then gather the wheat and bring it into my barn.'"

The Parables of the Mustard Seed and the Yeast

³¹He told them another parable: "The kingdom of heaven is like a mustard seed, which a man took and planted in his field. ³²Though it is the smallest of all your seeds, yet when it grows, it is the largest of garden plants and becomes a tree, so that the birds of the air come and perch in its branches."

³³He told them still another parable: "The kingdom of heaven is like yeast that a woman took and mixed into a large amount[a] of flour until it worked all through the dough."

³⁴Jesus spoke all these things to the crowd in parables; he did not say anything to them without using a parable. ³⁵So was fulfilled what was spoken through the prophet:

"I will open my mouth in parables,
I will utter things hidden since the creation of the world."[b]

The Parable of the Weeds Explained

³⁶Then he left the crowd and went into the house. His disciples came to him and said, "Explain to us the parable of the weeds in the field."

³⁷He answered, "The one who sowed the good seed is the Son of Man. ³⁸The field is the world, and the good seed stands for the sons of the kingdom. The weeds are the sons of the evil one, ³⁹and the enemy who sows them is the devil. The harvest is the end of the age, and the harvesters are angels.

⁴⁰"As the weeds are pulled up and burned in the fire, so it will be at the end of the age. ⁴¹The Son of Man will send out his angels, and they will weed out of his kingdom everything that causes sin and all who do evil. ⁴²They will throw them into the fiery furnace, where there will be weeping and gnashing of teeth. ⁴³Then the righteous will shine like the sun in the kingdom of their Father. He who has ears, let him hear.

The Parables of the Hidden Treasure and the Pearl

⁴⁴"The kingdom of heaven is like treasure hidden in a field. When a man found it, he hid it again, and then in his joy went and sold all he had and bought that field.

⁴⁵"Again, the kingdom of heaven is like a merchant looking for fine pearls. ⁴⁶When he found one of great value, he went away and sold everything he had and bought it.

a33 Greek *three satas* (probably about 1/2 bushel or 22 liters)   *b35* Psalm 78:2

The Parable of the Net

[47]"Once again, the kingdom of heaven is like a net that was let down into the lake and caught all kinds of fish. [48]When it was full, the fishermen pulled it up on the shore. Then they sat down and collected the good fish in baskets, but threw the bad away. [49]This is how it will be at the end of the age. The angels will come and separate the wicked from the righteous [50]and throw them into the fiery furnace, where there will be weeping and gnashing of teeth.

[51]"Have you understood all these things?" Jesus asked.

"Yes," they replied.

[52]He said to them, "Therefore every teacher of the law who has been instructed about the kingdom of heaven is like the owner of a house who brings out of his storeroom new treasures as well as old."

A Prophet Without Honor

[53]When Jesus had finished these parables, he moved on from there. [54]Coming to his hometown, he began teaching the people in their synagogue, and they were amazed. "Where did this man get this wisdom and these miraculous powers?" they asked. [55]"Isn't this the carpenter's son? Isn't his mother's name Mary, and aren't his brothers James, Joseph, Simon and Judas? [56]Aren't all his sisters with us? Where then did this man get all these things?" [57]And they took offense at him.

But Jesus said to them, "Only in his hometown and in his own house is a prophet without honor."

[58]And he did not do many miracles there because of their lack of faith.

John the Baptist Beheaded

14 At that time Herod the tetrarch heard the reports about Jesus, [2]and he said to his attendants, "This is John the Baptist; he has risen from the dead! That is why miraculous powers are at work in him."

[3]Now Herod had arrested John and bound him and put him in prison because of Herodias, his brother Philip's wife, [4]for John had been saying to him: "It is not lawful for you to have her." [5]Herod wanted to kill John, but he was afraid of the people, because they considered him a prophet.

[6]On Herod's birthday the daughter of Herodias danced for them and pleased Herod so much [7]that he promised with an oath to give her whatever she asked. [8]Prompted by her mother, she said, "Give me here on a platter the head of John the Baptist." [9]The king was distressed, but because of his oaths and his dinner guests, he ordered that her request be granted [10]and had John beheaded in the prison. [11]His head was brought in on a platter and given to the girl, who carried it to her mother. [12]John's disciples came and took his body and buried it. Then they went and told Jesus.

kingdom of heaven? **3.** How does it compare with the parable of the weeds? **4.** Who are the teachers of the old law who have been instructed in the new gospel (v.52)? **5.** How does the hometown crowd's response to Jesus (vv.54-58) differ from that of other Israelites? What do they "know"? How does this impede his ministry?

REFLECT: 1. Compared to the man and the merchant, how valuable is the kingdom to you and why: (a) It's worth more than anything else? (b) I think I'd miss too many of the other things? (c) I'm not ready to carry all this so far? What does it mean to "sell everything" for the kingdom? **2.** Of the parables in chapter 13, which one is still unclear? All too clear? **3.** "Familiarity breeds contempt" (for a hometown prophet) also applies to any of us who grow up "always knowing Jesus." What does this story teach us about assuming that we know all about Jesus? **4.** What relation does our faith have to Jesus' ability to be at work? Why does he look for faith?

OPEN: If promised "anything you ask for" at your next birthday, what would you want?

DIG: 1. What is Herod's fear after hearing reports of Jesus? What was Herod's fear during the life of John the Baptist? **2.** Why did Herod behead John? What does this say about his character? **3.** What does Herod seem to fear most: The fame of Jesus? The ghost of John? The reaction of his dinner guests? His wife?

REFLECT: What is one area in your life where your actions are often governed by fear of what others think? How could Jesus help you?

OPEN: 1. After a busy day, how do you like to unwind? 2. If you had to feed five thousand people at a picnic, what would you serve?

DIG: 1. Why does Jesus withdraw? How does he react to the interruption? 2. What sensitivity do the disciples show initially? How might they have felt after Jesus' statement in verse 16? 3. What is their likely reaction after the miracle? What new power do the disciples discover in Jesus? 4. What is the lesson here?

REFLECT: 1. What insight about Jesus will "stick to your ribs" from this story? 2. How have you seen Jesus stretch your resources beyond what you could imagine?

OPEN: 1. Of all your adventures in life, which was the most daring? 2. As a kid, who was your favorite ghost: Marley? Casper?

DIG: 1. Why did Jesus dismiss the disciples so abruptly? Why do you think Jesus wanted to pray alone? How might Jesus be tempted by his mounting popularity and the crowd's clamor for a king (see Jn 6:15)? 2. How does this temptation and Jesus' response to it resemble that of the temptations in 4:3-10? 3. Meanwhile, what happens out on the lake to rock the disciples' boat? To stir up their fear? To encourage their faith? 4. What do Peter's actions reveal about his personality? 5. Why do you think Jesus invites Peter (and us) to step out in faith? When did Peter begin to sink? Why then and not earlier? 6. What do the disciples conclude about Jesus as a result of this faith-stretching experience? 7. Once on land, how is the word about Jesus spread?

REFLECT: 1. Would you be more likely to stay in the boat or step out of it? Why? 2. What do you see in your own life that parallels Peter's attempt to walk on water?

Jesus Feeds the Five Thousand

[13]When Jesus heard what had happened, he withdrew by boat privately to a solitary place. Hearing of this, the crowds followed him on foot from the towns. [14]When Jesus landed and saw a large crowd, he had compassion on them and healed their sick.

[15]As evening approached, the disciples came to him and said, "This is a remote place, and it's already getting late. Send the crowds away, so they can go to the villages and buy themselves some food."

[16]Jesus replied, "They do not need to go away. You give them something to eat."

[17]"We have here only five loaves of bread and two fish," they answered.

[18]"Bring them here to me," he said. [19]And he directed the people to sit down on the grass. Taking the five loaves and the two fish and looking up to heaven, he gave thanks and broke the loaves. Then he gave them to the disciples, and the disciples gave them to the people. [20]They all ate and were satisfied, and the disciples picked up twelve basketfuls of broken pieces that were left over. [21]The number of those who ate was about five thousand men, besides women and children.

Jesus Walks on the Water

[22]Immediately Jesus made the disciples get into the boat and go on ahead of him to the other side, while he dismissed the crowd. [23]After he had dismissed them, he went up on a mountainside by himself to pray. When evening came, he was there alone, [24]but the boat was already a considerable distance[c] from land, buffeted by the waves because the wind was against it.

[25]During the fourth watch of the night Jesus went out to them, walking on the lake. [26]When the disciples saw him walking on the lake, they were terrified. "It's a ghost," they said, and cried out in fear.

[27]But Jesus immediately said to them: "Take courage! It is I. Don't be afraid."

[28]"Lord, if it's you," Peter replied, "tell me to come to you on the water."

[29]"Come," he said.

Then Peter got down out of the boat, walked on the water and came toward Jesus. [30]But when he saw the wind, he was afraid and, beginning to sink, cried out, "Lord, save me!"

[31]Immediately Jesus reached out his hand and caught him. "You of little faith," he said, "why did you doubt?"

[32]And when they climbed into the boat, the wind died down. [33]Then those who were in the boat worshiped him, saying, "Truly you are the Son of God."

[34]When they had crossed over, they landed at Gennesaret. [35]And when the men of that place recognized Jesus, they sent word to all the surrounding country. People brought all their sick to him [36]and begged him to let the sick just touch the edge of his cloak, and all who touched him were healed.

c24 Greek many stadia

LOOKING INTO THE SCRIPTURE/25 Minutes. Read Matthew 14:22-36 and discuss.

1. If you had been in the boat with the disciples when they saw someone walking on the water, what would you have said?
   a. I think I ate too many anchovies
   b. where's Jesus?
   c. I'm seeing things
   d. absolutely nothing
   e. let me out of here
   f. how does he do that?

2. What was Jesus saying when he cried out, "Take courage. It is I. Don't be afraid"?
   a. get yourself together
   b. Yoo-hoo! It's only me
   c. relax . . . believe in me
   d. why are you surprised? . . . you saw me feed 5,000 people today

3. When Peter replied, "If it's you, tell me to come to you on the water," what was he asking for?
   a. to have the same power
   b. to see a little proof
   c. to risk
   d. to show off
   e. to get to Jesus
   f. to test his own faith

4. What was the tone in Jesus' voice when he said, "you of little faith . . . why did you doubt?"
   a. disappointment: When are you ever going to learn?
   b. concern: What happened? You almost drowned!
   c. anguish: Oh Peter! I know what you are going through.
   d. anger: Don't ever do that again!
   e. reassurance: You almost made it. And with a little more faith, you will.

5. If Jesus knew Peter was going to sink, why did he invite him to "come"?
   a. to teach him a lesson
   b. to encourage him to take risks
   c. to test his faith
   d. to let him fail

6. If you could put in a good word for Peter, what would you say?
   a. at least he was willing to step out
   b. he learned
   c. he's my kind of person
   d. he had guts

MY OWN STORY/20 Minutes.

1. If you had to compare your strong point and weak point in terms of bones, what would be your strongest bone and weakest bone?
   a. crazy bone
   b. ham bone
   c. neck bone
   d. back bone
   e. wish bone

2. When it comes to risking, how would you describe yourself?
   a. cautious—hedge my bets
   b. impulsive—quick to leap
   c. calculating—play the odds
   d. procrastinating—put it off
   e. apprehensive—scared to death

3. If you had been Peter, how would you have responded if Jesus invited you to "Come"?
   a. fainted on the spot
   b. jumped at the chance
   c. asked for a guarantee bond
   d. said, "I'll go second."
   e. asked to think about it

4. Where do you feel that God is inviting you to "get out of the boat" right now?
   a. in my job/career—trying something risky
   b. in my family—starting over with someone
   c. in my spiritual walk—putting God first
   d. in my future planning—doing what I've been afraid to try

5. If God could help me deal with this situation, what would he do?
   a. be very gentle with me
   b. give me a push
   c. assure me that it is okay to fail
   d. give me a lot of support people
   e. get out of the boat with me

6. How could the group you are in help you?
   a. support me
   b. share their own risky plans
   c. hold each other accountable
   d. let me alone
   e. pray for me

Clean and Unclean

15 Then some Pharisees and teachers of the law came to Jesus from Jerusalem and asked, [2]"Why do your disciples break the tradition of the elders? They don't wash their hands before they eat!"

[3]Jesus replied, "And why do you break the command of God for the sake of your tradition? [4]For God said, 'Honor your father and mother'[d] and 'Anyone who curses his father or mother must be put to death.'[e] [5]But you say that if a man says to his father or mother, 'Whatever help you might otherwise have received from me is a gift devoted to God,' [6]he is not to 'honor his father'[f] with it. Thus you nullify the word of God for the sake of your tradition. [7]You hypocrites! Isaiah was right when he prophesied about you:

[8]" 'These people honor me with their lips,
　　but their hearts are far from me.
[9]They worship me in vain;
　　their teachings are but rules taught by men.'[g]"

[10]Jesus called the crowd to him and said, "Listen and understand. [11]What goes into a man's mouth does not make him 'unclean,' but what comes out of his mouth, that is what makes him 'unclean.' "

[12]Then the disciples came to him and asked, "Do you know that the Pharisees were offended when they heard this?"

[13]He replied, "Every plant that my heavenly Father has not planted will be pulled up by the roots. [14]Leave them; they are blind guides.[h] If a blind man leads a blind man, both will fall into a pit."

[15]Peter said, "Explain the parable to us."

[16]"Are you still so dull?" Jesus asked them. [17]"Don't you see that whatever enters the mouth goes into the stomach and then out of the body? [18]But the things that come out of the mouth come from the heart, and these make a man 'unclean.' [19]For out of the heart come evil thoughts, murder, adultery, sexual immorality, theft, false testimony, slander. [20]These are what make a man 'unclean'; but eating with unwashed hands does not make him 'unclean.' "

The Faith of the Canaanite Woman

[21]Leaving that place, Jesus withdrew to the region of Tyre and Sidon. [22]A Canaanite woman from that vicinity came to him, crying out, "Lord, Son of David, have mercy on me! My daughter is suffering terribly from demon-possession."

[23]Jesus did not answer a word. So his disciples came to him and urged him, "Send her away, for she keeps crying out after us."

[24]He answered, "I was sent only to the lost sheep of Israel."

[25]The woman came and knelt before him. "Lord, help me!" she said.

d4 Exodus 20:12; Deut. 5:16　　e4 Exodus 21:17; Lev. 20:9　　f6 Some manuscripts father or his mother　　g9 Isaiah 29:13　　h14 Some manuscripts guides of the blind

²⁶He replied, "It is not right to take the children's bread and toss it to their dogs."

²⁷"Yes, Lord," she said, "but even the dogs eat the crumbs that fall from their masters' table."

²⁸Then Jesus answered, "Woman, you have great faith! Your request is granted." And her daughter was healed from that very hour.

Jesus Feeds the Four Thousand

²⁹Jesus left there and went along the Sea of Galilee. Then he went up on a mountainside and sat down. ³⁰Great crowds came to him, bringing the lame, the blind, the crippled, the mute and many others, and laid them at his feet; and he healed them. ³¹The people were amazed when they saw the mute speaking, the crippled made well, the lame walking and the blind seeing. And they praised the God of Israel.

³²Jesus called his disciples to him and said, "I have compassion for these people; they have already been with me three days and have nothing to eat. I do not want to send them away hungry, or they may collapse on the way."

³³His disciples answered, "Where could we get enough bread in this remote place to feed such a crowd?"

³⁴"How many loaves do you have?" Jesus asked.

"Seven," they replied, "and a few small fish."

³⁵He told the crowd to sit down on the ground. ³⁶Then he took the seven loaves and the fish, and when he had given thanks, he broke them and gave them to the disciples, and they in turn to the people. ³⁷They all ate and were satisfied. Afterward the disciples picked up seven basketfuls of broken pieces that were left over. ³⁸The number of those who ate was four thousand, besides women and children. ³⁹After Jesus had sent the crowd away, he got into the boat and went to the vicinity of Magadan.

The Demand for a Sign

16 The Pharisees and Sadducees came to Jesus and tested him by asking him to show them a sign from heaven.

²He replied,ⁱ "When evening comes, you say, 'It will be fair weather, for the sky is red,' ³and in the morning, 'Today it will be stormy, for the sky is red and overcast.' You know how to interpret the appearance of the sky, but you cannot interpret the signs of the times. ⁴A wicked and adulterous generation looks for a miraculous sign, but none will be given it except the sign of Jonah." Jesus then left them and went away.

The Yeast of the Pharisees and Sadducees

⁵When they went across the lake, the disciples forgot to take bread. ⁶"Be careful," Jesus said to them. "Be on your guard against the yeast of the Pharisees and Sadducees."

⁷They discussed this among themselves and said, "It is because we didn't bring any bread."

⁸Aware of their discussion, Jesus asked, "You of little faith, why are you talking among yourselves about having no bread?

ⁱ2 Some early manuscripts do not have the rest of verse 2 and all of verse 3.

OPEN: What things (names, birthdays, keys, umbrellas, etc.) do you tend to forget? Why?

DIG: 1. What is Jesus doing along the Sea of Galilee (vv.29-31)? How does that compare with Jewish expectations of the Messiah (see Isa 35:3-6)? **2.** How does the feeding of this multitude compare with the previous one (see 14:13-21)? **3.** How do you account for the disciples' lack of insight and faith (v.33;see 14:15)? **4.** What is Jesus' reason for healing and feeding the crowds?

REFLECT: 1. When you face overwhelming situations now, how well do you remember God's provision for you in the past? **2.** What would stimulate your memory of God's mercy? **3.** How helpful is it for you to hear the stories of the way God has worked in the lives of other Christians? Why?

OPEN: Which would you rather have hot out of the oven: Hot bread with butter? Chocolate chip cookies? Homemade doughnuts?

DIG: 1. What do you think the Pharisees and Sadducees were actually hoping to see in the sky? How convincing would a sign have been for these religious leaders? **2.** In light of verses 1-4, what is the "yeast" about which Jesus warns the disciples? **3.** What was Jesus' point in the series of questions? **4.** Why are the disciples so slow in understanding Jesus?

REFLECT: 1. How is the "yeast of the Pharisees and Sadducees" in operation today? **2.** When you feel you just aren't "catching on" to Jesus, what helps you to keep on trying?

9Do you still not understand? Don't you remember the five loaves for the five thousand, and how many basketfuls you gathered? 10Or the seven loaves for the four thousand, and how many basketfuls you gathered? 11How is it you don't understand that I was not talking to you about bread? But be on your guard against the yeast of the Pharisees and Sadducees." 12Then they understood that he was not telling them to guard against the yeast used in bread, but against the teaching of the Pharisees and Sadducees.

Peter's Confession of Christ

13When Jesus came to the region of Caesarea Philippi, he asked his disciples, "Who do people say the Son of Man is?"

14They replied, "Some say John the Baptist; others say Elijah; and still others, Jeremiah or one of the prophets."

15"But what about you?" he asked. "Who do you say I am?"

16Simon Peter answered, "You are the Christ,^{j} the Son of the living God."

17Jesus replied, "Blessed are you, Simon son of Jonah, for this was not revealed to you by man, but by my Father in heaven. 18And I tell you that you are Peter,^{k} and on this rock I will build my church, and the gates of Hades^l will not overcome it.^{m} 19I will give you the keys of the kingdom of heaven; whatever you bind on earth will be^n bound in heaven, and whatever you loose on earth will be^n loosed in heaven." 20Then he warned his disciples not to tell anyone that he was the Christ.

Jesus Predicts His Death

21From that time on Jesus began to explain to his disciples that he must go to Jerusalem and suffer many things at the hands of the elders, chief priests and teachers of the law, and that he must be killed and on the third day be raised to life.

22Peter took him aside and began to rebuke him. "Never, Lord!" he said. "This shall never happen to you!"

23Jesus turned and said to Peter, "Get behind me, Satan! You are a stumbling block to me; you do not have in mind the things of God, but the things of men."

24Then Jesus said to his disciples, "If anyone would come after me, he must deny himself and take up his cross and follow me. 25For whoever wants to save his life^o will lose it, but whoever loses his life for me will find it. 26What good will it be for a man if he gains the whole world, yet forfeits his soul? Or what can a man give in exchange for his soul? 27For the Son of Man is going to come in his Father's glory with his angels, and then he will reward each person according to what he has done. 28I tell you the truth, some who are standing here will not taste death before they see the Son of Man coming in his kingdom."

OPEN: 1. If we polled two good friends from your late teen years, what adjective would they use to describe you? **2.** If you could "gain the world," where would you place your summer and winter castles?

DIG: 1. Why did people think that Jesus was John the Baptist, Elijah, or Jeremiah? **2.** What was significant about Peter's confession? **3.** How do you interpret the insight (v.17), power (v.18), and authority (v.19) given to Peter? What are the "keys" of the kingdom? What do they "bind" and "loose"? **4.** Why does Jesus change the direction of his teaching now? **5.** What kind of Messiah was Peter expecting? Why was Jesus' response to Peter so strong (see 4:1-11)? **6.** What activities and attitudes are at the heart of Christian discipleship? How does a Christian forfeit his life? What things tempt people to lose their life or exchange their soul? **7.** How might verse 28 relate to what happens next?

REFLECT: 1. When and how did you come to recognize Jesus as your Messiah? **2.** In what area does verse 24 strike home to you now? **3.** What perspective does Jesus' "gain and forfeit" argument (vv.25-26) give you on your current priorities?

---

j16 Or *Messiah*; also in verse 20   k18 *Peter* means *rock.*   l18 Or *hell*
m18 Or *not prove stronger than it*   n19 Or *have been*   o25 The Greek word
means either *life* or *soul; also in verse 26.*

LOOKING INTO THE SCRIPTURE/20 Minutes. Read Matthew 16:13-28 and discuss.

1. If you were to ask the average person where you work, "Who is Jesus Christ?" what would he say?
   a. a religious nut
   b. greatest man who ever lived
   c. Son of God
   d. a swear word
   e. an enigma (mystery)

2. "You are the Christ." When Peter answered this, what did he mean?
   a. long-awaited Messiah
   b. ruler of a new Israel
   c. sacrifice for sin
   d. answer to his deepest quest

3. Why did Peter get so upset when Jesus explained the cross?
   a. he didn't understand prophecy
   b. he didn't want Jesus to suffer
   c. he didn't want to suffer
   d. he didn't want to lose his leader
   e. he was just acting tough

4. What is Jesus saying? "If anyone would come after me, he must deny himself and take up his cross and follow me."
   a. following Jesus is no rose garden
   b. if you've got reservations, now is the time to get out
   c. it's gonna cost you everything
   d. shape up or ship out

5. What is Jesus saying here? "What good is it for a man to gain the whole world, yet forfeit his soul?"
   a. it's a question of personal priorities
   b. why pay the ultimate price for temporary happiness?
   c. it's all or nothing
   d. someday you'll have to answer for your choices

6. How do you think Peter felt after this experience?
   a. confused
   b. depressed
   c. scared to death
   d. ready to go

MY OWN STORY/25 Minutes.

1. For each period of your life, put a symbol to indicate how you experienced Jesus.

☐ K=Jesus is someone to KNOW about   ☐ L=Jesus is someone to LEARN about
☐ F=Jesus is someone to FOLLOW   ☐ A=Jesus is someone to AVOID

CHILDHOOD	TEENS	COLLEGE AGE	YOUNG ADULTHOOD	MIDDLE AGE	RETIRE- MENT	SENIOR CITIZEN

2. How would you compare where you are in your spiritual journey to a ball game? Are you right now . . .
   a. a spectator—in the grandstand
   b. a benchwarmer
   c. playing on the offensive team
   d. playing defense
   e. on the injury list

3. How would you describe your response to Jesus' call to deny yourself, take up your cross and follow him?
   a. I'm not ready for this
   b. I've got a long way to go
   c. I've come a long way
   d. There's a lot more to it than I bargained for
   e. Ask me tomorrow

4. For you, what would taking the next step in your spiritual life mean?
   a. remedial work in the basics—prayer, Bible reading, etc.
   b. turning to Jesus for guidance in daily decisions
   c. deeper commitment to the people in my small group
   d. reevaluating my goals and priorities

5. How can other members of your group help you?
   a. give me a kick in the pants when I need it
   b. pray for me
   c. keep quiet on discipleship while I think it through
   d. give me the support I need
   e. hold me accountable

OPEN: 1. What was one mountaintop experience in your life? 2.
Of all the places you call "God's
country," which is your favorite?

DIG: 1. It's been six days since
Peter confessed the Christ and
Jesus predicted his death. Why is
that context important for what
happens next? Who does Jesus
invite as a witness? Why only
three? Why these three? 2. What
does it mean to be "transfigured"?
3. What did Moses represent?
Elijah (see 11:13)? 4. Why was
Peter's response inappropriate?
5. What is significant in what the
voice from the cloud says about
Jesus? 6. Why does Jesus silence the disciples? 7. What do
the disciples learn about John the
Baptist (see Mal 4:5-6)? About
Jesus?

REFLECT: 1. How did you come
to realize that Jesus was the one
above all others that you should
listen to? 2. How has God said to
you, "This is my child, whom I
love, with whom I am well
pleased"?

OPEN: If you could move mountains, which one would you move
first: Mt. Everest? Your favorite
ski hill? Mountains of paper?

DIG: 1. Where was Jesus when
the disciples were trying to cast
out the demon? How does this
contribute to his anger? 2. Who is
Jesus describing in verse 17? Why
would he say such a thing? 3.
How would you paraphrase what
Jesus says in verse 20? 4. What
does the disciples' grief show
about their expectations?

REFLECT: 1. When has a mountaintop experience in your life been
followed by a valley experience?
Which builds up your faith more?
2. In which areas of your life do
you long to see more faith?

The Transfiguration

17 After six days Jesus took with him Peter, James and John the brother of James, and led them up a high mountain by themselves. [2]There he was transfigured before them. His face shone like the sun, and his clothes became as white as the light. [3]Just then there appeared before them Moses and Elijah, talking with Jesus.

[4]Peter said to Jesus, "Lord, it is good for us to be here. If you wish, I will put up three shelters—one for you, one for Moses and one for Elijah."

[5]While he was still speaking, a bright cloud enveloped them, and a voice from the cloud said, "This is my Son, whom I love; with him I am well pleased. Listen to him!"

[6]When the disciples heard this, they fell facedown to the ground, terrified. [7]But Jesus came and touched them. "Get up," he said. "Don't be afraid." [8]When they looked up, they saw no one except Jesus.

[9]As they were coming down the mountain, Jesus instructed them, "Don't tell anyone what you have seen, until the Son of Man has been raised from the dead."

[10]The disciples asked him, "Why then do the teachers of the law say that Elijah must come first?"

[11]Jesus replied, "To be sure, Elijah comes and will restore all things. [12]But I tell you, Elijah has already come, and they did not recognize him, but have done to him everything they wished. In the same way the Son of Man is going to suffer at their hands." [13]Then the disciples understood that he was talking to them about John the Baptist.

The Healing of a Boy With a Demon

[14]When they came to the crowd, a man approached Jesus and knelt before him. [15]"Lord, have mercy on my son," he said. "He has seizures and is suffering greatly. He often falls into the fire or into the water. [16]I brought him to your disciples, but they could not heal him."

[17]"O unbelieving and perverse generation," Jesus replied, "how long shall I stay with you? How long shall I put up with you? Bring the boy here to me." [18]Jesus rebuked the demon, and it came out of the boy, and he was healed from that moment.

[19]Then the disciples came to Jesus in private and asked, "Why couldn't we drive it out?"

[20]He replied, "Because you have so little faith. I tell you the truth, if you have faith as small as a mustard seed, you can say to this mountain, 'Move from here to there' and it will move. Nothing will be impossible for you. [p]"

[22]When they came together in Galilee, he said to them, "The Son of Man is going to be betrayed into the hands of men. [23]They will kill him, and on the third day he will be raised to life." And the disciples were filled with grief.

---

[p]20 Some manuscripts *you.* [21]*But this kind does not go out except by prayer and fasting.*

The Temple Tax

²⁴After Jesus and his disciples arrived in Capernaum, the collectors of the two-drachma tax came to Peter and asked, "Doesn't your teacher pay the temple tax*?"

²⁵"Yes, he does," he replied.

When Peter came into the house, Jesus was the first to speak. "What do you think, Simon?" he asked. "From whom do the kings of the earth collect duty and taxes—from their own sons or from others?"

²⁶"From others," Peter answered.

"Then the sons are exempt," Jesus said to him. ²⁷"But so that we may not offend them, go to the lake and throw out your line. Take the first fish you catch; open its mouth and you will find a four-drachma coin. Take it and give it to them for my tax and yours."

The Greatest in the Kingdom of Heaven

18 At that time the disciples came to Jesus and asked, "Who is the greatest in the kingdom of heaven?"

²He called a little child and had him stand among them. ³And he said: "I tell you the truth, unless you change and become like little children, you will never enter the kingdom of heaven. ⁴Therefore, whoever humbles himself like this child is the greatest in the kingdom of heaven.

⁵"And whoever welcomes a little child like this in my name welcomes me. ⁶But if anyone causes one of these little ones who believe in me to sin, it would be better for him to have a large millstone hung around his neck and to be drowned in the depths of the sea.

⁷"Woe to the world because of the things that cause people to sin! Such things must come, but woe to the man through whom they come! ⁸If your hand or your foot causes you to sin, cut it off and throw it away. It is better for you to enter life maimed or crippled than to have two hands or two feet and be thrown into eternal fire. ⁹And if your eye causes you to sin, gouge it out and throw it away. It is better for you to enter life with one eye than to have two eyes and be thrown into the fire of hell.

The Parable of the Lost Sheep

¹⁰"See that you do not look down on one of these little ones. For I tell you that their angels in heaven always see the face of my Father in heaven.ʳ

¹²"What do you think? If a man owns a hundred sheep, and one of them wanders away, will he not leave the ninety-nine on the hills and go to look for the one that wandered off? ¹³And if he finds it, I tell you the truth, he is happier about that one sheep than about the ninety-nine that did not wander off. ¹⁴In the same way your Father in heaven is not willing that any of these little ones should be lost.

OPEN: What wild "fish story" is retold in your family?

DIG: 1. What was the temple tax (see Ex 30:11-16)? Who was required to pay it? **2.** Why would Jesus say he was exempt from the tax? **3.** What lesson was Jesus teaching Peter by paying the tax anyway?

REFLECT: 1. Which freedoms do you enjoy most as a Christian? **2.** What is at stake when we offend someone?

OPEN: 1. Of the following, which "woe" would be the worst way to go: (a) Canoe going over a sudden 250-foot waterfall? (b) Parachute failing to open? (c) Running out of fuel in outer space? (d) Being a late-night snack for a pride of lions? **2.** Which would best describe you as a child: "Little angel" or "Holy terror"? Why?

DIG: 1. Why would the disciples want to be "the greatest"? What does this say about their understanding of the kingdom? **2.** What does it mean to humble oneself like a child? Why do you think this is important for Jesus' kingdom? **3.** Why is causing a child to sin such a serious offense? **4.** Although evil is inevitable (vv.7-9), how are we still responsible to care for others' spiritual welfare? **5.** What does the parable in verses 12-13 teach about God's attitude toward "little ones"? Toward "straying sheep"?

REFLECT: 1. What childlike quality do you need to recapture? Why? **2.** When have you felt like the sheep that wandered off? How did God get you back? **3.** What needs to change in your attitude toward those who "wander"? Toward the weak? The powerless? What could be an area in your life that causes problems for others? What will you do about it?

---

*24 Greek *the two drachmas*   ʳ10 Some manuscripts *heaven.* ¹¹*The Son of Man came to save what was lost.*

OPEN: How did your folks choose between you and your siblings when you wanted the same thing?

DIG: 1. Whom is Jesus addressing? For what desired result? 2. This reconciliation process involves what four stages? What obstacle frustrates the process? What authority is given to Jesus' followers to aid this process?

REFLECT: What happens when this process is short-circuited by "going public" right away?

OPEN: How many credit cards do you have? When does your credit card tempt you the most?

DIG: 1. Offenders in Jesus' day were forgiven up to three times; a fourth offense need not be forgiven. What does Jesus' answer say about forgiveness in the kingdom? 2. How does the parable of the unmerciful servant extend Jesus' teaching on forgiveness (vv.23-35)? In refusing to be merciful to others, what do we deny ourselves (vv.31-34)? 3. How does Jesus' point in verse 35 compare with 6:12? Do we forgive others so God will forgive us, or does God forgive us so that we will have a forgiving attitude? Explain. 4. Based on this parable, is God's forgiveness of us limited or unlimited? Conditional or unconditional? Likewise, our forgiveness of others? 5. In summary, what does Jesus teach in chapter 18 about sin and forgiveness?

REFLECT: 1. What has driven home the importance of forgiveness to you? How can we forgive, yet not encourage irresponsibility? 2. How can you forgive someone from the distant past who hurt you deeply? 3. What is the connection between forgiveness, health, and wholeness?

A Brother Who Sins Against You

[15]"If your brother sins against you,[s] go and show him his fault, just between the two of you. If he listens to you, you have won your brother over. [16]But if he will not listen, take one or two others along, so that 'every matter may be established by the testimony of two or three witnesses.'[t] [17]If he refuses to listen to them, tell it to the church; and if he refuses to listen even to the church, treat him as you would a pagan or a tax collector.

[18]"I tell you the truth, whatever you bind on earth will be[u] bound in heaven, and whatever you loose on earth will be[u] loosed in heaven.

[19]"Again, I tell you that if two of you on earth agree about anything you ask for, it will be done for you by my Father in heaven. [20]For where two or three come together in my name, there am I with them."

The Parable of the Unmerciful Servant

[21]Then Peter came to Jesus and asked, "Lord, how many times shall I forgive my brother when he sins against me? Up to seven times?"

[22]Jesus answered, "I tell you, not seven times, but seventy-seven times.[v]

[23]"Therefore, the kingdom of heaven is like a king who wanted to settle accounts with his servants. [24]As he began the settlement, a man who owed him ten thousand talents[w] was brought to him. [25]Since he was not able to pay, the master ordered that he and his wife and his children and all that he had be sold to repay the debt.

[26]"The servant fell on his knees before him. 'Be patient with me,' he begged, 'and I will pay back everything.' [27]The servant's master took pity on him, canceled the debt and let him go.

[28]"But when that servant went out, he found one of his fellow servants who owed him a hundred denarii.[x] He grabbed him and began to choke him. 'Pay back what you owe me!' he demanded.

[29]"His fellow servant fell to his knees and begged him, 'Be patient with me, and I will pay you back.'

[30]"But he refused. Instead, he went off and had the man thrown into prison until he could pay the debt. [31]When the other servants saw what had happened, they were greatly distressed and went and told their master everything that had happened.

[32]"Then the master called the servant in. 'You wicked servant,' he said, 'I canceled all that debt of yours because you begged me to. [33]Shouldn't you have had mercy on your fellow servant just as I had on you?' [34]In anger his master turned him over to the jailers to be tortured, until he should pay back all he owed.

[35]"This is how my heavenly Father will treat each of you unless you forgive your brother from your heart."

---

[s]15 Some manuscripts do not have *against you*.   [t]16 Deut. 19:15   [u]18 Or *have been*   [v]22 Or *seventy times seven*   [w]24 That is, millions of dollars   [x]28 That is, a few dollars

LOOKING INTO THE SCRIPTURE/25 Minutes. Read Matthew 18:21-35 and discuss.

1. Do you suppose Peter had a special reason for asking how many times he needed to forgive his brother and, if so, what was it?
   a. he was the type to keep score
   b. he couldn't forgive someone
   c. he was easily hurt
   d. he just wanted to know

2. What is the parable that Jesus told really about?
   a. how to deal with someone who owes you money
   b. how to deal with your own anger when you've been wronged
   c. how to keep your relationship with God fresh
   d. how to avoid getting trapped in grudges
   e. how to say thanks for God's forgiveness

3. How would you describe the attitude of the servant toward the one who had wronged him?
   a. business is business
   b. an eye for an eye
   c. don't let the scoundrel off the hook
   d. let him suffer

4. What's the principle for you as a Christian in dealing with someone who has wronged you?
   a. you can't out-forgive God
   b. scorekeepers end up getting hurt
   c. God expects you to be a "pushover"
   d. if you don't forgive others, God is going to refigure what you owe him
   e. unforgivers wind up in their own chains
   f. only the forgiven know how to forgive

MY OWN STORY/20 Minutes. Study the case history below and share how you would deal with the situation.

LITTLE BROTHER: You have been putting up with your little brother for years. When you were growing up, you had to share a bedroom, where he kept "his side" like a pig pen. He "borrowed" your clothes without asking, left the car a mess when he used it, and never thought of filling the tank with gas. Now, the two of you run the family business, but you have to keep the books, pay the bills, and come in on Saturdays while he coaches a Little League team. Recently, your doctor told you that you have an ulcer, and it is caused by deep-seated anger against your little brother.

1. What do you do?
   a. decide it's not worth getting sick over
   b. complain to his wife
   c. call your father and tell everything
   d. sweep it under the rug
   e. have it out with him
   f. take off for six months and leave the business to him

2. What have you found helpful in dealing with sour relationships?
   a. keep short accounts
   b. write a letter but don't mail it
   c. ask someone else to mediate
   d. have it out—right now
   e. sleep on it
   f. get away from the situation
   g. break off the relationship

3. Who is the easiest and hardest person for you to forgive?
   a. brother/sister
   b. spouse
   c. parents/kids
   d. neighbor/friend
   e. stranger
   f. yourself

4. How could you pass on God's forgiveness to those who have wronged you?
   a. pray for them
   b. think first about whether I've done anything wrong myself
   c. hold them accountable for the consequences of what they have done
   d. drop the issue and let them know it's past history
   e. look for ways to show kindness to them

Divorce

19 When Jesus had finished saying these things, he left Galilee and went into the region of Judea to the other side of the Jordan. [2]Large crowds followed him, and he healed them there.

[3]Some Pharisees came to him to test him. They asked, "Is it lawful for a man to divorce his wife for any and every reason?"

[4]"Haven't you read," he replied, "that at the beginning the Creator 'made them male and female,'[y] [5]and said, 'For this reason a man will leave his father and mother and be united to his wife, and the two will become one flesh'[z]? [6]So they are no longer two, but one. Therefore what God has joined together, let man not separate."

[7]"Why then," they asked, "did Moses command that a man give his wife a certificate of divorce and send her away?"

[8]Jesus replied, "Moses permitted you to divorce your wives because your hearts were hard. But it was not this way from the beginning. [9]I tell you that anyone who divorces his wife, except for marital unfaithfulness, and marries another woman commits adultery."

[10]The disciples said to him, "If this is the situation between a husband and wife, it is better not to marry."

[11]Jesus replied, "Not everyone can accept this word, but only those to whom it has been given. [12]For some are eunuchs because they were born that way; others were made that way by men; and others have renounced marriage[a] because of the kingdom of heaven. The one who can accept this should accept it."

The Little Children and Jesus

[13]Then little children were brought to Jesus for him to place his hands on them and pray for them. But the disciples rebuked those who brought them.

[14]Jesus said, "Let the little children come to me, and do not hinder them, for the kingdom of heaven belongs to such as these." [15]When he had placed his hands on them, he went on from there.

The Rich Young Man

[16]Now a man came up to Jesus and asked, "Teacher, what good thing must I do to get eternal life?"

[17]"Why do you ask me about what is good?" Jesus replied. "There is only One who is good. If you want to enter life, obey the commandments."

[18]"Which ones?" the man inquired.

Jesus replied, " 'Do not murder, do not commit adultery, do not steal, do not give false testimony, [19]honor your father and mother,'[b] and 'love your neighbor as yourself.'[c]"

[20]"All these I have kept," the young man said. "What do I still lack?"

---

y4 Gen. 1:27   *z* Gen. 2:24   *a12* Or *have made themselves eunuchs*
b19 Exodus 20:12-16; Deut. 5:16-20   *c19* Lev. 19:18

21Jesus answered, "If you want to be perfect, go, sell your possessions and give to the poor, and you will have treasure in heaven. Then come, follow me."

22When the young man heard this, he went away sad, because he had great wealth.

23Then Jesus said to his disciples, "I tell you the truth, it is hard for a rich man to enter the kingdom of heaven. 24Again I tell you, it is easier for a camel to go through the eye of a needle than for a rich man to enter the kingdom of God."

25When the disciples heard this, they were greatly astonished and asked, "Who then can be saved?"

26Jesus looked at them and said, "With man this is impossible, but with God all things are possible."

27Peter answered him, "We have left everything to follow you! What then will there be for us?"

28Jesus said to them, "I tell you the truth, at the renewal of all things, when the Son of Man sits on his glorious throne, you who have followed me will also sit on twelve thrones, judging the twelve tribes of Israel. 29And everyone who has left houses or brothers or sisters or father or mother*d* or children or fields for my sake will receive a hundred times as much and will inherit eternal life. 30But many who are first will be last, and many who are last will be first.

The Parable of the Workers in the Vineyard

20 "For the kingdom of heaven is like a landowner who went out early in the morning to hire men to work in his vineyard. 2He agreed to pay them a denarius for the day and sent them into his vineyard.

3"About the third hour he went out and saw others standing in the marketplace doing nothing. 4He told them, 'You also go and work in my vineyard, and I will pay you whatever is right.' 5So they went.

"He went out again about the sixth hour and the ninth hour and did the same thing. 6About the eleventh hour he went out and found still others standing around. He asked them, 'Why have you been standing here all day long doing nothing?'

7" 'Because no one has hired us,' they answered.

"He said to them, 'You also go and work in my vineyard.'

8"When evening came, the owner of the vineyard said to his foreman, 'Call the workers and pay them their wages, beginning with the last ones hired and going on to the first.'

9"The workers who were hired about the eleventh hour came and each received a denarius. 10So when those came who were hired first, they expected to receive more. But each one of them also received a denarius. 11When they received it, they began to grumble against the landowner. 12"These men who were hired last worked only one hour,' they said, 'and you have made them equal to us who have borne the burden of the work and the heat of the day.'

what basis is it possible for anyone, rich or poor, to enter (vv.26-30)? 7. According to verses 16-30, how are these four terms connected: *being saved*, *becoming a disciple*, *entering the kingdom of heaven*, and *inheriting eternal life*?

REFLECT: 1. Jesus hit this man where it hurt—in his wallet. If Jesus were to address you where it hurts, what would his hot topic be? 2. Why is Jesus so tough on riches? 3. What have you given up to follow Jesus? How is your life different as a result?

OPEN: Which folk do you believe work harder: (a) Mothers of young children? (b) Attorneys? (c) Door to door salesmen? (d) High school teachers? (e) Preachers? Why?

DIG: 1. To what is the kingdom of heaven compared? Why is this parable told here (see 19:30 and 20:16)? 2. Why are identical wages given to both early and late workers? Who is discontent and why (vv.10-12)? Is the landowner's practice unjust, generous, or both? Why? 3. How does this parable apply to the kingdom and to 19:30? Who gets any less of God: The "eleventh hour" converts (Gentiles)? Or those who should have known God all along from the "first hour" (the Jews)?

REFLECT: 1. If you had been the first hired, how would you feel about this system? 2. How do you feel realizing that those who are not "life long" believers will get the same benefits as you in the kingdom? 3. Would you recommend that people wait until just before they die to come to Christ, so that they won't have to work so hard or give up so much? Why?

*d*29 Some manuscripts *mother or wife*

OPEN: **1.** What did your parents want you to be when you grew up? What about you? **2.** What are some secret expectations you have for your children?

DIG: **1.** Why does Jesus once again predict his death? Why on this occasion? **2.** What in the request of the woman (vv.20-21) shows that the disciples' view of the kingdom was different from Jesus'? Of what are she (and they) ignorant? **3.** In order to share in his kingdom, what "cup" must the disciples share with Jesus (vv.18-19)? **4.** Why were the other ten disciples so outraged? Were their reactions any more commendable? **5.** What contrast does Jesus set up between how the Gentiles rule and how authority is exercised in God's kingdom? How does Jesus model this new way? **6.** How would you compare the blindness of the two men (vv.29-34) with that of the disciples (vv.20-28)? **7.** How do their requests differ? **8.** Why are these two singled out for healing? Once healed, what do they do? Why? How does this relate to the disciples' concern (vv.20-28)?

REFLECT: **1.** How significant do you feel in relation to God's kingdom? In what specific ways can you serve people, using Jesus as your model? **2.** In what ways do you feel spiritually blind? How is your sight better now than six months ago? **3.** If Jesus said, "What do you want me to do for you?", how would you answer?

[13]"But he answered one of them, 'Friend, I am not being unfair to you. Didn't you agree to work for a denarius? [14]Take your pay and go. I want to give the man who was hired last the same as I gave you. [15]Don't I have the right to do what I want with my own money? Or are you envious because I am generous?'

[16]"So the last will be first, and the first will be last."

Jesus Again Predicts His Death

[17]Now as Jesus was going up to Jerusalem, he took the twelve disciples aside and said to them, [18]"We are going up to Jerusalem, and the Son of Man will be betrayed to the chief priests and the teachers of the law. They will condemn him to death [19]and will turn him over to the Gentiles to be mocked and flogged and crucified. On the third day he will be raised to life!"

A Mother's Request

[20]Then the mother of Zebedee's sons came to Jesus with her sons and, kneeling down, asked a favor of him.

[21]"What is it you want?" he asked.

She said, "Grant that one of these two sons of mine may sit at your right and the other at your left in your kingdom."

[22]"You don't know what you are asking," Jesus said to them. "Can you drink the cup I am going to drink?"

"We can," they answered.

[23]Jesus said to them, "You will indeed drink from my cup, but to sit at my right or left is not for me to grant. These places belong to those for whom they have been prepared by my Father."

[24]When the ten heard about this, they were indignant with the two brothers. [25]Jesus called them together and said, "You know that the rulers of the Gentiles lord it over them, and their high officials exercise authority over them. [26]Not so with you. Instead, whoever wants to become great among you must be your servant, [27]and whoever wants to be first must be your slave— [28]just as the Son of Man did not come to be served, but to serve, and to give his life as a ransom for for many."

Two Blind Men Receive Sight

[29]As Jesus and his disciples were leaving Jericho, a large crowd followed him. [30]Two blind men were sitting by the roadside, and when they heard that Jesus was going by, they shouted, "Lord, Son of David, have mercy on us!"

[31]The crowd rebuked them and told them to be quiet, but they shouted all the louder, "Lord, Son of David, have mercy on us!"

[32]Jesus stopped and called them. "What do you want me to do for you?" he asked.

[33]"Lord," they answered, "we want our sight."

[34]Jesus had compassion on them and touched their eyes. Immediately they received their sight and followed him.

Matthew 20:20-28   **A MOTHER'S REQUEST**

LOOKING INTO THE SCRIPTURE/20 Minutes. Read Matthew 20:20-28 and discuss.

1. If you had been the mother, how would you have felt about Jesus' response to her question?
   a. confused
   b. disappointed
   c. angry
   d. insulted
   e. inspired

2. What do you think motivated the mother to ask a favor of Jesus?
   a. mother's love
   b. ambition for her sons
   c. she knew they would be best
   d. she wanted the best for her sons

3. What was the mother really wanting when she asked if her sons could "sit at your right . . . and left hand . . ."?
   a. close relationship with God
   b. power and position
   c. special recognition
   d. her own satisfaction
   e. spiritual security

4. What was Jesus really saying, "You don't know what you are asking"?
   a. you're embarrassing your sons
   b. you've got to be kidding
   c. your sons don't deserve it
   d. what you ask is impossible
   e. it's not my decision

5. What is Jesus referring to when he said, "Can you drink the cup I am going to drink?"
   a. royal silverware
   b. divine authority
   c. suffering and death
   d. God's plan for Jesus
   e. unreasonable expectations

6. What values did Jesus turn upside down when he met with the disciples?
   a. always listen to a boy's mother
   b. God gives special favors
   c. heaven rewards the powerful
   d. the great are the ones who are served
   e. get what you can out of life

MY OWN STORY/20 Minutes. Take a moment and share your experience.

1. Do/did your parents put any expectations on you?   ☐ Yes ☐ No ☐ Sometimes

2. Are/were you able to live up to those expectations?   ☐ Yes ☐ No ☐ Sometimes

3. Do/did you put any expectations on your children?   ☐ Yes ☐ No ☐ Sometimes

4. What would you desire for your children? (Top three)
   ☐ good health
   ☐ college education
   ☐ good friends
   ☐ spiritual fulfillment
   ☐ success in their field
   ☐ secure job
   ☐ lasting marriage
   ☐ life full of surprises
   ☐ star on athletic team
   ☐ amount to something
   ☐ good grades in school
   ☐ leader in school
   ☐ happiness
   ☐ life free of hardship
   ☐ financial independence

5. If you could pass on to your children three things, what would they be?
   ☐ moral courage
   ☐ sense of humor
   ☐ faith in God
   ☐ respect for country
   ☐ family pride
   ☐ lots of initiative
   ☐ good self-image
   ☐ money
   ☐ opportunity to get ahead
   ☐ your own values
   ☐ love of adventure
   ☐ concern for the poor
   ☐ peace of mind
   ☐ basic honesty
   ☐ hard work

OPEN: How would you arrange for the President to have maximum exposure in your town: What parades? What TV talk shows or radio call-in programs? Where would he eat? Stay the night?

DIG: 1. To what town has Jesus come? Why? **2.** Jesus comes on a donkey and not on a stallion. What kind of Messiah does that portray? **3.** Why such a large crowd at this time of year? What did they shout? Why? **4.** What kind of kingdom and king were the people expecting? How do their wishes compare with the reality of Jesus? **5.** How might that discrepancy account for the same crowd shouting later on, "Crucify him!"?

REFLECT: 1. What difference does it make to you that Jesus is a "gentle" king, and not like the one described in 20:25? **2.** How would you have reacted if you had been there to greet Jesus riding into town? Do you jump on political or religious bandwagons today? Why or why not? **3.** How do you reconcile Jesus' kingship with his humility? How are each of these traits important to you?

OPEN: When you see something wrong, are you more likely to act without thinking or think without acting?

DIG: 1. What upset Jesus so much about what he saw in the temple (see Isa 56:3-7)? **2.** Although the merchants once performed a useful role for out-of-towners, how had it become a block to the Jews' worship? To the Gentiles' ministry? **3.** In this passage, which groups of people did and did not recognize the significance of Jesus? How do you explain that? **4.** How is the fig tree incident a parable about what has happened in the temple and what is to come (see Hos 9:10-17)? **5.** What does this dramatized parable teach about faith? Prayer? Judgment? Jesus?

REFLECT: 1. If Jesus were to visit your church, where would he begin "turning over tables"? What about in your life? **2.** How could the promise of verse 22 be abused? On the other hand, how does it encourage you in your prayer?

The Triumphal Entry

21 As they approached Jerusalem and came to Bethphage on the Mount of Olives, Jesus sent two disciples, [2]saying to them, "Go to the village ahead of you, and at once you will find a donkey tied there, with her colt by her. Untie them and bring them to me. [3]If anyone says anything to you, tell him that the Lord needs them, and he will send them right away."

[4]This took place to fulfill what was spoken through the prophet:

[5]"Say to the Daughter of Zion,
  'See, your king comes to you,
gentle and riding on a donkey,
  on a colt, the foal of a donkey.' "[e]

[6]The disciples went and did as Jesus had instructed them. [7]They brought the donkey and the colt, placed their cloaks on them, and Jesus sat on them. [8]A very large crowd spread their cloaks on the road, while others cut branches from the trees and spread them on the road. [9]The crowds that went ahead of him and those that followed shouted,

"Hosanna[f] to the Son of David!"

"Blessed is he who comes in the name of the Lord!"[g]

"Hosanna[f] in the highest!"

[10]When Jesus entered Jerusalem, the whole city was stirred and asked, "Who is this?"

[11]The crowds answered, "This is Jesus, the prophet from Nazareth in Galilee."

Jesus at the Temple

[12]Jesus entered the temple area and drove out all who were buying and selling there. He overturned the tables of the money changers and the benches of those selling doves. [13]"It is written," he said to them, " 'My house will be called a house of prayer,'[h] but you are making it a 'den of robbers.'[i]"

[14]The blind and the lame came to him at the temple, and he healed them. [15]But when the chief priests and the teachers of the law saw the wonderful things he did and the children shouting in the temple area, "Hosanna to the Son of David," they were indignant.

[16]"Do you hear what these children are saying?" they asked him.

"Yes," replied Jesus, "have you never read,

" 'From the lips of children and infants
  you have ordained praise'[j]?"

[17]And he left them and went out of the city to Bethany, where he spent the night.

---

[e]5 Zech. 9:9   [f]9 A Hebrew expression meaning "Save!" which became an exclamation of praise; also in verse 15   [g]9 Psalm 118:26   [h]13 Isaiah 56:7   [i]13 Jer. 7:11   [j]16 Psalm 8:2

The Fig Tree Withers

¹⁸Early in the morning, as he was on his way back to the city, he was hungry. ¹⁹Seeing a fig tree by the road, he went up to it but found nothing on it except leaves. Then he said to it, "May you never bear fruit again!" Immediately the tree withered.

²⁰When the disciples saw this, they were amazed. "How did the fig tree wither so quickly?" they asked.

²¹Jesus replied, "I tell you the truth, if you have faith and do not doubt, not only can you do what was done to the fig tree, but also you can say to this mountain, 'Go, throw yourself into the sea,' and it will be done. ²²If you believe, you will receive whatever you ask for in prayer."

The Authority of Jesus Questioned

²³Jesus entered the temple courts, and, while he was teaching, the chief priests and the elders of the people came to him. "By what authority are you doing these things?" they asked. "And who gave you this authority?"

²⁴Jesus replied, "I will also ask you one question. If you answer me, I will tell you by what authority I am doing these things. ²⁵John's baptism—where did it come from? Was it from heaven, or from men?"

They discussed it among themselves and said, "If we say, 'From heaven,' he will ask, 'Then why didn't you believe him?' ²⁶But if we say, 'From men'—we are afraid of the people, for they all hold that John was a prophet."

²⁷So they answered Jesus, "We don't know."

Then he said, "Neither will I tell you by what authority I am doing these things.

The Parable of the Two Sons

²⁸"What do you think? There was a man who had two sons. He went to the first and said, 'Son, go and work today in the vineyard.'

²⁹" 'I will not,' he answered, but later he changed his mind and went.

³⁰"Then the father went to the other son and said the same thing. He answered, 'I will, sir,' but he did not go.

³¹"Which of the two did what his father wanted?"

"The first," they answered.

Jesus said to them, "I tell you the truth, the tax collectors and the prostitutes are entering the kingdom of God ahead of you. ³²For John came to you to show you the way of righteousness, and you did not believe him, but the tax collectors and the prostitutes did. And even after you saw this, you did not repent and believe him.

OPEN: In high school, with what big authority figure did you run into trouble? Why?

DIG: 1. With what issue is Jesus confronted? Why? What answers could Jesus have given? How would these have trapped him? **2.** How did Jesus' counter-question force the issue? **3.** How was Jesus' authority linked to John's?

REFLECT: When it comes right down to it, whose opinion do you care about more—God's or people's? How does that show?

OPEN: As a child, what kind of worker were you? How much did your parents have to yell and scream to get you to work?

DIG: 1. What links this parable to Jesus' encounter with the chief priests and elders (vv.23-27)? **2.** Describe the story. What is the father's request? What does each son say and do? Why? **3.** Which group is like which son? How? **4.** How do you suppose the religious leaders responded to this story?

REFLECT: Which son's story is most like your own? Why?

The Parable of the Tenants

[33]"Listen to another parable: There was a landowner who planted a vineyard. He put a wall around it, dug a winepress in it and built a watchtower. Then he rented the vineyard to some farmers and went away on a journey. [34]When the harvest time approached, he sent his servants to the tenants to collect his fruit.

[35]"The tenants seized his servants; they beat one, killed another, and stoned a third. [36]Then he sent other servants to them, more than the first time, and the tenants treated them the same way. [37]Last of all, he sent his son to them. 'They will respect my son,' he said.

[38]"But when the tenants saw the son, they said to each other, 'This is the heir. Come, let's kill him and take his inheritance.' [39]So they took him and threw him out of the vineyard and killed him.

[40]"Therefore, when the owner of the vineyard comes, what will he do to those tenants?"

[41]"He will bring those wretches to a wretched end," they replied, "and he will rent the vineyard to other tenants, who will give him his share of the crop at harvest time."

[42]Jesus said to them, "Have you never read in the Scriptures:

> " 'The stone the builders rejected
>   has become the capstone[k];
> the Lord has done this,
>   and it is marvelous in our eyes'[l]?

[43]"Therefore I tell you that the kingdom of God will be taken away from you and given to a people who will produce its fruit. [44]He who falls on this stone will be broken to pieces, but he on whom it falls will be crushed."[m]

[45]When the chief priests and the Pharisees heard Jesus' parables, they knew he was talking about them. [46]They looked for a way to arrest him, but they were afraid of the crowd because the people held that he was a prophet.

The Parable of the Wedding Banquet

22 Jesus spoke to them again in parables, saying: [2]"The kingdom of heaven is like a king who prepared a wedding banquet for his son. [3]He sent his servants to those who had been invited to the banquet to tell them to come, but they refused to come.

[4]"Then he sent some more servants and said, 'Tell those who have been invited that I have prepared my dinner: My oxen and fattened cattle have been butchered, and everything is ready. Come to the wedding banquet.'

[5]"But they paid no attention and went off—one to his field, another to his business. [6]The rest seized his servants, mistreated them and killed them. [7]The king was enraged. He sent his army and destroyed those murderers and burned their city.

[8]"Then he said to his servants, 'The wedding banquet is

---

k42 Or *cornerstone*   l42 Psalm 118:22,23   m44 Some manuscripts do not have verse 44.

ready, but those I invited did not deserve to come. [9]Go to the street corners and invite to the banquet anyone you find.' [10]So the servants went out into the streets and gathered all the people they could find, both good and bad, and the wedding hall was filled with guests.

[11]"But when the king came in to see the guests, he noticed a man there who was not wearing wedding clothes. [12]'Friend,' he asked, 'how did you get in here without wedding clothes?' The man was speechless.

[13]"Then the king told the attendants, 'Tie him hand and foot, and throw him outside, into the darkness, where there will be weeping and gnashing of teeth.'

[14]"For many are invited, but few are chosen."

Paying Taxes to Caesar

[15]Then the Pharisees went out and laid plans to trap him in his words. [16]They sent their disciples to him along with the Herodians. "Teacher," they said, "we know you are a man of integrity and that you teach the way of God in accordance with the truth. You aren't swayed by men, because you pay no attention to who they are. [17]Tell us then, what is your opinion? Is it right to pay taxes to Caesar or not?"

[18]But Jesus, knowing their evil intent, said, "You hypocrites, why are you trying to trap me? [19]Show me the coin used for paying the tax." They brought him a denarius, [20]and he asked them, "Whose portrait is this? And whose inscription?"

[21]"Caesar's," they replied.

Then he said to them, "Give to Caesar what is Caesar's, and to God what is God's."

[22]When they heard this, they were amazed. So they left him and went away.

Marriage at the Resurrection

[23]That same day the Sadducees, who say there is no resurrection, came to him with a question. [24]"Teacher," they said, "Moses told us that if a man dies without having children, his brother must marry the widow and have children for him. [25]Now there were seven brothers among us. The first one married and died, and since he had no children, he left his wife to his brother. [26]The same thing happened to the second and third brother, right on down to the seventh. [27]Finally, the woman died. [28]Now then, at the resurrection, whose wife will she be of the seven, since all of them were married to her?"

[29]Jesus replied, "You are in error because you do not know the Scriptures or the power of God. [30]At the resurrection people will neither marry nor be given in marriage; they will be like the angels in heaven. [31]But about the resurrection of the dead—have you not read what God said to you, [32]'I am the God of Abraham, the God of Isaac, and the God of Jacob'[n]? He is not the God of the dead but of the living."

[33]When the crowds heard this, they were astonished at his teaching.

REFLECT: 1. When did Jesus first call you to the banquet? How did you respond initially? How many other times did he invite you? **2.** With whom in this story do you identify most easily? Why? **3.** What can you do this week to encourage "full attendance" and "proper dress"?

OPEN: Who can guess how many times the word or numeral "one" is printed on a one dollar bill?

DIG: 1. How would the crowd respond if Jesus said simply, "Pay Caesar"? Why? How would the ruling government respond if Jesus said, "Don't pay"? **2.** What does Jesus mean by his answer (v.21)? What is it that should be given to God? What is he teaching about the relationship of Church and State? Which obligation is primary? Why?

REFLECT: 1. In your life, what belongs to Caesar ? To God? **2.** How well are you giving to each?

OPEN: In heaven, who or what on earth would you miss most?

DIG: 1. Who questions Jesus now? What do they believe? How does their question appear: Mocking? Serious? Scriptural (see Dt 25:5-10)? A trick? **2.** What aspects of their question does Jesus answer? Why is there no marriage in heaven? **3.** How does Exodus 3:6 "prove" the resurrection?

REFLECT: What hope does the fact of the resurrection give you? What one question would you like to ask Jesus about life after death?

[n]32 Exodus 3:6

OPEN: Who are the three people in this world who love you the most?

DIG: 1. How are these three loves (vv.38-39) related to each other? To the Law and the Prophets (see Dt 6:5 and Lev 19:18 in context)? To "situational ethics" today? **2.** Is love the only absolute? Why?

OPEN: Would you rather *ask* questions or *answer* them? Why?

DIG: 1. Were the Pharisees expecting the Messiah to be human or to be divine? What problem with this view does Jesus point out? **2.** Why would it take Jesus' death and resurrection to show that the Messiah is more than just David's son?

REFLECT: How has your view of Jesus been stretched by your study in Matthew?

OPEN: Growing up, what "hot buttons" did you push to get your parents mad? What "hot buttons" do your kids (if any) use on you?

DIG: 1. What was the seat of Moses? Given Jesus' remarks about the Pharisees in chapters 21-22, what is surprising about his remarks in 23:3? How does he limit his commendation of the Pharisees? **2.** As Jesus sees it, what is the main evil of the Pharisees? How are the disciples to avoid falling into the same evil? Why would it be important that the disciples not allow themselves to be called "Rabbi"? What distinction was Jesus trying to make between his followers and the Pharisees? **3.** Compare the path to greatness followed by the Pharisees with that taught by Jesus (vv.5-12). What do these two views of greatness teach us about the two views of the kingdom? **4.** Make a list of the seven charges Jesus makes against the Pharisees and the teachers of the Law (vv.13-32). How do they relate to what Jesus says in verses 2-7? Do you find anything common to all seven charges? How do each of these affect the common

The Greatest Commandment

³⁴Hearing that Jesus had silenced the Sadducees, the Pharisees got together. ³⁵One of them, an expert in the law, tested him with this question: ³⁶"Teacher, which is the greatest commandment in the Law?"

³⁷Jesus replied: " 'Love the Lord your God with all your heart and with all your soul and with all your mind.'ᵒ ³⁸This is the first and greatest commandment. ³⁹And the second is like it: 'Love your neighbor as yourself.'ᵖ ⁴⁰All the Law and the Prophets hang on these two commandments."

Whose Son Is the Christ?

⁴¹While the Pharisees were gathered together, Jesus asked them, ⁴²"What do you think about the Christ�q? Whose son is he?"

"The son of David," they replied.

⁴³He said to them, "How is it then that David, speaking by the Spirit, calls him 'Lord'? For he says,

⁴⁴" 'The Lord said to my Lord:
"Sit at my right hand
until I put your enemies
under your feet." 'ʳ

⁴⁵If then David calls him 'Lord,' how can he be his son?" ⁴⁶No one could say a word in reply, and from that day on no one dared to ask him any more questions.

Seven Woes

23 Then Jesus said to the crowds and to his disciples: ²"The teachers of the law and the Pharisees sit in Moses' seat. ³So you must obey them and do everything they tell you. But do not do what they do, for they do not practice what they preach. ⁴They tie up heavy loads and put them on men's shoulders, but they themselves are not willing to lift a finger to move them.

⁵"Everything they do is done for men to see: They make their phylacteriesˢ wide and the tassels on their garments long; ⁶they love the place of honor at banquets and the most important seats in the synagogues; ⁷they love to be greeted in the marketplaces and to have men call them 'Rabbi.'

⁸"But you are not to be called 'Rabbi,' for you have only one Master and you are all brothers. ⁹And do not call anyone on earth 'father,' for you have one Father, and he is in heaven. ¹⁰Nor are you to be called 'teacher,' for you have one Teacher, the Christ.q ¹¹The greatest among you will be your servant. ¹²For whoever exalts himself will be humbled, and whoever humbles himself will be exalted.

ᵒ37 Deut. 6:5   ᵖ39 Lev. 19:18   q42,10 Or *Messiah*   ʳ44 Psalm 110:1
ˢ5 That is, boxes containing Scripture verses, worn on forehead and arm

[13]"Woe to you, teachers of the law and Pharisees, you hypocrites! You shut the kingdom of heaven in men's faces. You yourselves do not enter, nor will you let those enter who are trying to. [1]

[15]"Woe to you, teachers of the law and Pharisees, you hypocrites! You travel over land and sea to win a single convert, and when he becomes one, you make him twice as much a son of hell as you are.

[16]"Woe to you, blind guides! You say, 'If anyone swears by the temple, it means nothing; but if anyone swears by the gold of the temple, he is bound by his oath.' [17]You blind fools! Which is greater: the gold, or the temple that makes the gold sacred? [18]You also say, 'If anyone swears by the altar, it means nothing; but if anyone swears by the gift on it, he is bound by his oath.' [19]You blind men! Which is greater: the gift, or the altar that makes the gift sacred? [20]Therefore, he who swears by the altar swears by it and by everything on it. [21]And he who swears by the temple swears by it and by the one who dwells in it. [22]And he who swears by heaven swears by God's throne and by the one who sits on it.

[23]"Woe to you, teachers of the law and Pharisees, you hypocrites! You give a tenth of your spices—mint, dill and cummin. But you have neglected the more important matters of the law—justice, mercy and faithfulness. You should have practiced the latter, without neglecting the former. [24]You blind guides! You strain out a gnat but swallow a camel.

[25]"Woe to you, teachers of the law and Pharisees, you hypocrites! You clean the outside of the cup and dish, but inside they are full of greed and self-indulgence. [26]Blind Pharisee! First clean the inside of the cup and dish, and then the outside also will be clean.

[27]"Woe to you, teachers of the law and Pharisees, you hypocrites! You are like whitewashed tombs, which look beautiful on the outside but on the inside are full of dead men's bones and everything unclean. [28]In the same way, on the outside you appear to people as righteous but on the inside you are full of hypocrisy and wickedness.

[29]"Woe to you, teachers of the law and Pharisees, you hypocrites! You build tombs for the prophets and decorate the graves of the righteous. [30]And you say, 'If we had lived in the days of our forefathers, we would not have taken part with them in shedding the blood of the prophets.' [31]So you testify against yourselves that you are the descendants of those who murdered the prophets. [32]Fill up, then, the measure of the sin of your forefathers!

[33]"You snakes! You brood of vipers! How will you escape being condemned to hell? [34]Therefore I am sending you prophets and wise men and teachers. Some of them you will kill and crucify; others you will flog in your synagogues and pursue from town to town. [35]And so upon you will come all the righteous

people? **5.** How have the religious leaders corrupted the practice of evangelism (vv.13-15)? Of oath-making (vv.16-22)? Of tithing (vv.23-24: see Mic 6:6-8)? Of integrity, where public image matches inner reality (vv.25-28)? **6.** In what way are these religious leaders condemned to repeat the past because of their failure to learn from their forefathers (vv.29-36)? How is the punishment in verses 33-36 appropriate to the crimes? **7.** What emotion does Jesus display in verses 37-39? How do you think he felt as he was teaching? Why?

REFLECT: 1. Where does Jesus catch your attention in this passage? What practices touch close-to-home in your life? How can you avoid what is preached against in this passage? **2.** How can you avoid making it hard for others to grow spiritually? **3.** What about today's church do you lament over (as Jesus did over Jerusalem)? **4.** From reading this passage, what should today's teachers and pastors be especially mindful of? How have you seen the "power of the pulpit" abused? **5.** Do you feel Jesus is a little too tough on the Pharisees? On you? Why or why not?

---

[1]13 Some manuscripts *to.* [14]*Woe to you, teachers of the law and Pharisees, you hypocrites! You devour widows' houses and for a show make lengthy prayers. Therefore you will be punished more severely.*

blood that has been shed on earth, from the blood of righteous Abel to the blood of Zechariah son of Berekiah, whom you murdered between the temple and the altar. ³⁶I tell you the truth, all this will come upon this generation.

³⁷"O Jerusalem, Jerusalem, you who kill the prophets and stone those sent to you, how often I have longed to gather your children together, as a hen gathers her chicks under her wings, but you were not willing. ³⁸Look, your house is left to you desolate. ³⁹For I tell you, you will not see me again until you say, 'Blessed is he who comes in the name of the Lord.'^u"

Signs of the End of the Age

24 Jesus left the temple and was walking away when his disciples came up to him to call his attention to its buildings. ²"Do you see all these things?" he asked. "I tell you the truth, not one stone here will be left on another; every one will be thrown down."

³As Jesus was sitting on the Mount of Olives, the disciples came to him privately. "Tell us," they said, "when will this happen, and what will be the sign of your coming and of the end of the age?"

⁴Jesus answered: "Watch out that no one deceives you. ⁵For many will come in my name, claiming, 'I am the Christ,'^v and will deceive many. ⁶You will hear of wars and rumors of wars, but see to it that you are not alarmed. Such things must happen, but the end is still to come. ⁷Nation will rise against nation, and kingdom against kingdom. There will be famines and earthquakes in various places. ⁸All these are the beginning of birth pains.

⁹"Then you will be handed over to be persecuted and put to death, and you will be hated by all nations because of me. ¹⁰At that time many will turn away from the faith and will betray and hate each other, ¹¹and many false prophets will appear and deceive many people. ¹²Because of the increase of wickedness, the love of most will grow cold, ¹³but he who stands firm to the end will be saved. ¹⁴And this gospel of the kingdom will be preached in the whole world as a testimony to all nations, and then the end will come.

¹⁵"So when you see standing in the holy place 'the abomination that causes desolation,'^w spoken of through the prophet Daniel—let the reader understand— ¹⁶then let those who are in Judea flee to the mountains. ¹⁷Let no one on the roof of his house go down to take anything out of the house. ¹⁸Let no one in the field go back to get his cloak. ¹⁹How dreadful it will be in those days for pregnant women and nursing mothers! ²⁰Pray that your flight will not take place in winter or on the Sabbath. ²¹For then there will be great distress, unequaled from the beginning of the world until now—and never to be equaled again. ²²If those days had not been cut short, no one would survive, but for the sake of the elect those days will be shortened. ²³At that time if anyone says to you, 'Look, here is the Christ!' or, 'There he is!' do not

OPEN: 1. When you were growing up, what were you like with building blocks (Lincoln logs, Tinker toys, Legos, etc.): (a) Meticulous in following the instructions step by step? (b) Innovative in designing your own structure? (c) Mischievous in destroying someone else's creation? **2.** How are you like that today in your "building projects"?

DIG: 1. What prompts Jesus' next lesson? **2.** What bombshell does he drop on his disciples? How do the Jewish people (including the disciples) feel about the temple? How must the disciples have felt when they heard Jesus' words in verse 2? **3.** What three questions do the disciples ask? **4.** What events might mislead the disciples into thinking the end had come (vv.4-7)? **5.** What would happen to the church after that (vv.9-12)? What does Jesus promise for those who endure and don't give in? What must the church continue doing (v.14)? **6.** What event would signal the start of the great distress? What does "the abomination that causes desolation" mean? (See Da 9:27 and 11:31 in context.) **7.** What should Christians do when this happens (vv.16-20)? Why? **8.** What dangerous deceptions would Christians need to guard against (vv.23-26)? Why would believers be susceptible to such rumors then? **9.** In contrast, what will mark the coming of the true Messiah (vv.27-29)? What will his second coming be like (vv.30-31)? **10.** What is the lesson from the fig tree? How does it apply to the disciples' question (v.3) and Jesus' answer (vv.33-35)?

REFLECT: 1. Some people think this passage anticipated the destruction of Jerusalem in A.D. 70, while others think it refers to the end of the world. What do you think? Could it be both? **2.** How is this passage meant to influence

^u*39* Psalm 118:26   ^v*5* Or *Messiah*; also in verse 23   ^w*15* Daniel 9:27; 11:31; 12:11

believe it. [24]For false Christs and false prophets will appear and perform great signs and miracles to deceive even the elect—if that were possible. [25]See, I have told you ahead of time.

[26]"So if anyone tells you, 'There he is, out in the desert,' do not go out; or, 'Here he is, in the inner rooms,' do not believe it. [27]For as lightning that comes from the east is visible even in the west, so will be the coming of the Son of Man. [28]Wherever there is a carcass, there the vultures will gather.

[29]"Immediately after the distress of those days

" 'the sun will be darkened,
   and the moon will not give its light;
the stars will fall from the sky,
   and the heavenly bodies will be shaken.'[x]

[30]"At that time the sign of the Son of Man will appear in the sky, and all the nations of the earth will mourn. They will see the Son of Man coming on the clouds of the sky, with power and great glory. [31]And he will send his angels with a loud trumpet call, and they will gather his elect from the four winds, from one end of the heavens to the other.

[32]"Now learn this lesson from the fig tree: As soon as its twigs get tender and its leaves come out, you know that summer is near. [33]Even so, when you see all these things, you know that it[y] is near, right at the door. [34]I tell you the truth, this generation[z] will certainly not pass away until all these things have happened. [35]Heaven and earth will pass away, but my words will never pass away.

The Day and Hour Unknown

[36]"No one knows about that day or hour, not even the angels in heaven, nor the Son,[a] but only the Father. [37]As it was in the days of Noah, so it will be at the coming of the Son of Man. [38]For in the days before the flood, people were eating and drinking, marrying and giving in marriage, up to the day Noah entered the ark; [39]and they knew nothing about what would happen until the flood came and took them all away. That is how it will be at the coming of the Son of Man. [40]Two men will be in the field; one will be taken and the other left. [41]Two women will be grinding with a hand mill; one will be taken and the other left.

[42]"Therefore keep watch, because you do not know on what day your Lord will come. [43]But understand this: If the owner of the house had known at what time of night the thief was coming, he would have kept watch and would not have let his house be broken into. [44]So you also must be ready, because the Son of Man will come at an hour when you do not expect him.

[45]"Who then is the faithful and wise servant, whom the master has put in charge of the servants in his household to give them their food at the proper time? [46]It will be good for that servant whose master finds him doing so when he returns. [47]I tell you the truth, he will put him in charge of all his possessions. [48]But suppose that servant is wicked and says to himself, 'My

your lifestyle? What gets in your way of taking this seriously? **3.** If you could ask Jesus one question about either the second coming or the end of the world, what would you ask? How do you think he would answer it? **4.** Do you see some of these signs being fulfilled today? In what way? How do you feel about this?

OPEN: 1. If Jesus returned at 7:00 PM this Tuesday, what would you be doing? **2.** As a child, what was your favorite time of day? Day of the week? Season of the year?

DIG: 1. In what ways is the Flood like the second coming of Christ? **2.** What does it mean, practically, to be ready for Jesus' return if we do not know when he will come? **3.** In view of Christ's second coming, what does the story of the faithful and wise servant teach you about readiness? About stewardship? Judgment? Responsibility for serving and witnessing to others? **4.** How does this story relate to 24:1-31? To 24:32-35? **5.** What is one thing you can say for certain about the day and the hour of the second coming of Christ?

REFLECT: 1. Specifically, how are you preparing for the Second Coming? **2.** How would you explain the end times and the Second Coming to a seeker? **3.** Over what has God given you stewardship? How would God evaluate the job you're doing?

---

[x]29 Isaiah 13:10; 34:4   [y]33 Or he   [z]34 Or race   [a]36 Some manuscripts do not have *nor the Son*.

master is staying away a long time,' [49]and he then begins to beat his fellow servants and to eat and drink with drunkards. [50]The master of that servant will come on a day when he does not expect him and at an hour he is not aware of. [51]He will cut him to pieces and assign him a place with the hypocrites, where there will be weeping and gnashing of teeth.

The Parable of the Ten Virgins

25 "At that time the kingdom of heaven will be like ten virgins who took their lamps and went out to meet the bridegroom. [2]Five of them were foolish and five were wise. [3]The foolish ones took their lamps but did not take any oil with them. [4]The wise, however, took oil in jars along with their lamps. [5]The bridegroom was a long time in coming, and they all became drowsy and fell asleep.

[6]"At midnight the cry rang out: 'Here's the bridegroom! Come out to meet him!'

[7]"Then all the virgins woke up and trimmed their lamps. [8]The foolish ones said to the wise, 'Give us some of your oil; our lamps are going out.'

[9]"'No,' they replied, 'there may not be enough for both us and you. Instead, go to those who sell oil and buy some for yourselves.'

[10]"But while they were on their way to buy the oil, the bridegroom arrived. The virgins who were ready went in with him to the wedding banquet. And the door was shut.

[11]"Later the others also came. 'Sir! Sir!' they said. 'Open the door for us!'

[12]"But he replied, 'I tell you the truth, I don't know you.'

[13]"Therefore keep watch, because you do not know the day or the hour.

The Parable of the Talents

[14]"Again, it will be like a man going on a journey, who called his servants and entrusted his property to them. [15]To one he gave five talents[b] of money, to another two talents, and to another one talent, each according to his ability. Then he went on his journey. [16]The man who had received the five talents went at once and put his money to work and gained five more. [17]So also, the one with the two talents gained two more. [18]But the man who had received the one talent went off, dug a hole in the ground and hid his master's money.

[19]"After a long time the master of those servants returned and settled accounts with them. [20]The man who had received the five talents brought the other five. 'Master,' he said, 'you entrusted me with five talents. See, I have gained five more.'

[21]"His master replied, 'Well done, good and faithful servant! You have been faithful with a few things; I will put you in charge of many things. Come and share your master's happiness!'

[22]"The man with the two talents also came. 'Master,' he said, 'you entrusted me with two talents; see, I have gained two more.'

[b]15 A talent was worth more than a thousand dollars.

OPEN: 1. If a meeting begins at 7:00 PM, do you get there at 6:45? 7:05? Plan to leave your house at 7:00? Hope everyone else will be late? **2.** How does your punctuality at today's Bible study illustrate this?

DIG: 1. How does this parable relate to Matthew 24? **2.** In what ways were the ten girls alike? Different? What unexpected event takes place (vv.5-6)? With what embarrassing consequence (v. 8)? **3.** What is the point of this parable (see also 24:42)? **4.** Why is readiness so important in regard to the Second Coming?

REFLECT: 1. At the final wedding banquet, where will you be standing? Why? **2.** What is the "oil" that keeps your "lamp" lit? **3.** Who are you most like in this story? Why?

OPEN: 1. Who was one of the most talented people you knew in school? What happened to that person? **2.** What were you known for in school—what talents did people recognize in you?

DIG: 1. In this parable, who does the master represent? The journey? The talents? The servants? **2.** What happens to the two servants who doubled their investment? To the servant who hides his talent? On what basis were they rewarded? **3.** How does the master's treatment of the one-talent servant seem to you: Fair? Harsh? Lenient? Why? **4.** Why do you think Jesus thought it necessary to repeat his point so many times and in so many different ways (as in ch.23-25)?

REFLECT: 1. If the Master returned today, what would he say about the way you've used what he gave you? How have you worked at developing it? What kind of responsibility do you feel

THE PARABLE OF THE TALENTS

LOOKING INTO THE SCRIPTURE/25 Minutes. Read Matthew 25:14-30 and discuss.

1. My opinion of the master is that
   a. he was too harsh with his servant
   b. he was not hard enough on the servant
   c. his reaction was justified
   d. I'm glad I don't work for him

2. When Jesus talks in this parable about "talents," what is he referring to?
   a. ability to make something of money
   b. natural abilities
   c. special spiritual gifts
   d. capital for investment

3. How would you have felt if you were the one to receive only one talent?
   a. jealous of the others who got more
   b. resigned to a life of obscurity
   c. relieved to have less responsibility
   d. invigorated to invest it wisely

4. What happened to the two servants who doubled their investment?
   a. they kept the profit
   b. they felt good about themselves
   c. the master split the profit with the servant that did nothing
   d. the master rewarded them

5. Why did the servant with one talent hide his talent?
   a. he was lazy
   b. he was afraid of his master
   c. he had no initiative
   d. he had low self-confidence

6. What was Jesus saying to the two servants who doubled their investment?
   a. I am proud of you
   b. you'll get your reward in heaven
   c. my investment in you paid off
   d. I can trust you with bigger things

7. Why was the master so hard on the servant who hid his talent?
   a. he didn't take responsibility for what was given him
   b. he wasted his opportunity
   c. he wasted his master's goods
   d. he wallowed in self-pity
   e. he did absolutely no good to anyone

MY OWN STORY/20 Minutes.

1. One of the best ways to figure out what God wants you to do with your life is to take a look at your abilities and assets. Finish the sentence by checking three or four things: "I am good at . . ."
   ☐ working with children
   ☐ listening/caring
   ☐ helping behind the scenes
   ☐ playing an instrument
   ☐ problem solving
   ☐ coaching/teaching
   ☐ organizing/administering
   ☐ acting/singing
   ☐ sharing my faith
   ☐ motivating/leading
   ☐ getting others involved
   ☐ crusading for a cause
   ☐ peacemaking/reconciling
   ☐ cooking/homemaking
   ☐ teaching the Bible
   ☐ running a business
   ☐ helping others start a business
   ☐ working with old people
   ☐ playing ball
   ☐ making people laugh
   ☐ sticking it out
   ☐ cheering others on
   ☐ hanging out with kids
   ☐ being sensitive to others
   ☐ raising money

2. Let the others in your group add two more things you are good at.

3. Now imagine how those abilities could be used to share Christ's love and do God's work in your circumstances. Be specific as you apply your strengths to "kingdom business."

4. What is your favorite excuse for not using your talents?
   a. I don't have any
   b. I'm tired
   c. I'm afraid I might fail
   d. I'm not as talented as . . .
   e. I've got a hang-up
   f. I want to be humble
   g. I don't have the time

5. What do you need to get you started?
   a. guarantee from God that I'll be successful
   b. self-confidence
   c. my priorities sorted out
   d. lots of support from friends
   e. a personal call from God
   f. energy
   g. a gentle push from group members

toward God regarding your talents? **2.** When, if ever, have you observed that the more you used a talent, the more talents God gave you? **3.** What will you do this week with the talents God has given you to prepare for his coming? What can your group do to help you in this regard?

OPEN: 1. Where do you keep your prized possessions? **2.** What award do you prize because it was given to you for special service or recognition?

DIG: 1. Does this story seem more like a parable or a prophecy? Why? **2.** List the six actions Jesus will use as the basis of judgment. What kinds of acts are these? For whom are they done now and ultimately (v.40)? How do they benefit the doer? **3.** How are those who don't do the acts and those who do them similar? Different? **4.** What does this section teach about Christian responsibility? Who, besides those mentioned here, might be considered "the least of these"? **5.** In summary, what did Jesus teach in chapters 23-25? How were Jesus and his opponents different in actions and attitudes? Is the judgment note in this section consistent with your view of Jesus? Why or why not?

REFLECT: 1. When have you been hungry, thirsty, a stranger, in need of clothes, sick or imprisoned, and someone reached out to you? When have you reached out to people in those conditions? **2.** In these six areas, where do you find yourself serving most naturally? In which areas do you have the most trouble reaching out?

²³"His master replied, 'Well done, good and faithful servant! You have been faithful with a few things; I will put you in charge of many things. Come and share your master's happiness!'

²⁴"Then the man who had received the one talent came. 'Master,' he said, 'I knew that you are a hard man, harvesting where you have not sown and gathering where you have not scattered seed. ²⁵So I was afraid and went out and hid your talent in the ground. See, here is what belongs to you.'

²⁶"His master replied, 'You wicked, lazy servant! So you knew that I harvest where I have not sown and gather where I have not scattered seed? ²⁷Well then, you should have put my money on deposit with the bankers, so that when I returned I would have received it back with interest.

²⁸" 'Take the talent from him and give it to the one who has the ten talents. ²⁹For everyone who has will be given more, and he will have an abundance. Whoever does not have, even what he has will be taken from him. ³⁰And throw that worthless servant outside, into the darkness, where there will be weeping and gnashing of teeth.'

The Sheep and the Goats

³¹"When the Son of Man comes in his glory, and all the angels with him, he will sit on his throne in heavenly glory. ³²All the nations will be gathered before him, and he will separate the people one from another as a shepherd separates the sheep from the goats. ³³He will put the sheep on his right and the goats on his left.

³⁴"Then the King will say to those on his right, 'Come, you who are blessed by my Father; take your inheritance, the kingdom prepared for you since the creation of the world. ³⁵For I was hungry and you gave me something to eat, I was thirsty and you gave me something to drink, I was a stranger and you invited me in, ³⁶I needed clothes and you clothed me, I was sick and you looked after me, I was in prison and you came to visit me.'

³⁷"Then the righteous will answer him, 'Lord, when did we see you hungry and feed you, or thirsty and give you something to drink? ³⁸When did we see you a stranger and invite you in, or needing clothes and clothe you? ³⁹When did we see you sick or in prison and go to visit you?'

⁴⁰"The King will reply, 'I tell you the truth, whatever you did for one of the least of these brothers of mine, you did for me.'

⁴¹"Then he will say to those on his left, 'Depart from me, you who are cursed, into the eternal fire prepared for the devil and his angels. ⁴²For I was hungry and you gave me nothing to eat, I was thirsty and you gave me nothing to drink, ⁴³I was a stranger and you did not invite me in, I needed clothes and you did not clothe me, I was sick and in prison and you did not look after me.'

⁴⁴"They also will answer, 'Lord, when did we see you hungry or thirsty or a stranger or needing clothes or sick or in prison, and did not help you?'

⁴⁵"He will reply, 'I tell you the truth, whatever you did not

do for one of the least of these, you did not do for me.'

46"Then they will go away to eternal punishment, but the righteous to eternal life."

The Plot Against Jesus

26 When Jesus had finished saying all these things, he said to his disciples, 2"As you know, the Passover is two days away—and the Son of Man will be handed over to be crucified."

3Then the chief priests and the elders of the people assembled in the palace of the high priest, whose name was Caiaphas, 4and they plotted to arrest Jesus in some sly way and kill him. 5"But not during the Feast," they said, "or there may be a riot among the people."

Jesus Anointed at Bethany

6While Jesus was in Bethany in the home of a man known as Simon the Leper, 7a woman came to him with an alabaster jar of very expensive perfume, which she poured on his head as he was reclining at the table.

8When the disciples saw this, they were indignant. "Why this waste?" they asked. 9"This perfume could have been sold at a high price and the money given to the poor."

10Aware of this, Jesus said to them, "Why are you bothering this woman? She has done a beautiful thing to me. 11The poor you will always have with you, but you will not always have me. 12When she poured this perfume on my body, she did it to prepare me for burial. 13I tell you the truth, wherever this gospel is preached throughout the world, what she has done will also be told, in memory of her."

Judas Agrees to Betray Jesus

14Then one of the Twelve—the one called Judas Iscariot— went to the chief priests 15and asked, "What are you willing to give me if I hand him over to you?" So they counted out for him thirty silver coins. 16From then on Judas watched for an opportunity to hand him over.

The Lord's Supper

17On the first day of the Feast of Unleavened Bread, the disciples came to Jesus and asked, "Where do you want us to make preparations for you to eat the Passover?"

18He replied, "Go into the city to a certain man and tell him, 'The Teacher says: My appointed time is near. I am going to celebrate the Passover with my disciples at your house.'" 19So the disciples did as Jesus had directed them and prepared the Passover.

20When evening came, Jesus was reclining at the table with the Twelve. 21And while they were eating, he said, "I tell you the truth, one of you will betray me."

22They were very sad and began to say to him one after the other, "Surely not I, Lord?"

23Jesus replied, "The one who has dipped his hand into the bowl with me will betray me. 24The Son of Man will go just as

OPEN: If you had a year's wages to blow on one special gift, what would you buy and for whom?

DIG: 1. Why was Passover an appropriate time for the events of verses 1-5 to unfold? Why might the timing be risky? **2.** What is significant about the setting for this woman's gift to Jesus? **3.** What context in Jesus' life (vv.11-12) justifies this woman's act? Why are the disciples indignant? **4.** What is Jesus trying to teach his disciples about priorities? **5.** How could this scene relate to what happens in verses 14-16?

REFLECT: 1. What "beautiful" thing could you do this week for Jesus (or "the least of these")? **2.** Whereas the woman (v.7) gave lavishly for Jesus, Judas wanted to see what he could get from him. In what ways are you like the woman? Like Judas?

OPEN: As a kid, what were mealtimes like in your family? Where did everyone sit around the table? What were the consequences for misbehavior at the table?

DIG: 1. What do you know about the Feast of Unleavened Bread (see Ex 12:1-30)? **2.** Why do you think Jesus was so secretive about his arrangements for the Passover meal? **3.** In what stages does Jesus reveal his betrayer (vv.21, 23,25)? Is Jesus warning Judas not to go through with his scheme? Or is Jesus predicting what will happen when he does? **4.** In what ways do the bread and wine relate to his body and blood? **5.** Are the disciples singing their final hymn together (v.30) in a major or minor key? Why do you think that?

77

REFLECT: 1. What does Communion mean to you? **2.** How steadily do you know God's forgiveness of your sins? Why do many Christians struggle with guilt if Jesus provides the forgiveness of sins? **3.** What impresses you most about Jesus at the Last Supper?

it is written about him. But woe to that man who betrays the Son of Man! It would be better for him if he had not been born."

[25]Then Judas, the one who would betray him, said, "Surely not I, Rabbi?"

Jesus answered, "Yes, it is you."[c]

[26]While they were eating, Jesus took bread, gave thanks and broke it, and gave it to his disciples, saying, "Take and eat; this is my body."

[27]Then he took the cup, gave thanks and offered it to them, saying, "Drink from it, all of you. [28]This is my blood of the[d] covenant, which is poured out for many for the forgiveness of sins. [29]I tell you, I will not drink of this fruit of the vine from now on until that day when I drink it anew with you in my Father's kingdom."

[30]When they had sung a hymn, they went out to the Mount of Olives.

Jesus Predicts Peter's Denial

OPEN: What very sincere promise did you once make but failed to deliver on: (a) To *always* clean up your room? (b) Always get your homework in *on time*? (c) Marry the one you *first* loved? (d) Have a *daily* quiet time? (e) Other:_____?

DIG: What emotions and motives accompany Jesus' next prediction? Peter's vow? Jesus' reply? Peter's follow-up vow?

REFLECT: When have you felt betrayed? How did you deal with it?

[31]Then Jesus told them, "This very night you will all fall away on account of me, for it is written:

> " 'I will strike the shepherd,
>   and the sheep of the flock will be scattered.'[e]

[32]But after I have risen, I will go ahead of you into Galilee."

[33]Peter replied, "Even if all fall away on account of you, I never will."

[34]"I tell you the truth," Jesus answered, "this very night, before the rooster crows, you will disown me three times."

[35]But Peter declared, "Even if I have to die with you, I will never disown you." And all the other disciples said the same.

Gethsemane

OPEN: What was the longest night of your life: Delivering your first child? Waiting up for your teenager? Deciding to call it quits?

DIG: 1. What are the various emotions Jesus must have felt in Gethsemane? What does he ask of the disciples? What does he ask of God? **2.** What is God's will (vv.39,42)? What model for our prayers does Jesus provide here? What obstacles to prayer does Jesus face? Likewise, his disciples?

REFLECT: 1. What has been your "Gethsemane"—a place where you really wrestled with God? What was the issue? What do you learn from Jesus' example about praying at those times? **2.** Who would you want to "watch and pray" with you next time you face a "Gethsemane"? **3.** What do you appreciate most about Jesus from this story?

[36]Then Jesus went with his disciples to a place called Gethsemane, and he said to them, "Sit here while I go over there and pray." [37]He took Peter and the two sons of Zebedee along with him, and he began to be sorrowful and troubled. [38]Then he said to them, "My soul is overwhelmed with sorrow to the point of death. Stay here and keep watch with me."

[39]Going a little farther, he fell with his face to the ground and prayed, "My Father, if it is possible, may this cup be taken from me. Yet not as I will, but as you will."

[40]Then he returned to his disciples and found them sleeping. "Could you men not keep watch with me for one hour?" he asked Peter. [41]"Watch and pray so that you will not fall into temptation. The spirit is willing, but the body is weak."

[42]He went away a second time and prayed, "My Father, if it is not possible for this cup to be taken away unless I drink it, may your will be done."

[43]When he came back, he again found them sleeping, because their eyes were heavy. [44]So he left them and went away once more and prayed the third time, saying the same thing.

[c]25 Or *"You yourself have said it"*   [d]28 Some manuscripts *the new*
[e]31 Zech. 13:7

⁴⁵Then he returned to the disciples and said to them, "Are you still sleeping and resting? Look, the hour is near, and the Son of Man is betrayed into the hands of sinners. ⁴⁶Rise, let us go! Here comes my betrayer!"

Jesus Arrested

⁴⁷While he was still speaking, Judas, one of the Twelve, arrived. With him was a large crowd armed with swords and clubs, sent from the chief priests and the elders of the people. ⁴⁸Now the betrayer had arranged a signal with them: "The one I kiss is the man; arrest him." ⁴⁹Going at once to Jesus, Judas said, "Greetings, Rabbi!" and kissed him.

⁵⁰Jesus replied, "Friend, do what you came for."ᶠ

Then the men stepped forward, seized Jesus and arrested him. ⁵¹With that, one of Jesus' companions reached for his sword, drew it out and struck the servant of the high priest, cutting off his ear.

⁵²"Put your sword back in its place," Jesus said to him, "for all who draw the sword will die by the sword. ⁵³Do you think I cannot call on my Father, and he will at once put at my disposal more than twelve legions of angels? ⁵⁴But how then would the Scriptures be fulfilled that say it must happen in this way?"

⁵⁵At that time Jesus said to the crowd, "Am I leading a rebellion, that you have come out with swords and clubs to capture me? Every day I sat in the temple courts teaching, and you did not arrest me. ⁵⁶But this has all taken place that the writings of the prophets might be fulfilled." Then all the disciples deserted him and fled.

Before the Sanhedrin

⁵⁷Those who had arrested Jesus took him to Caiaphas, the high priest, where the teachers of the law and the elders had assembled. ⁵⁸But Peter followed him at a distance, right up to the courtyard of the high priest. He entered and sat down with the guards to see the outcome.

⁵⁹The chief priests and the whole Sanhedrin were looking for false evidence against Jesus so that they could put him to death. ⁶⁰But they did not find any, though many false witnesses came forward.

Finally two came forward ⁶¹and declared, "This fellow said, 'I am able to destroy the temple of God and rebuild it in three days.' "

⁶²Then the high priest stood up and said to Jesus, "Are you not going to answer? What is this testimony that these men are bringing against you?" ⁶³But Jesus remained silent.

The high priest said to him, "I charge you under oath by the living God: Tell us if you are the Christ,ᵍ the Son of God."

⁶⁴"Yes, it is as you say," Jesus replied. "But I say to all of you: In the future you will see the Son of Man sitting at the right hand of the Mighty One and coming on the clouds of heaven."

OPEN: How did your favorite adventure hero respond to danger?

DIG: 1. What kind of Messiah was the large, armed crowd expecting to arrest? Was the sword-wielding disciple's expectation essentially the same as theirs? Why or why not? **2.** What does Jesus' response to Judas, the crowd, and the disciple show about the type of Messiah he is?

REFLECT: 1. Knowing yourself, how would you have reacted if you had been with Jesus in this scene? **2.** How does your ideal of a heroic messiah correspond to the reality of Jesus in this passage?

OPEN: Have you ever been in a court of law or situation where you felt unfairly treated or felt the judge violated your rights?

DIG: 1. Who are the Sanhedrin (or senate body of elders), and what kind of cases were brought before them (see Ac 4,5,22-24)? **2.** Why take Jesus to the high priest? Why do you think Peter followed? Why would the priests knowingly accept false evidence? Why two witnesses (v.60; see Dt 19:15)? **3.** What is unusual about Jesus' self-defense? How does he view these proceedings? How does he view God's kingdom? **4.** What is blasphemy? Why would the priests think Jesus was guilty of this? Why don't they press their case?

REFLECT: 1. What impresses you most about Jesus here? **2.** Ever "defend your faith"? How well did you do? How could you give a better answer for the hope you have (1Pe 3:15-16)? **3.** How do you know when to keep silent and when to talk about your faith?

ᶠ50 Or "Friend, why have you come?"   ᵍ63 Or Messiah; also in verse 68

[65]Then the high priest tore his clothes and said, "He has spoken blasphemy! Why do we need any more witnesses? Look, now you have heard the blasphemy. [66]What do you think?"

"He is worthy of death," they answered.

[67]Then they spit in his face and struck him with their fists. Others slapped him [68]and said, "Prophesy to us, Christ. Who hit you?"

Peter Disowns Jesus

[69]Now Peter was sitting out in the courtyard, and a servant girl came to him. "You also were with Jesus of Galilee," she said.

[70]But he denied it before them all. "I don't know what you're talking about," he said.

[71]Then he went out to the gateway, where another girl saw him and said to the people there, "This fellow was with Jesus of Nazareth."

[72]He denied it again, with an oath: "I don't know the man!"

[73]After a little while, those standing there went up to Peter and said, "Surely you are one of them, for your accent gives you away."

[74]Then he began to call down curses on himself and he swore to them, "I don't know the man!"

Immediately a rooster crowed. [75]Then Peter remembered the word Jesus had spoken: "Before the rooster crows, you will disown me three times." And he went outside and wept bitterly.

Judas Hangs Himself

27 Early in the morning, all the chief priests and the elders of the people came to the decision to put Jesus to death. [2]They bound him, led him away and handed him over to Pilate, the governor.

[3]When Judas, who had betrayed him, saw that Jesus was condemned, he was seized with remorse and returned the thirty silver coins to the chief priests and the elders. [4]"I have sinned," he said, "for I have betrayed innocent blood."

"What is that to us?" they replied. "That's your responsibility."

[5]So Judas threw the money into the temple and left. Then he went away and hanged himself.

[6]The chief priests picked up the coins and said, "It is against the law to put this into the treasury, since it is blood money." [7]So they decided to use the money to buy the potter's field as a burial place for foreigners. [8]That is why it has been called the Field of Blood to this day. [9]Then what was spoken by Jeremiah the prophet was fulfilled: "They took the thirty silver coins, the price set on him by the people of Israel, [10]and they used them to buy the potter's field, as the Lord commanded me."[h]

OPEN: In high school, when did you really disappoint yourself?

DIG: 1. So far in Matthew, what character traits has Peter exhibited? Here, how do his actions reveal his character? Which character trait dominates this story? **2.** When did Peter realize what was happening? Why then? Why cry?

REFLECT: When have you felt like Peter? What was the "rooster" in your life that made you realize what was happening? How did you make a comeback?

OPEN: Ever wish you could erase words once written, or retrieve words once spoken? Illustrate.

DIG: 1. Why is Judas suddenly seized with remorse? Was he was expecting a different outcome? If so, what? **2.** What in verse 4 helps to explain the priests' actions in verses 1-2? Why do you think they avoid taking direct responsibility for Jesus' death?

REFLECT: 1. Both Peter and Judas caved in under pressure, yet history has treated them very differently. Why? **2.** Have you ever felt like you were beyond redemption? Why? To whom did (or can) you turn in this situation?

h10 See Zech. 11:12,13; Jer. 19:1-13; 32:6-9.

LOOKING INTO THE SCRIPTURE/20 Minutes. Read Matthew 26:69-75 and discuss.

1. How do you react to Peter in this story?
   a. I probably would have done the same thing
   b. he was a coward
   c. with pity
   d. disbelief that he could do something so dumb
   e. I was angry

2. Why do you think Peter followed Jesus to the scene of the trial?
   a. to satisfy his curiosity
   b. to rescue him
   c. to keep his promise
   d. to be near Jesus
   e. to record the events for the other disciples

3. What made Peter claim that he did not know Jesus?
   a. fear for his life
   b. spiritual weakness
   c. momentary insanity
   d. no guts

4. If you could put in a good word for Peter, what would it be?
   a. he meant well
   b. he couldn't help it
   c. he came back
   d. he's only human
   e. he was confused

5. After this, why do you think Jesus chose Peter and changed his name from Simon (sinking sand) to Peter (the rock)?
   a. Peter was the best one available
   b. Jesus believed in positive thinking
   c. belief that despite his flaws, Peter would do fine
   d. to illustrate the power of God

6. What impact do you think this failure had upon the future of Peter's life?
   a. it probably made him less cocky
   b. it probably made him less self-confident
   c. it probably made him a more sensitive person
   d. it probably made him into the man of God that he became

7. If Peter were the only disciple present beside Jesus during this incident, he must have shared this experience about his failure with others. Why?
   a. to get it off his chest
   b. to ask forgiveness from the others
   c. to help someone else who had done the same
   d. to show how God uses failure

MY OWN STORY/20 Minutes.

1. How do you usually react to failure?
   a. kick myself for days
   b. run away from the situation
   c. hide my feelings from everyone
   d. ask forgiveness and move on
   e. try to be extra nice

2. When you blow it, what have you found helpful?
   a. talk it over with a friend
   b. do penance
   c. forget about it
   d. try to learn from the mistake
   e. take some time off to get back on track
   f. write myself a long letter
   g. spend time with God

3. What have you found helpful in dealing with a friend who has experienced failure?
   a. keep my mouth shut
   b. share some of my failures
   c. let your friend talk it out
   d. do something crazy together
   e. refuse to let the person dwell on it

4. In the light of this lesson, how would you describe your life this past week in terms of a weather report?
   a. sunny and bright
   b. patchy fog and clouds
   c. stormy
   d. hurricane warnings
   e. cold and gloomy

OPEN: When have you been in a *wild* crowd: Rock concert? Football game? Protest march? Public hearing? Serendipity group?

DIG: 1. At this time in history, it was against Roman law to proclaim yourself Messiah (it was considered treason). The punishment for breaking this law was death. What does this tell us about the Roman view of what a Messiah was? How does this help explain Pilate's interest in Jesus? **2.** What is Pilate's overriding concern in this trial: Identifying the Messiah? Hearing out Jesus? Exchanging prisoners? Doing justice? Appeasement? **3.** Is Pilate more concerned about appeasing the crowd? His wife? His conscience? Why? In this regard, how do his actions compare with those of the chief priests (vv.1-4)? **4.** What is Pilate's motive in offering the crowd a prisoner exchange? How concerned is Pilate that Jesus is innocent? **5.** Who is ultimately on trial here? For what?

REFLECT: 1. When, if ever, have you been caught up in the enthusiasm of a group and done what you would have preferred not to do? How can you more effectively be your own person? **2.** On a scale of 1 (=easiest) to 10 (=toughest), how difficult is it for you to accept responsibility? **3.** With whom do you identify in this story: Pilate, Pilate's wife, the crowd, the chief priests, or Barabbas? Why?

OPEN: 1. Which of these violent deaths do you remember the most: (a) John F. Kennedy, (b) Martin Luther King, or (c) John Lennon? **2.** Which death affected you the most? **3.** Ultimately, which of these people will be remembered most? Why?

DIG: 1. Why were the soldiers so cruel in this case? What does that say about their view of Jesus? Of themselves? **2.** Why does Jesus need Simon's help? What shape

Jesus Before Pilate

[11]Meanwhile Jesus stood before the governor, and the governor asked him, "Are you the king of the Jews?"

"Yes, it is as you say," Jesus replied.

[12]When he was accused by the chief priests and the elders, he gave no answer. [13]Then Pilate asked him, "Don't you hear the testimony they are bringing against you?" [14]But Jesus made no reply, not even to a single charge—to the great amazement of the governor.

[15]Now it was the governor's custom at the Feast to release a prisoner chosen by the crowd. [16]At that time they had a notorious prisoner, called Barabbas. [17]So when the crowd had gathered, Pilate asked them, "Which one do you want me to release to you: Barabbas, or Jesus who is called Christ?" [18]For he knew it was out of envy that they had handed Jesus over to him.

[19]While Pilate was sitting on the judge's seat, his wife sent him this message: "Don't have anything to do with that innocent man, for I have suffered a great deal today in a dream because of him."

[20]But the chief priests and the elders persuaded the crowd to ask for Barabbas and to have Jesus executed.

[21]"Which of the two do you want me to release to you?" asked the governor.

"Barabbas," they answered.

[22]"What shall I do, then, with Jesus who is called Christ?" Pilate asked.

They all answered, "Crucify him!"

[23]"Why? What crime has he committed?" asked Pilate.

But they shouted all the louder, "Crucify him!"

[24]When Pilate saw that he was getting nowhere, but that instead an uproar was starting, he took water and washed his hands in front of the crowd. "I am innocent of this man's blood," he said. "It is your responsibility!"

[25]All the people answered, "Let his blood be on us and on our children!"

[26]Then he released Barabbas to them. But he had Jesus flogged, and handed him over to be crucified.

The Soldiers Mock Jesus

[27]Then the governor's soldiers took Jesus into the Praetorium and gathered the whole company of soldiers around him. [28]They stripped him and put a scarlet robe on him, [29]and then twisted together a crown of thorns and set it on his head. They put a staff in his right hand and knelt in front of him and mocked him. "Hail, king of the Jews!" they said. [30]They spit on him, and took the staff and struck him on the head again and again. [31]After they had mocked him, they took off the robe and put his own clothes on him. Then they led him away to crucify him.

LOOKING INTO THE SCRIPTURE/25 Minutes. Read Matthew 27:11-26 and discuss.

1. Each person in this passage looked upon Jesus from a different perspective and saw a different thing. Match the people with their viewpoint of Jesus.

☐ Pilate/Roman Governor   ☐ troublemaker
☐ wife of Pilate   ☐ threat to Roman Empire
☐ chief priests   ☐ threat to religious establishment
☐ Barabbas   ☐ imposter
☐ crowd   ☐ innocent person
                           ☐ Messiah/God's Son
                           ☐ stranger who took my place
                           ☐ yesterday's hero

2. Why did the religious authorities bring Jesus to Pilate, the Roman governor?
   a. to place the blame on Pilate
   b. they knew Pilate would give in
   c. they were afraid of the crowd
   d. their law forbade killing
   e. only the Roman governor could give the death sentence

3. Why did the Roman governor offer to release a prisoner chosen by the crowd?
   a. to avoid making a decision about Jesus
   b. to check out their motives
   c. to expose their hypocrisy
   d. to get Jesus off the hook
   e. to keep everybody happy

4. How would you describe Pilate?
   a. pragmatist—what works is right
   b. absolutist—what is right is right
   c. relativist—it all depends on the situation
   d. pantywaisted powder puff

5. How would you portray Pilate if you were a film director?
   a. smooth politician
   b. wimp
   c. victim of circumstances
   d. realist

6. Do you think Pilate knew that Jesus was innocent?
   a. it's hard to say
   b. probably so
   c. absolutely
   d. if he didn't, he was blind

7. Who ended up the biggest winner and who ended up the biggest loser in this situation?
   a. Pilate
   b. wife of Pilate
   c. chief priests
   d. Barabbas
   e. crowd

MY OWN STORY/20 Minutes.

1. How do you react to conflicting pressures from different sources?
   a. bury my head in the sand
   b. get stubborn and do my own thing
   c. listen to each one and make a decision
   d. look for more options
   e. try to avoid making a decision

2. Faced with a similar dilemma, how would you describe yourself?
   a. pragmatist—what works is right
   b. absolutist—what is right is right
   c. relativist—it all depends on the situation
   d. broad-minded escapist—there are too many issues to decide
   e. pantywaisted powder puff—whatever keeps the peace
   f. procrastinator—ask me tomorrow

3. If you had been in Pilate's shoes, what would you have done?
   a. the same thing
   b. referred the problem to Rome
   c. deferred making a decision until studying the facts some more
   d. stood up against the pressure and dismissed the charges
   e. I don't know

4. Who in this story would best describe the way you respond to the radical claims of Jesus Christ?
   a. Pilate
   b. wife of Pilate
   c. chief priests
   d. Barabbas
   e. crowd

is he in? **3.** For what "official" reason is Jesus crucified? **4.** What three groups taunt Jesus? Why these particular insults? **5.** What supreme irony do you see here in the cry for Jesus to come down from the cross? If he had, would they believe? If there's no cross, would they ever be saved? **6.** How has Jesus' experience with the Tempter prepared him for such a time as this (v.40; see 4:3,6)?

REFLECT: 1. If Jesus came today, who would "crucify" him? What would be the charge against him? Where would you be? **2.** In what way does the agony of these insults deepen your appreciation of what Christ did for you in his death? **3.** Write a note to Jesus expressing your feelings about his crucifixion.

OPEN: What is the saddest funeral you ever experienced—one where a friend, family member or national figure was taken suddenly and unexpectedly? How did you feel?

DIG: 1. Why does Jesus cry out in verse 46? What is the significance of this for Jesus? For you? **2.** What do the sympathizers see? Hear? Feel? Do? **3.** What is the significance of each of the supernatural events accompanying Jesus' death? What effect did they have on the centurion? **4.** What might the disciples believe about Jesus now? **5.** In asking for the body of Jesus, what risks is Joseph taking with Pilate and the Sanhedrin? **6.** By posting the guards at the tomb, do the leaders really believe Jesus will rise again? Or do they think that the disciples will steal the body? Or do they fear something else? Why? What would it cost the Roman guards if Jesus "escaped"?

The Crucifixion

[32]As they were going out, they met a man from Cyrene, named Simon, and they forced him to carry the cross. [33]They came to a place called Golgotha (which means The Place of the Skull). [34]There they offered Jesus wine to drink, mixed with gall; but after tasting it, he refused to drink it. [35]When they had crucified him, they divided up his clothes by casting lots.[i] [36]And sitting down, they kept watch over him there. [37]Above his head they placed the written charge against him: THIS IS JESUS, THE KING OF THE JEWS. [38]Two robbers were crucified with him, one on his right and one on his left. [39]Those who passed by hurled insults at him, shaking their heads [40]and saying, "You who are going to destroy the temple and build it in three days, save yourself! Come down from the cross, if you are the Son of God!"

[41]In the same way the chief priests, the teachers of the law and the elders mocked him. [42]"He saved others," they said, "but he can't save himself! He's the King of Israel! Let him come down now from the cross, and we will believe in him. [43]He trusts in God. Let God rescue him now if he wants him, for he said, 'I am the Son of God.'" [44]In the same way the robbers who were crucified with him also heaped insults on him.

The Death of Jesus

[45]From the sixth hour until the ninth hour darkness came over all the land. [46]About the ninth hour Jesus cried out in a loud voice, *"Eloi, Eloi,*[j] *lama sabachthani?"*—which means, "My God, my God, why have you forsaken me?"[k]

[47]When some of those standing there heard this, they said, "He's calling Elijah." [48]Immediately one of them ran and got a sponge. He filled it with wine vinegar, put it on a stick, and offered it to Jesus to drink. [49]The rest said, "Now leave him alone. Let's see if Elijah comes to save him."

[50]And when Jesus had cried out again in a loud voice, he gave up his spirit.

[51]At that moment the curtain of the temple was torn in two from top to bottom. The earth shook and the rocks split. [52]The tombs broke open and the bodies of many holy people who had died were raised to life. [53]They came out of the tombs, and after Jesus' resurrection they went into the holy city and appeared to many people.

[54]When the centurion and those with him who were guarding Jesus saw the earthquake and all that had happened, they were terrified, and exclaimed, "Surely he was the Son[l] of God!"

[55]Many women were there, watching from a distance. They had followed Jesus from Galilee to care for his needs. [56]Among them were Mary Magdalene, Mary the mother of James and Joses, and the mother of Zebedee's sons.

---

[i]35 A few late manuscripts *lots that the word spoken by the prophet might be fulfilled: "They divided my garments among themselves and cast lots for my clothing"* (Psalm 22:18)
[j]46 Some manuscripts *Eli, Eli*   [k]46 Psalm 22:1   [l]54 Or *a son*

LOOKING INTO THE SCRIPTURE/25 Minutes. Read Matthew 27:45-56 and discuss.

1. If you were the editor of the *Jerusalem Times,* what headline would you pick to describe the events of the Scripture passage the next day?
   a. strange darkness descends
   b. earthquake rocks city
   c. temple curtain ruined
   d. dead people reported seen
   e. spiritual leader killed
   f. three thieves crucified

2. How would you describe Jesus in his obituary?
   a. prominent civic leader
   b. controversial teacher
   c. troublemaker
   d. failure
   e. innocent victim
   f. the so-called Messiah
   g. mysterious miracle worker

3. Of Jesus' own followers, how many do you think understood what was happening to Jesus on the day he died?
   a. not one
   b. maybe the women
   c. the centurion
   d. only his disciples

4 Why did darkness cover the land for three hours?
   a. just a coincidence
   b. an eclipse of the sun
   c. God was mad at the world
   d. the darkness of sin reigned

5. What caused Jesus to cry out, "My God, my God, why have you forsaken me?"
   a. the physical pain he was suffering
   b. the feeling that God had deserted him
   c. God really did turn his back on him at that moment
   d. God did not send his angels to rescue him as he expected
   e. he thought the whole world had turned against him
   f. he was angry at God

6. What is so significant about the curtain in the temple being torn in two?
   a. the barrier between God and man was taken away
   b. everyone can approach God directly now
   c. no more need for mystery
   d. fellowship restored between God and mankind

MY OWN STORY/20 Minutes.

1. When you think about the death of Jesus, what person in this story best describes you?
   a. the temple crowd—detached, cynical
   b. the one who brought the sponge—hostile jokester
   c. one of the people raised from the dead
   d. the centurion—terrified but awed
   e. women followers—sympathetic and caring

2. What remains a mystery to you about the death of Jesus?
   a. why it ever happened
   b. how God could let it happen
   c. why nobody came to his rescue
   d. why the disciples didn't understand
   e. how the earthquake and the darkness happened

3. At what point in your life did you come to realize that Jesus died for you?
   a. as a child
   b. years ago
   c. just recently
   d. don't know that I have

4. How would you describe the way the death of Jesus has impacted your life, lifestyle and whole system of values?
   a. a little bit
   b. a whole lot
   c. not as much as it should
   d. a lot more than it used to
   e. I'm not sure

REFLECT: 1. Why was Jesus separated from the Father when he was on the cross? For whose sins did he go to the cross? 2. How do you explain the *necessity* of Jesus' death to a nonbeliever? 3. Is Jesus' death for you more a dispassionate fact, or an emotional experience? Why? 4. How have you tried to "guard" against God breaking through in your life? Why? What happened?

The Burial of Jesus

⁵⁷As evening approached, there came a rich man from Arimathea, named Joseph, who had himself become a disciple of Jesus. ⁵⁸Going to Pilate, he asked for Jesus' body, and Pilate ordered that it be given to him. ⁵⁹Joseph took the body, wrapped it in a clean linen cloth, ⁶⁰and placed it in his own new tomb that he had cut out of the rock. He rolled a big stone in front of the entrance to the tomb and went away. ⁶¹Mary Magdalene and the other Mary were sitting there opposite the tomb.

The Guard at the Tomb

⁶²The next day, the one after Preparation Day, the chief priests and the Pharisees went to Pilate. ⁶³"Sir," they said, "we remember that while he was still alive that deceiver said, 'After three days I will rise again.' ⁶⁴So give the order for the tomb to be made secure until the third day. Otherwise, his disciples may come and steal the body and tell the people that he has been raised from the dead. This last deception will be worse than the first."

⁶⁵"Take a guard," Pilate answered. "Go, make the tomb as secure as you know how." ⁶⁶So they went and made the tomb secure by putting a seal on the stone and posting the guard.

The Resurrection

28 After the Sabbath, at dawn on the first day of the week, Mary Magdalene and the other Mary went to look at the tomb.

²There was a violent earthquake, for an angel of the Lord came down from heaven and, going to the tomb, rolled back the stone and sat on it. ³His appearance was like lightning, and his clothes were white as snow. ⁴The guards were so afraid of him that they shook and became like dead men.

⁵The angel said to the women, "Do not be afraid, for I know that you are looking for Jesus, who was crucified. ⁶He is not here; he has risen, just as he said. Come and see the place where he lay. ⁷Then go quickly and tell his disciples: 'He has risen from the dead and is going ahead of you into Galilee. There you will see him.' Now I have told you."

⁸So the women hurried away from the tomb, afraid yet filled with joy, and ran to tell his disciples. ⁹Suddenly Jesus met them. "Greetings," he said. They came to him, clasped his feet and worshiped him. ¹⁰Then Jesus said to them, "Do not be afraid. Go and tell my brothers to go to Galilee; there they will see me."

The Guards' Report

¹¹While the women were on their way, some of the guards went into the city and reported to the chief priests everything that had happened. ¹²When the chief priests had met with the elders and devised a plan, they gave the soldiers a large sum of money, ¹³telling them, "You are to say, 'His disciples came during the night and stole him away while we were asleep.' ¹⁴If this report gets to the governor, we will satisfy him and keep you

OPEN: 1. What do you like to do first thing Sunday morning? Why? 2. Of "all the news that's fit to print," what section of the newspaper do you read first? 3. Which do you believe more: (a) What you hear? (b) What you see? (c) What you want?

DIG: 1. Who visits the tomb? When? Why now (see Mt 6:1; also Lk 23:56-24:1)? 2. How were they feeling on their way to the tomb? What problems do they expect to confront (see 27:60,65-66)? 3. How do you think they felt as they left the tomb? As they met Jesus? 4. Why did Jesus appear to these women before he appeared to his own disciples? In light of 4:10, what is the significance of the fact that they worshiped Jesus? 5. How might the guards' report have differed from the women's report? 6. Why would the chief priests and others prefer to believe the falsified story? 7. Upon seeing the resurrected Jesus, how do the disciples respond? Why is doubt mingled with their worship? What do they doubt? 8. How does Jesus' commission here compare with his earlier one in 10:5-7? 9. Of the four actions commanded of the disciples (vv.19-20), which one is central? How are they to make disciples? Of whom? With what resources? Toward what end?

out of trouble." [15]So the soldiers took the money and did as they were instructed. And this story has been widely circulated among the Jews to this very day.

The Great Commission

[16]Then the eleven disciples went to Galilee, to the mountain where Jesus had told them to go. [17]When they saw him, they worshiped him; but some doubted. [18]Then Jesus came to them and said, "All authority in heaven and on earth has been given to me. [19]Therefore go and make disciples of all nations, baptizing them in[m] the name of the Father and of the Son and of the Holy Spirit, [20]and teaching them to obey everything I have commanded you. And surely I am with you always, to the very end of the age."

REFLECT: 1. How did the reality of Jesus' resurrection "dawn" upon you? Were you more of a "quick believer" or a "slow doubter"? Why? **2.** How would you argue against the ideas that:(a) The disciples stole the body? (b) That Jesus only "swooned" on the cross, and revived in the cool tomb? (c) That the resurrection was a legend that caught on? **3.** In what ways can you fulfill the Great Commission in the context of your family? Work? Community? What hope does this passage give you as you seek to follow Jesus? **4.** How has the Book of Matthew changed your views of: Jesus as the Messiah? The kingdom of God? Jesus' ministry? Your ministry?

---

[m]19 Or *into;* see Acts 8:16; 19:5; Romans 6:3; 1 Cor. 1:13; 10:2 and Gal. 3:27.

MARK

INTRODUCTION

Author

From the Bible, we discover that Mark's full name is John Mark, that he was the son of Mary, and that their home was used as a meeting place by the disciples. Peter went there directly after his miraculous release from prison (Acts 12:1-17). Consequently, as a young man, Mark was immersed in the life of the newly forming church.

In particular, Mark was close to Peter. Peter referred to him as "my son Mark" (1 Peter 5:13). Many hold that Mark was Peter's secretary and that his gospel reflects Peter's view of the events. Writing in A.D. 140, Bishop Papias says: "Mark, having become the interpreter of Peter, wrote down accurately all that he remembered of the things said and done by our Lord, but not, however, in order."

Mark was also connected closely with Paul. Along with his cousin Barnabas, Mark accompanied the great apostle on the first missionary journey. Mark unaccountably left the party at Perga when they turned inland to Asia. Because of this, Paul refused to allow Mark to go on the second missionary journey, so Barnabas went with Mark to Cyprus while Paul teamed up with Silas. For years Mark dropped out of sight. Tradition says he founded the church at Alexandria, Egypt. Eventually, Paul and Mark were reconciled, so much so that Mark became Paul's companion during his imprisonment in a Roman jail.

Date and Audience

The ten years between A.D. 60 and A.D. 70 when Mark wrote his gospel were not good ones for the Christians living in Rome. For a long time they had hardly been noticed — they were just another exotic religious sect. But then Nero burned down Rome in A.D. 64 and had to find someone to blame. The Christians were nominated, and an era of persecution began. Nero threw them to the animals in the coliseum and burned them as human torches at his garden parties. It is into this atmosphere of persecution, to these Christians who were dying for Jesus' name, that Mark directed his gospel.

This was the first written account of Jesus' life. Thus it was, according to William Barclay, "the most important book in the world." Mark's collection of hitherto word-of-mouth stories was widely circulated and was used by Matthew and Luke when they wrote their gospels. In fact, all but 24 verses of Mark's gospel are found in their accounts.

Characteristics

In the shortest of the gospels, Mark races breathlessly through Jesus' life by connecting together a series of little stories. His sentences are almost childlike. He makes a simple statement and then connects it to another by using "and." Yet this gospel is the richest and most vivid in eyewitness detail. For example, when speaking of Jesus blessing the children, Mark alone tells us that Jesus first took them in his arms (Mark 10:13-16).

Overview Study Questions

1. Trace, in order, the following references to Mark and then write a "portrait" of this gospel writer: Acts 12:12; Acts 12:25; Acts 13:5; Acts 15:36-41; (here Mark disappears from sight); Colossians 4:10; Philemon 24; 2 Timothy 4:11; and 1 Peter 5:13.
2. Read through all of Mark's gospel in one sitting. It won't take long. It is only the length of a magazine article. As you read, notice the major divisions of thought.
3. As you study Mark, make a detailed outline. Title each section.

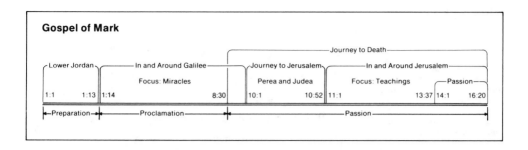

Gospel of Mark

			Journey to Death	
Lower Jordan	In and Around Galilee	Journey to Jerusalem	In and Around Jerusalem	
	Focus: Miracles	Perea and Judea	Focus: Teachings	Passion
1:1 1:13	1:14 8:30	10:1 10:52	11:1 13:37	14:1 16:20
←—Preparation—→	—Proclamation—		—Passion—	

Mark

OPEN: 1. When the mail comes, what do you open and read first? **2.** When you buy clothes, are you more interested in low price or high quality?

DIG: 1. What do the contexts of the quotes (Mal 3:1; Isa 40:3) teach about the "coming one"? **2.** Why is John's ministry so popular (vv.4-5)? **3.** What does John's clothing and diet say about him (v.6; see 2Ki 1:8; Mal 4:5)? **4.** Given John's message (vv.7-8), what type of person is the crowd anticipating (see Isa 32:15-20)? How do these expectations account for the crowd's reception of John, despite his hard message? **5.** What do you think the dove and voice (vv.10-11) meant to Jesus as he came out of the water? As he entered the desert? During his temptations? How would all this prepare him?

REFLECT: 1. What from your life illustrates what it means to repent? **2.** When did Jesus Christ become more than just a religious figure or "cuss word" to you? **3.** What "spiritual wilderness" has God sent you into? How has that confirmed his love or mission?

OPEN: Where did you go the first time you really "left home"?

DIG: What is the "good news" according to Jesus? What might this kingdom mean to the disciples?

REFLECT: If the disciples show what it means to "repent and believe," where are you: (a) Still fishing? (b) Keeping the old business going and spending nights and weekends with Jesus? (c) Swimming to shore? Explain.

John the Baptist Prepares the Way

1 The beginning of the gospel about Jesus Christ, the Son of God. [a]

[2] It is written in Isaiah the prophet:

"I will send my messenger ahead of you,
who will prepare your way" [b]—
[3] "a voice of one calling in the desert,
'Prepare the way for the Lord,
make straight paths for him.' " [c]

[4] And so John came, baptizing in the desert region and preaching a baptism of repentance for the forgiveness of sins. [5] The whole Judean countryside and all the people of Jerusalem went out to him. Confessing their sins, they were baptized by him in the Jordan River. [6] John wore clothing made of camel's hair, with a leather belt around his waist, and he ate locusts and wild honey. [7] And this was his message: "After me will come one more powerful than I, the thongs of whose sandals I am not worthy to stoop down and untie. [8] I baptize you with [d] water, but he will baptize you with the Holy Spirit."

The Baptism and Temptation of Jesus

[9] At that time Jesus came from Nazareth in Galilee and was baptized by John in the Jordan. [10] As Jesus was coming up out of the water, he saw heaven being torn open and the Spirit descending on him like a dove. [11] And a voice came from heaven: "You are my Son, whom I love; with you I am well pleased."

[12] At once the Spirit sent him out into the desert, [13] and he was in the desert forty days, being tempted by Satan. He was with the wild animals, and angels attended him.

The Calling of the First Disciples

[14] After John was put in prison, Jesus went into Galilee, proclaiming the good news of God. [15] "The time has come," he said. "The kingdom of God is near. Repent and believe the good news!"

[16] As Jesus walked beside the Sea of Galilee, he saw Simon and his brother Andrew casting a net into the lake, for they were fishermen. [17] "Come, follow me," Jesus said, "and I will make you fishers of men." [18] At once they left their nets and followed him.

[19] When he had gone a little farther, he saw James son of Zebedee and his brother John in a boat, preparing their nets. [20] Without delay he called them, and they left their father Zebedee in the boat with the hired men and followed him.

---

a1 Some manuscripts do not have *the Son of God.*   *b2* Mal. 3:1   *c3* Isaiah 40:3
d8 Or *in*

LOOKING INTO THE SCRIPTURE/25 Minutes. Read Mark 1:1-8 and discuss. Answer YES, NO or MAYBE to these situations:

1. JOHN THE BAPTIST WAS THE KIND OF GUY THAT I WOULD LIKE TO . . .

Y	N	M	take shopping
Y	N	M	rock me to sleep
Y	N	M	get stuck with in an elevator
Y	N	M	invite to a black tie dinner
Y	N	M	drive with for 500 miles keeping within the speed limit
Y	N	M	send to convert my hard-hearted sister in the hospital
Y	N	M	sit with at an all-you-can-eat buffet

2. Why did the people flock to John the Baptist instead of avoiding him?
   a. he was the first prophet in 300 years
   b. he was more interesting than a circus
   c. anyone will come to see a fire burn
   d. he spoke to the reality of their hearts
   e. he talked about sin and forgiveness

3. In modern words, what was the message of John?
   a. you can have it all
   b. look out for number one
   c. turn or burn
   d. you only go around once, so reach for the gusto
   e. pay me now or pay me later
   f. there's a new day coming

4. Why was the establishment so upset with John?
   a. his popularity
   b. his simple life
   c. his preaching
   d. his attack on sin
   e. his call for change

5. What role did John the Baptist play in the overall plan of God?
   a. shake up the establishment
   b. bridge the Old to New Testament
   c. prepare folks for coming of Jesus
   d. baptize Jesus
   e. alert sinners to the need for a Savior

MY OWN STORY/20 Minutes.

1. If John the Baptist came to your town with this message, how would he be received?
   a. the media would love it
   b. people would flock to him
   c. church people would be polite
   d. everybody would run for cover
   e. people would ignore him

2. Who played the part of John the Baptist in your life—who "prepared the way" for Jesus?
   a. my parents
   b. a Sunday school teacher
   c. a coach/counselor/teacher
   d. a special friend
   e. a whole lot of people
   f. nobody yet

3. How would you describe your relationship with Jesus right now?
   a. just beginning
   b. nowhere
   c. holding
   d. struggling
   e. roller-coaster
   f. going great

4. What would it take to move you on in your relationship with God?
   a. a little support
   b. a deeper commitment
   c. some spiritual discipline
   d. a big change
   e. a miracle
   f. a strong belief that God loves even me

OPEN: Who's one of the best teachers you've had? What made that person so good?

DIG: 1. Why do you suppose Jesus started his public ministry in a synagogue? What two things about Jesus amazed the people? Why? 2. What does it mean to teach "with authority"? What was the nature and source of Jesus' authority?

REFLECT: 1. What insights about the kingdom of God do you see here? 2. On a scale of one to ten, how much authority does Jesus have in your life? What would he have to cast out to rate a ten?

OPEN: 1. As a child, were you sickly or robust? 2. What is your solitary place?

DIG: 1. How does Jesus' healing (vv.30-31) compare with his exorcism (v.25)? What new realm of authority is seen here? 2. How do you picture the scene in verses 32-34? Why does he silence the demons? 3. After a day like this (vv.29-34), what pressures could Jesus feel as a new day dawns? What might he pray about? How might this relate to his decision (v.38)? 4. As Simon, how do you feel about that decision?

REFLECT: 1. In your experience, how do actions on behalf of God and meditation with God affect one another? 2. What insight do you see in these stories about Jesus and the kingdom?

OPEN: When caught in a crowd (rush hour, Christmas crunch, or other traffic), what do you do?

DIG: Why is the leper unsure of Jesus' desire to help (see Lev 13)? What is significant about Jesus touching the leper prior to healing him? What do the crowds expect?

REFLECT: What would it mean for Jesus to "touch" you? Where do you need his special touch this week? How can you "touch lepers" in your community?

Jesus Drives Out an Evil Spirit

21They went to Capernaum, and when the Sabbath came, Jesus went into the synagogue and began to teach. 22The people were amazed at his teaching, because he taught them as one who had authority, not as the teachers of the law. 23Just then a man in their synagogue who was possessed by an evil*e* spirit cried out, 24"What do you want with us, Jesus of Nazareth? Have you come to destroy us? I know who you are—the Holy One of God!"

25"Be quiet!" said Jesus sternly. "Come out of him!" 26The evil spirit shook the man violently and came out of him with a shriek.

27The people were all so amazed that they asked each other, "What is this? A new teaching—and with authority! He even gives orders to evil spirits and they obey him." 28News about him spread quickly over the whole region of Galilee.

Jesus Heals Many

29As soon as they left the synagogue, they went with James and John to the home of Simon and Andrew. 30Simon's mother-in-law was in bed with a fever, and they told Jesus about her. 31So he went to her, took her hand and helped her up. The fever left her and she began to wait on them.

32That evening after sunset the people brought to Jesus all the sick and demon-possessed. 33The whole town gathered at the door, 34and Jesus healed many who had various diseases. He also drove out many demons, but he would not let the demons speak because they knew who he was.

Jesus Prays in a Solitary Place

35Very early in the morning, while it was still dark, Jesus got up, left the house and went off to a solitary place, where he prayed. 36Simon and his companions went to look for him, 37and when they found him, they exclaimed: "Everyone is looking for you!"

38Jesus replied, "Let us go somewhere else—to the nearby villages—so I can preach there also. That is why I have come." 39So he traveled throughout Galilee, preaching in their synagogues and driving out demons.

A Man With Leprosy

40A man with leprosy*f* came to him and begged him on his knees, "If you are willing, you can make me clean."

41Filled with compassion, Jesus reached out his hand and touched the man. "I am willing," he said. "Be clean!" 42Immediately the leprosy left him and he was cured.

43Jesus sent him away at once with a strong warning: 44"See that you don't tell this to anyone. But go, show yourself to the priest and offer the sacrifices that Moses commanded for your cleansing, as a testimony to them." 45Instead he went out and

---

e23 Greek *unclean*; also in verses 26 and 27   *f40* The Greek word was used for various diseases affecting the skin—not necessarily leprosy.

began to talk freely, spreading the news. As a result, Jesus could no longer enter a town openly but stayed outside in lonely places. Yet the people still came to him from everywhere.

Jesus Heals a Paralytic

2 A few days later, when Jesus again entered Capernaum, the people heard that he had come home. ²So many gathered that there was no room left, not even outside the door, and he preached the word to them. ³Some men came, bringing to him a paralytic, carried by four of them. ⁴Since they could not get him to Jesus because of the crowd, they made an opening in the roof above Jesus and, after digging through it, lowered the mat the paralyzed man was lying on. ⁵When Jesus saw their faith, he said to the paralytic, "Son, your sins are forgiven."

⁶Now some teachers of the law were sitting there, thinking to themselves, ⁷"Why does this fellow talk like that? He's blaspheming! Who can forgive sins but God alone?"

⁸Immediately Jesus knew in his spirit that this was what they were thinking in their hearts, and he said to them, "Why are you thinking these things? ⁹Which is easier: to say to the paralytic, 'Your sins are forgiven,' or to say, 'Get up, take your mat and walk'? ¹⁰But that you may know that the Son of Man has authority on earth to forgive sins . . . ." He said to the paralytic, ¹¹"I tell you, get up, take your mat and go home." ¹²He got up, took his mat and walked out in full view of them all. This amazed everyone and they praised God, saying, "We have never seen anything like this!"

The Calling of Levi

¹³Once again Jesus went out beside the lake. A large crowd came to him, and he began to teach them. ¹⁴As he walked along, he saw Levi son of Alphaeus sitting at the tax collector's booth. "Follow me," Jesus told him, and Levi got up and followed him.

¹⁵While Jesus was having dinner at Levi's house, many tax collectors and "sinners" were eating with him and his disciples, for there were many who followed him. ¹⁶When the teachers of the law who were Pharisees saw him eating with the "sinners" and tax collectors, they asked his disciples: "Why does he eat with tax collectors and 'sinners'?"

¹⁷On hearing this, Jesus said to them, "It is not the healthy who need a doctor, but the sick. I have not come to call the righteous, but sinners."

Jesus Questioned About Fasting

¹⁸Now John's disciples and the Pharisees were fasting. Some people came and asked Jesus, "How is it that John's disciples and the disciples of the Pharisees are fasting, but yours are not?"

¹⁹Jesus answered, "How can the guests of the bridegroom fast while he is with them? They cannot, so long as they have him with them. ²⁰But the time will come when the bridegroom will be taken from them, and on that day they will fast.

²¹"No one sews a patch of unshrunk cloth on an old garment. If he does, the new piece will pull away from the old, making

---

OPEN: If in a crisis, even at 3:00 AM, which four friends would you call?

DIG: 1. What would you be seeing and feeling if you were in this crowd (vv.1-4)? What was going on in the mind of the owner of the house? The paralytic? The teachers of the law? **2.** Why are the teachers so upset? In their minds, how are sin and the authority of God linked (see Jn 9:1-3)? **3.** Why didn't Jesus just heal the man like everyone expected? What new insight about the kingdom and himself is he revealing?

REFLECT: 1. In what ways is sin like paralysis? What freedoms has Jesus' word of forgiveness given to you? Where do you need to hear that word again? **2.** In this story, do you identify more with the paralytic, his friends, or the teachers? Why?

OPEN: If your salary was suddenly tripled, what would you do with the extra money?

DIG: 1. The fishermen disciples (1:16-19) may have paid inflated taxes to Levi for years. How would they feel when Jesus called him? Why did he do so? What did it cost him? **2.** What does Jesus say is needed to enter God's kingdom?

REFLECT: 1. How "sick" were you before you saw your need for a spiritual doctor? **2.** When Jesus calls, how will you respond?

OPEN: Do you "fix and mend" or "toss and replace"? Why?

DIG: 1. Why did John's disciples and the Pharisees fast? Jesus' disciples did not fast—what does that imply? **2.** How do the three mini-parables (vv.19-22) answer the question? What is the new wine? The old wineskins?

---

the tear worse. ²²And no one pours new wine into old wineskins.
If he does, the wine will burst the skins, and both the wine and
the wineskins will be ruined. No, he pours new wine into new
wineskins."

Lord of the Sabbath

²³One Sabbath Jesus was going through the grainfields, and
as his disciples walked along, they began to pick some heads of
grain. ²⁴The Pharisees said to him, "Look, why are they doing
what is unlawful on the Sabbath?"

²⁵He answered, "Have you never read what David did when
he and his companions were hungry and in need? ²⁶In the days
of Abiathar the high priest, he entered the house of God and ate
the consecrated bread, which is lawful only for priests to eat.
And he also gave some to his companions."

²⁷Then he said to them, "The Sabbath was made for man, not
man for the Sabbath. ²⁸So the Son of Man is Lord even of the
Sabbath."

3 Another time he went into the synagogue, and a man with
a shriveled hand was there. ²Some of them were looking for
a reason to accuse Jesus, so they watched him closely to see if
he would heal him on the Sabbath. ³Jesus said to the man with
the shriveled hand, "Stand up in front of everyone."

⁴Then Jesus asked them, "Which is lawful on the Sabbath:
to do good or to do evil, to save life or to kill?" But they
remained silent.

⁵He looked around at them in anger and, deeply distressed at
their stubborn hearts, said to the man, "Stretch out your hand."
He stretched it out, and his hand was completely restored.
⁶Then the Pharisees went out and began to plot with the Herodians how they might kill Jesus.

Crowds Follow Jesus

⁷Jesus withdrew with his disciples to the lake, and a large
crowd from Galilee followed. ⁸When they heard all he was
doing, many people came to him from Judea, Jerusalem, Idu-
mea, and the regions across the Jordan and around Tyre and
Sidon. ⁹Because of the crowd he told his disciples to have a small
boat ready for him, to keep the people from crowding him. ¹⁰For
he had healed many, so that those with diseases were pushing
forward to touch him. ¹¹Whenever the evil^g spirits saw him, they
fell down before him and cried out, "You are the Son of God."
¹²But he gave them strict orders not to tell who he was.

The Appointing of the Twelve Apostles

¹³Jesus went up on a mountainside and called to him those he
wanted, and they came to him. ¹⁴He appointed twelve—designating them apostles^h—that they might be with him and that he
might send them out to preach ¹⁵and to have authority to drive
out demons. ¹⁶These are the twelve he appointed: Simon (to
whom he gave the name Peter); ¹⁷James son of Zebedee and his

---

g11 Greek unclean; also in verse 30   *h14 Some manuscripts do not have
designating them apostles.*

brother John (to them he gave the name Boanerges, which means Sons of Thunder); [18]Andrew, Philip, Bartholomew, Matthew, Thomas, James son of Alphaeus, Thaddaeus, Simon the Zealot [19]and Judas Iscariot, who betrayed him.

Jesus and Beelzebub

[20]Then Jesus entered a house, and again a crowd gathered, so that he and his disciples were not even able to eat. [21]When his family heard about this, they went to take charge of him, for they said, "He is out of his mind."

[22]And the teachers of the law who came down from Jerusalem said, "He is possessed by Beelzebub[i]! By the prince of demons he is driving out demons."

[23]So Jesus called them and spoke to them in parables: "How can Satan drive out Satan? [24]If a kingdom is divided against itself, that kingdom cannot stand. [25]If a house is divided against itself, that house cannot stand. [26]And if Satan opposes himself and is divided, he cannot stand; his end has come. [27]In fact, no one can enter a strong man's house and carry off his possessions unless he first ties up the strong man. Then he can rob his house. [28]I tell you the truth, all the sins and blasphemies of men will be forgiven them. [29]But whoever blasphemes against the Holy Spirit will never be forgiven; he is guilty of an eternal sin."

[30]He said this because they were saying, "He has an evil spirit."

Jesus' Mother and Brothers

[31]Then Jesus' mother and brothers arrived. Standing outside, they sent someone in to call him. [32]A crowd was sitting around him, and they told him, "Your mother and brothers are outside looking for you."

[33]"Who are my mother and my brothers?" he asked.

[34]Then he looked at those seated in a circle around him and said, "Here are my mother and my brothers! [35]Whoever does God's will is my brother and sister and mother."

The Parable of the Sower

4 Again Jesus began to teach by the lake. The crowd that gathered around him was so large that he got into a boat and sat in it out on the lake, while all the people were along the shore at the water's edge. [2]He taught them many things by parables, and in his teaching said: [3]"Listen! A farmer went out to sow his seed. [4]As he was scattering the seed, some fell along the path, and the birds came and ate it up. [5]Some fell on rocky places, where it did not have much soil. It sprang up quickly, because the soil was shallow. [6]But when the sun came up, the plants were scorched, and they withered because they had no root. [7]Other seed fell among thorns, which grew up and choked the plants, so that they did not bear grain. [8]Still other seed fell on good soil. It came up, grew and produced a crop, multiplying thirty, sixty, or even a hundred times."

OPEN: 1. What crazy stunt or notorious behavior from your high school days are your classmates likely to remember you by? 2. What is one "pet peeve" your parents or siblings have against you?

DIG: 1. Why was Jesus' family worried about him? What type of conversation must they have had before deciding to get him? 2. What is the significance of where these Pharisees were from? What tensions might these uneducated people feel when they hear what these respected, educated leaders say about Jesus? 3. How do Jesus' parables answer the charge? How do they relate to verse 29? 4. What did the crowd expect in verses 31-32? What did Jesus say is the basis for a family relationship with him? Is doing God's will an action or a belief (see Lk 6:46; Jn 6:29)?

REFLECT: 1. How can you tell if a person's mistaken ideas about Jesus stem from misunderstanding or a hard heart? 2. How has Jesus plundered Satan's kingdom in your life? 3. What would be true of a kingdom where the king viewed his subjects as his brothers and sisters? How does that reflect Jesus' relationship with you? 4. Of the responses to Jesus in this chapter (3:6,8,21,22, 34-35), which best describes your relationship to him now? Why?

OPEN: 1. Who told you the best stories when you were a kid? What made them memorable? 2. What experience, if any, have you had farming or gardening? Do house plants tend to thrive or die under your care?

DIG: 1. What are the four types of soil on which these seeds fall? What kind of growth occurred in each soil type? 2. How might this crowd have responded to such a parable? How are the parables like a spiritual "hearing test"? What blocks understanding? What distinguishes those who are told "the secret of the kingdom" from those

i22 Greek Beezeboul or Beelzeboul

LOOKING INTO THE SCRIPTURE/15 Minutes. Read Mark 4:1-20 and discuss.

1. If you had been in the crowd when Jesus shared this parable, how would you have felt?
   a. what's he saying?
   b. wonder which soil I am?
   c. is he trying to say something to me?
   d. who does he think he is?

2. Why do you think Jesus used this illustration to expain how people receive his message?
   a. he was sick and tired of people tagging along and doing nothing
   b. they were sitting in a wheat field
   c. everybody understood farming
   d. he deliberately wanted to keep some people in the dark

3. What is the "crop" that the seed is supposed to produce?
   a. wheat
   b. the lifestyle of Jesus
   c. new converts to the faith
   d. spirituality

4. What is Jesus really saying in this parable?
   a. if you can't hear, turn up the volume
   b. paint or get off the ladder
   c. if you are not producing, it's not the fault of the seed
   d. God is making a list and checking it twice

MY OWN STORY/30 Minutes.

1. If you had to divide your life from BIRTH to RIGHT NOW into four quarters (like the four quarters of a football game), how would you describe each quarter as far as your responsiveness to the *spiritual values* that Jesus preached and lived? On the line below, fill in the four quarters of your life—starting with CHILDHOOD as your first quarter. Then, for each *quarter,* jot down one of the four soils:

P=PATH   R=ROCKY   T=THORNY   G=GOOD

CHILDHOOD

First Quarter   Second Quarter   Third Quarter   Fourth Quarter

2. In the period of your life where you indicated the best crop, what was the contributing factor?
   a. I was around a spiritual community of people
   b. I was daily seeking the will of God
   c. I had very few distractions in my life
   d. I had my priorities in order
   e. I was communicating with God regularly

3. In the period of your life where you indicated the poorest crop, what was the contributing factor?
   a. I had a whole lot of problems
   b. I didn't know anything about Christ
   c. I knew about Christ, but I was taken up with other things
   d. I didn't have a supportive community
   e. I was living life my way

4. If you were to take God seriously for 30 days, what would it mean in practical terms?
   a. plowing up the soil and starting over
   b. removing a few rocks
   c. doing some serious weeding
   d. letting God do his thing

5. Which of these "farm trivia" facts would encourage you the most as you "sow" the "seed" of the gospel?
   a. seed can germinate after being stored for centuries
   b. a seed of grain can yield 100 times its weight
   c. spring wheat is planted in the fall
   d. the crop yield cannot be determined as the seed is planted

⁹Then Jesus said, "He who has ears to hear, let him hear."

¹⁰When he was alone, the Twelve and the others around him asked him about the parables. ¹¹He told them, "The secret of the kingdom of God has been given to you. But to those on the outside everything is said in parables ¹²so that,

" 'they may be ever seeing but never perceiving,
and ever hearing but never understanding;
otherwise they might turn and be forgiven!'ʲ"

¹³Then Jesus said to them, "Don't you understand this parable? How then will you understand any parable? ¹⁴The farmer sows the word. ¹⁵Some people are like seed along the path, where the word is sown. As soon as they hear it, Satan comes and takes away the word that was sown in them. ¹⁶Others, like seed sown on rocky places, hear the word and at once receive it with joy. ¹⁷But since they have no root, they last only a short time. When trouble or persecution comes because of the word, they quickly fall away. ¹⁸Still others, like seed sown among thorns, hear the word; ¹⁹but the worries of this life, the deceitfulness of wealth and the desires for other things come in and choke the word, making it unfruitful. ²⁰Others, like seed sown on good soil, hear the word, accept it, and produce a crop—thirty, sixty or even a hundred times what was sown."

A Lamp on a Stand

²¹He said to them, "Do you bring in a lamp to put it under a bowl or a bed? Instead, don't you put it on its stand? ²²For whatever is hidden is meant to be disclosed, and whatever is concealed is meant to be brought out into the open. ²³If anyone has ears to hear, let him hear."

²⁴"Consider carefully what you hear," he continued. "With the measure you use, it will be measured to you—and even more. ²⁵Whoever has will be given more; whoever does not have, even what he has will be taken from him."

The Parable of the Growing Seed

²⁶He also said, "This is what the kingdom of God is like. A man scatters seed on the ground. ²⁷Night and day, whether he sleeps or gets up, the seed sprouts and grows, though he does not know how. ²⁸All by itself the soil produces grain—first the stalk, then the head, then the full kernel in the head. ²⁹As soon as the grain is ripe, he puts the sickle to it, because the harvest has come."

The Parable of the Mustard Seed

³⁰Again he said, "What shall we say the kingdom of God is like, or what parable shall we use to describe it? ³¹It is like a mustard seed, which is the smallest seed you plant in the ground. ³²Yet when planted, it grows and becomes the largest of all garden plants, with such big branches that the birds of the air can perch in its shade."

³³With many similar parables Jesus spoke the word to them,

"outside"? **3.** Why does the word not take root at all in some people? What causes the second plant to wither? What three things choked off the third plant? **4.** In the context of chapter 3, how does this parable explain the various responses to Jesus? **5.** What modern analogy would you use to explain this parable to city kids who have never seen a farm?

REFLECT: 1. Which soil would best describe your response to the gospel when you first heard it? What kind of crop have you been producing lately? How does one become the good soil? **2.** In your circle of acquaintances, which kind of "soil" do you most often see in their hearts? **3.** What does this parable teach you about failure and success in evangelism?

OPEN: 1. As a child, what "big dream" did you have about what you would be when you grew up? **2.** What is your favorite TV game show? Do you try to figure out the questions, or just wait for the answers? Why?

DIG: 1. If Jesus is the lamp (v.21), what is he revealing (see also vv.11-12)? **2.** What is the secret of receiving more from Jesus? **3.** In verses 26-29, what part (if any) do people play in the growing kingdom? How does this parable complement the one in verses 3-20? **4.** What does the contrasting seed and bush teach about the kingdom (vv.30-32)? **5.** Taken together, what do all of the parables show about God's kingdom?

REFLECT: 1. In terms of the light of Christ that you shed, are you a 20-, 60-, 100-, or 200-watt light bulb? Or burned out? Why? **2.** Does knowing that the growth of the kingdom is ultimately in God's hands cause you to rest or to work more? Why? **3.** Taking verses 28 and 31 personally, at what stage is the kingdom in your life now: Still a seed? Sprouting? Outgrowing the "weeds"? Producing a harvest? **4.** What hope do these parables give you when you feel that you, your church, or your work for Christ is insignificant?

j12 Isaiah 6:9,10

as much as they could understand. ³⁴He did not say anything to them without using a parable. But when he was alone with his own disciples, he explained everything.

Jesus Calms the Storm

³⁵That day when evening came, he said to his disciples, "Let us go over to the other side." ³⁶Leaving the crowd behind, they took him along, just as he was, in the boat. There were also other boats with him. ³⁷A furious squall came up, and the waves broke over the boat, so that it was nearly swamped. ³⁸Jesus was in the stern, sleeping on a cushion. The disciples woke him and said to him, "Teacher, don't you care if we drown?"

³⁹He got up, rebuked the wind and said to the waves, "Quiet! Be still!" Then the wind died down and it was completely calm.

⁴⁰He said to his disciples, "Why are you so afraid? Do you still have no faith?"

⁴¹They were terrified and asked each other, "Who is this? Even the wind and the waves obey him!"

The Healing of a Demon-possessed Man

5 They went across the lake to the region of the Gerasenes.ᵏ ²When Jesus got out of the boat, a man with an evilˡ spirit came from the tombs to meet him. ³This man lived in the tombs, and no one could bind him any more, not even with a chain. ⁴For he had often been chained hand and foot, but he tore the chains apart and broke the irons on his feet. No one was strong enough to subdue him. ⁵Night and day among the tombs and in the hills he would cry out and cut himself with stones.

⁶When he saw Jesus from a distance, he ran and fell on his knees in front of him. ⁷He shouted at the top of his voice, "What do you want with me, Jesus, Son of the Most High God? Swear to God that you won't torture me!" ⁸For Jesus had said to him, "Come out of this man, you evil spirit!"

⁹Then Jesus asked him, "What is your name?"

"My name is Legion," he replied, "for we are many." ¹⁰And he begged Jesus again and again not to send them out of the area.

¹¹A large herd of pigs was feeding on the nearby hillside. ¹²The demons begged Jesus, "Send us among the pigs; allow us to go into them." ¹³He gave them permission, and the evil spirits came out and went into the pigs. The herd, about two thousand in number, rushed down the steep bank into the lake and were drowned.

¹⁴Those tending the pigs ran off and reported this in the town and countryside, and the people went out to see what had happened. ¹⁵When they came to Jesus, they saw the man who had been possessed by the legion of demons, sitting there, dressed and in his right mind; and they were afraid. ¹⁶Those who had seen it told the people what had happened to the demon-possessed man—and told about the pigs as well. ¹⁷Then the people began to plead with Jesus to leave their region.

¹⁸As Jesus was getting into the boat, the man who had been

OPEN: What terrifying storm or movie can you still recall vividly?

DIG: 1. What emotions did the disciples feel as this storm raged on and on? What did they want from Jesus? How do you picture their faces in verses 39-41? Which would frighten you more—the storm or Jesus? **2.** What was Jesus showing them about himself in all this?

REFLECT: How do you react to Jesus when he seems to be asleep in your life?

OPEN: 1. When did a vacation turn into something unpleasant you never expected? **2.** Do you like horror films/books? Why?

DIG: 1. How are the disciples feeling as they cross the lake? After a ride like theirs, how would it feel to be accosted by this man in the cemetery at night? **2.** What do we learn about demons from the actions of the possessed man? **3.** How does the healing take place? What is the man like afterwards? **4.** Why do you think the people reacted as they did? Why were they afraid (v.15) after seeing the man "dressed and in his right mind"? What does this story say about their values? **5.** What was the ethnic background of those in the Decapolis? How might that explain the charge to witness (v.19), when previously Jesus ordered silence (1:43-44)? **6.** What do you suppose the demoniac said to his family? **7.** What did the disciples learn about Jesus on this day (4:35-5:20)?

REFLECT: 1. When have you felt like the demoniac—torn by so many conflicting voices and feelings? How did Jesus bring peace into that chaos? How do you need to hear his word of peace right now? **2.** When have you felt like the townspeople, wishing Jesus would leave because he changes things too much?

ᵏ1 Some manuscripts *Gadarenes;* other manuscripts *Gergesenes*   ˡ2 Greek *unclean;* also in verses 8 and 13

Mark 4:35-41   **JESUS CALMS THE STORM**

LOOKING INTO THE SCRIPTURE/25 Minutes. Read Mark 4:35-41 and discuss.

1. If you had been one of these disciples, what would you have told your wife that evening?
     a. I almost got killed!
     b. that Jesus is sure a sound sleeper
     c. I can't figure Jesus out
     d. only God can do what I saw today

2. Why do you think Jesus suggested that they take a boat trip across the lake?
     a. to get a little rest
     b. to get away from people
     c. to put the disciples through this test
     d. to be alone with his disciples

3. Why did Jesus let the storm come up?
     a. he didn't. It was natural
     b. he was sleeping
     c. he wanted to teach them a lesson
     d. he didn't send the storm, but he used it to stretch their faith
     e. he didn't know what was going on

4. Why do you think the disciples awakened Jesus?
     a. concern for their lives
     b. they needed help bailing water
     c. they resented his sleeping during the crisis
     d. they expected a miracle

5. What was the tone in Jesus' voice when he said, "You of little faith. Why are you so afraid?"
     a. put down: "You scaredicats"
     b. puzzlement: "Why would you worry when I am in the boat"
     c. empathy: "I feel what you're feeling"
     d. disappointment: "You've disappointed me. I wish you had more faith"

MY OWN STORY/20 Minutes.

1. What is your typical response to storms in your life?
     a. help: What do I do?
     b. anger: Why did this happen to me?
     c. brave front: I can tough it out.
     d. turn to God: Help me out of this, Lord!
     e. punt: I give up.

2. How would you compare your life now to the storm in the Scripture?
     a. smooth sailing—enjoying the ride
     b. choppy water—rough ride
     c. cloud burst—danger signals
     d. storm over—cleaning up the mess

3. What brings storms in your life?
     a. financial difficulties
     b. hassles with relationships
     c. insecurity: job/future
     d. failure: feeling a failure
     e. tragedy: sickness/death

4. "Quiet! Be still!" For the storm you're facing, what would this mean?
     a. don't panic
     b. quit rocking the boat
     c. accept the storm as a gift
     d. don't sweat the small stuff
     e. God has it under control

5. If you have time, take and discuss this stress test. Circle those events you have experienced within the past 12 months. Total your score. If you score more than 150 points, you are probably living under a whole lot of stress.

EVENT	STRESS POINTS	EVENT	STRESS POINTS	EVENT	STRESS POINTS
Death of spouse	100	Health problem	44	Foreclosure on mort./loan	30
Divorce	73	Pregnancy	40	Change in work	29
Marital separation	65	Sex difficulties	39	Son/daughter leaving home	29
Jail term	63	Gain of new family member	39	Trouble with in-laws	29
Death of family member	63	Business readjustment	39	Major achievement	28
Personal injury or illness	53	Change in financial state	38	Wife starting/stopping work	26
Marriage	50	Death of a close friend	37	Change in living conditions	25
Loss of job	47	Change in line of work	36	Revision of personal habits	24
Marital reconciliation	45	Arguments with spouse	35	Trouble with boss	23
Retirement	45	Large mortgage taken out	31	Change in work hours	20

demon-possessed begged to go with him. [19]Jesus did not let him, but said, "Go home to your family and tell them how much the Lord has done for you, and how he has had mercy on you." [20]So the man went away and began to tell in the Decapolis *m*how much Jesus had done for him. And all the people were amazed.

A Dead Girl and a Sick Woman

[21]When Jesus had again crossed over by boat to the other side of the lake, a large crowd gathered around him while he was by the lake. [22]Then one of the synagogue rulers, named Jairus, came there. Seeing Jesus, he fell at his feet [23]and pleaded earnestly with him, "My little daughter is dying. Please come and put your hands on her so that she will be healed and live." [24]So Jesus went with him.

A large crowd followed and pressed around him. [25]And a woman was there who had been subject to bleeding for twelve years. [26]She had suffered a great deal under the care of many doctors and had spent all she had, yet instead of getting better she grew worse. [27]When she heard about Jesus, she came up behind him in the crowd and touched his cloak, [28]because she thought, "If I just touch his clothes, I will be healed." [29]Immediately her bleeding stopped and she felt in her body that she was freed from her suffering.

[30]At once Jesus realized that power had gone out from him. He turned around in the crowd and asked, "Who touched my clothes?"

[31]"You see the people crowding against you," his disciples answered, "and yet you can ask, 'Who touched me?' "

[32]But Jesus kept looking around to see who had done it. [33]Then the woman, knowing what had happened to her, came and fell at his feet and, trembling with fear, told him the whole truth. [34]He said to her, "Daughter, your faith has healed you. Go in peace and be freed from your suffering."

[35]While Jesus was still speaking, some men came from the house of Jairus, the synagogue ruler. "Your daughter is dead," they said. "Why bother the teacher any more?"

[36]Ignoring what they said, Jesus told the synagogue ruler, "Don't be afraid; just believe."

[37]He did not let anyone follow him except Peter, James and John the brother of James. [38]When they came to the home of the synagogue ruler, Jesus saw a commotion, with people crying and wailing loudly. [39]He went in and said to them, "Why all this commotion and wailing? The child is not dead but asleep." [40]But they laughed at him.

After he put them all out, he took the child's father and mother and the disciples who were with him, and went in where the child was. [41]He took her by the hand and said to her, *"Talitha koum!"* (which means, "Little girl, I say to you, get up!"). [42]Immediately the girl stood up and walked around (she was twelve years old). At this they were completely astonished. [43]He gave strict orders not to let anyone know about this, and told them to give her something to eat.

m20 That is, the Ten Cities

OPEN: 1. What would you do if the phone rang, the doorbell chimed, your child called for help, and the oven alarm went off all at the same time? **2.** What does it take to get you out of bed? What are you like when you awake?

DIG: 1. Of all the people pressing for Jesus' attention, two get through to him in this story—how so? **2.** What impressions do you get of the sick woman (vv.25-26)? This illness made her ceremonially unclean and thus unable to have contact with other people. What do you think it took for her to touch Jesus? Why do you think Jesus makes the sick woman reveal herself? How was her faith obvious to Jesus? **3.** What is the relationship (here) between faith and healing? In what ways, other than physical, was this woman healed and given new peace? **4.** What impressions do you get of Jairus (vv.22-23)? How is his situation similar to that of the sick woman? How is it different? **5.** What is Jesus' reaction to the news that the child is dead? Jairus' reaction? Why did Jesus say the child was asleep? As Jairus, what would you say to the crowd outside your house after Jesus left? **6.** What new things did the disciples learn about the power of Jesus? What do the stories in 4:35-5:43 have in common?

REFLECT: What is the relationship between crisis and faith in your life? How have you been like the woman or like Jairus? The men in verse 35? The mourners in verse 40?

A Prophet Without Honor

6 Jesus left there and went to his hometown, accompanied by his disciples. [2]When the Sabbath came, he began to teach in the synagogue, and many who heard him were amazed.

"Where did this man get these things?" they asked. "What's this wisdom that has been given him, that he even does miracles! [3]Isn't this the carpenter? Isn't this Mary's son and the brother of James, Joseph,[n] Judas and Simon? Aren't his sisters here with us?" And they took offense at him.

[4]Jesus said to them, "Only in his hometown, among his relatives and in his own house is a prophet without honor." [5]He could not do any miracles there, except lay his hands on a few sick people and heal them. [6]And he was amazed at their lack of faith.

Jesus Sends Out the Twelve

Then Jesus went around teaching from village to village. [7]Calling the Twelve to him, he sent them out two by two and gave them authority over evil[o] spirits.

[8]These were his instructions: "Take nothing for the journey except a staff—no bread, no bag, no money in your belts. [9]Wear sandals but not an extra tunic. [10]Whenever you enter a house, stay there until you leave that town. [11]And if any place will not welcome you or listen to you, shake the dust off your feet when you leave, as a testimony against them."

[12]They went out and preached that people should repent. [13]They drove out many demons and anointed many sick people with oil and healed them.

John the Baptist Beheaded

[14]King Herod heard about this, for Jesus' name had become well known. Some were saying,[p] "John the Baptist has been raised from the dead, and that is why miraculous powers are at work in him."

[15]Others said, "He is Elijah."

And still others claimed, "He is a prophet, like one of the prophets of long ago."

[16]But when Herod heard this, he said, "John, the man I beheaded, has been raised from the dead!"

[17]For Herod himself had given orders to have John arrested, and he had him bound and put in prison. He did this because of Herodias, his brother Philip's wife, whom he had married. [18]For John had been saying to Herod, "It is not lawful for you to have your brother's wife." [19]So Herodias nursed a grudge against John and wanted to kill him. But she was not able to, [20]because Herod feared John and protected him, knowing him to be a righteous and holy man. When Herod heard John, he was greatly puzzled[q]; yet he liked to listen to him.

[21]Finally the opportune time came. On his birthday Herod gave a banquet for his high officials and military commanders

OPEN: What childhood escapade of yours do you hear about most often when you visit family?

DIG: After these four "power" miracles, what happens when Jesus goes home? Why? What do the four questions (vv.2-3) reveal? How is Jesus' ministry limited in Nazareth?

REFLECT: 1. How has familiarity with Jesus blocked you from really seeing who he is? What helps you get a fresh look? **2.** How does your family react to your faith in Christ? How does that affect you?

OPEN: Who in your family packs too much?

DIG: 1. What was the significance of the disciples' assignment for the kingdom of God? What impact would this have on the villages? On the opposition movement (3:6, 22)? **2.** How is the disciples' message like that of John (1:4) and Jesus (1:14-15)?

REFLECT: Where has God sent you to tell about the kingdom? How is it going?

OPEN: 1. If you were granted one wish for your next birthday present, what would it be? **2.** If a king promised you whatever you wanted, what would you ask for?

DIG: 1. Why include this "flashback" to Herod in between sending out the disciples (vv.6-13) and their return (vv.30-31)? **2.** What drew Herod's attention to Jesus? What was the significance of Elijah and John the Baptist to the people of Jesus' day (see Mt 17:9-13)? Why might people mistake Jesus for one of them? **3.** Why does Herod jail John? What does that reveal about Herod? About John? About Herodias? **4.** What kind of leader do you think Herod was? What is at stake for him here? How powerful do you think he felt when he went to bed that night? What kind of soil (4:13-20) does he represent? **5.** How do the two "kings"—Jesus and Herod—differ in terms of their kingdoms, character, popularity, and use of power?

---

[n]3 Greek *Joses*, a variant of *Joseph*   [o]7 Greek *unclean*   [p]14 Some early manuscripts *He was saying*   [q]20 Some early manuscripts *he did many things*

REFLECT: 1. What would this story say to someone facing persecution, then and now? **2.** When have you felt like Herod—attracted to the truth but afraid to follow through with it? What happened? In contrast, how might you grow in reflecting John's courage?

and the leading men of Galilee. ²²When the daughter of Herodias came in and danced, she pleased Herod and his dinner guests.

The king said to the girl, "Ask me for anything you want, and I'll give it to you." ²³And he promised her with an oath, "Whatever you ask I will give you, up to half my kingdom."

²⁴She went out and said to her mother, "What shall I ask for?"

"The head of John the Baptist," she answered.

²⁵At once the girl hurried in to the king with the request: "I want you to give me right now the head of John the Baptist on a platter."

²⁶The king was greatly distressed, but because of his oaths and his dinner guests, he did not want to refuse her. ²⁷So he immediately sent an executioner with orders to bring John's head. The man went, beheaded John in the prison, ²⁸and brought back his head on a platter. He presented it to the girl, and she gave it to her mother. ²⁹On hearing of this, John's disciples came and took his body and laid it in a tomb.

Jesus Feeds the Five Thousand

³⁰The apostles gathered around Jesus and reported to him all they had done and taught. ³¹Then, because so many people were coming and going that they did not even have a chance to eat, he said to them, "Come with me by yourselves to a quiet place and get some rest."

³²So they went away by themselves in a boat to a solitary place. ³³But many who saw them leaving recognized them and ran on foot from all the towns and got there ahead of them. ³⁴When Jesus landed and saw a large crowd, he had compassion on them, because they were like sheep without a shepherd. So he began teaching them many things.

³⁵By this time it was late in the day, so his disciples came to him. "This is a remote place," they said, "and it's already very late. ³⁶Send the people away so they can go to the surrounding countryside and villages and buy themselves something to eat."

³⁷But he answered, "You give them something to eat."

They said to him, "That would take eight months of a man's wages⸍! Are we to go and spend that much on bread and give it to them to eat?"

³⁸"How many loaves do you have?" he asked. "Go and see."

When they found out, they said, "Five—and two fish."

³⁹Then Jesus directed them to have all the people sit down in groups on the green grass. ⁴⁰So they sat down in groups of hundreds and fifties. ⁴¹Taking the five loaves and the two fish and looking up to heaven, he gave thanks and broke the loaves. Then he gave them to his disciples to set before the people. He also divided the two fish among them all. ⁴²They all ate and were satisfied, ⁴³and the disciples picked up twelve basketfuls of broken pieces of bread and fish. ⁴⁴The number of the men who had eaten was five thousand.

OPEN: 1. After a busy day, how do you like to unwind? **2.** For what occasion would you have an open house party with a big spread?

DIG: 1. Why did Jesus decide to take the disciples away? What happened as soon as they left? How did the disciples and Jesus differ in the way they viewed the problem? How would you have felt about this intrusion? **2.** What emotions might have been expressed by the disciples in verse 37? **3.** What would you feel as a disciple when you gathered the leftovers? What was the purpose of doing so? **4.** How does this dinner party of Jesus compare to that of Herod (6:21-29)? What does this story imply about Jesus' identity? His mission?

REFLECT: How has Jesus "fed" you when you've been spiritually hungry lately? When you sense that hunger, do you come searching for him, or do you usually try to "fill up" on something else first? If so, what? Why?

⸍37 Greek *take two hundred denarii*

JESUS FEEDS THE FIVE THOUSAND

LOOKING INTO THE SCRIPTURE/25 Minutes. Read Mark 6:30-44 and discuss.

1. Which three from the following list will ruin a *restful* vacation for you the most?
   ☐ running into acquaintances from home   ☐ phone calls from the office
   ☐ mosquitoes/jellyfish/ants   ☐ surprises
   ☐ car trouble   ☐ losing your wallet
   ☐ 7 straight days of rain   ☐ standing in long lines
   ☐ losing luggage   ☐ tight time schedule
   ☐ unfinished business at work   ☐ having relatives along

2. "Come with me by yourself to a quiet place and get some rest." If you were one of the disciples, what would you expect?
   a. a quiet little vacation
   b. time to be with Jesus
   c. a fun time
   d. anything but people

3. Surprise. There are 5,000 waiting on the shore. How do you feel?
   a. delighted
   b. "Oh no"
   c. compassion
   d. anger/frustration
   e. whipped

4. "You give them something to eat." Why did the disciples object?
   a. they were "on empty"
   b. they didn't like welfare
   c. they were mad because their vacation was blown
   d. they were afraid of attracting loafers

5. "How many loaves do you have?" What was Jesus asking the disciples to do?
   a. take inventory of their resources
   b. stop thinking of their own self-interests
   c. see how impossible it really was
   d. start with what they had
   e. trust that he had a plan

MY OWN STORY/20 Minutes. Read the Scripture again and share your feelings.

1. How do you react when you are faced with an overwhelming sense of need?
   a. panicked
   b. inadequate
   c. let's do something
   d. I can't do anything
   e. hold back and feel guilty later

2. How does it make you feel when you realize that you have special gifts to contribute to the world's needs?
   a. lump in my throat
   b. scared stiff
   c. pretty responsible
   d. eager to do something
   e. mixed feelings
   f. question God's choice of me

3. What is your favorite way of avoiding your responsibility?
   a. claim problem is too big
   b. blame everybody else
   c. wait for someone to go first
   d. say I can't make a difference
   e. turn on the TV and ignore the issue
   f. get busy with something else

4. If you could pool the resources of your group to do something about the needs of your community, what would be your biggest strength?
   a. financial
   b. leadership
   c. political connections
   d. community action
   e. spiritual motivation
   f. genuine concern

5. Where are you now in listening to God's call for action? (Put a dot somewhere between the two extremes).

GOD IS ON   I MAKE SURE
THE PHONE   I'M NOT AT HOME
RIGHT NOW _____ WHEN GOD CALLS

OPEN: In school, what subject did you have the most trouble learning: Math? Spelling? Phys. Ed.?

DIG: 1. What new problem do the disciples encounter on this day? How would you react in their place? **2.** What is the significance of Jesus' walking on the water and his response to their terror (see Isa 43:1-3; 44:8)? How do you think the disciples understood it? **3.** What should they have perceived in the "lesson of the loaves" that would have prepared them for this? Who is he revealing himself to be? Why is he doing it this way, rather than telling them directly? **4.** How do the crowds (vv.53-56) view him?

REFLECT: Where are you "straining at the oars"? How do Jesus' words (v.50) speak to that storm?

OPEN: 1. In your family, how were you punished for a "foul mouth"? **2.** What's the most fun you ever had getting dirty? **3.** To what foods did you grow up saying "yecchh!"?

DIG: 1. What is the issue debated by the Pharisees and Jesus? Given this debate, how would each define what it means to be spiritual? How does the quote from Isaiah address the issue at hand? **2.** Although the traditions were established to help people obey the law, how is it that they ended up overshadowing that law (vv.8-9)? **3.** Something declared "Corban" meant it was dedicated to God, thus it was no longer able to be given away. What does this illustration show about how traditions twisted the law? **4.** How does Jesus' idea of being unclean differ from that of the Pharisees? Why doesn't Jesus offer any solution to the problem at this time?

REFLECT: 1. What in your religious life is comparable to the "tradition of the elders" (i.e., rules or regulations not from Scripture but from your tradition and culture)? How could these rules

Jesus Walks on the Water

[45]Immediately Jesus made his disciples get into the boat and go on ahead of him to Bethsaida, while he dismissed the crowd. [46]After leaving them, he went up on a mountainside to pray.

[47]When evening came, the boat was in the middle of the lake, and he was alone on land. [48]He saw the disciples straining at the oars, because the wind was against them. About the fourth watch of the night he went out to them, walking on the lake. He was about to pass by them, [49]but when they saw him walking on the lake, they thought he was a ghost. They cried out, [50]because they all saw him and were terrified.

Immediately he spoke to them and said, "Take courage! It is I. Don't be afraid." [51]Then he climbed into the boat with them, and the wind died down. They were completely amazed, [52]for they had not understood about the loaves; their hearts were hardened.

[53]When they had crossed over, they landed at Gennesaret and anchored there. [54]As soon as they got out of the boat, people recognized Jesus. [55]They ran throughout that whole region and carried the sick on mats to wherever they heard he was. [56]And wherever he went—into villages, towns or countryside—they placed the sick in the marketplaces. They begged him to let them touch even the edge of his cloak, and all who touched him were healed.

Clean and Unclean

7 The Pharisees and some of the teachers of the law who had come from Jerusalem gathered around Jesus and [2]saw some of his disciples eating food with hands that were "unclean," that is, unwashed. [3](The Pharisees and all the Jews do not eat unless they give their hands a ceremonial washing, holding to the tradition of the elders. [4]When they come from the marketplace they do not eat unless they wash. And they observe many other traditions, such as the washing of cups, pitchers and kettles. [s])

[5]So the Pharisees and teachers of the law asked Jesus, "Why don't your disciples live according to the tradition of the elders instead of eating their food with 'unclean' hands?"

[6]He replied, "Isaiah was right when he prophesied about you hypocrites; as it is written:

" 'These people honor me with their lips,
    but their hearts are far from me.
[7]They worship me in vain;
    their teachings are but rules taught by men.'[t]

[8]You have let go of the commands of God and are holding on to the traditions of men."

[9]And he said to them: "You have a fine way of setting aside the commands of God in order to observe[u] your own traditions! [10]For Moses said, 'Honor your father and your mother,'[v] and, 'Anyone who curses his father or mother must be put to death.'[w]

---

[s]4 Some early manuscripts *pitchers, kettles and dining couches*   [t]6,7 Isaiah 29:13
[u]9 Some manuscripts *set up*   [v]10 Exodus 20:12; Deut. 5:16
[w]10 Exodus 21:17; Lev. 20:9

[11]But you say that if a man says to his father or mother: 'Whatever help you might otherwise have received from me is Corban' (that is, a gift devoted to God), [12]then you no longer let him do anything for his father or mother. [13]Thus you nullify the word of God by your tradition that you have handed down. And you do many things like that."

[14]Again Jesus called the crowd to him and said, "Listen to me, everyone, and understand this. [15]Nothing outside a man can make him 'unclean' by going into him. Rather, it is what comes out of a man that makes him 'unclean.'[x]"

[17]After he had left the crowd and entered the house, his disciples asked him about this parable. [18]"Are you so dull?" he asked. "Don't you see that nothing that enters a man from the outside can make him 'unclean'? [19]For it doesn't go into his heart but into his stomach, and then out of his body." (In saying this, Jesus declared all foods "clean.")

[20]He went on: "What comes out of a man is what makes him 'unclean.' [21]For from within, out of men's hearts, come evil thoughts, sexual immorality, theft, murder, adultery, [22]greed, malice, deceit, lewdness, envy, slander, arrogance and folly. [23]All these evils come from inside and make a man 'unclean.' "

The Faith of a Syrophoenician Woman

[24]Jesus left that place and went to the vicinity of Tyre.[y] He entered a house and did not want anyone to know it; yet he could not keep his presence secret. [25]In fact, as soon as she heard about him, a woman whose little daughter was possessed by an evil[z] spirit came and fell at his feet. [26]The woman was a Greek, born in Syrian Phoenicia. She begged Jesus to drive the demon out of her daughter.

[27]"First let the children eat all they want," he told her, "for it is not right to take the children's bread and toss it to their dogs."

[28]"Yes, Lord," she replied, "but even the dogs under the table eat the children's crumbs."

[29]Then he told her, "For such a reply, you may go; the demon has left your daughter."

[30]She went home and found her child lying on the bed, and the demon gone.

The Healing of a Deaf and Mute Man

[31]Then Jesus left the vicinity of Tyre and went through Sidon, down to the Sea of Galilee and into the region of the Decapolis.[a] [32]There some people brought to him a man who was deaf and could hardly talk, and they begged him to place his hand on the man.

[33]After he took him aside, away from the crowd, Jesus put his fingers into the man's ears. Then he spit and touched the man's tongue. [34]He looked up to heaven and with a deep sigh said to him, *"Ephphatha!"* (which means, "Be opened!"). [35]At this, the

OPEN: For what would you walk 100 miles out of your way? Why?

DIG: 1. What is Jesus' point in going to Tyre (a Gentile area) after the discussion in 7:1-23? **2.** Were Jesus' words harsh or a play on words? How does this woman take it? How does her reply show faith? **3.** What message is Jesus giving by this healing?

REFLECT: If Jesus came to your community, who are the "unclean" he would care for? How might you be his hands and feet for them?

OPEN: If you became deaf, what three sounds would you not miss?

DIG: 1. What is significant about where this healing occurred (5:1-20)? How does it relate to the debate in 7:1-23? **2.** Why do you think Jesus used this method to heal the man? **3.** How is the response of these Gentiles (v.37) like that of the Jews (1:27; 2:12) and the Twelve (4:41)? What is Mark's point in emphasizing this?

actually block someone from God? How might they mask evil in a "religious" disguise? **2.** How would you decide whether someone was really "spiritual" or not? How has your view of spirituality changed over the past few years? Why? **3.** Verses 20-23 represent an evil heart, whereas 12:30 represents a pure, whole heart. How can you strengthen that second kind of heart? What do you do when the evil heart wins out?

---

[x]15 Some early manuscripts 'unclean.' [16]If anyone has ears to hear, let him hear.
[y]24 Many early manuscripts Tyre and Sidon   [z]25 Greek unclean   [a]31 That is, the Ten Cities

REFLECT: 1. How has your grasp of who Jesus is changed over the past five years? 2. What can you do this week to show friendship to someone who is alone?

OPEN: How did your parents complete this sentence when you were a child: "How many times do I have to tell you,…"?

DIG: 1. How does this feeding compare and contrast with that of 6:30-44? 2. In light of all the miracles that Jesus had already done, why would the Pharisees "demand a sign from heaven"? How might they have responded if Jesus had provided one? 3. From what you have seen of the Pharisees and Herod so far, what does Jesus mean by his warning in verse 15? How does their "yeast" differ from Jesus' "bread"? How do the disciples take Jesus' comments? 4. With what tone of voice do you hear Jesus saying verses 17-21? Why? 5. How are the numbers "12" and "7" used elsewhere in the Bible? What is Jesus' point in highlighting these numbers? What should the disciples understand about Jesus by these numbers and feedings? How are they like and unlike the Pharisees (vv.11-12)?

REFLECT: 1. Do you sometimes doubt Jesus' ability to meet your needs? How so? How are you discovering that he really can shepherd you? In what areas are you still unsure about that? 2. How can you recognize where the "yeast of the Pharisees and Herod" is still active today? How does it show in the way people relate to God? To one another? 3. What does "hardness of heart" mean to you? How has Jesus made your heart softer? What part is still hard?

man's ears were opened, his tongue was loosened and he began to speak plainly.

[36]Jesus commanded them not to tell anyone. But the more he did so, the more they kept talking about it. [37]People were overwhelmed with amazement. "He has done everything well," they said. "He even makes the deaf hear and the mute speak."

Jesus Feeds the Four Thousand

8 During those days another large crowd gathered. Since they had nothing to eat, Jesus called his disciples to him and said, [2]"I have compassion for these people; they have already been with me three days and have nothing to eat. [3]If I send them home hungry, they will collapse on the way, because some of them have come a long distance."

[4]His disciples answered, "But where in this remote place can anyone get enough bread to feed them?"

[5]"How many loaves do you have?" Jesus asked.

"Seven," they replied.

[6]He told the crowd to sit down on the ground. When he had taken the seven loaves and given thanks, he broke them and gave them to his disciples to set before the people, and they did so. [7]They had a few small fish as well; he gave thanks for them also and told the disciples to distribute them. [8]The people ate and were satisfied. Afterward the disciples picked up seven basketfuls of broken pieces that were left over. [9]About four thousand men were present. And having sent them away, [10]he got into the boat with his disciples and went to the region of Dalmanutha.

[11]The Pharisees came and began to question Jesus. To test him, they asked him for a sign from heaven. [12]He sighed deeply and said, "Why does this generation ask for a miraculous sign? I tell you the truth, no sign will be given to it." [13]Then he left them, got back into the boat and crossed to the other side.

The Yeast of the Pharisees and Herod

[14]The disciples had forgotten to bring bread, except for one loaf they had with them in the boat. [15]"Be careful," Jesus warned them. "Watch out for the yeast of the Pharisees and that of Herod."

[16]They discussed this with one another and said, "It is because we have no bread."

[17]Aware of their discussion, Jesus asked them: "Why are you talking about having no bread? Do you still not see or understand? Are your hearts hardened? [18]Do you have eyes but fail to see, and ears but fail to hear? And don't you remember? [19]When I broke the five loaves for the five thousand, how many basketfuls of pieces did you pick up?"

"Twelve," they replied.

[20]"And when I broke the seven loaves for the four thousand, how many basketfuls of pieces did you pick up?"

They answered, "Seven."

[21]He said to them, "Do you still not understand?"

The Healing of a Blind Man at Bethsaida

²²They came to Bethsaida, and some people brought a blind man and begged Jesus to touch him. ²³He took the blind man by the hand and led him outside the village. When he had spit on the man's eyes and put his hands on him, Jesus asked, "Do you see anything?"

²⁴He looked up and said, "I see people; they look like trees walking around."

²⁵Once more Jesus put his hands on the man's eyes. Then his eyes were opened, his sight was restored, and he saw everything clearly. ²⁶Jesus sent him home, saying, "Don't go into the village.ᵇ"

Peter's Confession of Christ

²⁷Jesus and his disciples went on to the villages around Caesarea Philippi. On the way he asked them, "Who do people say I am?"

²⁸They replied, "Some say John the Baptist; others say Elijah; and still others, one of the prophets."

²⁹"But what about you?" he asked. "Who do you say I am?" Peter answered, "You are the Christ.ᶜ"

³⁰Jesus warned them not to tell anyone about him.

Jesus Predicts His Death

³¹He then began to teach them that the Son of Man must suffer many things and be rejected by the elders, chief priests and teachers of the law, and that he must be killed and after three days rise again. ³²He spoke plainly about this, and Peter took him aside and began to rebuke him.

³³But when Jesus turned and looked at his disciples, he rebuked Peter. "Get behind me, Satan!" he said. "You do not have in mind the things of God, but the things of men."

³⁴Then he called the crowd to him along with his disciples and said: "If anyone would come after me, he must deny himself and take up his cross and follow me. ³⁵For whoever wants to save his lifeᵈ will lose it, but whoever loses his life for me and for the gospel will save it. ³⁶What good is it for a man to gain the whole world, yet forfeit his soul? ³⁷Or what can a man give in exchange for his soul? ³⁸If anyone is ashamed of me and my words in this adulterous and sinful generation, the Son of Man will be ashamed of him when he comes in his Father's glory with the holy angels."

9 And he said to them, "I tell you the truth, some who are standing here will not taste death before they see the kingdom of God come with power."

ᵇ26 Some manuscripts *Don't go and tell anyone in the village*   ᶜ29 Or *Messiah*.
"The Christ" (Greek) and "the Messiah" (Hebrew) both mean "the Anointed One."
ᵈ35 The Greek word means either *life* or *soul*; also in verse 36.

OPEN: Of all the places called "God's country," which one is your favorite for sight-seeing, camping, or a stroll down memory lane?

DIG: 1. What is the connection between 9:1 and this event? 2. What do you imagine this scene was like? What is the significance of Moses' and Elijah's presence? Of the voice (see 1:11)? Why would this be important for Jesus at this stage of his ministry? Why would it be important for the disciples? 3. Why did Jesus take the three if he didn't want them to tell anyone what happened (see also 8:32)? 4. Who played the role of Elijah (see Mt 17:10-13)? With what result (6:14-29)? How could John the Baptist's experience help the disciples understand the nature of Jesus' Messiahship?

REFLECT: 1. What spot for you is most like the Mount of Transfiguration—where you grasped a bit of Jesus' glory in a special way? 2. How does the picture of a suffering Messiah shape your view of what the Christian life is all about?

_____

OPEN: 1. When you were a child, what issues were most likely to trigger an argument within your family? 2. Are you more gullible (like Winnie the Pooh), cynical (like Eeyore), helter-skelter (like Odie, the dog), or calculating (like Garfield)? Likewise, how would you characterize your children (if any)? Give examples.

DIG: 1. While the three disciples were up on the mountain, what problem were the other nine having? How did they deal with it? How might verses 2-3 account for the "wonder" with which the others greeted Jesus? What do you think the argument was about in verse 14? 2. As the boy's father, how would you feel during this argument? 3. How do the contrasts between this story and the transfiguration account for Jesus' response (v.19)? 4. What is the major difference between Jesus' teaching in 8:31 and 9:30-32? What is significant about this difference?

REFLECT: 1. When have you felt like the father in verse 24? How

The Transfiguration

[2]After six days Jesus took Peter, James and John with him and led them up a high mountain, where they were all alone. There he was transfigured before them. [3]His clothes became dazzling white, whiter than anyone in the world could bleach them. [4]And there appeared before them Elijah and Moses, who were talking with Jesus.

[5]Peter said to Jesus, "Rabbi, it is good for us to be here. Let us put up three shelters—one for you, one for Moses and one for Elijah." [6](He did not know what to say, they were so frightened.)

[7]Then a cloud appeared and enveloped them, and a voice came from the cloud: "This is my Son, whom I love. Listen to him!"

[8]Suddenly, when they looked around, they no longer saw anyone with them except Jesus.

[9]As they were coming down the mountain, Jesus gave them orders not to tell anyone what they had seen until the Son of Man had risen from the dead. [10]They kept the matter to themselves, discussing what "rising from the dead" meant.

[11]And they asked him, "Why do the teachers of the law say that Elijah must come first?"

[12]Jesus replied, "To be sure, Elijah does come first, and restores all things. Why then is it written that the Son of Man must suffer much and be rejected? [13]But I tell you, Elijah has come, and they have done to him everything they wished, just as it is written about him."

The Healing of a Boy With an Evil Spirit

[14]When they came to the other disciples, they saw a large crowd around them and the teachers of the law arguing with them. [15]As soon as all the people saw Jesus, they were overwhelmed with wonder and ran to greet him.

[16]"What are you arguing with them about?" he asked.

[17]A man in the crowd answered, "Teacher, I brought you my son, who is possessed by a spirit that has robbed him of speech. [18]Whenever it seizes him, it throws him to the ground. He foams at the mouth, gnashes his teeth and becomes rigid. I asked your disciples to drive out the spirit, but they could not."

[19]"O unbelieving generation," Jesus replied, "how long shall I stay with you? How long shall I put up with you? Bring the boy to me."

[20]So they brought him. When the spirit saw Jesus, it immediately threw the boy into a convulsion. He fell to the ground and rolled around, foaming at the mouth.

[21]Jesus asked the boy's father, "How long has he been like this?"

"From childhood," he answered. [22]"It has often thrown him into fire or water to kill him. But if you can do anything, take pity on us and help us."

[23]"'If you can'?" said Jesus. "Everything is possible for him who believes."

LOOKING INTO THE SCRIPTURE/25 Minutes. Read Mark 9:2-13 and discuss.

1. What impresses you about Peter in this story?
  - a. his enthusiasm
  - b. quick thinking in a threatening situation
  - c. willingness to act on his faith
  - d. "foot in mouth" disease

2. Why do you think Jesus took time for this long trip into the mountains just a few weeks before his death?
  - a. to spend time with God
  - b. to prepare himself for the cross
  - c. to strengthen his disciples
  - d. to sort out his thoughts

3. If you had been Peter when Moses and Elijah appeared, how would you have felt?
  - a. scared spitless
  - b. totally awed
  - c. out of place
  - d. on a high
  - e. like hiding

4. Why did Peter want to build three shelters?
  - a. to honor Elijah, Moses, and Jesus
  - b. to remember the occasion
  - c. to keep the mountaintop feeling
  - d. he couldn't think of anything better to do
  - e. to expend nervous energy

5. What is the meaning of the words, "This is my Son, whom I love. Listen to him."
  - a. shut up a minute
  - b. forget about building anything
  - c. "Be still and know that I am God"
  - d. the splendor you have seen is proof that Jesus is my son

6. If you had been Peter after this experience, how would you have felt?
  - a. subdued
  - b. awed
  - c. put down
  - d. elated/ecstatic
  - e. very special

MY OWN STORY/20 Minutes. Read the Scripture and share your own experience.

1. On the line below, put a mark and an event or place to indicate the time you remember having your first mountaintop experience with God.
BIRTH _____ NOW

2. What is your most recent mountaintop experience?
  - a. years ago
  - b. quite recently
  - c. right now
  - d. hasn't happened yet

3. What helps you to feel close to God?
  - a. nature
  - b. music
  - c. being alone with Christ
  - d. real Christian fellowship
  - e. the Lord's Supper
  - f. remembering His love for you

4. How do you feel when you are on the mountaintop?
  - a. like being awed
  - b. like the other shoe is about to drop
  - c. like nothing else matters
  - d. like conquering the world
  - e. like staying forever

5. How would you describe your relationship with God now?
  - a. on the mountaintop
  - b. down off the mountain
  - c. in the valley
  - d. in a quandry
  - e. in the desert
  - f. in mid-climb

do prayer and faith relate for you at those times? **2.** Where do you learn more—during spiritual highs or lows? **3.** How can you live with the full reality of evil and yet with strong awareness of God's transforming power? In what way do you feel that tension now? **4.** What possibilities and what abuses come to mind when you ponder the fact that "everything is possible for him who believes" (v.23)?

²⁴Immediately the boy's father exclaimed, "I do believe; help me overcome my unbelief!"

²⁵When Jesus saw that a crowd was running to the scene, he rebuked the evil*ᵉ* spirit. "You deaf and mute spirit," he said, "I command you, come out of him and never enter him again."

²⁶The spirit shrieked, convulsed him violently and came out. The boy looked so much like a corpse that many said, "He's dead." ²⁷But Jesus took him by the hand and lifted him to his feet, and he stood up.

²⁸After Jesus had gone indoors, his disciples asked him privately, "Why couldn't we drive it out?"

²⁹He replied, "This kind can come out only by prayer.*ᶠ*"

³⁰They left that place and passed through Galilee. Jesus did not want anyone to know where they were, ³¹because he was teaching his disciples. He said to them, "The Son of Man is going to be betrayed into the hands of men. They will kill him, and after three days he will rise." ³²But they did not understand what he meant and were afraid to ask him about it.

Who Is the Greatest?

³³They came to Capernaum. When he was in the house, he asked them, "What were you arguing about on the road?" ³⁴But they kept quiet because on the way they had argued about who was the greatest.

³⁵Sitting down, Jesus called the Twelve and said, "If anyone wants to be first, he must be the very last, and the servant of all."

³⁶He took a little child and had him stand among them. Taking him in his arms, he said to them, ³⁷"Whoever welcomes one of these little children in my name welcomes me; and whoever welcomes me does not welcome me but the one who sent me."

Whoever Is Not Against Us Is for Us

³⁸"Teacher," said John, "we saw a man driving out demons in your name and we told him to stop, because he was not one of us."

³⁹"Do not stop him," Jesus said. "No one who does a miracle in my name can in the next moment say anything bad about me, ⁴⁰for whoever is not against us is for us. ⁴¹I tell you the truth, anyone who gives you a cup of water in my name because you belong to Christ will certainly not lose his reward.

Causing to Sin

⁴²"And if anyone causes one of these little ones who believe in me to sin, it would be better for him to be thrown into the sea with a large millstone tied around his neck. ⁴³If your hand causes you to sin, cut it off. It is better for you to enter life maimed than with two hands to go into hell, where the fire never goes out.*ᵍ* ⁴⁵And if your foot causes you to sin, cut it off. It is

OPEN: What one childhood quality would you like to recapture?

DIG: 1. As a disciple, how would you feel when Jesus asked about the argument? Why does Jesus use the child as an object lesson on true greatness in the kingdom? **2.** What is ironic in verses 38-41 (see 9:18)? Why are these exorcists a problem for John? **3.** What does it mean to do something "in Jesus' name"?

REFLECT: 1. How does success "Jesus-style" differ from the ideas of success pressing on you from the world? What would it mean for you to reflect verses 35-37 in your family? In your work? What is the surprising incentive to do so? **2.** What Christian groups do you tend to "bad-mouth" because they are "not one of us"? Why? What is Jesus' point for you here?

OPEN: If you had to give up a hand, a foot, or an eye, which would you give up and why?

DIG: 1. What four things does Jesus say are "better"? What is his point in using this hyperbole? How does this relate to his other teachings about discipleship in 9:33-41? In 8:34? What is critical? **2.** How does the admonition to be at peace relate to verses 42-49?

ᵉ25 Greek unclean   ᶠ29 Some manuscripts prayer and fasting   ᵍ43 Some manuscripts out, ⁴⁴where / " 'their worm does not die, / and the fire is not quenched.'

better for you to enter life crippled than to have two feet and be thrown into hell. *h* 47And if your eye causes you to sin, pluck it out. It is better for you to enter the kingdom of God with one eye than to have two eyes and be thrown into hell, 48where

" 'their worm does not die,
and the fire is not quenched.' *i*

49Everyone will be salted with fire.

50"Salt is good, but if it loses its saltiness, how can you make it salty again? Have salt in yourselves, and be at peace with each other."

Divorce

10 Jesus then left that place and went into the region of Judea and across the Jordan. Again crowds of people came to him, and as was his custom, he taught them.

2Some Pharisees came and tested him by asking, "Is it lawful for a man to divorce his wife?"

3"What did Moses command you?" he replied.

4They said, "Moses permitted a man to write a certificate of divorce and send her away."

5"It was because your hearts were hard that Moses wrote you this law," Jesus replied. 6"But at the beginning of creation God 'made them male and female.' *j* 7"For this reason a man will leave his father and mother and be united to his wife, *k* 8and the two will become one flesh.' *l* So they are no longer two, but one. 9Therefore what God has joined together, let man not separate."

10When they were in the house again, the disciples asked Jesus about this. 11He answered, "Anyone who divorces his wife and marries another woman commits adultery against her. 12And if she divorces her husband and marries another man, she commits adultery."

The Little Children and Jesus

13People were bringing little children to Jesus to have him touch them, but the disciples rebuked them. 14When Jesus saw this, he was indignant. He said to them, "Let the little children come to me, and do not hinder them, for the kingdom of God belongs to such as these. 15I tell you the truth, anyone who will not receive the kingdom of God like a little child will never enter it." 16And he took the children in his arms, put his hands on them and blessed them.

The Rich Young Man

17As Jesus started on his way, a man ran up to him and fell on his knees before him. "Good teacher," he asked, "what must I do to inherit eternal life?"

18"Why do you call me good?" Jesus answered. "No one is good—except God alone. 19You know the commandments: 'Do not murder, do not commit adultery, do not steal, do not give

REFLECT: 1. What does verse 42 imply about our relationships with those we perceive as weak? **2.** What can you do to "salt" your relationships with peace this week?

OPEN: What do you like best and least about weddings?

DIG: 1. How were the Pharisees trying to test Jesus by their question? What was their viewpoint on divorce? **2.** Instead of answering their question, how does Jesus put them to the test by emphasizing God's intent for marriage? **3.** In light of the political situation (6:17-19), what risks was Jesus taking in stating verses 11-12?

REFLECT: 1. How can you apply the principles of marriage underlined here? **2.** Do you think Jesus would respond the same to someone in a troubled marriage who sincerely asking the question in verse 2? Why or why not?

OPEN: 1. What really bugs you about kids? What is really great about them? **2.** Did you choose the job you are in for (a) money, (b) fulfillment, or (c) the chance to make a contribution ?

DIG: 1. Why would the disciples want to keep the children away from Jesus? What childlike qualities was Jesus commending (vv.13-16)? **2.** How does the man's question (v.17) compare with what Jesus had just taught about the kingdom (v.15)? What was his assumption about how one gains the kingdom? **3.** What is Jesus trying to drive home by responding to the way the man addressed him? **4.** Jesus quizzes the man on only a partial list of the Ten Commandments (see Ex 20). How well might the man have obeyed the ones relating directly to God? **5.** Why does Jesus

---

h45 Some manuscripts hell, 46where / " 'their worm does not die, / and the fire is not quenched.' *i48 Isaiah 66:24* *j6 Gen. 1:27* *k7 Some early manuscripts do not have and be united to his wife.* *l8 Gen. 2:24* command the man as he does (v.21; see also 8:34)? What does his response reveal which had been hidden by his good works? **6.** What does the disciples' shock reveal about them? On what basis is it possible for anyone to receive the kingdom? **7.** How is the promise (vv.29-30) to come true for believers?

REFLECT: **1.** Are you more like the man or the children (vv.13-16) in terms of the way you approach God? Why? **2.** What has helped you to see the impossibility of "earning" the kingdom? As a result, how have you experienced the gift of the kingdom as described in verses 29-30? **3.** What in your life could Jesus point to as something that is preventing you from receiving the kingdom?

OPEN: **1.** What did your parents want you to be when you grew up? **2.** What career ambition did you have at age 12? Age 20? Age 30?

DIG: **1.** Why would going to Jerusalem cause the disciples to be astonished and afraid? **2.** What impresses you about Jesus' resolve with the Twelve and with James and John? **3.** What view of the kingdom are James and John still clinging to? How could they respond like this in light of verses 33-34? **4.** What is the *cup*, the *baptism*, and the *glory* as each applies to Jesus? As each applies to the disciples? **5.** What made the other disciples indignant? **6.** How does Jesus use this uproar to convey new insights into what greatness is? **7.** How does Jesus practice what he preached? In this context, what is a "ransom for many"? How is the death of Christ the ultimate service to all? **8.** How does 10:45 answer the question recorded in 8:37?

false testimony, do not defraud, honor your father and mother.'[m]"

²⁰"Teacher," he declared, "all these I have kept since I was a boy."

²¹Jesus looked at him and loved him. "One thing you lack," he said. "Go, sell everything you have and give to the poor, and you will have treasure in heaven. Then come, follow me."

²²At this the man's face fell. He went away sad, because he had great wealth.

²³Jesus looked around and said to his disciples, "How hard it is for the rich to enter the kingdom of God!"

²⁴The disciples were amazed at his words. But Jesus said again, "Children, how hard it is[n] to enter the kingdom of God! ²⁵It is easier for a camel to go through the eye of a needle than for a rich man to enter the kingdom of God."

²⁶The disciples were even more amazed, and said to each other, "Who then can be saved?"

²⁷Jesus looked at them and said, "With man this is impossible, but not with God; all things are possible with God."

²⁸Peter said to him, "We have left everything to follow you!"

²⁹"I tell you the truth," Jesus replied, "no one who has left home or brothers or sisters or mother or father or children or fields for me and the gospel ³⁰will fail to receive a hundred times as much in this present age (homes, brothers, sisters, mothers, children and fields—and with them, persecutions) and in the age to come, eternal life. ³¹But many who are first will be last, and the last first."

Jesus Again Predicts His Death

³²They were on their way up to Jerusalem, with Jesus leading the way, and the disciples were astonished, while those who followed were afraid. Again he took the Twelve aside and told them what was going to happen to him. ³³"We are going up to Jerusalem," he said, "and the Son of Man will be betrayed to the chief priests and teachers of the law. They will condemn him to death and will hand him over to the Gentiles, ³⁴who will mock him and spit on him, flog him and kill him. Three days later he will rise."

The Request of James and John

³⁵Then James and John, the sons of Zebedee, came to him. "Teacher," they said, "we want you to do for us whatever we ask."

³⁶"What do you want me to do for you?" he asked.

³⁷They replied, "Let one of us sit at your right and the other at your left in your glory."

³⁸"You don't know what you are asking," Jesus said. "Can you drink the cup I drink or be baptized with the baptism I am baptized with?"

³⁹"We can," they answered.

Jesus said to them, "You will drink the cup I drink and be

---

m19 Exodus 20:12-16; Deut. 5:16-20   *n24* Some manuscripts *is for those who trust in riches* baptized with the baptism I am baptized with, [40]but to sit at my right or left is not for me to grant. These places belong to those for whom they have been prepared."

[41]When the ten heard about this, they became indignant with James and John. [42]Jesus called them together and said, "You know that those who are regarded as rulers of the Gentiles lord it over them, and their high officials exercise authority over them. [43]Not so with you. Instead, whoever wants to become great among you must be your servant, [44]and whoever wants to be first must be slave of all. [45]For even the Son of Man did not come to be served, but to serve, and to give his life as a ransom for many."

Blind Bartimaeus Receives His Sight

[46]Then they came to Jericho. As Jesus and his disciples, together with a large crowd, were leaving the city, a blind man, Bartimaeus (that is, the Son of Timaeus), was sitting by the roadside begging. [47]When he heard that it was Jesus of Nazareth, he began to shout, "Jesus, Son of David, have mercy on me!"

[48]Many rebuked him and told him to be quiet, but he shouted all the more, "Son of David, have mercy on me!"

[49]Jesus stopped and said, "Call him."

So they called to the blind man, "Cheer up! On your feet! He's calling you." [50]Throwing his cloak aside, he jumped to his feet and came to Jesus.

[51]"What do you want me to do for you?" Jesus asked him. The blind man said, "Rabbi, I want to see."

[52]"Go," said Jesus, "your faith has healed you." Immediately he received his sight and followed Jesus along the road.

The Triumphal Entry

11 As they approached Jerusalem and came to Bethphage and Bethany at the Mount of Olives, Jesus sent two of his disciples, [2]saying to them, "Go to the village ahead of you, and just as you enter it, you will find a colt tied there, which no one has ever ridden. Untie it and bring it here. [3]If anyone asks you, 'Why are you doing this?' tell him, 'The Lord needs it and will send it back here shortly.' "

[4]They went and found a colt outside in the street, tied at a doorway. As they untied it, [5]some people standing there asked, "What are you doing, untying that colt?" [6]They answered as Jesus had told them to, and the people let them go. [7]When they brought the colt to Jesus and threw their cloaks over it, he sat on it. [8]Many people spread their cloaks on the road, while others spread branches they had cut in the fields. [9]Those who went ahead and those who followed shouted,

"Hosanna![o]"

"Blessed is he who comes in the name of the Lord!"[p]

REFLECT: 1. How and why do you find yourself desiring the first chair in God's orchestra? 2. How does Jesus' life as a servant influence your view of spiritual power? Your view of relationships? Your use of spiritual gifts? 3. What one way could you serve this week?

OPEN: How do you respond when a beggar approaches you on the street? Why?

DIG: 1. What is significant about the way Bartimaeus addresses Jesus? About the way this beggar is treated by the crowd? How does he evidence faith (while the crowd does not)? 2. How is Bartimaeus different from the young man in 10:17-22? 3. Why is there no "order of silence" (as in 7:36)?

REFLECT: If Jesus asked you, "What do you want me to do for you?", what would you say? What would be your part and God's part in fulfilling your desire?

OPEN: 1. What is the closest you have come to seeing something like the Rose Bowl Parade? 2. What is the closest you have come to meeting a world leader or celebrity? What did you do to celebrate the event?

DIG: 1. How did the manner in which Jesus entered Jerusalem confirm his character (see Zec 9:9)? 2. In light of the response he received, what were the expectations of the crowd? The disciples (see 10:37)? Jesus? 3. What do you find most significant about the triumphal entry into Jerusalem?

REFLECT: 1. How did Jesus ride into your life: As a conquering hero forcing you into submission? As a gentle king bearing peace? As a white knight rescuing you? How about now? 2. Have you ever misunderstood Jesus' purposes, praising him one day and despairing the next? Explain.

---

*o*9 A Hebrew expression meaning "Save!" which became an exclamation of praise; also in verse 10   *p*9 Psalm 118:25,26   *q*17 Isaiah 56:7

¹⁰"Blessed is the coming kingdom of our father David!"

"Hosanna in the highest!"

¹¹Jesus entered Jerusalem and went to the temple. He looked around at everything, but since it was already late, he went out to Bethany with the Twelve.

Jesus Clears the Temple

¹²The next day as they were leaving Bethany, Jesus was hungry. ¹³Seeing in the distance a fig tree in leaf, he went to find out if it had any fruit. When he reached it, he found nothing but leaves, because it was not the season for figs. ¹⁴Then he said to the tree, "May no one ever eat fruit from you again." And his disciples heard him say it.

¹⁵On reaching Jerusalem, Jesus entered the temple area and began driving out those who were buying and selling there. He overturned the tables of the money changers and the benches of those selling doves, ¹⁶and would not allow anyone to carry merchandise through the temple courts. ¹⁷And as he taught them, he said, "Is it not written:

" 'My house will be called
a house of prayer for all nations'ʳ?

But you have made it 'a den of robbers.'ʳ'"

¹⁸The chief priests and the teachers of the law heard this and began looking for a way to kill him, for they feared him, because the whole crowd was amazed at his teaching.

¹⁹When evening came, theyˢ went out of the city.

The Withered Fig Tree

²⁰In the morning, as they went along, they saw the fig tree withered from the roots. ²¹Peter remembered and said to Jesus, "Rabbi, look! The fig tree you cursed has withered!"

²²"Haveᵗ faith in God," Jesus answered. ²³"I tell you the truth, if anyone says to this mountain, 'Go, throw yourself into the sea,' and does not doubt in his heart but believes that what he says will happen, it will be done for him. ²⁴Therefore I tell you, whatever you ask for in prayer, believe that you have received it, and it will be yours. ²⁵And when you stand praying, if you hold anything against anyone, forgive him, so that your Father in heaven may forgive you your sins.ᵘ'"

The Authority of Jesus Questioned

²⁷They arrived again in Jerusalem, and while Jesus was walking in the temple courts, the chief priests, the teachers of the law and the elders came to him. ²⁸"By what authority are you doing these things?" they asked. "And who gave you authority to do this?"

²⁹Jesus replied, "I will ask you one question. Answer me, and I will tell you by what authority I am doing these things. ³⁰John's baptism—was it from heaven, or from men? Tell me!"

OPEN: When is the last time you got so mad about injustice or fraud that you did something about it?

DIG: 1. How does the story of the fig tree relate to the clearing of the temple (vv.13-14, 20-21)? In what ways did the Pharisees cover their fruitlessness with flashy foliage? **2.** This profiteering on the sale of sacrificial animals took place in the only area where Gentiles could worship. Why would that especially anger Jesus (see Isa 56:6-8)? What was Jesus threatening when he called the temple a "den of robbers" (see Jer 7:9-15)? What does this event say about Jesus? **3.** Why did the priests and teachers have to be so crafty in their plot? **4.** Why was Peter amazed (vv.20-21)? Should he have been? What conditions for effective prayer are upheld here?

REFLECT: 1. If you were a tree, what would help you produce more fruit: Pruning? Watering? Staking? Transplanting? Fertilizing? Why? **2.** What does this story and 9:42 show you about what angers Jesus most? How could this relate to your religious practices? **3.** Of the conditions for prayer here, which stretch you the most? Why? In light of how Jesus uses power, what other conditions may there be? **4.** What are your major prayer requests now?

OPEN: What authority figures do you still trust implicitly? Which do you now distrust? Why?

DIG: 1. Why were the leaders concerned about authority? In their eyes, who had legitimate authority? **2.** What dilemma does this question pose for Jesus? Why doesn't he answer them directly? How does he cause the leaders' trickery to backfire on them?

REFLECT: In what way does the honor of God compete with "the praise of men" in your life?

ʳ17 Jer. 7:11   ˢ19 Some early manuscripts *he*   ᵗ22 Some early manuscripts *If you have*   ᵘ25 Some manuscripts *sins. ²⁶But if you do not forgive, neither will your Father who is in heaven forgive your sins.*

LOOKING INTO THE SCRIPTURE/25 Minutes. Read Mark 11:12-19 and discuss.

Divide into groups of four or five and share how angry each of the following situations makes you by choosing a number from 1 to 5 (1 being NO SWEAT, 2 being MIFFED, 3 being LOW GROWL, 4 being FLARING NOSTRILS and 5 being BLOOD BOILS)

1	2	3	4	5	Getting the run-around/red tape
1	2	3	4	5	Car boils over during 5 o'clock rush
1	2	3	4	5	Political scandals
1	2	3	4	5	Mistreatment of others/bigotry
1	2	3	4	5	Criticism from your mother
1	2	3	4	5	No time left for yourself/someone intrudes on your time
1	2	3	4	5	Violation of your rights
1	2	3	4	5	God is commercialized
1	2	3	4	5	Sunday morning paper gets wet
1	2	3	4	5	Favorite sweater lost at drycleaners
1	2	3	4	5	Preacher preaches past noon
1	2	3	4	5	Cold food in a restaurant
1	2	3	4	5	Lose money in a vending machine

2. How would you describe the behavior of Jesus in this passage?
   a. politician
   b. umpire
   c. Marine sergeant
   d. pussycat
   e. tyrant
   f. bull in a china shop
   g. county sheriff
   h. superman
   i. bouncer

3. Do you think Jesus overreacted in this situation?   □ Yes □ No

4. Why did the chief priests and the teachers of the law start looking for a way to kill Jesus?
   a. he intruded on their turf
   b. he threatened their authority
   c. he exposed them as a bunch of thieves
   d. he ruined their business

5. If Jesus came to clean up your town, where would he start?
   a. city hall
   b. high school
   c. porno shops
   d. church
   e. newspapers
   f. your room

MY OWN STORY/20 Minutes. Take a moment and think about your own reaction to social wrongs or abuse.

1. How would you describe your own response to injustice, abuse, or moral corruption?
   a. pussycat
   b. bull in a china shop
   c. politician
   d. pistol-packing mama
   e. the three stooges

2. When are you more likely to get involved or take action?
   a. when my interests are threatened
   b. when my friends are involved
   c. when a moral principle I believe in strongly is involved
   d. when God tells me
   e. when I think I can make a difference

3. What have you found most effective in changing the behavior of society for the good?
   a. appeal to people's sense of fairness
   b. work on changing the heart first
   c. change the law
   d. work quietly behind the scenes
   e. overturning a few tables

4. Where is God calling you now to get involved?
   a. winning people to Christ
   b. reaching leaders in the community
   c. getting involved in community programs to assist the poor, underprivileged, or abused
   d. forming a political action task force

[31]They discussed it among themselves and said, "If we say, 'From heaven,' he will ask, 'Then why didn't you believe him?' [32]But if we say, 'From men'. . . ." (They feared the people, for everyone held that John really was a prophet.)

[33]So they answered Jesus, "We don't know."

Jesus said, "Neither will I tell you by what authority I am doing these things."

The Parable of the Tenants

12 He then began to speak to them in parables: "A man planted a vineyard. He put a wall around it, dug a pit for the winepress and built a watchtower. Then he rented the vineyard to some farmers and went away on a journey. [2]At harvest time he sent a servant to the tenants to collect from them some of the fruit of the vineyard. [3]But they seized him, beat him and sent him away empty-handed. [4]Then he sent another servant to them; they struck this man on the head and treated him shamefully. [5]He sent still another, and that one they killed. He sent many others; some of them they beat, others they killed.

[6]"He had one left to send, a son, whom he loved. He sent him last of all, saying, 'They will respect my son.'

[7]"But the tenants said to one another, 'This is the heir. Come, let's kill him, and the inheritance will be ours.' [8]So they took him and killed him, and threw him out of the vineyard.

[9]"What then will the owner of the vineyard do? He will come and kill those tenants and give the vineyard to others. [10]Haven't you read this scripture:

" 'The stone the builders rejected
    has become the capstone[v];
[11]the Lord has done this,
    and it is marvelous in our eyes'[w]?"

[12]Then they looked for a way to arrest him because they knew he had spoken the parable against them. But they were afraid of the crowd; so they left him and went away.

Paying Taxes to Caesar

[13]Later they sent some of the Pharisees and Herodians to Jesus to catch him in his words. [14]They came to him and said, "Teacher, we know you are a man of integrity. You aren't swayed by men, because you pay no attention to who they are; but you teach the way of God in accordance with the truth. Is it right to pay taxes to Caesar or not? [15]Should we pay or shouldn't we?"

But Jesus knew their hypocrisy. "Why are you trying to trap me?" he asked. "Bring me a denarius and let me look at it." [16]They brought the coin, and he asked them, "Whose portrait is this? And whose inscription?"

"Caesar's," they replied.

[17]Then Jesus said to them, "Give to Caesar what is Caesar's and to God what is God's."

And they were amazed at him.

OPEN: 1. If you owned a garden or an orchard, what would you grow? **2.** If you had to entrust your business or belongings to someone outside your family, whom would you choose? Why?

DIG: 1. What does the vineyard represent? Who is the owner? The son? Who are the tenants? The servants? What was Jesus prophesying by telling this story? **2.** How does the Scripture Jesus quotes relate to the parable? Who were the builders? Who is the capstone? **3.** What impact did this parable have on its first hearers? How did it answer the question about Jesus' authority (11:28)?

REFLECT: 1. How do you make Jesus feel welcome in your life each day? What actions of yours might make him feel unwelcome? **2.** Does Jesus seem more like a *millstone* (weight), or a *capstone* (one who holds everything together) in your life? Give an example of each, if you can.

OPEN: When do you feel right about paying taxes? For what?

DIG: 1. What was dangerous about this trap? Why do the Herodians (allied to Rome) and the Pharisees make strange partners? How was Jesus a threat to each? **2.** What if Jesus had just said yes? If he had said no? What did Jesus' answer probably do to their partnership?

REFLECT: If it's the coin that you give to "Caesar," what do you give to God? What often prevents you from giving to God what is God's?

[v]10 Or *cornerstone*   [w]11 Psalm 118:22,23

Marriage at the Resurrection

[18]Then the Sadducees, who say there is no resurrection, came to him with a question. [19]"Teacher," they said, "Moses wrote for us that if a man's brother dies and leaves a wife but no children, the man must marry the widow and have children for his brother. [20]Now there were seven brothers. The first one married and died without leaving any children. [21]The second one married the widow, but he also died, leaving no child. It was the same with the third. [22]In fact, none of the seven left any children. Last of all, the woman died too. [23]At the resurrection[x] whose wife will she be, since the seven were married to her?"

[24]Jesus replied, "Are you not in error because you do not know the Scriptures or the power of God? [25]When the dead rise, they will neither marry nor be given in marriage; they will be like the angels in heaven. [26]Now about the dead rising—have you not read in the book of Moses, in the account of the bush, how God said to him, 'I am the God of Abraham, the God of Isaac, and the God of Jacob'[y]? [27]He is not the God of the dead, but of the living. You are badly mistaken!"

The Greatest Commandment

[28]One of the teachers of the law came and heard them debating. Noticing that Jesus had given them a good answer, he asked him, "Of all the commandments, which is the most important?"

[29]"The most important one," answered Jesus, "is this: 'Hear, O Israel, the Lord our God, the Lord is one.[z] [30]Love the Lord your God with all your heart and with all your soul and with all your mind and with all your strength.'[a] [31]The second is this: 'Love your neighbor as yourself.'[b] There is no commandment greater than these."

[32]"Well said, teacher," the man replied. "You are right in saying that God is one and there is no other but him. [33]To love him with all your heart, with all your understanding and with all your strength, and to love your neighbor as yourself is more important than all burnt offerings and sacrifices."

[34]When Jesus saw that he had answered wisely, he said to him, "You are not far from the kingdom of God." And from then on no one dared ask him any more questions.

Whose Son Is the Christ?

[35]While Jesus was teaching in the temple courts, he asked, "How is it that the teachers of the law say that the Christ[c] is the son of David? [36]David himself, speaking by the Holy Spirit, declared:

" 'The Lord said to my Lord:
"Sit at my right hand
until I put your enemies
under your feet." '[d]

OPEN: What aspects of earthly life would you like to see remain the same in heaven?

DIG: 1. What was odd about the Sadducees' question? Why ask it? **2.** What is the source of the Sadducees' false assumption? **3.** What characterizes "resurrection life"? How does Exodus 3:6 (quoted in v.26) demonstrate the fact of the resurrection?

REFLECT: 1. Which do you know more about—the Scriptures, or the power of God? What are your hopes for growing in the other area? **2.** What is most important to you about this promise?

OPEN: What subject is guaranteed to spark a debate your house? Sports? Politics? Religion? Other:_____?

DIG: 1. Why are these two commandments the greatest? How do the Ten Commandments relate to these two? **2.** How was this teacher's attitude different from that of many others who questioned Jesus (11:28; 12:13-14; 12:18-19)? What does Jesus' response to this man teach you about Jesus? About the kingdom? **3.** Why do you think Jesus' answer silenced his enemies? What else were they thinking but didn't say?

REFLECT: In the three possibilities of love relationships (with God, neighbors, and self), where are you the strongest? The weakest? What have you found that helps love to grow in each area?

---

[x]23 Some manuscripts *resurrection, when men rise from the dead,*   [y]26 Exodus 3:6
[z]29 Or *the Lord our God is one Lord*   [a]30 Deut. 6:4,5   [b]31 Lev. 19:18
[c]35 Or *Messiah*   [d]36 Psalm 110:1

³⁷David himself calls him 'Lord.' How then can he be his son?" The large crowd listened to him with delight.

³⁸As he taught, Jesus said, "Watch out for the teachers of the law. They like to walk around in flowing robes and be greeted in the marketplaces, ³⁹and have the most important seats in the synagogues and the places of honor at banquets. ⁴⁰They devour widows' houses and for a show make lengthy prayers. Such men will be punished most severely."

The Widow's Offering

⁴¹Jesus sat down opposite the place where the offerings were put and watched the crowd putting their money into the temple treasury. Many rich people threw in large amounts. ⁴²But a poor widow came and put in two very small copper coins,ᵉ worth only a fraction of a penny.ᶠ

⁴³Calling his disciples to him, Jesus said, "I tell you the truth, this poor widow has put more into the treasury than all the others. ⁴⁴They all gave out of their wealth; but she, out of her poverty, put in everything—all she had to live on."

Signs of the End of the Age

13 As he was leaving the temple, one of his disciples said to him, "Look, Teacher! What massive stones! What magnificent buildings!"

²"Do you see all these great buildings?" replied Jesus. "Not one stone here will be left on another; every one will be thrown down."

³As Jesus was sitting on the Mount of Olives opposite the temple, Peter, James, John and Andrew asked him privately, ⁴"Tell us, when will these things happen? And what will be the sign that they are all about to be fulfilled?"

⁵Jesus said to them: "Watch out that no one deceives you. ⁶Many will come in my name, claiming, 'I am he,' and will deceive many. ⁷When you hear of wars and rumors of wars, do not be alarmed. Such things must happen, but the end is still to come. ⁸Nation will rise against nation, and kingdom against kingdom. There will be earthquakes in various places, and famines. These are the beginning of birth pains.

⁹"You must be on your guard. You will be handed over to the local councils and flogged in the synagogues. On account of me you will stand before governors and kings as witnesses to them. ¹⁰And the gospel must first be preached to all nations. ¹¹Whenever you are arrested and brought to trial, do not worry beforehand about what to say. Just say whatever is given you at the time, for it is not you speaking, but the Holy Spirit.

¹²"Brother will betray brother to death, and a father his child. Children will rebel against their parents and have them put to death. ¹³All men will hate you because of me, but he who stands firm to the end will be saved.

OPEN: 1. If you could take two things with you to heaven, what would they be? **2.** In school or at work, did you ever "get burned" because you stood by the truth or refused to go along with the crowd? Was it worth it? Why or why not? **3.** Who pulled off the best surprise party, secret gift, or serendipity on you? How so?

DIG: 1. Why do you think that Jesus used the discussion about the temple to begin his discourse about the end of the age? What made the temple so significant for the disciples? What would its destruction symbolize for them? **2.** Upon hearing this bombshell, what two questions do the disciples ask (v.4)? What events might deceive them into thinking the end times had come (vv.5-8)? Of what will these events be a sign? **3.** After that, what things will happen to the disciples and the early church (vv.9-13)? To governors, kings and "all nations"? What comfort and advocate will aid them to endure their trials? **4.** What dreadful event (v.14; see Da 9:26; 11:31; 12:11) will bring "days of distress" unequalled in human history? What deceptive signs will accompany that distress (vv. 21-22)? **5.** How will the Son of Man come (vv.24-27)? **6.** How does the "fig tree" lesson (vv.28-29) answer the disciples' questions

ᵉ42 Greek *two lepta*   ᶠ42 Greek *kodrantes*   ᵍ14 Daniel 9:27; 11:31; 12:11
ʰ14 Or *he*; also in verse 29

14"When you see 'the abomination that causes desolation'[g] standing where it[h] does not belong—let the reader understand— then let those who are in Judea flee to the mountains. 15Let no one on the roof of his house go down or enter the house to take anything out. 16Let no one in the field go back to get his cloak. 17How dreadful it will be in those days for pregnant women and nursing mothers! 18Pray that this will not take place in winter, 19because those will be days of distress unequaled from the beginning, when God created the world, until now—and never to be equaled again. 20If the Lord had not cut short those days, no one would survive. But for the sake of the elect, whom he has chosen, he has shortened them. 21At that time if anyone says to you, 'Look, here is the Christ[i]!' or, 'Look, there he is!' do not believe it. 22For false Christs and false prophets will appear and perform signs and miracles to deceive the elect—if that were possible. 23So be on your guard; I have told you everything ahead of time.

24"But in those days, following that distress,

" 'the sun will be darkened,
    and the moon will not give its light;
25the stars will fall from the sky,
    and the heavenly bodies will be shaken.'[j]

26"At that time men will see the Son of Man coming in clouds with great power and glory. 27And he will send his angels and gather his elect from the four winds, from the ends of the earth to the ends of the heavens.

28"Now learn this lesson from the fig tree: As soon as its twigs get tender and its leaves come out, you know that summer is near. 29Even so, when you see these things happening, you know that it is near, right at the door. 30I tell you the truth, this generation[k] will certainly not pass away until all these things have happened. 31Heaven and earth will pass away, but my words will never pass away.

The Day and Hour Unknown

32"No one knows about that day or hour, not even the angels in heaven, nor the Son, but only the Father. 33Be on guard! Be alert[l]! You do not know when that time will come. 34It's like a man going away: He leaves his house and puts his servants in charge, each with his assigned task, and tells the one at the door to keep watch.

35"Therefore keep watch because you do not know when the owner of the house will come back—whether in the evening, or at midnight, or when the rooster crows, or at dawn. 36If he comes suddenly, do not let him find you sleeping. 37What I say to you, I say to everyone: 'Watch!' "

from verse 4 (also 11:12-14, 20-21)? **7.** What promises does Jesus give in verses 30-31? How would this comfort (or discomfort) the disciples? What impact do these promises have on you, 20 centuries later? **8.** What visions in the past, present, and future do you see in these various *signs*: (a) "Wars and rumors of wars"? (b) Earthquakes and famines? (c) Trials and persecutions? (d) Family divisions? (e) World-wide evangelization? (f) False Christs and false prophets? **9.** Why do you think the Father has kept the time secret (v.32)? What is the responsibility of believers in the meantime?

REFLECT: 1. When you see the forces of evil apparently winning, do you feel like withdrawing from the battle and perching on the rooftop? Or rolling up your sleeves and getting into the fray? How does this passage encourage you? **2.** What is the most exciting thing to you about the Second Coming? The most distressing? What questions would you like to ask Jesus about it? **3.** Specifically, how can you fulfill verses 34 and 37: "Be on guard! Be alert... Watch!"?

---

[i]21 Or *Messiah*   [j]25 Isaiah 13:10; 34:4   [k]30 Or *race*
[l]33 Some manuscripts *alert and pray*

OPEN: 1. If you had a year's wages to blow on friends, which would you choose: (a) Big party for all? (b) Glorious trip for a few? or (c) Extravagant gift for one? 2. What one gift you received stands out in your memory? Why?

DIG: 1. What was significant about this time of year? How might this cause the fear expressed by Jesus' opponents? 2. How does this woman's action (v.3) strike you: Thoughtful, but misguided? Tasteful, but extravagant? Wasteful, no buts about it? Honoring to the nth degree? 3. Do you think the perfume could have been better spent? Why? How was her action justified by Jesus (vv.6-9) and used by Judas (vv.10-11)?

REFLECT: 1. What "beautiful thing" (v.6) would you like to do for Jesus that some might see as wasteful? 2. How do you balance giving to Christ through support of your church and through caring for the poor?

OPEN: 1. What is one of your favorite places to eat? What makes it special? 2. What favorite meal does Mom prepare to celebrate your homecoming?

DIG: 1. How does this meal relate to the Passover (see Ex 12)? 2. Why would secrecy be needed as this meal was planned? What risk was involved? 3. What does Jesus say about his betrayer? How do the disciples react to that bombshell? 4. What new meaning did Jesus give to the Passover bread? The wine? What vow did he make? 5. How much do you think the disciples understood when Jesus spoke about his body and blood? What clue to the meaning of Jesus' death and resurrection would later be provided by reference to the first Passover (see Ex 12)? 6. Were the disciples singing their last hymn together (v.26) in a minor or major key? Why do you think so?

REFLECT: 1. How would you have felt if you had been at that meal? 2. What is your focus when you partake of Communion? Why is Communion important to the body of believers?

Jesus Anointed at Bethany

14 Now the Passover and the Feast of Unleavened Bread were only two days away, and the chief priests and the teachers of the law were looking for some sly way to arrest Jesus and kill him. [2]"But not during the Feast," they said, "or the people may riot."

[3]While he was in Bethany, reclining at the table in the home of a man known as Simon the Leper, a woman came with an alabaster jar of very expensive perfume, made of pure nard. She broke the jar and poured the perfume on his head.

[4]Some of those present were saying indignantly to one another, "Why this waste of perfume? [5]It could have been sold for more than a year's wages[m] and the money given to the poor." And they rebuked her harshly.

[6]"Leave her alone," said Jesus. "Why are you bothering her? She has done a beautiful thing to me. [7]The poor you will always have with you, and you can help them any time you want. But you will not always have me. [8]She did what she could. She poured perfume on my body beforehand to prepare for my burial. [9]I tell you the truth, wherever the gospel is preached throughout the world, what she has done will also be told, in memory of her."

[10]Then Judas Iscariot, one of the Twelve, went to the chief priests to betray Jesus to them. [11]They were delighted to hear this and promised to give him money. So he watched for an opportunity to hand him over.

The Lord's Supper

[12]On the first day of the Feast of Unleavened Bread, when it was customary to sacrifice the Passover lamb, Jesus' disciples asked him, "Where do you want us to go and make preparations for you to eat the Passover?"

[13]So he sent two of his disciples, telling them, "Go into the city, and a man carrying a jar of water will meet you. Follow him. [14]Say to the owner of the house he enters, 'The Teacher asks: Where is my guest room, where I may eat the Passover with my disciples?' [15]He will show you a large upper room, furnished and ready. Make preparations for us there."

[16]The disciples left, went into the city and found things just as Jesus had told them. So they prepared the Passover.

[17]When evening came, Jesus arrived with the Twelve. [18]While they were reclining at the table eating, he said, "I tell you the truth, one of you will betray me—one who is eating with me."

[19]They were saddened, and one by one they said to him, "Surely not I?"

[20]"It is one of the Twelve," he replied, "one who dips bread into the bowl with me. [21]The Son of Man will go just as it is written about him. But woe to that man who betrays the Son of Man! It would be better for him if he had not been born."

[22]While they were eating, Jesus took bread, gave thanks and broke it, and gave it to his disciples, saying, "Take it; this is my body."

m5 Greek than three hundred denarii

LOOKING INTO THE SCRIPTURE/20 Minutes. Read Mark 14:1-11 and discuss.

1. When you want to give a special gift to someone you love, which kind of thing do you look for?

Totally frivolous . . . . Very practical
Something I like . . . . Something she/he would like
Expensive . . . . Inexpensive, but creative
Something you use . . . . Something you look at
Responding to current need . . . . Anticipating future need

2. Why do you think the woman spent a year's wages on perfume?
   a. to express devotion to Jesus
   b. to show off
   c. to get to heaven
   d. on an impulse

3. Why were Jesus' friends so upset?
   a. she crashed the party
   b. she wasted money
   c. she made everybody look cheap
   d. she was a known prostitute
   e. she was a little weird

4. If you had been one of the disciples, what would you have said to the woman?
   a. let's save the money for the poor
   b. do what you want—it's your money
   c. what a waste
   d. beat it!

5. What was the motive of the people who criticized the woman?
   a. concern for the poor
   b. greed
   c. jealousy toward the woman
   d. hope of embarrassing Jesus

6. What was Jesus really saying when he defended the action of the woman?
   a. extravagance is okay
   b. her motive made it okay
   c. don't worry about the poor
   d. don't judge another's motives

7. For Judas, this was the last straw. Why?
   a. Jesus fraternized with a woman
   b. Jesus didn't care about the poor
   c. Jesus predicted his own death
   d. Jesus thought himself pretty important

MY OWN STORY/20 Minutes. Read the Scripture again and share your experience.

1. When you spend money on another person, what concerns you?
   a. can I afford it?
   b. am I buying a friendship?
   c. will it do some good?
   d. will that person feel obligated to return with a similar gift?
   e. have I spent enough to show my feelings are serious?
   f. will s/he like what I got?
   g. should I have given this to someone else?

2. What is the biggest problem you have in making money decisions?
   a. never enough to go around
   b. no financial plan
   c. no clear priorities
   d. too many credit cards

3. If you had ten times the amount of money you now have to give away, would you do a better job with your giving?
   a. I would like to think so
   b. I would sure try
   c. probably not
   d. ask me tomorrow

4. When it comes to giving money, what factors do you consider?
   a. IRS deduction
   b. how great the need is
   c. how will it be used
   d. what others will think
   e. my commitment to that cause

[23]Then he took the cup, gave thanks and offered it to them, and they all drank from it.

[24]"This is my blood of the[n] covenant, which is poured out for many," he said to them. [25]"I tell you the truth, I will not drink again of the fruit of the vine until that day when I drink it anew in the kingdom of God."

[26]When they had sung a hymn, they went out to the Mount of Olives.

Jesus Predicts Peter's Denial

[27]"You will all fall away," Jesus told them, "for it is written:

" 'I will strike the shepherd,
  and the sheep will be scattered.'[o]

[28]But after I have risen, I will go ahead of you into Galilee."
[29]Peter declared, "Even if all fall away, I will not."

[30]"I tell you the truth," Jesus answered, "today—yes, tonight—before the rooster crows twice[p] you yourself will disown me three times."

[31]But Peter insisted emphatically, "Even if I have to die with you, I will never disown you." And all the others said the same.

Gethsemane

[32]They went to a place called Gethsemane, and Jesus said to his disciples, "Sit here while I pray." [33]He took Peter, James and John along with him, and he began to be deeply distressed and troubled. [34]"My soul is overwhelmed with sorrow to the point of death," he said to them. "Stay here and keep watch."

[35]Going a little farther, he fell to the ground and prayed that if possible the hour might pass from him. [36]"Abba,[q] Father," he said, "everything is possible for you. Take this cup from me. Yet not what I will, but what you will."

[37]Then he returned to his disciples and found them sleeping. "Simon," he said to Peter, "are you asleep? Could you not keep watch for one hour? [38]Watch and pray so that you will not fall into temptation. The spirit is willing, but the body is weak."

[39]Once more he went away and prayed the same thing. [40]When he came back, he again found them sleeping, because their eyes were heavy. They did not know what to say to him.

[41]Returning the third time, he said to them, "Are you still sleeping and resting? Enough! The hour has come. Look, the Son of Man is betrayed into the hands of sinners. [42]Rise! Let us go! Here comes my betrayer!"

Jesus Arrested

[43]Just as he was speaking, Judas, one of the Twelve, appeared. With him was a crowd armed with swords and clubs, sent from the chief priests, the teachers of the law, and the elders. [44]Now the betrayer had arranged a signal with them: "The one I kiss is the man; arrest him and lead him away under guard." [45]Going at once to Jesus, Judas said, "Rabbi!" and

OPEN: Where do you go (or what do you do) when you're facing difficult situations? Do you prefer to be alone at these times, or in the company of close friends?

DIG: 1. How does Peter see himself in relation to the other disciples? How might the others feel about that? 2. Why do you think Jesus warned the disciples (especially Peter) of their upcoming denial? 3. Why did Jesus take Peter, James, and John with him to pray (v.33)? 4. Why don't the disciples share Jesus' sense of urgency? How does this relate to their statements in the previous passage? 5. What did Jesus desire most of all? Yet how did he pray? Why? 6. Why did Jesus urge Peter specifically to "watch and pray"? 7. From this story, what key thing do you learn about Jesus? About affirming God's will?

REFLECT: 1. How do you feel, realizing that Jesus knows your weaknesses and failures too? 2. When, if ever, have you faced a "Gethsemane"? What happened? 3. What determines for whom and what you pray? How will the Gethsemane story change the way you pray this week?

OPEN: How would you react if one of your kids (or parents!) was arrested?

DIG: 1. Why is the crowd armed (v.48)? What does this tell you about Judas' misunderstanding of Jesus' mission? 2. How do you account for the disciples' reactions (vv.47,50,51)?

LOOKING INTO THE SCRIPTURE/20 Minutes. Read Mark 14:32-42 and share.

1. If you knew that you had only a few days to live, what would you do with the time? Choose three.

☐ not tell anyone
☐ straighten out my affairs
☐ throw a big party
☐ spend time with loved ones
☐ write all my friends
☐ have as much fun as possible
☐ plan my funeral
☐ isolate myself from everyone
☐ give away all my possessions

☐ travel around
☐ offer myself for science
☐ spend time with God
☐ reminisce with my old buddies
☐ go fishing
☐ do what I've always wanted to do
☐ gamble everything in Las Vegas
☐ do nothing different
☐ call friends and family to say "Good-by"

2. Why did Jesus take Peter, James, and John along with him?
   a. he needed their fellowship
   b. to test their endurance
   c. to experience his grief so they could write about it
   d. to pray for him

3. From Jesus' perspective, what was the test?
   a. to do God's will or his own
   b. to take the easy way out
   c. to keep his emotions from showing
   d. to say "no" to Satan

4. For the disciples, what was the test?
   a. to stay awake and pray
   b. to be present with Jesus in his agony
   c. to keep from giving advice
   d. to watch Jesus suffer

5. From the standpoint of God, the Father, what was the test?
   a. to stand by and let his Son make the decision
   b. to call off the mission and save his Son
   c. to keep from lashing out against Satan
   d. to stick to the game plan for saving mankind from judgment

---

MY OWN STORY/40 Minutes.

1. With what decision are you struggling at the moment?
   a. what to do with my life
   b. what does God want
   c. should I make a change in job
   d. how can I improve my marriage
   e. what should I do for my kids
   f. how can I make Christ a part of my lifestyle
   g. how can I get out of the mess I'm in
   h. how can I be a Christian and a success

2. Where are you now in this decision?
   a. still praying about it
   b. torn between several alternatives
   c. waiting on a phone call from God
   d. starting to act on my decision
   e. just barely coping
   f. not sure God is listening

3. What is harder for you?
   a. to struggle to know God's will
   b. to do what I know God wants
   c. to go through this struggle with someone I love
   d. to keep open and available to God for change of direction

4. Who do you call on when you need help in knowing God's will?
   a. no one but God
   b. someone who will listen and not give advice
   c. someone who has been through struggles
   d. someone completely objective
   e. someone good at giving advice

5. How do you know when you've identified God's will for you?
   a. I feel peaceful about the decision
   b. My friends agree with my decision
   c. Scripture tells me what is God's will in this situation
   d. Circumstances work out according to God's will
   e. I'm not sure I ever really know God's will
   f. In hindsight I can see what God's will was

kissed him. ⁴⁶The men seized Jesus and arrested him. ⁴⁷Then one of those standing near drew his sword and struck the servant of the high priest, cutting off his ear.

⁴⁸"Am I leading a rebellion," said Jesus, "that you have come out with swords and clubs to capture me? ⁴⁹Every day I was with you, teaching in the temple courts, and you did not arrest me. But the Scriptures must be fulfilled." ⁵⁰Then everyone deserted him and fled.

⁵¹A young man, wearing nothing but a linen garment, was following Jesus. When they seized him, ⁵²he fled naked, leaving his garment behind.

Before the Sanhedrin

⁵³They took Jesus to the high priest, and all the chief priests, elders and teachers of the law came together. ⁵⁴Peter followed him at a distance, right into the courtyard of the high priest. There he sat with the guards and warmed himself at the fire.

⁵⁵The chief priests and the whole Sanhedrin were looking for evidence against Jesus so that they could put him to death, but they did not find any. ⁵⁶Many testified falsely against him, but their statements did not agree.

⁵⁷Then some stood up and gave this false testimony against him: ⁵⁸"We heard him say, 'I will destroy this man-made temple and in three days will build another, not made by man.' " ⁵⁹Yet even then their testimony did not agree.

⁶⁰Then the high priest stood up before them and asked Jesus, "Are you not going to answer? What is this testimony that these men are bringing against you?" ⁶¹But Jesus remained silent and gave no answer.

Again the high priest asked him, "Are you the Christ,ʳ the Son of the Blessed One?"

⁶²"I am," said Jesus. "And you will see the Son of Man sitting at the right hand of the Mighty One and coming on the clouds of heaven."

⁶³The high priest tore his clothes. "Why do we need any more witnesses?" he asked. ⁶⁴"You have heard the blasphemy. What do you think?"

They all condemned him as worthy of death. ⁶⁵Then some began to spit at him; they blindfolded him, struck him with their fists, and said, "Prophesy!" And the guards took him and beat him.

Peter Disowns Jesus

⁶⁶While Peter was below in the courtyard, one of the servant girls of the high priest came by. ⁶⁷When she saw Peter warming himself, she looked closely at him.

"You also were with that Nazarene, Jesus," she said.

⁶⁸But he denied it. "I don't know or understand what you're talking about," he said, and went out into the entryway.ˢ

⁶⁹When the servant girl saw him there, she said again to those standing around, "This fellow is one of them." ⁷⁰Again he denied it.

ʳ61 Or *Messiah*   ˢ68 Some early manuscripts *entryway and the rooster crowed*

After a little while, those standing near said to Peter, "Surely you are one of them, for you are a Galilean."

71He began to call down curses on himself, and he swore to them, "I don't know this man you're talking about."

72Immediately the rooster crowed the second time.' Then Peter remembered the word Jesus had spoken to him: "Before the rooster crows twice" you will disown me three times." And he broke down and wept.

Jesus Before Pilate

15 Very early in the morning, the chief priests, with the elders, the teachers of the law and the whole Sanhedrin, reached a decision. They bound Jesus, led him away and handed him over to Pilate.

2"Are you the king of the Jews?" asked Pilate.

"Yes, it is as you say," Jesus replied.

3The chief priests accused him of many things. 4So again Pilate asked him, "Aren't you going to answer? See how many things they are accusing you of."

5But Jesus still made no reply, and Pilate was amazed.

6Now it was the custom at the Feast to release a prisoner whom the people requested. 7A man called Barabbas was in prison with the insurrectionists who had committed murder in the uprising. 8The crowd came up and asked Pilate to do for them what he usually did.

9"Do you want me to release to you the king of the Jews?" asked Pilate, 10knowing it was out of envy that the chief priests had handed Jesus over to him. 11But the chief priests stirred up the crowd to have Pilate release Barabbas instead.

12"What shall I do, then, with the one you call the king of the Jews?" Pilate asked them.

13"Crucify him!" they shouted.

14"Why? What crime has he committed?" asked Pilate.

But they shouted all the louder, "Crucify him!"

15Wanting to satisfy the crowd, Pilate released Barabbas to them. He had Jesus flogged, and handed him over to be crucified.

The Soldiers Mock Jesus

16The soldiers led Jesus away into the palace (that is, the Praetorium) and called together the whole company of soldiers. 17They put a purple robe on him, then twisted together a crown of thorns and set it on him. 18And they began to call out to him, "Hail, king of the Jews!" 19Again and again they struck him on the head with a staff and spit on him. Falling on their knees, they paid homage to him. 20And when they had mocked him, they took off the purple robe and put his own clothes on him. Then they led him out to crucify him.

REFLECT: 1. When, if ever, have you felt that your failures had made it impossible for Christ to use you again? **2.** What "rooster" reminds you of failure and guilt? What helps then?

OPEN: 1. As a kid, would you rather have been punished by Mom or by Dad? Why? **2.** In grade school, were you the champion of the underdog, or the underdog?

DIG: 1. What insights into Pilate's and Jesus' character does this story offer? Why is Pilate indecisive? Why is Jesus silent? **2.** Why do the people, after witnessing Jesus' miracles, hearing his teachings, and praising him with hosannas, now demand that Jesus be crucified? **3.** Why does Pilate grant their request? **4.** What insights into the gospel do you see in the release of Barabbas in exchange for Jesus (see 8:37; 10:45)? **5.** What mental, physical, and emotional brutality do the soldiers inflict on Jesus? Why? Does their mockery stem from fear, anger, unbelief, or what?

REFLECT: 1. Why did Jesus go through this trial and torture when he could easily have used his great powers and escaped? How does this make you feel? What does it make you want to do? **2.** Have your actions ever mocked the name of Jesus? What can you do to resist this kind of behavior? **3.** What do you think you would have done in Pilate's place? In Barabbas' place? In the soldiers' place?

---

t72 Some early manuscripts do not have *the second time*.   u72 Some early manuscripts do not have *twice*.

OPEN: 1. Have you ever sat with someone who was dying? What was it like? 2. How do you feel deep down when you attend funerals and burials?

DIG: 1. Why is Simon needed to carry Jesus' cross (see 14:65; 15:15,19)? How might that affect him? 2. What kinds of people were usually crucified (v.27)? How is Jesus like them? 3. What further insults are added to injury (vv.29-32)? 4. What ironies do you see here: In the places occupied by the robbers (see 10:37)? In the call for Jesus to save himself by coming down from the cross? In the officially posted reason for Jesus' death? 5. What aspect of the crucifixion was the worst for Jesus: The physical pain? The spiritual separation from God? Why? What causes his separation from the Father (see Hab 1:13)? What does this say about our part in his crucifixion? 6. How are the cry of Jesus (v.34; also Ps 22:1), the tearing of the temple curtain (v.38; see Heb 10:19-22), and the faith of the centurion (v.39) all related? 7. What do you learn about Joseph (vv.43-46)? What risks does a man of his status take by this action? 8. What is significant about the centurion's confirmation of Jesus' death? About the eyewitnesses of his burial (Mt 28:11-15)?

REFLECT: 1. Read Isaiah 53:12. How would you paraphrase it to explain what Jesus' death was all about? 2. What "curtain" do you feel still separates you from God? How does Jesus' death relate to that? 3. What is the riskiest thing you have ever done because of your faith in Jesus? Why did you do it?

The Crucifixion

[21]A certain man from Cyrene, Simon, the father of Alexander and Rufus, was passing by on his way in from the country, and they forced him to carry the cross. [22]They brought Jesus to the place called Golgotha (which means The Place of the Skull). [23]Then they offered him wine mixed with myrrh, but he did not take it. [24]And they crucified him. Dividing up his clothes, they cast lots to see what each would get.

[25]It was the third hour when they crucified him. [26]The written notice of the charge against him read: THE KING OF THE JEWS. [27]They crucified two robbers with him, one on his right and one on his left. [v] [29]Those who passed by hurled insults at him, shaking their heads and saying, "So! You who are going to destroy the temple and build it in three days, [30]come down from the cross and save yourself!"

[31]In the same way the chief priests and the teachers of the law mocked him among themselves. "He saved others," they said, "but he can't save himself! [32]Let this Christ, [w]this King of Israel, come down now from the cross, that we may see and believe." Those crucified with him also heaped insults on him.

The Death of Jesus

[33]At the sixth hour darkness came over the whole land until the ninth hour. [34]And at the ninth hour Jesus cried out in a loud voice, *"Eloi, Eloi, lama sabachthani?"*—which means, "My God, my God, why have you forsaken me?" [x]

[35]When some of those standing near heard this, they said, "Listen, he's calling Elijah."

[36]One man ran, filled a sponge with wine vinegar, put it on a stick, and offered it to Jesus to drink. "Now leave him alone. Let's see if Elijah comes to take him down," he said.

[37]With a loud cry, Jesus breathed his last.

[38]The curtain of the temple was torn in two from top to bottom. [39]And when the centurion, who stood there in front of Jesus, heard his cry and[y] saw how he died, he said, "Surely this man was the Son[z] of God!"

[40]Some women were watching from a distance. Among them were Mary Magdalene, Mary the mother of James the younger and of Joses, and Salome. [41]In Galilee these women had followed him and cared for his needs. Many other women who had come up with him to Jerusalem were also there.

The Burial of Jesus

[42]It was Preparation Day (that is, the day before the Sabbath). So as evening approached, [43]Joseph of Arimathea, a prominent member of the Council, who was himself waiting for the kingdom of God, went boldly to Pilate and asked for Jesus' body. [44]Pilate was surprised to hear that he was already dead. Summoning the centurion, he asked him if Jesus had already died. [45]When he learned from the centurion that it was so, he gave the

---

[v]27 Some manuscripts *left,* [28]*and the scripture was fulfilled which says,* "*He was counted with the lawless ones*" (Isaiah 53:12)   [w]32 Or *Messiah*   [x]34 Psalm 22:1   [y]39 Some manuscripts do not have *heard his cry and.*   [z]39 Or *a son*

body to Joseph. [46]So Joseph bought some linen cloth, took down the body, wrapped it in the linen, and placed it in a tomb cut out of rock. Then he rolled a stone against the entrance of the tomb. [47]Mary Magdalene and Mary the mother of Joses saw where he was laid.

The Resurrection

16 When the Sabbath was over, Mary Magdalene, Mary the mother of James, and Salome bought spices so that they might go to anoint Jesus' body. [2]Very early on the first day of the week, just after sunrise, they were on their way to the tomb [3]and they asked each other, "Who will roll the stone away from the entrance of the tomb?"

[4]But when they looked up, they saw that the stone, which was very large, had been rolled away. [5]As they entered the tomb, they saw a young man dressed in a white robe sitting on the right side, and they were alarmed.

[6]"Don't be alarmed," he said. "You are looking for Jesus the Nazarene, who was crucified. He has risen! He is not here. See the place where they laid him. [7]But go, tell his disciples and Peter, 'He is going ahead of you into Galilee. There you will see him, just as he told you.' "

[8]Trembling and bewildered, the women went out and fled from the tomb. They said nothing to anyone, because they were afraid.

[The most reliable early manuscripts and other ancient witnesses do not have Mark 16:9-20.]

[9]When Jesus rose early on the first day of the week, he appeared first to Mary Magdalene, out of whom he had driven seven demons. [10]She went and told those who had been with him and who were mourning and weeping. [11]When they heard that Jesus was alive and that she had seen him, they did not believe it.

[12]Afterward Jesus appeared in a different form to two of them while they were walking in the country. [13]These returned and reported it to the rest; but they did not believe them either.

[14]Later Jesus appeared to the Eleven as they were eating; he rebuked them for their lack of faith and their stubborn refusal to believe those who had seen him after he had risen.

[15]He said to them, "Go into all the world and preach the good news to all creation. [16]Whoever believes and is baptized will be saved, but whoever does not believe will be condemned. [17]And these signs will accompany those who believe: In my name they will drive out demons; they will speak in new tongues; [18]they will pick up snakes with their hands; and when they drink deadly poison, it will not hurt them at all; they will place their hands on sick people, and they will get well."

[19]After the Lord Jesus had spoken to them, he was taken up into heaven and he sat at the right hand of God. [20]Then the disciples went out and preached everywhere, and the Lord worked with them and confirmed his word by the signs that accompanied it.

OPEN: 1. What do you like to do on Sunday mornings? **2.** What "incredible" event would you disbelieve were it not that you saw it with your own two eyes? Try now to convince your small group that it really happened, even though they weren't there to see it for themselves. What difficulties do you experience in the re-telling of your eyewitness account?

DIG: 1. Why do you think the women go to the tomb at the time they do? What does this say about them? Where have their thoughts been since Friday? **2.** What potential problem looms ahead? What do they find instead? What do they fear? Seeing the empty tomb and the man sitting beside it, what thoughts are racing through their heads? **3.** Do you think they believed the man? How do their actions support your answer? **4.** Why do you think the angel asked them specifically to speak to Peter? What does this tell you about Jesus' plans for Peter?

REFLECT: 1. Would you have had trouble believing the angel's words? Why or why not? **2.** Who did Jesus send to you to tell you he had risen? Did you have trouble believing that person? How were you finally convinced of Jesus' resurrection? **3.** To whom is Jesus sending you with this message? How will you accomplish this mission? **4.** Where is your spiritual life focused these days: On Good Friday? Easter Sunday? Or in between? **5.** What will you remember most from the gospel of Mark to sharpen your focus of who Jesus really is?

LUKE

INTRODUCTION

Author

Although no author is named in the third Gospel, there is a tradition dating from the second century that Luke was the writer. There is good ground to accept Luke as author simply because he was *not* an apostle, nor was he particularly famous in the first-century church. In fact, he was a Gentile — the only non-Jewish author in the New Testament. Therefore, it is highly unlikely that anyone would have attached his name to this gospel had he not actually written it.

Internal evidence supports the testimony of tradition. For one thing, it is clear that the same man wrote both the third Gospel and the Book of Acts. Both books are dedicated to Theophilus. The books are similar in style, language, and interests. The author of Acts begins by saying, "In my former book," which is surely the Gospel. Since Acts was traditionally associated with Luke, the evidence that both books came from the same pen strengthens the tradition that Luke wrote the gospel bearing his name.

It is also interesting to note that the author of the third Gospel uses the language we would expect from a doctor (Luke was a physician). He describes illnesses with more precision than is found in Matthew and Mark (4:38; 5:12). He also omits the comment in Mark 5:26 that the woman who was subject to bleeding "had suffered a great deal under the care of many doctors and had spent all she had, yet instead of getting better she grew worse." Professional ethics prevailed in that day as well as in our own!

Little is known about Luke from the New Testament except that he was a doctor beloved by Paul (Col. 4:14) and that he was a coworker with Paul (2 Tim. 4:11; Philem. 24). However, in the Book of Acts, Luke describes experiences he shared while traveling with Paul (in the so-called *we* passages), though even here it is Paul, not Luke, who is front and center. One early non-canonical document, the *Prologue to Luke,* states that Luke was a physician, that he was unmarried and childless, and that he died at the age of 84. Beyond this, we know Luke only through his two eloquent documents published in the New Testament.

Date

There is no strong evidence as to when Luke's gospel was written. Many scholars date it between A.D. 75 and 85, although this is by no means conclusive. In fact, since Acts ends with Paul awaiting trial in Rome (probably before A.D. 67), if Luke wrote his gospel before he wrote Acts, then a date in the early sixties is likely.

Audience

Luke was a Gentile who wrote the story of Jesus for other Gentiles. This fact about the third Gospel gives it its distinctive flavor. The Gentile character of the manuscript begins in the preface, in which Luke dedicates the book to Theophilus, probably a high-ranking Roman government official (this title "most excellent" was normally reserved for such officials). Luke then dates the conception and birth of John the Baptist and Jesus with reference to the Roman rulers governing at the time (1:5; 2:1-2). Throughout the book, Luke makes a habit of translating Hebrew words into their Greek equivalents so that his Gentile readers will understand. For example, Luke never refers to Jesus as "Rabbi," the Hebrew title for a teacher, but always by the Greek equivalent, "Master." Luke identifies the place where Jesus was crucified not as *Golgotha,* its Hebrew name, but as *Kranion,* the Greek equivalent for "the place of the skull."

The Gentile character of the third Gospel is also seen in its identification of Jesus' lineage. Luke traces him back to Adam, the founder of the human race, and not, as Matthew does, back to Abraham, the founder of the Jewish race. Also in contrast to Matthew, Luke seldom quotes the Old Testament or demonstrates how Jesus fulfills Old Testament prophecy. This is a Gentile book about the Jewish Messiah who died for the whole world.

Characteristics

Luke's account of the life of Jesus is a unique document. For one thing, it is the longest book in the New Testament. Therefore, it contains more information about Jesus than any other book in the Bible. For another thing, Luke's gospel is extraordinarily joyful. It begins and ends with rejoicing (1:46-47 and 24:52-53), and in the account itself, Luke uses the words "joy" (6:23), "laughter" (6:21), and "celebration" (15:23, 32). Luke is also the only writer to record the four great canticles of joy and worship: *Magnificat* (1:46-55), *Benedictus* (1:68-79), *Gloria in Excelsis* (2:4), and *Nunc Dimittis* (2:29-32).

Why is Luke so filled with joy? He is overwhelmed with the thought that Jesus is the Savior of the whole world. He is astonished that Jesus came to seek and to save not just his kinsfolk, the Jews, but all people regardless of race, age, or culture.

Jesus came, for example, for the Gentiles. This is clear in Luke's gospel. In Luke, we hear Simeon prophesy that Jesus will be "a light for revelation to the Gentiles" (2:32). We hear Jesus praise the widow in Zarephath and Naaman the Syrian, two Gentiles whose stories are told in the Old Testament (4:25-27), and we hear Jesus single out the faith of a Roman centurion as an example of how people should respond to him (7:9).

Jesus came even for the hated Samaritans. As we see in the parable of the Good Samaritan (10:25-37), he places them on a par with the Jews in regard to God's kingdom. Luke has a lot to say about social outcasts in general. Women, children, and the poor — often treated badly by first-century society — are treated with special compassion by Luke. It is not accidental that Luke alone recounts the birth narratives from *Mary's* point of view. Luke mentions thirteen women not named in other gospel accounts. His special concern for children is clearly seen in his careful record of Jesus' childhood; Luke is the only gospel writer to record this information. As for the poor, Luke makes it clear that Jesus came to minister to them (4:18; 7:22; see also 1:53; 6:30; 14:11-13; 21; 16:19-31). Luke also takes great pains to warn about the danger of riches (1:53; 6:24; 12:1-34; 16:1-31; 18:18-30; 19:1-10; 21:1-4). From Luke's perspective, then, it does not matter who you are — you are welcome in God's kingdom. How well this is expressed in the beloved parable of the Prodigal Son (15:11-32), which occurs only in Luke's gospel. In Jesus' own words: "People will come from east and west and north and south, and will take their places at the feast in the kingdom of God" (13:29).

In addition to Luke's universality (Christ has come for all people) and his fascination with people (especially the outcasts), several other themes distinguish Luke. For example, Luke records more of Jesus' teaching about prayer than is found anywhere else in the Bible. He records nine of Jesus' own prayers. Luke also has more to say than the other gospels about the Holy Spirit (4:1, 14; 10:21; 24:49). He will pick up and expand on this emphasis of the Holy Spirit's active ministry in the companion volume to the third Gospel, the Book of Acts.

Structure

Luke was obviously well-educated, as we would expect a doctor to be. His training is reflected in his style.

Language

His prologue (1:1-4) is a fine example of first-rate classical Greek. Luke is capable of this quality of writing. The rest of chapters 1 and 2, however, have a strong Jewish flavor to them, almost as if Luke is translating from Jewish sources as he describes Jesus' birth and infancy. Then in chapter 3 he begins to write in the language of the people — good *koine* (popular) Greek.

Historical Detail

Luke writes very carefully. As he indicates in the prologue, his aim is to produce "an orderly account" (1: 3), which is exactly what he does. This book gives evidence of his meticulous research. For example, he dates the beginning of John the Baptist's ministry by reference to *six* historical facts (3:1-2). Another example of Luke's care as a historian is his practice of stating the exact titles of various Roman officials, even though these were notoriously difficult to get straight. Sir William Ramsay, the famous British scholar, once undertook to reseach the accuracy of Luke's writing. When he began he thought that Luke was a poor historian. His research, however, convinced him that exactly the opposite was true. He wrote:

> No writer is correct by mere chance, or accurate sporadically. He is accurate by virtue of a certain habit of mind. Some men are accurate by nature: a permissible view that a writer is accurate occasionally and inaccurate in other parts of his work which is produced by his moral and intellectual character. . . . The present writer takes the view that Luke's history is unsurpassed in respect of its trustworthiness. (W. Ramsay, *The Bearing of Recent Discovery on the Trustworthiness of the New Testament*, p. 80).

Zest

Yet for all the author's care and meticulous nature, Luke's gospel is no dry, pedantic document. It sparkles with life and vitality. Luke's portraits of people are particularly vivid and compassionate. People like Zacchaeus and Cleopas, Mary and Martha, Elizabeth and Mary the mother of Jesus all spring to life through his talented pen. Luke's gospel tells a rare and unforgettable story.

Outline

Luke's prologue to Theophilus (1:1-4) is followed by the comparatively long infancy narratives (1:5-2:52). Jesus' baptism and temptations are presented in the section on his preparation for ministry (3:1-4:13). Next come three sections on Jesus' ministry, divided according to location: ministry in Galilee (4:14-9:50), from Galilee to Jerusalem (9:51-19:44), and ministry in Jerusalem (19:45-21:38). Luke's gospel concludes with an account of Jesus' death and resurrection (22:1-24; 53).

Overview Study Questions

1. Write a short biography of Luke using the references found in the New Testament. These include three from Paul's writings (Col. 4:14; 2 Tim. 4:11; Philem. 24) and the so-called "we-sections" in Acts, when Luke accompanied Paul (Acts 16:10-17; 20:5-21:18; 27:1-28:16).
2. Skim through Luke, using the outline above to guide you. What themes do you detect? What are the major points Luke makes about Jesus?
3. Luke's account contains four great canticles (hymns) of praise. These have often been set to music and used in prayer books. Read them over and use them to write your own worship service. Perhaps you will also want to write music for one of them; draw a picture (abstract or realistic) inspired by a canticle; paraphrase the words; or pray them as part of your own worship. These canticles are: the *Magnificat* (1:46-55), *Benedictus* (1:68-79), *Gloria in Excelsis* (2:14), *Nunc Dimittis* (2:29-32).

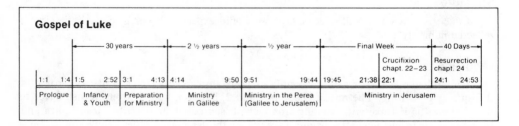

Luke

Introduction

1 Many have undertaken to draw up an account of the things that have been fulfilled[a] among us, [2]just as they were handed down to us by those who from the first were eyewitnesses and servants of the word. [3]Therefore, since I myself have carefully investigated everything from the beginning, it seemed good also to me to write an orderly account for you, most excellent Theophilus, [4]so that you may know the certainty of the things you have been taught.

The Birth of John the Baptist Foretold

[5]In the time of Herod king of Judea there was a priest named Zechariah, who belonged to the priestly division of Abijah; his wife Elizabeth was also a descendant of Aaron. [6]Both of them were upright in the sight of God, observing all the Lord's commandments and regulations blamelessly. [7]But they had no children, because Elizabeth was barren; and they were both well along in years.

[8]Once when Zechariah's division was on duty and he was serving as priest before God, [9]he was chosen by lot, according to the custom of the priesthood, to go into the temple of the Lord and burn incense. [10]And when the time for the burning of incense came, all the assembled worshipers were praying outside.

[11]Then an angel of the Lord appeared to him, standing at the right side of the altar of incense. [12]When Zechariah saw him, he was startled and was gripped with fear. [13]But the angel said to him: "Do not be afraid, Zechariah; your prayer has been heard. Your wife Elizabeth will bear you a son, and you are to give him the name John. [14]He will be a joy and delight to you, and many will rejoice because of his birth, [15]for he will be great in the sight of the Lord. He is never to take wine or other fermented drink, and he will be filled with the Holy Spirit even from birth.[b] [16]Many of the people of Israel will he bring back to the Lord their God. [17]And he will go on before the Lord, in the spirit and power of Elijah, to turn the hearts of the fathers to their children and the disobedient to the wisdom of the righteous—to make ready a people prepared for the Lord."

[18]Zechariah asked the angel, "How can I be sure of this? I am an old man and my wife is well along in years."

[19]The angel answered, "I am Gabriel. I stand in the presence of God, and I have been sent to speak to you and to tell you this good news. [20]And now you will be silent and not able to speak until the day this happens, because you did not believe my words, which will come true at their proper time."

[21]Meanwhile, the people were waiting for Zechariah and wondering why he stayed so long in the temple. [22]When he came out,

OPEN: 1. How are you at writing exciting narrative? (a) I'm another Hemingway, (b) As good as most newspaper reporters, (c) I'd starve as a writer. **2.** Have you drawn up your last will and testament? What important facts did you include? Who would you choose as the biographer of your life story, and why? **3.** What is a recent surprise that your family has experienced: A job promotion? A new addition to the family? Your child got all "A's"? You got into this Bible study?

DIG: 1. What do you learn from verses 1-4 about Luke? About the reason he wrote this gospel? About where he got his sources? **2.** What stands out to you about Zechariah and Elizabeth (vv.5-7)? Barrenness was seen as a sign of God's disfavor and a legitimate reason for divorce. What feelings must the couple have had in light of their barrenness? **3.** What was the significance of the task for which Zechariah was chosen (see 1Ch 23:13)? Since many priests never had this opportunity, what might he be feeling as he prepares for it? How about when the angel appears? **4.** How would the birth of this son affect Zechariah and Elizabeth? How would you describe his mission in your own words? Why would Zechariah doubt? **5.** In the meantime, how were the people feeling (v.21)? What did they think when Zechariah emerged from the temple, mute?

REFLECT: 1. In what ways do you feel spiritually barren? How might this account of Elizabeth and Zechariah affect your feelings of barrenness? **2.** Of the major characters in this story—Zechariah, Elizabeth, John—with whom do you identify most? Why? With whom do you identify least? Why? How is John's mission a model for your mission today? How might you "prepare" people for the Lord? **3.** When was the last time you doubted God? What caused your doubt?

---

a1 Or been surely believed   *b15 Or from his mother's womb* he could not speak to them. They realized he had seen a vision in the temple, for he kept making signs to them but remained unable to speak.

²³When his time of service was completed, he returned home. ²⁴After this his wife Elizabeth became pregnant and for five months remained in seclusion. ²⁵"The Lord has done this for me," she said. "In these days he has shown his favor and taken away my disgrace among the people."

The Birth of Jesus Foretold

²⁶In the sixth month, God sent the angel Gabriel to Nazareth, a town in Galilee, ²⁷to a virgin pledged to be married to a man named Joseph, a descendant of David. The virgin's name was Mary. ²⁸The angel went to her and said, "Greetings, you who are highly favored! The Lord is with you."

²⁹Mary was greatly troubled at his words and wondered what kind of greeting this might be. ³⁰But the angel said to her, "Do not be afraid, Mary, you have found favor with God. ³¹You will be with child and give birth to a son, and you are to give him the name Jesus. ³²He will be great and will be called the Son of the Most High. The Lord God will give him the throne of his father David, ³³and he will reign over the house of Jacob forever; his kingdom will never end."

³⁴"How will this be," Mary asked the angel, "since I am a virgin?"

³⁵The angel answered, "The Holy Spirit will come upon you, and the power of the Most High will overshadow you. So the holy one to be born will be calledᶜ the Son of God. ³⁶Even Elizabeth your relative is going to have a child in her old age, and she who was said to be barren is in her sixth month. ³⁷For nothing is impossible with God."

³⁸"I am the Lord's servant," Mary answered. "May it be to me as you have said." Then the angel left her.

Mary Visits Elizabeth

³⁹At that time Mary got ready and hurried to a town in the hill country of Judea, ⁴⁰where she entered Zechariah's home and greeted Elizabeth. ⁴¹When Elizabeth heard Mary's greeting, the baby leaped in her womb, and Elizabeth was filled with the Holy Spirit. ⁴²In a loud voice she exclaimed: "Blessed are you among women, and blessed is the child you will bear! ⁴³But why am I so favored, that the mother of my Lord should come to me? ⁴⁴As soon as the sound of your greeting reached my ears, the baby in my womb leaped for joy. ⁴⁵Blessed is she who has believed that what the Lord has said to her will be accomplished!"

Mary's Song

⁴⁶And Mary said:

"My soul glorifies the Lord
⁴⁷ and my spirit rejoices in God my Savior,
⁴⁸for he has been mindful
    of the humble state of his servant.

ᶜ35 Or So the child to be born will be called holy,

OPEN: If told that you (or your parents) were to have a child this year, how would you react?

DIG: 1. How does Gabriel's word to Mary compare with his word to Zechariah (1:13-17)? **2.** How does Mary (vv.34,38) respond differently than Zechariah (vv.12,18)? **3.** What truths about Jesus are emphasized here? What expectations must have been raised in Mary? What risks is she asked to take? **4.** How does Elizabeth's pregnancy encourage Mary?

REFLECT: 1. What would it mean to doubt and fear God? When were you recently fearful but believing? How did God meet you? **2.** In what area of your life do you need to believe that "nothing is impossible with God"? What keeps you from believing this?

OPEN: Who do you call first when you have special news to share?

DIG: How might Mary have felt when Elizabeth greeted her like this? How is she "blessed" and encouraged?

REFLECT: What does Mary's faith (vv.38-45) model for you?

OPEN: What tunes do you carry around in your head, ready to burst forth in the car, shower, or wherever? What type of music do you and your kids play around the house? Any clashes there? Why?

DIG: 1. For what does Mary praise God in this song? What contrasts does she make in verses 51-53? How do these reflect her feelings

From now on all generations will call me blessed,

⁴⁹ for the Mighty One has done great things for me—
holy is his name.

⁵⁰His mercy extends to those who fear him,
from generation to generation.

⁵¹He has performed mighty deeds with his arm;
he has scattered those who are proud in their inmost
thoughts.

⁵²He has brought down rulers from their thrones
but has lifted up the humble.

⁵³He has filled the hungry with good things
but has sent the rich away empty.

⁵⁴He has helped his servant Israel,
remembering to be merciful

⁵⁵to Abraham and his descendants forever,
even as he said to our fathers.''

⁵⁶Mary stayed with Elizabeth for about three months and then
returned home.

The Birth of John the Baptist

⁵⁷When it was time for Elizabeth to have her baby, she gave
birth to a son. ⁵⁸Her neighbors and relatives heard that the Lord
had shown her great mercy, and they shared her joy.

⁵⁹On the eighth day they came to circumcise the child, and
they were going to name him after his father Zechariah, ⁶⁰but
his mother spoke up and said, "No! He is to be called John."

⁶¹They said to her, "There is no one among your relatives who
has that name."

⁶²Then they made signs to his father, to find out what he
would like to name the child. ⁶³He asked for a writing tablet,
and to everyone's astonishment he wrote, "His name is John."
⁶⁴Immediately his mouth was opened and his tongue was loosed,
and he began to speak, praising God. ⁶⁵The neighbors were all
filled with awe, and throughout the hill country of Judea people
were talking about all these things. ⁶⁶Everyone who heard this
wondered about it, asking, "What then is this child going to
be?" For the Lord's hand was with him.

Zechariah's Song

⁶⁷His father Zechariah was filled with the Holy Spirit and
prophesied:

⁶⁸"Praise be to the Lord, the God of Israel,
because he has come and has redeemed his people.

⁶⁹He has raised up a horn^d of salvation for us
in the house of his servant David

⁷⁰(as he said through his holy prophets of long ago),

⁷¹salvation from our enemies
and from the hand of all who hate us—

⁷²to show mercy to our fathers
and to remember his holy covenant,

⁷³ the oath he swore to our father Abraham:

---

^d69 *Horn* here symbolizes strength.

---

about God? About herself? **2.** Who are the "proud," the "rulers," and the "rich," whose overthrow she celebrates? How will Jesus fulfill the themes of this song? **3.** What would a diary from this 3-month visit reveal (v.56)?

REFLECT: 1. Of the attributes of God celebrated in Mary's song, which do you appreciate the most? Which challenges you the most? Why? **2.** How does your life reflect God's concern for justice, mercy, and deliverance? Would Mary consider you "God's humble servant" or a "proud, rich ruler"? Why?

OPEN: What is your nickname and how did you get it?

DIG: 1. How did John's birth fulfill the words of the angel in verses 13-17? **2.** How did the neighbors and relatives respond to these events? How does all this begin to promote the gospel? **3.** As Zechariah's neighbor, what would you be thinking about his new son?

REFLECT: What does it mean to you that "the Lord's hand" is with someone: Success? Courage? Wealth? Endurance? Holiness? How was "the Lord's hand" seen in John's life? What does that mean to you?

OPEN: (For parents:) When your first child was born, what did you do to celebrate? (For non-parents:) How would you celebrate that event?

DIG: 1. Make a list of the things for which Zechariah praises God. How does his song compare and contrast with Mary's (vv.46-55)? **2.** What does it mean that Zechariah was "filled with the Holy Spirit"? Do you think it was the same experience of the Spirit that believers experience today? Why or why not? **3.** What, according to this song, is the purpose of salvation? How does Zechariah's song show God's unfolding plan from OT days to the coming of the Messiah?

74to rescue us from the hand of our enemies,
    and to enable us to serve him without fear
75 in holiness and righteousness before him all our days.

76And you, my child, will be called a prophet of the Most
    High;
    for you will go on before the Lord to prepare the way
    for him,
77to give his people the knowledge of salvation
    through the forgiveness of their sins,
78because of the tender mercy of our God,
    by which the rising sun will come to us from heaven
79to shine on those living in darkness
    and in the shadow of death,
    to guide our feet into the path of peace."

80And the child grew and became strong in spirit; and he lived in the desert until he appeared publicly to Israel.

The Birth of Jesus

2 In those days Caesar Augustus issued a decree that a census should be taken of the entire Roman world. 2(This was the first census that took place while Quirinius was governor of Syria.) 3And everyone went to his own town to register.

4So Joseph also went up from the town of Nazareth in Galilee to Judea, to Bethlehem the town of David, because he belonged to the house and line of David. 5He went there to register with Mary, who was pledged to be married to him and was expecting a child. 6While they were there, the time came for the baby to be born, 7and she gave birth to her firstborn, a son. She wrapped him in cloths and placed him in a manger, because there was no room for them in the inn.

The Shepherds and the Angels

8And there were shepherds living out in the fields nearby, keeping watch over their flocks at night. 9An angel of the Lord appeared to them, and the glory of the Lord shone around them, and they were terrified. 10But the angel said to them, "Do not be afraid. I bring you good news of great joy that will be for all the people. 11Today in the town of David a Savior has been born to you; he is Christ*e* the Lord. 12This will be a sign to you: You will find a baby wrapped in cloths and lying in a manger."

13Suddenly a great company of the heavenly host appeared with the angel, praising God and saying,

14"Glory to God in the highest,
    and on earth peace to men on whom his favor rests."

15When the angels had left them and gone into heaven, the shepherds said to one another, "Let's go to Bethlehem and see this thing that has happened, which the Lord has told us about."

16So they hurried off and found Mary and Joseph, and the baby, who was lying in the manger. 17When they had seen him,

e11 Or Messiah. "The Christ" (Greek) and "the Messiah" (Hebrew) both mean "the Anointed One"; also in verse 26.

Luke 2:8-20   **THE SHEPHERDS AND THE ANGELS**

LOOKING INTO THE SCRIPTURE/20 Minutes. Read Luke 2:8-20 and discuss.

1. What do you remember about Christmas time when you were a child? Ask the first person in your group to answer the first question. The second person the next question, etc., until you have answered all of the questions below.

☐ Where were you living when you were seven years old?
☐ What was the weather like around Christmas time?
☐ Who did most of the decorating of the tree?
☐ What special tradition did your family observe at Christmas?
☐ What is your earliest memory of a Christmas morning?
☐ When and where did you open your presents?
☐ What Christmas present stands out in your memory?
☐ Who was the person in your family who made Christmas special?
☐ What tradition would you like to continue with your children?

2. Why do you think God chose to announce the birth of his Son to shepherds?
   a. only ones listening
   b. lowliest of people
   c. lived close to nature/God
   d. they were open and receptive

3. What do you think the good news, "a Savior has been born . . . Christ the Lord," meant to the shepherds?
   a. very little
   b. something special
   c. the long-awaited Messiah had arrived
   d. life will be different
   e. there was hope for them
   f. God was alive

4. How would you have felt if you had been there when a "great company of heavenly angels appeared . . ."?
   a. totally awed
   b. scared to death
   c. blown away
   d. like crawling in a hole

5. Do you think Mary and Joseph understood the cosmic significance of the child they had just given birth to?
   a. probably not
   b. they must have
   c. Mary could have
   d. up to a point
   e. they couldn't have

MY OWN STORY/20 Minutes.

1. How would you announce the birth of your kids?
   a. chocolate candy and cigars
   b. telegrams and phone calls
   c. throw a party
   d. big banner on the front door
   e. save the money for college

2. When did the Christmas story take on real significance for you?
   a. when I was a child
   b. years ago
   c. quite recently
   d. not sure it ever has

3. How would you compare your spiritual awakening to the shepherds?
   a. not quite so dramatic
   b. different, but just as real
   c. more intellectual
   d. just as confusing
   e. more gradual

4. How would you describe your relationship to God right now?
   a. nowhere
   b. up and down
   c. in a holding pattern
   d. on the injured list
   e. great
   f. doing better

they spread the word concerning what had been told them about this child, [18]and all who heard it were amazed at what the shepherds said to them. [19]But Mary treasured up all these things and pondered them in her heart. [20]The shepherds returned, glorifying and praising God for all the things they had heard and seen, which were just as they had been told.

Jesus Presented in the Temple

[21]On the eighth day, when it was time to circumcise him, he was named Jesus, the name the angel had given him before he had been conceived.

[22]When the time of their purification according to the Law of Moses had been completed, Joseph and Mary took him to Jerusalem to present him to the Lord [23](as it is written in the Law of the Lord, "Every firstborn male is to be consecrated to the Lord"[f]), [24]and to offer a sacrifice in keeping with what is said in the Law of the Lord: "a pair of doves or two young pigeons."[g]

[25]Now there was a man in Jerusalem called Simeon, who was righteous and devout. He was waiting for the consolation of Israel, and the Holy Spirit was upon him. [26]It had been revealed to him by the Holy Spirit that he would not die before he had seen the Lord's Christ. [27]Moved by the Spirit, he went into the temple courts. When the parents brought in the child Jesus to do for him what the custom of the Law required, [28]Simeon took him in his arms and praised God, saying:

> [29]"Sovereign Lord, as you have promised,
>   you now dismiss[h] your servant in peace.
> [30]For my eyes have seen your salvation,
> [31] which you have prepared in the sight of all people,
> [32]a light for revelation to the Gentiles
>   and for glory to your people Israel."

[33]The child's father and mother marveled at what was said about him. [34]Then Simeon blessed them and said to Mary, his mother: "This child is destined to cause the falling and rising of many in Israel, and to be a sign that will be spoken against, [35]so that the thoughts of many hearts will be revealed. And a sword will pierce your own soul too."

[36]There was also a prophetess, Anna, the daughter of Phanuel, of the tribe of Asher. She was very old; she had lived with her husband seven years after her marriage, [37]and then was a widow until she was eighty-four.[i] She never left the temple but worshiped night and day, fasting and praying. [38]Coming up to them at that very moment, she gave thanks to God and spoke about the child to all who were looking forward to the redemption of Jerusalem.

[39]When Joseph and Mary had done everything required by the Law of the Lord, they returned to Galilee to their own town of Nazareth. [40]And the child grew and became strong; he was filled with wisdom, and the grace of God was upon him.

OPEN: 1. When you were growing up, what teacher, coach, or relative made you feel special? How did that person make you feel so good? **2.** Who helps you feel special now? **3.** Who is the oldest person you know?

DIG: 1. What Mosaic laws are being fulfilled by this presentation (see Lev 12:1-8, Ex 13:2, 12,13; Nu 18:15,16)? How do these events parallel Jesus' mission? What does his name mean? **2.** What does this temple ceremony reveal about the parents of Jesus: They were very poor? Religious? Proud? Dedicated? Fearful of their salvation? **3.** In Simeon's two prophecies (vv.29-32,34-25), what was he predicting about the work of Jesus? The fate of the nations? The pain of his parents? **4.** Know anyone like dear old, saintly Anna? How does she complement Simeon's prophecy? **5.** What impact would these startling predictions by Simeon and Anna have on all who were listening that day? On the parents of Jesus as they returned home (vv.33,39)? On Jesus as he was growing up (v.40)? **6.** In summary, what do you learn about Mary and Joseph in this passage? About Jesus? About God?

REFLECT: 1. How has Christ brought "light" to your life? How is he still the cause of "the falling and rising" of people throughout the world? **2.** How did your parents dedicate you to the Lord, if at all? How do you feel about the fact that you were or weren't dedicated? How did your parents help you mature spiritually? **3.** When has God brought along a "Simeon" and "Anna" to confirm something in your life? How did this make you feel?

---

[f]23 Exodus 13:2,12   [g]24 Lev. 12:8   [h]29 Or promised, / now dismiss
[i]37 Or widow for eighty-four years

LOOKING INTO THE SCRIPTURE/20 Minutes. Read Luke 2:21-40 and discuss.

1. What does this story reveal about the parents of Jesus?
    a. they were very poor
    b. they were religious
    c. they were very young
    d. they knew their son was very special

2. Why do you suppose this was such a meaningful occasion for Simeon?
    a. he had waited so long for this moment
    b. he expected to see the Christ (God's Anointed One)
    c. God had not forgotten his promise
    d. he marvelled at how God could use a baby to bring his salvation

3. Put yourself in Joseph and Mary's shoes. How would you have felt if two old people came to you and gave startling predictions about your son?
    a. proud
    b. scared
    c. confused
    d. overwhelmed

4. In Simeon's prophecy about the child, what was he predicting?
    a. Roman Empire would collapse
    b. Israel would reject God's Messiah
    c. national bloodshed
    d. the parents would experience pain

5. Do you think the parents of Jesus understood what was going to happen to their son?
    a. maybe a little
    b. probably not
    c. not at first
    d. his mother probably did
    e. I would like to think so

6. What strikes you as significant about Anna and Simeon?
    a. they were both old
    b. they both spent all their time at the temple
    c. they were very close to their God
    d. they lived life expecting to see God at work
    e. they were both concerned about the welfare of Isreal
    f. they recognized their need for a Savior

MY OWN STORY/25 Minutes.

1. Briefly tell your "roots," what your parents were like when you were born:
    a. financially
    b. religiously
    c. socially

2. What do you know about your baptism or dedication as an infant?
    a. don't know anything about it
    b. I have a certificate/pictures in my baby book
    c. we did not go to church then
    d. it was a big family affair

3. Do you think your parents understand what is going on in your life now?
    a. I hope not
    b. probably
    c. maybe a little bit
    d. for sure
    e. no, but I'd like them to

4. Do you think God has a plan and purpose for your life like he did for Mary and Joseph?
    a. not at all
    b. in a way
    c. maybe, but not the same plan
    d. definitely

5. How open are you to God's will for your life at the moment?
    a. a little bit
    b. a whole lot
    c. just don't send me to Africa
    d. ask me tomorrow

6. What would be the crowning joy for you in your old age?
    a. to see my children's children
    b. to strike it rich
    c. to look back on a life full of surprises
    d. to leave the world a better place to live in
    f. to feel I have done God's will

OPEN: 1. What was your best family trip? **2.** Ever get lost as a child? What happened?

DIG: 1. What was the significance of this feast, which was an annual tradition with Jesus' parents (see Ex 23:15; Dt 16:1-6)? **2.** Make a list of Jesus' character traits revealed in this passage. What do they tell us about the kind of child Jesus was? **3.** How much does he seem to know about his mission? How much do his parents know? **4.** Why do you think Luke included this episode of Jesus' life?

REFLECT: In balancing hunger for God with your daily responsibilities, do you err more on the side of neglecting God or the other concerns? Why? What would a proper balance look like for you?

OPEN: 1. You are producing a play, with someone from your family or small group in the role of a fiery street preacher. Who would you cast in that role, and why? **2.** If you were an advertising executive and your firm had been chosen to prepare the way for the President's' arrival in your hometown, what would you do?

DIG: 1. How much time passes between appearances of John the Baptist here and in 1:80? What do you suppose John was doing in those intervening years? Why? **2.** Why does Luke list all the political and religious figures in verses 1-2? **3.** How would you describe John's message and style (see also Mt 3:1-12; Mk 1:1-18; Jn 1:6-8,19-28)? **4.** What's radical about John's message? What does the "root" and "fruit" signify? Is he advocating social upheaval? Or inner transformation? Is he "preaching" or "meddling"? Why? Why would anyone go out of their way to hear such a preacher? **5.** How does John's message to the people (vv.7-14) illustrate the kind of repentance he is calling for? What does John say about the *need for* and *outcome of* repentance? **6.** Why is John confused with Christ (v.15; Jn 1:19-28)? By contrast, how does John differentiate himself and his ministry? What does the "wheat" and "chaff"

The Boy Jesus at the Temple

41Every year his parents went to Jerusalem for the Feast of the Passover. 42When he was twelve years old, they went up to the Feast, according to the custom. 43After the Feast was over, while his parents were returning home, the boy Jesus stayed behind in Jerusalem, but they were unaware of it. 44Thinking he was in their company, they traveled on for a day. Then they began looking for him among their relatives and friends. 45When they did not find him, they went back to Jerusalem to look for him. 46After three days they found him in the temple courts, sitting among the teachers, listening to them and asking them questions. 47Everyone who heard him was amazed at his understanding and his answers. 48When his parents saw him, they were astonished. His mother said to him, "Son, why have you treated us like this? Your father and I have been anxiously searching for you."

49"Why were you searching for me?" he asked. "Didn't you know I had to be in my Father's house?" 50But they did not understand what he was saying to them.

51Then he went down to Nazareth with them and was obedient to them. But his mother treasured all these things in her heart. 52And Jesus grew in wisdom and stature, and in favor with God and men.

John the Baptist Prepares the Way

3 In the fifteenth year of the reign of Tiberius Caesar—when Pontius Pilate was governor of Judea, Herod tetrarch of Galilee, his brother Philip tetrarch of Iturea and Traconitis, and Lysanias tetrarch of Abilene— 2during the high priesthood of Annas and Caiaphas, the word of God came to John son of Zechariah in the desert. 3He went into all the country around the Jordan, preaching a baptism of repentance for the forgiveness of sins. 4As is written in the book of the words of Isaiah the prophet:

"A voice of one calling in the desert,
'Prepare the way for the Lord,
make straight paths for him.
5Every valley shall be filled in,
every mountain and hill made low.
The crooked roads shall become straight,
the rough ways smooth.
6And all mankind will see God's salvation.' "*j*

7John said to the crowds coming out to be baptized by him, "You brood of vipers! Who warned you to flee from the coming wrath? 8Produce fruit in keeping with repentance. And do not begin to say to yourselves, 'We have Abraham as our father.' For I tell you that out of these stones God can raise up children for Abraham. 9The ax is already at the root of the trees, and every tree that does not produce good fruit will be cut down and thrown into the fire."

10"What should we do then?" the crowd asked.

j6 Isaiah 40:3-5

LOOKING INTO THE SCRIPTURE/20 Minutes. Read Luke 2:41-52 and discuss.

1. How do you think Jesus' parents felt while they were searching for three to five days for Jesus?
    a. hysterical
    b. calm and collected
    c. angry and terrified
    d. relaxed and confident

2. When they found him in the temple, what did they say?
    a. just wait until you get home!
    b. you're not coming next year!
    c. where in the world have you been?
    d. we're proud of you.
    e. do you realize how worried we've been?

3. What was the problem, from the parents' point of view?
    a. Jesus wandered off in a big crowd at Passover
    b. Jesus embarassed his parents in public
    c. Jesus had gone too far in his religious activity
    d. Jesus hardly seemed like their son anymore

4. What was the situation from Jesus' perspective?
    a. his parents were too protective
    b. he was growing up and had more important things to do
    c. there were people here he could help
    d. he had found his real "home" in the temple

5. As a result of this incident, what do you think changed in the relationship between Jesus and his parents?
    a. Joseph and Mary had lots to think about
    b. Jesus knew more than his parents, and they knew it
    c. they were more alert to Jesus' spiritual growth
    d. it probably happened again, but without the fireworks
    e. they had more confidence that Jesus would grow up to be a responsible adult
    f. they all probably had more understanding for each others' feelings

6. How do you feel about the possibility that Jesus' parents were not spared the struggle of most parents?
    a. reassured
    b. there's no hope for me then
    c. more "normal"
    d. inspired to keep going
    e. wondering about my expectations of parenthood

MY OWN STORY/20 Minutes.

1. What kind of preparation did your parents have to raise you?
    a. they had Dr. Spock's book
    b. their parents were good role models
    c. absolutely no preparation
    d. family life classes at school

2. Do you think your parents understood what they were getting in for when they had you?
    a. they wanted twelve children until they had me
    b. they thought child-raising would be cheaper
    c. they knew life was tough but had lots of love to share
    d. they weren't counting on my teenage rebellion
    e. they trusted God would help them through the surprises

3. What do you cherish most about your parents?
    a. unconditional love/acceptance
    b. old-fashioned values
    c. spiritual direction
    d. fun times together
    e. closeness/togetherness

4. What are you going to do differently in raising your children?
    a. give them more freedom
    b. give them less freedom
    c. spend more time with them
    d. show more affection
    e. enjoy them
    f. give them more guidance

5. If you could pass on one or two things to your children, what would they be?
    a. spiritual direction
    b. self-respect
    c. drive/ambition
    d. concern/compassion
    e. value of hard work
    f. good memories
    g. money/wealth

signify? **7.** What is the beginning of the end for John's ministry (vv.19-20)? What does this illustrate about John?

REFLECT: **1.** Who have been "John the Baptists" in your life—people who have shown you the way, led you to Christ, encouraged you, and given you a kick in the pants? **2.** What would John say you could do specifically to show Christian love and repentance? **3.** What one action will you take this week to "produce fruit in keeping with your repentance"?

OPEN: **1.** Who's the family historian in your extended family? What has he/she done to help you know more about your ancestors? **2.** If you were to explore in more detail the life of one of your ancestors, whose life would you investigate? Why? **3.** Who is the hero in your genealogy? Who is the black sheep? Why?

DIG: **1.** What is significant about Jesus being baptized at the same time as all the people? What three things happen at Jesus' baptism that make it unlike the others'? What meaning do you think these events have for Jesus? **2.** How does this account of Jesus' baptism compare and contrast with the other accounts (Mt 3:13-17; Mk 1:9-11; Jn 1:32-34)? **3.** If Matthew's genealogy starts with *Abraham* to demonstrate God's working through the chosen people (Mt 1:1-17), what is Luke's point in going all the way back to *Adam* (v.38)? What do Adam and Jesus have in common? Why else might Luke include this genealogy (see 1:27, 32, 69)? **4.** In this genealogy, which names stand out to you? What do you remember about them? What can you conclude about Jesus' "earthly ancestry" from what you know of these people?

[11]John answered, "The man with two tunics should share with him who has none, and the one who has food should do the same."

[12]Tax collectors also came to be baptized. "Teacher," they asked, "what should we do?"

[13]"Don't collect any more than you are required to," he told them.

[14]Then some soldiers asked him, "And what should we do?"

He replied, "Don't extort money and don't accuse people falsely—be content with your pay."

[15]The people were waiting expectantly and were all wondering in their hearts if John might possibly be the Christ.[k] [16]John answered them all, "I baptize you with[l] water. But one more powerful than I will come, the thongs of whose sandals I am not worthy to untie. He will baptize you with the Holy Spirit and with fire. [17]His winnowing fork is in his hand to clear his threshing floor and to gather the wheat into his barn, but he will burn up the chaff with unquenchable fire." [18]And with many other words John exhorted the people and preached the good news to them.

[19]But when John rebuked Herod the tetrarch because of Herodias, his brother's wife, and all the other evil things he had done, [20]Herod added this to them all: He locked John up in prison.

The Baptism and Genealogy of Jesus

[21]When all the people were being baptized, Jesus was baptized too. And as he was praying, heaven was opened [22]and the Holy Spirit descended on him in bodily form like a dove. And a voice came from heaven: "You are my Son, whom I love; with you I am well pleased."

[23]Now Jesus himself was about thirty years old when he began his ministry. He was the son, so it was thought, of Joseph,

> the son of Heli, [24]the son of Matthat,
> the son of Levi, the son of Melki,
> the son of Jannai, the son of Joseph,
> [25]the son of Mattathias, the son of Amos,
> the son of Nahum, the son of Esli,
> the son of Naggai, [26]the son of Maath,
> the son of Mattathias, the son of Semein,
> the son of Josech, the son of Joda,
> [27]the son of Joanan, the son of Rhesa,
> the son of Zerubbabel, the son of Shealtiel,
> the son of Neri, [28]the son of Melki,
> the son of Addi, the son of Cosam,
> the son of Elmadam, the son of Er,
> [29]the son of Joshua, the son of Eliezer,
> the son of Jorim, the son of Matthat,
> the son of Levi, [30]the son of Simeon,
> the son of Judah, the son of Joseph,
> the son of Jonam, the son of Eliakim,

k15 Or Messiah   l16 Or in

³¹the son of Melea, the son of Menna,
  the son of Mattatha, the son of Nathan,
  the son of David, ³²the son of Jesse,
  the son of Obed, the son of Boaz,
  the son of Salmon,ᵐ the son of Nahshon,
³³the son of Amminadab, the son of Ram,ⁿ
  the son of Hezron, the son of Perez,
  the son of Judah, ³⁴the son of Jacob,
  the son of Isaac, the son of Abraham,
  the son of Terah, the son of Nahor,
³⁵the son of Serug, the son of Reu,
  the son of Peleg, the son of Eber,
  the son of Shelah, ³⁶the son of Cainan,
  the son of Arphaxad, the son of Shem,
  the son of Noah, the son of Lamech,
³⁷the son of Methuselah, the son of Enoch,
  the son of Jared, the son of Mahalalel,
  the son of Kenan, ³⁸the son of Enosh,
  the son of Seth, the son of Adam,
  the son of God.

The Temptation of Jesus

4 Jesus, full of the Holy Spirit, returned from the Jordan and was led by the Spirit in the desert, ²where for forty days he was tempted by the devil. He ate nothing during those days, and at the end of them he was hungry.

³The devil said to him, "If you are the Son of God, tell this stone to become bread."

⁴Jesus answered, "It is written: 'Man does not live on bread alone.'ᵒ"

⁵The devil led him up to a high place and showed him in an instant all the kingdoms of the world. ⁶And he said to him, "I will give you all their authority and splendor, for it has been given to me, and I can give it to anyone I want to. ⁷So if you worship me, it will all be yours."

⁸Jesus answered, "It is written: 'Worship the Lord your God and serve him only.'ᵖ"

⁹The devil led him to Jerusalem and had him stand on the highest point of the temple. "If you are the Son of God," he said, "throw yourself down from here. ¹⁰For it is written:

" 'He will command his angels concerning you
  to guard you carefully;
¹¹they will lift you up in their hands,
  so that you will not strike your foot against a stone.'�q"

¹²Jesus answered, "It says: 'Do not put the Lord your God to the test.'ʳ"

¹³When the devil had finished all this tempting, he left him until an opportune time.

OPEN: 1. When "you deserve a break today," what fast-food restaurant do you run out to? Why? **2.** What's one of your all-time favorite foods? How often do you eat it?

DIG: 1. Under what circumstances (vv.1-2) was Jesus tempted: After a spiritual high? At a weak moment? Apart from God? **2.** In each temptation, what was its appeal? Its price? How does Jesus resist them? How does Satan's use of Scripture differ from the way Jesus uses it? **3.** How are the three temptations similar? Different? **4.** Why were the temptations all directed against the divine Sonship of Jesus, when this had just been confirmed at Jesus' baptism (3:21-22)? Why did God allow Jesus to go through this?

REFLECT: 1. If the devil had three "shots" at you, what three temptations would he use? How do these compare to Jesus' temptations? **2.** What can help you resist these appeals to self-interest, power, and spiritual pride? What encouragement do you find here?

REFLECT: 1. How has Jesus been like a "new Adam" for you—giving you a fresh start at life? How does Jesus' sonship (v.22) form the basis for the way the Father sees you? What kinship do you sense with Jesus? **2.** What means the most to you about your own baptism? **3.** At what time(s) in your life have you felt God's special touch, as if something new was beginning for you? What happened?

ᵐ32 Some early manuscripts *Sala*   ⁿ33 Some manuscripts *Amminadab, the son of Admin, the son of Arni;* other manuscripts vary widely.   ᵒ4 Deut. 8:3
ᵖ8 Deut. 6:13   q11 Psalm 91:11,12   ʳ12 Deut. 6:16

OPEN: 1. What do you like best about the hometown where you grew up? **2.** What was the symbol or sign of having "made it" in your hometown: e.g., big house, star player, member of right club, being from one of the "old families"?

DIG: 1. Compare 3:21; 4:1,14, 18. What is the common element in each of these verses? What does this tell us about the source of Jesus' power? **2.** What is significant about the time, place, and posture (vv.16, 21-22) for Jesus' discourse from Isaiah? **3.** What is Jesus' five-fold mission (vv.18-19)? How does he fulfill it literally? Spiritually? Then? Now? **4.** What expectations stirred in the people as a result of Jesus' claim (vv.21-22)? **5.** What is Jesus saying through the proverb (v.23)? Through the Elijah and Elisha stories (vv.24-27)? Why does this turn their amazement (v.22) into anger (vv.28-29)? How does all this relate to the prophetic statements in 2:14, 2:32 and 3:67?

REFLECT: 1. Jesus refers to five goals of his mission. If all five are to be carried on by the church as a whole, which area of concern do you give priority to and which do you tend to neglect: (a) Preaching the gospel? (b) Helping people to be free to really live? (c) Performing acts of mercy? (d) Working for fair and just social structures? (e) Celebrating God's grace to disheartened people? **2.** Who are the "Gentiles" God desires you to care for? How might you do so?

OPEN: Who was your favorite teacher in high school? Why?

DIG: 1. How is this story related to the one before, especially verses 18-19? What similarities and differences do you see? **2.** What about Jesus' teaching impressed the people most? Why?

REFLECT: 1. How has Jesus' authority grabbed your attention recently? **2.** How is his authority bringing freedom to you?

Jesus Rejected at Nazareth

¹⁴Jesus returned to Galilee in the power of the Spirit, and news about him spread through the whole countryside. ¹⁵He taught in their synagogues, and everyone praised him.

¹⁶He went to Nazareth, where he had been brought up, and on the Sabbath day he went into the synagogue, as was his custom. And he stood up to read. ¹⁷The scroll of the prophet Isaiah was handed to him. Unrolling it, he found the place where it is written:

¹⁸"The Spirit of the Lord is on me,
because he has anointed me
to preach good news to the poor.
He has sent me to proclaim freedom for the prisoners
and recovery of sight for the blind,
to release the oppressed,
¹⁹   to proclaim the year of the Lord's favor." ˢ

²⁰Then he rolled up the scroll, gave it back to the attendant and sat down. The eyes of everyone in the synagogue were fastened on him, ²¹and he began by saying to them, "Today this scripture is fulfilled in your hearing."

²²All spoke well of him and were amazed at the gracious words that came from his lips. "Isn't this Joseph's son?" they asked.

²³Jesus said to them, "Surely you will quote this proverb to me: 'Physician, heal yourself! Do here in your hometown what we have heard that you did in Capernaum.'"

²⁴"I tell you the truth," he continued, "no prophet is accepted in his hometown. ²⁵I assure you that there were many widows in Israel in Elijah's time, when the sky was shut for three and a half years and there was a severe famine throughout the land. ²⁶Yet Elijah was not sent to any of them, but to a widow in Zarephath in the region of Sidon. ²⁷And there were many in Israel with leprosy ᵗ in the time of Elisha the prophet, yet not one of them was cleansed—only Naaman the Syrian."

²⁸All the people in the synagogue were furious when they heard this. ²⁹They got up, drove him out of the town, and took him to the brow of the hill on which the town was built, in order to throw him down the cliff. ³⁰But he walked right through the crowd and went on his way.

Jesus Drives Out an Evil Spirit

³¹Then he went down to Capernaum, a town in Galilee, and on the Sabbath began to teach the people. ³²They were amazed at his teaching, because his message had authority.

³³In the synagogue there was a man possessed by a demon, an evil ᵘ spirit. He cried out at the top of his voice, ³⁴"Ha! What do you want with us, Jesus of Nazareth? Have you come to destroy us? I know who you are—the Holy One of God!"

³⁵"Be quiet!" Jesus said sternly. "Come out of him!" Then the demon threw the man down before them all and came out without injuring him.

ˢ*19* Isaiah 61:1,2   ᵗ*27* The Greek word was used for various diseases affecting the skin—not necessarily leprosy.   ᵘ*33* Greek *unclean*; also in verse 36

LOOKING INTO THE SCRIPTURE/20 Minutes. Read Luke 4:14-30 and discuss.

1. How would you describe the reception Jesus got in his hometown?
   a. thunderous applause
   b. faint praise
   c. mixed reviews
   d. a few snickers
   e. a change in public opinion

2. Why do you think his hometown had a problem accepting Jesus?
   a. rumors about Mary's pregnancy
   b. he came from the lower class
   c. they accepted the notion that "nothing good could come out of Nazareth"
   d. spiritual blindness
   e. they didn't understand prophecy

3. Why didn't Jesus wow them with a miracle?
   a. he was warned of this temptation by Satan
   b. they didn't have faith
   c. he was not a crowd pleaser
   d. that was not his purpose
   e. they still would not have believed
   f. he had nothing to prove

4. Why would Jesus' hometown neighbors be so furious?
   a. he discounted them
   b. he made them look bad
   c. he was just a carpenter's son
   d. he thought he was better than they were
   e. he would rather go to the non-Jews who would accept him

---

MY OWN STORY/25 Minutes.

1. Where do you find it hardest to be accepted as a person of worth and special value?
   a. around strangers
   b. around school/work
   c. around home
   d. around church
   e. around my friends

2. How do you deal with feelings of rejection?
   a. turn cold and indifferent
   b. get bitter and nasty
   c. crawl into a shell and mope
   d. laugh it off
   e. share openly, "I feel I have been discounted. . . ."

3. This story suggests several ways of coping with feelings of rejection. Which one(s) makes sense to you right now?
   a. I can accept the fact that my kin might praise me, but not really take me seriously
   b. there are others in the world who need me
   c. God can give me courage to do what's right despite criticism
   d. rejection might help me examine my life and make corrections as needed
   e. acceptance from my peers is not as important as God's love and acceptance of me

4. In Luke 4:18-19, Jesus applied five Old Testament promises to his mission on earth. Which of these five forms of rejection can you connect with the gospel in your life today?

☐ POVERTY (downtrodden, underprivileged): to receive hope and dignity
☐ IMPRISONMENT (physically, psychologically or politically captive): to receive freedom from bondage
☐ BLINDNESS (physical disability often meaning spiritual darkness): to receive new sight to recognize God's perspective and new life
☐ OPPRESSION (political and economic disadvantage): to receive release and new freedom from forces holding you down
☐ DEBT (every 50 years all debts were canceled): to receive the Jubilee Year's release from debt of every sort

[36]All the people were amazed and said to each other, "What is this teaching? With authority and power he gives orders to evil spirits and they come out!" [37]And the news about him spread throughout the surrounding area.

Jesus Heals Many

[38]Jesus left the synagogue and went to the home of Simon. Now Simon's mother-in-law was suffering from a high fever, and they asked Jesus to help her. [39]So he bent over her and rebuked the fever, and it left her. She got up at once and began to wait on them.

[40]When the sun was setting, the people brought to Jesus all who had various kinds of sickness, and laying his hands on each one, he healed them. [41]Moreover, demons came out of many people, shouting, "You are the Son of God!" But he rebuked them and would not allow them to speak, because they knew he was the Christ. [v]

[42]At daybreak Jesus went out to a solitary place. The people were looking for him and when they came to where he was, they tried to keep him from leaving them. [43]But he said, "I must preach the good news of the kingdom of God to the other towns also, because that is why I was sent." [44]And he kept on preaching in the synagogues of Judea. [w]

The Calling of the First Disciples

5 One day as Jesus was standing by the Lake of Gennesaret, [x] with the people crowding around him and listening to the word of God, [2]he saw at the water's edge two boats, left there by the fishermen, who were washing their nets. [3]He got into one of the boats, the one belonging to Simon, and asked him to put out a little from shore. Then he sat down and taught the people from the boat.

[4]When he had finished speaking, he said to Simon, "Put out into deep water, and let down [y] the nets for a catch."

[5]Simon answered, "Master, we've worked hard all night and haven't caught anything. But because you say so, I will let down the nets."

[6]When they had done so, they caught such a large number of fish that their nets began to break. [7]So they signaled their partners in the other boat to come and help them, and they came and filled both boats so full that they began to sink.

[8]When Simon Peter saw this, he fell at Jesus' knees and said, "Go away from me, Lord; I am a sinful man!" [9]For he and all his companions were astonished at the catch of fish they had taken, [10]and so were James and John, the sons of Zebedee, Simon's partners.

Then Jesus said to Simon, "Don't be afraid; from now on you will catch men." [11]So they pulled their boats up on shore, left everything and followed him.

OPEN: When you need a break from pressure, where do you go? What do you do?

DIG: 1. How has Jesus' life changed since 4:1-13? What in this section shows that Jesus is beginning to feel the effects of this change? **2.** What do you imagine the scene was like in verses 40-41? **3.** Why does Jesus find it necessary to retreat at this time (vv.42-44)? What pressure is he facing? What are his priorities? **4.** What do you see about the kingdom of God from the stories in chapter 4?

REFLECT: Jesus is obviously busy and in high demand, yet he takes time to be alone. How do you discern God's *long-range* call to you amidst all the shouting of the *urgent* claims?

OPEN: What was it like the first time you left home (for college, the military, a job, marriage, etc.)?

DIG: 1. Picture yourself as Simon. What are you thinking, doing, feeling in verses 1-3? When Jesus speaks directly to you in verse 4? Why do you go along with his odd request? **2.** How did this miracle affect Peter? Why does this have a more profound effect on him than the healing of his mother-in-law? What is he beginning to grasp about Jesus? About sin? About belief in himself?

REFLECT: In *your* "fishing business," how do you see Jesus: (a) Interesting, but slightly irrelevant teacher? (b) Potentially a great business partner, if you could only get him to work for you? (c) The one who calls all the shots? Why?

v41 Or *Messiah*   *w44* Or *the land of the Jews;* some manuscripts *Galilee*
x1 That is, Sea of Galilee   *y4* The Greek verb is plural.

Luke 5:1-11   CALLING THE FIRST DISCIPLES

LOOKING INTO THE SCRIPTURE/20 Minutes. Read Luke 5:1-11 and discuss.

1. What gets your attention about this first meeting of Jesus and Simon?
   a. it was a terrific coincidence
   b. it was more than coincidental
   c. Jesus trusted a stranger to help him
   d. how Jesus showed his interest in Simon's work

2. If you had been Simon Peter when Jesus asked him to "Put out into deep water, and let down the nets for a catch," what would you have done?
   a. what Peter did
   b. made some excuse
   c. politely told Jesus to stick to his preaching
   d. suggested another time when the fish were biting
   e. gone ahead grudgingly
   f. wondered who this person thought he was

3. When they "caught such a large number of fish that their nets began to break," how do you think Simon Peter felt?
   a. overjoyed
   b. terrible about what he had said to Jesus
   c. dumbfounded
   d. aware of who Jesus was

4. When Simon Peter said, "Go away from me, Lord; I am a sinful man!" what did he mean?
   a. You embarrass me because you know more about fishing than I do
   b. I feel uncomfortable being around you because of my sinful life
   c. I know you are all that you say you are, but I am not ready to follow
   d. Stop bugging me. Get out of my life
   e. I'm confused. If I say "yes," I know that it will mean changing my life and I don't think I can measure up

5. "They left everything and followed Him." Why?
   a. they wanted Jesus to become their fishing partner
   b. they followed him in blind faith
   c. they were confused and needed time to figure him out
   d. they were attracted to his message
   e. they were intrigued by the thought of becoming "fishers of men"
   f. they were irresponsible
   g. they knew then and there that he was the Messiah

MY OWN STORY/20 Minutes. Share some of your own spiritual journey with your group.

1. In comparison to Simon Peter's call, how would you explain your spiritual beginning?
   a. tame
   b. more intellectual
   c. just as confusing
   d. even crazier
   e. different, but just as real
   f. not sure

2. What is the condition of your spiritual boat right now?
   a. sinking
   b. out for repairs in dry dock
   c. dead in the water
   d. sailing at a fast clip
   e. sailing in the wrong direction
   f. battered by the heavy waves

3. Where do you think Jesus is, in relationship to your spiritual boat?
   a. on the shore watching
   b. swimming out to meet me
   c. climbing on board
   d. aboard, but not doing anything
   e. casting out the nets
   f. pulling in the catch

4. How does the idea of "putting out into deep water and letting down your nets for a catch" sound to you?
   a. scary
   b. crazy
   c. okay, but . . .
   d. fine, if someone will join me
   e. just the invitation I've been waiting for
   f. not sure what you mean

5. What is it going to take to get you going?
   a. time to consider the cost
   b. a little support from others
   c. a good kick in the pants
   d. time to get myself together
   e. help to clean up my life
   f. frankly, I don't know

OPEN: What illness are you most afraid of catching? Why?

DIG: 1. By touching the man before he heals him, what is Jesus saying? 2. Why does Jesus try to silence the man?

REFLECT: 1. When have you felt shunned, like a leper? How did Jesus "touch" you then? Did he use someone in the process? 2. Who are the "lepers" where you live? What would it mean for you to touch them for Christ?

_____

OPEN: Who were your four closest friends in high school? What was one memorable prank you pulled off with their help?

DIG: 1. What is significant about these Pharisees and teachers? 2. What might they be thinking about Jesus in verses 17-19? In verse 20? Why would Jesus risk upsetting them? 3. The friends came for healing, so why did Jesus raise the issue of forgiveness? How would the friends react to Jesus' words (v.20)? To his actions (v.24)? 4. What new realm of Jesus' authority is demonstrated here? 5. What motivates the people, friends, man, and Pharisees to each respond as they do?

REFLECT: 1. Who are you most like in this story, and why? 2. Where are you a little paralyzed right now—emotionally, spiritually, relationally? What needs to happen for you to "take your mat and go home"?

_____

OPEN: A famous person you want to meet is coming to dine with you tomorrow. What would you do to get ready?

DIG: 1. Tax collectors lined their pockets with money collected from fish taxes, road taxes, etc. How might Simon and his friends (5:1-11) feel about Jesus' choice? About the Pharisees' complaint (v.30)? 2. Why choose Levi? What is the irony here (vv.31-32)? 3. Why is Jesus questioned about fasting (v.33)? 4. What is Jesus implying by the parable in verses 34-35? In verses 36-39? How

The Man With Leprosy

¹²While Jesus was in one of the towns, a man came along who was covered with leprosy.ᶻ When he saw Jesus, he fell with his face to the ground and begged him, "Lord, if you are willing, you can make me clean."

¹³Jesus reached out his hand and touched the man. "I am willing," he said. "Be clean!" And immediately the leprosy left him.

¹⁴Then Jesus ordered him, "Don't tell anyone, but go, show yourself to the priest and offer the sacrifices that Moses commanded for your cleansing, as a testimony to them."

¹⁵Yet the news about him spread all the more, so that crowds of people came to hear him and to be healed of their sicknesses. ¹⁶But Jesus often withdrew to lonely places and prayed.

Jesus Heals a Paralytic

¹⁷One day as he was teaching, Pharisees and teachers of the law, who had come from every village of Galilee and from Judea and Jerusalem, were sitting there. And the power of the Lord was present for him to heal the sick. ¹⁸Some men came carrying a paralytic on a mat and tried to take him into the house to lay him before Jesus. ¹⁹When they could not find a way to do this because of the crowd, they went up on the roof and lowered him on his mat through the tiles into the middle of the crowd, right in front of Jesus.

²⁰When Jesus saw their faith, he said, "Friend, your sins are forgiven."

²¹The Pharisees and the teachers of the law began thinking to themselves, "Who is this fellow who speaks blasphemy? Who can forgive sins but God alone?"

²²Jesus knew what they were thinking and asked, "Why are you thinking these things in your hearts? ²³Which is easier: to say, 'Your sins are forgiven,' or to say, 'Get up and walk'? ²⁴But that you may know that the Son of Man has authority on earth to forgive sins. . . ." He said to the paralyzed man, "I tell you, get up, take your mat and go home." ²⁵Immediately he stood up in front of them, took what he had been lying on and went home praising God. ²⁶Everyone was amazed and gave praise to God. They were filled with awe and said, "We have seen remarkable things today."

The Calling of Levi

²⁷After this, Jesus went out and saw a tax collector by the name of Levi sitting at his tax booth. "Follow me," Jesus said to him, ²⁸and Levi got up, left everything and followed him.

²⁹Then Levi held a great banquet for Jesus at his house, and a large crowd of tax collectors and others were eating with them. ³⁰But the Pharisees and the teachers of the law who belonged to their sect complained to his disciples, "Why do you eat and drink with tax collectors and 'sinners'?"

³¹Jesus answered them, "It is not the healthy who need a doctor, but the sick. ³²I have not come to call the righteous, but sinners to repentance."

ᶻ12 The Greek word was used for various diseases affecting the skin—not necessarily leprosy.

LOOKING INTO THE SCRIPTURE/15 Minutes. Read Luke 5:17-26 and discuss.

1. If you had been the paralytic when your friends decided to take you up on the roof, remove the tiles, and lower you into the room, how would you have felt?
   a. reluctant: You're going to embarrass me
   b. scared: You're going to drop me
   c. dubious: You guys are crazy
   d. grateful: I appreciate your concern
   e. apprehensive: They are going to throw us out
   f. mixed: I don't think it is going to work, but I'm willing to trust you guys

2. What would it have taken for you to lower your paralytic friend down through the roof?
   a. organization
   b. courage
   c. a good sense of humor
   d. physical strength
   e. good timing
   f. desperation
   g. the right equipment

3. When the crowd heard all of the commotion on the roof and saw the paralytic being lowered into the room, how do you think the bystanders felt?
   a. annoyed: Don't these guys have any respect?
   b. amused: This is the best show in town
   c. angry: Throw them out
   d. sympathy: These guys are really concerned for their friend.

4. When Jesus said to the paralytic, "Friend, your sins are forgiven," what do you think the Pharisees and teachers of the law were thinking?
   a. who does this guy think he is?
   b. you have no right to assume his paralysis is caused by sin
   c. this Jesus ought to be sued for malpractice
   d. wait a minute. This guy has not sinned. He's just sick
   e. Jesus is trying to say that spiritual and physical illness are interrelated

5. If something like this ever happened in your church, what would the people say?
   a. this is the most excitement we've seen in years
   b. who is going to pay for the roof?
   c. whatever it takes to get someone healed is fine with us
   d. we're used to these things
   e. let's see this never happens again

MY OWN STORY/20 Minutes.

1. Take a moment and think about the major areas of your life. Then, for each area, put a dot to indicate your fitness—somewhere between ON THE INJURY LIST and PERFECT FITNESS. The midpoint on the line would be normal—you're not bad enough to ask for help, but you're not feeling great in this area either.

	ON THE INJURY LIST	PERFECT FITNESS
BODY: feeling physically fit		
MIND: feeling no stress/no pain		
SPIRIT: feeling close to God		
JOB/SCHOOL: doing what I like		
RELATIONSHIPS: getting along at home		
FUTURE: feeling good and secure		

2. What would you like to have from the group you are in right now to help you in the area where you indicated the greatest need? Go around and let each person in your group finish this sentence: "The way in which you could help me most is . . ."
   a. organization
   b. courage and faith
   c. a good sense of humor
   d. physical strength
   e. faithfulness in prayer
   f. desperation
   g. the right equipment

does this relate to Levi's call and to the disciples' not fasting? **5.** What is the new cloth? Old garment? New wine? Old wineskins?

REFLECT: 1. In this story, what do you have to do to qualify as a disciple? **2.** In the way you relate to "undesirable types," are you more like Levi (inviting them to your party), the Pharisees (looking down on them), or the disciples (unsure what to do)? Why?

OPEN: What rules did your family have that, as a kid, you thought were stupid? How do you view those rules now?

DIG: 1. How are things developing in the Pharisees' ongoing investigation of Jesus (5:17,30,33)? What is the main issue here for the Pharisees? For Jesus? **2.** How does the story of David (see vv.3-4; 1Sa 21:1-6) apply to Jesus and his disciples? **3.** How does Jesus clarify the Sabbath issue (vv.5,9)? **4.** Why does Jesus provoke the Pharisees' wrath by healing on the Sabbath? Couldn't he wait a day? **5.** What do you learn about the differences between Jesus and formalized religion in the events of 5:27-6:10?

REFLECT: 1. When have you felt the tension between obeying religious *principles* and doing something to help *people*? What causes that tension? **2.** What impresses you about Jesus in this scene? As you try to follow Jesus, do you sense you are becoming more free to love others, or becoming more constrained by religious rules? Why?

OPEN: What was one of the best teams you ever belonged to?

DIG: In the context of chapter 6, what is significant about Jesus calling these men? What do you know about them? Who are brothers? Buddies? Antagonists?

Jesus Questioned About Fasting

[33]They said to him, "John's disciples often fast and pray, and so do the disciples of the Pharisees, but yours go on eating and drinking."

[34]Jesus answered, "Can you make the guests of the bridegroom fast while he is with them? [35]But the time will come when the bridegroom will be taken from them; in those days they will fast."

[36]He told them this parable: "No one tears a patch from a new garment and sews it on an old one. If he does, he will have torn the new garment, and the patch from the new will not match the old. [37]And no one pours new wine into old wineskins. If he does, the new wine will burst the skins, the wine will run out and the wineskins will be ruined. [38]No, new wine must be poured into new wineskins. [39]And no one after drinking old wine wants the new, for he says, 'The old is better.' "

Lord of the Sabbath

6 One Sabbath Jesus was going through the grainfields, and his disciples began to pick some heads of grain, rub them in their hands and eat the kernels. [2]Some of the Pharisees asked, "Why are you doing what is unlawful on the Sabbath?"

[3]Jesus answered them, "Have you never read what David did when he and his companions were hungry? [4]He entered the house of God, and taking the consecrated bread, he ate what is lawful only for priests to eat. And he also gave some to his companions." [5]Then Jesus said to them, "The Son of Man is Lord of the Sabbath."

[6]On another Sabbath he went into the synagogue and was teaching, and a man was there whose right hand was shriveled. [7]The Pharisees and the teachers of the law were looking for a reason to accuse Jesus, so they watched him closely to see if he would heal on the Sabbath. [8]But Jesus knew what they were thinking and said to the man with the shriveled hand, "Get up and stand in front of everyone." So he got up and stood there.

[9]Then Jesus said to them, "I ask you, which is lawful on the Sabbath: to do good or to do evil, to save life or to destroy it?"

[10]He looked around at them all, and then said to the man, "Stretch out your hand." He did so, and his hand was completely restored. [11]But they were furious and began to discuss with one another what they might do to Jesus.

The Twelve Apostles

[12]One of those days Jesus went out to a mountainside to pray, and spent the night praying to God. [13]When morning came, he called his disciples to him and chose twelve of them, whom he also designated apostles: [14]Simon (whom he named Peter), his brother Andrew, James, John, Philip, Bartholomew, [15]Matthew, Thomas, James son of Alphaeus, Simon who was called the Zealot, [16]Judas son of James, and Judas Iscariot, who became a traitor.

Blessings and Woes

[17]He went down with them and stood on a level place. A large crowd of his disciples was there and a great number of people from all over Judea, from Jerusalem, and from the coast of Tyre and Sidon, [18]who had come to hear him and to be healed of their diseases. Those troubled by evil[a] spirits were cured, [19]and the people all tried to touch him, because power was coming from him and healing them all.

[20]Looking at his disciples, he said:

"Blessed are you who are poor,
    for yours is the kingdom of God.
[21]Blessed are you who hunger now,
    for you will be satisfied.
Blessed are you who weep now,
    for you will laugh.
[22]Blessed are you when men hate you,
    when they exclude you and insult you
    and reject your name as evil,
        because of the Son of Man.

[23]"Rejoice in that day and leap for joy, because great is your reward in heaven. For that is how their fathers treated the prophets.

[24]"But woe to you who are rich,
    for you have already received your comfort.
[25]Woe to you who are well fed now,
    for you will go hungry.
Woe to you who laugh now,
    for you will mourn and weep.
[26]Woe to you when all men speak well of you,
    for that is how their fathers treated the false prophets.

Love for Enemies

[27]"But I tell you who hear me: Love your enemies, do good to those who hate you, [28]bless those who curse you, pray for those who mistreat you. [29]If someone strikes you on one cheek, turn to him the other also. If someone takes your cloak, do not stop him from taking your tunic. [30]Give to everyone who asks you, and if anyone takes what belongs to you, do not demand it back. [31]Do to others as you would have them do to you.

[32]"If you love those who love you, what credit is that to you? Even 'sinners' love those who love them. [33]And if you do good to those who are good to you, what credit is that to you? Even 'sinners' do that. [34]And if you lend to those from whom you expect repayment, what credit is that to you? Even 'sinners' lend to 'sinners,' expecting to be repaid in full. [35]But love your enemies, do good to them, and lend to them without expecting to get anything back. Then your reward will be great, and you will be sons of the Most High, because he is kind to the ungrateful and wicked. [36]Be merciful, just as your Father is merciful.

OPEN: What one campaign promise do you remember from the last major election? Why that one? (Did you bank on it? Was it kept?)

DIG: 1. Who's in the crowd? Why have they come? How does Jesus meet their needs? How do his actions (vv.18-19) relate to his teaching (vv.20-22)? **2.** What four qualities ought to characterize kingdom people (vv.20-22)? How would you define each of these? What blessing is promised for each? When are these blessings to be experienced: Now? In the future? Both? **3.** Who may Jesus be thinking of in verses 24-26 (see v.11)? How would you define each warning he gives here? **4.** What is taught here about God's kingdom?

REFLECT: 1. How do the values Jesus talks about here compare with the values you are sold every day on TV? Which set of values do you and your family buy into? Which promise means the most to you now? Why? Which warning seems most personal? Why? **2.** If you could add another "blessed" and another "woe" to counteract the values on TV, what would you add?

OPEN: Who were the good guys and the bad guys on your favorite Saturday morning cartoons or TV show?

DIG: 1. What's the significance of the shift Jesus has made in the object of love (see Lev 19:18)? What specifically are we to do to enemies? Why? **2.** Since applying verses 29-30 literally could only reinforce someone's bad behavior (think of raising your child like this!), what is Jesus' point (see vv.31,36)?

REFLECT: 1. How does this description of love challenge you? **2.** How can that be a model for relating to someone you find difficult?

[a]18 Greek unclean

OPEN: 1. Would you rather be a movie director or a movie critic? Why? 2. Where would you like to locate your "dream house"? Why?

DIG: 1. What two activities does Jesus condemn and commend (vv.37-38)? What does the promise (v.38) mean in this context? 2. What's the point of this parable (vv.39-40) in this context? 3. What is the point of the speck and the plank? 4. How does the tree and its fruit (vv.43-45) help you recognize a kingdom person? How does this relate to verses 37-42? 5. Compare the two houses and their owner-builders (vv.46-49). How does this lesson relate to the other two?

REFLECT: 1. In light of this three-fold passage, how would you recommend approaching people who need help or correction? How do you normally do so? 2. What quality of "fruit" would your family say you are producing: Grade A-1? So-so? Wormy? Why? What would Jesus need to do to make it good? 3. During the last "storm" to hit your life, what did you learn about your life's "foundation"? 4. What "building blocks" from 6:27-45 do you need to add to your foundation? How can your group help you do so?

OPEN: What's the most dramatic "near death" experience you've ever had: An accident? Illness? Showing your father a bad report card? Bottom fell out of the stock market? The sky fell in on you?

DIG: 1. How are Roman centurions portrayed here and elsewhere in Scripture (see Mt 27:26,54; 28:4,11-15; Ac 10:2; 23:17-18; 27:43)? In what way is this related to 6:43-45? 2. On what basis do the elders request Jesus' help? How does their approach differ from the centurion's (vv.6-8)? How does this relate to Jesus' commandment (v.9)? 3. What quality of faith is exhibited here?

Judging Others

37"Do not judge, and you will not be judged. Do not condemn, and you will not be condemned. Forgive, and you will be forgiven. 38Give, and it will be given to you. A good measure, pressed down, shaken together and running over, will be poured into your lap. For with the measure you use, it will be measured to you."

39He also told them this parable: "Can a blind man lead a blind man? Will they not both fall into a pit? 40A student is not above his teacher, but everyone who is fully trained will be like his teacher.

41"Why do you look at the speck of sawdust in your brother's eye and pay no attention to the plank in your own eye? 42How can you say to your brother, 'Brother, let me take the speck out of your eye,' when you yourself fail to see the plank in your own eye? You hypocrite, first take the plank out of your eye, and then you will see clearly to remove the speck from your brother's eye.

A Tree and Its Fruit

43"No good tree bears bad fruit, nor does a bad tree bear good fruit. 44Each tree is recognized by its own fruit. People do not pick figs from thornbushes, or grapes from briers. 45The good man brings good things out of the good stored up in his heart, and the evil man brings evil things out of the evil stored up in his heart. For out of the overflow of his heart his mouth speaks.

The Wise and Foolish Builders

46"Why do you call me, 'Lord, Lord,' and do not do what I say? 47I will show you what he is like who comes to me and hears my words and puts them into practice. 48He is like a man building a house, who dug down deep and laid the foundation on rock. When a flood came, the torrent struck that house but could not shake it, because it was well built. 49But the one who hears my words and does not put them into practice is like a man who built a house on the ground without a foundation. The moment the torrent struck that house, it collapsed and its destruction was complete."

The Faith of the Centurion

7 When Jesus had finished saying all this in the hearing of the people, he entered Capernaum. 2There a centurion's servant, whom his master valued highly, was sick and about to die. 3The centurion heard of Jesus and sent some elders of the Jews to him, asking him to come and heal his servant. 4When they came to Jesus, they pleaded earnestly with him, "This man deserves to have you do this, 5because he loves our nation and has built our synagogue." 6So Jesus went with them.

He was not far from the house when the centurion sent friends to say to him: "Lord, don't trouble yourself, for I do not deserve to have you come under my roof. 7That is why I did not even consider myself worthy to come to you. But say the word, and my servant will be healed. 8For I myself am a man under authority, with soldiers under me. I tell this one, 'Go,' and he goes; and that one, 'Come,' and he comes. I say to my servant, 'Do this,' and he does it.''

⁹When Jesus heard this, he was amazed at him, and turning to the crowd following him, he said, "I tell you, I have not found such great faith even in Israel.'' ¹⁰Then the men who had been sent returned to the house and found the servant well.

Jesus Raises a Widow's Son

¹¹Soon afterward, Jesus went to a town called Nain, and his disciples and a large crowd went along with him. ¹²As he approached the town gate, a dead person was being carried out—the only son of his mother, and she was a widow. And a large crowd from the town was with her. ¹³When the Lord saw her, his heart went out to her and he said, "Don't cry.''

¹⁴Then he went up and touched the coffin, and those carrying it stood still. He said, "Young man, I say to you, get up!'' ¹⁵The dead man sat up and began to talk, and Jesus gave him back to his mother.

¹⁶They were all filled with awe and praised God. "A great prophet has appeared among us,'' they said. "God has come to help his people.'' ¹⁷This news about Jesus spread throughout Judea[b] and the surrounding country.

Jesus and John the Baptist

¹⁸John's disciples told him about all these things. Calling two of them, ¹⁹he sent them to the Lord to ask, "Are you the one who was to come, or should we expect someone else?''

²⁰When the men came to Jesus, they said, "John the Baptist sent us to you to ask, 'Are you the one who was to come, or should we expect someone else?' ''

²¹At that very time Jesus cured many who had diseases, sicknesses and evil spirits, and gave sight to many who were blind. ²²So he replied to the messengers, "Go back and report to John what you have seen and heard: The blind receive sight, the lame walk, those who have leprosy[c] are cured, the deaf hear, the dead are raised, and the good news is preached to the poor. ²³Blessed is the man who does not fall away on account of me.''

²⁴After John's messengers left, Jesus began to speak to the crowd about John: "What did you go out into the desert to see? A reed swayed by the wind? ²⁵If not, what did you go out to see? A man dressed in fine clothes? No, those who wear expensive clothes and indulge in luxury are in palaces. ²⁶But what did you go out to see? A prophet? Yes, I tell you, and more than a prophet. ²⁷This is the one about whom it is written:

" 'I will send my messenger ahead of you,
who will prepare your way before you.'[d]

²⁸I tell you, among those born of women there is no one greater than John; yet the one who is least in the kingdom of God is greater than he.''

REFLECT: In living out the Christian life, what practical difference does it make whether you live by confidence in your goodness, or by trust in Christ's power? How does this reveal itself, especially in a crisis?

OPEN: What national hero or liberating event do you associate with the "good ol' days"? Why?

DIG: This story resembles the one in 2 Kings 4:8-37. In light of that, why did Jesus perform this miracle in Nain (near Shunem)? What did he reveal about himself? What impact did he have on others?

REFLECT: How do you see yourself fitting into this story and the one in 7:1-10? How does Jesus' love and authority affect you?

OPEN: 1. (For the married:) When did you know that the person you married was "the one"? (For the unmarried:) What is the sign you are looking for as that decisive signal? **2.** What recent situation has frustrated you because you weren't sure what to do?

DIG: 1. How does John receive information about Jesus? Why can't he get it firsthand (see 3:20)? What question does he tell his men to ask Jesus (v.20)? Why? What is John's probable expectation of the way a Messiah ought to act (see 3:16-17)? **2.** How does Jesus answer the question (vv.21-23)? Why doesn't he answer directly? What six things characterize his ministry? **3.** From Isaiah 29:18-19; 35:5-6; 61:1, how might John interpret Jesus' reply? How might he take Jesus' added blessing (v.23)? **4.** What questions does Jesus put to the people? How does Jesus affirm John? **5.** As great as John was, who is greater? Why? **6.** How does the people's response to John contrast to that of the Pharisees? How are the followers of the Pharisees like children bickering over which game to play (vv.31-32)? How are the followers of John and Jesus like children proving God's wisdom is right (v.35)?

b17 Or *the land of the Jews*   *c22* The Greek word was used for various diseases affecting the skin—not necessarily leprosy.   *d27* Mal. 3:1

REFLECT: 1. When did you come to the place in your spiritual pilgrimage when you knew Jesus was "the one" you were looking for? How did you come to this understanding? What difference has it made? 2. Looking at verses 33-34, are you more like John or Jesus in your lifestyle? Would you be more effective if you lived differently? Why or why not? 3. If you could ask Jesus one question today about a decision you are facing, what would it be?

OPEN: 1. What is one special gift you've received from your kids or parents? 2. What parties do you like to go to? Hate going to?

DIG: 1. What risk was this woman taking in coming to the house of a Pharisee? What does this tell you about her emotional state? 2. What is your impression of Simon? What do you think Jesus' purpose was in telling the parable in verses 41-43? Why didn't he just accuse Simon of not loving enough? What does this tell you about Jesus? 3. What does Jesus see in this woman that Simon does not? How does this affect Jesus' actions toward her? In this passage, what seems to be Jesus' main concern? Simon's concern? 4. How important would it be to this woman that Jesus forgives her? What does this tell you about Jesus?

REFLECT: 1. How difficult is it for you to be demonstrative in a relationship with Jesus? What hinders you from being more open with your love? 2. When it comes to relationships, are you a "big forgiver" or a "stingy one"? Why? How does this tie in with your relationship with God? 3. What do you learn from this story that could apply this week?

[29](All the people, even the tax collectors, when they heard Jesus' words, acknowledged that God's way was right, because they had been baptized by John. [30]But the Pharisees and experts in the law rejected God's purpose for themselves, because they had not been baptized by John.)

[31]"To what, then, can I compare the people of this generation? What are they like? [32]They are like children sitting in the marketplace and calling out to each other:

" 'We played the flute for you,
　　and you did not dance;
we sang a dirge,
　　and you did not cry.'

[33]For John the Baptist came neither eating bread nor drinking wine, and you say, 'He has a demon.' [34]The Son of Man came eating and drinking, and you say, 'Here is a glutton and a drunkard, a friend of tax collectors and "sinners." ' [35]But wisdom is proved right by all her children."

Jesus Anointed by a Sinful Woman

[36]Now one of the Pharisees invited Jesus to have dinner with him, so he went to the Pharisee's house and reclined at the table. [37]When a woman who had lived a sinful life in that town learned that Jesus was eating at the Pharisee's house, she brought an alabaster jar of perfume, [38]and as she stood behind him at his feet weeping, she began to wet his feet with her tears. Then she wiped them with her hair, kissed them and poured perfume on them.

[39]When the Pharisee who had invited him saw this, he said to himself, "If this man were a prophet, he would know who is touching him and what kind of woman she is—that she is a sinner."

[40]Jesus answered him, "Simon, I have something to tell you."

"Tell me, teacher," he said.

[41]"Two men owed money to a certain moneylender. One owed him five hundred denarii,[e] and the other fifty. [42]Neither of them had the money to pay him back, so he canceled the debts of both. Now which of them will love him more?"

[43]Simon replied, "I suppose the one who had the bigger debt canceled."

"You have judged correctly," Jesus said.

[44]Then he turned toward the woman and said to Simon, "Do you see this woman? I came into your house. You did not give me any water for my feet, but she wet my feet with her tears and wiped them with her hair. [45]You did not give me a kiss, but this woman, from the time I entered, has not stopped kissing my feet. [46]You did not put oil on my head, but she has poured perfume on my feet. [47]Therefore, I tell you, her many sins have been forgiven—for she loved much. But he who has been forgiven little loves little."

[48]Then Jesus said to her, "Your sins are forgiven."

e41 A denarius was a coin worth about a day's wages.

LOOKING INTO THE SCRIPTURE/20 Minutes. Read Luke 7:36-50 and discuss.

1. Do you think the Pharisee was aware of the social custom to greet guests with a kiss and wash their feet?
    a. yes
    b. no

2. Do you think Jesus was aware of the purification law prohibiting anyone to "touch" a prostitute?
    a. yes
    b. no

3. Why do you think the sinful woman came to the Pharisee's house?
    a. to upset the Pharisee
    b. to ruin the party
    c. to seek forgiveness
    d. to minister to Jesus
    e. to confront her oppressors

4. What made the Pharisee so upset?
    a. her reputation
    b. his reputation
    c. Jesus' acceptance of the woman

5. How did the Pharisee feel when the sinful woman "touched" Jesus?
    a. contaminated
    b. humiliated
    c. angry
    d. sympathetic
    e. hysterical

6. "If this man were a prophet, he would know who is touching him and what kind of woman she is—that she is a sinner." Which possibility comes closest to your understanding of Jesus?
    a. Jesus was not a prophet and didn't know who the woman was
    b. Jesus knew who the woman was but didn't care about the Law
    c. Jesus cared about the Law but cared about the person more
    d. Jesus, because he really was a prophet, was able to see the "sinful woman" as clean and forgiven

7. In the story about the two men who owed money, what was Jesus saying to Simon?
    a. You can't know grace because you have never thought of yourself as a sinner
    b. You are a bigger sinner than the woman but you don't know it
    c. The more you have sinned the more your love for God
    d. The more you have been forgiven the more your love for God

8. What was the tone in Jesus' voice when he said to the woman, "Your faith has saved you; go in peace."
    a. judicial: like a judge
    b. clinical: like a psychiatrist
    c. pastoral: like a priest
    d. paternal: like a father
    e. authoritative: like a sergeant

MY OWN STORY/25 Minutes.

1. Who was the prophet in your life who believed in you and saw beauty in you before you believed in yourself?
    a. my mom/dad
    b. a special teacher/coach
    c. one special friend
    d. a pastor/youth leader

2. How did this affect your life?
    a. I could deal with my own negative feelings
    b. I could accept God's forgiveness
    c. I started to believe in myself
    d. I started to act differently

⁴⁹The other guests began to say among themselves, "Who is this who even forgives sins?"

⁵⁰Jesus said to the woman, "Your faith has saved you; go in peace."

The Parable of the Sower

8 After this, Jesus traveled about from one town and village to another, proclaiming the good news of the kingdom of God. The Twelve were with him, ²and also some women who had been cured of evil spirits and diseases: Mary (called Magdalene) from whom seven demons had come out; ³Joanna the wife of Cuza, the manager of Herod's household; Susanna; and many others. These women were helping to support them out of their own means.

⁴While a large crowd was gathering and people were coming to Jesus from town after town, he told this parable: ⁵"A farmer went out to sow his seed. As he was scattering the seed, some fell along the path; it was trampled on, and the birds of the air ate it up. ⁶Some fell on rock, and when it came up, the plants withered because they had no moisture. ⁷Other seed fell among thorns, which grew up with it and choked the plants. ⁸Still other seed fell on good soil. It came up and yielded a crop, a hundred times more than was sown."

When he said this, he called out, "He who has ears to hear, let him hear."

⁹His disciples asked him what this parable meant. ¹⁰He said, "The knowledge of the secrets of the kingdom of God has been given to you, but to others I speak in parables, so that,

" 'though seeing, they may not see;
though hearing, they may not understand.'ᶠ

¹¹"This is the meaning of the parable: The seed is the word of God. ¹²Those along the path are the ones who hear, and then the devil comes and takes away the word from their hearts, so that they may not believe and be saved. ¹³Those on the rock are the ones who receive the word with joy when they hear it, but they have no root. They believe for a while, but in the time of testing they fall away. ¹⁴The seed that fell among thorns stands for those who hear, but as they go on their way they are choked by life's worries, riches and pleasures, and they do not mature. ¹⁵But the seed on good soil stands for those with a noble and good heart, who hear the word, retain it, and by persevering produce a crop.

A Lamp on a Stand

¹⁶"No one lights a lamp and hides it in a jar or puts it under a bed. Instead, he puts it on a stand, so that those who come in can see the light. ¹⁷For there is nothing hidden that will not be disclosed, and nothing concealed that will not be known or brought out into the open. ¹⁸Therefore consider carefully how you listen. Whoever has will be given more; whoever does not have, even what he thinks he has will be taken from him."

ᶠ10 Isaiah 6:9

OPEN: 1. What's one of the best groups (teammates, hikers, tourists) you've ever traveled with? Why? **2.** What kind of luck have you had with growing things? Are you a "green thumb" or a "brown thumb"? What is your secret of success (or reason for failure)?

DIG: 1. What is Jesus' ministry style here (v.1)? Who travels with him? What strikes you about this "crew"? **2.** What is the setting for this parable (v.4)? What is a parable? What does verse 10 reveal about the purpose of the parable? **3.** What is the reason why the disciples receive an explanation, while the others do not? How would the parable help the disciples to better understand what is happening in their ministry? **4.** In Jesus' explanation of this parable, what is the seed? The soils? The fruit? The farmer? **5.** What does it really mean to "hear"? How would you explain this parable to city kids who had never seen a field? What modern analogy would you use?

REFLECT: 1. What kind of "soil" best represents you now? What kind of soil would have represented you five years ago? **2.** When it comes to "hearing" God right now, are you: (a) "Locked in" on the station? (b) Getting a lot of static? (c) Barely picking up the signal? Why? **3.** What help do you get from this parable about sharing your faith with others?

OPEN: If I looked under your bed right now, what would I find?

DIG: 1. If Jesus and his message are the lamp of truth, what is this parable saying about the kingdom of God? What is the promise for those who do and don't listen? **2.** How does Jesus expand on this in verses 19-21?

Jesus' Mother and Brothers

[19]Now Jesus' mother and brothers came to see him, but they were not able to get near him because of the crowd. [20]Someone told him, "Your mother and brothers are standing outside, wanting to see you."

[21]He replied, "My mother and brothers are those who hear God's word and put it into practice."

Jesus Calms the Storm

[22]One day Jesus said to his disciples, "Let's go over to the other side of the lake." So they got into a boat and set out. [23]As they sailed, he fell asleep. A squall came down on the lake, so that the boat was being swamped, and they were in great danger.

[24]The disciples went and woke him, saying, "Master, Master, we're going to drown!"

He got up and rebuked the wind and the raging waters; the storm subsided, and all was calm. [25]"Where is your faith?" he asked his disciples.

In fear and amazement they asked one another, "Who is this? He commands even the winds and the water, and they obey him."

The Healing of a Demon-possessed Man

[26]They sailed to the region of the Gerasenes,[g] which is across the lake from Galilee. [27]When Jesus stepped ashore, he was met by a demon-possessed man from the town. For a long time this man had not worn clothes or lived in a house, but had lived in the tombs. [28]When he saw Jesus, he cried out and fell at his feet, shouting at the top of his voice, "What do you want with me, Jesus, Son of the Most High God? I beg you, don't torture me!" [29]For Jesus had commanded the evil[h] spirit to come out of the man. Many times it had seized him, and though he was chained hand and foot and kept under guard, he had broken his chains and had been driven by the demon into solitary places.

[30]Jesus asked him, "What is your name?"

"Legion," he replied, because many demons had gone into him. [31]And they begged him repeatedly not to order them to go into the Abyss.

[32]A large herd of pigs was feeding there on the hillside. The demons begged Jesus to let them go into them, and he gave them permission. [33]When the demons came out of the man, they went into the pigs, and the herd rushed down the steep bank into the lake and was drowned.

[34]When those tending the pigs saw what had happened, they ran off and reported this in the town and countryside, [35]and the people went out to see what had happened. When they came to Jesus, they found the man from whom the demons had gone out, sitting at Jesus' feet, dressed and in his right mind; and they were afraid. [36]Those who had seen it told the people how the demon-possessed man had been cured. [37]Then all the people of

REFLECT: How do you "receive" from Jesus or get "near" him? Are you sensing that kinship with him now? Why or why not?

OPEN: What is the worst storm you remember?

DIG: 1. What is Jesus teaching his disciples by ignoring and then rebuking the storm? **2.** Why is Jesus upset? **3.** What emotions hinder faith? Accompany it? Why?

REFLECT: Comparing your life to a storm, what would it be like right now: Partly cloudy? Lightening? Raging? Clearing up? What do you wish Jesus would do for you?

OPEN: 1. Where do you go to "get away from it all"? What do you do for "kicks"? **2.** When did a vacation turn into something you never expected? What happened?

DIG: 1. After 8:22-25, how might the disciples be feeling: As they arrive on the other side of the lake? Once they realize they are in a graveyard? As the demoniac runs toward them? **2.** How does Jesus treat the man differently than the way others have? What is the net result? **3.** How do the pig farmers respond? The townspeople? Of what are they afraid? Why? **4.** The man wants to go with Jesus, but is turned down. Why? What happens instead?

REFLECT: 1. In your life right now, what is the thing that wears on you, that makes you feel like a "legion" (6,000 soldiers) is marching through your head, keeping you awake at night or torn at work? **2.** When, if ever, have you wanted Jesus to leave you alone? To get out of your life? To let you hurt yourself? **3.** Have you ever been like the townspeople who don't want to listen to the claims of Christ if it means a big change in life? **4.** When you first "met" Jesus, how did he treat you? How was this different from the way others treat you?

---

g26 Some manuscripts *Gadarenes*; other manuscripts *Gergesenes;* also in verse 37
h29 Greek *unclean*

the region of the Gerasenes asked Jesus to leave them, because they were overcome with fear. So he got into the boat and left.

38The man from whom the demons had gone out begged to go with him, but Jesus sent him away, saying, 39"Return home and tell how much God has done for you." So the man went away and told all over town how much Jesus had done for him.

A Dead Girl and a Sick Woman

40Now when Jesus returned, a crowd welcomed him, for they were all expecting him. 41Then a man named Jairus, a ruler of the synagogue, came and fell at Jesus' feet, pleading with him to come to his house 42because his only daughter, a girl of about twelve, was dying.

As Jesus was on his way, the crowds almost crushed him. 43And a woman was there who had been subject to bleeding for twelve years, [i] but no one could heal her. 44She came up behind him and touched the edge of his cloak, and immediately her bleeding stopped.

45"Who touched me?" Jesus asked.

When they all denied it, Peter said, "Master, the people are crowding and pressing against you."

46But Jesus said, "Someone touched me; I know that power has gone out from me."

47Then the woman, seeing that she could not go unnoticed, came trembling and fell at his feet. In the presence of all the people, she told why she had touched him and how she had been instantly healed. 48Then he said to her, "Daughter, your faith has healed you. Go in peace."

49While Jesus was still speaking, someone came from the house of Jairus, the synagogue ruler. "Your daughter is dead," he said. "Don't bother the teacher any more."

50Hearing this, Jesus said to Jairus, "Don't be afraid; just believe, and she will be healed."

51When he arrived at the house of Jairus, he did not let anyone go in with him except Peter, John and James, and the child's father and mother. 52Meanwhile, all the people were wailing and mourning for her. "Stop wailing," Jesus said. "She is not dead but asleep."

53They laughed at him, knowing that she was dead. 54But he took her by the hand and said, "My child, get up!" 55Her spirit returned, and at once she stood up. Then Jesus told them to give her something to eat. 56Her parents were astonished, but he ordered them not to tell anyone what had happened.

Jesus Sends Out the Twelve

9 When Jesus had called the Twelve together, he gave them power and authority to drive out all demons and to cure diseases, 2and he sent them out to preach the kingdom of God and to heal the sick. 3He told them: "Take nothing for the journey—no staff, no bag, no bread, no money, no extra tunic. 4Whatever house you enter, stay there until you leave that town. 5If people do not welcome you, shake the dust off your feet when

i43 Many manuscripts *years, and she had spent all she had on doctors* you leave their town, as a testimony against them." [6]So they set out and went from village to village, preaching the gospel and healing people everywhere.

[7]Now Herod the tetrarch heard about all that was going on. And he was perplexed, because some were saying that John had been raised from the dead, [8]others that Elijah had appeared, and still others that one of the prophets of long ago had come back to life. [9]But Herod said, "I beheaded John. Who, then, is this I hear such things about?" And he tried to see him.

Jesus Feeds the Five Thousand

[10]When the apostles returned, they reported to Jesus what they had done. Then he took them with him and they withdrew by themselves to a town called Bethsaida, [11]but the crowds learned about it and followed him. He welcomed them and spoke to them about the kingdom of God, and healed those who needed healing.

[12]Late in the afternoon the Twelve came to him and said, "Send the crowd away so they can go to the surrounding villages and countryside and find food and lodging, because we are in a remote place here."

[13]He replied, "You give them something to eat."

They answered, "We have only five loaves of bread and two fish—unless we go and buy food for all this crowd." [14](About five thousand men were there.)

But he said to his disciples, "Have them sit down in groups of about fifty each." [15]The disciples did so, and everybody sat down. [16]Taking the five loaves and the two fish and looking up to heaven, he gave thanks and broke them. Then he gave them to the disciples to set before the people. [17]They all ate and were satisfied, and the disciples picked up twelve basketfuls of broken pieces that were left over.

Peter's Confession of Christ

[18]Once when Jesus was praying in private and his disciples were with him, he asked them, "Who do the crowds say I am?"

[19]They replied, "Some say John the Baptist; others say Elijah; and still others, that one of the prophets of long ago has come back to life."

[20]"But what about you?" he asked. "Who do you say I am?"

Peter answered, "The Christ[j] of God."

[21]Jesus strictly warned them not to tell this to anyone. [22]And he said, "The Son of Man must suffer many things and be rejected by the elders, chief priests and teachers of the law, and he must be killed and on the third day be raised to life."

[23]Then he said to them all: "If anyone would come after me, he must deny himself and take up his cross daily and follow me. [24]For whoever wants to save his life will lose it, but whoever loses his life for me will save it. [25]What good is it for a man to gain the whole world, and yet lose or forfeit his very self? [26]If anyone is ashamed of me and my words, the Son of Man will

REFLECT: 1. Who is someone you admire because they dared to give their life to a mission? **2.** What is your mission in life, other than to keep food on the table? How does God's kingdom fit in?

OPEN: How do you unwind when you return from work or a trip: Eat? Read? Sleep? Play? TV?

DIG: 1. Why does Jesus take his disciples away with him upon their return? **2.** What tones of voice do you hear in verse 12? Verse 13? How do you account for the differences in the way Jesus and the disciples view the crowd? **3.** What thoughts must the disciples have as they collect the leftovers?

REFLECT: From what do you need a rest: Work hassles? Kids? Church activities? Community activities? School deadlines? How would you cope if God gave you a new challenge instead?

OPEN: When you were a teenager, how did peer pressure affect your choice of clothes? Music?

DIG: 1. Why would Jesus be interested in this opinion poll? **2.** Why does Jesus focus his follow-up question (v.20)? **3.** Why doesn't Jesus want them to tell anyone he is the Christ? **4.** What lies ahead for Jesus? For his disciples? **5.** What activities or attitudes are key to following Christ (v.23)? **6.** How do these three sections (vv.18-20, 21-22, 23-27) flow together?

REFLECT: 1. When did Jesus become more than just a name in the history books to you? **2.** What does it mean specifically to you to: (a) deny yourself, (b) take up your cross daily, (c) follow Christ, and (d) lose your life? **3.** Knowing what you do now, would you reconsider your commitment to Christ? Why or why not?

be ashamed of him when he comes in his glory and in the glory of the Father and of the holy angels. [27]I tell you the truth, some who are standing here will not taste death before they see the kingdom of God."

The Transfiguration

[28]About eight days after Jesus said this, he took Peter, John and James with him and went up onto a mountain to pray. [29]As he was praying, the appearance of his face changed, and his clothes became as bright as a flash of lightning. [30]Two men, Moses and Elijah, [31]appeared in glorious splendor, talking with Jesus. They spoke about his departure, which he was about to bring to fulfillment at Jerusalem. [32]Peter and his companions were very sleepy, but when they became fully awake, they saw his glory and the two men standing with him. [33]As the men were leaving Jesus, Peter said to him, "Master, it is good for us to be here. Let us put up three shelters—one for you, one for Moses and one for Elijah." (He did not know what he was saying.)

[34]While he was speaking, a cloud appeared and enveloped them, and they were afraid as they entered the cloud. [35]A voice came from the cloud, saying, "This is my Son, whom I have chosen; listen to him." [36]When the voice had spoken, they found that Jesus was alone. The disciples kept this to themselves, and told no one at that time what they had seen.

The Healing of a Boy With an Evil Spirit

[37]The next day, when they came down from the mountain, a large crowd met him. [38]A man in the crowd called out, "Teacher, I beg you to look at my son, for he is my only child. [39]A spirit seizes him and he suddenly screams; it throws him into convulsions so that he foams at the mouth. It scarcely ever leaves him and is destroying him. [40]I begged your disciples to drive it out, but they could not."

[41]"O unbelieving and perverse generation," Jesus replied, "how long shall I stay with you and put up with you? Bring your son here."

[42]Even while the boy was coming, the demon threw him to the ground in a convulsion. But Jesus rebuked the evil[k] spirit, healed the boy and gave him back to his father. [43]And they were all amazed at the greatness of God.

While everyone was marveling at all that Jesus did, he said to his disciples, [44]"Listen carefully to what I am about to tell you: The Son of Man is going to be betrayed into the hands of men." [45]But they did not understand what this meant. It was hidden from them, so that they did not grasp it, and they were afraid to ask him about it.

---

[k]42 Greek *unclean*

Who Will Be the Greatest?

[46]An argument started among the disciples as to which of them would be the greatest. [47]Jesus, knowing their thoughts, took a little child and had him stand beside him. [48]Then he said to them, "Whoever welcomes this little child in my name welcomes me; and whoever welcomes me welcomes the one who sent me. For he who is least among you all—he is the greatest."

[49]"Master," said John, "we saw a man driving out demons in your name and we tried to stop him, because he is not one of us."

[50]"Do not stop him," Jesus said, "for whoever is not against you is for you."

Samaritan Opposition

[51]As the time approached for him to be taken up to heaven, Jesus resolutely set out for Jerusalem. [52]And he sent messengers on ahead, who went into a Samaritan village to get things ready for him; [53]but the people there did not welcome him, because he was heading for Jerusalem. [54]When the disciples James and John saw this, they asked, "Lord, do you want us to call fire down from heaven to destroy them[l]?" [55]But Jesus turned and rebuked them, [56]and[m] they went to another village.

The Cost of Following Jesus

[57]As they were walking along the road, a man said to him, "I will follow you wherever you go."

[58]Jesus replied, "Foxes have holes and birds of the air have nests, but the Son of Man has no place to lay his head."

[59]He said to another man, "Follow me."

But the man replied, "Lord, first let me go and bury my father."

[60]Jesus said to him, "Let the dead bury their own dead, but you go and proclaim the kingdom of God."

[61]Still another said, "I will follow you, Lord; but first let me go back and say good-by to my family."

[62]Jesus replied, "No one who puts his hand to the plow and looks back is fit for service in the kingdom of God."

Jesus Sends Out the Seventy-two

10 After this the Lord appointed seventy-two[n] others and sent them two by two ahead of him to every town and place where he was about to go. [2]He told them, "The harvest is plentiful, but the workers are few. Ask the Lord of the harvest, therefore, to send out workers into his harvest field. [3]Go! I am sending you out like lambs among wolves. [4]Do not take a purse or bag or sandals; and do not greet anyone on the road.

[5]"When you enter a house, first say, 'Peace to this house.' [6]If a man of peace is there, your peace will rest on him; if not, it will return to you. [7]Stay in that house, eating and drinking

---

[l]54 Some manuscripts *them, even as Elijah did*   [m]55,56 Some manuscripts *them. And he said, "You do not know what kind of spirit you are of, for the Son of Man did not come to destroy men's lives, but to save them." 56And*   [n]1 Some manuscripts *seventy*; also in verse 17

OPEN: 1. Ever been "the greatest" at anything, with your kids or among your peers? **2.** Will Rogers had no enemies, only "friends he hadn't met." How about you?

DIG: 1. In chapter 9, how are the disciples gauging "greatness"? How does Jesus do so? **2.** In John's concern (v.49), what's the root desire? The irony (see v.40)? **3.** How does Jesus' "timetable" meet further resistance (vv.51-56)? Why from the Samaritans? Why from his own disciples? How must Jesus be feeling by now?

REFLECT: 1. How did you picture "greatness" as a kid? As an adult? **2.** What impresses you about Jesus in these two stories? How has prejudice blinded you to God's work at times? How have resolute priorities kept you on track?

OPEN: What's your favorite excuse for not doing something (e.g., "dog ate my homework")?

DIG: How does Jesus respond to the excuses offered by these prospective followers? In your own words, what do each of Jesus' sayings mean? What's his point?

REFLECT: If Jesus were to say to you "Follow me—*today*," and you were to use one of your favorite excuses for putting things off, what would happen?

OPEN: 1. If you had to sell something "door to door," what would you choose: Fuller brushes? Encyclopedias? Jewelry? Magazine subscriptions? Serendipity Bibles? Why? **2.** What territory or city would you choose: New York City high-rises? Deep South? Appalachian mountains? California beach resorts?

DIG: 1. Why does he send the disciples out two-by-two? Why does he send them ahead of him? **2.** How is the Christian disciple like a "worker in the harvest"? A "lamb among wolves"? **3.** What was the purpose of traveling light (v.4)? Of praying first, going later? **4.** What kind of household guests are they to be (v.5)? Why? **5.** How are they related to the town of which they are a part (vv.8-12)? What is their basic message? **6.** How do verses 1-12 show the urgency Jesus himself senses for evangelism? What is the reason for this urgency? **7.** What do you know about Sodom (see Ge 19:24-28)? Korazin and Bethsaida? About Capernaum (see Mt 4:13)? Why are they worse off than Tyre and Sidon? **8.** What is the comfort and the danger of aligning oneself with Jesus (v.16)? **9.** Upon their return, what does Jesus say to them (vv.18-20)? What in their report gives Jesus reason for joy (v.21)? **10.** What does he mean by his blessing in verse 23?

REFLECT: 1. How do you feel about the harvest where you live? Are people ripe for the gospel? What would it take for you to be more involved in the harvest? **2.** When have you felt like a lamb among wolves? What did you learn from that experience? **3.** What do these verses show you about the privileges you have in Jesus Christ? Of these privileges, which are you experiencing now? **4.** How does a sense of being blessed by knowing Jesus (v.23) influence your response to God?

OPEN: What part of your city (or campus, or neighborhood) is considered unsafe to walk alone at night? Why? Would you provide escort service or help a distressed person in this area? Why or why not?

DIG: 1. Who's testing whom in this story? **2.** Does the lawyer seem to think he has passed the test in verse 28? How so? **3.** Why does Jesus answer with a story instead of a straight answer? **4.** How might one justify the actions of the priest and the Levite (see Lev 21:1-3; Nu 19:11-22)? **5.** Given the divisions between Jews

whatever they give you, for the worker deserves his wages. Do not move around from house to house.

8"When you enter a town and are welcomed, eat what is set before you. 9Heal the sick who are there and tell them, 'The kingdom of God is near you.' 10But when you enter a town and are not welcomed, go into its streets and say, 11'Even the dust of your town that sticks to our feet we wipe off against you. Yet be sure of this: The kingdom of God is near.' 12I tell you, it will be more bearable on that day for Sodom than for that town.

13"Woe to you, Korazin! Woe to you, Bethsaida! For if the miracles that were performed in you had been performed in Tyre and Sidon, they would have repented long ago, sitting in sackcloth and ashes. 14But it will be more bearable for Tyre and Sidon at the judgment than for you. 15And you, Capernaum, will you be lifted up to the skies? No, you will go down to the depths. °

16"He who listens to you listens to me; he who rejects you rejects me; but he who rejects me rejects him who sent me."

17The seventy-two returned with joy and said, "Lord, even the demons submit to us in your name."

18He replied, "I saw Satan fall like lightning from heaven. 19I have given you authority to trample on snakes and scorpions and to overcome all the power of the enemy; nothing will harm you. 20However, do not rejoice that the spirits submit to you, but rejoice that your names are written in heaven."

21At that time Jesus, full of joy through the Holy Spirit, said, "I praise you, Father, Lord of heaven and earth, because you have hidden these things from the wise and learned, and revealed them to little children. Yes, Father, for this was your good pleasure.

22"All things have been committed to me by my Father. No one knows who the Son is except the Father, and no one knows who the Father is except the Son and those to whom the Son chooses to reveal him."

23Then he turned to his disciples and said privately, "Blessed are the eyes that see what you see. 24For I tell you that many prophets and kings wanted to see what you see but did not see it, and to hear what you hear but did not hear it."

The Parable of the Good Samaritan

25On one occasion an expert in the law stood up to test Jesus. "Teacher," he asked, "what must I do to inherit eternal life?"

26"What is written in the Law?" he replied. "How do you read it?"

27He answered: " 'Love the Lord your God with all your heart and with all your soul and with all your strength and with all your mind'ᵖ; and, 'Love your neighbor as yourself.'ᵠ"

28"You have answered correctly," Jesus replied. "Do this and you will live."

29But he wanted to justify himself, so he asked Jesus, "And who is my neighbor?"

º15 Greek Hades   ᵖ27 Deut. 6:5   ᵠ27 Lev. 19:18

LOOKING INTO THE SCRIPTURE/20 Minutes. Read Luke 10:25-37 and discuss.

1. Do you think Jesus knew about the Samaritans—that they were social outcasts because they had intermarried with the wrong people? □ Yes □ No

2. Do you think Jesus knew about the road from Jerusalem to Jericho—that it was the most dangerous road in Judea with robbers posing as wounded people? □ Yes □ No

3. Do you think Jesus knew about the Old Testament rule that anyone who touched a dead person was "unclean" for several days? □ Yes □ No

4. If there was a good chance that the wounded person was only "playing dead" in order to trap the priest and Levite, do you think they were justified in passing by on the other side? □ Yes □ No

5. If the priest and Levite were taking the dangerous road because they were in a rush to get to their religious duties in Jericho, do you think they could be justified in passing by the wounded man? □ Yes □ No

6. Why do you think the Samaritan stopped when the others "passed by on the other side"?
   a. he was more sensitive
   b. he didn't care about the religious problem of touching a dead corpse
   c. he knew what it meant to be a hurting person and have people pass by
   d. he didn't have much to lose

7. Why do you think Jesus told this parable in response to the lawyer's question, "Who is my neighbor?"
   a. to let the lawyer answer his own question
   b. to catch the lawyer in a moral dilemma
   c. to use a "case history" approach that lawyers use

MY OWN STORY/20 Minutes.

1. What do you do when people come up to you on a street corner asking for a handout?
   a. ignore them
   b. take a look at what they are wearing
   c. give them money without any questions
   d. get to know their situations and then decide
   e. assume I'm being conned
   f. find some excuse not to give
   g. offer to take them to the grocery store and buy what they need
   h. share the gospel with them and pray for them
   i. take them to your pastor who is better equipped to handle the problem
   j. report them to the police

2. Now that you've read this parable, who would you say is your "neighbor"?
   a. someone like me with a need
   b. anyone who approaches me with a need
   c. only reputable charitable organizations
   d. those I have reasonable hope of helping
   e. the ones I'm most afraid of helping

3. If you had to call upon someone outside of your family at 3 o'clock in the morning because of a deep personal problem, on whom would you call?
   a. my pastor/priest
   b. professional counselor
   c. my friend _____
   d. someone who had the same problem
   e. someone who had conquered this problem
   f. someone who didn't know me

and Samaritans (see Jn 4), what's unusual about the plot twist in this story? What is Jesus' point here?

REFLECT: 1. With whom do you identify most in this story? Why? 2. Who have been Good Samaritans in your life? What makes a Good Samaritan really *good* ? 3. To whom will you be a Good Samaritan this week?

OPEN: What is one trait that all your family members share?

DIG: How do these two sisters differ? Why is Mary's choice better? What is Jesus' point?

REFLECT: In your opinion, what are the good points and the blind spots of both Mary and Martha? Who are you most like?

OPEN: 1. As a child, did you have a standard prayer that you recited? If so, how much can you remember? 2. What's the funniest prayer you've heard a child say?

DIG: 1. What motivates the disciples to ask about prayer at this point (v.1)? 2. In Jesus' model prayer (vv.2-4), what two concerns related to God come first? Why? What personal concerns then follow? How do prayer and forgiveness relate? 3. What does the parable in verses 5-8 teach about prayer? How do verses 9-10 relate to the parable? How could verses 9-10 be misunderstood or misapplied? How do verses 11-13 clarify the intent of verses 9-10? 4. What does this teach you about God's kingdom? About God's goodness?

---

[30]In reply Jesus said: "A man was going down from Jerusalem to Jericho, when he fell into the hands of robbers. They stripped him of his clothes, beat him and went away, leaving him half dead. [31]A priest happened to be going down the same road, and when he saw the man, he passed by on the other side. [32]So too, a Levite, when he came to the place and saw him, passed by on the other side. [33]But a Samaritan, as he traveled, came where the man was; and when he saw him, he took pity on him. [34]He went to him and bandaged his wounds, pouring on oil and wine. Then he put the man on his own donkey, took him to an inn and took care of him. [35]The next day he took out two silver coins[r] and gave them to the innkeeper. 'Look after him,' he said, 'and when I return, I will reimburse you for any extra expense you may have.'

[36]"Which of these three do you think was a neighbor to the man who fell into the hands of robbers?"

[37]The expert in the law replied, "The one who had mercy on him."

Jesus told him, "Go and do likewise."

At the Home of Martha and Mary

[38]As Jesus and his disciples were on their way, he came to a village where a woman named Martha opened her home to him. [39]She had a sister called Mary, who sat at the Lord's feet listening to what he said. [40]But Martha was distracted by all the preparations that had to be made. She came to him and asked, "Lord, don't you care that my sister has left me to do the work by myself? Tell her to help me!"

[41]"Martha, Martha," the Lord answered, "you are worried and upset about many things, [42]but only one thing is needed.[s] Mary has chosen what is better, and it will not be taken away from her."

Jesus' Teaching on Prayer

11 One day Jesus was praying in a certain place. When he finished, one of his disciples said to him, "Lord, teach us to pray, just as John taught his disciples."

[2]He said to them, "When you pray, say:

" 'Father,[t]
hallowed be your name,
your kingdom come.[u]
[3]Give us each day our daily bread.
[4]Forgive us our sins,
    for we also forgive everyone who sins against us.[v]
And lead us not into temptation.[w] ' "

[5]Then he said to them, "Suppose one of you has a friend, and he goes to him at midnight and says, 'Friend, lend me three loaves of bread, [6]because a friend of mine on a journey has come to me, and I have nothing to set before him.'

---

[r]35 Greek *two denarii*　　[s]42 Some manuscripts *but few things are needed—or only one*
[t]2 Some manuscripts *Our Father in heaven*　　[u]2 Some manuscripts *come. May your will be done on earth as it is in heaven.*　　[v]4 Greek *everyone who is indebted to us*
[w]4 Some manuscripts *temptation but deliver us from the evil one*

Luke 10:38-42   **AT THE HOME OF MARTHA AND MARY**

LOOKING INTO THE STORY/20 Minutes. Read Luke 10:38-42 and discuss.

1. Why do you think Jesus went to Martha and Mary's house?
   a. they were close friends
   b. he had nowhere else to go
   c. he liked their cooking
   d. he needed their fellowship

2. What do you think Jesus meant when he said, "Mary has chosen what is better"?
   a. Martha had her priorities messed up
   b. people who let their housework go are more spiritual
   c. people are more important than a clean house
   d. fussing over little things is a sign of spiritual immaturity
   e. spiritual matters come first

3. If you had been Martha, how would you have responded to Jesus' remark?
   a. gone to my room and pouted
   b. thought to myself: "He doesn't have to live with my sister"
   c. flown off-the-handle
   d. felt put down
   e. accepted the rebuke
   f. sat down with Jesus and let the supper burn

4. Why do you think Jesus said it?
   a. Martha was picking on Mary
   b. Martha was getting on his nerves
   c. he knew her well enough to say this without hurting her
   d. he knew he had one more week and he wanted to spend the time with them

---

MY OWN STORY/25 Minutes.

1. How do you see yourself . . . somewhere between the two extremes.

ON HOUSEWORK: dirty dishes everywhere _____ slippers at the door
ON TEMPERAMENT: easygoing _____ high strung
ON TAKING RESPONSIBILITY: little sister _____ big sister
ON ORGANIZING MY LIFE: a day late and a dollar short _____ ten minutes early
ON HURT FEELINGS: let's have it out _____ sweep it under the rug

2. If you had to choose between Mary and Martha for the following situations, who would you choose?

MARY	MARTHA	
☐	☐	For a roommate
☐	☐	For a close friend
☐	☐	To work for
☐	☐	To work for you
☐	☐	To be your next-door neighbor
☐	☐	To be the executor of your estate
☐	☐	To be your pastor
☐	☐	To go to with a problem

3. If you had Mary as a sister, what would you do?
   a. try to change her
   b. move out
   c. accept her as she is
   d. learn from her spirituality
   e. accept myself as different
   f. try to change myself

4. If you were the parents of these two sisters, what would you do?
   a. try to affirm them for their uniqueness
   b. let them keep their rooms as they wish
   c. set some rules for everybody
   d. move out and leave the house to them
   e. accept them as they are
   f. help them appreciate each other's unique temperaments

5. What would Jesus likely say to you if he dropped in on your home today?
   a. turn down the music
   b. turn off the TV
   c. reorganize your time
   d. enjoy the people in your life
   e. slow down and appreciate the little things
   f. set aside time for God daily
   g. take a look at your expectations of yourself
   h. _____

REFLECT: 1. What should be the relationship between this prayer and our own? How do you usually pray? Do you have a set time? A set place? Or are you more spontaneous when you pray? **2.** What do you use to prepare for prayer: Read a psalm? A devotional guide? A hymn? **3.** What concerns occupy most of your time in prayer: Praise? Confession? Petition? Why? In which area do you want to grow? **4.** When have you felt like God was not listening? What do you do then? **5.** What one thing would you like to seek the Father for?

OPEN: 1. When you were in high school, who was the arch rival to your school in sports? Who generally won? **2.** How well did you keep your bedroom when you were growing up? Have your habits improved any with age?

DIG: 1. How does the crowd react to Jesus' miracle (vv.14-16)? **2.** How does Jesus show the foolishness of the claim that he drives out demons by Beelzebub? What does Jesus' ability to drive out demons say about the kingdom of God (v.20)? **3.** How do you reconcile verse 23 with 9:50? **4.** What is Jesus' point in verses 24-26? To whom is the point addressed? Why is the final condition worse than the first? **5.** How and why does Jesus turn around the blessing shouted to him in verse 27? What is he emphasizing here?

REFLECT: If you compared your life right now to a fortress, what is it like: (a) The Rock of Gibraltar? (b) Slowly eroding? (c) Quickly crumbling? Are you spiritually "on the attack" or feeling besieged? How's the battle going?

⁷"Then the one inside answers, 'Don't bother me. The door is already locked, and my children are with me in bed. I can't get up and give you anything.' ⁸I tell you, though he will not get up and give him the bread because he is his friend, yet because of the man's boldnessˣ he will get up and give him as much as he needs.

⁹"So I say to you: Ask and it will be given to you; seek and you will find; knock and the door will be opened to you. ¹⁰For everyone who asks receives; he who seeks finds; and to him who knocks, the door will be opened.

¹¹"Which of you fathers, if your son asks forʸ a fish, will give him a snake instead? ¹²Or if he asks for an egg, will give him a scorpion? ¹³If you then, though you are evil, know how to give good gifts to your children, how much more will your Father in heaven give the Holy Spirit to those who ask him!"

Jesus and Beelzebub

¹⁴Jesus was driving out a demon that was mute. When the demon left, the man who had been mute spoke, and the crowd was amazed. ¹⁵But some of them said, "By Beelzebub,ᶻ the prince of demons, he is driving out demons." ¹⁶Others tested him by asking for a sign from heaven.

¹⁷Jesus knew their thoughts and said to them: "Any kingdom divided against itself will be ruined, and a house divided against itself will fall. ¹⁸If Satan is divided against himself, how can his kingdom stand? I say this because you claim that I drive out demons by Beelzebub. ¹⁹Now if I drive out demons by Beelzebub, by whom do your followers drive them out? So then, they will be your judges. ²⁰But if I drive out demons by the finger of God, then the kingdom of God has come to you.

²¹"When a strong man, fully armed, guards his own house, his possessions are safe. ²²But when someone stronger attacks and overpowers him, he takes away the armor in which the man trusted and divides up the spoils.

²³"He who is not with me is against me, and he who does not gather with me, scatters.

²⁴"When an evilᵃ spirit comes out of a man, it goes through arid places seeking rest and does not find it. Then it says, 'I will return to the house I left.' ²⁵When it arrives, it finds the house swept clean and put in order. ²⁶Then it goes and takes seven other spirits more wicked than itself, and they go in and live there. And the final condition of that man is worse than the first."

²⁷As Jesus was saying these things, a woman in the crowd called out, "Blessed is the mother who gave you birth and nursed you."

²⁸He replied, "Blessed rather are those who hear the word of God and obey it."

ˣ8 Or *persistence*   ʸ11 Some manuscripts *for bread, will give him a stone; or if he asks for*
ᶻ15 Greek *Beezeboul* or *Beelzeboul*; also in verses 18 and 19   ᵃ24 Greek *unclean*

The Sign of Jonah

²⁹As the crowds increased, Jesus said, "This is a wicked generation. It asks for a miraculous sign, but none will be given it except the sign of Jonah. ³⁰For as Jonah was a sign to the Ninevites, so also will the Son of Man be to this generation. ³¹The Queen of the South will rise at the judgment with the men of this generation and condemn them; for she came from the ends of the earth to listen to Solomon's wisdom, and now one*ᵇ* greater than Solomon is here. ³²The men of Nineveh will stand up at the judgment with this generation and condemn it; for they repented at the preaching of Jonah, and now one greater than Jonah is here.

OPEN: What does the roadside sign nearest your house say? Are you sure?

DIG: 1. Why is Jesus upset about "this generation"? 2. What is the sign of Jonah? How is Jesus like that? 3. Who is this Queen (1Ki 10:1-15)? Who condemns whom? 4. What is Jesus' point here?

REFLECT: What "sign" would it take for your generation to turn to God? What's the problem with relying on "signs" to do the trick?

The Lamp of the Body

³³"No one lights a lamp and puts it in a place where it will be hidden, or under a bowl. Instead he puts it on its stand, so that those who come in may see the light. ³⁴Your eye is the lamp of your body. When your eyes are good, your whole body also is full of light. But when they are bad, your body also is full of darkness. ³⁵See to it, then, that the light within you is not darkness. ³⁶Therefore, if your whole body is full of light, and no part of it dark, it will be completely lighted, as when the light of a lamp shines on you."

OPEN: How many flashlights do you own? How many work?

DIG: What is Jesus' point in this analogy (v.34)? What do the eye and body represent? How is spiritual truth perceived?

REFLECT: How would you score on a spiritual sight exam: 20/20? 20/80? Color-blind? Why?

Six Woes

³⁷When Jesus had finished speaking, a Pharisee invited him to eat with him; so he went in and reclined at the table. ³⁸But the Pharisee, noticing that Jesus did not first wash before the meal, was surprised.

³⁹Then the Lord said to him, "Now then, you Pharisees clean the outside of the cup and dish, but inside you are full of greed and wickedness. ⁴⁰You foolish people! Did not the one who made the outside make the inside also? ⁴¹But give what is inside the dish*ᶜ* to the poor, and everything will be clean for you.

⁴²"Woe to you Pharisees, because you give God a tenth of your mint, rue and all other kinds of garden herbs, but you neglect justice and the love of God. You should have practiced the latter without leaving the former undone.

⁴³"Woe to you Pharisees, because you love the most important seats in the synagogues and greetings in the marketplaces.

⁴⁴"Woe to you, because you are like unmarked graves, which men walk over without knowing it."

⁴⁵One of the experts in the law answered him, "Teacher, when you say these things, you insult us also."

⁴⁶Jesus replied, "And you experts in the law, woe to you, because you load people down with burdens they can hardly carry, and you yourselves will not lift one finger to help them.

⁴⁷"Woe to you, because you build tombs for the prophets, and it was your forefathers who killed them. ⁴⁸So you testify that you approve of what your forefathers did; they killed the prophets, and you build their tombs. ⁴⁹Because of this, God in his wisdom

OPEN: When you were a child, who insisted that you "wash up" before meals? Who insisted that you wear "clean" clothes? How did you react to this fussing?

DIG: 1. What is the natural and the surprising thing Jesus does to open this scene? 2. How does the Lord turn the tables on his host? What is his basic point about the Pharisees (vv.39-41)? 3. In your own words, what is the meaning of these three woes directed at the Pharisees (vv.42-44)? Given the Pharisees' view of tombs and the dead (see Nu 19:16), what is the significance of the unmarked graves (v.44)? 4. What is the point of these criticisms? 5. In your own words, what is the meaning of the next three woes (vv.46-52)? In the sixth woe (v.52), what does Jesus mean by the key of knowledge? 6. What is the main point of these accusations directed at lawyers? 7. How does this Pharisee dinner compare with the first dinner in 7:36-50? Why the difference?

REFLECT: 1. Typically, Jesus is thought of as "meek and mild." What is the significance of this passage's presentation of Jesus for you? 2. Of the three woes

---

ᵇ31 Or something; also in verse 32   *ᶜ41 Or what you have* directed to the Pharisees, which one is Jesus directing most to you? Why? **3.** Of the three woes directed to the lawyers, which one has your name on it? Why? **4.** How would you like your life to change in light of what you've read here? What specifically would you like to see happen this week?

OPEN: As a kid, who was the disciplinarian at home? If discovered, what secret sin was "unpardonable": Drinking? Smoking? Lying? Playing hooky? Out too late? Tinkling on the toilet seat?

DIG: 1. Why does this crowd grow? **2.** What warnings (vv.1-3) does Jesus issue the disciples? **3.** How does hypocrisy work like yeast (see 11:37-54)? **4.** Why does Jesus encourage his disciples to fear, yet be fearless (vv.4-7)? **5.** What does it mean to "blaspheme against the Holy Spirit" (v.10)? How is the contrite person assured of not having done this? **6.** What does Jesus teach about the believer's security in: (a) Facing human opposition? (b) Facing God's judgment?

REFLECT: 1. How do you feel knowing that everything done in secret will someday be revealed? **2.** When have you felt like you took a real risk and stood for Jesus in a public way? What did you learn from that?

OPEN: What did you like to collect as a kid? Now? What collection were (are) you most proud of?

DIG: 1. In response to the man's plea, Jesus tells a parable. What is the man's problem? His solution? Why is he a fool? **2.** In your own words, what is the punch line of this parable?

REFLECT: 1. When have you been like the man in this story? **2.** Advertising is dedicated to making us think verse 15 is wrong. What differences in lifestyle result

said, 'I will send them prophets and apostles, some of whom they will kill and others they will persecute.' ⁵⁰Therefore this generation will be held responsible for the blood of all the prophets that has been shed since the beginning of the world, ⁵¹from the blood of Abel to the blood of Zechariah, who was killed between the altar and the sanctuary. Yes, I tell you, this generation will be held responsible for it all.

⁵²"Woe to you experts in the law, because you have taken away the key to knowledge. You yourselves have not entered, and you have hindered those who were entering."

⁵³When Jesus left there, the Pharisees and the teachers of the law began to oppose him fiercely and to besiege him with questions, ⁵⁴waiting to catch him in something he might say.

Warnings and Encouragements

12 Meanwhile, when a crowd of many thousands had gathered, so that they were trampling on one another, Jesus began to speak first to his disciples, saying: "Be on your guard against the yeast of the Pharisees, which is hypocrisy. ²There is nothing concealed that will not be disclosed, or hidden that will not be made known. ³What you have said in the dark will be heard in the daylight, and what you have whispered in the ear in the inner rooms will be proclaimed from the roofs.

⁴"I tell you, my friends, do not be afraid of those who kill the body and after that can do no more. ⁵But I will show you whom you should fear: Fear him who, after the killing of the body, has power to throw you into hell. Yes, I tell you, fear him. ⁶Are not five sparrows sold for two pennies^d? Yet not one of them is forgotten by God. ⁷Indeed, the very hairs of your head are all numbered. Don't be afraid; you are worth more than many sparrows.

⁸"I tell you, whoever acknowledges me before men, the Son of Man will also acknowledge him before the angels of God. ⁹But he who disowns me before men will be disowned before the angels of God. ¹⁰And everyone who speaks a word against the Son of Man will be forgiven, but anyone who blasphemes against the Holy Spirit will not be forgiven.

¹¹"When you are brought before synagogues, rulers and authorities, do not worry about how you will defend yourselves or what you will say, ¹²for the Holy Spirit will teach you at that time what you should say."

The Parable of the Rich Fool

¹³Someone in the crowd said to him, "Teacher, tell my brother to divide the inheritance with me."

¹⁴Jesus replied, "Man, who appointed me a judge or an arbiter between you?" ¹⁵Then he said to them, "Watch out! Be on your guard against all kinds of greed; a man's life does not consist in the abundance of his possessions."

¹⁶And he told them this parable: "The ground of a certain rich man produced a good crop. ¹⁷He thought to himself, 'What shall I do? I have no place to store my crops.'

---

^d6 Greek *two assaria*

LOOKING INTO THE SCRIPTURE/15 Minutes. Read Luke 12:13-21 and discuss.

1. In verse 13, what was the man in the crowd really saying to Jesus?
   a. my brother is treating me poorly
   b. I want my share of the action
   c. would you straighten out this mess?
   d. my brother is greedy
   e. what does the Jewish law say about inheritance?

2. In his reply, what was Jesus telling the crowd?
   a. greed will get you into trouble
   b. I am not a judge or an arbiter
   c. money, wealth, and material goods are not important
   d. concern for money and wealth can easily get out of control

3. In the parable, what is Jesus saying about wealth and the pursuit of wealth?
   a. wealth can make us greedy
   b. wealth will make us better people
   c. wealth can be used to further the kingdom of God
   d. wealth can make us self-indulgent

4. Why is God's response to the rich man so harsh?
   a. because God is intolerant of self-indulgent people
   b. because God has so much compassion for the poor
   c. because God wanted him to use his resources more wisely
   d. because God is jealous of other "gods" such as wealth

5. What does it mean to be "rich toward God"?
   a. seek first the kingdom of God
   b. give most of your money to the poor
   c. use your abilities and resources to further God's kingdom
   d. invest in church lotteries

6. If Jesus commented on our view of wealth today, what do you think he would say?
   a. "Lifestyles of the Rich and Famous" is not the way to go
   b. you are grabbing for it all but missing the true meaning of life
   c. it is difficult to see the difference between Christian values and secular values today
   d. you have so much but you are spiritually bankrupt

MY OWN STORY/30 Minutes.

1. Where are your riches? (Name two)
   a. in my children
   b. in my friends
   c. in my bank account
   d. in my education
   e. in my job advancement
   f. in a good self-image
   g. in a strong body
   h. in some beautiful memories
   i. in my family

2. What are three priorities for your life right now?
   a. a good time
   b. a good marriage/family
   c. having nice things
   d. getting ahead
   e. being true to myself
   f. finding spiritual fulfillment
   g. making a contribution to mankind
   h. making lots of money

3. How would you like to be remembered?
   a. as the one who had a lot
   b. as the one who gave a lot
   c. as the one who built it all single-handedly
   d. as the one who enjoyed what he/she had
   e. as the one who lost it all to be rich toward God

4. Where would you like to leave your riches?
   a. to my family
   b. to a charitable cause that I believe in
   c. to build a memorial at my church
   d. to my college/school
   e. to overseas missions
   f. to the government

from believing Jesus versus the advertisements? **3.** In planning an investment portfolio to become "rich toward God," what will you do this week? This year?

OPEN: Which situation is most worrisome to you: Overdrawn at the bank? Gained 10 pounds? Child expelled? Nobody called all weekend? Mother-in-law stays two weeks? Business folds?

DIG: 1. How does this section relate to the preceding parable about riches? **2.** What does Jesus tell the disciples *not* to do? Why? What does Jesus urge them to do instead? Why? What will result? **3.** What does Jesus teach here about seeking the kingdom?

REFLECT: 1. On a scale from 1 to 10 (1= "no sweat" and 10= "panic"), what is the worry quotient in your life right now? Why? **2.** How can you transfer your "treasure" from "Wall Street" to "Heaven's Gate"? **3.** Who is more severe: The man in verses 16-19, or the kingdom-seeking disciples in verse 33? Why? Which example best describes you now?

OPEN: 1. In high school, what caused you to be "grounded": Missing curfew? Bad report card? Throwing a party when the folks were away? **2.** Are you a night owl or an early bird? Ever fall asleep at the wheel? On a date? On duty?

DIG: 1. What is the relationship between the watchfulness of this passage and the worry of verses 22-34? What are the major concerns of these passages? **2.** Why does Peter ask the question in verse 41? Why does Jesus answer as he does? **3.** Why does Jesus say they should be ready (vv.39-40)? Who is the thief? **4.** What should be the attitude and

---

[18]"Then he said, 'This is what I'll do. I will tear down my barns and build bigger ones, and there I will store all my grain and my goods. [19]And I'll say to myself, "You have plenty of good things laid up for many years. Take life easy; eat, drink and be merry." '

[20]"But God said to him, 'You fool! This very night your life will be demanded from you. Then who will get what you have prepared for yourself?'

[21]"This is how it will be with anyone who stores up things for himself but is not rich toward God."

Do Not Worry

[22]Then Jesus said to his disciples: "Therefore I tell you, do not worry about your life, what you will eat; or about your body, what you will wear. [23]Life is more than food, and the body more than clothes. [24]Consider the ravens: They do not sow or reap, they have no storeroom or barn; yet God feeds them. And how much more valuable you are than birds! [25]Who of you by worrying can add a single hour to his life[e]? [26]Since you cannot do this very little thing, why do you worry about the rest?

[27]"Consider how the lilies grow. They do not labor or spin. Yet I tell you, not even Solomon in all his splendor was dressed like one of these. [28]If that is how God clothes the grass of the field, which is here today, and tomorrow is thrown into the fire, how much more will he clothe you, O you of little faith! [29]And do not set your heart on what you will eat or drink; do not worry about it. [30]For the pagan world runs after all such things, and your Father knows that you need them. [31]But seek his kingdom, and these things will be given to you as well.

[32]"Do not be afraid, little flock, for your Father has been pleased to give you the kingdom. [33]Sell your possessions and give to the poor. Provide purses for yourselves that will not wear out, a treasure in heaven that will not be exhausted, where no thief comes near and no moth destroys. [34]For where your treasure is, there your heart will be also.

Watchfulness

[35]"Be dressed ready for service and keep your lamps burning, [36]like men waiting for their master to return from a wedding banquet, so that when he comes and knocks they can immediately open the door for him. [37]It will be good for those servants whose master finds them watching when he comes. I tell you the truth, he will dress himself to serve, will have them recline at the table and will come and wait on them. [38]It will be good for those servants whose master finds them ready, even if he comes in the second or third watch of the night. [39]But understand this: If the owner of the house had known at what hour the thief was coming, he would not have let his house be broken into. [40]You also must be ready, because the Son of Man will come at an hour when you do not expect him."

---

[e]25 Or *single cubit to his height*

41Peter asked, "Lord, are you telling this parable to us, or to everyone?"

42The Lord answered, "Who then is the faithful and wise manager, whom the master puts in charge of his servants to give them their food allowance at the proper time? 43It will be good for that servant whom the master finds doing so when he returns. 44I tell you the truth, he will put him in charge of all his possessions. 45But suppose the servant says to himself, 'My master is taking a long time in coming,' and he then begins to beat the menservants and maidservants and to eat and drink and get drunk. 46The master of that servant will come on a day when he does not expect him and at an hour he is not aware of. He will cut him to pieces and assign him a place with the unbelievers.

47"That servant who knows his master's will and does not get ready or does not do what his master wants will be beaten with many blows. 48But the one who does not know and does things deserving punishment will be beaten with few blows. From everyone who has been given much, much will be demanded; and from the one who has been entrusted with much, much more will be asked.

Not Peace but Division

49"I have come to bring fire on the earth, and how I wish it were already kindled! 50But I have a baptism to undergo, and how distressed I am until it is completed! 51Do you think I came to bring peace on earth? No, I tell you, but division. 52From now on there will be five in one family divided against each other, three against two and two against three. 53They will be divided, father against son and son against father, mother against daughter and daughter against mother, mother-in-law against daughter-in-law and daughter-in-law against mother-in-law."

Interpreting the Times

54He said to the crowd: "When you see a cloud rising in the west, immediately you say, 'It's going to rain,' and it does. 55And when the south wind blows, you say, 'It's going to be hot,' and it is. 56Hypocrites! You know how to interpret the appearance of the earth and the sky. How is it that you don't know how to interpret this present time?

57"Why don't you judge for yourselves what is right? 58As you are going with your adversary to the magistrate, try hard to be reconciled to him on the way, or he may drag you off to the judge, and the judge turn you over to the officer, and the officer throw you into prison. 59I tell you, you will not get out until you have paid the last penny.*"

actions of the faithful and wise manager (vv.42-43)? What could tempt the manager to do wrong (v.45)? **5.** How does Jesus summarize this passage (v.48)? How would the disciples have interpreted it?

REFLECT: 1. What dangers is Jesus warning you about in this section? Which danger is most likely to be a problem for you? **2.** What has God entrusted to you as his manager? If you knew that in 30 days' time Jesus was returning, what would you do to get things ready for inspection?

OPEN: What divisive subjects are no longer fit for discussion at your family table or at family reunions?

DIG: 1. Of what "fire" is Jesus speaking? What "baptism"? What division? How and why does Jesus bring division? How does this relate to 12:31-34? How do you reconcile this with the fact that Jesus brings peace? **2.** From verses 49-53, how has the crowd "misread" Jesus? In what way are they hypocrites? What does the warning (vv.57-59) mean?

REFLECT: 1. What has Christ brought to your family and friends: division or peace? Why? **2.** How can you tell if it is your faith that strains a relationship, or the way you express that faith? **3.** What signs in your own life indicate how you're doing? Using a weather map to describe your spiritual life, what does it forecast?

59 Greek lepton

Repent or Perish

13 Now there were some present at that time who told Jesus about the Galileans whose blood Pilate had mixed with their sacrifices. ²Jesus answered, "Do you think that these Galileans were worse sinners than all the other Galileans because they suffered this way? ³I tell you, no! But unless you repent, you too will all perish. ⁴Or those eighteen who died when the tower in Siloam fell on them—do you think they were more guilty than all the others living in Jerusalem? ⁵I tell you, no! But unless you repent, you too will all perish."

⁶Then he told this parable: "A man had a fig tree, planted in his vineyard, and he went to look for fruit on it, but did not find any. ⁷So he said to the man who took care of the vineyard, 'For three years now I've been coming to look for fruit on this fig tree and haven't found any. Cut it down! Why should it use up the soil?'

⁸" 'Sir,' the man replied, 'leave it alone for one more year, and I'll dig around it and fertilize it. ⁹If it bears fruit next year, fine! If not, then cut it down.' "

A Crippled Woman Healed on the Sabbath

¹⁰On a Sabbath Jesus was teaching in one of the synagogues, ¹¹and a woman was there who had been crippled by a spirit for eighteen years. She was bent over and could not straighten up at all. ¹²When Jesus saw her, he called her forward and said to her, "Woman, you are set free from your infirmity." ¹³Then he put his hands on her, and immediately she straightened up and praised God.

¹⁴Indignant because Jesus had healed on the Sabbath, the synagogue ruler said to the people, "There are six days for work. So come and be healed on those days, not on the Sabbath."

¹⁵The Lord answered him, "You hypocrites! Doesn't each of you on the Sabbath untie his ox or donkey from the stall and lead it out to give it water? ¹⁶Then should not this woman, a daughter of Abraham, whom Satan has kept bound for eighteen long years, be set free on the Sabbath day from what bound her?"

¹⁷When he said this, all his opponents were humiliated, but the people were delighted with all the wonderful things he was doing.

The Parables of the Mustard Seed and the Yeast

¹⁸Then Jesus asked, "What is the kingdom of God like? What shall I compare it to? ¹⁹It is like a mustard seed, which a man took and planted in his garden. It grew and became a tree, and the birds of the air perched in its branches."

²⁰Again he asked, "What shall I compare the kingdom of God to? ²¹It is like yeast that a woman took and mixed into a large amount⁸ of flour until it worked all through the dough."

---

⁸21 Greek *three satas* (probably about 1/2 bushel or 22 liters)

The Narrow Door

²²Then Jesus went through the towns and villages, teaching as he made his way to Jerusalem. ²³Someone asked him, "Lord, are only a few people going to be saved?"

He said to them, ²⁴"Make every effort to enter through the narrow door, because many, I tell you, will try to enter and will not be able to. ²⁵Once the owner of the house gets up and closes the door, you will stand outside knocking and pleading, 'Sir, open the door for us.'

"But he will answer, 'I don't know you or where you come from.'

²⁶"Then you will say, 'We ate and drank with you, and you taught in our streets.'

²⁷"But he will reply, 'I don't know you or where you come from. Away from me, all you evildoers!'

²⁸"There will be weeping there, and gnashing of teeth, when you see Abraham, Isaac and Jacob and all the prophets in the kingdom of God, but you yourselves thrown out. ²⁹People will come from east and west and north and south, and will take their places at the feast in the kingdom of God. ³⁰Indeed there are those who are last who will be first, and first who will be last."

Jesus' Sorrow for Jerusalem

³¹At that time some Pharisees came to Jesus and said to him, "Leave this place and go somewhere else. Herod wants to kill you."

³²He replied, "Go tell that fox, 'I will drive out demons and heal people today and tomorrow, and on the third day I will reach my goal.' ³³In any case, I must keep going today and tomorrow and the next day—for surely no prophet can die outside Jerusalem!

³⁴"O Jerusalem, Jerusalem, you who kill the prophets and stone those sent to you, how often I have longed to gather your children together, as a hen gathers her chicks under her wings, but you were not willing! ³⁵Look, your house is left to you desolate. I tell you, you will not see me again until you say, 'Blessed is he who comes in the name of the Lord.' ʰ"

Jesus at a Pharisee's House

14 One Sabbath, when Jesus went to eat in the house of a prominent Pharisee, he was being carefully watched. ²There in front of him was a man suffering from dropsy. ³Jesus asked the Pharisees and experts in the law, "Is it lawful to heal on the Sabbath or not?" ⁴But they remained silent. So taking hold of the man, he healed him and sent him away.

⁵Then he asked them, "If one of you has a sonⁱ or an ox that falls into a well on the Sabbath day, will you not immediately pull him out?" ⁶And they had nothing to say.

⁷When he noticed how the guests picked the places of honor at the table, he told them this parable: ⁸"When someone invites you to a wedding feast, do not take the place of honor, for a

OPEN: What happened the last time you were locked out of your house or car? How did you get in?

DIG: 1. According to Jesus, who will make it through the narrow door and who won't? **2.** If God wants all kinds of people (v.29) to know him, why isn't the door wider? In the context of Luke, who are the ones outside (11:23, 37-53; 12:9,21,45-46; 13:3)? Why isn't eating and drinking with Jesus enough? **3.** In the end, do you think only "a few" or "many" or "all" people will be saved? Why?

REFLECT: How do you know whether you are "inside" or "outside" the kingdom? How would you get "in" (see 11:9; 12:31-32)?

OPEN: What place do you identify with your spiritual roots?

DIG: 1. What does Jesus reveal here (vv.32-33) about his intentions? What does his response reveal about him? **2.** What strikes you about Jesus' prophecy?

REFLECT: What concerns you about the spiritual condition of your nation? Your church? You? What would it mean for each to gather under Jesus' wings?

OPEN: If you could have the best seats in the house, what would you choose: Super Bowl? A rock concert? Philharmonic orchestra? Indy 500? Royal wedding?

DIG: 1. What's the situation here: The day? Host? Atmosphere? Do you suppose the man with dropsy was planted there to trap Jesus? **2.** What does Jesus do to heal the man and to trap the Pharisees (vv.3-5)? What does their silence mean? **3.** Why do the guests' actions (v.7) attract Jesus' attention? How do you imagine this scene? How does Jesus' view of honor vary from that held by others at the meal? **4.** What does this

ʰ35 Psalm 118:26   ⁱ5 Some manuscripts *donkey*

teach you about kingdom values vs. social values and their application at the final banquet? At your next party?

REFLECT: 1. How do things like customs and status get in the way of loving others in your family? Church? Work place? Community? 2. If you threw a party for the "poor," "crippled," "lame," and "blind" in your world, who would you invite? How might you do this?

OPEN: What was one of your best birthday parties? How so?

DIG: 1. Do you think that the man in verse 15 understood Jesus' teaching and blessing in the previous passage? Why or why not? 2. In this parable, who are the invited guests? Why don't they come? What happens to them? Who eventually comes? 3. On what basis is one invited? How might Jesus' servant fulfil the command of verse 23? What does this parable teach about the kingdom?

REFLECT: From your experience, why do so many say "No" to God's "banquet"? What can you say or do to help people overcome their hesitation?

OPEN: If you were on a TV game show, would you try for the $50,000 grand prize, even though you might lose the $25,000 you had won so far? Why?

DIG: 1. What does Jesus say to the crowds about family? In this context, what does he mean by "hate"? By carrying a cross? 2. How do each of the three parables here relate to the necessity of giving our primary love and loyalty to Jesus? 3. What does the salt analogy emphasize about discipleship? 4. In summary, what

person more distinguished than you may have been invited. ⁹If so, the host who invited both of you will come and say to you, 'Give this man your seat.' Then, humiliated, you will have to take the least important place. ¹⁰But when you are invited, take the lowest place, so that when your host comes, he will say to you, 'Friend, move up to a better place.' Then you will be honored in the presence of all your fellow guests. ¹¹For everyone who exalts himself will be humbled, and he who humbles himself will be exalted."

¹²Then Jesus said to his host, "When you give a luncheon or dinner, do not invite your friends, your brothers or relatives, or your rich neighbors; if you do, they may invite you back and so you will be repaid. ¹³But when you give a banquet, invite the poor, the crippled, the lame, the blind, ¹⁴and you will be blessed. Although they cannot repay you, you will be repaid at the resurrection of the righteous."

The Parable of the Great Banquet

¹⁵When one of those at the table with him heard this, he said to Jesus, "Blessed is the man who will eat at the feast in the kingdom of God."

¹⁶Jesus replied: "A certain man was preparing a great banquet and invited many guests. ¹⁷At the time of the banquet he sent his servant to tell those who had been invited, 'Come, for everything is now ready.'

¹⁸"But they all alike began to make excuses. The first said, 'I have just bought a field, and I must go and see it. Please excuse me.'

¹⁹"Another said, 'I have just bought five yoke of oxen, and I'm on my way to try them out. Please excuse me.'

²⁰"Still another said, 'I just got married, so I can't come.'

²¹"The servant came back and reported this to his master. Then the owner of the house became angry and ordered his servant, 'Go out quickly into the streets and alleys of the town and bring in the poor, the crippled, the blind and the lame.'

²²" 'Sir,' the servant said, 'what you ordered has been done, but there is still room.'

²³"Then the master told his servant, 'Go out to the roads and country lanes and make them come in, so that my house will be full. ²⁴I tell you, not one of those men who were invited will get a taste of my banquet.' "

The Cost of Being a Disciple

²⁵Large crowds were traveling with Jesus, and turning to them he said: ²⁶"If anyone comes to me and does not hate his father and mother, his wife and children, his brothers and sisters—yes, even his own life—he cannot be my disciple. ²⁷And anyone who does not carry his cross and follow me cannot be my disciple.

²⁸"Suppose one of you wants to build a tower. Will he not first sit down and estimate the cost to see if he has enough money to complete it? ²⁹For if he lays the foundation and is not able to finish it, everyone who sees it will ridicule him, ³⁰saying, 'This fellow began to build and was not able to finish.'

LOOKING INTO THE SCRIPTURE/20 Minutes. Read Luke 14:15-24 and discuss.

1. How do you feel when someone declines your invitation to dinner?
   a. no problem
   b. hurt feelings
   c. wonder what the real reason is
   d. resentment for the trouble I went to
   e. embarrassment
   f. understanding

2. To what is the "great banquet" referring?
   a. the kingdom of God
   b. deeper spiritual things
   c. Jesus himself
   d. the marriage banquet at the return of Christ
   e. restoration of the Jewish nation

3. Why did the three people who were originally invited refuse to come?
   a. they didn't like banquets
   b. too busy with other things
   c. not interested in being with God
   d. unaware of what they were missing
   e. they didn't realize this was the last invitation

4. "Go out quickly into the streets and alleys . . . bring in the poor, the crippled, the blind and the lame." Who are these people?
   a. the losers
   b. outcasts of society
   c. people hungry for spiritual things
   d. Gentiles outside of the covenant
   e. everybody who knows they do not deserve God's grace

5. "I tell you, not one of those men who were invited will get a taste of my banquet." Why?
   a. they blew their chance
   b. committed the "unforgivable sin"
   c. chose not to receive God's grace
   d. rejected Jesus as the Messiah

6. If God invited you to a banquet as his special guest (to spend time together) what would you do?
   a. probably make some excuse
   b. ask who else is coming
   c. wonder what God was up to
   d. go reluctantly
   e. jump at the chance
   f. don't know

MY OWN STORY/25 Minutes.

1. How would you describe your spiritual diet right now?
   a. baby food
   b. TV dinners
   c. meat and potatoes
   d. junk food except on Sunday
   e. dehydrated food (dried out)
   f. gourmet feast
   g. pure Bread and Wine

2. What can you expect at God's banquet?
   a. all my needs will be met
   b. the company will be interesting
   c. it's a once-in-a-lifetime event
   d. it will take commitment to stay and eat
   e. I will always be welcome
   f. in order not to get fat I will be asked to share the banquet with others

3. When it comes to experiencing God's spiritual feast, what will help you enjoy it more?
   a. spiritual hunger
   b. recognition that it is not a pot-luck— God provides all the food
   c. eating on a regular schedule rather than gorging once a week
   d. assurance that I can eat whenever I'm hungry

4. What would it take to get you to come to the banquet of God's deeper things?
   a. an adjustment in my schedule
   b. an invitation direct from God
   c. a few friends to join me
   d. lively entertainment and fun
   e. a little more spiritual hunger

kingdom values are taught? Why such tough talk from Jesus?

REFLECT: 1. When did you realize that following Jesus was costly? How so? **2.** Ever wonder since then if the cost was worth it? What keeps you going?

OPEN: As for "lost and found" items, do you lose more than you find? How so? Which items are still lost? Recently found?

DIG: 1. Who is in Jesus' "mixed audience"? How do they respond to him? **2.** How does Jesus' parable of the sheep relate to the muttering of the Pharisees? What is Jesus' point? **3.** How do you picture the woman searching for her money (vv.8-9)? What is Jesus' point here?

REFLECT: 1. When did you stray from the Christian faith? What did God use to bring you back? **2.** How do these stories make you feel about your value to God? **3.** How could these stories affect your relationships with those you know who wander from the faith?

OPEN: 1. Did you ever run away from home? Where did you go? What happened? **2.** Who was (or is) the "obedient" type in your family? The "wild one"? Which were (or are) you? How did (or do) these types get along?

DIG: 1. What stages does the younger son go through on his pilgrimage? What brings him to his senses? What does he realize then? With what sort of attitude does he approach his father? **2.** From your understanding of the father, what do you think he was doing while his son was away? Why do you think that? How does he receive his son? **3.** How does the older brother feel about his younger brother's return? Why? How does the father answer the older brother's objection? **4.**

³¹"Or suppose a king is about to go to war against another king. Will he not first sit down and consider whether he is able with ten thousand men to oppose the one coming against him with twenty thousand? ³²If he is not able, he will send a delegation while the other is still a long way off and will ask for terms of peace. ³³In the same way, any of you who does not give up everything he has cannot be my disciple.

³⁴"Salt is good, but if it loses its saltiness, how can it be made salty again? ³⁵It is fit neither for the soil nor for the manure pile; it is thrown out.

"He who has ears to hear, let him hear."

The Parable of the Lost Sheep

15 Now the tax collectors and "sinners" were all gathering around to hear him. ²But the Pharisees and the teachers of the law muttered, "This man welcomes sinners and eats with them."

³Then Jesus told them this parable: ⁴"Suppose one of you has a hundred sheep and loses one of them. Does he not leave the ninety-nine in the open country and go after the lost sheep until he finds it? ⁵And when he finds it, he joyfully puts it on his shoulders ⁶and goes home. Then he calls his friends and neighbors together and says, 'Rejoice with me; I have found my lost sheep.' ⁷I tell you that in the same way there will be more rejoicing in heaven over one sinner who repents than over ninety-nine righteous persons who do not need to repent.

The Parable of the Lost Coin

⁸"Or suppose a woman has ten silver coins^j and loses one. Does she not light a lamp, sweep the house and search carefully until she finds it? ⁹And when she finds it, she calls her friends and neighbors together and says, 'Rejoice with me; I have found my lost coin.' ¹⁰In the same way, I tell you, there is rejoicing in the presence of the angels of God over one sinner who repents."

The Parable of the Lost Son

¹¹Jesus continued: "There was a man who had two sons. ¹²The younger one said to his father, 'Father, give me my share of the estate.' So he divided his property between them.

¹³"Not long after that, the younger son got together all he had, set off for a distant country and there squandered his wealth in wild living. ¹⁴After he had spent everything, there was a severe famine in that whole country, and he began to be in need. ¹⁵So he went and hired himself out to a citizen of that country, who sent him to his fields to feed pigs. ¹⁶He longed to fill his stomach with the pods that the pigs were eating, but no one gave him anything.

¹⁷"When he came to his senses, he said, 'How many of my father's hired men have food to spare, and here I am starving to death! ¹⁸I will set out and go back to my father and say to him: Father, I have sinned against heaven and against you. ¹⁹I am no

---

j8 Greek ten drachmas, each worth about a day's wages

Luke 15:11-32   **THE PARABLE OF THE LOST SON (PRODIGAL)**

LOOKING INTO THE SCRIPTURE/20 Minutes. Read Luke 15:11-32 and discuss.

1. Why do you think the Prodigal Son decided to leave home?
    a. to grow up
    b. to get away from his father's values
    c. he wasn't appreciated at home
    d. to try to make it on his own
    e. to get away from his older brother

2. What was it that caused the Prodigal Son to come to his senses?
    a. homesickness
    b. guilt for what he had done
    c. feeling sorry for himself
    d. feeling sorry for his father
    e. hunger pangs
    f. realization that he was stupid
    g. he "hit bottom"

3. When the Prodigal Son returned home, what was his father's attitude?
    a. come on in but you're grounded
    b. you have disgraced the family
    c. where's the money
    d. I don't approve of what you've done, but you are still my son
    e. welcome home, son, I love you

4. When the older brother (who had been good) heard music and dancing, what was his attitude?
    a. it's unfair
    b. don't expect me to forgive him
    c. no use being good
    d. he blew his inheritance and now he's blowing mine

5. Do you think that the father was wise to give his son his inheritance when he knew his son would probably blow it? ☐ Yes ☐ No

6. If the father had a pretty good idea where his son had gone, do you think he should have gone after him? ☐ Yes ☐ No

7. Do you think it was wise for the father to "kill the fatted calf" and throw a party when his son came home? ☐ Yes ☐ No

8. Do you think the father split his inheritance a second time so that the Prodigal Son could have some spending money? ☐ I hope so ☐ I hope not

---

MY OWN STORY/20 Minutes. Share some of your own story through this parable.

1. By temperament and experience, whom do you identify with in this story?
    a. Prodigal Son
    b. Older Brother
    c. The Father

2. If you had to compare your spiritual journey to the Prodigal's journey, where are you now?
    a. at home, but not too happy
    b. in a far country
    c. coming to my senses
    d. on my way home, but not sure what I'll find
    e. I've just arrived/feeling great
    f. enjoying the fattened calf and the party

3. When it comes to spiritual things, what is your response to God's "party"?
    a. denial: there's no party in this life
    b. party pooper: sorry, I'm too busy
    c. party lover: I'm ready, let's party
    d. wallflower: I'm there, but I can't dance

4. What's the lesson for you in this parable?
    a. you've got to let your children go, even though you know they will probably blow it
    b. God's love has no strings
    c. waiting for your children to come home is painful
    d. older brothers have trouble enjoying the party
    e. Love overcomes mistakes

What's Jesus' point with this parable? What does this story teach about sin, repentance, and God's love? Could you make a case for re-titling this parable "The Waiting Father" or "The Elder Brother"? How so? **5.** In summary, how do these three parables answer the Pharisees' objection in verse 2? What does Jesus want to teach the Pharisees in verses 25-31? In light of the context (v.2), why does Jesus leave the story open-ended as to how the older brother responded to his father's plea?

REFLECT: 1. Comparing yourself to the two brothers in this story, who are you most like? Why? Are you quietly "at home"? Living only for today? Paying the consequences for yesterday? On the way home? Whom would you have identified with ten years ago, or in your youth? **2.** How have you experienced God as this father? **3.** When have you been like the older brother, quietly resentful of God's lavishness to "less deserving" people? Why? **4.** If we only had Jesus' words in 14:25-35 without the parables in chapter 15, how would you feel about God? Likewise, if we only had the parables without that warning, how would you feel?

OPEN: 1. Which job would *best* fit your personality: Ringmaster at a circus? Owner of a video store? Construction worker? Librarian? Skydiving instructor? Gourmet chef? Church pastor? **2.** Which of these jobs would *least* fit? Why?

DIG: 1. Why would it be important for Jesus' disciples to hear this parable? **2.** In what crisis does the manager find himself? What plan does he devise? In light of this deceit, why does the owner commend the manager (v.8)? **3.** How does Jesus summarize this parable (v.9)? What do you think he's commending here? How do verses 10-12 help you understand his point? **4.** What's the problem with trying to serve two masters (v.13)? What characterizes the attitude of the Pharisees who are listening in? How does he use the parable to speak to them (v.15)?

longer worthy to be called your son; make me like one of your hired men.' [20]So he got up and went to his father.

"But while he was still a long way off, his father saw him and was filled with compassion for him; he ran to his son, threw his arms around him and kissed him.

[21]"The son said to him, 'Father, I have sinned against heaven and against you. I am no longer worthy to be called your son. [k]'

[22]"But the father said to his servants, 'Quick! Bring the best robe and put it on him. Put a ring on his finger and sandals on his feet. [23]Bring the fattened calf and kill it. Let's have a feast and celebrate. [24]For this son of mine was dead and is alive again; he was lost and is found.' So they began to celebrate.

[25]"Meanwhile, the older son was in the field. When he came near the house, he heard music and dancing. [26]So he called one of the servants and asked him what was going on. [27]'Your brother has come,' he replied, 'and your father has killed the fattened calf because he has him back safe and sound.'

[28]"The older brother became angry and refused to go in. So his father went out and pleaded with him. [29]But he answered his father, 'Look! All these years I've been slaving for you and never disobeyed your orders. Yet you never gave me even a young goat so I could celebrate with my friends. [30]But when this son of yours who has squandered your property with prostitutes comes home, you kill the fattened calf for him!'

[31]" 'My son,' the father said, 'you are always with me, and everything I have is yours. [32]But we had to celebrate and be glad, because this brother of yours was dead and is alive again; he was lost and is found.' "

The Parable of the Shrewd Manager

16 Jesus told his disciples: "There was a rich man whose manager was accused of wasting his possessions. [2]So he called him in and asked him, 'What is this I hear about you? Give an account of your management, because you cannot be manager any longer.'

[3]"The manager said to himself, 'What shall I do now? My master is taking away my job. I'm not strong enough to dig, and I'm ashamed to beg— [4]I know what I'll do so that, when I lose my job here, people will welcome me into their houses.'

[5]"So he called in each one of his master's debtors. He asked the first, 'How much do you owe my master?'

[6]" 'Eight hundred gallons[l] of olive oil,' he replied.

"The manager told him, 'Take your bill, sit down quickly, and make it four hundred.'

[7]"Then he asked the second, 'And how much do you owe?'

" 'A thousand bushels[m] of wheat,' he replied.

"He told him, 'Take your bill and make it eight hundred.'

[8]"The master commended the dishonest manager because he had acted shrewdly. For the people of this world are more shrewd in dealing with their own kind than are the people of the

---

[k]21 Some early manuscripts *son. Make me like one of your hired men.*
[l]6 Greek *one hundred batous* (probably about 3 kiloliters)   [m]7 Greek *one hundred korous* (probably about 35 kiloliters)

light. [9]I tell you, use worldly wealth to gain friends for yourselves, so that when it is gone, you will be welcomed into eternal dwellings.

[10]"Whoever can be trusted with very little can also be trusted with much, and whoever is dishonest with very little will also be dishonest with much. [11]So if you have not been trustworthy in handling worldly wealth, who will trust you with true riches? [12]And if you have not been trustworthy with someone else's property, who will give you property of your own?

[13]"No servant can serve two masters. Either he will hate the one and love the other, or he will be devoted to the one and despise the other. You cannot serve both God and Money."

[14]The Pharisees, who loved money, heard all this and were sneering at Jesus. [15]He said to them, "You are the ones who justify yourselves in the eyes of men, but God knows your hearts. What is highly valued among men is detestable in God's sight.

Additional Teachings

[16]"The Law and the Prophets were proclaimed until John. Since that time, the good news of the kingdom of God is being preached, and everyone is forcing his way into it. [17]It is easier for heaven and earth to disappear than for the least stroke of a pen to drop out of the Law.

[18]"Anyone who divorces his wife and marries another woman commits adultery, and the man who marries a divorced woman commits adultery.

The Rich Man and Lazarus

[19]"There was a rich man who was dressed in purple and fine linen and lived in luxury every day. [20]At his gate was laid a beggar named Lazarus, covered with sores [21]and longing to eat what fell from the rich man's table. Even the dogs came and licked his sores.

[22]"The time came when the beggar died and the angels carried him to Abraham's side. The rich man also died and was buried. [23]In hell,[n] where he was in torment, he looked up and saw Abraham far away, with Lazarus by his side. [24]So he called to him, 'Father Abraham, have pity on me and send Lazarus to dip the tip of his finger in water and cool my tongue, because I am in agony in this fire.'

[25]"But Abraham replied, 'Son, remember that in your lifetime you received your good things, while Lazarus received bad things, but now he is comforted here and you are in agony. [26]And besides all this, between us and you a great chasm has been fixed, so that those who want to go from here to you cannot, nor can anyone cross over from there to us.'

[27]"He answered, 'Then I beg you, father, send Lazarus to my father's house, [28]for I have five brothers. Let him warn them, so that they will not also come to this place of torment.'

REFLECT: 1. How do you view your money: (a) It's mine, keep your hands off? (b) It's my creditors'? (c) It's God's—I just manage it? Why? How could you use it for the sake of the kingdom? 2. Who (or what) are some of the masters you've served in the past? What masters scream at you for allegiance now? How do you deal with these voices in light of your commitment to Christ?

DIG: How has the coming of the kingdom supplanted the law? Reinforced it? How might verse 18 illustrate how the Pharisees were the ones subverting the law?

REFLECT: To clarify this passage, what would you ask Jesus?

OPEN: 1. For what occasions do you feel like dressing to the hilt? When are you permitted and content to dress just in rags? 2. Do you like it when a dog licks you constantly? Why or why not?

DIG: 1. How do the lives of the rich man and Lazarus compare on earth (vv.19-21)? After death (vv.22-24)? 2. What determines who enters heaven? Why does this poor man qualify while the rich man is kept out? 3. What does this story teach you about human nature? Why is it so difficult for people to be convinced of God's ways? How does verse 31 relate to verse 13? 4. In sum, what ought we do with our lives on earth?

REFLECT: 1. On a scale of one (the rich man and his brothers) to ten (Lazarus), where do you stand? Why there? How can you move closer to a ten? 2. Since lack of knowledge is not the brothers' problem, what is? How do you see that tendency in yourself? 3. How do you feel about discussing "the Judgment" with friends?

[n]23 Greek *Hades*

177

²⁹"Abraham replied, 'They have Moses and the Prophets; let them listen to them.'

³⁰" 'No, father Abraham,' he said, 'but if someone from the dead goes to them, they will repent.'

³¹"He said to him, 'If they do not listen to Moses and the Prophets, they will not be convinced even if someone rises from the dead.' "

Sin, Faith, Duty

17 Jesus said to his disciples: "Things that cause people to sin are bound to come, but woe to that person through whom they come. ²It would be better for him to be thrown into the sea with a millstone tied around his neck than for him to cause one of these little ones to sin. ³So watch yourselves.

"If your brother sins, rebuke him, and if he repents, forgive him. ⁴If he sins against you seven times in a day, and seven times comes back to you and says, 'I repent,' forgive him."

⁵The apostles said to the Lord, "Increase our faith!"

⁶He replied, "If you have faith as small as a mustard seed, you can say to this mulberry tree, 'Be uprooted and planted in the sea,' and it will obey you.

⁷"Suppose one of you had a servant plowing or looking after the sheep. Would he say to the servant when he comes in from the field, 'Come along now and sit down to eat'? ⁸Would he not rather say, 'Prepare my supper, get yourself ready and wait on me while I eat and drink; after that you may eat and drink'? ⁹Would he thank the servant because he did what he was told to do? ¹⁰So you also, when you have done everything you were told to do, should say, 'We are unworthy servants; we have only done our duty.' "

Ten Healed of Leprosy

¹¹Now on his way to Jerusalem, Jesus traveled along the border between Samaria and Galilee. ¹²As he was going into a village, ten men who had leprosy° met him. They stood at a distance ¹³and called out in a loud voice, "Jesus, Master, have pity on us!"

¹⁴When he saw them, he said, "Go, show yourselves to the priests." And as they went, they were cleansed.

¹⁵One of them, when he saw he was healed, came back, praising God in a loud voice. ¹⁶He threw himself at Jesus' feet and thanked him—and he was a Samaritan.

¹⁷Jesus asked, "Were not all ten cleansed? Where are the other nine? ¹⁸Was no one found to return and give praise to God except this foreigner?" ¹⁹Then he said to him, "Rise and go; your faith has made you well."

OPEN: As a child, what was a sure-fire way that your sister or brother (or parents!) could "get your goat"?

DIG: 1. What might be an example of what Jesus means in verse 1? In this context, what does it mean to "watch yourself"? **2.** How could you practice verses 3-4 without reinforcing someone's bad behavior? Is Jesus being realistic, idealistic, or what? **3.** How might the disciples' plea (v.5) relate to Jesus' statement (vv.3-4)? What does Jesus' response (v.6) really mean? **4.** What attitudes should Jesus' followers have in serving him (vv.7-10)?

REFLECT: Which quality of a disciple do you have the most difficulty with? How might dealing with this affect the other qualities?

OPEN: As for writing "thank you" notes, do you: (a) Prepare a card before opening the gift? (b) Get to it "soon"? (c) Feel guilty for doing nothing? (d) Feel nothing? Why?

DIG: 1. What was it like to be a leper? What would their healing mean for them? **2.** As one of the nine, how would you rationalize not going back to Jesus to say "thanks"? **3.** What is significant about the one being a Samaritan?

REFLECT: How has Jesus healed you spiritually? Physically? Emotionally?

°12 The Greek word was used for various diseases affecting the skin—not necessarily leprosy.

The Coming of the Kingdom of God

[20]Once, having been asked by the Pharisees when the kingdom of God would come, Jesus replied, "The kingdom of God does not come with your careful observation, [21]nor will people say, 'Here it is,' or 'There it is,' because the kingdom of God is within[p] you."

[22]Then he said to his disciples, "The time is coming when you will long to see one of the days of the Son of Man, but you will not see it. [23]Men will tell you, 'There he is!' or 'Here he is!' Do not go running off after them. [24]For the Son of Man in his day[q] will be like the lightning, which flashes and lights up the sky from one end to the other. [25]But first he must suffer many things and be rejected by this generation.

[26]"Just as it was in the days of Noah, so also will it be in the days of the Son of Man. [27]People were eating, drinking, marrying and being given in marriage up to the day Noah entered the ark. Then the flood came and destroyed them all.

[28]"It was the same in the days of Lot. People were eating and drinking, buying and selling, planting and building. [29]But the day Lot left Sodom, fire and sulfur rained down from heaven and destroyed them all.

[30]"It will be just like this on the day the Son of Man is revealed. [31]On that day no one who is on the roof of his house, with his goods inside, should go down to get them. Likewise, no one in the field should go back for anything. [32]Remember Lot's wife! [33]Whoever tries to keep his life will lose it, and whoever loses his life will preserve it. [34]I tell you, on that night two people will be in one bed; one will be taken and the other left. [35]Two women will be grinding grain together; one will be taken and the other left.[r]"

[37]"Where, Lord?" they asked.

He replied, "Where there is a dead body, there the vultures will gather."

The Parable of the Persistent Widow

18 Then Jesus told his disciples a parable to show them that they should always pray and not give up. [2]He said: "In a certain town there was a judge who neither feared God nor cared about men. [3]And there was a widow in that town who kept coming to him with the plea, 'Grant me justice against my adversary.'

[4]"For some time he refused. But finally he said to himself, 'Even though I don't fear God or care about men, [5]yet because this widow keeps bothering me, I will see that she gets justice, so that she won't eventually wear me out with her coming!' "

[6]And the Lord said, "Listen to what the unjust judge says. [7]And will not God bring about justice for his chosen ones, who cry out to him day and night? Will he keep putting them off? [8]I tell you, he will see that they get justice, and quickly. However, when the Son of Man comes, will he find faith on the earth?"

OPEN: Looking back over the various transition periods of your life, which would you characterize as a period of "eating and drinking"? Of "buying and selling"? Of "planting and building"?

DIG: 1. In answering the Pharisees' question, what does Jesus say about the kingdom—as to when, how, or where it is? Does he view the kingdom as an inward, spiritual reality *within* people? Or an outward, social manifestation *among* them? Or is he speaking of their failure to recognize who he is? **2.** What did Jesus mean by "one of the days of the Son of Man"? **3.** How will those days be like the days of Noah and Lot? In light of the unexpected nature of his coming, how are his followers to live? What is meant by the warning about Lot's wife (vv.32-33; see Ge 19:17,26)? **4.** Verse 37 was a common proverb, implying that something will happen in its proper time. Why does Jesus answer like this? **5.** How do the kingdom of God and the days of the Son of Man differ?

REFLECT: While you live "in the kingdom" waiting for "the Son of Man" to come, what do you see in this section about the way you ought to apply verses 32-33?

OPEN: What did you use to do to get your way with your parents: Sulk? Cry? Bribery? Persistence? Force? Wit? What worked best?

DIG: 1. Since Roman judges were noted for their openness to bribes, what did this poor woman use? What is Jesus' point here? **2.** How is God like and unlike the judge?

REFLECT: 1. As for prayer, are you more likely to give up or hang tough? Why? **2.** Does this story mean I should *keep* praying to win "Megabucks," or to see the coming of God's kingdom? Why?

[p]21 Or *among*   [q]24 Some manuscripts do not have *in his day.*   [r]35 Some manuscripts *left.* [36]*Two men will be in the field; one will be taken and the other left.*

The Parable of the Pharisee and the Tax Collector

⁹To some who were confident of their own righteousness and looked down on everybody else, Jesus told this parable: ¹⁰"Two men went up to the temple to pray, one a Pharisee and the other a tax collector. ¹¹The Pharisee stood up and prayed about[f] himself: 'God, I thank you that I am not like other men—robbers, evildoers, adulterers—or even like this tax collector. ¹²I fast twice a week and give a tenth of all I get.'

¹³"But the tax collector stood at a distance. He would not even look up to heaven, but beat his breast and said, 'God, have mercy on me, a sinner.'

¹⁴"I tell you that this man, rather than the other, went home justified before God. For everyone who exalts himself will be humbled, and he who humbles himself will be exalted."

The Little Children and Jesus

¹⁵People were also bringing babies to Jesus to have him touch them. When the disciples saw this, they rebuked them. ¹⁶But Jesus called the children to him and said, "Let the little children come to me, and do not hinder them, for the kingdom of God belongs to such as these. ¹⁷I tell you the truth, anyone who will not receive the kingdom of God like a little child will never enter it."

The Rich Ruler

¹⁸A certain ruler asked him, "Good teacher, what must I do to inherit eternal life?"

¹⁹"Why do you call me good?" Jesus answered. "No one is good—except God alone. ²⁰You know the commandments: 'Do not commit adultery, do not murder, do not steal, do not give false testimony, honor your father and mother.'[g]"

²¹"All these I have kept since I was a boy," he said.

²²When Jesus heard this, he said to him, "You still lack one thing. Sell everything you have and give to the poor, and you will have treasure in heaven. Then come, follow me."

²³When he heard this, he became very sad, because he was a man of great wealth. ²⁴Jesus looked at him and said, "How hard it is for the rich to enter the kingdom of God! ²⁵Indeed, it is easier for a camel to go through the eye of a needle than for a rich man to enter the kingdom of God."

²⁶Those who heard this asked, "Who then can be saved?"

²⁷Jesus replied, "What is impossible with men is possible with God."

²⁸Peter said to him, "We have left all we had to follow you!"

²⁹"I tell you the truth," Jesus said to them, "no one who has left home or wife or brothers or parents or children for the sake of the kingdom of God ³⁰will fail to receive many times as much in this age and, in the age to come, eternal life."

ᶠ11 Or *to*   ᵍ20 Exodus 20:12-16; Deut. 5:16-20

Luke 18:9-14   THE PARABLE OF THE PHARISEE AND TAX COLLECTOR

LOOKING INTO THE SCRIPTURE/20 Minutes. Read Luke 18:9-14 and discuss.

1. How do you feel about the Pharisee in the story?
   a. like punching him in the nose
   b. I agree with him
   c. I feel like putting him in his place
   d. I feel sorry for him

2. Why do you think the Pharisee acted this way?
   a. gratitude to God
   b. peer pressure from friends
   c. sincere desire to please God
   d. fear of letting anybody know what he's really feeling
   e. he was self-righteous

3. How do you feel about the tax collector?
   a. at least he's honest
   b. he's more aware of who he is
   c. I can relate to this guy
   d. after cheating us, he has his nerve

4. Why do you think the tax collector acted the way he did?
   a. he knew he had done wrong
   b. he wanted sympathy
   c. he had a poor self-image
   d. he was plea bargaining with God
   e. he felt like dirt

MY OWN STORY/20 Minutes.

1. How much of your own problems could you share with each of these people? Put a dot on the line to indicate your response.

WITH THE PHARISEE, I COULD SHARE
Everything _____ Nothing

WITH THE TAX COLLECTOR, I COULD SHARE
Everything _____ Nothing

2. For the person with whom you could share the most in the previous questions, why do you feel this way?
   a. he is more spiritual
   b. more honest
   c. more like me
   d. more like the person I want to be
   e. more likely to understand me

3. If the tax collector in the parable came to your group, how would he be received?
   a. with open arms
   b. with suspicion
   c. with disgust
   d. like a fellow-sinner

4. If the Pharisee in the parable showed up at your group, how would he be received?
   a. with open arms
   b. with raised eyebrows
   c. with a few snickers
   d. with cold stares
   e. with sympathy

5. What is the reason you have for receiving one of these people better than another?
   a. fewer surface problems to hassle
   b. less emotional healing needed
   c. we don't tolerate sinners
   d. we don't tolerate phonies
   e. one would fit into our group better
   f. there really isn't a good reason

6. What would it take for you to receive either of these people into your group?
   a. a lot of patience
   b. a thick skin
   c. compassion
   d. tough love

DIG: In light of all the talk about the kingdom of God coming, why is this new teaching misunderstood (see also 9:22,45)?

REFLECT: When facing a tough spiritual battle, who do you trust? What do you do if they don't understand?

OPEN: As a child, how did you feel when told "you can't do that—you're too little"? Did you rise to the occasion anyway? How so?

DIG: 1. What do the disciples still fail to see about Jesus (v.39; compare 18:15)? About his kingdom? 2. From this story, what do you know of the beggar's handicap? His faith? His intensity? How does his blindness compare with that of the disciples (v.34)?

REFLECT: 1. Have you ever felt Jesus was too busy for you? Why? How do we inadvertently communicate that idea to children or people with chronic needs? 2. If Jesus asked, "What do you want me to do for you?" (v.41), what would you say?

OPEN: If you could pick an ideal height, how tall would you be?

DIG: 1. How does Zacchaeus compare with the rich ruler (18:18-30) in his approach and response to Jesus? 2. Why does Jesus dine with him? Why does this bother others? Do you think Jesus' words (vv.9-10) stopped the crowd's muttering? Why or why not? On what basis does Jesus confirm Zacchaeus' salvation?

REFLECT: 1. Where did Jesus first find you? (Up a tree? Out on a limb?) 2. How did he get you to join him: With coaxing? Big scare? An invitation you couldn't refuse?

OPEN: With $1,000 to spare, what would you do: (a) Buy a paper-folding machine and sell door-to-door with big potential profit? (b) Bank the cash, collect a modest but sure interest? (c) Stuff it in a mattress because the stock market might crash?

Jesus Again Predicts His Death

[31] Jesus took the Twelve aside and told them, "We are going up to Jerusalem, and everything that is written by the prophets about the Son of Man will be fulfilled. [32] He will be handed over to the Gentiles. They will mock him, insult him, spit on him, flog him and kill him. [33] On the third day he will rise again."

[34] The disciples did not understand any of this. Its meaning was hidden from them, and they did not know what he was talking about.

A Blind Beggar Receives His Sight

[35] As Jesus approached Jericho, a blind man was sitting by the roadside begging. [36] When he heard the crowd going by, he asked what was happening. [37] They told him, "Jesus of Nazareth is passing by."

[38] He called out, "Jesus, Son of David, have mercy on me!"

[39] Those who led the way rebuked him and told him to be quiet, but he shouted all the more, "Son of David, have mercy on me!"

[40] Jesus stopped and ordered the man to be brought to him. When he came near, Jesus asked him, [41] "What do you want me to do for you?"

"Lord, I want to see," he replied.

[42] Jesus said to him, "Receive your sight; your faith has healed you." [43] Immediately he received his sight and followed Jesus, praising God. When all the people saw it, they also praised God.

Zacchaeus the Tax Collector

19 Jesus entered Jericho and was passing through. [2] A man was there by the name of Zacchaeus; he was a chief tax collector and was wealthy. [3] He wanted to see who Jesus was, but being a short man he could not, because of the crowd. [4] So he ran ahead and climbed a sycamore-fig tree to see him, since Jesus was coming that way.

[5] When Jesus reached the spot, he looked up and said to him, "Zacchaeus, come down immediately. I must stay at your house today." [6] So he came down at once and welcomed him gladly.

[7] All the people saw this and began to mutter, "He has gone to be the guest of a 'sinner.' "

[8] But Zacchaeus stood up and said to the Lord, "Look, Lord! Here and now I give half of my possessions to the poor, and if I have cheated anybody out of anything, I will pay back four times the amount."

[9] Jesus said to him, "Today salvation has come to this house, because this man, too, is a son of Abraham. [10] For the Son of Man came to seek and to save what was lost."

The Parable of the Ten Minas

[11] While they were listening to this, he went on to tell them a parable, because he was near Jerusalem and the people thought that the kingdom of God was going to appear at once. [12] He said: "A man of noble birth went to a distant country to have himself appointed king and then to return. [13] So he called ten of his

Luke 19:1-10   **ZACCHAEUS THE TAX COLLECTOR**

LOOKING INTO THE SCRIPTURE/20 Minutes. Read Luke 19:1-10 and discuss.

1. What impresses you about Zacchaeus?
   a. his wealth
   b. his agility
   c. his curiosity
   d. his flexibility
   e. his change of heart

2. What was it about Zacchaeus that Jesus singled him out?
   a. the worst sinner in town
   b. sold out to Roman authorities
   c. guilty of fraud and thievery
   d. hungry for something more in life
   e. he was so short

3. What do you suppose was Jesus' facial expression when he said, "Zacchaeus, come down immediately . . ."?
   a. stern
   b. delighted
   c. relieved to find a dinner companion
   d. sympathetic
   e. matter-of-fact

4. Why do you think Jesus invited himself to Zacchaeus' house for dinner?
   a. he felt sorry for him
   b. he wanted to talk to him about his shady business
   c. he needed a spectacular miracle to gain credibility in the town
   d. he knew he had what Zacchaeus was seeking

5. What do you think they talked about over dinner?
   a. the weather
   b. how Zach was really feeling
   c. God's plan for his life
   d. how to pay back what he had stolen from the people

6. "Today salvation has come to this house, because this man, too, is a son of Abraham...." What is Jesus saying about Zach here?
   a. Zach is a newborn person
   b. accept Zach as a brother Jew
   c. Zach has followed in the tradition of Abraham's faith
   d. Zach is no worse than any of you
   e. give Zach a chance to pay back what he has stolen

7. Do you think the meeting between Zacchaeus and Jesus was coincidental or all part of the plan and purpose of God?
   a. coincidental
   b. more than coincidental
   c. don't know

8. How do you think Zacchaeus felt when he left Jesus?
   a. loved and accepted
   b. relieved and restored
   c. clean and beautiful
   d. a part of God's family again

MY OWN STORY/20 Minutes. Suppose Jesus were to invite himself to your house. Bob Munger, in his little booklet "My Heart—Christ's Home," describes the areas of life as the rooms of a house. Take an inventory of your own life, then give yourself a grade on each room as follows: A = excellent rating; B = good rating; C = passing, but needs a little dusting; and D = barely passing, needs a lot of cleaning.

☐ LIBRARY: This room is your mind—what you allow to go into it and come out of it. It is the "control room" of the entire house.

☐ DINING ROOM: Appetites, desires, those things that your mind and spirit feed on for nourishment.

☐ DRAWING ROOM: This room is where you draw close to God, seek time with him daily, not just in times of distress or need.

☐ WORKSHOP: This room is where your gifts, talents, skills are put to work for God . . . by the power of the Spirit.

☐ RUMPUS ROOM: The social area of your life—the things you do to amuse yourself and others.

☐ HALL CLOSET: The one secret place that no one knows about, but is a real stumbling block in your walk in the Spirit.

servants and gave them ten minas. " 'Put this money to work,' he said, 'until I come back.'

¹⁴"But his subjects hated him and sent a delegation after him to say, 'We don't want this man to be our king.'

¹⁵"He was made king, however, and returned home. Then he sent for the servants to whom he had given the money, in order to find out what they had gained with it.

¹⁶"The first one came and said, 'Sir, your mina has earned ten more.'

¹⁷" 'Well done, my good servant!' his master replied. 'Because you have been trustworthy in a very small matter, take charge of ten cities.'

¹⁸"The second came and said, 'Sir, your mina has earned five more.'

¹⁹"His master answered, 'You take charge of five cities.'

²⁰"Then another servant came and said, 'Sir, here is your mina; I have kept it laid away in a piece of cloth. ²¹I was afraid of you, because you are a hard man. You take out what you did not put in and reap what you did not sow.'

²²"His master replied, 'I will judge you by your own words, you wicked servant! You knew, did you, that I am a hard man, taking out what I did not put in, and reaping what I did not sow? ²³Why then didn't you put my money on deposit, so that when I came back, I could have collected it with interest?'

²⁴"Then he said to those standing by, 'Take his mina away from him and give it to the one who has ten minas.'

²⁵" 'Sir,' they said, 'he already has ten!'

²⁶"He replied, 'I tell you that to everyone who has, more will be given, but as for the one who has nothing, even what he has will be taken away. ²⁷But those enemies of mine who did not want me to be king over them—bring them here and kill them in front of me.' "

The Triumphal Entry

²⁸After Jesus had said this, he went on ahead, going up to Jerusalem. ²⁹As he approached Bethphage and Bethany at the hill called the Mount of Olives, he sent two of his disciples, saying to them, ³⁰"Go to the village ahead of you, and as you enter it, you will find a colt tied there, which no one has ever ridden. Untie it and bring it here. ³¹If anyone asks you, 'Why are you untying it?' tell him, 'The Lord needs it.' "

³²Those who were sent ahead went and found it just as he had told them. ³³As they were untying the colt, its owners asked them, "Why are you untying the colt?"

³⁴They replied, "The Lord needs it."

³⁵They brought it to Jesus, threw their cloaks on the colt and put Jesus on it. ³⁶As he went along, people spread their cloaks on the road.

³⁷When he came near the place where the road goes down the Mount of Olives, the whole crowd of disciples began joyfully to praise God in loud voices for all the miracles they had seen:

ᵘ13 A mina was about three months' wages.

[38]"Blessed is the king who comes in the name of the Lord!"[v]

"Peace in heaven and glory in the highest!"

[39]Some of the Pharisees in the crowd said to Jesus, "Teacher, rebuke your disciples!"

[40]"I tell you," he replied, "if they keep quiet, the stones will cry out."

[41]As he approached Jerusalem and saw the city, he wept over it [42]and said, "If you, even you, had only known on this day what would bring you peace—but now it is hidden from your eyes. [43]The days will come upon you when your enemies will build an embankment against you and encircle you and hem you in on every side. [44]They will dash you to the ground, you and the children within your walls. They will not leave one stone on another, because you did not recognize the time of God's coming to you."

Jesus at the Temple

[45]Then he entered the temple area and began driving out those who were selling. [46]"It is written," he said to them, " 'My house will be a house of prayer'[w]; but you have made it 'a den of robbers.'[x]"

[47]Every day he was teaching at the temple. But the chief priests, the teachers of the law and the leaders among the people were trying to kill him. [48]Yet they could not find any way to do it, because all the people hung on his words.

The Authority of Jesus Questioned

20 One day as he was teaching the people in the temple courts and preaching the gospel, the chief priests and the teachers of the law, together with the elders, came up to him. [2]"Tell us by what authority you are doing these things," they said. "Who gave you this authority?"

[3]He replied, "I will also ask you a question. Tell me, [4]John's baptism—was it from heaven, or from men?"

[5]They discussed it among themselves and said, "If we say, 'From heaven,' he will ask, 'Why didn't you believe him?' [6]But if we say, 'From men,' all the people will stone us, because they are persuaded that John was a prophet."

[7]So they answered, "We don't know where it was from."

[8]Jesus said, "Neither will I tell you by what authority I am doing these things."

The Parable of the Tenants

[9]He went on to tell the people this parable: "A man planted a vineyard, rented it to some farmers and went away for a long time. [10]At harvest time he sent a servant to the tenants so they would give him some of the fruit of the vineyard. But the tenants beat him and sent him away empty-handed. [11]He sent another servant, but that one also they beat and treated shamefully and

(vv.39-40) imply about him? **6.** How do verses 45-48 relate to Jesus' concern about Jerusalem? Why does he take such extreme action?

REFLECT: 1. What kind of reception would Jesus get: (a) If he rode into your town today? (b) After the people heard the message? **2.** How would he be treated by the local media? By elected officials? The guys in the tavern? The ladies in the bridge club? **3.** Where (or who) is your "Jerusalem"—the place (or person) you yearn to see come to God? **4.** How has Jesus "turned over tables" in your life? What has he been cleaning out recently?

OPEN: As a teenager, what authority figure (parent, teacher, minister) upset you most? Why?

DIG: 1. What "things" (v.2) has Jesus been doing? What about these things would worry the chief priests? **2.** What vested interests are they trying to protect from Jesus' probing question? For Jesus' own sake, why does he evade their question?

REFLECT: What people, things, or events led you to recognize Jesus' authority? What is his authority changing in your life now?

OPEN: When have you recently experienced "three-strikes-and-you're-out": Employment? Dating? School? Baseball? How do you handle such rejection?

DIG: 1. How does this parable relate to the question of authority raised in verses 1-8? **2.** What does the landowner do? How do the tenants respond? Why? **3.** What do the landowner, the tenants, the servants, and the son represent? **4.** How does the

[v]38 Psalm 118:26   [w]46 Isaiah 56:7   [x]46 Jer. 7:11

quoted Scripture relate to the parable? Who are the builders? The capstone? **5.** How does the parable and the quote affect the religious leaders? Why don't they act? Why choose this time to tell such a parable?

REFLECT: 1. At different times in your life, how have you received Jesus? What is your reception like now? **2.** Is Jesus more like a *millstone* (weight) or a *capstone* (one that holds everything together) in your life? Why? **3.** Whom do you feel most like in this story? Why? How could your Christian friends encourage you this week?

sent away empty-handed. [12]He sent still a third, and they wounded him and threw him out.

[13]"Then the owner of the vineyard said, 'What shall I do? I will send my son, whom I love; perhaps they will respect him.'

[14]"But when the tenants saw him, they talked the matter over. 'This is the heir,' they said. 'Let's kill him, and the inheritance will be ours.' [15]So they threw him out of the vineyard and killed him.

"What then will the owner of the vineyard do to them? [16]He will come and kill those tenants and give the vineyard to others."

When the people heard this, they said, "May this never be!"

[17]Jesus looked directly at them and asked, "Then what is the meaning of that which is written:

" 'The stone the builders rejected
has become the capstone[y][z]?

[18]Everyone who falls on that stone will be broken to pieces, but he on whom it falls will be crushed."

[19]The teachers of the law and the chief priests looked for a way to arrest him immediately, because they knew he had spoken this parable against them. But they were afraid of the people.

Paying Taxes to Caesar

[20]Keeping a close watch on him, they sent spies, who pretended to be honest. They hoped to catch Jesus in something he said so that they might hand him over to the power and authority of the governor. [21]So the spies questioned him: "Teacher, we know that you speak and teach what is right, and that you do not show partiality but teach the way of God in accordance with the truth. [22]Is it right for us to pay taxes to Caesar or not?"

[23]He saw through their duplicity and said to them, [24]"Show me a denarius. Whose portrait and inscription are on it?"

[25]"Caesar's," they replied.

He said to them, "Then give to Caesar what is Caesar's, and to God what is God's."

[26]They were unable to trap him in what he had said there in public. And astonished by his answer, they became silent.

The Resurrection and Marriage

[27]Some of the Sadducees, who say there is no resurrection, came to Jesus with a question. [28]"Teacher," they said, "Moses wrote for us that if a man's brother dies and leaves a wife but no children, the man must marry the widow and have children for his brother. [29]Now there were seven brothers. The first one married a woman and died childless. [30]The second [31]and then the third married her, and in the same way the seven died, leaving no children. [32]Finally, the woman died too. [33]Now then, at the resurrection whose wife will she be, since the seven were married to her?"

[34]Jesus replied, "The people of this age marry and are given in marriage. [35]But those who are considered worthy of taking part in that age and in the resurrection from the dead will neither

OPEN: When do you pay your taxes: Early, late, or never? Why?

DIG: 1. Why ask this question (v.22)? **2.** What's the trap here: If Jesus had said, "Pay Caesar," what would have happened to his crowd support (19:36,48; 20:19)? If Jesus had said, "Don't pay," how would the rulers have responded? **3.** What's so insightful about Jesus' response?

REFLECT: In giving yourself to God, are you in the 15%, 28%, 45%, or 100% "tax bracket"? Why?

OPEN: What was the last "big exam" you had to really prepare for? How did you do?

DIG: 1. Given that the Sadducees were status quo politicians and strict materialists (see Ac 23:8), how do you imagine they questioned Jesus? With what address? Tone of voice? **2.** How seriously does Jesus treat this absurd question? What if he had ridiculed it? **3.** What does Jesus teach about life after death? **4.** How does he then "prove" the resurrection? (Note the verb tense in this Ex 3:6 quote and recall *when* this burning bush incident took place.) **5.** How do the teachers of the law differ in their response? Why?

y17 Or *cornerstone*   *z17* Psalm 118:22

186

marry nor be given in marriage, [36]and they can no longer die; for they are like the angels. They are God's children, since they are children of the resurrection. [37]But in the account of the bush, even Moses showed that the dead rise, for he calls the Lord 'the God of Abraham, and the God of Isaac, and the God of Jacob.'[a] [38]He is not the God of the dead, but of the living, for to him all are alive."

[39]Some of the teachers of the law responded, "Well said, teacher!" [40]And no one dared to ask him any more questions.

Whose Son Is the Christ?

[41]Then Jesus said to them, "How is it that they say the Christ[b] is the Son of David? [42]David himself declares in the Book of Psalms:

" 'The Lord said to my Lord:
"Sit at my right hand
[43]until I make your enemies
a footstool for your feet." '[c]

[44]David calls him 'Lord.' How then can he be his son?"

[45]While all the people were listening, Jesus said to his disciples, [46]"Beware of the teachers of the law. They like to walk around in flowing robes and love to be greeted in the marketplaces and have the most important seats in the synagogues and the places of honor at banquets. [47]They devour widows' houses and for a show make lengthy prayers. Such men will be punished most severely."

The Widow's Offering

21 As he looked up, Jesus saw the rich putting their gifts into the temple treasury. [2]He also saw a poor widow put in two very small copper coins.[d] [3]"I tell you the truth," he said, "this poor widow has put in more than all the others. [4]All these people gave their gifts out of their wealth; but she out of her poverty put in all she had to live on."

Signs of the End of the Age

[5]Some of his disciples were remarking about how the temple was adorned with beautiful stones and with gifts dedicated to God. But Jesus said, [6]"As for what you see here, the time will come when not one stone will be left on another; every one of them will be thrown down."

[7]"Teacher," they asked, "when will these things happen? And what will be the sign that they are about to take place?"

[8]He replied: "Watch out that you are not deceived. For many will come in my name, claiming, 'I am he,' and, 'The time is near.' Do not follow them. [9]When you hear of wars and revolutions, do not be frightened. These things must happen first, but the end will not come right away."

[10]Then he said to them: "Nation will rise against nation, and

REFLECT: How do you deal with someone who wants to argue a point in the Bible? What if the person has honest questions and you don't have the answer?

OPEN: As a child, what "hot buttons" did you push to make your parents mad?

DIG: 1. Given the issue of authority in this chapter, why is Jesus asking questions (and pushing hot buttons) now? **2.** What things undermine the authority of the religious leaders? **3.** How does the poor widow differ from these leaders? What is Jesus' point in making this contrast?

REFLECT: 1. When have you "used" religion to get something for yourself (attention, respect, good feelings) rather than for love of God? What helps get you back on track? **2.** Do you give to God off the top (at the outset of the month), or from what is left over (at month's end)? Explain.

OPEN: What is the tallest building you have been in? What could you see from the top?

DIG: 1. What prompts Jesus' next lesson? **2.** What bombshell does he drop on his disciples (v.6)? How did the Jewish people (including the disciples) feel about the temple? How must they have felt when they heard Jesus' words? **3.** The disciples identified the destruction of the temple with the end times, but Jesus separates them. In verses 8-19, which is he teaching about? **4.** What will happen to the disciples and the church before the end? What comfort will come in the midst of

a37 Exodus 3:6   b41 Or Messiah   c43 Psalm 110:1   d2 Greek two lepta these trials? What should the attitude of the disciples be during that time? **5.** In A.D. 70, Jerusalem was destroyed by the Romans. Why would Jesus warn of this event in verses 20-24? Why will Jerusalem be devastated (see 11:49-51; 13:34-35 and 19:41-44)? How does Jesus describe this time (vv.21-24)? What does he tell the people to do? Why? **6.** In verses 25-28, which event (the coming of the end or Jerusalem's destruction) is in view? What do the two events have in common? What is significant about the way the Son of Man will come (v.27; see Da 7:13-14)? What should be the attitude of believers when they see the Son of Man coming? **7.** What is the lesson of the fig tree (vv.29-31)? How does the fig tree answer the disciples' question from verse 7? **8.** How would the promises (vv.32-33) have been a comfort to the disciples? A discomfort? What impact do they have on you, 20 centuries later? **9.** In the midst of this heavy news and heavy times, how does Jesus caution his followers (vv.34-35)? Why? **10.** During this time, what is Jesus' schedule? The schedule of the people? What is significant about these schedules to you?

REFLECT: 1. Have you ever felt that verses 12-19 were the story of your life? What happened? How did God protect you through this time of hardship? **2.** When reading the parable of the fig tree today, how near is the fig tree to sprouting? What makes you think this? How does this affect the way you live your life? **3.** How well does your life reflect verse 36? What will you do this week to become better at watching and praying?

kingdom against kingdom. ¹¹There will be great earthquakes, famines and pestilences in various places, and fearful events and great signs from heaven.

¹²"But before all this, they will lay hands on you and persecute you. They will deliver you to synagogues and prisons, and you will be brought before kings and governors, and all on account of my name. ¹³This will result in your being witnesses to them. ¹⁴But make up your mind not to worry beforehand how you will defend yourselves. ¹⁵For I will give you words and wisdom that none of your adversaries will be able to resist or contradict. ¹⁶You will be betrayed even by parents, brothers, relatives and friends, and they will put some of you to death. ¹⁷All men will hate you because of me. ¹⁸But not a hair of your head will perish. ¹⁹By standing firm you will gain life.

²⁰"When you see Jerusalem being surrounded by armies, you will know that its desolation is near. ²¹Then let those who are in Judea flee to the mountains, let those in the city get out, and let those in the country not enter the city. ²²For this is the time of punishment in fulfillment of all that has been written. ²³How dreadful it will be in those days for pregnant women and nursing mothers! There will be great distress in the land and wrath against this people. ²⁴They will fall by the sword and will be taken as prisoners to all the nations. Jerusalem will be trampled on by the Gentiles until the times of the Gentiles are fulfilled.

²⁵"There will be signs in the sun, moon and stars. On the earth, nations will be in anguish and perplexity at the roaring and tossing of the sea. ²⁶Men will faint from terror, apprehensive of what is coming on the world, for the heavenly bodies will be shaken. ²⁷At that time they will see the Son of Man coming in a cloud with power and great glory. ²⁸When these things begin to take place, stand up and lift up your heads, because your redemption is drawing near."

²⁹He told them this parable: "Look at the fig tree and all the trees. ³⁰When they sprout leaves, you can see for yourselves and know that summer is near. ³¹Even so, when you see these things happening, you know that the kingdom of God is near.

³²"I tell you the truth, this generation ᵉ will certainly not pass away until all these things have happened. ³³Heaven and earth will pass away, but my words will never pass away.

³⁴"Be careful, or your hearts will be weighed down with dissipation, drunkenness and the anxieties of life, and that day will close on you unexpectedly like a trap. ³⁵For it will come upon all those who live on the face of the whole earth. ³⁶Be always on the watch, and pray that you may be able to escape all that is about to happen, and that you may be able to stand before the Son of Man."

³⁷Each day Jesus was teaching at the temple, and each evening he went out to spend the night on the hill called the Mount of Olives, ³⁸and all the people came early in the morning to hear him at the temple.

ᵉ32 Or race

Judas Agrees to Betray Jesus

22 Now the Feast of Unleavened Bread, called the Passover, was approaching, [2]and the chief priests and the teachers of the law were looking for some way to get rid of Jesus, for they were afraid of the people. [3]Then Satan entered Judas, called Iscariot, one of the Twelve. [4]And Judas went to the chief priests and the officers of the temple guard and discussed with them how he might betray Jesus. [5]They were delighted and agreed to give him money. [6]He consented, and watched for an opportunity to hand Jesus over to them when no crowd was present.

The Last Supper

[7]Then came the day of Unleavened Bread on which the Passover lamb had to be sacrificed. [8]Jesus sent Peter and John, saying, "Go and make preparations for us to eat the Passover."

[9]"Where do you want us to prepare for it?" they asked.

[10]He replied, "As you enter the city, a man carrying a jar of water will meet you. Follow him to the house that he enters, [11]and say to the owner of the house, 'The Teacher asks: Where is the guest room, where I may eat the Passover with my disciples?' [12]He will show you a large upper room, all furnished. Make preparations there."

[13]They left and found things just as Jesus had told them. So they prepared the Passover.

[14]When the hour came, Jesus and his apostles reclined at the table. [15]And he said to them, "I have eagerly desired to eat this Passover with you before I suffer. [16]For I tell you, I will not eat it again until it finds fulfillment in the kingdom of God."

[17]After taking the cup, he gave thanks and said, "Take this and divide it among you. [18]For I tell you I will not drink again of the fruit of the vine until the kingdom of God comes."

[19]And he took bread, gave thanks and broke it, and gave it to them, saying, "This is my body given for you; do this in remembrance of me."

[20]In the same way, after the supper he took the cup, saying, "This cup is the new covenant in my blood, which is poured out for you. [21]But the hand of him who is going to betray me is with mine on the table. [22]The Son of Man will go as it has been decreed, but woe to that man who betrays him." [23]They began to question among themselves which of them it might be who would do this.

[24]Also a dispute arose among them as to which of them was considered to be greatest. [25]Jesus said to them, "The kings of the Gentiles lord it over them; and those who exercise authority over them call themselves Benefactors. [26]But you are not to be like that. Instead, the greatest among you should be like the youngest, and the one who rules like the one who serves. [27]For who is greater, the one who is at the table or the one who serves? Is it not the one who is at the table? But I am among you as one who serves. [28]You are those who have stood by me in my trials. [29]And I confer on you a kingdom, just as my Father conferred one on me, [30]so that you may eat and drink at my table in my kingdom and sit on thrones, judging the twelve tribes of Israel.

OPEN: 1. Where is one of your favorite places to eat as a family? What makes the place so good? **2.** When you were growing up, what were mealtimes like? Where did everyone sit around the table? What's one vivid memory you have about each family member at that time?

DIG: 1. What was the significance of Passover? The Passover lamb (see Ex 12:1-13,21-28)? **2.** In light of 19:28-48, why are the priests and teachers so determined to kill Jesus? How does that relate to the roundabout way Jesus has the disciples arrange for the Passover feast? **3.** Besides the desire to be with friends, why might Jesus "eagerly desire" to share this particular Passover feast with the disciples? How will Passover really be "fulfilled" in the kingdom of God (v.16)? How does Jesus' use of the bread and wine change the emphasis of Passover? What new meaning does he give to it? From Jeremiah 31:31-33, how would you describe the "new covenant" Jesus brought about (see also Heb 10:11-18)? **4.** If you were there, how would you have reacted to the news about Jesus' unnamed betrayer (vv.21-22)? How might that lead to the argument in verse 24? How does Jesus resolve that argument (vv.25-27)? What does he mean by the promise in verses 28-30? **5.** How must Peter feel in verses 31-34? What are the differences between Judas (vv.1-6) and Peter, since both turned away from Jesus? **6.** What is Jesus trying to impress upon Peter and the others in verses 35-38: (a) They should fight? (b) They really will be left on their own once he's gone? (c) He is indeed going to die, and will not be able to care for them? or (d) Other: _____? Why?

REFLECT: 1. What does sharing in Communion or the Lord's Supper mean to you? What do you think about during it? **2.** What would it mean to apply Jesus' words about service (v.27) in your family life? Work or school relationships? Political views? Use of money? What makes it hard for you to apply this principle in those areas? What motive is there for you to do so? **3.** With which disciple do you identify most and why: (a) Judas—I've sold out on Jesus? (b) Those arguing—I want to follow Jesus, but I still want to be successful in the eyes of others? or (c) Peter—I am passionately committed to Jesus, but sometimes I fall flat on my face?

OPEN: In times of crisis, do you stay cool, get hot, panic, or dig in? Where do you go to get away from it all?

DIG: 1. What strikes you about Jesus' prayer? In saying, "your will be done," is Jesus: (a) Helplessly submitting to fate? (b) Admitting defeat before a power that beat him? (c) Bitterly resigning himself to the inevitable? or (d) Quietly trusting in God's love even still? **2.** Why is the crowd so large and armed (v.52)? What do they fear? Why are their fears unfounded? **3.** What is the irony in Judas' betrayal? In Peter's use of the sword? How must the servant—first attacked and then healed—feel about what's going on? **4.** What does Jesus mean by "your hour" (v.53; in contrast to his own, v.42)?

REFLECT: 1. What do *you* mean when you pray, "your will be done"? **2.** How would you compare Jesus' attitudes and actions with those of his disciples? His enemies? What impresses you most about him?

³¹"Simon, Simon, Satan has asked to sift you*ʲ* as wheat. ³²But I have prayed for you, Simon, that your faith may not fail. And when you have turned back, strengthen your brothers."

³³But he replied, "Lord, I am ready to go with you to prison and to death."

³⁴Jesus answered, "I tell you, Peter, before the rooster crows today, you will deny three times that you know me."

³⁵Then Jesus asked them, "When I sent you without purse, bag or sandals, did you lack anything?"

"Nothing," they answered.

³⁶He said to them, "But now if you have a purse, take it, and also a bag; and if you don't have a sword, sell your cloak and buy one. ³⁷It is written: 'And he was numbered with the transgressors'*ᵍ*; and I tell you that this must be fulfilled in me. Yes, what is written about me is reaching its fulfillment."

³⁸The disciples said, "See, Lord, here are two swords."

"That is enough," he replied.

Jesus Prays on the Mount of Olives

³⁹Jesus went out as usual to the Mount of Olives, and his disciples followed him. ⁴⁰On reaching the place, he said to them, "Pray that you will not fall into temptation." ⁴¹He withdrew about a stone's throw beyond them, knelt down and prayed, ⁴²"Father, if you are willing, take this cup from me; yet not my will, but yours be done." ⁴³An angel from heaven appeared to him and strengthened him. ⁴⁴And being in anguish, he prayed more earnestly, and his sweat was like drops of blood falling to the ground.*ʰ*

⁴⁵When he rose from prayer and went back to the disciples, he found them asleep, exhausted from sorrow. ⁴⁶"Why are you sleeping?" he asked them. "Get up and pray so that you will not fall into temptation."

Jesus Arrested

⁴⁷While he was still speaking a crowd came up, and the man who was called Judas, one of the Twelve, was leading them. He approached Jesus to kiss him, ⁴⁸but Jesus asked him, "Judas, are you betraying the Son of Man with a kiss?"

⁴⁹When Jesus' followers saw what was going to happen, they said, "Lord, should we strike with our swords?" ⁵⁰And one of them struck the servant of the high priest, cutting off his right ear.

⁵¹But Jesus answered, "No more of this!" And he touched the man's ear and healed him.

⁵²Then Jesus said to the chief priests, the officers of the temple guard, and the elders, who had come for him, "Am I leading a rebellion, that you have come with swords and clubs? ⁵³Every day I was with you in the temple courts, and you did not lay a hand on me. But this is your hour—when darkness reigns."

ʲ31 The Greek is plural.   *ᵍ37* Isaiah 53:12   *ʰ44* Some early manuscripts do not have verses 43 and 44.

Peter Disowns Jesus

⁵⁴Then seizing him, they led him away and took him into the house of the high priest. Peter followed at a distance. ⁵⁵But when they had kindled a fire in the middle of the courtyard and had sat down together, Peter sat down with them. ⁵⁶A servant girl saw him seated there in the firelight. She looked closely at him and said, "This man was with him."

⁵⁷But he denied it. "Woman, I don't know him," he said. ⁵⁸A little later someone else saw him and said, "You also are one of them."

"Man, I am not!" Peter replied.

⁵⁹About an hour later another asserted, "Certainly this fellow was with him, for he is a Galilean."

⁶⁰Peter replied, "Man, I don't know what you're talking about!" Just as he was speaking, the rooster crowed. ⁶¹The Lord turned and looked straight at Peter. Then Peter remembered the word the Lord had spoken to him: "Before the rooster crows today, you will disown me three times." ⁶²And he went outside and wept bitterly.

The Soldiers Mock Jesus

⁶³The men who were guarding Jesus began mocking and beating him. ⁶⁴They blindfolded him and demanded, "Prophesy! Who hit you?" ⁶⁵And they said many other insulting things to him.

Jesus Before Pilate and Herod

⁶⁶At daybreak the council of the elders of the people, both the chief priests and teachers of the law, met together, and Jesus was led before them. ⁶⁷"If you are the Christ,ⁱ" they said, "tell us."

Jesus answered, "If I tell you, you will not believe me, ⁶⁸and if I asked you, you would not answer. ⁶⁹But from now on, the Son of Man will be seated at the right hand of the mighty God."

⁷⁰They all asked, "Are you then the Son of God?"

He replied, "You are right in saying I am."

⁷¹Then they said, "Why do we need any more testimony? We have heard it from his own lips."

23 Then the whole assembly rose and led him off to Pilate. ²And they began to accuse him, saying, "We have found this man subverting our nation. He opposes payment of taxes to Caesar and claims to be Christ,ʲ a king."

³So Pilate asked Jesus, "Are you the king of the Jews?"

"Yes, it is as you say," Jesus replied.

⁴Then Pilate announced to the chief priests and the crowd, "I find no basis for a charge against this man."

⁵But they insisted, "He stirs up the people all over Judeaᵏ by his teaching. He started in Galilee and has come all the way here."

⁶On hearing this, Pilate asked if the man was a Galilean. ⁷When he learned that Jesus was under Herod's jurisdiction, he sent him to Herod, who was also in Jerusalem at that time.

ⁱ67 Or Messiah   ʲ2 Or Messiah; also in verses 35 and 39   ᵏ5 Or over the land of the Jews

REFLECT: 1. In 19:45, Jesus confronted injustice with action, but here he was silent. What particular form of injustice makes your blood boil? How do you decide when to fight for what is right, and when not to? How has that decision faced you recently? 2. What contrasts do you see between Jesus' kingship and the authority of Pilate and Herod? What difference does it make to you that Jesus is not the type of king they were? 3. How does the story of Barabbas illustrate what Jesus has done for you?

8When Herod saw Jesus, he was greatly pleased, because for a long time he had been wanting to see him. From what he had heard about him, he hoped to see him perform some miracle. 9He plied him with many questions, but Jesus gave him no answer. 10The chief priests and the teachers of the law were standing there, vehemently accusing him. 11Then Herod and his soldiers ridiculed and mocked him. Dressing him in an elegant robe, they sent him back to Pilate. 12That day Herod and Pilate became friends—before this they had been enemies.

13Pilate called together the chief priests, the rulers and the people, 14and said to them, "You brought me this man as one who was inciting the people to rebellion. I have examined him in your presence and have found no basis for your charges against him. 15Neither has Herod, for he sent him back to us; as you can see, he has done nothing to deserve death. 16Therefore, I will punish him and then release him.'"

18With one voice they cried out, "Away with this man! Release Barabbas to us!" 19(Barabbas had been thrown into prison for an insurrection in the city, and for murder.)

20Wanting to release Jesus, Pilate appealed to them again. 21But they kept shouting, "Crucify him! Crucify him!"

22For the third time he spoke to them: "Why? What crime has this man committed? I have found in him no grounds for the death penalty. Therefore I will have him punished and then release him."

23But with loud shouts they insistently demanded that he be crucified, and their shouts prevailed. 24So Pilate decided to grant their demand. 25He released the man who had been thrown into prison for insurrection and murder, the one they asked for, and surrendered Jesus to their will.

The Crucifixion

26As they led him away, they seized Simon from Cyrene, who was on his way in from the country, and put the cross on him and made him carry it behind Jesus. 27A large number of people followed him, including women who mourned and wailed for him. 28Jesus turned and said to them, "Daughters of Jerusalem, do not weep for me; weep for yourselves and for your children. 29For the time will come when you will say, 'Blessed are the barren women, the wombs that never bore and the breasts that never nursed!' 30Then

" 'they will say to the mountains, "Fall on us!"
and to the hills, "Cover us!" 'm

31For if men do these things when the tree is green, what will happen when it is dry?"

32Two other men, both criminals, were also led out with him to be executed. 33When they came to the place called the Skull, there they crucified him, along with the criminals—one on his right, the other on his left. 34Jesus said, "Father, forgive them,

OPEN: Of all your childhood chores (doing laundry, cleaning your room, mowing the lawn, caring for pets, doing the dishes), which was your least favorite? Most favorite? Which one did you have to be forced to do?

DIG: 1. By now, how is Jesus faring (see Mk 14:65; 15:15-19)? Why would someone have to help Jesus carry the cross? 2. Why would Jesus rather have no one weep for him (vv.28-31; see 21:20-24)? How might the crowds feel about what he said? How would you paraphrase what he meant by the proverb in verse 31? 3. What attitudes and motives do you see in the crowd following this death-march? In the rulers? The criminals? The soldiers? The sign (v.38)? In Jesus? 4. What aspects of the gospel message do you see in verses 40-43? 5. Do you think the written notice (put there at Pilate's request) hints at sarcasm or truth on Pilate's part? Why?

l16 Some manuscripts him." 17Now he was obliged to release one man to them at the Feast.   m30 Hosea 10:8

for they do not know what they are doing."[n] And they divided up his clothes by casting lots.

[35]The people stood watching, and the rulers even sneered at him. They said, "He saved others; let him save himself if he is the Christ of God, the Chosen One."

[36]The soldiers also came up and mocked him. They offered him wine vinegar [37]and said, "If you are the king of the Jews, save yourself."

[38]There was a written notice above him, which read: THIS IS THE KING OF THE JEWS.

[39]One of the criminals who hung there hurled insults at him: "Aren't you the Christ? Save yourself and us!"

[40]But the other criminal rebuked him. "Don't you fear God," he said, "since you are under the same sentence? [41]We are punished justly, for we are getting what our deeds deserve. But this man has done nothing wrong."

[42]Then he said, "Jesus, remember me when you come into your kingdom[o]."

[43]Jesus answered him, "I tell you the truth, today you will be with me in paradise."

Jesus' Death

[44]It was now about the sixth hour, and darkness came over the whole land until the ninth hour, [45]for the sun stopped shining. And the curtain of the temple was torn in two. [46]Jesus called out with a loud voice, "Father, into your hands I commit my spirit." When he had said this, he breathed his last.

[47]The centurion, seeing what had happened, praised God and said, "Surely this was a righteous man." [48]When all the people who had gathered to witness this sight saw what took place, they beat their breasts and went away. [49]But all those who knew him, including the women who had followed him from Galilee, stood at a distance, watching these things.

Jesus' Burial

[50]Now there was a man named Joseph, a member of the Council, a good and upright man, [51]who had not consented to their decision and action. He came from the Judean town of Arimathea and he was waiting for the kingdom of God. [52]Going to Pilate, he asked for Jesus' body. [53]Then he took it down, wrapped it in linen cloth and placed it in a tomb cut in the rock, one in which no one had yet been laid. [54]It was Preparation Day, and the Sabbath was about to begin.

[55]The women who had come with Jesus from Galilee followed Joseph and saw the tomb and how his body was laid in it. [56]Then they went home and prepared spices and perfumes. But they rested on the Sabbath in obedience to the commandment.

REFLECT: 1. How do you view the crucifixion: Necessary evil? Common tragedy? Cruel and unusual punishment? Sacrifice for sin? Triumph over injustice? Why? 2. When did the meaning of the death of Christ begin to make sense to you? How would you explain the necessity of the crucifixion to a non-Christian friend? What hope does Christ's death give you? 3. Who in this story do you identify with most? With least? Why? 4. What impresses you about Jesus here?

OPEN: 1. Whose death (family, friend or national figure) has affected you most? Why? 2. When was the last time you took a big risk, not knowing how things would turn out?

DIG: 1. What is the meaning of the darkness (see 22:53; 1 Jn 1:5)? The torn curtain (Heb 9:1-4, 6-8, 11-12,25-28;10:19-20)? Jesus' prayer (Ps 31:5)? The centurion's confession (Jn 12:32)? 2. What do you learn about Joseph? Why would he risk his reputation and status at this point?

REFLECT: 1. From the elements here, how would you describe to someone what Jesus' death was all about? How does it make a difference in your view of sin and failure? Your confidence in God's love? 2. Jesus had apparently failed, but Joseph and the women did not abandon him. What do you learn from this for your life?

---

[n]34 Some early manuscripts do not have this sentence.   [o]42 Some manuscripts *come with your kingly power*

OPEN: What time do you normally have to get up in the morning? How about on a day off?

DIG: 1. Given what all these women have experienced in the last few days (19:37ff; 23:26-49, 55), how would they feel as they prepare to go to the tomb? When they find it empty? When the two men spoke to them? 2. Why wouldn't the Eleven believe them? What must be going through Peter's mind?

REFLECT: 1. How did the meaning of the resurrection first "dawn" upon you? What difference does the resurrection make to you? 2. Where is your spiritual life focused these days: On Good Friday? Easter Sunday? Or in between?

OPEN: If you got laid off from work today or your job was "terminated," where would you go to "get yourself together"?

DIG: 1. Eavesdrop on these two disciples: What things are they likely talking about as they walk (see vv.19-24)? What tones of voice do you hear? What hopes are dashed? What plans might they be making? How do they react to the "stranger"? 2. From your knowledge of OT prophecy and law, what passages might "the stranger" have discussed with them in verses 25-27? Why did Jesus do this roundabout Bible study rather than just reveal his identity immediately and directly? 3. How does the time at dinner open their eyes? What happens to Jesus when they recognize him? Why do you think he leaves? 4. What has happened to the other disciples that has caused them to change their minds from verse 11? Why a special appearance to Peter? What expectations must they have now (see also Ac 1:6)?

REFLECT: 1. Where is your "Road to Emmaus"—the place where Jesus surprised you recently? What happened? 2. How well do you think you can explain the life, death, and resurrection of

The Resurrection

24 On the first day of the week, very early in the morning, the women took the spices they had prepared and went to the tomb. ²They found the stone rolled away from the tomb, ³but when they entered, they did not find the body of the Lord Jesus. ⁴While they were wondering about this, suddenly two men in clothes that gleamed like lightning stood beside them. ⁵In their fright the women bowed down with their faces to the ground, but the men said to them, "Why do you look for the living among the dead? ⁶He is not here; he has risen! Remember how he told you, while he was still with you in Galilee: ⁷'The Son of Man must be delivered into the hands of sinful men, be crucified and on the third day be raised again.' " ⁸Then they remembered his words.

⁹When they came back from the tomb, they told all these things to the Eleven and to all the others. ¹⁰It was Mary Magdalene, Joanna, Mary the mother of James, and the others with them who told this to the apostles. ¹¹But they did not believe the women, because their words seemed to them like nonsense. ¹²Peter, however, got up and ran to the tomb. Bending over, he saw the strips of linen lying by themselves, and he went away, wondering to himself what had happened.

On the Road to Emmaus

¹³Now that same day two of them were going to a village called Emmaus, about seven miles*ᵖ* from Jerusalem. ¹⁴They were talking with each other about everything that had happened. ¹⁵As they talked and discussed these things with each other, Jesus himself came up and walked along with them; ¹⁶but they were kept from recognizing him.

¹⁷He asked them, "What are you discussing together as you walk along?"

They stood still, their faces downcast. ¹⁸One of them, named Cleopas, asked him, "Are you only a visitor to Jerusalem and do not know the things that have happened there in these days?"

¹⁹"What things?" he asked.

"About Jesus of Nazareth," they replied. "He was a prophet, powerful in word and deed before God and all the people. ²⁰The chief priests and our rulers handed him over to be sentenced to death, and they crucified him; ²¹but we had hoped that he was the one who was going to redeem Israel. And what is more, it is the third day since all this took place. ²²In addition, some of our women amazed us. They went to the tomb early this morning ²³but didn't find his body. They came and told us that they had seen a vision of angels, who said he was alive. ²⁴Then some of our companions went to the tomb and found it just as the women had said, but him they did not see."

²⁵He said to them, "How foolish you are, and how slow of heart to believe all that the prophets have spoken! ²⁶Did not the Christ*ᵠ* have to suffer these things and then enter his glory?" ²⁷And beginning with Moses and all the Prophets, he explained to them what was said in all the Scriptures concerning himself.

ᵖ13 Greek sixty stadia (about 11 kilometers)   *ᵠ26 Or Messiah; also in verse 46*

Luke 24:13-35   ON THE ROAD TO EMMAUS

LOOKING INTO THE SCRIPTURE/20 Minutes. Read Luke 24:13-35 and discuss.

1. Why did the two men take off for Emmaus?
   a. scared stiff
   b. work the next day
   c. running away
   d. disillusionment over the events of the last week

2. Why didn't the two men recognize Jesus when he joined them?
   a. they refused to believe their eyes
   b. they were too occupied
   c. Jesus was invisible in his resurrection body
   d. they didn't look up to see who it was
   e. they were kept from recognizing him

3. When they heard the report from the women about the empty tomb, what did they assume?
   a. the worst
   b. Jesus was alive
   c. someone had stolen the body
   d. the authorities were arresting everybody

4. Why did Jesus begin with Moses and the prophets in explaining what happened?
   a. the guys knew about them
   b. Moses gave the Law and the prophets predicted the coming Messiah
   c. to understand Jesus, you have to understand the Old Testament
   d. to show them they were on the right track about Jesus

5. What opened the eyes of the two men?
   a. burst of insight
   b. the way Jesus "took bread . . . and broke it"
   c. the Holy Spirit
   d. putting two and two together

6. Why did the two men want to return to Jerusalem?
   a. to join the party
   b. to confirm the women's report
   c. to make amends
   d. to be with their friends
   e. to tell everybody the good news
   f. to rejoin Jesus' team they had quit

MY OWN STORY/25 Minutes.

1. Take a moment and indicate from 1 to 10 how you would cope with the following stress situations. 1 is NO ANXIETY; 10 is HIGH ANXIETY.

_____ DEATH: Your closest friend suddenly dies
_____ SECURITY: One day your boss tells you that you are fired
_____ HOPE SHATTERED: The dreams you had for the future are dashed
_____ LODGING: You don't have a place to sleep tonight
_____ REPUTATION: You risked everything and the cause you believed in turns sour
_____ FRIENDS: The old gang breaks up, including most of your friends
_____ SUICIDE: One of your friends hangs himself
_____ BETRAYAL: You feel let down by the one person in the world you trusted
_____ SHAME: The people in town laugh at you and think you've wasted your life

2. Have you ever felt like running away or throwing in the towel spiritually?
   a. maybe once or twice
   b. often
   c. never

3. What is the thing that triggers a spiritual crisis in your experience?
   a. financial panic
   b. anger with God over personal tragedy
   c. disappointment in a relationship
   d. domestic problems/hassles
   e. questions/doubts about my faith
   f. disillusionment with my church
   g. lack of direction from God

4. What has helped you recognize Jesus walking alongside you when you are down spiritually?
   a. time alone with God
   b. talking it out with someone
   c. fellowship with other strugglers
   d. getting away from the situation
   e. Communion
   f. reading familiar Scripture
   g. a favorite hymn

Jesus Christ, and the way a person can have a relationship with him? Try rehearsing or role playing this in your group. Who could you communicate these truths with "for real" today?

OPEN: What favorite slogan or "pep" talk do you recall from your mentors (parents, a coach, music teacher, etc.)? How were you treated when you blew it?

DIG: 1. How is "peace be with you" a good summary of the gospel? 2. Why are the disciples having such difficulty believing: (a) Not using their eyes? (b) Not enough evidence? (c) Not enough faith? (d) Too much joy? Why was it necessary for them to see that Jesus was not a ghost? 3. What interpretation from Jesus helps them to believe? 4. What task does he give them? With what promise? How must they have felt? 5. Why do the disciples react so differently when Jesus is taken away now (vv.50-53; compare when he was taken away by the crucifixion)?

REFLECT: 1. Why is it important to you that Jesus' mission was anticipated far beforehand in the Old Testament? What OT hopes for the Messiah are especially significant for you? 2. How would you live differently if Jesus was not currently reigning in heaven, but was only another noble martyr? 3. In light of your circumstances, where is the "mission field" Jesus has sent you? Who are some of the people in that "field"? How can you be a witness to them by your life? By your words? 4. How do you respond to his mission for you: (a) Let's get going!? (b) I couldn't possibly do that!? (c) He didn't mean me? (d) I'm scared, but I'll trust him? Why? 5. What has been the high point in this study for you?

28As they approached the village to which they were going, Jesus acted as if he were going farther. 29But they urged him strongly, "Stay with us, for it is nearly evening; the day is almost over." So he went in to stay with them.

30When he was at the table with them, he took bread, gave thanks, broke it and began to give it to them. 31Then their eyes were opened and they recognized him, and he disappeared from their sight. 32They asked each other, "Were not our hearts burning within us while he talked with us on the road and opened the Scriptures to us?"

33They got up and returned at once to Jerusalem. There they found the Eleven and those with them, assembled together 34and saying, "It is true! The Lord has risen and has appeared to Simon." 35Then the two told what had happened on the way, and how Jesus was recognized by them when he broke the bread.

Jesus Appears to the Disciples

36While they were still talking about this, Jesus himself stood among them and said to them, "Peace be with you."

37They were startled and frightened, thinking they saw a ghost. 38He said to them, "Why are you troubled, and why do doubts rise in your minds? 39Look at my hands and my feet. It is I myself! Touch me and see; a ghost does not have flesh and bones, as you see I have."

40When he had said this, he showed them his hands and feet. 41And while they still did not believe it because of joy and amazement, he asked them, "Do you have anything here to eat?" 42They gave him a piece of broiled fish, 43and he took it and ate it in their presence.

44He said to them, "This is what I told you while I was still with you: Everything must be fulfilled that is written about me in the Law of Moses, the Prophets and the Psalms."

45Then he opened their minds so they could understand the Scriptures. 46He told them, "This is what is written: The Christ will suffer and rise from the dead on the third day, 47and repentance and forgiveness of sins will be preached in his name to all nations, beginning at Jerusalem. 48You are witnesses of these things. 49I am going to send you what my Father has promised; but stay in the city until you have been clothed with power from on high."

The Ascension

50When he had led them out to the vicinity of Bethany, he lifted up his hands and blessed them. 51While he was blessing them, he left them and was taken up into heaven. 52Then they worshiped him and returned to Jerusalem with great joy. 53And they stayed continually at the temple, praising God.

JOHN

INTRODUCTION

Author—The Disciple Whom Jesus Loved

The writer of the fourth Gospel does not name himself in the text. Like the other three gospels, the fourth Gospel is anonymous. The inscription "The Gospel According to John" or "According to John" (as found in some ancient manuscripts) was added to the text by early Christians.

Yet in a curious way the fourth Gospel is less anonymous than the other three because the writer identifies himself in the final chapter by way of a title. He calls himself "the disciple whom Jesus loved" (21:20-24; see also 13:23-25; 19:26-27; 20:2-8; 21:7). Who then is this mysterious disciple who wanted to be known only in terms of his relationship to Jesus?

One of the Twelve

He must have been one of the twelve original disciples because he was present at the Last Supper (13:23-25; 21:20). In fact, the beloved disciple was "reclining next to" Jesus (13:23). This gives us a valuable clue as to his identity: He was probably one of the three (occasionally four) disciples who were closest to Jesus—Peter, James, John and sometimes Andrew. We know that the person reclining next to Jesus was not Peter, because Peter asked this disciple a question (13:24). The person was probably not Andrew, since Andrew is explicitly named several times in the text (1:40, 44; 6:8; 12:22); it would be strange to name a disciple in some places and to list him anonymously in others as "the disciple whom Jesus loved." Most of the other disciples are also named in this gospel. Some have suggested Lazarus as author of the fourth Gospel because in 11:5 Jesus is said to have loved him, but Lazarus is named in chapters 11-12. Of all the possible candidates, only the sons of Zebedee (James and John) are not named in the fourth Gospel. The beloved disciple could not have been James, since he died at the hands of Herod Agrippa I (Acts 12:2) early in the development of the church, and the fourth Gospel was written years after his death. Therefore, the most likely candidate is his brother John.

Indeed, early church tradition is unanimous that John the apostle, the son of Zebedee, wrote the fourth Gospel. For example, toward the end of the second century Irenaeus wrote: "Afterwards, John, the disciple of the Lord, who also had leaned upon His breast, did himself publish a Gospel during his residence at Ephesus in Asia."

John's Biography

What, then, do we know about John the apostle? First, we know that he and his brother James, along with Peter and his brother Andrew, were the first four disciples called by Jesus (Mark 1:19). Furthermore, James and John seem inseparable. On only one occasion is John recorded as acting alone (Luke 9:49-50). Together the two brothers want to call down fire on a village (Luke 9:54). Together they earn the title from Jesus of "Sons of Thunder" (Mark 3:17). The two of them request to be seated on Jesus' right and left in the coming kingdom (Mark 10:37). They are both with Jesus on the Mount of Transfiguration (Mark 9:2), in Gethsemane (Mark 14:33), and when Jairus' daughter is raised from the dead (Mark 5:37). John is right at the heart of Jesus' life and ministry. He of all the disciples is qualified to give the world a glimpse of Jesus' deepest thoughts and profound concerns.

Date

As is so often the case with books of the Bible, it is not possible to give an exact date for the writing of John's gospel. Most scholars agree that it was the last of the four gospels to be written. It was probably composed in A.D. 80 or 90, though it may have been written shortly after the fall of Jerusalem in A.D. 70.

Characteristics

For those familiar with the synoptic Gospels (Matthew, Mark, Luke), what strikes one so forcibly about John's gospel is how *different* it is. Despite their different emphases, the Synoptics tell the same story (probably because Matthew and Luke both build upon Mark's account). They are telling one part of Jesus' story. John, however, tells another part of that story. This is not to say that John's account contradicts the Synoptics. Rather, John makes explicit what Matthew, Mark, and Luke only hint at. He leaves out a lot of material covered in the Synoptics, but he adds information about aspects of Jesus' ministry not discussed elsewhere. And he records for us not just Jesus' pithy statements, so prominent in the Synoptics, but also his longer discourses.

The Omissions

In John's gospel, we find no information about Jesus' birth; his baptism is only alluded to; and his temptation is not even mentioned. In the fourth Gospel, Jesus casts out no demons, cures no lepers, almost never speaks in parables, and does not emphasize the idea of the kingdom of God. John does not mention the institution of the Lord's Supper or Jesus' agony in the Garden of Gethsemane.

The Conclusion

Instead, in John's gospel we are told about portions of Jesus' ministry not discussed in the Synoptics. We hear about Jesus' ministry before John the Baptist's imprisonment. We hear of Jesus' visits to Jerusalem before his final visit when he was crucified. Perhaps most importantly, in the fourth Gospel we are given details of Jesus' ministry in Judea (the Synoptic gospels focus on his Galilean ministry). John's gospel is particularly rich when it comes to the teachings of Jesus. Here we find his long discourses on great themes such as light, love, life, truth, and abiding. Here in the great *I Am* sections we listen to Jesus reveal who he is.

John also records for us some of the most beloved stories about Jesus. Only in the fourth Gospel can we read about the wedding feast at Cana of Galilee (2:1-11), the night visit of Nicodemus (3:1-15), the conversation with the woman at the well (4:4-42), the raising of Lazarus from the dead (11:1-44), and the washing of the disciples' feet (13:1-17). In John's gospel, we find the bulk of our Lord's teaching about the Holy Spirit and here the mysterious "I" in the Sermon on the Mount ("You have heard that it was said . . . but I tell you. . . .") becomes the majestic "I am" who is God's own Son.

Style

John writes in very simple Greek. He does not use a wide range of vocabulary. He often repeats words and phrases. Yet the end result is a compelling document whose very simplicity makes it impressive.

The fourth Gospel was written by a man with an adequate but not extensive education in Greek. In fact, some scholars suggest that this Greek sounds acquired, not native. Furthermore, the writing has a strong Jewish flavoring. This is exactly what one would expect of John, the son of Zebedee—a Jew who had lived for a long time in Galilee, an area whose population included more Gentiles than Jews.

Theme

Why did John write as he did about Jesus? What was his purpose in gathering together this account? Two of his own statements provide the answer to this question.

First, John asserts in his first epistle: "This we proclaim concerning the Word of life. The life appeared; we have seen it and testify to it. . . . We proclaim to you what we have seen and heard, so that you also may have fellowship with us" (1 John 1:1-3). Second, John states at the end of his gospel: "These are written that you may believe that Jesus is the Christ, the Son of God, and that by believing you may have life in his name" (John 20:31). John's gospel, therefore, like the other three gospels, is a witness document. He tells us Jesus' story so that we will understand who Jesus is, put our faith in him as the unique Son of God, and so experience life in Christ and fellowship with other believers.

Structure

It is not clear how John's gospel ought to be subdivided. It is an incredibly rich, complex, and fluid piece of writing in which various themes operate at different levels.

Still, most scholars agree that John's gospel begins with a distinct prologue (1:1-18) and then divides into two major parts. The first part of the gospel concentrates on Jesus' *public ministry*. It is organized around his miracles, "signs" that reveal who he really is. This part covers most of the three years of Jesus' ministry.

In the second part, the focus shifts from the crowds to the disciples and Jesus' *private ministry* among them. The theme in this section is the *glory* that is revealed in Jesus' crucifixion and resurrection. The time period of this part is short: from the Thursday night of the Last Supper through Jesus' postresurrection appearances.

Additional themes run through the book. For example, the material is grouped around the major Jewish feasts. Also, the idea of the passion of Jesus is present throughout. The chart below illustrates the structural complexity of this gospel.

Overview Study Questions

1. The author of the fourth Gospel never names himself. Yet you can figure out who he is. Look up all the references given above in the section entitled "Author" and then summarize how we know John wrote this book.
2. Read the stories about John in Mark's gospel and write a short biography. See Mark 1:16-20; 3:13-19; 5:37; 9:2-13; 9:38-41; 10:35-45; 13:3-4; and 14:32-42.
3. Skim John's gospel. What picture of Jesus emerges from these pages?

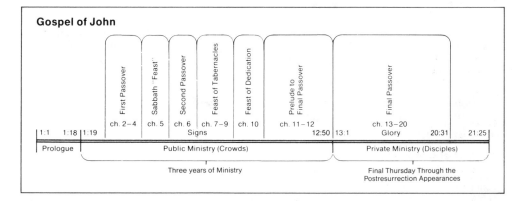

John

OPEN : 1. What is your full name? How did your parents come up with it? **2.** What is your nick-name? How did you get that?

DIG: 1. Why does this gospel begin "in the beginning" rather than at Jesus' birth? **2.** What facts about "the Word" can you find in verses 1-5? Verses 10-18? **3.** What is John the Baptist's role as a witness? **4.** Who or what fails to comprehend the light (vv.5,10, 11)? Why? **5.** From the image of "receiving" someone (v.12), how would you explain what faith is about? What is the result of this type of faith? **6.** How would someone "full of grace and truth" treat others? In light of that, why are John (v.15) and Moses (v.17) given "second-billing"? **7.** From this passage, how can a person come to know God?

REFLECT: 1. How much have you allowed Jesus to "dwell" with you? Are you keeping him at the door? In the living room? Or have you given him the keys? Why? **2.** What strikes you most about Jesus in this passage? Why?

OPEN: 1. As a child, were you ever kept after school or sent to the principal's office? What for? **2.** Have you ever been embarrassed by mistaking a stranger for a friend? What happened?

DIG: 1. What questions do the priests and Levites ask John? What do these questions reveal about the reason why they were sent? **2.** Why does John respond so abruptly? What would you have said in his situation? **3.** What is John's goal in life (vv.22-23,26-27; also Isa 40:3-5)? **4.** Since baptism only applied to Gentile converts to Judaism, what is behind the Pharisees' cynical

The Word Became Flesh

1 In the beginning was the Word, and the Word was with God, and the Word was God. [2]He was with God in the beginning.

[3]Through him all things were made; without him nothing was made that has been made. [4]In him was life, and that life was the light of men. [5]The light shines in the darkness, but the darkness has not understood[a] it.

[6]There came a man who was sent from God; his name was John. [7]He came as a witness to testify concerning that light, so that through him all men might believe. [8]He himself was not the light; he came only as a witness to the light. [9]The true light that gives light to every man was coming into the world.[b]

[10]He was in the world, and though the world was made through him, the world did not recognize him. [11]He came to that which was his own, but his own did not receive him. [12]Yet to all who received him, to those who believed in his name, he gave the right to become children of God— [13]children born not of natural descent,[c] nor of human decision or a husband's will, but born of God.

[14]The Word became flesh and made his dwelling among us. We have seen his glory, the glory of the One and Only,[d] who came from the Father, full of grace and truth.

[15]John testifies concerning him. He cries out, saying, "This was he of whom I said, 'He who comes after me has surpassed me because he was before me.' " [16]From the fullness of his grace we have all received one blessing after another. [17]For the law was given through Moses; grace and truth came through Jesus Christ. [18]No one has ever seen God, but God the One and Only,[d] [e]who is at the Father's side, has made him known.

John the Baptist Denies Being the Christ

[19]Now this was John's testimony when the Jews of Jerusalem sent priests and Levites to ask him who he was. [20]He did not fail to confess, but confessed freely, "I am not the Christ.[f]"

[21]They asked him, "Then who are you? Are you Elijah?" He said, "I am not."

"Are you the Prophet?" He answered, "No."

[22]Finally they said, "Who are you? Give us an answer to take back to those who sent us. What do you say about yourself?"

[23]John replied in the words of Isaiah the prophet, "I am the voice of one calling in the desert, 'Make straight the way for the Lord.' "[g]

[24]Now some Pharisees who had been sent [25]questioned him,

---

[a]5 Or *darkness, and the darkness has not overcome* [b]9 Or *This was the true light that gives light to every man who comes into the world* [c]13 Greek of *bloods* [d]14,18 Or *the Only Begotten* [e]18 Some manuscripts *but the only* (or *only begotten*) *Son* [f]20 Or *Messiah.* "The Christ" (Greek) and "the Messiah" (Hebrew) both mean "the Anointed One"; also in verse 25. [g]23 Isaiah 40:3

LOOKING INTO THE SCRIPTURE/20 Minutes. Read John 1:1-18 and discuss.

1. If you really wanted to explain to someone how much you loved them, what would you do?
    a. rent a billboard
    b. send a video
    c. flood the city with leaflets
    d. send someone to explain
    e. go myself

2. How would you describe the opening of this gospel?
    a. looking down the barrel of time
    b. the curtain rising on a great drama
    c. the music from a space odyssey
    d. walking into a movie that has already started
    e. reading the last page of a great novel before you read the book

3. What do you think is the theme of this introduction?
    a. the Creator of the world has come to redeem his creation
    b. God who created the world has become flesh
    c. the battle for the control of the world has started
    d. life and salvation is for everyone

4. How would you describe John the Baptist's role?
    a. pre-game show
    b. press box announcer
    c. first act
    d. the clue to the mystery
    e. a footnote in history

5. What is the invitation in verse 12?
    a. to live a good life
    b. to learn how to be successful
    c. to get yourself together
    d. to join the family of God

6. When does this life begin?
    a. when you die and go to heaven
    b. whenever you take God at his word
    c. when you win the lottery
    d. when you clean up your life

7. What impresses me most about God is that:
    a. he has always existed
    b. he is the light (nothing is hidden from him)
    c. he sent his son to live with us as a human being (the Incarnation)
    d. he gave us the right to become his children
    e. he really wants us to know him
    f. he is the Creator & Sustainer of life

MY OWN STORY/25 Minutes.

1. When did Jesus become the Word of God to you?
    a. years ago
    b. just recently
    c. never has
    d. not sure what you mean

2. If you had to compare your relationship with God right now to a ball game, where would you be?
    a. sitting in the grandstands
    b. on the team/benchwarming
    c. playing defense
    d. playing offense
    e. on the injury list
    f. halftime in the locker room
    g. trying to figure out the game
    h. giving it all I've got

3. What if Jesus told you that you were his personal representative in the world today. How would that make you feel?
    a. you've got to be kidding
    b. scared
    c. OK, if I'm not the only one
    d. OK, but I don't like the idea that those closest to me might not accept me
    e. I'm not ready to be a servant
    f. not sure what this means
    g. eager to start

question (vv.24-25) and John's evasive answer (vv.26-27)? **5.** How does John finally answer their question about his baptism (vv.30-31)? What does he mean by calling Jesus the "Lamb of God" (v.29; see Ex 12:1-13; Isa 53:7) and the "Son of God" (v.34)? What proof supports these claims?

REFLECT: 1. What is your goal in life? How would you compare your goals to a cooked steak: Half-cooked? Medium rare? Medium well? Well done? **2.** Of the titles for Jesus given so far (the Word, the Light, the Christ, the Lamb of God, the Son of God), which means the most to you? Why? **3.** What is one "evidence" that has led you to faith in Jesus?

OPEN: 1. When you get some good news, who is the first person you want to share it with? Why? **2.** As a kid, what would it take to get you to believe something your brother or sister told you?

DIG: 1. In light of verses 30-31, how do you think John felt when his disciples left him to follow Jesus? What does this say about John? **2.** What motivated the disciples of John to follow Jesus? What motivated Andrew to tell Simon about him? **3.** What are the titles used in this passage to describe Jesus? What do they mean? **4.** How do you think Simon felt when Jesus changed his name to Cephas (meaning "rock")? **5.** What did Philip have in common with Andrew? What insight about Jesus excites Philip? **6.** What type of person is Nathanael? Why might he find it hard to believe Philip's statement? Why would Jesus call Philip and Nathanael in such different ways? How do you think Nathanael felt when Jesus spoke to him? **7.** Of the five people in verses 35-48 who followed Jesus, answer this: (a) How was the contact made for each one? (b) How much did each one know about Jesus when he decided to follow him? (c) How does each "decision for Christ" illustrate the point of the prologue about the light of John and the true light of Christ?

"Why then do you baptize if you are not the Christ, nor Elijah, nor the Prophet?"

[26]"I baptize with[h] water," John replied, "but among you stands one you do not know. [27]He is the one who comes after me, the thongs of whose sandals I am not worthy to untie."

[28]This all happened at Bethany on the other side of the Jordan, where John was baptizing.

Jesus the Lamb of God

[29]The next day John saw Jesus coming toward him and said, "Look, the Lamb of God, who takes away the sin of the world! [30]This is the one I meant when I said, 'A man who comes after me has surpassed me because he was before me.' [31]I myself did not know him, but the reason I came baptizing with water was that he might be revealed to Israel."

[32]Then John gave this testimony: "I saw the Spirit come down from heaven as a dove and remain on him. [33]I would not have known him, except that the one who sent me to baptize with water told me, 'The man on whom you see the Spirit come down and remain is he who will baptize with the Holy Spirit.' [34]I have seen and I testify that this is the Son of God."

Jesus' First Disciples

[35]The next day John was there again with two of his disciples. [36]When he saw Jesus passing by, he said, "Look, the Lamb of God!"

[37]When the two disciples heard him say this, they followed Jesus. [38]Turning around, Jesus saw them following and asked, "What do you want?"

They said, "Rabbi" (which means Teacher), "where are you staying?"

[39]"Come," he replied, "and you will see."

So they went and saw where he was staying, and spent that day with him. It was about the tenth hour.

[40]Andrew, Simon Peter's brother, was one of the two who heard what John had said and who had followed Jesus. [41]The first thing Andrew did was to find his brother Simon and tell him, "We have found the Messiah" (that is, the Christ). [42]And he brought him to Jesus.

Jesus looked at him and said, "You are Simon son of John. You will be called Cephas" (which, when translated, is Peter[i]).

Jesus Calls Philip and Nathanael

[43]The next day Jesus decided to leave for Galilee. Finding Philip, he said to him, "Follow me."

[44]Philip, like Andrew and Peter, was from the town of Bethsaida. [45]Philip found Nathanael and told him, "We have found the one Moses wrote about in the Law, and about whom the prophets also wrote—Jesus of Nazareth, the son of Joseph."

[46]"Nazareth! Can anything good come from there?" Nathanael asked.

---

[h]26 Or *in*; also in verses 31 and 33   [i]42 Both *Cephas* (Aramaic) and *Peter* (Greek) mean *rock*.

LOOKING INTO THE SCRIPTURE/20 Minutes. Read the Scripture passage aloud in your group, then answer the questions below.

1. What was John the Baptist saying about Jesus when he described him as the "Lamb of God"?
    a. he was to be the ruler of the restored kingdom of Judah
    b. he was the promised sacrifice for the sin of the world
    c. he was meek and gentle like a sheep

2. How do you react to the disciples following Jesus for the day?
    a. they were irresponsible
    b. Jesus must have been irresistable
    c. they didn't have anything better to do
    d. etiquette was not their strong point
    e. they had no idea what they were in for

3. What is Jesus inviting the two disciples of John the Baptist to do?
    a. switch their allegiance to him
    b. examine the evidence for themselves
    c. tag along for the fun of it
    d. give him a chance to prove himself

4. "We have found the Messiah." What was Andrew, Simon Peter's brother, really saying?
    a. Jesus will help them to overthrow the Roman Empire
    b. Jesus is a great teacher
    c. Jesus is the future king of Israel
    d. Jesus will take away their sin

5. "You are Simon son of John. You will be Cephas." Why did Jesus change his name from Simon (meaning "sinking sand") to Peter (meaning "the rock")?
    a. he wanted Simon to feel good about himself
    b. he saw a strength in Simon that justified changing his name
    c. he wanted to start the process of changing Simon's self image
    d. he saw ahead to what Simon would be some day

MY OWN STORY/25 Minutes.

1. What was your name when you first felt drawn to Jesus?
    a. Desperate David
    b. Guilty Gus
    c. Much Afraid
    d. Lonely Larry
    e. Confused Connie
    f. _____

2. What was it about Jesus that drew you to him?
    a. historical evidence
    b. being around my parents
    c. my own personal yearning
    d. the changed life of a friend
    e. peer pressure
    f. search for the truth
    g. desire to find meaning for my life

3. If you were given a "nickname" right now to describe your spiritual condition, what would it be?
    a. Slippery: on a greasy slide going downhill
    b. Rocky II: the comeback kid
    c. Barely: never triumphant/just somehow
    d. Refrigerator: taking it all in
    e. Grace: thankful for what God did
    f. Patience: God is doing his thing
    g. Spacey: out to lunch
    h. _____

4. What is the biggest obstacle to your spiritual growth right now?
    a. not knowing what God wants
    b. keeping a daily discipline
    c. feeling all alone
    d. fear of failing
    e. _____

REFLECT: 1. What was your motive for following Jesus originally? What were the circumstances that led you to do so? How much did you know about him? 2. Who was the John or Andrew in your life?

"Come and see," said Philip.

[47]When Jesus saw Nathanael approaching, he said of him, "Here is a true Israelite, in whom there is nothing false."

[48]"How do you know me?" Nathanael asked.

Jesus answered, "I saw you while you were still under the fig tree before Philip called you."

[49]Then Nathanael declared, "Rabbi, you are the Son of God; you are the King of Israel."

[50]Jesus said, "You believe[j] because I told you I saw you under the fig tree. You shall see greater things than that." [51]He then added, "I tell you[k] the truth, you[k] shall see heaven open, and the angels of God ascending and descending on the Son of Man."

Jesus Changes Water to Wine

OPEN: What is the funniest thing you've witnessed at a wedding?

DIG: 1. Jesus is not known as a miracle-worker, so why does Mary approach him (v.3)? What do you learn about Jesus and his mother from verses 3-5? 2. Given their social customs, how would you feel as the host (v.3)? As a servant (vv.6-8)? As the host in verses 9-10? As the groom? 3. What part does the function and size of the jars play in this story? How does the quantity and quality of the wine demonstrate Jesus' glory? 4. How does this sign relate to the "time" he refers to in verse 4 (see also 7:6,8; 12:33; 17:1)?

REFLECT: Where is the "wine" level (zest for life) in your life right now: Full? Half full? Empty? What is draining you? What area seems like stale water in an old jug? How could Jesus renew that?

2 On the third day a wedding took place at Cana in Galilee. Jesus' mother was there, [2]and Jesus and his disciples had also been invited to the wedding. [3]When the wine was gone, Jesus' mother said to him, "They have no more wine."

[4]"Dear woman, why do you involve me?" Jesus replied, "My time has not yet come."

[5]His mother said to the servants, "Do whatever he tells you."

[6]Nearby stood six stone water jars, the kind used by the Jews for ceremonial washing, each holding from twenty to thirty gallons.[l]

[7]Jesus said to the servants, "Fill the jars with water"; so they filled them to the brim.

[8]Then he told them, "Now draw some out and take it to the master of the banquet."

They did so, [9]and the master of the banquet tasted the water that had been turned into wine. He did not realize where it had come from, though the servants who had drawn the water knew. Then he called the bridegroom aside [10]and said, "Everyone brings out the choice wine first and then the cheaper wine after the guests have had too much to drink; but you have saved the best till now."

[11]This, the first of his miraculous signs, Jesus performed in Cana of Galilee. He thus revealed his glory, and his disciples put their faith in him.

Jesus Clears the Temple

OPEN: 1. How are you at keeping your room (kitchen, desktop, car) clean? 2. What guest would cause you to get busy and clean house: The "boss"? Your pastor? A celebrity? Your in-laws?

DIG: 1. Originally the sellers and money-changers were set up to provide sacrificial animals for sale at the temple as a help to Jews from far away. How might this once-useful practice have deteriorated into a racket? Why else was Jesus angry? 2. As one of the sellers, how would you feel about Jesus' actions? As one of the disciples, how would you feel? 3. How is Jesus challenged? Why?

[12]After this he went down to Capernaum with his mother and brothers and his disciples. There they stayed for a few days.

[13]When it was almost time for the Jewish Passover, Jesus went up to Jerusalem. [14]In the temple courts he found men selling cattle, sheep and doves, and others sitting at tables exchanging money. [15]So he made a whip out of cords, and drove all from the temple area, both sheep and cattle; he scattered the coins of the money changers and overturned their tables. [16]To those who sold doves he said, "Get these out of here! How dare you turn my Father's house into a market!"

---

[j]50 Or Do you believe...?   [k]51 The Greek is plural.   [l]6 Greek two to three metretes (probably about 75 to 115 liters)

John 2:1-11   **JESUS CHANGES WATER TO WINE**

LOOKING INTO THE SCRIPTURE/20 Minutes. Read John 2:1-11 and discuss.

1. If you could choose any miracle to start you off in a new job or ministry, what would it be?
   a. healing the multitudes
   b. negotiating a peace treaty between superpowers
   c. paying off the national debt in one day at no one's expense
   d. raising a sunken ship and saving the passengers
   e. leading a national revival
   f. _____

2. Why do you think Jesus went to the wedding?
   a. to please his mother
   b. the whole village was invited
   c. it was the fun place to be
   d. to perform a miracle

3. When they ran out of wine, why did the mother of Jesus try to get Jesus involved?
   a. concern for the guests
   b. to get the bridegroom out of a jam
   c. she was catering the party
   d. she knew Jesus could do something

4. How do you think Jesus felt?
   a. upset
   b. annoyed
   c. embarrassed
   d. reluctant
   e. willing

5. Why did Jesus go about solving the problem as he did?
   a. to keep from embarrassing the groom
   b. to remain anonymous
   c. he didn't know if it would work
   d. to surprise everyone

6. How do you think the bridegroom felt when he heard about the new wine?
   a. perplexed
   b. intrigued
   c. delighted
   d. amazed

7. Why do you think Jesus performed his first miracle at a wedding feast?
   a. it just happened that way
   b. his mother asked him
   c. he saw a need and met it
   d. wine had special significance
   e. weddings had special significance

MY OWN STORY/25 Minutes.

1. Where do you need to see the water turned into wine in your life right now? Choose two or three.
   ☐ SELF-ESTEEM: feeling blah, worthless, useless, and out of it
   ☐ FAMILY: feeling hassled, haggard, strung out, and put through the wringer
   ☐ WORK/SCHOOL: feeling pushed, pressed, and overloaded
   ☐ APPEARANCE: feeling ugly, zits, braces, frizzy hair, and overweight
   ☐ SPIRITUAL LIFE: feeling lonely, dry, and out of sync with God and his family
   ☐ PHYSICAL LIFE: feeling worn out, used up, drained, and ready to retire
   ☐ MENTAL LIFE: feeling dumb, stupid, like my brain has taken a vacation

2. In the most difficult area above that you checked, how would you describe your situation in terms of the story of the Scripture?
   a. the wine has run out completely
   b. there's new wine available but I'm not drinking
   c. I've tried the new wine and nothing has changed
   d. I'm not sure the new wine is any better

3. What role do you see individual members of your group playing to make the miracle happen in your life?
   a. JESUS' MOTHER: Intercessor
   b. SERVANTS: Labor under Jesus' direction
   c. BANQUET MAITRE D': Witness of the change
   d. DISCIPLES: Walking the road with me
   e. JESUS: Resource manager

What effect does his response have on them? **4.** Why doesn't Jesus entrust himself to the crowds in verses 23-25?

REFLECT: If you compare your spiritual life to the rooms of a house, which room do you think Jesus might want to clean up: (a) Library—the reading room? (b) Dining room—appetites, desires? (c) Workshop—where you keep your gifts, skills and talents? (d) Recreation room—where you hang out after work? (e) Family room—where most of your relationships are lived out? or (f) Closet—where your hang-ups are? Do you resist or welcome Jesus' "clean up" operation in your life? How so?

OPEN: 1. Where were you first told that babies came from? How old were you when you learned the real story? **2.** How do you react when someone turns on the light when you are sleeping?

DIG: 1. What can you find out about Nicodemus in verses 1-2? What is significant about his coming to Jesus? Why at night (see vv.19-20)? Why was Jesus so direct with him? **2.** What two ideas about birth are Jesus and Nicodemus thinking of? What point is Jesus making by comparing spiritual birth to the wind? How does Jesus account for Nicodemus' lack of understanding? **3.** What does Jesus claim about himself in verses 13-15? How does the "snake in the desert" (Nu 21:4-9) illustrate what he has come to do? **4.** From verses 16-18, what stands out to you about God? About what he wants to do? About how a person is condemned? How will belief show itself (vv.15-21)? **5.** How is Jesus' use of the words "born again" similar to and different from the way it is used today? How would you define what it means to a person who had never heard the phrase?

REFLECT: 1. What first aroused your interest in Jesus? Why? **2.** Where are you right now in the birthing process of spiritual life: Not yet conceived? Developing, but not so anyone could tell? Heavy with child and waiting? Kicking and screaming like an infant? Growing daily? Explain.

[17] His disciples remembered that it is written: "Zeal for your house will consume me." [m]

[18] Then the Jews demanded of him, "What miraculous sign can you show us to prove your authority to do all this?"

[19] Jesus answered them, "Destroy this temple, and I will raise it again in three days."

[20] The Jews replied, "It has taken forty-six years to build this temple, and you are going to raise it in three days?" [21] But the temple he had spoken of was his body. [22] After he was raised from the dead, his disciples recalled what he had said. Then they believed the Scripture and the words that Jesus had spoken.

[23] Now while he was in Jerusalem at the Passover Feast, many people saw the miraculous signs he was doing and believed in his name. [n] [24] But Jesus would not entrust himself to them, for he knew all men. [25] He did not need man's testimony about man, for he knew what was in a man.

Jesus Teaches Nicodemus

3 Now there was a man of the Pharisees named Nicodemus, a member of the Jewish ruling council. [2] He came to Jesus at night and said, "Rabbi, we know you are a teacher who has come from God. For no one could perform the miraculous signs you are doing if God were not with him."

[3] In reply Jesus declared, "I tell you the truth, no one can see the kingdom of God unless he is born again. [o]"

[4] "How can a man be born when he is old?" Nicodemus asked. "Surely he cannot enter a second time into his mother's womb to be born!"

[5] Jesus answered, "I tell you the truth, no one can enter the kingdom of God unless he is born of water and the Spirit. [6] Flesh gives birth to flesh, but the Spirit [p] gives birth to spirit. [7] You should not be surprised at my saying, 'You [q] must be born again.' [8] The wind blows wherever it pleases. You hear its sound, but you cannot tell where it comes from or where it is going. So it is with everyone born of the Spirit."

[9] "How can this be?" Nicodemus asked.

[10] "You are Israel's teacher," said Jesus, "and do you not understand these things? [11] I tell you the truth, we speak of what we know, and we testify to what we have seen, but still you people do not accept our testimony. [12] I have spoken to you of earthly things and you do not believe; how then will you believe if I speak of heavenly things? [13] No one has ever gone into heaven except the one who came from heaven—the Son of Man. [r] [14] Just as Moses lifted up the snake in the desert, so the Son of Man must be lifted up, [15] that everyone who believes in him may have eternal life. [s]

[16] "For God so loved the world that he gave his one and only Son, [t] that whoever believes in him shall not perish but have eternal life. [17] For God did not send his Son into the world to condemn the world, but to save the world through him. [18] Who-

---

m17 Psalm 69:9   *n23* Or *and believed in him*   *o3* Or *born from above*; also in verse 7   *p6* Or *but spirit*   *q7* The Greek is plural.   *r13* Some manuscripts *Man, who is in heaven*   *s15* Or *believes may have eternal life in him*   *t16* Or *his only begotten Son*

John 3:1-21   **JESUS TEACHES NICODEMUS**

LOOKING INTO THE SCRIPTURE/20 Minutes. Read John 3:1-21 and discuss.

1. Why did Nicodemus come to Jesus by night?
   a. he couldn't wait until morning
   b. he worked during the day
   c. he was afraid of being seen
   d. he wanted time alone with Jesus

2. Of the three levels of communication, how did the conversation start out?
   a. mouth to mouth—polite talk
   b. head to head—intellectual talk
   c. heart to heart—deep sharing

3. When Jesus explained, ". . . unless a man is born again . . ." what happened?
   a. Nicodemus got defensive
   b. Nicodemus got curious
   c. Nicodemus got interested
   d. Nicodemus got confused

4. In the conversation that followed, what is the issue?
   a. religion versus new life
   b. what Jesus' kingdom is all about
   c. why religious people don't understand
   d. how to get into the kingdom

5. "Just as Moses lifted up the snake in the desert, so the Son of Man must be lifted up. . . ." To what is Jesus referring here?
   a. Numbers 21:4-9 in the Old Testament
   b. the death of Jesus on the cross
   c. the resurrection of Jesus
   d. the second coming of Jesus

6. What is the condition for obtaining eternal life according to verses 16-18?
   a. feeling sorry for yourself
   b. feeling sorry for your sins
   c. living a clean life
   d. going to church every Sunday
   e. receiving God's free gift by faith

7. How do you think Nicodemus came away from this conversation with Jesus?
   a. totally confused
   b. enlightened
   c. a silent follower of Jesus
   d. intellectually convinced
   e. with "food" for thought

8. Do you think Jesus could have been more kind to the religion teacher?   ☐ Yes ☐ No

---

MY OWN STORY/25 Minutes.

1. The chart below shows thirteen stages of conversion in the spiritual journey of a person. Where are you now in your own spiritual journey?

	I. QUEST STAGE		II. COMMITMENT STAGE			III. INTEGRATION STAGE		
Totally alienated from God	Atheist *(I know there is no God)*	Seeker *(I'm searching for God)*	Commitment to ethics *(clean living)*		Discovery of Christian fellowship and community	Changes in my world view and purpose in life	**Totally reconciled to God**
Spiritual "death"				Personal encounter			**Spiritual maturity**
Distorted self	Indifference *(who cares)*	Agnostic *(I don't know if there is a God)*	Commitment to ideas *(my church's teachings)*	Commitment to persons *(doing good)*	Growth in truth *(understanding of my faith)*	Changes in my relationship with others	**True self** **Wholeness**

2. What is the Spirit's "wind" like in your life right now?
   a. still as a summer night
   b. a few little gusts
   c. howling
   d. full sail
   e. _____

3. Where is the "wind" of the Spirit carrying you?
   a. to a safe harbor
   b. out to the rough waters
   c. I'm not sure, but it is exciting
   d. nowhere that I know
   e. _____

ever believes in him is not condemned, but whoever does not believe stands condemned already because he has not believed in the name of God's one and only Son. *u* [19]This is the verdict: Light has come into the world, but men loved darkness instead of light because their deeds were evil. [20]Everyone who does evil hates the light, and will not come into the light for fear that his deeds will be exposed. [21]But whoever lives by the truth comes into the light, so that it may be seen plainly that what he has done has been done through God." *v*

John the Baptist's Testimony About Jesus

[22]After this, Jesus and his disciples went out into the Judean countryside, where he spent some time with them, and baptized. [23]Now John also was baptizing at Aenon near Salim, because there was plenty of water, and people were constantly coming to be baptized. [24](This was before John was put in prison.) [25]An argument developed between some of John's disciples and a certain Jew *w* over the matter of ceremonial washing. [26]They came to John and said to him, "Rabbi, that man who was with you on the other side of the Jordan—the one you testified about—well, he is baptizing, and everyone is going to him."

[27]To this John replied, "A man can receive only what is given him from heaven. [28]You yourselves can testify that I said, 'I am not the Christ *x* but am sent ahead of him.' [29]The bride belongs to the bridegroom. The friend who attends the bridegroom waits and listens for him, and is full of joy when he hears the bridegroom's voice. That joy is mine, and it is now complete. [30]He must become greater; I must become less.

[31]"The one who comes from above is above all; the one who is from the earth belongs to the earth, and speaks as one from the earth. The one who comes from heaven is above all. [32]He testifies to what he has seen and heard, but no one accepts his testimony. [33]The man who has accepted it has certified that God is truthful. [34]For the one whom God has sent speaks the words of God, for God *y* gives the Spirit without limit. [35]The Father loves the Son and has placed everything in his hands. [36]Whoever believes in the Son has eternal life, but whoever rejects the Son will not see life, for God's wrath remains on him." *z*

Jesus Talks With a Samaritan Woman

4 The Pharisees heard that Jesus was gaining and baptizing more disciples than John, [2]although in fact it was not Jesus who baptized, but his disciples. [3]When the Lord learned of this, he left Judea and went back once more to Galilee.

[4]Now he had to go through Samaria. [5]So he came to a town in Samaria called Sychar, near the plot of ground Jacob had given to his son Joseph. [6]Jacob's well was there, and Jesus, tired as he was from the journey, sat down by the well. It was about the sixth hour.

OPEN: 1. What did you and your brother or sister often fight about? How would you try to get your way? 2. At family reunions, what subject (e.g., politics or religion) is bound to start an argument?

DIG: 1. Given the different ideas about baptisms, what do you think had happened at the river? What do you think the "certain Jew" had said? How would you have felt if you had been one of John's disciples at this point? 2. How does John the Baptist respond? What is the point of the allegory or story about the bride and bridegroom? What does John's response tell you about him? 3. What facts about Jesus does John bring out in verses 31-36? 4. How does the phrase "rejecting the Son" stand in contrast to what "belief" really means? What are the results of each response to him?

REFLECT: 1. Other than the way John the Baptist did, how will *you* express the role and place of Jesus in your life? 2. In a scientific world in which everything must be measured or proven, what proof can you put forward for your hope of eternal life?

OPEN: 1. When you were growing up, who were the people you were told not to associate with? What part of the city or country would you be warned about? What would have happened if you had gone there? 2. Where was the "watering hole" in your home town, where everybody went to "hang out"?

DIG: 1. From 1:19-28 and 3:22-26, why might Jesus decide to "get out of town" in a hurry? 2. As someone taught from birth to despise the Samaritans, how would you feel when Jesus decided to go through Samaria instead of taking the long way home? 3. Since "nice" girls did not come to

u18 Or *God's only begotten Son*   *v21* Some interpreters end the quotation after verse 15.
w25 Some manuscripts *and certain Jews*   *x28* Or *Messiah*   *y34* Greek *he*
z36 Some interpreters end the quotation after verse 30.

LOOKING INTO THE SCRIPTURE/15 Minutes. Read John 4:1-26 and walk through the spiritual encounter with the Samaritan woman.

1. What was the Samaritan woman really saying in reply to Jesus' question, "will you give me a drink?"
   a. do you know who I am (an outcast)?
   b. why would you talk to me?
   c. you're giving me too much attention. What do you want?
   d. you're threatening me

2. What was the woman's response when Jesus said, "If you knew the gift of God and who it is that asks you for a drink, you would have asked him and he would have given you living water."
   a. stumbling for an answer at first
   b. arousing of a spiritual desire for something
   c. curious: "Is it possible this is the thing I've been looking for?"
   d. skeptical: "Who do you think you are?"

3. How does the woman respond when Jesus explains, ". . . the water I give will become a spring of water welling up to eternal life . . ."
   a. puzzled: "Are you kidding me?"
   b. desirous: "I'd love to have it."
   c. open: "I'm ready."

4. Why didn't the woman give up on this conversation when Jesus told her, "Go, call your husband and come back?"
   a. she was intrigued by his willingness to talk
   b. she realized she had nothing to hide
   c. what Jesus offered appealed to her
   d. he treated her with respect
   e. she knew he spoke the truth and that he could help her
   f. she didn't want to lose the chance to get her questions answered

5. When Jesus declared that "the time is coming . . . when true worshipers will worship the Father in spirit and truth . . ." what was her response?
   a. deep desire: "I want that myself"
   b. awareness: "I think I understand"
   c. commitment: "I'm sold"
   d. clarification: "What are you trying to say?"

6. What do you imagine was the look on her face when Jesus said, "I who speak to you am he."
   a. mouth open: surprise
   b. furrowed brow: puzzlement
   c. flashing eyes: anger
   d. laughter: delight

MY OWN STORY/25 Minutes. Share your own experience.

1. How do you respond when someone speaks to you unexpectedly?
   a. pretend I didn't hear
   b. try to be courteous
   c. look around at who's there
   d. move away quickly
   e. answer any questions

2. How would you compare your own spiritual beginnings with God to that of the woman at the well?
   a. more intellectual
   b. different, but just as real
   c. even more crazy
   d. I'll have to think about that

3. In your own experience, do you think the circumstances surrounding your own encounter were coincidental or part of the plan and purpose of God?
   a. purely coincidental
   b. more than coincidental
   c. still trying to figure this out

4. If Jesus were to stop by the "watering hole" where you hang out, what would he probably ask you right now? (be honest).
   a. what are you doing with your life?
   b. are you satisfied with what you're doing?
   c. are you looking for the real thing?
   d. other _____

5. How would you describe the way God is working in your life right now?
   a. master architect
   b. construction foreman
   c. coach on sidelines
   d. big boss in grandstands
   e. trainer
   f. cheerleader
   g. blocker/running interference
   h. Monday morning quarterback
   i. sculptor

the water well at noontime ("the sixth hour"), why do think Jesus risked his reputation to ask a favor of this woman? **4.** How would you describe the woman's response? **5.** How did Jesus turn the tables on her in verse 10? **6.** In the woman's reply, what is she really saying? How is she like Nicodemus? **7.** Why does Jesus change the topic of conversation so abruptly to her personal life (v.16)? What strikes you about the way he responds to her claim not to have a husband? **8.** Why do you think this woman changed the conversation to focus on a religious controversy? In the context of this scene, what does Jesus mean by telling her that God is interested in worshipers who will do so in "spirit and truth"? **9.** What is significant about Jesus choosing this woman as the first person to whom he revealed himself (see also vv.39-42)?

REFLECT: 1. What social, ethnic, or religious barriers are difficult for you to break through? How would Jesus relate to these people you find difficult? **2.** What aspects of Jesus' conversation could you use as a model for your own discussions with searching friends?

OPEN: What causes you to skip a meal unknowingly? To eat too much unknowingly?

DIG: 1. Why were the disciples surprised to find Jesus with this woman? **2.** What does "leaving her water jar" reveal about Jesus' impact on the woman? How did she affect others? **3.** How is Jesus' figurative speech once again misunderstood (see 2:19; 3:3; 4:10)? Why does he continue to speak like this? In what ways is

[7]When a Samaritan woman came to draw water, Jesus said to her, "Will you give me a drink?" [8](His disciples had gone into the town to buy food.)

[9]The Samaritan woman said to him, "You are a Jew and I am a Samaritan woman. How can you ask me for a drink?" (For Jews do not associate with Samaritans. [a])

[10]Jesus answered her, "If you knew the gift of God and who it is that asks you for a drink, you would have asked him and he would have given you living water."

[11]"Sir," the woman said, "you have nothing to draw with and the well is deep. Where can you get this living water? [12]Are you greater than our father Jacob, who gave us the well and drank from it himself, as did also his sons and his flocks and herds?"

[13]Jesus answered, "Everyone who drinks this water will be thirsty again, [14]but whoever drinks the water I give him will never thirst. Indeed, the water I give him will become in him a spring of water welling up to eternal life."

[15]The woman said to him, "Sir, give me this water so that I won't get thirsty and have to keep coming here to draw water."

[16]He told her, "Go, call your husband and come back."

[17]"I have no husband," she replied.

Jesus said to her, "You are right when you say you have no husband. [18]The fact is, you have had five husbands, and the man you now have is not your husband. What you have just said is quite true."

[19]"Sir," the woman said, "I can see that you are a prophet. [20]Our fathers worshiped on this mountain, but you Jews claim that the place where we must worship is in Jerusalem."

[21]Jesus declared, "Believe me, woman, a time is coming when you will worship the Father neither on this mountain nor in Jerusalem. [22]You Samaritans worship what you do not know; we worship what we do know, for salvation is from the Jews. [23]Yet a time is coming and has now come when the true worshipers will worship the Father in spirit and truth, for they are the kind of worshipers the Father seeks. [24]God is spirit, and his worshipers must worship in spirit and in truth."

[25]The woman said, "I know that Messiah" (called Christ) "is coming. When he comes, he will explain everything to us."

[26]Then Jesus declared, "I who speak to you am he."

The Disciples Rejoin Jesus

[27]Just then his disciples returned and were surprised to find him talking with a woman. But no one asked, "What do you want?" or "Why are you talking with her?"

[28]Then, leaving her water jar, the woman went back to the town and said to the people, [29]"Come, see a man who told me everything I ever did. Could this be the Christ[b]?" [30]They came out of the town and made their way toward him.

[31]Meanwhile his disciples urged him, "Rabbi, eat something."

a9 Or do not use dishes Samaritans have used   *b29 Or Messiah*

32But he said to them, "I have food to eat that you know nothing about."

33Then his disciples said to each other, "Could someone have brought him food?"

34"My food," said Jesus, "is to do the will of him who sent me and to finish his work. 35Do you not say, 'Four months more and then the harvest'? I tell you, open your eyes and look at the fields! They are ripe for harvest. 36Even now the reaper draws his wages, even now he harvests the crop for eternal life, so that the sower and the reaper may be glad together. 37Thus the saying 'One sows and another reaps' is true. 38I sent you to reap what you have not worked for. Others have done the hard work, and you have reaped the benefits of their labor."

Many Samaritans Believe

39Many of the Samaritans from that town believed in him because of the woman's testimony, "He told me everything I ever did." 40So when the Samaritans came to him, they urged him to stay with them, and he stayed two days. 41And because of his words many more became believers.

42They said to the woman, "We no longer believe just because of what you said; now we have heard for ourselves, and we know that this man really is the Savior of the world."

Jesus Heals the Official's Son

43After the two days he left for Galilee. 44(Now Jesus himself had pointed out that a prophet has no honor in his own country.) 45When he arrived in Galilee, the Galileans welcomed him. They had seen all that he had done in Jerusalem at the Passover Feast, for they also had been there.

46Once more he visited Cana in Galilee, where he had turned the water into wine. And there was a certain royal official whose son lay sick at Capernaum. 47When this man heard that Jesus had arrived in Galilee from Judea, he went to him and begged him to come and heal his son, who was close to death.

48"Unless you people see miraculous signs and wonders," Jesus told him, "you will never believe."

49The royal official said, "Sir, come down before my child dies."

50Jesus replied, "You may go. Your son will live."

The man took Jesus at his word and departed. 51While he was still on the way, his servants met him with the news that his boy was living. 52When he inquired as to the time when his son got better, they said to him, "The fever left him yesterday at the seventh hour."

53Then the father realized that this was the exact time at which Jesus had said to him, "Your son will live." So he and all his household believed.

54This was the second miraculous sign that Jesus performed, having come from Judea to Galilee.

God's will like food for him? **4.** How does the parable of harvesting apply to the disciples? **5.** Given the social barriers between Jews and Samaritans, what do verses 40-42 teach you about Jesus? As a disciple, how would you feel about spending two days as a guest of people against whom you were prejudiced?

REFLECT: 1. Considering your interest in spiritual things this week, have you been more like the disciples or the woman? Why? What distracts you from spiritual things? **2.** How does obeying the will of God supply the same essentials in your life that food does? **3.** What do you learn about being a witness from the woman? From the parable (vv.35-38)?

OPEN: When you were a child, what was the most serious illness or injury you ever had?

DIG: 1. Now that Jesus is back home again, what motivates the people to welcome him? **2.** How do you account for the contrast between the crowd's welcome (v.45) and Jesus' comments in verses 44 and 48? How are the Galileans like and unlike the Samaritans in verses 39-42? Why? **3.** What motivates the royal official to travel so far? How would you have responded to what Jesus told him to do? What was the result of his action? **4.** What does this "miraculous sign" point to about Jesus? How does it add to what was demonstrated by his first sign (see 2:1-11)?

REFLECT: 1. When you bring your problem to God (such as a sickness in the family), do you tend to accept his word or keep fretting and fussing? **2.** When have you taken God at his word (even though the circumstances were seemingly impossible), and discovered that God did exactly what he promised?

OPEN: When you get sick, what are you like: A puppy? Superman? Rip Van Winkle?

DIG: 1. How do you picture the setting of this story (vv.2-4)? What is the smell? The noises? The atmosphere? How would you feel in a place like this? 2. How would you picture the invalid (vv.5-7)? What does Jesus mean by his question in verse 6? What did the invalid hope Jesus might do? 3. As the invalid, what do you feel in verses 8-9? In verses 10-12? In verse 13? In verse 14? 4. Why were the leaders so upset? How do you suppose they responded to his medical update (v.15)?

REFLECT: 1. In what ways do people today try to be healed spiritually outside of Christ? How would you respond to someone who said all sickness is a result of sin? 2. Has your joy in God ever been squashed by someone's concern over religious rituals and traditions? What did that do to you? Have you ever responded to someone in that way? How so?

OPEN: 1. What mannerisms of your parents have you picked up? 2. As you get older, do you find yourself becoming more, or less, like your parents?

DIG: 1. What was the result for Jesus of healing the man in verses 1-15? 2. How did his response to the Jewish leaders only heighten their opposition? Why would Jesus do this? 3. In what ways is Jesus equal with the Father? What terms are used to show the kind of relationship between the two? How does this relate to 1:1 and 1:18? 4. What claims does Jesus make about himself in verse 24? What is the promise? When does someone start to possess this promise? 5. What happens to those who hear and believe (vv.24-30)? To those who do not? 6. How would you describe the business that God the Father and God the Son are in? What is the offer God is making to humanity?

The Healing at the Pool

5 Some time later, Jesus went up to Jerusalem for a feast of the Jews. [2]Now there is in Jerusalem near the Sheep Gate a pool, which in Aramaic is called Bethesda[c] and which is surrounded by five covered colonnades. [3]Here a great number of disabled people used to lie—the blind, the lame, the paralyzed.[d] [5]One who was there had been an invalid for thirty-eight years. [6]When Jesus saw him lying there and learned that he had been in this condition for a long time, he asked him, "Do you want to get well?"

[7]"Sir," the invalid replied, "I have no one to help me into the pool when the water is stirred. While I am trying to get in, someone else goes down ahead of me."

[8]Then Jesus said to him, "Get up! Pick up your mat and walk." [9]At once the man was cured; he picked up his mat and walked.

The day on which this took place was a Sabbath, [10]and so the Jews said to the man who had been healed, "It is the Sabbath; the law forbids you to carry your mat."

[11]But he replied, "The man who made me well said to me, 'Pick up your mat and walk.'"

[12]So they asked him, "Who is this fellow who told you to pick it up and walk?"

[13]The man who was healed had no idea who it was, for Jesus had slipped away into the crowd that was there.

[14]Later Jesus found him at the temple and said to him, "See, you are well again. Stop sinning or something worse may happen to you." [15]The man went away and told the Jews that it was Jesus who had made him well.

Life Through the Son

[16]So, because Jesus was doing these things on the Sabbath, the Jews persecuted him. [17]Jesus said to them, "My Father is always at his work to this very day, and I, too, am working." [18]For this reason the Jews tried all the harder to kill him; not only was he breaking the Sabbath, but he was even calling God his own Father, making himself equal with God.

[19]Jesus gave them this answer: "I tell you the truth, the Son can do nothing by himself; he can do only what he sees his Father doing, because whatever the Father does the Son also does. [20]For the Father loves the Son and shows him all he does. Yes, to your amazement he will show him even greater things than these. [21]For just as the Father raises the dead and gives them life, even so the Son gives life to whom he is pleased to give it. [22]Moreover, the Father judges no one, but has entrusted all judgment to the Son, [23]that all may honor the Son just as they honor the Father. He who does not honor the Son does not honor the Father, who sent him.

[c]2 Some manuscripts Bethzatha; other manuscripts Bethsaida   [d]3 Some less important manuscripts paralyzed—and they waited for the moving of the waters. [4]From time to time an angel of the Lord would come down and stir up the waters. The first one into the pool after each such disturbance would be cured of whatever disease he had.

LOOKING INTO THE SCRIPTURE/20 Minutes. Read John 5:1-15 and discuss.

1. Do you think the paralytic was really sick or playing sick?
   - a. he was really sick
   - b. he thought he was sick
   - c. he was sick to avoid taking responsibility for his life
   - d. he was sick, but it was in his mind

2. Who do you think brought this man to the pool each morning?
   - a. family/friends
   - b. wife/children
   - c. community volunteers
   - d. people who felt sorry for him

3. Why do you think this man wanted to go to the pool?
   - a. to meet his buddies
   - b. to be in the place of healing
   - c. to be healed
   - d. to get away from responsibility

4. When Jesus asked him the question, "Do you want to get well?", how would you paraphrase his answer?
   - a. are you crazy? Would I be lying here for 38 years if I could walk?
   - b. oh, poor me! I'm really so helpless
   - c. others that I rely on have failed me
   - d. I've been sick so long I don't think I can accept responsibility for my life

5. How would you paraphrase Jesus' reply?
   - a. if you really want to get well, you can
   - b. don't blame others for your problems
   - c. I'm sick of your whining. Move it
   - d. getting well may cost you your excuses. Are you willing to risk it?

6. Do you think Jesus was being harsh or cruel with this man?
   - a. yes
   - b. no

MY OWN STORY/25 Minutes.

1. Honestly, how many years have you been lying next to your healing place while manipulating others with your problems?
   - a. now, wait a minute. I don't do that
   - b. not sure what you mean
   - c. I don't know how to get over my paralysis
   - d. quite a few

2. What is your favorite excuse for avoiding responsibility for your life?
   - a. I've got an inferiority complex
   - b. my parents overprotected me
   - c. I never got any breaks
   - d. I've had a bad year
   - e. the last time I tried, I failed
   - f. I don't have any support at home
   - g. my church isn't going anywhere
   - h. nobody else will join me

3. If Jesus were to pass by your "pool" today, what would he say or do if he knew your deepest need at the moment?
   - a. stop and be with me
   - b. ask me "what's going on?"
   - c. assure me that "it's okay"
   - d. put his arms around me
   - e. tell me to "get off my duff"
   - f. get me started in his "Word"
   - g. lift me into the healing pool
   - h. remove the thing that is crippling me
   - i. help me to deal with the thing that is crippling me
   - j. get me out of the situation I'm in
   - k. crack a few jokes
   - l. throw away my crutches
   - m. tell me "he's proud to have me on his team"
   - n. pass on without saying a word

REFLECT: 1. If you had to explain to someone what verse 24 means in your own words, how would you put it? **2.** In your own spiritual journey, when did you come to understand this truth? How did it effect your self-image? Your lifestyle? Your life goals?

OPEN: Who was one of your heroes when you were a kid and is still someone you admire? Who was a hero that has since turned out to be a disappointment?

DIG: 1. Have someone read aloud verses 24-30, pretentiously making those self-assertions. How does this person make the rest of you feel? **2.** Who or what testifies in favor of Jesus? How do you think the religious leaders felt when Jesus refers to these witnesses (already discounted by these authorities)? **3.** How does Jesus throw back at the religious leaders their own Scriptures? Since lack of information was not their problem, what was?

REFLECT: 1. What "witnesses" have convinced you that Jesus is indeed the one who gives life? **2.** How do you see these leaders' attitudes and misuse of Scripture reflected today? How can you use Scripture to cultivate the love of God in you?

OPEN: Do you prefer to socialize at large parties, dinner for four, or a quiet evening to yourself? Why?

DIG: 1. Why did the crowd follow Jesus? What did they think about him? **2.** What was the test that Jesus was using on Philip? How might the wedding at Cana (2:1-11) be a factor in this test? From their responses, what grades would you give Philip and

---

[24]"I tell you the truth, whoever hears my word and believes him who sent me has eternal life and will not be condemned; he has crossed over from death to life. [25]I tell you the truth, a time is coming and has now come when the dead will hear the voice of the Son of God and those who hear will live. [26]For as the Father has life in himself, so he has granted the Son to have life in himself. [27]And he has given him authority to judge because he is the Son of Man.

[28]"Do not be amazed at this, for a time is coming when all who are in their graves will hear his voice [29]and come out—those who have done good will rise to live, and those who have done evil will rise to be condemned. [30]By myself I can do nothing; I judge only as I hear, and my judgment is just, for I seek not to please myself but him who sent me.

Testimonies About Jesus

[31]"If I testify about myself, my testimony is not valid. [32]There is another who testifies in my favor, and I know that his testimony about me is valid.

[33]"You have sent to John and he has testified to the truth. [34]Not that I accept human testimony; but I mention it that you may be saved. [35]John was a lamp that burned and gave light, and you chose for a time to enjoy his light.

[36]"I have testimony weightier than that of John. For the very work that the Father has given me to finish, and which I am doing, testifies that the Father has sent me. [37]And the Father who sent me has himself testified concerning me. You have never heard his voice nor seen his form, [38]nor does his word dwell in you, for you do not believe the one he sent. [39]You diligently study*e* the Scriptures because you think that by them you possess eternal life. These are the Scriptures that testify about me, [40]yet you refuse to come to me to have life.

[41]"I do not accept praise from men, [42]but I know you. I know that you do not have the love of God in your hearts. [43]I have come in my Father's name, and you do not accept me; but if someone else comes in his own name, you will accept him. [44]How can you believe if you accept praise from one another, yet make no effort to obtain the praise that comes from the only God*f*?

[45]"But do not think I will accuse you before the Father. Your accuser is Moses, on whom your hopes are set. [46]If you believed Moses, you would believe me, for he wrote about me. [47]But since you do not believe what he wrote, how are you going to believe what I say?"

Jesus Feeds the Five Thousand

6 Some time after this, Jesus crossed to the far shore of the Sea of Galilee (that is, the Sea of Tiberias), [2]and a great crowd of people followed him because they saw the miraculous signs he had performed on the sick. [3]Then Jesus went up on a mountainside and sat down with his disciples. [4]The Jewish Passover Feast was near.

e39 Or Study diligently (the imperative)   f44 Some early manuscripts the Only One

⁵When Jesus looked up and saw a great crowd coming toward him, he said to Philip, "Where shall we buy bread for these people to eat?" ⁶He asked this only to test him, for he already had in mind what he was going to do.

⁷Philip answered him, "Eight months' wages^g would not buy enough bread for each one to have a bite!"

⁸Another of his disciples, Andrew, Simon Peter's brother, spoke up, ⁹"Here is a boy with five small barley loaves and two small fish, but how far will they go among so many?"

¹⁰Jesus said, "Have the people sit down." There was plenty of grass in that place, and the men sat down, about five thousand of them. ¹¹Jesus then took the loaves, gave thanks, and distributed to those who were seated as much as they wanted. He did the same with the fish.

¹²When they had all had enough to eat, he said to his disciples, "Gather the pieces that are left over. Let nothing be wasted." ¹³So they gathered them and filled twelve baskets with the pieces of the five barley loaves left over by those who had eaten.

¹⁴After the people saw the miraculous sign that Jesus did, they began to say, "Surely this is the Prophet who is to come into the world." ¹⁵Jesus, knowing that they intended to come and make him king by force, withdrew again to a mountain by himself.

Jesus Walks on the Water

¹⁶When evening came, his disciples went down to the lake, ¹⁷where they got into a boat and set off across the lake for Capernaum. By now it was dark, and Jesus had not yet joined them. ¹⁸A strong wind was blowing and the waters grew rough. ¹⁹When they had rowed three or three and a half miles,^h they saw Jesus approaching the boat, walking on the water; and they were terrified. ²⁰But he said to them, "It is I; don't be afraid." ²¹Then they were willing to take him into the boat, and immediately the boat reached the shore where they were heading.

²²The next day the crowd that had stayed on the opposite shore of the lake realized that only one boat had been there, and that Jesus had not entered it with his disciples, but that they had gone away alone. ²³Then some boats from Tiberias landed near the place where the people had eaten the bread after the Lord had given thanks. ²⁴Once the crowd realized that neither Jesus nor his disciples were there, they got into the boats and went to Capernaum in search of Jesus.

Jesus the Bread of Life

²⁵When they found him on the other side of the lake, they asked him, "Rabbi, when did you get here?"

²⁶Jesus answered, "I tell you the truth, you are looking for me, not because you saw miraculous signs but because you ate the loaves and had your fill. ²⁷Do not work for food that spoils, but for food that endures to eternal life, which the Son of Man will give you. On him God the Father has placed his seal of approval."

Andrew? **3.** What is the significance of the fact that there was more left over after the feeding than there was food to start with? What truths about Jesus does this miracle show? **4.** How could the nearness of the Passover feast (when Jews from all over the empire would flock to Jerusalem) fuel the desires of the people (vv.14-15)? What does Jesus' response indicate about his idea of his kingship?

REFLECT: 1. When have you seen God stretch your limited resources (physically or emotionally) far beyond what you could have imagined? In what way do you need to trust him to do so now? **2.** How are you like Philip and Andrew—failing to remember something about Jesus when you face a difficult situation?

OPEN: What was one of your greatest childhood fears: Bugs? High places? Darkness? Water?

DIG: 1. On a dark and stormy night, weary from rowing and afraid of capsizing, how would you have reacted if you saw Jesus on the water? When he climbed aboard? **2.** What did the disciples fail to see in the feeding of the 5,000 that could have helped them here?

REFLECT: How do you respond when storms whip up in your life? What difference does this story make as you face those times?

OPEN: 1. What type of bread are you today: All natural? "Rye"? Moldy? Crusty? Fresh? Easy to "butter up"? **2.** Who is the easiest in your family for you to communicate with? With which person are you often misunderstood?

DIG: 1. Why are the crowds still searching for Jesus (vv.24-26)?

^g7 Greek *two hundred denarii*   ^h19 Greek *rowed twenty-five or thirty stadia* (about 5 or 6 kilometers)

215

2. How does Jesus' response to their question show the difference between his interests and theirs? **3.** How are they to work for the food that leads to eternal life? **4.** What does the crowd ask Jesus to do in order that they can believe him? What is their real interest? **5.** How does Jesus use their interest in food to illustrate what he wants them to understand? What are the similarities and differences between manna and the "bread of life" (v.35)? **6.** What claims does Jesus make in verses 35-40? What do these claims emphasize about his being the bread of life? About the will of the Father? **7.** In verses 41-42, how do the crowds respond to his claims? How is the principle of the hometown prophet (see 4:44) played out here? **8.** What part is played by God and by the people in the process of coming to know Jesus (vv.44-45)? What promise is repeated three times for those who do come to him? Why the emphasis on this? **9.** How is the "bread" he gives greater than that of Moses (vv.32,49)? **10.** On what level are the people responding to his comments? Given their misunderstanding, why does Jesus develop the illustration even more graphically (vv.53-58)? **11.** From the passage as a whole, what does Jesus mean by "eating his flesh" and "drinking his blood" (compare v.40 with v.54)? How does the image of eating and drinking clarify what he means by believing in him?

REFLECT: 1. In your culture, what is the main reason for following Jesus? What was *your* original motive? **2.** How would you describe your daily spiritual diet: Junk food? Frozen food? Baby food? TV microwave food? Leftovers? Meat and potatoes? Pure bread and wine? **3.** Has your familiarity with Jesus (raised on Sunday School stories, parochial school, etc.) ever kept you from seeing who he really is? What can help remove the blinders?

[28]Then they asked him, "What must we do to do the works God requires?"

[29]Jesus answered, "The work of God is this: to believe in the one he has sent."

[30]So they asked him, "What miraculous sign then will you give that we may see it and believe you? What will you do? [31]Our forefathers ate the manna in the desert; as it is written: 'He gave them bread from heaven to eat.'[i]"

[32]Jesus said to them, "I tell you the truth, it is not Moses who has given you the bread from heaven, but it is my Father who gives you the true bread from heaven. [33]For the bread of God is he who comes down from heaven and gives life to the world."

[34]"Sir," they said, "from now on give us this bread."

[35]Then Jesus declared, "I am the bread of life. He who comes to me will never go hungry, and he who believes in me will never be thirsty. [36]But as I told you, you have seen me and still you do not believe. [37]All that the Father gives me will come to me, and whoever comes to me I will never drive away. [38]For I have come down from heaven not to do my will but to do the will of him who sent me. [39]And this is the will of him who sent me, that I shall lose none of all that he has given me, but raise them up at the last day. [40]For my Father's will is that everyone who looks to the Son and believes in him shall have eternal life, and I will raise him up at the last day."

[41]At this the Jews began to grumble about him because he said, "I am the bread that came down from heaven." [42]They said, "Is this not Jesus, the son of Joseph, whose father and mother we know? How can he now say, 'I came down from heaven'?"

[43]"Stop grumbling among yourselves," Jesus answered. [44]"No one can come to me unless the Father who sent me draws him, and I will raise him up at the last day. [45]It is written in the Prophets: 'They will all be taught by God.'[j] Everyone who listens to the Father and learns from him comes to me. [46]No one has seen the Father except the one who is from God; only he has seen the Father. [47]I tell you the truth, he who believes has everlasting life. [48]I am the bread of life. [49]Your forefathers ate the manna in the desert, yet they died. [50]But here is the bread that comes down from heaven, which a man may eat and not die. [51]I am the living bread that came down from heaven. If anyone eats of this bread, he will live forever. This bread is my flesh, which I will give for the life of the world."

[52]Then the Jews began to argue sharply among themselves, "How can this man give us his flesh to eat?"

[53]Jesus said to them, "I tell you the truth, unless you eat the flesh of the Son of Man and drink his blood, you have no life in you. [54]Whoever eats my flesh and drinks my blood has eternal life, and I will raise him up at the last day. [55]For my flesh is real food and my blood is real drink. [56]Whoever eats my flesh and drinks my blood remains in me, and I in him. [57]Just as the living Father sent me and I live because of the Father, so the one who

i31 Exodus 16:4; Neh. 9:15; Psalm 78:24,25   *j45* Isaiah 54:13

feeds on me will live because of me. 58This is the bread that came down from heaven. Your forefathers ate manna and died, but he who feeds on this bread will live forever." 59He said this while teaching in the synagogue in Capernaum.

Many Disciples Desert Jesus

60On hearing it, many of his disciples said, "This is a hard teaching. Who can accept it?"

61Aware that his disciples were grumbling about this, Jesus said to them, "Does this offend you? 62What if you see the Son of Man ascend to where he was before! 63The Spirit gives life; the flesh counts for nothing. The words I have spoken to you are spirit *k* and they are life. 64Yet there are some of you who do not believe." For Jesus had known from the beginning which of them did not believe and who would betray him. 65He went on to say, "This is why I told you that no one can come to me unless the Father has enabled him."

66From this time many of his disciples turned back and no longer followed him.

67"You do not want to leave too, do you?" Jesus asked the Twelve.

68Simon Peter answered him, "Lord, to whom shall we go? You have the words of eternal life. 69We believe and know that you are the Holy One of God."

70Then Jesus replied, "Have I not chosen you, the Twelve? Yet one of you is a devil!" 71(He meant Judas, the son of Simon Iscariot, who, though one of the Twelve, was later to betray him.)

Jesus Goes to the Feast of Tabernacles

7 After this, Jesus went around in Galilee, purposely staying away from Judea because the Jews there were waiting to take his life. 2But when the Jewish Feast of Tabernacles was near, 3Jesus' brothers said to him, "You ought to leave here and go to Judea, so that your disciples may see the miracles you do. 4No one who wants to become a public figure acts in secret. Since you are doing these things, show yourself to the world." 5For even his own brothers did not believe in him.

6Therefore Jesus told them, "The right time for me has not yet come; for you any time is right. 7The world cannot hate you, but it hates me because I testify that what it does is evil. 8You go to the Feast. I am not yet *l* going up to this Feast, because for me the right time has not yet come." 9Having said this, he stayed in Galilee.

10However, after his brothers had left for the Feast, he went also, not publicly, but in secret. 11Now at the Feast the Jews were watching for him and asking, "Where is that man?"

12Among the crowds there was widespread whispering about him. Some said, "He is a good man."

Others replied, "No, he deceives the people." 13But no one would say anything publicly about him for fear of the Jews.

OPEN: How did you feel when you received your first "Dear John" letter?

DIG: 1. What teaching do Jesus' followers find so unacceptable (6:54-56)? How has their attitude changed since verses 14-15? **2.** Do you think they turned away because they did—or did not— really understand what he meant? Why? **3.** Why do you think Peter and the others decided to stay? How does this relate to verse 65?

REFLECT: 1. When times are hard, what keeps you from junking your faith and going on to something else? **2.** How do people today make Jesus into an "errand boy" to meet their own personal agendas? In what way have you been tempted to do so?

OPEN: Were you ever dared by your brothers or sisters to do something that turned out to be dangerous? What happened?

DIG: 1. Why did the religious leaders want to kill Jesus (see 5:18)? **2.** In urging Jesus to attend this feast, are the brothers being sincere or sarcastic (vv.2-5; see 6:42,66)? Explain. **3.** What does Jesus say is the difference between him and his brothers? What does he realize about public reaction to him? **4.** What rumors are circulating about Jesus in Jerusalem? Hence, why do you think he chose to go secretly?

REFLECT: 1. Do you face any family opposition to or ridicule of your faith? How do you deal with it? How does Jesus' situation help? **2.** Are you more likely to be cautious or daring in sharing your faith with your family? Why?

*k*63 Or *Spirit*   *l*8 Some early manuscripts do not have *yet.*

217

OPEN: From your school days, what rule seemed most arbitrary or silly? Did you break it?

DIG: 1. Given the risk, why does Jesus go to the Passover? How do the people react to Jesus' teaching? Why? **2.** What do Jesus' responses reveal about his authority? About their authority? Their objections to his healing? Their judgments? **3.** How would you respond if you were in the crowd? If you were one of Jesus' brothers (vv.3-5)? **4.** What point are the leaders missing?

REFLECT: 1. Have you ever been really impressed with Jesus one moment, only to turn from him the next? Why does that happen? **2.** When have you seen religious principles put ahead of love?

OPEN: When you played "hide and seek" as a kid (or with your kids), did you prefer hiding or seeking? Where was one of your best hiding spots? Did you stay hidden long, or did you jump out to scare the one seeking you?

DIG: 1. Who is saying what about Jesus in this passage? What is causing the confusion? **2.** Why does Jesus' teaching in verses 14-29 provoke the responses of verses 30-31? How do you account for the wide range of opinions about him? For the "timing" involved? **3.** Every day at this feast, water would be poured out as a symbol of thanks for God's provision. In this context, what does Jesus' statement in verses 37-38 mean? What are some ways that the Spirit's work is like water (compare 4:13-14)? How is the Spirit received? **4.** How does the confusion over Jesus' birthplace (vv.41-42) cloud the issue of his identity even more?

REFLECT: 1. Has the flow of the Spirit in your life lately felt more like a refreshing spring or a clogged faucet? What have you found helpful in releasing the stream of the Spirit's water in your life? **2.** What is the relationship for

Jesus Teaches at the Feast

[14]Not until halfway through the Feast did Jesus go up to the temple courts and begin to teach. [15]The Jews were amazed and asked, "How did this man get such learning without having studied?"

[16]Jesus answered, "My teaching is not my own. It comes from him who sent me. [17]If anyone chooses to do God's will, he will find out whether my teaching comes from God or whether I speak on my own. [18]He who speaks on his own does so to gain honor for himself, but he who works for the honor of the one who sent him is a man of truth; there is nothing false about him. [19]Has not Moses given you the law? Yet not one of you keeps the law. Why are you trying to kill me?"

[20]"You are demon-possessed," the crowd answered. "Who is trying to kill you?"

[21]Jesus said to them, "I did one miracle, and you are all astonished. [22]Yet, because Moses gave you circumcision (though actually it did not come from Moses, but from the patriarchs), you circumcise a child on the Sabbath. [23]Now if a child can be circumcised on the Sabbath so that the law of Moses may not be broken, why are you angry with me for healing the whole man on the Sabbath? [24]Stop judging by mere appearances, and make a right judgment."

Is Jesus the Christ?

[25]At that point some of the people of Jerusalem began to ask, "Isn't this the man they are trying to kill? [26]Here he is, speaking publicly, and they are not saying a word to him. Have the authorities really concluded that he is the Christ[m]? [27]But we know where this man is from; when the Christ comes, no one will know where he is from."

[28]Then Jesus, still teaching in the temple courts, cried out, "Yes, you know me, and you know where I am from. I am not here on my own, but he who sent me is true. You do not know him, [29]but I know him because I am from him and he sent me."

[30]At this they tried to seize him, but no one laid a hand on him, because his time had not yet come. [31]Still, many in the crowd put their faith in him. They said, "When the Christ comes, will he do more miraculous signs than this man?"

[32]The Pharisees heard the crowd whispering such things about him. Then the chief priests and the Pharisees sent temple guards to arrest him.

[33]Jesus said, "I am with you for only a short time, and then I go to the one who sent me. [34]You will look for me, but you will not find me; and where I am, you cannot come."

[35]The Jews said to one another, "Where does this man intend to go that we cannot find him? Will he go where our people live scattered among the Greeks, and teach the Greeks? [36]What did he mean when he said, 'You will look for me, but you will not find me,' and 'Where I am, you cannot come'?"

[37]On the last and greatest day of the Feast, Jesus stood and

[m]26 Or *Messiah*; also in verses 27, 31, 41 and 42

said in a loud voice, "If anyone is thirsty, let him come to me and drink. [38]Whoever believes in me, as[n] the Scripture has said, streams of living water will flow from within him." [39]By this he meant the Spirit, whom those who believed in him were later to receive. Up to that time the Spirit had not been given, since Jesus had not yet been glorified.

[40]On hearing his words, some of the people said, "Surely this man is the Prophet."

[41]Others said, "He is the Christ."

Still others asked, "How can the Christ come from Galilee? [42]Does not the Scripture say that the Christ will come from David's family[o] and from Bethlehem, the town where David lived?" [43]Thus the people were divided because of Jesus. [44]Some wanted to seize him, but no one laid a hand on him.

Unbelief of the Jewish Leaders

[45]Finally the temple guards went back to the chief priests and Pharisees, who asked them, "Why didn't you bring him in?"

[46]"No one ever spoke the way this man does," the guards declared.

[47]"You mean he has deceived you also?" the Pharisees retorted. [48]"Has any of the rulers or of the Pharisees believed in him? [49]No! But this mob that knows nothing of the law—there is a curse on them."

[50]Nicodemus, who had gone to Jesus earlier and who was one of their own number, asked, [51]"Does our law condemn anyone without first hearing him to find out what he is doing?"

[52]They replied, "Are you from Galilee, too? Look into it, and you will find that a prophet[p] does not come out of Galilee."

[The earliest and most reliable manuscripts and other ancient witnesses do not have John 7:53-8:11.]

[53]Then each went to his own home.

8 But Jesus went to the Mount of Olives. [2]At dawn he appeared again in the temple courts, where all the people gathered around him, and he sat down to teach them. [3]The teachers of the law and the Pharisees brought in a woman caught in adultery. They made her stand before the group [4]and said to Jesus, "Teacher, this woman was caught in the act of adultery. [5]In the Law Moses commanded us to stone such women. Now what do you say?" [6]They were using this question as a trap, in order to have a basis for accusing him.

But Jesus bent down and started to write on the ground with his finger. [7]When they kept on questioning him, he straightened up and said to them, "If any one of you is without sin, let him be the first to throw a stone at her." [8]Again he stooped down and wrote on the ground.

OPEN: 1. Do you jump to conclusions quickly, or only after much deliberation? Do people read you like a book, or does it take a while to know you? 2. When has someone jumped to a wrong conclusion about you? How did you feel?

DIG: 1. Why do the guards keep hands off? What tensions do they feel? 2. What justification do the Pharisees offer in refuting the guards? Nicodemus? Why would Nicodemus risk defending Jesus?

REFLECT: When have you been ridiculed because of your faith? What did you do?

OPEN: Ever been kept after school? Interrogated by police? Caught at the wrong place? Were you guilty or acquitted?

DIG: 1. How is this situation a trap for Jesus? What would the Pharisees accuse Jesus of if he told them to let her go? If he told them to stone her? How does he spring the trap? 2. How would the woman just caught in adultery have felt? What then would be the significance of Jesus' question in verse 10? 3. How does Jesus' response to the woman exemplify "grace and truth" (1:17)?

n37,38 Or / If anyone is thirsty, let him come to me. / And let him drink, 38who believes in me. / As o42 Greek seed p52 Two early manuscripts the Prophet

LOOKING INTO THE SCRIPTURE/20 Minutes. Read John 7:58-8:11 and discuss.

1. Which to you is the grossest sin?
   a. cheating on income tax
   b. having premarital/extramarital sex
   c. selling pornography
   d. cutting shady business deals
   e. child abuse

2. Who would you have trouble forgiving?
   a. a rapist
   b. a drug dealer
   c. a crooked politician
   d. an adulterer
   e. a Nazi war criminal

3. If you had been in the crowd when the woman caught in adultery was brought to Jesus, what would you have done?
   a. blushed
   b. stood up for the woman
   c. looked the other way
   d. picked up a stone
   e. prayed for the woman

4. Why do you think Jesus bent down and wrote on the ground?
   a. to let the men think
   b. to take the attention away from the woman
   c. to write something for the teachers to read—like their names
   d. to collect his thoughts
   e. to doodle something
   f. to keep from getting so angry with the accusers

5. What was Jesus really saying by these words, "If any one of you is without sin, let him be the first to throw a stone at her"?
   a. deal with your own sin first
   b. judgmentalism is a worse sin
   c. everyone of you has committed adultery
   d. you see in others your own sin

6. In the last thing Jesus said to the woman, what was the tone in his voice and what did it mean?
   a. guilt trip: You've been bad, and I'm ashamed of you
   b. warning: I'll let you off this time but don't do it again
   c. affirmation: You're a beautiful person and you don't have to put yourself down
   d. support: You may fail again and again, but let's go for it
   e. understanding: You're free to live differently

MY OWN STORY/25 Minutes.

1. What's the hardest thing about forgiving?
   a. they might think I'm condoning their behavior
   b. when their sin is something I don't have trouble with
   c. fear they might consider me a patsy
   d. resisting the temptation to take revenge
   e. letting go of the hurt feelings

2. Why do you think more people confess their sins to the bartender than a pastor/priest?
   a. it's easier to talk when you're drunk
   b. bartenders are more understanding
   c. people are more at home in a bar
   d. bartenders never judge you
   e. everybody in a bar has failed

3. When it comes to forgiving yourself when you blow it, put a dot on the line to indicate where you are between these two extremes.

I ALWAYS PUT
MYSELF DOWN _____
I HAVE LEARNED TO ACCEPT
GOD'S FORGIVENESS

4. What do you do when you blow it?
   a. crawl into a hole
   b. try to be extra good
   c. confess it to God and move on
   d. confess it to my pastor or priest
   e. shrug it off

5. Who are the people in your life that accept you no matter what you've done?
   a. my parents
   b. my friends
   c. one special person
   d. my support group

9At this, those who heard began to go away one at a time, the older ones first, until only Jesus was left, with the woman still standing there. 10Jesus straightened up and asked her, "Woman, where are they? Has no one condemned you?"

11"No one, sir," she said.

"Then neither do I condemn you," Jesus declared. "Go now and leave your life of sin."

The Validity of Jesus' Testimony

12When Jesus spoke again to the people, he said, "I am the light of the world. Whoever follows me will never walk in darkness, but will have the light of life."

13The Pharisees challenged him, "Here you are, appearing as your own witness; your testimony is not valid."

14Jesus answered, "Even if I testify on my own behalf, my testimony is valid, for I know where I came from and where I am going. But you have no idea where I come from or where I am going. 15You judge by human standards; I pass judgment on no one. 16But if I do judge, my decisions are right, because I am not alone. I stand with the Father, who sent me. 17In your own Law it is written that the testimony of two men is valid. 18I am one who testifies for myself; my other witness is the Father, who sent me."

19Then they asked him, "Where is your father?"

"You do not know me or my Father," Jesus replied. "If you knew me, you would know my Father also." 20He spoke these words while teaching in the temple area near the place where the offerings were put. Yet no one seized him, because his time had not yet come.

21Once more Jesus said to them, "I am going away, and you will look for me, and you will die in your sin. Where I go, you cannot come."

22This made the Jews ask, "Will he kill himself? Is that why he says, 'Where I go, you cannot come'?"

23But he continued, "You are from below; I am from above. You are of this world; I am not of this world. 24I told you that you would die in your sins; if you do not believe that I am ⌐the one I claim to be,¬q you will indeed die in your sins."

25"Who are you?" they asked.

"Just what I have been claiming all along," Jesus replied. 26"I have much to say in judgment of you. But he who sent me is reliable, and what I have heard from him I tell the world."

27They did not understand that he was telling them about his Father. 28So Jesus said, "When you have lifted up the Son of Man, then you will know that I am ⌐the one I claim to be¬ and that I do nothing on my own but speak just what the Father has taught me. 29The one who sent me is with me; he has not left me alone, for I always do what pleases him." 30Even as he spoke, many put their faith in him.

q24 Or I am he; also in verse 28

OPEN: 1. Where did your ancestors come from? How did they get to this country? **2.** Who is one of the more colorful characters in your family tree? **3.** Who is revered as the spiritual giant or founding father/mother in your spiritual family or church circles?

DIG: 1. What does Jesus want to stress to the people who "believed" him? What does he mean by *disciples*? *Truth*? *Freedom*? **2.** What false assumptions confuse the issue of spiritual freedom for Abraham's descendants? How does Jesus undermine their base of confidence? What issues does he force them to confront (vv.34-41)? **3.** How does Jesus undermine their claim in verse 41? What does he say is the ultimate test to show who "belongs to God" (v.47)? How does he account for their misunderstanding of him (vv.37,43,45,47)? **4.** In verse 48, why do the people use these terms to insult Jesus (see 4:29)? What accounts for their antagonism (vv.24-27,44)? **5.** What is the critical question raised by his claim in verse 51 (also v.24)? How is this issue central to the whole argument in 7:4-8:58? How does Jesus use their loyalty to Abraham against them? Why does Jesus' final claim cause such an outrage (see Ex 3:14)?

REFLECT: 1. What are you proud of in your religious heritage? In what ways has it been a handicap? **2.** How can you be sure that there is room in your life for his word? What needs to be cleaned out so there is room? **3.** Of the four claims Jesus makes in this chapter (vv.12,32,51,58), which means the most to you now? Why? **4.** From this passage, what can you do for someone who is honestly seeking God? What in your spiritual journey might help?

The Children of Abraham

[31]To the Jews who had believed him, Jesus said, "If you hold to my teaching, you are really my disciples. [32]Then you will know the truth, and the truth will set you free."

[33]They answered him, "We are Abraham's descendants[r] and have never been slaves of anyone. How can you say that we shall be set free?"

[34]Jesus replied, "I tell you the truth, everyone who sins is a slave to sin. [35]Now a slave has no permanent place in the family, but a son belongs to it forever. [36]So if the Son sets you free, you will be free indeed. [37]I know you are Abraham's descendants. Yet you are ready to kill me, because you have no room for my word. [38]I am telling you what I have seen in the Father's presence, and you do what you have heard from your father.[s]"

[39]"Abraham is our father," they answered.

"If you were Abraham's children," said Jesus, "then you would[t] do the things Abraham did. [40]As it is, you are determined to kill me, a man who has told you the truth that I heard from God. Abraham did not do such things. [41]You are doing the things your own father does."

"We are not illegitimate children," they protested. "The only Father we have is God himself."

The Children of the Devil

[42]Jesus said to them, "If God were your Father, you would love me, for I came from God and now am here. I have not come on my own; but he sent me. [43]Why is my language not clear to you? Because you are unable to hear what I say. [44]You belong to your father, the devil, and you want to carry out your father's desire. He was a murderer from the beginning, not holding to the truth, for there is no truth in him. When he lies, he speaks his native language, for he is a liar and the father of lies. [45]Yet because I tell the truth, you do not believe me! [46]Can any of you prove me guilty of sin? If I am telling the truth, why don't you believe me? [47]He who belongs to God hears what God says. The reason you do not hear is that you do not belong to God."

The Claims of Jesus About Himself

[48]The Jews answered him, "Aren't we right in saying that you are a Samaritan and demon-possessed?"

[49]"I am not possessed by a demon," said Jesus, "but I honor my Father and you dishonor me. [50]I am not seeking glory for myself; but there is one who seeks it, and he is the judge. [51]I tell you the truth, if anyone keeps my word, he will never see death."

[52]At this the Jews exclaimed, "Now we know that you are demon-possessed! Abraham died and so did the prophets, yet you say that if anyone keeps your word, he will never taste

---

[r]33 Greek seed; also in verse 37   *[s]38 Or presence. Therefore do what you have heard from the Father.*   *[t]39 Some early manuscripts "If you are Abraham's children," said Jesus, "then*

death. [53]Are you greater than our father Abraham? He died, and so did the prophets. Who do you think you are?"

[54]Jesus replied, "If I glorify myself, my glory means nothing. My Father, whom you claim as your God, is the one who glorifies me. [55]Though you do not know him, I know him. If I said I did not, I would be a liar like you, but I do know him and keep his word. [56]Your father Abraham rejoiced at the thought of seeing my day; he saw it and was glad."

[57]"You are not yet fifty years old," the Jews said to him, "and you have seen Abraham!"

[58]"I tell you the truth," Jesus answered, "before Abraham was born, I am!" [59]At this, they picked up stones to stone him, but Jesus hid himself, slipping away from the temple grounds.

Jesus Heals a Man Born Blind

9 As he went along, he saw a man blind from birth. [2]His disciples asked him, "Rabbi, who sinned, this man or his parents, that he was born blind?"

[3]"Neither this man nor his parents sinned," said Jesus, "but this happened so that the work of God might be displayed in his life. [4]As long as it is day, we must do the work of him who sent me. Night is coming, when no one can work. [5]While I am in the world, I am the light of the world."

[6]Having said this, he spit on the ground, made some mud with the saliva, and put it on the man's eyes. [7]"Go," he told him, "wash in the Pool of Siloam" (this word means Sent). So the man went and washed, and came home seeing.

[8]His neighbors and those who had formerly seen him begging asked, "Isn't this the same man who used to sit and beg?" [9]Some claimed that he was.

Others said, "No, he only looks like him."

But he himself insisted, "I am the man."

[10]"How then were your eyes opened?" they demanded.

[11]He replied, "The man they call Jesus made some mud and put it on my eyes. He told me to go to Siloam and wash. So I went and washed, and then I could see."

[12]"Where is this man?" they asked him.

"I don't know," he said.

The Pharisees Investigate the Healing

[13]They brought to the Pharisees the man who had been blind. [14]Now the day on which Jesus had made the mud and opened the man's eyes was a Sabbath. [15]Therefore the Pharisees also asked him how he had received his sight. "He put mud on my eyes," the man replied, "and I washed, and now I see."

[16]Some of the Pharisees said, "This man is not from God, for he does not keep the Sabbath."

But others asked, "How can a sinner do such miraculous signs?" So they were divided.

[17]Finally they turned again to the blind man, "What have you to say about him? It was your eyes he opened."

The man replied, "He is a prophet."

[18]The Jews still did not believe that he had been blind and had received his sight until they sent for the man's parents. [19]"Is this

were his father or mother? **3.** Note the conflicting claims to knowledge and certainty on the part of the Pharisees, the parents, and the man born blind. What is each party sure of? Not sure of? **4.** In the course of this investigation, what is the man able to see about Jesus (vv.12,17,25,27,30-33, also 36,38)? About the Pharisees? How is his attitude changing as well? **5.** In contrast to the man's growing spiritual insight, how are the Pharisees progressing? **6.** What is the Pharisees' real motive in questioning the man (vv.28, 34)? What in the man's response finally puts them "over the top"?

REFLECT: 1. Who has been the toughest person for you to explain your faith to? Why? What have you found to be helpful in dealing with people who ridicule your faith? **2.** Has your faith in Jesus led to your exclusion from any group? How has this hurt or helped you?

OPEN: What one day in your life qualifies for the "roller-coaster" award (most highs and lows in 24 hours)?

DIG: 1. Why does Jesus wait until now to fully present himself? How is the man, only now, able to affirm Jesus as Lord? **2.** How has this chapter illustrated verse 39? What blindness is the result of sin (vv.39-41)? How do such guilty people "see" again?

REFLECT: How would you score your own spiritual sight: 20/20? 20/800? A few "blind spots"? Why? What could correct this?

your son?" they asked. "Is this the one you say was born blind? How is it that now he can see?"

[20]"We know he is our son," the parents answered, "and we know he was born blind. [21]But how he can see now, or who opened his eyes, we don't know. Ask him. He is of age; he will speak for himself." [22]His parents said this because they were afraid of the Jews, for already the Jews had decided that anyone who acknowledged that Jesus was the Christ[u] would be put out of the synagogue. [23]That was why his parents said, "He is of age; ask him."

[24]A second time they summoned the man who had been blind. "Give glory to God,[v]" they said. "We know this man is a sinner."

[25]He replied, "Whether he is a sinner or not, I don't know. One thing I do know. I was blind but now I see!"

[26]Then they asked him, "What did he do to you? How did he open your eyes?"

[27]He answered, "I have told you already and you did not listen. Why do you want to hear it again? Do you want to become his disciples, too?"

[28]Then they hurled insults at him and said, "You are this fellow's disciple! We are disciples of Moses! [29]We know that God spoke to Moses, but as for this fellow, we don't even know where he comes from."

[30]The man answered, "Now that is remarkable! You don't know where he comes from, yet he opened my eyes. [31]We know that God does not listen to sinners. He listens to the godly man who does his will. [32]Nobody has ever heard of opening the eyes of a man born blind. [33]If this man were not from God, he could do nothing."

[34]To this they replied, "You were steeped in sin at birth; how dare you lecture us!" And they threw him out.

Spiritual Blindness

[35]Jesus heard that they had thrown him out, and when he found him, he said, "Do you believe in the Son of Man?"

[36]"Who is he, sir?" the man asked. "Tell me so that I may believe in him."

[37]Jesus said, "You have now seen him; in fact, he is the one speaking with you."

[38]Then the man said, "Lord, I believe," and he worshiped him.

[39]Jesus said, "For judgment I have come into this world, so that the blind will see and those who see will become blind."

[40]Some Pharisees who were with him heard him say this and asked, "What? Are we blind too?"

[41]Jesus said, "If you were blind, you would not be guilty of sin; but now that you claim you can see, your guilt remains.

[u]22 Or *Messiah*   [v]24 A solemn charge to tell the truth (see Joshua 7:19)

The Shepherd and His Flock

10 "I tell you the truth, the man who does not enter the sheep pen by the gate, but climbs in by some other way, is a thief and a robber. ²The man who enters by the gate is the shepherd of his sheep. ³The watchman opens the gate for him, and the sheep listen to his voice. He calls his own sheep by name and leads them out. ⁴When he has brought out all his own, he goes on ahead of them, and his sheep follow him because they know his voice. ⁵But they will never follow a stranger; in fact, they will run away from him because they do not recognize a stranger's voice." ⁶Jesus used this figure of speech, but they did not understand what he was telling them.

⁷Therefore Jesus said again, "I tell you the truth, I am the gate for the sheep. ⁸All who ever came before me were thieves and robbers, but the sheep did not listen to them. ⁹I am the gate; whoever enters through me will be saved. *ʷ*He will come in and go out, and find pasture. ¹⁰The thief comes only to steal and kill and destroy; I have come that they may have life, and have it to the full.

¹¹"I am the good shepherd. The good shepherd lays down his life for the sheep. ¹²The hired hand is not the shepherd who owns the sheep. So when he sees the wolf coming, he abandons the sheep and runs away. Then the wolf attacks the flock and scatters it. ¹³The man runs away because he is a hired hand and cares nothing for the sheep.

¹⁴"I am the good shepherd; I know my sheep and my sheep know me— ¹⁵just as the Father knows me and I know the Father—and I lay down my life for the sheep. ¹⁶I have other sheep that are not of this sheep pen. I must bring them also. They too will listen to my voice, and there shall be one flock and one shepherd. ¹⁷The reason my Father loves me is that I lay down my life—only to take it up again. ¹⁸No one takes it from me, but I lay it down of my own accord. I have authority to lay it down and authority to take it up again. This command I received from my Father."

¹⁹At these words the Jews were again divided. ²⁰Many of them said, "He is demon-possessed and raving mad. Why listen to him?"

²¹But others said, "These are not the sayings of a man possessed by a demon. Can a demon open the eyes of the blind?"

The Unbelief of the Jews

²²Then came the Feast of Dedication*ˣ* at Jerusalem. It was winter, ²³and Jesus was in the temple area walking in Solomon's Colonnade. ²⁴The Jews gathered around him, saying, "How long will you keep us in suspense? If you are the Christ,*ʸ* tell us plainly."

²⁵Jesus answered, "I did tell you, but you do not believe. The miracles I do in my Father's name speak for me, ²⁶but you do not believe because you are not my sheep. ²⁷My sheep listen to my voice; I know them, and they follow me. ²⁸I give them

OPEN: As a kid, what was your favorite pet? How did this pet respond when it heard your voice?

DIG: 1. What do the sheep, shepherd, and stranger represent? How does the story in chapter 9 provide one example of what this parable is about? **2.** What is the relationship of the shepherd to his sheep? How do the sheep respond to the shepherd? How does this relate to the Pharisees' difficulty in understanding Jesus? **3.** What does Jesus mean by likening himself to a gate for the sheepfold? How is he unlike the "thieves and robbers" (vv.8-10)? In this context, who are these "thieves and robbers"? **4.** How does Jesus identify himself with the "good shepherd" (vv.11-15)? How does Jesus' death relate to his promise in verse 10? **5.** Who are the "other sheep" he must bring also? What characterizes his flock? **6.** What final claim does Jesus make (vv.17-18)? Why do his listeners respond as they do? How would you have responded?

REFLECT: 1. What turning point was significant for you in terms of hearing "God's voice" and responding? **2.** How do you discern his voice from those of so many others that vie for your attention?

OPEN: 1. What is the big annual "feast day" for your family? Who usually comes? What is served? What is the big "pastime"? **2.** What family traditions are you going to preserve for your kids?

DIG: 1. Given the meaning of Hanukkah (when Jews celebrate their deliverance during the Maccabean revolt), what feelings about Rome's authority might surface among the crowds? How

---

ʷ9 Or *kept safe*   *ˣ22* That is, Hanukkah   *ʸ24* Or *Messiah* would the Roman authorities prepare for this feast? Given these tensions, what might be the real intent of the Pharisees' question in verse 24? **2.** How does Jesus push things even further? Why? How does he diagnose their problem? **3.** How do the leaders interpret Jesus' claim to be one with God? How does Jesus sidetrack them (v.34; Ps 82:6)? What evidence does he offer? **4.** What could account for the difference in reception Jesus received across the Jordan (vv.40-42)?

REFLECT: 1. What has convinced you that Jesus is the Messiah? What "old ways" of looking at Jesus must you overcome by faith? **2.** What difference does it make that Jesus is God and not just a man? Would the promise of verse 28 mean much otherwise?

OPEN: What is the saddest funeral you ever experienced where a friend, family member, or national figure was taken suddenly and unexpectedly? How did you feel at the time?

DIG: 1. How would you describe Jesus' relationship with this family (vv.1-5)? Why does Jesus deliberately delay (v.6)? **2.** Given his disciples' objection (v.8), what do you think Jesus means by his parable (vv.9-10)? **3.** Why is Jesus returning to Lazarus at this time (vv.11-15)? What do the disciples fear instead (vv.8,16)?

REFLECT: 1. Have you ever felt like God was not listening when you prayed? How did you deal with this? How does the way in which Jesus postponed his response to the sisters' request help you in understanding your own prayer life? **2.** Have you, like Thomas (v.16), ever felt Jesus was calling you to do something very risky? What happened?

eternal life, and they shall never perish; no one can snatch them out of my hand. [29]My Father, who has given them to me, is greater than all[z]; no one can snatch them out of my Father's hand. [30]I and the Father are one."

[31]Again the Jews picked up stones to stone him, [32]but Jesus said to them, "I have shown you many great miracles from the Father. For which of these do you stone me?"

[33]"We are not stoning you for any of these," replied the Jews, "but for blasphemy, because you, a mere man, claim to be God."

[34]Jesus answered them, "Is it not written in your Law, 'I have said you are gods'[a]? [35]If he called them 'gods,' to whom the word of God came—and the Scripture cannot be broken— [36]what about the one whom the Father set apart as his very own and sent into the world? Why then do you accuse me of blasphemy because I said, 'I am God's Son'? [37]Do not believe me unless I do what my Father does. [38]But if I do it, even though you do not believe me, believe the miracles, that you may know and understand that the Father is in me, and I in the Father." [39]Again they tried to seize him, but he escaped their grasp.

[40]Then Jesus went back across the Jordan to the place where John had been baptizing in the early days. Here he stayed [41]and many people came to him. They said, "Though John never performed a miraculous sign, all that John said about this man was true." [42]And in that place many believed in Jesus.

The Death of Lazarus

11 Now a man named Lazarus was sick. He was from Bethany, the village of Mary and her sister Martha. [2]This Mary, whose brother Lazarus now lay sick, was the same one who poured perfume on the Lord and wiped his feet with her hair. [3]So the sisters sent word to Jesus, "Lord, the one you love is sick."

[4]When he heard this, Jesus said, "This sickness will not end in death. No, it is for God's glory so that God's Son may be glorified through it." [5]Jesus loved Martha and her sister and Lazarus. [6]Yet when he heard that Lazarus was sick, he stayed where he was two more days.

[7]Then he said to his disciples, "Let us go back to Judea."

[8]"But Rabbi," they said, "a short while ago the Jews tried to stone you, and yet you are going back there?"

[9]Jesus answered, "Are there not twelve hours of daylight? A man who walks by day will not stumble, for he sees by this world's light. [10]It is when he walks by night that he stumbles, for he has no light."

[11]After he had said this, he went on to tell them, "Our friend Lazarus has fallen asleep; but I am going there to wake him up."

[12]His disciples replied, "Lord, if he sleeps, he will get better."

[13]Jesus had been speaking of his death, but his disciples thought he meant natural sleep.

---

[z]29 Many early manuscripts *What my Father has given me is greater than all*
[a]34 Psalm 82:6

LOOKING INTO THE SCRIPTURE/20 Minutes. Read John 11:1-44 and discuss.

1. If your best friend did not come when you needed him/her, how would you feel?
   a. very angry
   b. deserted
   c. hurt
   d. assume there was good reason
   e. terrible, but I would never show it

2. Why do you think Jesus delayed two days before setting out to see Lazarus?
   a. he knew he couldn't make it before Lazarus' death
   b. he was warned that people were out to kill him
   c. he needed time to prepare himself
   d. God had a greater purpose in mind

3. Why do you think Jesus told his disciples that Lazarus was sleeping at first when he knew Lazarus was dead?
   a. he didn't want to deal with their shock
   b. he wanted to deal with their shock at a later time
   c. he needed time to work through his own feelings first
   d. he didn't want them to think the situation was hopeless

4. Jesus did not cry when he got word of Lazarus' death, but he did cry when he went with Mary to the tomb. Why?
   a. he knew he could raise Lazarus, but he felt for the mourners
   b. the reality didn't sink in until he saw the tomb personally
   c. he was glad Lazarus was dead so he could show his power, but death is horrible even so
   d. he cried because Mary was crying

5. Of the five stages of grief, where were (1) Thomas, (2) Martha on his arrival, (3) Mary at the tomb, (4) some of the Jews (v. 37)?
   a. denial/isolation: He is not really dead
   b. anger: He's dead and you let him die
   c. bargaining: If you'll do this, I'll do that
   d. depression: I don't want to talk about it
   e. acceptance: He's dead and there's nothing we can do about it

6. If you had been there and saw Jesus crying, how would you have felt?
   a. embarrassed for him: Grown men don't cry
   b. relieved: It's okay to cry
   c. awkward: Let's get on with it
   d. mad: You could have done something if you had gotten here earlier and now all you can do is blubber
   e. comforted: He really cared

7. Why did Jesus ask the friends to "Take away the stone" (v. 38) and "Take off the grave clothes and let him go"?
   a. he needed their help
   b. he didn't like the smell
   c. he wanted to convince them that Lazarus had really been dead
   d. he wanted them to be part of the healing process
   e. he always works in cooperation with human instruments

MY OWN STORY/25 Minutes. Share how this story touches on some of your own experience.

1. How do you handle grief—particularly unexpected death?
   a. pretend nothing has happened
   b. keep everything inside
   c. get angry at God
   d. isolate myself from everybody
   e. call my friends and talk, talk, talk
   f. try to put on a brave front
   g. keep busy
   h. let it all out

2. What have you found helpful when you are called upon to help a friend who is undergoing grief?
   a. share some Scripture
   b. just be present and say nothing
   c. wait three days and call
   d. bring food/flowers/book
   e. take this person away for a day in the mountains
   f. do a lot of hugging/touching
   g. listen to their reminiscences
   h. encourage them to say what they're really feeling

[14]So then he told them plainly, "Lazarus is dead, [15]and for your sake I am glad I was not there, so that you may believe. But let us go to him."

[16]Then Thomas (called Didymus) said to the rest of the disciples, "Let us also go, that we may die with him."

Jesus Comforts the Sisters

[17]On his arrival, Jesus found that Lazarus had already been in the tomb for four days. [18]Bethany was less than two miles[b] from Jerusalem, [19]and many Jews had come to Martha and Mary to comfort them in the loss of their brother. [20]When Martha heard that Jesus was coming, she went out to meet him, but Mary stayed at home.

[21]"Lord," Martha said to Jesus, "if you had been here, my brother would not have died. [22]But I know that even now God will give you whatever you ask."

[23]Jesus said to her, "Your brother will rise again."

[24]Martha answered, "I know he will rise again in the resurrection at the last day."

[25]Jesus said to her, "I am the resurrection and the life. He who believes in me will live, even though he dies; [26]and whoever lives and believes in me will never die. Do you believe this?"

[27]"Yes, Lord," she told him, "I believe that you are the Christ,[c] the Son of God, who was to come into the world."

[28]And after she had said this, she went back and called her sister Mary aside. "The Teacher is here," she said, "and is asking for you." [29]When Mary heard this, she got up quickly and went to him. [30]Now Jesus had not yet entered the village, but was still at the place where Martha had met him. [31]When the Jews who had been with Mary in the house, comforting her, noticed how quickly she got up and went out, they followed her, supposing she was going to the tomb to mourn there.

[32]When Mary reached the place where Jesus was and saw him, she fell at his feet and said, "Lord, if you had been here, my brother would not have died."

[33]When Jesus saw her weeping, and the Jews who had come along with her also weeping, he was deeply moved in spirit and troubled. [34]"Where have you laid him?" he asked.

"Come and see, Lord," they replied.

[35]Jesus wept.

[36]Then the Jews said, "See how he loved him!"

[37]But some of them said, "Could not he who opened the eyes of the blind man have kept this man from dying?"

Jesus Raises Lazarus From the Dead

[38]Jesus, once more deeply moved, came to the tomb. It was a cave with a stone laid across the entrance. [39]"Take away the stone," he said.

"But, Lord," said Martha, the sister of the dead man, "by this time there is a bad odor, for he has been there four days."

[40]Then Jesus said, "Did I not tell you that if you believed, you would see the glory of God?"

[b]18 Greek *fifteen stadia* (about 3 kilometers)   [c]27 Or *Messiah*

OPEN: 1. Which of your siblings (if any) are you closest to? Why that one? Which friend of yours has been closer than a brother? **2.** If you could raise one person from the dead, who would it be? Why?

DIG: 1. How long had Lazarus been dead by the time Jesus arrived? How would you feel if you were Martha or Mary and you heard that Jesus had finally come? **2.** What do you learn about Martha from the way she talks with Jesus in verses 21-27? How does Jesus stretch her faith by his claim in verse 25? How does this relate to his claim in 10:9? **3.** What does Martha's statement (v.27) sound like to you: (a) Stab in the dark? (b) Hope against hope? (c) Intellectual assent? (d) Active commitment? Why do you think so? **4.** How is Mary's greeting like and unlike Martha's? Since Jesus knew he was going to raise Lazarus (11:11), how do you account for his weeping (vv.33-35)? **5.** What lies behind the comments of the mourners in verses 36-37? **6.** How does Martha's objection in verse 39 contrast with her confidence in verse 22? **7.** Putting yourself in the drama, how would you feel as Martha? As Lazarus? As the mourners?

REFLECT: 1. When have you been faced with a tough situation recently that ended up stretching your faith? What would have been different for you if that struggle had simply been avoided? **2.** Have you ever attended a funeral where there was no sense of eternal life, as in verses 25-26? How did you go away from that experience? What difference does this hope make for you? **3.** How does Jesus' response to Lazarus' death and Mary's weeping (v.35) help you to trust him more? **4.** Spiritually, do you feel like you are: Still in the grave? Alive, but wearing the old grave clothes? Alive and set free? Why? **5.** What are some "old grave clothes" that still must be shed for you to feel truly free in Christ? **6.** What death of a relationship, emotional scars, or other practical concerns, and past hurts now block your faith in Jesus?

⁴¹So they took away the stone. Then Jesus looked up and said, "Father, I thank you that you have heard me. ⁴²I knew that you always hear me, but I said this for the benefit of the people standing here, that they may believe that you sent me."

⁴³When he had said this, Jesus called in a loud voice, "Lazarus, come out!" ⁴⁴The dead man came out, his hands and feet wrapped with strips of linen, and a cloth around his face.

Jesus said to them, "Take off the grave clothes and let him go."

The Plot to Kill Jesus

⁴⁵Therefore many of the Jews who had come to visit Mary, and had seen what Jesus did, put their faith in him. ⁴⁶But some of them went to the Pharisees and told them what Jesus had done. ⁴⁷Then the chief priests and the Pharisees called a meeting of the Sanhedrin.

"What are we accomplishing?" they asked. "Here is this man performing many miraculous signs. ⁴⁸If we let him go on like this, everyone will believe in him, and then the Romans will come and take away both our place *d* and our nation."

⁴⁹Then one of them, named Caiaphas, who was high priest that year, spoke up, "You know nothing at all! ⁵⁰You do not realize that it is better for you that one man die for the people than that the whole nation perish."

⁵¹He did not say this on his own, but as high priest that year he prophesied that Jesus would die for the Jewish nation, ⁵²and not only for that nation but also for the scattered children of God, to bring them together and make them one. ⁵³So from that day on they plotted to take his life.

⁵⁴Therefore Jesus no longer moved about publicly among the Jews. Instead he withdrew to a region near the desert, to a village called Ephraim, where he stayed with his disciples.

⁵⁵When it was almost time for the Jewish Passover, many went up from the country to Jerusalem for their ceremonial cleansing before the Passover. ⁵⁶They kept looking for Jesus, and as they stood in the temple area they asked one another, "What do you think? Isn't he coming to the Feast at all?" ⁵⁷But the chief priests and Pharisees had given orders that if anyone found out where Jesus was, he should report it so that they might arrest him.

Jesus Anointed at Bethany

12 Six days before the Passover, Jesus arrived at Bethany, where Lazarus lived, whom Jesus had raised from the dead. ²Here a dinner was given in Jesus' honor. Martha served, while Lazarus was among those reclining at the table with him. ³Then Mary took about a pint *e* of pure nard, an expensive perfume; she poured it on Jesus' feet and wiped his feet with her hair. And the house was filled with the fragrance of the perfume.

⁴But one of his disciples, Judas Iscariot, who was later to betray him, objected, ⁵"Why wasn't this perfume sold and the

---

OPEN: 1. Have you seen "wheels of justice" grind exceedingly slow, not at all, or come unhinged altogether? When? Relatively speaking, which council works more efficiently and justly: Your company board, city council, or your church council? **2.** When have you challenged "company policy"?

DIG: 1. What responses does the Lazarus miracle produce? Why? What does it show about their view of Jesus? **2.** What are the chief concerns of the leaders? What do they fail to see in this story? How does Caiaphas propose to solve "the Jesus problem"? How does Caiaphas' murderous threat unwittingly convey prophetic truth about Jesus' death (see 3:16)? **3.** How does Jesus respond to this new situation? What do you think the crowds would be expecting as Passover approached?

REFLECT: 1. What would you have done if you had been on the Sanhedrin? Would politics or truth win out with you? **2.** How have you tried to keep Jesus in line with your religious traditions? What have you done when traditions have kept you from Jesus?

OPEN: If you had a year's wages to blow on friends, which would you choose: (a) Big party? (b) Glorious trip for a few? or (c) Extravagant gift for one?

DIG: 1. Given the value of the perfume (v.5), how would you have reacted as you watched Mary? Why? **2.** How does Jesus interpret Mary's action? How is his comment in verse 8 especially applicable to Judas? **3.** How is the blindness of the priests shown by their reaction to Lazarus?

---

d48 Or temple   *e3* Greek *a* litra (probably about 0.5 liter)

REFLECT: If you had a year's salary or time to use for Christ, how would you use it? How is that reflected in your budget and priorities now?

money given to the poor? It was worth a year's wages.*ƒ*" ⁶He did not say this because he cared about the poor but because he was a thief; as keeper of the money bag, he used to help himself to what was put into it.

⁷"Leave her alone," Jesus replied. "It was intended, that she should save this perfume for the day of my burial. ⁸You will always have the poor among you, but you will not always have me."

⁹Meanwhile a large crowd of Jews found out that Jesus was there and came, not only because of him but also to see Lazarus, whom he had raised from the dead. ¹⁰So the chief priests made plans to kill Lazarus as well, ¹¹for on account of him many of the Jews were going over to Jesus and putting their faith in him.

DIG: 1. How would you set this opening scene for TV? What "flashbacks" (e.g., the raising of Lazarus from the dead) would you use as the TV producer to show the crowd now so whipped up, but once so confused and divided (as in 7:40-43; 10:19-21)? **2.** How could you tie in their hope that Jesus will do at *this* Passover what God did at the *first* Passover? **3.** Why a lowly donkey for Jesus (see Zec 9:9)? **4.** According to your script, what would the crowds, the disciples, and Jewish leaders be feeling now? One week later? Had you been there, what would you be feeling: Fanaticism, fickleness, faith, or fear? Why?

REFLECT: 1. What convinced you that Jesus is your King? What is the best thing you've seen about the type of king he is? **2.** Is your worship life like a hero's victory or a funeral dirge? Why?

The Triumphal Entry

¹²The next day the great crowd that had come for the Feast heard that Jesus was on his way to Jerusalem. ¹³They took palm branches and went out to meet him, shouting,

"Hosanna!*ᵍ*"

"Blessed is he who comes in the name of the Lord!"*ʰ*

"Blessed is the King of Israel!"

¹⁴Jesus found a young donkey and sat upon it, as it is written,

¹⁵"Do not be afraid, O Daughter of Zion;
  see, your king is coming,
  seated on a donkey's colt."*ⁱ*

¹⁶At first his disciples did not understand all this. Only after Jesus was glorified did they realize that these things had been written about him and that they had done these things to him. ¹⁷Now the crowd that was with him when he called Lazarus from the tomb and raised him from the dead continued to spread the word. ¹⁸Many people, because they had heard that he had given this miraculous sign, went out to meet him. ¹⁹So the Pharisees said to one another, "See, this is getting us nowhere. Look how the whole world has gone after him!"

Jesus Predicts His Death

OPEN: Are you more likely to panic in the *big* crises or the *little* ones? Explain.

DIG: 1. What brings *Gentiles* to Jerusalem during a time of *Jewish* patriotism? **2.** What was so unique about their request that Philip would first filter it through Andrew? **3.** Jesus said several times that "his time had not come" (2:4; 7:6,30). What regarding this request caused him to say that now it has come? **4.** In his parable (v.24), who is the kernel of wheat?

²⁰Now there were some Greeks among those who went up to worship at the Feast. ²¹They came to Philip, who was from Bethsaida in Galilee, with a request. "Sir," they said, "we would like to see Jesus." ²²Philip went to tell Andrew; Andrew and Philip in turn told Jesus.

²³Jesus replied, "The hour has come for the Son of Man to be glorified. ²⁴I tell you the truth, unless a kernel of wheat falls to the ground and dies, it remains only a single seed. But if it dies, it produces many seeds. ²⁵The man who loves his life will lose it, while the man who hates his life in this world will keep

ƒ5 Greek *three hundred denarii* became an exclamation of praise   *ᵍ13* A Hebrew expression meaning "Save!" which   *ʰ13* Psalm 118:25, 26   *ⁱ15* Zech. 9:9

it for eternal life. ²⁶Whoever serves me must follow me; and where I am, my servant also will be. My Father will honor the one who serves me.

²⁷"Now my heart is troubled, and what shall I say? 'Father, save me from this hour'? No, it was for this very reason I came to this hour. ²⁸Father, glorify your name!"

Then a voice came from heaven, "I have glorified it, and will glorify it again." ²⁹The crowd that was there and heard it said it had thundered; others said an angel had spoken to him. ³⁰Jesus said, "This voice was for your benefit, not mine. ³¹Now is the time for judgment on this world; now the prince of this world will be driven out. ³²But I, when I am lifted up from the earth, will draw all men to myself." ³³He said this to show the kind of death he was going to die.

³⁴The crowd spoke up, "We have heard from the Law that the Christ[j] will remain forever, so how can you say, 'The Son of Man must be lifted up'? Who is this 'Son of Man'?"

³⁵Then Jesus told them, "You are going to have the light just a little while longer. Walk while you have the light, before darkness overtakes you. The man who walks in the dark does not know where he is going. ³⁶Put your trust in the light while you have it, so that you may become sons of light." When he had finished speaking, Jesus left and hid himself from them.

The Jews Continue in Their Unbelief

³⁷Even after Jesus had done all these miraculous signs in their presence, they still would not believe in him. ³⁸This was to fulfill the word of Isaiah the prophet:

"Lord, who has believed our message
   and to whom has the arm of the Lord been
      revealed?"[k]

³⁹For this reason they could not believe, because, as Isaiah says elsewhere:

⁴⁰"He has blinded their eyes
   and deadened their hearts,
so they can neither see with their eyes,
   nor understand with their hearts,
   nor turn—and I would heal them."[l]

⁴¹Isaiah said this because he saw Jesus' glory and spoke about him.

⁴²Yet at the same time many even among the leaders believed in him. But because of the Pharisees they would not confess their faith for fear they would be put out of the synagogue; ⁴³for they loved praise from men more than praise from God.

⁴⁴Then Jesus cried out, "When a man believes in me, he does not believe in me only, but in the one who sent me. ⁴⁵When he looks at me, he sees the one who sent me. ⁴⁶I have come into the world as a light, so that no one who believes in me should stay in darkness.

How is this related to the Gentiles' re-quest? **5.** What is he calling his disciples to do in verses 25-26? What promise do they receive? **6.** In verses 27-32, what is about to occur "now"? How does this affect Jesus? How is the story of Lazarus related to verse 28? How is this word for the people's benefit? **7.** What causes the crowd's initial support (in 12:13) to waver here (vv.32-34)? What happened to their celebration?

REFLECT: 1. Where is Jesus calling you to *die* so that you might *live*? What do you tend to hold on to rather than follow Jesus? **2.** Do you feel like you are walking in the dark, the light, or in some shadow land right now? Why?

———————

OPEN: Are you more like the salesman who could "sell an ice-box to an Eskimo," or more like the Eskimo that buys one? Any examples?

DIG: 1. What are some of the miraculous signs that Jesus has done in this gospel? How do the prophecies from Isaiah 5:31 and 6:10 account for the people's disbelief in spite of these signs? Do you think the prophecy from Isaiah 6:10 is a statement of irony, or of God's intent? Why? **2.** What is the author implying about Jesus in verse 41 (see 8:58)? **3.** What inhibits the leaders from speaking up? How does this illustrate 12:25-26? If you were in their shoes, what would you be saying to yourself as you faced this dilemma? **4.** What is Jesus claiming in verses 44-45? How do verses 44-46 relate to 1:1-5? How is Jesus like a light? **5.** What does Jesus emphasize in verses 47-50? As a last public statement, why is this one especially appropriate? How is it that Jesus' words can either judge a person or lead one to life?

---

j34 Or Messiah   *k38 Isaiah 53:1*   *l40 Isaiah 6:10*

REFLECT: 1. Where do you find it most difficult to live your faith: At home or work? Why? **2.** When have you felt pressured by fear to keep quiet about your faith? What happened? **3.** What have you found most helpful in letting people know where you stand with God?

OPEN: 1. What were the "special" meals in your family: Thanksgiving? Sunday lunch? Birthday dinners? Christmas? What was usually served? **2.** Who would you nominate for the "Mother Teresa Award" in your family or church for selfless, tireless servanthood?

DIG: 1. What does Jesus *know* that escapes the disciples' attention (vv.1,3,11)? Hence, what impresses you about Jesus washing their feet? **2.** If you were Peter, would you have reacted as he did? Why or why not? While Peter is taking the washing of his feet literally, what do you think Jesus meant by his statement in verse 8? In verse 10? What new meaning would these statements take on after Jesus' death and resurrection? **3.** How does Jesus challenge their idea of what it means to be the chief followers of the Messiah (vv.12-17)? What role reversals do you see here?

REFLECT: 1. In your spiritual life, who is one person who has demonstrated what it means to "wash feet"? What did he or she do? **2.** Specifically, how will you put Jesus' teaching into practice in at least one relationship this week at home, work, or church?

[47]"As for the person who hears my words but does not keep them, I do not judge him. For I did not come to judge the world, but to save it. [48]There is a judge for the one who rejects me and does not accept my words; that very word which I spoke will condemn him at the last day. [49]For I did not speak of my own accord, but the Father who sent me commanded me what to say and how to say it. [50]I know that his command leads to eternal life. So whatever I say is just what the Father has told me to say."

Jesus Washes His Disciples' Feet

13 It was just before the Passover Feast. Jesus knew that the time had come for him to leave this world and go to the Father. Having loved his own who were in the world, he now showed them the full extent of his love.[m]

[2]The evening meal was being served, and the devil had already prompted Judas Iscariot, son of Simon, to betray Jesus. [3]Jesus knew that the Father had put all things under his power, and that he had come from God and was returning to God; [4]so he got up from the meal, took off his outer clothing, and wrapped a towel around his waist. [5]After that, he poured water into a basin and began to wash his disciples' feet, drying them with the towel that was wrapped around him.

[6]He came to Simon Peter, who said to him, "Lord, are you going to wash my feet?"

[7]Jesus replied, "You do not realize now what I am doing, but later you will understand."

[8]"No," said Peter, "you shall never wash my feet."

Jesus answered, "Unless I wash you, you have no part with me."

[9]"Then, Lord," Simon Peter replied, "not just my feet but my hands and my head as well!"

[10]Jesus answered, "A person who has had a bath needs only to wash his feet; his whole body is clean. And you are clean, though not every one of you." [11]For he knew who was going to betray him, and that was why he said not every one was clean.

[12]When he had finished washing their feet, he put on his clothes and returned to his place. "Do you understand what I have done for you?" he asked them. [13]"You call me 'Teacher' and 'Lord,' and rightly so, for that is what I am. [14]Now that I, your Lord and Teacher, have washed your feet, you also should wash one another's feet. [15]I have set you an example that you should do as I have done for you. [16]I tell you the truth, no servant is greater than his master, nor is a messenger greater than the one who sent him. [17]Now that you know these things, you will be blessed if you do them.

[m]1 Or *he loved them to the last*

John 13:1-17   **JESUS WASHES HIS DISCIPLES' FEET**

LOOKING INTO THE SCRIPTURE/20 Minutes. Read John 13:1-17 and discuss.

1. What do you look for in a leader? Rank these qualities in order of their importance from 1 to 10. Then go back and put an * next to those qualities you think Peter would demonstrate as a leader.

_____ toleration: accepts differences of opinion
_____ motivation: able too inspire confidence
_____ courage: willing to take risks
_____ initiative: self-starter
_____ intelligence: high I.Q.

_____ task oriented: dedicated to reaching goals
_____ unselfish: puts others first
_____ flexible: able to make midcourse corrections
_____ pragmatic: practical and resourceful
_____ action oriented: try anything once

2. Assuming the disciples were aware of the custom of footwashing, why didn't they wash their feet when entering the home?
   a. you can't wash your own feet
   b. they forgot
   c. it was the servant's job
   d. it would be humiliating

3. Why do you think Jesus washed his disciples' feet?
   a. to shame them
   b. to show his deep love for them
   c. to teach them a lesson in servanthood
   d. to give them a new model for their lives together
   e. to show them real leadership

4. Why was Peter so upset with Jesus?
   a. he felt guilty
   b. he didn't want to see Jesus degrading himself
   c. he thought one of the other disciples should do it
   d. he thought his feet were clean enough
   e. he didn't understand what Jesus was doing

5. "A person who has had a bath needs only to wash his feet; his whole body is clean. . . ." What is the point Jesus is making here?
   a. this is just a ritual to observe
   b. your feet are the important part of the body
   c. If you've taken a bath before starting out, all you need to clean are your feet
   d. spiritually, once you have been cleansed of sin, all you need to have is the feet washed of daily dirt.

6. How did Jesus expect the disciples to follow his example?
   a. by washing each other's feet
   b. by serving each other and those for whom the message is intended
   c. by counting themselves no better than Jesus
   d. by being willing to suffer all the shame Jesus would suffer

---

MY OWN STORY/25 Minutes.

1. If Jesus were to wash your feet today in a new and meaningful way (knowing your needs as he does), what would Jesus do?
   a. wash my feet
   b. ask "how can I help you?" and do it
   c. tell me he was proud to have me on the team
   d. put his arms around me and hold me
   e. forgive my sin

2. Why do you think people in the church do not regularly practice the equivalent of footwashing?
   a. we don't want to get too close
   b. we're too busy meeting our own needs
   c. it's not really okay to have needs
   d. overwhelmed and don't know where to start
   e. we're too proud to serve one another

3. In your family relationships, what would it mean to practice footwashing?
   a. to be available to meet needs
   b. to consider no job too menial
   c. to be sensitive to someone who is having a bad day
   d. to show our affection more
   e. to spend time just listening
   f. to be patient and forgiving

OPEN: 1. Which childhood hero later let you down? Why? **2.** When you are troubled, what symptoms show on your face? In your spirit?

DIG: 1. If you were a movie director, how would you capture the drama of verses 18-22? If you had been sitting at this table, what would you be feeling? Saying? **2.** In foretelling his betrayal, what do you sense in Jesus: Resolution? Resignation? Restlessness? What do you sense in his disciples? In Judas? **3.** Is Judas to be excused or held responsible when "the Devil made him do it" (v.27; also 6:70; 12:4-6; 13:2)? **4.** How is the reference to "the poor" and to "night" (vv.29-30) ironic?

REFLECT: 1. If you knew ahead of time that someone would "stab you in the back," how would you treat that person? How does Jesus show what an "in spite of" type of love is all about? **2.** Given three years of very intimate fellowship with Jesus, how *could* Judas turn around and betray him?

OPEN: What trait do you share with other family members?

DIG: 1. Why did Jesus wait until Judas had gone to share what he does here? **2.** What does he call the disciples to do? From 13:1-17, how would you define love? From 3:16 and 13:1, why is love the best evidence that they are Jesus' fol-lowers? **3.** What type of person is Peter (vv.6-9,36-37)? How do you think he felt after verse 38?

REFLECT: 1. How do your "good intentions" compare to Peter's? **2.** On a scale from 1 to 10, how does your spiritual community rank against the standard of love? How could you increase its score?

Jesus Predicts His Betrayal

[18]"I am not referring to all of you; I know those I have chosen. But this is to fulfill the scripture: 'He who shares my bread has lifted up his heel against me.'[n]

[19]"I am telling you now before it happens, so that when it does happen you will believe that I am He. [20]I tell you the truth, whoever accepts anyone I send accepts me; and whoever accepts me accepts the one who sent me."

[21]After he had said this, Jesus was troubled in spirit and testified, "I tell you the truth, one of you is going to betray me."

[22]His disciples stared at one another, at a loss to know which of them he meant. [23]One of them, the disciple whom Jesus loved, was reclining next to him. [24]Simon Peter motioned to this disciple and said, "Ask him which one he means."

[25]Leaning back against Jesus, he asked him, "Lord, who is it?"

[26]Jesus answered, "It is the one to whom I will give this piece of bread when I have dipped it in the dish." Then, dipping the piece of bread, he gave it to Judas Iscariot, son of Simon. [27]As soon as Judas took the bread, Satan entered into him.

"What you are about to do, do quickly," Jesus told him, [28]but no one at the meal understood why Jesus said this to him. [29]Since Judas had charge of the money, some thought Jesus was telling him to buy what was needed for the Feast, or to give something to the poor. [30]As soon as Judas had taken the bread, he went out. And it was night.

Jesus Predicts Peter's Denial

[31]When he was gone, Jesus said, "Now is the Son of Man glorified and God is glorified in him. [32]If God is glorified in him,[o] God will glorify the Son in himself, and will glorify him at once.

[33]"My children, I will be with you only a little longer. You will look for me, and just as I told the Jews, so I tell you now: Where I am going, you cannot come.

[34]"A new command I give you: Love one another. As I have loved you, so you must love one another. [35]By this all men will know that you are my disciples, if you love one another."

[36]Simon Peter asked him, "Lord, where are you going?"

Jesus replied, "Where I am going, you cannot follow now, but you will follow later."

[37]Peter asked, "Lord, why can't I follow you now? I will lay down my life for you."

[38]Then Jesus answered, "Will you really lay down your life for me? I tell you the truth, before the rooster crows, you will disown me three times!

[n]18 Psalm 41:9   [o]32 Many early manuscripts do not have *If God is glorified in him.*

Jesus Comforts His Disciples

14 "Do not let your hearts be troubled. Trust in God*p*; trust also in me. ²In my Father's house are many rooms; if it were not so, I would have told you. I am going there to prepare a place for you. ³And if I go and prepare a place for you, I will come back and take you to be with me that you also may be where I am. ⁴You know the way to the place where I am going."

Jesus the Way to the Father

⁵Thomas said to him, "Lord, we don't know where you are going, so how can we know the way?"

⁶Jesus answered, "I am the way and the truth and the life. No one comes to the Father except through me. ⁷If you really knew me, you would know*q* my Father as well. From now on, you do know him and have seen him."

⁸Philip said, "Lord, show us the Father and that will be enough for us."

⁹Jesus answered: "Don't you know me, Philip, even after I have been among you such a long time? Anyone who has seen me has seen the Father. How can you say, 'Show us the Father'? ¹⁰Don't you believe that I am in the Father, and that the Father is in me? The words I say to you are not just my own. Rather, it is the Father, living in me, who is doing his work. ¹¹Believe me when I say that I am in the Father and the Father is in me; or at least believe on the evidence of the miracles themselves. ¹²I tell you the truth, anyone who has faith in me will do what I have been doing. He will do even greater things than these, because I am going to the Father. ¹³And I will do whatever you ask in my name, so that the Son may bring glory to the Father. ¹⁴You may ask me for anything in my name, and I will do it.

Jesus Promises the Holy Spirit

¹⁵"If you love me, you will obey what I command. ¹⁶And I will ask the Father, and he will give you another Counselor to be with you forever— ¹⁷the Spirit of truth. The world cannot accept him, because it neither sees him nor knows him. But you know him, for he lives with you and will be*r* in you. ¹⁸I will not leave you as orphans; I will come to you. ¹⁹Before long, the world will not see me anymore, but you will see me. Because I live, you also will live. ²⁰On that day you will realize that I am in my Father, and you are in me, and I am in you. ²¹Whoever has my commands and obeys them, he is the one who loves me. He who loves me will be loved by my Father, and I too will love him and show myself to him."

²²Then Judas (not Judas Iscariot) said, "But, Lord, why do you intend to show yourself to us and not to the world?"

²³Jesus replied, "If anyone loves me, he will obey my teaching. My Father will love him, and we will come to him and make

OPEN: 1. Can you remember a time when you got lost? What happened? **2.** What is your favorite room in the house? Why?

DIG: 1. What comfort does Jesus offer his disciples? **2.** Look at Peter's question in 13:36, Thomas' in 14:5, Philip's in 14:8, and Judas' in 14:22. What problems are the disciples struggling with? **3.** Put Jesus' statement in 14:6-7 in your own words. What is the force of the claims Jesus makes here? **4.** How does 1:18 relate to what Jesus says in 14:9? With what tone of voice do you imagine Jesus speaking in verses 9-14? What evidence does Jesus give for his claims? **5.** Do you think the promises Jesus makes in verses 12-14 are "blank check" promises about prayer? Or are there some conditions to them? If so, what? Does he mean the church will do works greater in *power*? Greater in *scope*? How could this be?

REFLECT: 1. If Jesus is the way, do you feel you are on a bumpy dead-end street, or on a four-lane highway? Why? **2.** In light of 14:6, how would you respond to someone who says, "there are many ways to God"? **3.** In troubled times, what promises of God give you hope and courage?

OPEN: Who was the best counselor you ever had? What was it about this person that made him or her so special?

DIG: 1. How are the disciples to show love to each other (13:34)? To Jesus (14:15)? Why is this idea repeated four times (vv.15, 21,23, 24)? **2.** How does Jesus set the example for us in verse 31? **3.** What do you learn about the Spirit in verses 16-17 and 25-27? What is the relationship of the Father, Jesus, and the Spirit to the believer? To each other? **4.** What is the difference between how *Jesus* gives peace and how the *world* does? **5.** Since Satan has no power over Jesus, why must Jesus die (see 3:14-15; 6:53-54; 10:15-18)?

---

p1 Or *You trust in God*   *q7* Some early manuscripts *If you really have known me, you will know*   *r17* Some early manuscripts *and is* our home with him. ²⁴He who does not love me will not obey my teaching. These words you hear are not my own; they belong to the Father who sent me.

²⁵"All this I have spoken while still with you. ²⁶But the Counselor, the Holy Spirit, whom the Father will send in my name, will teach you all things and will remind you of everything I have said to you. ²⁷Peace I leave with you; my peace I give you. I do not give to you as the world gives. Do not let your hearts be troubled and do not be afraid.

²⁸"You heard me say, 'I am going away and I am coming back to you.' If you loved me, you would be glad that I am going to the Father, for the Father is greater than I. ²⁹I have told you now before it happens, so that when it does happen you will believe. ³⁰I will not speak with you much longer, for the prince of this world is coming. He has no hold on me, ³¹but the world must learn that I love the Father and that I do exactly what my Father has commanded me.

"Come now; let us leave.

The Vine and the Branches

15 "I am the true vine, and my Father is the gardener. ²He cuts off every branch in me that bears no fruit, while every branch that does bear fruit he prunes[s] so that it will be even more fruitful. ³You are already clean because of the word I have spoken to you. ⁴Remain in me, and I will remain in you. No branch can bear fruit by itself; it must remain in the vine. Neither can you bear fruit unless you remain in me.

⁵"I am the vine; you are the branches. If a man remains in me and I in him, he will bear much fruit; apart from me you can do nothing. ⁶If anyone does not remain in me, he is like a branch that is thrown away and withers; such branches are picked up, thrown into the fire and burned. ⁷If you remain in me and my words remain in you, ask whatever you wish, and it will be given you. ⁸This is to my Father's glory, that you bear much fruit, showing yourselves to be my disciples.

⁹"As the Father has loved me, so have I loved you. Now remain in my love. ¹⁰If you obey my commands, you will remain in my love, just as I have obeyed my Father's commands and remain in his love. ¹¹I have told you this so that my joy may be in you and that your joy may be complete. ¹²My command is this: Love each other as I have loved you. ¹³Greater love has no one than this, that he lay down his life for his friends. ¹⁴You are my friends if you do what I command. ¹⁵I no longer call you servants, because a servant does not know his master's business. Instead, I have called you friends, for everything that I learned from my Father I have made known to you. ¹⁶You did not choose me, but I chose you and appointed you to go and bear fruit—fruit that will last. Then the Father will give you whatever you ask in my name. ¹⁷This is my command: Love each other.

ˢ2 The Greek for *prunes* also means *cleans*.

LOOKING INTO THE SCRIPTURE/20 Minutes. Read John 15:1-17 and discuss.

1. Take this test and share your answers TRUE or FALSE.

T F The life of the grape is in the branch
T F You can't judge a grapevine by its looks
T F A good gardener is a tough pruner
T F Pruning a vine will not hurt it
T F It's the job of the branch to stay connected to the vine
T F A vine without fruit is worthless

2. Why did Jesus use the illustration of a vine?
  a. everybody could understand
  b. to explain spiritual principles
  c. to threaten spiritual non-producers
  d. he was passing through a vineyard

3. Where does this illustration fit into the larger discourse on the Holy Spirit's ministry?
  a. it explains how the Father, Son, and Holy Spirit work together
  b. it shows the Father as a loving caretaker
  c. it shows the Son as the vine
  d. it shows the importance of the believer abiding in the vine

4. What do the branch that bears no fruit and the fruitful branch have in common?
  a. they both start out tapped into the vine
  b. they both get cut off, but for different reasons
  c. one is dead, the other is growing
  d. neither bears fruit because the buds are cut off

5. If you had been one of the disciples hearing this illustration for the first time, what would you have learned?
  a. very little at the time
  b. to cling to Christ
  c. to trust God
  d. to depend upon the Holy Spirit
  e. life brings with it humbling experiences

6. What is the Christian promised for remaining in the vine?
  a. success in everything he/she does
  b. a life full of happiness
  c. the fragrance of Christ in his/her life
  d. eternal life
  e. the ability to do God's work

MY OWN STORY/25 Minutes.

1. What kind of fruit would you like to see in your Christian life?
  a. love for my family
  b. compassion for the needy
  c. obedience to God
  d. willingness to serve others
  e. ability to share my faith

2. On those days when your vine is wilted, how do you get your spiritual energy back?
  a. drink some water: spend time alone with God
  b. cultivate the soil: seek encouragement from friends
  c. fertilize: sign up for a retreat or Bible study
  d. take out of the hot sun: get away from the stress
  e. submit to pruning: admit where I've been wrong
  f. wait for evening's cool: get some sleep

3. If God could get his hands on you, what would he do?
  a. I'm afraid to think
  b. prune off a few things
  c. do some radical surgery
  d. care for me very tenderly
  e. nothing

4. Where do you struggle to "remain in the vine?"
  a. busy: no time for cultivation
  b. distracted: my work/school comes first
  c. tired: the fruit is too heavy
  d. disappointed: God hasn't come through in my life
  e. defeated: it's hard to be obedient to God's will
  f. lonely: I feel like I'm the only branch on the vine

OPEN: Have you ever been to a large group or reunion of someone else's family? How did you feel? How did you try to fit in?

DIG: 1. Since the emphasis in 15:9-17 was on love, why does Jesus now talk about hate? How is the relationship of the disciples to the world like that of Jesus' relationship to it? What does Jesus mean here by "the world"? **2.** What lesson did Jesus teach by the phrase "no servant is greater than his master" in 13:16? How does the lesson here compare to that one? What do you see in the relationship between the Father, Jesus, and the disciples? **3.** How has Jesus' coming highlighted the reality and evil of sin (vv.22,24)?

REFLECT: When have you found that speaking truth and showing love can lead to hostility from others? How do you explain that?

The World Hates the Disciples

[18]"If the world hates you, keep in mind that it hated me first. [19]If you belonged to the world, it would love you as its own. As it is, you do not belong to the world, but I have chosen you out of the world. That is why the world hates you. [20]Remember the words I spoke to you: 'No servant is greater than his master.'[t] If they persecuted me, they will persecute you also. If they obeyed my teaching, they will obey yours also. [21]They will treat you this way because of my name, for they do not know the One who sent me. [22]If I had not come and spoken to them, they would not be guilty of sin. Now, however, they have no excuse for their sin. [23]He who hates me hates my Father as well. [24]If I had not done among them what no one else did, they would not be guilty of sin. But now they have seen these miracles, and yet they have hated both me and my Father. [25]But this is to fulfill what is written in their Law: 'They hated me without reason.'[u]

[26]"When the Counselor comes, whom I will send to you from the Father, the Spirit of truth who goes out from the Father, he will testify about me. [27]And you also must testify, for you have been with me from the beginning.

16 "All this I have told you so that you will not go astray. [2]They will put you out of the synagogue; in fact, a time is coming when anyone who kills you will think he is offering a service to God. [3]They will do such things because they have not known the Father or me. [4]I have told you this, so that when the time comes you will remember that I warned you. I did not tell you this at first because I was with you.

OPEN: 1. How are you at saying "goodbye"? **2.** Is it harder for you to be the one leaving home, or the one left behind? Explain.

DIG: 1. What are the disciples feeling now? What is their grief keeping them from understanding? **2.** How would you paraphrase the three goals of the Spirit's work (vv.8-11)? What other roles does the Spirit play (14:16-17,26-27; 16:7-11,13-15)? Therefore, why is it good that Jesus goes away? **3.** If you were a disciple, how would you feel after hearing verse 16?

REFLECT: Of the various roles of the Holy Spirit described here, which one have you come to appreciate recently? How so?

The Work of the Holy Spirit

[5]"Now I am going to him who sent me, yet none of you asks me, 'Where are you going?' [6]Because I have said these things, you are filled with grief. [7]But I tell you the truth: It is for your good that I am going away. Unless I go away, the Counselor will not come to you; but if I go, I will send him to you. [8]When he comes, he will convict the world of guilt[v] in regard to sin and righteousness and judgment: [9]in regard to sin, because men do not believe in me; [10]in regard to righteousness, because I am going to the Father, where you can see me no longer; [11]and in regard to judgment, because the prince of this world now stands condemned.

[12]"I have much more to say to you, more than you can now bear. [13]But when he, the Spirit of truth, comes, he will guide you into all truth. He will not speak on his own; he will speak only what he hears, and he will tell you what is yet to come. [14]He will bring glory to me by taking from what is mine and making it known to you. [15]All that belongs to the Father is mine. That is why I said the Spirit will take from what is mine and make it known to you.

[16]"In a little while you will see me no more, and then after a little while you will see me."

---

[t]20 John 13:16   [u]25 Psalms 35:19; 69:4   [v]8 Or *will expose the guilt of the world*

The Disciples' Grief Will Turn to Joy

[17]Some of his disciples said to one another, "What does he mean by saying, 'In a little while you will see me no more, and then after a little while you will see me,' and 'Because I am going to the Father'?" [18]They kept asking, "What does he mean by 'a little while'? We don't understand what he is saying."

[19]Jesus saw that they wanted to ask him about this, so he said to them, "Are you asking one another what I meant when I said, 'In a little while you will see me no more, and then after a little while you will see me'? [20]I tell you the truth, you will weep and mourn while the world rejoices. You will grieve, but your grief will turn to joy. [21]A woman giving birth to a child has pain because her time has come; but when her baby is born she forgets the anguish because of her joy that a child is born into the world. [22]So with you: Now is your time of grief, but I will see you again and you will rejoice, and no one will take away your joy. [23]In that day you will no longer ask me anything. I tell you the truth, my Father will give you whatever you ask in my name. [24]Until now you have not asked for anything in my name. Ask and you will receive, and your joy will be complete.

[25]"Though I have been speaking figuratively, a time is coming when I will no longer use this kind of language but will tell you plainly about my Father. [26]In that day you will ask in my name. I am not saying that I will ask the Father on your behalf. [27]No, the Father himself loves you because you have loved me and have believed that I came from God. [28]I came from the Father and entered the world; now I am leaving the world and going back to the Father."

[29]Then Jesus' disciples said, "Now you are speaking clearly and without figures of speech. [30]Now we can see that you know all things and that you do not even need to have anyone ask you questions. This makes us believe that you came from God."

[31]"You believe at last!"[w] Jesus answered. [32]"But a time is coming, and has come, when you will be scattered, each to his own home. You will leave me all alone. Yet I am not alone, for my Father is with me.

[33]"I have told you these things, so that in me you may have peace. In this world you will have trouble. But take heart! I have overcome the world."

Jesus Prays for Himself

17 After Jesus said this, he looked toward heaven and prayed:

"Father, the time has come. Glorify your Son, that your Son may glorify you. [2]For you granted him authority over all people that he might give eternal life to all those you have given him. [3]Now this is eternal life: that they may know you, the only true God, and Jesus Christ, whom you have sent. [4]I have brought you glory on earth by completing the

OPEN: 1. How scattered is your family? How often do you get together for family reunions? **2.** Did your parents ever tell you about your birth experience? What was it like for them?

DIG: 1. What tones of voice do you hear in verses 17-18? If you were there, would Jesus' answer encourage you, or confuse you more? **2.** What event is Jesus referring to in verses 20-22? In what ways does the world's "joy" (v.20) contrast with the joy the disciples will experience (v.22)? How is this similar to what Jesus said about dying (12:24)? About peace (14:27)? **3.** What characterizes the relationship we can have with the Father because of Jesus (vv.23-27)? **4.** Do you think the disciples truly grasp what Jesus says in verse 28? Why? **5.** Why would the disciples be both alarmed and relieved (vv.29-33)?

REFLECT: 1. Both Jesus and the world offer a form of peace (14:27; 16:33), joy (15:11; 16:22-24) and love (13:34-35; 15:9-19). How have you experienced each type? What is different between them? **2.** How do you deal with change? Moves? Job transfers? Transitions from one stage in your life to another? How has "pain" helped you to grow up? **3.** From your experience, how could you comfort someone going through change?

OPEN: 1. What was one task you accomplished as a child that made you feel really good, even older than your age? **2.** What going-away gift have you received or given that still warms your heart or brings a smile? **3.** What is the best reason you have heard for not believing in Christianity?

DIG: 1. What event is it now "time" for (v.1; 12:23-24)? **2.** What does

[w]31 Or "Do you now believe?"

it mean to "glorify" someone (vv.4-5,10,22,24? How is Jesus' deity emphasized here? **3.** Who or what is the focal point of Jesus' prayer in verses 6-19? Why? If you had to file a report to the Father on Jesus' activities, how would you illustrate verses 6-8? **4.** What is Jesus' concern in verses 11 and 15? What does he mean by "the name you gave me" (see 8:58; Ex 3:14)? What do the events surrounding the original revelation of this name (Ex 3:7-10) show about its power to save? **5.** What does he mean by his request in verse 17? What is its purpose? **6.** Who or what is the focus of Jesus' prayer in verses 20-26? Toward what end? What kind of unity exists between God and Jesus that we should copy? **7.** How does this affect others (vv.21,23)? **8.** What does Jesus' ultimate desire (v.24) reveal about his love for us? **9.** How do verses 25-26 sum up the major concerns of Jesus in chapters 13-16?

REFLECT: 1. This week, whom have you glorified by the way you lived? How so? **2.** What two phrases sum up your goal for the past year? How does this relate to God's purpose? **3.** How are your prayers for others like and unlike Jesus' prayer? Do your prayers reflect the short-term urgent, or the long-term important needs that people have? **4.** If Jesus prayed only for the urgent needs of his disciples, how would this prayer be different? **5.** If paid $10.00/hour for consciously working at loving others, how much money would you have made this past week? What is one way you will "earn" more this week?

work you gave me to do. [5]And now, Father, glorify me in your presence with the glory I had with you before the world began.

Jesus Prays for His Disciples

[6]"I have revealed you[x] to those whom you gave me out of the world. They were yours; you gave them to me and they have obeyed your word. [7]Now they know that everything you have given me comes from you. [8]For I gave them the words you gave me and they accepted them. They knew with certainty that I came from you, and they believed that you sent me. [9]I pray for them. I am not praying for the world, but for those you have given me, for they are yours. [10]All I have is yours, and all you have is mine. And glory has come to me through them. [11]I will remain in the world no longer, but they are still in the world, and I am coming to you. Holy Father, protect them by the power of your name—the name you gave me—so that they may be one as we are one. [12]While I was with them, I protected them and kept them safe by that name you gave me. None has been lost except the one doomed to destruction so that Scripture would be fulfilled.

[13]"I am coming to you now, but I say these things while I am still in the world, so that they may have the full measure of my joy within them. [14]I have given them your word and the world has hated them, for they are not of the world any more than I am of the world. [15]My prayer is not that you take them out of the world but that you protect them from the evil one. [16]They are not of the world, even as I am not of it. [17]Sanctify[y] them by the truth; your word is truth. [18]As you sent me into the world, I have sent them into the world. [19]For them I sanctify myself, that they too may be truly sanctified.

Jesus Prays for All Believers

[20]"My prayer is not for them alone. I pray also for those who will believe in me through their message, [21]that all of them may be one, Father, just as you are in me and I am in you. May they also be in us so that the world may believe that you have sent me. [22]I have given them the glory that you gave me, that they may be one as we are one: [23]I in them and you in me. May they be brought to complete unity to let the world know that you sent me and have loved them even as you have loved me.

[24]"Father, I want those you have given me to be with me where I am, and to see my glory, the glory you have given me because you loved me before the creation of the world.

[25]"Righteous Father, though the world does not know you, I know you, and they know that you have sent me. [26]I have made you known to them, and will continue to make you known in order that the love you have for me may be in them and that I myself may be in them."

---

x6 Greek *your name;* also in verse 26   y17 Greek *hagiazo (set apart for sacred use* or *make holy);* also in verse 19

Jesus Arrested

18 When he had finished praying, Jesus left with his disciples and crossed the Kidron Valley. On the other side there was an olive grove, and he and his disciples went into it.

²Now Judas, who betrayed him, knew the place, because Jesus had often met there with his disciples. ³So Judas came to the grove, guiding a detachment of soldiers and some officials from the chief priests and Pharisees. They were carrying torches, lanterns and weapons.

⁴Jesus, knowing all that was going to happen to him, went out and asked them, "Who is it you want?"

⁵"Jesus of Nazareth," they replied.

"I am he," Jesus said. (And Judas the traitor was standing there with them.) ⁶When Jesus said, "I am he," they drew back and fell to the ground.

⁷Again he asked them, "Who is it you want?"

And they said, "Jesus of Nazareth."

⁸"I told you that I am he," Jesus answered. "If you are looking for me, then let these men go." ⁹This happened so that the words he had spoken would be fulfilled: "I have not lost one of those you gave me."ᶻ

¹⁰Then Simon Peter, who had a sword, drew it and struck the high priest's servant, cutting off his right ear. (The servant's name was Malchus.)

¹¹Jesus commanded Peter, "Put your sword away! Shall I not drink the cup the Father has given me?"

Jesus Taken to Annas

¹²Then the detachment of soldiers with its commander and the Jewish officials arrested Jesus. They bound him ¹³and brought him first to Annas, who was the father-in-law of Caiaphas, the high priest that year. ¹⁴Caiaphas was the one who had advised the Jews that it would be good if one man died for the people.

Peter's First Denial

¹⁵Simon Peter and another disciple were following Jesus. Because this disciple was known to the high priest, he went with Jesus into the high priest's courtyard, ¹⁶but Peter had to wait outside at the door. The other disciple, who was known to the high priest, came back, spoke to the girl on duty there and brought Peter in.

¹⁷"You are not one of this man's disciples, are you?" the girl at the door asked Peter.

He replied, "I am not."

¹⁸It was cold, and the servants and officials stood around a fire they had made to keep warm. Peter also was standing with them, warming himself.

OPEN: Where do you go when you need to prepare yourself for a very stressful time?

DIG: 1. Why do you suppose the Pharisees want to take advantage of the night to arrest Jesus (see 3:19-20; 12:35; 13:30)? **2.** How do you think the disciples felt when they saw these menacing-looking people coming? How do you account for the soldiers' deference (v.6; see also 1:5)? **3.** Seeing how he deals with the soldiers (vv.4, 8) and Peter (v.11), what do you learn about Jesus? **4.** How does Peter show he still doesn't grasp what is going on? As a soldier, how would you feel after Jesus said what he did in verse 11? **5.** What is "the cup" which Jesus must drink? **6.** Given his pacifism (vv.6,11), why is Jesus bound (v.12)? Who's afraid of whom here? Why?

REFLECT: 1. When have you felt you had a better way to deal with things than Jesus? What happened? **2.** How does Jesus' decision to "drink the cup" (v.11) help you in your obedience to God? What issue of obedience is challenging you now?

OPEN: 1. When have you embarrassed yourself by forgetting the name of the person you were talking to, or the friend you meant to introduce? **2.** As a child, what was one "big" thing you really messed up on: Missing the catch for the final out? Forgetting the crucial line in the school play? Leaving something behind, never to be recovered? **3.** After forgetting a name or messing up, what did you do?

DIG: 1. What do you think Peter and the other disciple hoped to

---

ᶻ9 John 6:39

do? How do you account for the difference between Peter here (v.17) and in the garden (18:10)? **2.** What is ironic about the high priest's questioning of Jesus? What do you imagine he was asking? **3.** How do Jesus' answers expose this trial as a mockery? If you were there, what would you have done on Jesus' behalf? **4.** What feelings must Peter have had after the rooster crowed (v.27; see 13:37-38)? What do you suppose Peter did at that point?

REFLECT: 1. How does the story of Peter both humble and encourage you? When have you felt like Peter? **2.** When have you dealt with someone whose mind was so made up that the facts didn't matter? How do you deal with this when it relates to your faith?

OPEN: As a child, were you ever set up to be blamed for something you didn't do? How did you react?

DIG: 1. Where is Jesus brought next? When? Why are the Jewish leaders rushing this trial through so fast? **2.** What is so ironic about the religious leaders in verse 28? How do their actions illustrate Jesus' charges against them in 5:39-40 and 7:24? **3.** What reason do they finally give to Pilate for bringing Jesus to him (vv.33-34)? Why would Pilate take this seriously? How are Pilate's fears like those of the Jewish leaders in 11:48? **4.** What does Jesus tell Pilate about his kingdom (vv.36-37)? Who is included in it? What do you think Pilate meant by his concerns in verse 38? **5.** In his pursuit of "truth," is Pilate trying to absolve himself, Jesus, or Barabbas? Why do you think so?

REFLECT: 1. Since both Peter and Pilate "caved in" under pressure, why do we tend to scorn Pilate but honor Peter? **2.** Do you see any of Pilate's qualities in yourself? **3.** How does Barabbas' freedom at Christ's expense illustrate the whole point of the gospel? **4.** From verses 11 and 36, how are we to advance God's kingdom (see also 17:18)?

The High Priest Questions Jesus

[19]Meanwhile, the high priest questioned Jesus about his disciples and his teaching.

[20]"I have spoken openly to the world," Jesus replied. "I always taught in synagogues or at the temple, where all the Jews come together. I said nothing in secret. [21]Why question me? Ask those who heard me. Surely they know what I said."

[22]When Jesus said this, one of the officials nearby struck him in the face. "Is this the way you answer the high priest?" he demanded.

[23]"If I said something wrong," Jesus replied, "testify as to what is wrong. But if I spoke the truth, why did you strike me?" [24]Then Annas sent him, still bound, to Caiaphas the high priest. [a]

Peter's Second and Third Denials

[25]As Simon Peter stood warming himself, he was asked, "You are not one of his disciples, are you?"

He denied it, saying, "I am not."

[26]One of the high priest's servants, a relative of the man whose ear Peter had cut off, challenged him, "Didn't I see you with him in the olive grove?" [27]Again Peter denied it, and at that moment a rooster began to crow.

Jesus Before Pilate

[28]Then the Jews led Jesus from Caiaphas to the palace of the Roman governor. By now it was early morning, and to avoid ceremonial uncleanness the Jews did not enter the palace; they wanted to be able to eat the Passover. [29]So Pilate came out to them and asked, "What charges are you bringing against this man?"

[30]"If he were not a criminal," they replied, "we would not have handed him over to you."

[31]Pilate said, "Take him yourselves and judge him by your own law."

"But we have no right to execute anyone," the Jews objected. [32]This happened so that the words Jesus had spoken indicating the kind of death he was going to die would be fulfilled.

[33]Pilate then went back inside the palace, summoned Jesus and asked him, "Are you the king of the Jews?"

[34]"Is that your own idea," Jesus asked, "or did others talk to you about me?"

[35]"Am I a Jew?" Pilate replied. "It was your people and your chief priests who handed you over to me. What is it you have done?"

[36]Jesus said, "My kingdom is not of this world. If it were, my servants would fight to prevent my arrest by the Jews. But now my kingdom is from another place."

[37]"You are a king, then!" said Pilate.

[a]24 Or (Now Annas had sent him, still bound, to Caiaphas the high priest.)

Jesus answered, "You are right in saying I am a king. In fact, for this reason I was born, and for this I came into the world, to testify to the truth. Everyone on the side of truth listens to me."

³⁸"What is truth?" Pilate asked. With this he went out again to the Jews and said, "I find no basis for a charge against him. ³⁹But it is your custom for me to release to you one prisoner at the time of the Passover. Do you want me to release 'the king of the Jews'?"

⁴⁰They shouted back, "No, not him! Give us Barabbas!" Now Barabbas had taken part in a rebellion.

Jesus Sentenced to be Crucified

19 Then Pilate took Jesus and had him flogged. ²The soldiers twisted together a crown of thorns and put it on his head. They clothed him in a purple robe ³and went up to him again and again, saying, "Hail, king of the Jews!" And they struck him in the face.

⁴Once more Pilate came out and said to the Jews, "Look, I am bringing him out to you to let you know that I find no basis for a charge against him." ⁵When Jesus came out wearing the crown of thorns and the purple robe, Pilate said to them, "Here is the man!"

⁶As soon as the chief priests and their officials saw him, they shouted, "Crucify! Crucify!"

But Pilate answered, "You take him and crucify him. As for me, I find no basis for a charge against him."

⁷The Jews insisted, "We have a law, and according to that law he must die, because he claimed to be the Son of God."

⁸When Pilate heard this, he was even more afraid, ⁹and he went back inside the palace. "Where do you come from?" he asked Jesus, but Jesus gave him no answer. ¹⁰"Do you refuse to speak to me?" Pilate said. "Don't you realize I have power either to free you or to crucify you?"

¹¹Jesus answered, "You would have no power over me if it were not given to you from above. Therefore the one who handed me over to you is guilty of a greater sin."

¹²From then on, Pilate tried to set Jesus free, but the Jews kept shouting, "If you let this man go, you are no friend of Caesar. Anyone who claims to be a king opposes Caesar."

¹³When Pilate heard this, he brought Jesus out and sat down on the judge's seat at a place known as the Stone Pavement (which in Aramaic is Gabbatha). ¹⁴It was the day of Preparation of Passover Week, about the sixth hour.

"Here is your king," Pilate said to the Jews.

¹⁵But they shouted, "Take him away! Take him away! Crucify him!"

"Shall I crucify your king?" Pilate asked.

"We have no king but Caesar," the chief priests answered.

¹⁶Finally Pilate handed him over to them to be crucified.

OPEN: As a kid, were you more likely to gang up on, actively defend, or simply welcome the "new kid on the block"? Were you ever the one ganged up on? Why?

DIG: 1. In view of Pilate's convictions (see 18:38; 19:4,6), why would he allow Jesus to be hit? Put yourself in the place of the soldiers (vv.1,3). Are you cruel, or are there deeper hates and fears involved? **2.** Why do the Jewish leaders clamor for Jesus to be crucified? What does Pilate's fearful response to that charge show about him? How might his conversation with Jesus in 18:33-37 contribute to this growing fear? **3.** How do Pilate's actions so far back up his claim in verse 10? Why do you think Jesus responds to that claim, but not his question in verse 9? **4.** What is the implied threat to Pilate in verse 12? What does the priests' reply (v.15) indicate about their spiritual condition? Why is this especially ironic (see 8:33,41)? **6.** Pretend you are Pilate. How would you explain to your wife that night why you finally let Jesus be killed?

REFLECT: When have you made a decision based on fear and ambition, rather than on what is right? How do you feel about that now? How can you guard against it in the future?

OPEN: 1. What movie or book (such as "Jesus Christ Superstar," "Godspell," or "The Last Temptation") brought home to you most vividly the events of the crucifixion? **2.** Which of these assassinations affected you the most: John Kennedy? Martin Luther King? John Lennon? What do you remember about the tragedy?

DIG: 1. According to the sign on Jesus' cross, for what "official" reason was he crucified? What meaning does this title have for Pilate (18:33-37)? For the soldiers (19:14-15)? The chief priests (19:14-15)? Is this title being used here sincerely or mockingly? Why is it in all three common languages (see also 12:32)? **2.** As Jesus may have recited Psalm 22 from the cross (Mt 27:46), how might he have felt as he watched the soldiers take his clothes (vv.23-24)? **3.** Given Jesus' mother's faith in him at the outset of his public ministry (2:3-5), what must she be feeling now at the end? **4.** From here and throughout John's gospel, we see that Jesus' death has special paradoxical meaning: In what sense was Jesus' death necessary, yet voluntary? Triumphant, yet tragic? Preordained, yet avoidable? Lifted up, yet laid down? Unjust, yet just? Finished, yet ongoing? **5.** What might "the flow of blood and water" mean (v.34; see Ex 12:7, 12-13; Jn 4:10; 7:37-38)?

REFLECT: 1. If Jesus preached the same gospel today that he preached in the first century, who might be the "chief priests," the "Peters," and "Pilates" now? Who would you be? **2.** How could you explain the need for the crucifixion to someone who really wanted to understand (see 3:14-16)? **3.** How did the meaning of Jesus' death become real to you? **4.** How have Jesus' "blood" and "water" touched your life? What would your life be like without them?

The Crucifixion

So the soldiers took charge of Jesus. [17]Carrying his own cross, he went out to the place of the Skull (which in Aramaic is called Golgotha). [18]Here they crucified him, and with him two others—one on each side and Jesus in the middle.

[19]Pilate had a notice prepared and fastened to the cross. It read: JESUS OF NAZARETH, THE KING OF THE JEWS. [20]Many of the Jews read this sign, for the place where Jesus was crucified was near the city, and the sign was written in Aramaic, Latin and Greek. [21]The chief priests of the Jews protested to Pilate, "Do not write 'The King of the Jews,' but that this man claimed to be king of the Jews."

[22]Pilate answered, "What I have written, I have written."

[23]When the soldiers crucified Jesus, they took his clothes, dividing them into four shares, one for each of them, with the undergarment remaining. This garment was seamless, woven in one piece from top to bottom.

[24]"Let's not tear it," they said to one another. "Let's decide by lot who will get it."

This happened that the scripture might be fulfilled which said,

> "They divided my garments among them
> and cast lots for my clothing."[b]

So this is what the soldiers did.

[25]Near the cross of Jesus stood his mother, his mother's sister, Mary the wife of Clopas, and Mary Magdalene. [26]When Jesus saw his mother there, and the disciple whom he loved standing nearby, he said to his mother, "Dear woman, here is your son," [27]and to the disciple, "Here is your mother." From that time on, this disciple took her into his home.

The Death of Jesus

[28]Later, knowing that all was now completed, and so that the Scripture would be fulfilled, Jesus said, "I am thirsty.' [29]A jar of wine vinegar was there, so they soaked a sponge in it, put the sponge on a stalk of the hyssop plant, and lifted it to Jesus' lips. [30]When he had received the drink, Jesus said, "It is finished." With that, he bowed his head and gave up his spirit.

[31]Now it was the day of Preparation, and the next day was to be a special Sabbath. Because the Jews did not want the bodies left on the crosses during the Sabbath, they asked Pilate to have the legs broken and the bodies taken down. [32]The soldiers therefore came and broke the legs of the first man who had been crucified with Jesus, and then those of the other. [33]But when they came to Jesus and found that he was already dead, they did not break his legs. [34]Instead, one of the soldiers pierced Jesus' side with a spear, bringing a sudden flow of blood and water. [35]The man who saw it has given testimony, and his testimony is true. He knows that he tells the truth, and he testifies so that

[b]24 Psalm 22:18

you also may believe. [36]These things happened so that the scripture would be fulfilled: "Not one of his bones will be broken,"[c] [37]and, as another scripture says, "They will look on the one they have pierced."[d]

The Burial of Jesus

[38]Later, Joseph of Arimathea asked Pilate for the body of Jesus. Now Joseph was a disciple of Jesus, but secretly because he feared the Jews. With Pilate's permission, he came and took the body away. [39]He was accompanied by Nicodemus, the man who earlier had visited Jesus at night. Nicodemus brought a mixture of myrrh and aloes, about seventy-five pounds.[e] [40]Taking Jesus' body, the two of them wrapped it, with the spices, in strips of linen. This was in accordance with Jewish burial customs. [41]At the place where Jesus was crucified, there was a garden, and in the garden a new tomb, in which no one had ever been laid. [42]Because it was the Jewish day of Preparation and since the tomb was nearby, they laid Jesus there.

The Empty Tomb

20 Early on the first day of the week, while it was still dark, Mary Magdalene went to the tomb and saw that the stone had been removed from the entrance. [2]So she came running to Simon Peter and the other disciple, the one Jesus loved, and said, "They have taken the Lord out of the tomb, and we don't know where they have put him!"

[3]So Peter and the other disciple started for the tomb. [4]Both were running, but the other disciple outran Peter and reached the tomb first. [5]He bent over and looked in at the strips of linen lying there but did not go in. [6]Then Simon Peter, who was behind him, arrived and went into the tomb. He saw the strips of linen lying there, [7]as well as the burial cloth that had been around Jesus' head. The cloth was folded up by itself, separate from the linen. [8]Finally the other disciple, who had reached the tomb first, also went inside. He saw and believed. [9](They still did not understand from Scripture that Jesus had to rise from the dead.)

Jesus Appears to Mary Magdalene

[10]Then the disciples went back to their homes, [11]but Mary stood outside the tomb crying. As she wept, she bent over to look into the tomb [12]and saw two angels in white, seated where Jesus' body had been, one at the head and the other at the foot.

[13]They asked her, "Woman, why are you crying?"

"They have taken my Lord away," she said, "and I don't know where they have put him." [14]At this, she turned around and saw Jesus standing there, but she did not realize that it was Jesus.

[15]"Woman," he said, "why are you crying? Who is it you are looking for?"

DIG: 1. As a secret believer like Joseph or Nicodemus, why would you risk public exposure now? **2.** Some say Jesus did not really die, but revived in the tomb. How would 19:1,18,32-34 and 40 argue against this idea?

REFLECT: 1. How does your fear of others and your love for Jesus sometimes conflict? **2.** In spite of past failures and fears, what will you do this week to show your love for Jesus?

OPEN: When something upsets you, who is the first one you tell?

DIG: 1. As Mary, having seen Jesus' tortuous death, what is your emotional state two days later? Why do you visit the tomb so early? Realizing the body is gone, how do you react? **2.** What does "the other disciple" (likely John, the author) believe? Why?

REFLECT: 1. When someone you love dies, how does the resurrection of Jesus help you to deal with your pain? **2.** What do you rely on for evidence that Jesus rose from the dead?

OPEN: What do you believe about UFOs? Have you ever seen any?

DIG: 1. Given the disciples' response (v.8), why is Mary crying? Would you have responded more like Mary or like the men? Why? **2.** Does Mary appear to be quietly grieving, or more hysterical? What finally breaks through her grief and confusion? How does her return to the disciples here contrast to that in verse 2? **3.** What term does Jesus use for his disciples here? What is new in their relationship from now on (see 15:15)?

---

c36 Exodus 12:46; Num. 9:12; Psalm 34:20   d37 Zech. 12:10   e39 Greek *a hundred litrai* (about 34 kilograms)

Thinking he was the gardener, she said, "Sir, if you have carried him away, tell me where you have put him, and I will get him."

¹⁶Jesus said to her, "Mary."

She turned toward him and cried out in Aramaic, "Rabboni!" (which means Teacher).

¹⁷Jesus said, "Do not hold on to me, for I have not yet returned to the Father. Go instead to my brothers and tell them, 'I am returning to my Father and your Father, to my God and your God.' "

¹⁸Mary Magdalene went to the disciples with the news: "I have seen the Lord!" And she told them that he had said these things to her.

Jesus Appears to His Disciples

¹⁹On the evening of that first day of the week, when the disciples were together, with the doors locked for fear of the Jews, Jesus came and stood among them and said, "Peace be with you!" ²⁰After he said this, he showed them his hands and side. The disciples were overjoyed when they saw the Lord.

²¹Again Jesus said, "Peace be with you! As the Father has sent me, I am sending you." ²²And with that he breathed on them and said, "Receive the Holy Spirit. ²³If you forgive anyone his sins, they are forgiven; if you do not forgive them, they are not forgiven."

Jesus Appears to Thomas

²⁴Now Thomas (called Didymus), one of the Twelve, was not with the disciples when Jesus came. ²⁵So the other disciples told him, "We have seen the Lord!"

But he said to them, "Unless I see the nail marks in his hands and put my finger where the nails were, and put my hand into his side, I will not believe it."

²⁶A week later his disciples were in the house again, and Thomas was with them. Though the doors were locked, Jesus came and stood among them and said, "Peace be with you!" ²⁷Then he said to Thomas, "Put your finger here; see my hands. Reach out your hand and put it into my side. Stop doubting and believe."

²⁸Thomas said to him, "My Lord and my God!"

²⁹Then Jesus told him, "Because you have seen me, you have believed; blessed are those who have not seen and yet have believed."

³⁰Jesus did many other miraculous signs in the presence of his disciples, which are not recorded in this book. ³¹But these are written that you may ͥ believe that Jesus is the Christ, the Son of God, and that by believing you may have life in his name.

ͥ31 Some manuscripts *may continue to*

LOOKING INTO THE SCRIPTURE/20 Minutes. Read John 20:24-31 and discuss these questions.

1. How do you feel when you find the last page of your mystery novel missing?
   a. cheated
   b. agitated
   c. indifferent
   d. creative: (write my own ending)
   e. driven: (who else has read it?)
   f. inconvenienced: (have to go to the library)
   g. defeated

2. Why do you think Thomas was not with the rest of the disciples on Easter night when Jesus appeared to them in the Upper Room?
   a. he had run away
   b. he was a loner
   c. he was sorting out things
   d. he thought it was all over

3. "Unless I see the nail marks in his hands and put my finger where the nails were, and put my hand into his side, I will not believe." What is Thomas saying here?
   a. you guys are crazy
   b. I want to believe, but . . .
   c. don't break my heart a second time . . .
   d. I need proof (seeing is believing)

4. Why did Jesus wait seven days to appear to Thomas?
   a. he was busy
   b. he wanted Thomas to think about it
   c. he wanted to wait until Thomas was ready
   d. he gave his disciples a chance to convince him

5. How did Jesus deal with Thomas?
   a. tenderly
   b. in his own way
   c. with the evidence he asked for

6. What did Jesus mean when he said, "blessed are those who have not seen and yet have believed"?
   a. those who do not doubt will be happier
   b. you don't have to see to believe
   c. God calls us to be faithful even when we can't see
   d. you blew it, Thomas

MY OWN STORY/25 Minutes.

1. When you have spiritual doubts, what does that indicate?
   a. my faith is weak
   b. I need some more information
   c. growth may be taking place
   d. someone needs to understand me
   e. I need a spiritual "check up"

2. What kind of spiritual "proof" do you need?
   a. pragmatic—if it works, it must be true
   b. empirical—firsthand experience
   c. faith—a leap in the dark
   d. historical—evidence of his working in the past
   e. rational—it makes sense

3. If you could ask God one question about your own faith, what would it be?
   a. how do you deal with doubt
   b. what happens when you don't feel like a Christian
   c. how do you know when you have "touched" God
   d. do I have faith even when I don't think about God during the day?

4. What have you found helpful in times of doubt?
   a. the fact the Bible says it
   b. the evidence of past miracles
   c. historical evidence
   d. the faith of others
   e. go back to the bare essentials

OPEN: 1. What has been the best fishing (hunting or camping) trip you have ever been on? 2. What is your favorite spot for a "cook-out"?

DIG: 1. Where are these seven disciples now? How far away (in miles and time) from the place where Jesus was killed and rose again? 2. In fishing all night using nets, do you think Peter just wants something to do, or is he returning to his old business? 3. Compare this story with Luke 5:1-11. Why do you think Jesus might repeat this type of miracle now? What effect would it have on Peter? 4. Where did Jesus get the fish in verse 9? How would you feel when you saw them if you had been fishing with the disciples all night? How does his preparation of breakfast relate to what he did for them in 13:1-17?

REFLECT: 1. Where do you go to get away from it all? How does God meet you there? 2. What does God use to get your attention and get through to you when he needs to reestablish contact?

OPEN: 1. Have you ever been kicked off the team, out of the club, out of the house, or out of school? Why? 2. Who was expected to do the most chores around your house when you were a kid? Who got off the easiest?

DIG: 1. Why do you think Jesus repeated the same question and charge to Peter three times? How is Peter supposed to demonstrate his love and loyalty to Jesus now? In light of 10:15, what would Jesus' "shepherd" image mean to Peter? 2. What does Jesus mean by his prediction in verse 18? Why did Peter ask about John right away? 3. What is the crucial issue revealed in Jesus' response to Peter (v.22)? How is this linked with verses 15-17?

Jesus and the Miraculous Catch of Fish

21 Afterward Jesus appeared again to his disciples, by the Sea of Tiberias.[g] It happened this way: ²Simon Peter, Thomas (called Didymus), Nathanael from Cana in Galilee, the sons of Zebedee, and two other disciples were together. ³"I'm going out to fish," Simon Peter told them, and they said, "We'll go with you." So they went out and got into the boat, but that night they caught nothing.

⁴Early in the morning, Jesus stood on the shore, but the disciples did not realize that it was Jesus.

⁵He called out to them, "Friends, haven't you any fish?"

"No," they answered.

⁶He said, "Throw your net on the right side of the boat and you will find some." When they did, they were unable to haul the net in because of the large number of fish.

⁷Then the disciple whom Jesus loved said to Peter, "It is the Lord!" As soon as Simon Peter heard him say, "It is the Lord," he wrapped his outer garment around him (for he had taken it off) and jumped into the water. ⁸The other disciples followed in the boat, towing the net full of fish, for they were not far from shore, about a hundred yards.[h] ⁹When they landed, they saw a fire of burning coals there with fish on it, and some bread.

¹⁰Jesus said to them, "Bring some of the fish you have just caught."

¹¹Simon Peter climbed aboard and dragged the net ashore. It was full of large fish, 153, but even with so many the net was not torn. ¹²Jesus said to them, "Come and have breakfast." None of the disciples dared ask him, "Who are you?" They knew it was the Lord. ¹³Jesus came, took the bread and gave it to them, and did the same with the fish. ¹⁴This was now the third time Jesus appeared to his disciples after he was raised from the dead.

Jesus Reinstates Peter

¹⁵When they had finished eating, Jesus said to Simon Peter, "Simon son of John, do you truly love me more than these?"

"Yes, Lord," he said, "you know that I love you."

Jesus said, "Feed my lambs."

¹⁶Again Jesus said, "Simon son of John, do you truly love me?"

He answered, "Yes, Lord, you know that I love you."

Jesus said, "Take care of my sheep."

¹⁷The third time he said to him, "Simon son of John, do you love me?"

Peter was hurt because Jesus asked him the third time, "Do you love me?" He said, "Lord, you know all things; you know that I love you."

---

g1 That is, Sea of Galilee   h8 Greek *about two hundred cubits* (about 90 meters)

LOOKING INTO THE SCRIPTURE/20 Minutes. Read John 21:15-25 and discuss.

1. Why do you think John included this story in his gospel?
   a. to explain how Jesus forgave his friend Peter
   b. to explain where Peter got his motivation to spread the Good News
   c. to explain why he lived to a ripe old age when Peter didn't

2. From the previous story, why do you think Peter was back fishing again?
   a. for recreation
   b. it was his livelihood
   c. he was waiting for further instructions
   d. he had given up on his commitment to follow Christ

3. Why did Jesus press Peter three times with the question, "Do you love me unconditionally . . . truly love me unconditionally . . . do you love me (like a brother)?"
   a. he was trying to make a point
   b. to get his attention
   c. to rub it in
   d. to shame him with his past failure

4. If you had been Peter by the end of the third question, how would you have felt?
   a. mad
   b. hurt
   c. humiliated
   d. like a buck private

5. "Feed my lambs . . . Take care of my sheep . . . Feed my sheep." What is Jesus saying here?
   a. your job is to take care of my followers
   b. show me that you love me
   c. keep the movement going
   d. don't blow it again

6. At this point in Peter's life, would you have nominated Peter to be a leader in the church?
   a. absolutely not
   b. maybe, but on probation
   c. I think so, because he learned from his failure
   d. I hope so, because I have done worse

MY OWN STORY/25 Minutes.

1. If you were asked the same question that Jesus asked Peter, how would you respond?
   a. yes—all of the time
   b. yes—most of the time
   c. yes—some of the time
   d. huh?
   e. ask me tomorrow

2. "Take care of my sheep." If Jesus said this to you three times, what would this mean for you now?
   a. get going
   b. I'm counting on you
   c. get your eyes off yourself
   d. consider the whole world
   e. seek first the kingdom of God

3. When you blow it, how do you feel afterwards?
   a. like running away
   b. like returning to familiar surroundings
   c. like trying again
   d. like committing myself even more next time
   e. I chalk it up to experience
   f. doubt—like maybe God is changing my direction because of my failure in one area
   g. angry at myself

4. How do you think God can help you overcome a recent failure in your life?
   a. by sending me friends who've gone through the same thing
   b. by showing where I went wrong so I learn from it
   c. by helping me face the consequences
   d. by just loving me
   e. by giving me a new job to do
   f. he can't do anything

5. In the past few months, where have you seen the most progress in your life?
   a. personal discipline
   b. spiritual development
   c. self-confidence
   d. concern for others
   e. family relationships
   f. moral courage
   g. Bible understanding
   h. openness to God's will
   i. change in priorities
   j. attitude about work/school
   k. ability to relax/unwind
   l. _____

REFLECT: 1. What is the closest you have come to blowing it so badly that you thought God was never going to speak to you again? What did you discover about God in that experience? **2.** When have you compared yourself with someone else and wondered why his or her life was the way it was? How did that affect your desire to do what you were supposed to do? **3.** Who do you know that needs to feel forgiven by God? By you? What will you do today to tell them they are forgiven? **4.** If you were writing a book about Jesus' work in your life, what would be some of the chapter titles? **5.** What has been "brought to light" for you through studying John's gospel?

Jesus said, "Feed my sheep. [18]I tell you the truth, when you were younger you dressed yourself and went where you wanted; but when you are old you will stretch out your hands, and someone else will dress you and lead you where you do not want to go." [19]Jesus said this to indicate the kind of death by which Peter would glorify God. Then he said to him, "Follow me!"

[20]Peter turned and saw that the disciple whom Jesus loved was following them. (This was the one who had leaned back against Jesus at the supper and had said, "Lord, who is going to betray you?") [21]When Peter saw him, he asked, "Lord, what about him?"

[22]Jesus answered, "If I want him to remain alive until I return, what is that to you? You must follow me." [23]Because of this, the rumor spread among the brothers that this disciple would not die. But Jesus did not say that he would not die; he only said, "If I want him to remain alive until I return, what is that to you?"

[24]This is the disciple who testifies to these things and who wrote them down. We know that his testimony is true.

[25]Jesus did many other things as well. If every one of them were written down, I suppose that even the whole world would not have room for the books that would be written.

ACTS

INTRODUCTION

Author

Although Luke is nowhere named within Acts as author, there is a strong and ancient tradition that he did, indeed, write this book as a companion piece to the third Gospel.

Little is known of Luke. He is mentioned only three times in the New Testament (Col. 4:14; Philem. 24; 2 Tim. 4:11). From these references, it can be deduced that Luke was a physician, a valued companion of Paul, and a Gentile.

A Physician

Luke's medical background is corroborated by his use of medical terms (especially in his gospel), for example, in recounting the story of the camel and the needle's eye. "For the word needle both Mark and Matthew use the Greek word *raphis,* which is the ordinary word for a tailor's or a household needle. Luke alone uses the word *belone,* which is the technical word for a surgeons' needle" (William Barclay, *The Acts of the Apostles,* p. XIV).

Paul's Companion

Luke's role as Paul's traveling companion is evident in the Book of Acts. In the four so-called *we* sections, the author suddenly switches from saying "They did this" to "We did that" (Acts 16:10-17; 20: 5-6; 21:1-18; 27:1-28:16). At these points in Paul's journeys, Luke joined him as a colleague in ministry.

A Gentile

We learn that Luke was a Gentile from the list of greetings with which Paul concludes Colossians. First Paul records the greetings sent by "the only Jews among my fellow workers" (Col. 4:10-11). Then in verse 12 he begins a second set of greetings presumably from the Gentiles in the party. Luke's name is included in this latter list.

Characteristics

The Book of Acts is the bridge between the Gospels and the Epistles. It is no accident that modern Bibles are arranged with the life of Jesus on one side of Acts and the correspondence of the apostles on the other. This is because, on the one hand, Acts completes the story of Jesus. It shows how his life, death, and resurrection brought a whole new community into existence: the church. On the other hand, Acts sets the stage for the correspondence to this church; the letters make up the rest of the New Testament. At many points it would be difficult to get the full sense of what the Epistles are saying without the data found in Acts.

Luke tells the story of the development of the church, not by strictly chronicling every event that occurred as the church spread from Jerusalem to Rome — the sheer volume of the data prevented this — but rather by opening a series of windows that allows us to glimpse important (and representative) developments in its growth.

1. Key Figure—The Holy Spirit

One thing that characterizes the entire story is the work of the Holy Spirit. There is little question in Luke's mind how the church spread: The Holy Spirit did it. So we see the church come into being as a result of the baptism of the Holy Spirit (2:38-41). First as only a handful of disciples, it turned suddenly into a full-fledged movement. We then see the Holy Spirit gently but directly guide the early church (13:2 and 16:7). In fact, the presence of the Holy Spirit signals that a church is authentic and not spurious (19:1-6). Some have suggested that this book ought to have been labeled *The Acts of the Holy Spirit* and not *The Acts of the Apostles*!

2. Leading Roles—Peter and Paul

This latter designation is inaccurate for yet another reason. The whole apostolic band is not really in view here. The Book of Acts is the story of only two apostles—Peter and Paul. Peter's story is told first. In the initial 12 chapters, he is the central figure. But in chapter 13, the spotlight shifts to Paul, and he holds center stage until Acts concludes.

The stories of these two men are not dissimilar. In fact, there are a surprising number of common elements. Both heal cripples (3:1-10; 14:8-12); both have the experience of seeing cures brought about in unusual ways (5:15-16; 19:11-12); both bring people back to life (9:36-42; 20:9-12); both meet a magician (8:9-25; 13:6-12); and both are released from prison as the result of a miracle (12:7; 16:26-28).

The reason for this focus on Peter and on Paul is not hard to guess. They were the key leaders of the two main elements of the early church: Peter was the chief apostle to the Jews, while Paul was the chief apostle to the Gentiles. So in hearing their stories, we hear the story of the unfolding of the whole church.

3. Key Sources

Where did Luke get his information about the growth of the church? The source of the second half of the book (chapters 13-28) is clear. Luke got this information directly from his friend and companion Paul. We know Luke was actually with Paul during some of this period (the *we* sections), and he may well have kept a journal. We can also guess that during the long days of travel, and during Paul's confinement in prison, the great apostle probably recounted his many adventures to Luke. But what about the first twelve chapters that center around Peter? Here is where Luke's skill as a historian is especially evident. Luke tells us in his prologue to the third Gospel that he "carefully investigated everything from the beginning" (Luke 1:3). How? Probably by talking to many individuals he may have met via Paul. For example, Luke knew Mark. Both men were with Paul when he wrote Colossians (Col. 4:10, 14). From Mark he would have received valuable information about the growth of the church in Jerusalem and about Peter's role in this. (Many feel Mark's gospel reflects Peter's perspective.) And certainly Luke would have listened to the stories about Peter that were repeated in the churches he visited. Finally, he may well have had access to the official records (written and oral) of the key churches mentioned in the first twelve chapters—the church at Jerusalem (from Mark and others); the church at Caesarea (Philip and his daughters entertained Luke and Paul according to Acts 21:8, and Philip was associated with Stephen and the events of Acts 6:1-8:3); and the church at Antioch (many feel Luke's home was Antioch).

4. Keen Historian

Luke's accuracy as a historian was called into question by certain scholars until the archaeological research of Sir William Ramsay demonstrated Luke's exact and detailed knowledge of the political and social conditions of the times. For example, although a number of different titles were given to Roman officials, Luke always seems to have got it right. When Paul was in Cyprus (Acts 13:7), Luke tells us a proconsul was in charge, although this was only briefly the case. At Malta (Acts 28:7), the ruler is correctly called the "chief man" or "chief official" *protos*. At Ephesus (Acts 19:35), Luke identifies the official who quieted the crowd as the "city clerk" *grammateus*. In Thessolonica (Acts 17:6), he identifies the leaders as "city officials" *politarches*, even though this was an unusual office with no parallel elsewhere in the Roman Empire and only recently verified by inscriptions. Luke had the mind of a researcher: He was careful and paid attention to details. Thus when reading his story of the early church, we have confidence that what Luke tells us is just what happened.

Theme

Why did Luke write the Book of Acts? One reason must have been his desire to commend Christianity to the Gentile world in general and to the Roman government in particular. Certainly there was much about Christianity that would have appealed to Gentiles. For one thing, Jesus came for all people and not just for his Jewish kinfolk. So one finds in Acts the same universality present in Luke's gospel. The good news about Jesus is not just for Jews but for all people. Not surprisingly, therefore, we find in Acts not only Jews turning to Jesus (three thousand on the Day of Pentecost, Acts 2:41) but also Gentiles. We see Peter (the Apostle to the Jews) welcoming Cornelius, the Roman centurion, into the church. We see Philip preaching to the Samaritans and Jewish believers and evangelizing Gentiles in Antioch. In particular, we find Paul called by Christ to be the Apostle to the Gentiles, setting up churches across the Roman Empire. Finally in Acts 15, there is formal affirmation that Gentiles are accepted in the church of Jesus Christ on equal terms with Jews (they do not first have to become Jewish converts). Acts is an eloquent testimony to the universal appeal of Jesus.

Luke's response to the Roman government is fascinating. He seemed to go out of his way to show that Christians were loyal citizens and not lawbreakers and criminals (18:14; 19:37; 23:29; 25:25). He also took pains to point out that Roman officials had always treated Christians fairly and courteously (13:12; 16:35-40; 18:12-17; 19:31). This was important to state lest Christianity be perceived as a political movement and therefore a threat to the Roman Empire. His writing did, after all, talk about the kingdom and about Jesus as Lord (the imperial title).

However, commending Christianity to Gentiles was probably not Luke's central aim. His main purpose is implicit in 1:8. "But you will receive power when the Holy Spirit comes on you; and you will be my witnesses in Jerusalem, and in all Judea and Samaria, and to the ends of the earth." Luke's aim was to show how, in thirty short years, Christianity had spread from Jerusalem to Rome.

Structure

Luke accomplished his purpose by describing six phases of growth (as charted by C. H. Turner and noted in Barclay, *The Acts of the Apostles*, p. xviii):

1. *The church at Jerusalem* (1:1-6:7). Summary statement: "So the word of God spread. The number of disciples in Jerusalem increased rapidly, and a large number of priests became obedient to the faith" (6:7).
2. *From Jerusalem to Palestine* (6:8-9:31). Summary statement: "Then the church throughout Judea, Galilee and Samaria enjoyed a time of peace . . . it grew in numbers . . ." (9:31).
3. *From Palestine to Antioch, gateway to the Gentile world* (9:32-12:24). Summary statement: "The word of God continued to increase and spread" (12:24).
4. *From Antioch to Asia* (12:25-16:5). Summary statement: "So the churches were strengthened in the faith and grew daily in numbers" (16:5).
5. *From Asia to Europe* (16:6-19:20). Summary statement: "In this way the word of the Lord spread widely and grew in power" (19:20).
6. *From Europe in general to Rome in particular* (19:21-28:31). Summary statement: "Therefore I want you to know that God's salvation has been sent to the Gentiles, and they will listen!" (28:28).

Acts

Jesus Taken Up Into Heaven

1 In my former book, Theophilus, I wrote about all that Jesus began to do and to teach ²until the day he was taken up to heaven, after giving instructions through the Holy Spirit to the apostles he had chosen. ³After his suffering, he showed himself to these men and gave many convincing proofs that he was alive. He appeared to them over a period of forty days and spoke about the kingdom of God. ⁴On one occasion, while he was eating with them, he gave them this command: "Do not leave Jerusalem, but wait for the gift my Father promised, which you have heard me speak about. ⁵For John baptized with ͣ water, but in a few days you will be baptized with the Holy Spirit."

⁶So when they met together, they asked him, "Lord, are you at this time going to restore the kingdom to Israel?"

⁷He said to them: "It is not for you to know the times or dates the Father has set by his own authority. ⁸But you will receive power when the Holy Spirit comes on you; and you will be my witnesses in Jerusalem, and in all Judea and Samaria, and to the ends of the earth."

⁹After he said this, he was taken up before their very eyes, and a cloud hid him from their sight.

¹⁰They were looking intently up into the sky as he was going, when suddenly two men dressed in white stood beside them. ¹¹"Men of Galilee," they said, "why do you stand here looking into the sky? This same Jesus, who has been taken from you into heaven, will come back in the same way you have seen him go into heaven."

Matthias Chosen to Replace Judas

¹²Then they returned to Jerusalem from the hill called the Mount of Olives, a Sabbath day's walk ͣ from the city. ¹³When they arrived, they went upstairs to the room where they were staying. Those present were Peter, John, James and Andrew; Philip and Thomas, Bartholomew and Matthew; James son of Alphaeus and Simon the Zealot, and Judas son of James. ¹⁴They all joined together constantly in prayer, along with the women and Mary the mother of Jesus, and with his brothers.

¹⁵In those days Peter stood up among the believers ͨ (a group numbering about a hundred and twenty) ¹⁶and said, "Brothers, the Scripture had to be fulfilled which the Holy Spirit spoke long ago through the mouth of David concerning Judas, who served as guide for those who arrested Jesus— ¹⁷he was one of our number and shared in this ministry."

¹⁸(With the reward he got for his wickedness, Judas bought a field; there he fell headlong, his body burst open and all his intestines spilled out. ¹⁹Everyone in Jerusalem heard about this, so they called that field in their language Akeldama, that is, Field of Blood.)

ͣ5 Or *in*   *ͣ12* That is, about 3/4 mile (about 1,100 meters)   *ͨ15* Greek *brothers*

20"For," said Peter, "it is written in the book of Psalms,

" 'May his place be deserted;
let there be no one to dwell in it,'[d]

and,

" 'May another take his place of leadership.'[e]

21Therefore it is necessary to choose one of the men who have been with us the whole time the Lord Jesus went in and out among us, 22beginning from John's baptism to the time when Jesus was taken up from us. For one of these must become a witness with us of his resurrection."

23So they proposed two men: Joseph called Barsabbas (also known as Justus) and Matthias. 24Then they prayed, "Lord, you know everyone's heart. Show us which of these two you have chosen 25to take over this apostolic ministry, which Judas left to go where he belongs." 26Then they cast lots, and the lot fell to Matthias; so he was added to the eleven apostles.

The Holy Spirit Comes at Pentecost

2 When the day of Pentecost came, they were all together in one place. 2Suddenly a sound like the blowing of a violent wind came from heaven and filled the whole house where they were sitting. 3They saw what seemed to be tongues of fire that separated and came to rest on each of them. 4All of them were filled with the Holy Spirit and began to speak in other tongues[f] as the Spirit enabled them.

5Now there were staying in Jerusalem God-fearing Jews from every nation under heaven. 6When they heard this sound, a crowd came together in bewilderment, because each one heard them speaking in his own language. 7Utterly amazed, they asked: "Are not all these men who are speaking Galileans? 8Then how is it that each of us hears them in his own native language? 9Parthians, Medes and Elamites; residents of Mesopotamia, Judea and Cappadocia, Pontus and Asia, 10Phrygia and Pamphylia, Egypt and the parts of Libya near Cyrene; visitors from Rome 11(both Jews and converts to Judaism); Cretans and Arabs—we hear them declaring the wonders of God in our own tongues!" 12Amazed and perplexed, they asked one another, "What does this mean?"

13Some, however, made fun of them and said, "They have had too much wine.[g]"

Peter Addresses the Crowd

14Then Peter stood up with the Eleven, raised his voice and addressed the crowd: "Fellow Jews and all of you who live in Jerusalem, let me explain this to you; listen carefully to what I say. 15These men are not drunk, as you suppose. It's only nine in the morning! 16No, this is what was spoken by the prophet Joel:

---

d20 Psalm 69:25   e20 Psalm 109:8   f4 Or *languages*; also in verse 11
g13 Or *sweet wine*

REFLECT: 1. What have been your best experiences in group prayer? How can praying with others for a common mission (one that is beyond your natural ability) enhance your own prayer life? How does verse 8 provide that for you? 2. How does the pattern of decision-making here compare with the way you, your family, or your church make important decisions? Which of the ingredients listed here do you need to utilize more?

OPEN: What parts of the world have you traveled where you wish you knew the native tongue?

DIG: 1. Why did God wait until Pentecost (a celebrative harvest festival, Dt 16:9-10) to give the Holy Spirit? 2. How far have these pilgrims come (vv.9-11)? What attracts them to the disciples? How does *being filled* with the Spirit relate to *bearing witness* to Jesus? 3. If you had been there, what would you have seen, heard, and felt? Would you respond more like those in verse 12, or those in verse 13? Why?

REFLECT: When have you experienced an empowering from God to witness about Christ? What will you do this week to be better prepared for God's use?

OPEN: What are you usually doing at 9:00 in the morning on a Saturday? On Sunday? Midweek?

DIG: 1. Compare Peter and the other disciples in John 18:25-27 and 20:19 with their actions here: What accounts for the great difference? 2. In what way is Luke 24:44-49 reflected in this sermon? Given the audience, why would Peter use so many quotes from the Old Testament? 3. What is the point Peter wants the people to understand about current events (vv.13,17,18)? Since the prophets used dramatic, figurative language to indicate God was going to deal with his people in a new way, how do you understand verses 19-21? What tells you Joel's prophecy is coming true *now*? **4.** How familiar were these people with the events of Jesus' life? How might they be dealing with the rumors of the empty tomb? Given that, why does Peter emphasize the resurrection (vv.24, 31,32)? **5.** What are the implications of the resurrection and ascension for Jesus (vv.24,30-31, 33-36)? For the people? What would it mean to the people that Jesus is a spiritual king far greater than their greatest earthly king (v.37)? **6.** How would you use Peter's answer (vv.38-40) to explain to someone what it means to become a Christian? What is required? What is promised? **7.** Remembering where these 3,000 came from (vv.8-11), in what way is 1:8 partially fulfilled here? What news will the people be bringing home with them?

REFLECT: 1. To repent and be baptized in Jesus' name meant to turn away from all other loyalties and affirm allegiance to Jesus. In what ways does that call still present a challenge to you? How have you experienced the reality of God's promises to those who answer that call? **2.** From Peter's sermon, what facts about Jesus would be key for non-believers to understand? **3.** When did you make your initial commitment to Christ? Who was influential in that process? What convinced you of your need for him? **4.** What difference does it make to you that Jesus truly is the reigning King over all? How does that truth affect your daily life? **5.** In chapter 2, what roles do the apostles and God have in witnessing? How does that encourage you in your witness for Christ? **6.** When was the last time you seized an opportunity to witness for Jesus? What happened? Who stood with you at that time? How are you like Peter? Unlike him? What encourages you as you watch Peter? Why?

[17] " 'In the last days, God says,
  I will pour out my Spirit on all people.
 Your sons and daughters will prophesy,
  your young men will see visions,
  your old men will dream dreams.
[18] Even on my servants, both men and women,
  I will pour out my Spirit in those days,
  and they will prophesy.
[19] I will show wonders in the heaven above
  and signs on the earth below,
  blood and fire and billows of smoke.
[20] The sun will be turned to darkness
  and the moon to blood
  before the coming of the great and glorious day of the Lord.
[21] And everyone who calls
  on the name of the Lord will be saved.' [h]

[22] "Men of Israel, listen to this: Jesus of Nazareth was a man accredited by God to you by miracles, wonders and signs, which God did among you through him, as you yourselves know. [23] This man was handed over to you by God's set purpose and foreknowledge; and you, with the help of wicked men,[i] put him to death by nailing him to the cross. [24] But God raised him from the dead, freeing him from the agony of death, because it was impossible for death to keep its hold on him. [25] David said about him:

 " 'I saw the Lord always before me.
  Because he is at my right hand,
  I will not be shaken.
[26] Therefore my heart is glad and my tongue rejoices;
  my body also will live in hope,
[27] because you will not abandon me to the grave,
  nor will you let your Holy One see decay.
[28] You have made known to me the paths of life;
  you will fill me with joy in your presence.'[j]

[29] "Brothers, I can tell you confidently that the patriarch David died and was buried, and his tomb is here to this day. [30] But he was a prophet and knew that God had promised him on oath that he would place one of his descendants on his throne. [31] Seeing what was ahead, he spoke of the resurrection of the Christ,[k] that he was not abandoned to the grave, nor did his body see decay. [32] God has raised this Jesus to life, and we are all witnesses of the fact. [33] Exalted to the right hand of God, he has received from the Father the promised Holy Spirit and has poured out what you now see and hear. [34] For David did not ascend to heaven, and yet he said,

 " 'The Lord said to my Lord:
  "Sit at my right hand

---

h21 Joel 2:28-32   *i23* Or *of those not having the law* (that is, Gentiles)
j28 Psalm 16:8-11   *k31* Or *Messiah.* "The Christ" (Greek) and "the Messiah" (Hebrew) both mean "the Anointed One"; also in verse 36.

[35]until I make your enemies
a footstool for your feet.' '[1]

[36]"Therefore let all Israel be assured of this: God has made this Jesus, whom you crucified, both Lord and Christ."

[37]When the people heard this, they were cut to the heart and said to Peter and the other apostles, "Brothers, what shall we do?"

[38]Peter replied, "Repent and be baptized, every one of you, in the name of Jesus Christ for the forgiveness of your sins. And you will receive the gift of the Holy Spirit. [39]The promise is for you and your children and for all who are far off—for all whom the Lord our God will call."

[40]With many other words he warned them; and he pleaded with them, "Save yourselves from this corrupt generation." [41]Those who accepted his message were baptized, and about three thousand were added to their number that day.

The Fellowship of the Believers

[42]They devoted themselves to the apostles' teaching and to the fellowship, to the breaking of bread and to prayer. [43]Everyone was filled with awe, and many wonders and miraculous signs were done by the apostles. [44]All the believers were together and had everything in common. [45]Selling their possessions and goods, they gave to anyone as he had need. [46]Every day they continued to meet together in the temple courts. They broke bread in their homes and ate together with glad and sincere hearts, [47]praising God and enjoying the favor of all the people. And the Lord added to their number daily those who were being saved.

Peter Heals the Crippled Beggar

3 One day Peter and John were going up to the temple at the time of prayer—at three in the afternoon. [2]Now a man crippled from birth was being carried to the temple gate called Beautiful, where he was put every day to beg from those going into the temple courts. [3]When he saw Peter and John about to enter, he asked them for money. [4]Peter looked straight at him, as did John. Then Peter said, "Look at us!" [5]So the man gave them his attention, expecting to get something from them.

[6]Then Peter said, "Silver or gold I do not have, but what I have I give you. In the name of Jesus Christ of Nazareth, walk." [7]Taking him by the right hand, he helped him up, and instantly the man's feet and ankles became strong. [8]He jumped to his feet and began to walk. Then he went with them into the temple courts, walking and jumping, and praising God. [9]When all the people saw him walking and praising God, [10]they recognized him as the same man who used to sit begging at the temple gate called Beautiful, and they were filled with wonder and amazement at what had happened to him.

OPEN: What do you devote yourself to *daily*? Anything that would pass for a "daily devotion"?

DIG: What do these 3,000 converts end up doing? How is God with them?

REFLECT: How is your church fellowship like and unlike the fellowship here? How does this make you feel? What could you do to help your church be more like this? How will this example affect the way you pray for your church?

OPEN: What are you usually doing at 3:00 in the afternoon on a Saturday? On Sunday? Midweek?

DIG: 1. As the cripple, what would you write as a diary entry for a typical day? **2.** When Peter grabs your hand, what thoughts flood your mind? **3.** What do you write in your diary after the events here? **4.** What was the purpose of miracles at this time (see 2:19,22)?

REFLECT: 1. How is Jesus healing some crippled area of your life? **2.** Would you do the same thing as Peter did, or would you ask John for a dime? Why? What might increase your trust in God to work through you?

*l*35 Psalm 110:1

OPEN: As a teen, whose name stirred up great emotion in you? What would you have been willing to do in the name of this person, or to get closer to this person?

DIG: 1. How is this situation like the one in 2:1-12? **2.** List all the facts about Jesus which Peter mentions here. How does this profile of Jesus compare with the one in 2:22-24? **3.** A person's name meant his or her whole character. What then does verse 16 mean? **4.** What does Peter say about the people? How would you feel being accused: "You killed..."? **5.** From Peter's second recorded sermon, how would you sum up what it means to become a Christian? **6.** Despite what Peter says about them (vv.13-15), how does he give the people hope in verses 24-26? How are *blessing* and *turning* related?

REFLECT: 1. Of all the truths about Jesus which Peter emphasizes here, which one strikes you the hardest? Why? **2.** When is it proper to come on strong against a person's sin, like Peter did in verses 13-15? In coming to Christ, did you need to be hit over the head with your sin first? How did it happen? **3.** If you had to explain the meaning of Jesus using only the OT, what passages would you use? What does Peter's use of the OT indicate about its benefits to your faith in Christ? How will you start to increase your knowledge of it?

OPEN: 1. Looking back, what "act of kindness" from an unsuspected source was redemptive in your formative years? **2.** When have you found it necessary to disobey civil authority for ethical reasons?

DIG: 1. What roles did the priests, the captain of the guard, and the Sadducees play in the ministry of Jesus (see Lk 20:27-40;22:6, 52)? Why would the Sadducees oppose the disciples' preaching? What would you feel if you were one of the believers who saw Peter and John taken away? If you were Peter or John? **2.** What is the high priest's family trying to do (v.7)—search for information, or intimidate the disciples? Why (see v.2; 3:16)? **3.** If you were one of the

Peter Speaks to the Onlookers

[11]While the beggar held on to Peter and John, all the people were astonished and came running to them in the place called Solomon's Colonnade. [12]When Peter saw this, he said to them: "Men of Israel, why does this surprise you? Why do you stare at us as if by our own power or godliness we had made this man walk? [13]The God of Abraham, Isaac and Jacob, the God of our fathers, has glorified his servant Jesus. You handed him over to be killed, and you disowned him before Pilate, though he had decided to let him go. [14]You disowned the Holy and Righteous One and asked that a murderer be released to you. [15]You killed the author of life, but God raised him from the dead. We are witnesses of this. [16]By faith in the name of Jesus, this man whom you see and know was made strong. It is Jesus' name and the faith that comes through him that has given this complete healing to him, as you can all see.

[17]"Now, brothers, I know that you acted in ignorance, as did your leaders. [18]But this is how God fulfilled what he had foretold through all the prophets, saying that his Christ[m] would suffer. [19]Repent, then, and turn to God, so that your sins may be wiped out, that times of refreshing may come from the Lord, [20]and that he may send the Christ, who has been appointed for you—even Jesus. [21]He must remain in heaven until the time comes for God to restore everything, as he promised long ago through his holy prophets. [22]For Moses said, 'The Lord your God will raise up for you a prophet like me from among your own people; you must listen to everything he tells you. [23]Anyone who does not listen to him will be completely cut off from among his people.'[n]

[24]"Indeed, all the prophets from Samuel on, as many as have spoken, have foretold these days. [25]And you are heirs of the prophets and of the covenant God made with your fathers. He said to Abraham, 'Through your offspring all peoples on earth will be blessed.'[o] [26]When God raised up his servant, he sent him first to you to bless you by turning each of you from your wicked ways."

Peter and John Before the Sanhedrin

4 The priests and the captain of the temple guard and the Sadducees came up to Peter and John while they were speaking to the people. [2]They were greatly disturbed because the apostles were teaching the people and proclaiming in Jesus the resurrection of the dead. [3]They seized Peter and John, and because it was evening, they put them in jail until the next day. [4]But many who heard the message believed, and the number of men grew to about five thousand.

[5]The next day the rulers, elders and teachers of the law met in Jerusalem. [6]Annas the high priest was there, and so were Caiaphas, John, Alexander and the other men of the high priest's family. [7]They had Peter and John brought before them and began to question them: "By what power or what name did you do this?"

---

m18 Or *Messiah*; also in verse 20   *n23* Deut. 18:15,18,19   *o25* Gen. 22:18; 26:4

[8]Then Peter, filled with the Holy Spirit, said to them: "Rulers and elders of the people! [9]If we are being called to account today for an act of kindness shown to a cripple and are asked how he was healed, [10]then know this, you and all the people of Israel: It is by the name of Jesus Christ of Nazareth, whom you crucified but whom God raised from the dead, that this man stands before you healed. [11]He is

> " 'the stone you builders rejected,
> which has become the capstone.[p][q]

[12]Salvation is found in no one else, for there is no other name under heaven given to men by which we must be saved."

[13]When they saw the courage of Peter and John and realized that they were unschooled, ordinary men, they were astonished and they took note that these men had been with Jesus. [14]But since they could see the man who had been healed standing there with them, there was nothing they could say. [15]So they ordered them to withdraw from the Sanhedrin and then conferred together. [16]"What are we going to do with these men?" they asked. "Everybody living in Jerusalem knows they have done an outstanding miracle, and we cannot deny it. [17]But to stop this thing from spreading any further among the people, we must warn these men to speak no longer to anyone in this name."

[18]Then they called them in again and commanded them not to speak or teach at all in the name of Jesus. [19]But Peter and John replied, "Judge for yourselves whether it is right in God's sight to obey you rather than God. [20]For we cannot help speaking about what we have seen and heard."

[21]After further threats they let them go. They could not decide how to punish them, because all the people were praising God for what had happened. [22]For the man who was miraculously healed was over forty years old.

The Believers' Prayer

[23]On their release, Peter and John went back to their own people and reported all that the chief priests and elders had said to them. [24]When they heard this, they raised their voices together in prayer to God. "Sovereign Lord," they said, "you made the heaven and the earth and the sea, and everything in them. [25]You spoke by the Holy Spirit through the mouth of your servant, our father David:

> " 'Why do the nations rage
> and the peoples plot in vain?
> [26]The kings of the earth take their stand
> and the rulers gather together
> against the Lord
> and against his Anointed One.[r][s]

[27]Indeed Herod and Pontius Pilate met together with the Gentiles and the people[t] of Israel in this city to conspire against your holy servant Jesus, whom you anointed. [28]They did what your

authorities, what would be your reaction to Peter's bold answer? How does Peter's filling with the Holy Spirit (vv.8-12) compare with the purpose of the filling in 2:4 (see also Lk 21:12-13)? **4.** How is the leader's response similar to their response to the Lazarus episode (see Jn 11:45-53; 12:10-11)? Why are they reacting like this?

REFLECT: 1. When, if ever, do you feel that Peter's response to his political and religious leaders would be appropriate for a Christian today? How do you reconcile this passage with Romans 13:1-4? **2.** What is the most persecution you have experienced due to your faith? How did you take it? **3.** On a scale of 1 (low) to 10 (high), how sure are you of Peter's statement in verse 12? What has built your assurance the most? What doubts still linger? **4.** How has knowing Jesus shaped your character so that people will notice you have "been with Jesus"?

OPEN: What *bold* move are you contemplating: Dating someone new? Singing a solo? Leading a group? New career? Other?

DIG: 1. How do the Sanhedrin (4:15-17) and the disciples each view themselves and God? **2.** Why would the disciples begin the prayer by recalling God's sovereignty (vv.24-28)? **3.** What does it mean that Jesus' death was not simply the plan of his enemies (v.28; see 2:23; 3:17-18)? **4.** How might 1:8 be shaping the disciples' prayer in verses 29-30? **5.** What is one purpose of the Spirit's filling (see 2:4; 4:8,31)?

REFLECT: 1. How are your prayers in crises like and unlike this prayer? Why would it be beneficial to recall God's character and actions in history? **2.** In times of trouble, do

---

[p]11 Or *cornerstone*   [q]11 Psalm 118:22   [r]26 That is, Christ or Messiah
[s]26 Psalm 2:1,2   [t]27 The Greek is plural.

you respond more like the *Sanhedrin* (trying to figure out for yourself what to do), or like the *disciples* (coming to God in earnest prayer)?

OPEN: 1. At what point and with what group have you sensed the most unity: Athletic team? Army unit? Fraternity? Bible study? Music Group? Your family? Prison mates? 2. What religious practice did you once do "just because everyone else did it that way," but you have since "outgrown"?

DIG: 1. Compare verses 32-35 with 2:42-47. What qualities mark this church? 2. Were Ananias and Sapphira required to sell the land and lay all the money at the apostles' feet? Why or why not? What was their sin? 3. What would Ananias and Sapphira gain by lying about the money they received? How is your answer related to verses 32-37? 4. Given that we *all* do bad things, why do you think God punished Ananias and Sapphira so severely? How might "great fear" be useful to God at this point? 5. How would the incident with Ananias and Sapphira lead to the response of people in verses 13-14? What words might outsiders use to describe this church? 6. Sociologically, how do you account for the increasing numbers and vitality of this church?

REFLECT: 1. If you were to describe your church, which of the phrases here would you use to do so? Which ones would not fit now? Why? 2. How well does verse 32 describe your relationship with others in your church? What would have to change for such sharing to be possible? 3. When have you tried to "fool" God? What happened? 4. How have you experienced the "fear of the Lord"? How has that changed your life?

power and will had decided beforehand should happen. [29]Now, Lord, consider their threats and enable your servants to speak your word with great boldness. [30]Stretch out your hand to heal and perform miraculous signs and wonders through the name of your holy servant Jesus."

[31]After they prayed, the place where they were meeting was shaken. And they were all filled with the Holy Spirit and spoke the word of God boldly.

The Believers Share Their Possessions

[32]All the believers were one in heart and mind. No one claimed that any of his possessions was his own, but they shared everything they had. [33]With great power the apostles continued to testify to the resurrection of the Lord Jesus, and much grace was upon them all. [34]There were no needy persons among them. For from time to time those who owned lands or houses sold them, brought the money from the sales [35]and put it at the apostles' feet, and it was distributed to anyone as he had need.

[36]Joseph, a Levite from Cyprus, whom the apostles called Barnabas (which means Son of Encouragement), [37]sold a field he owned and brought the money and put it at the apostles' feet.

Ananias and Sapphira

5 Now a man named Ananias, together with his wife Sapphira, also sold a piece of property. [2]With his wife's full knowledge he kept back part of the money for himself, but brought the rest and put it at the apostles' feet.

[3]Then Peter said, "Ananias, how is it that Satan has so filled your heart that you have lied to the Holy Spirit and have kept for yourself some of the money you received for the land? [4]Didn't it belong to you before it was sold? And after it was sold, wasn't the money at your disposal? What made you think of doing such a thing? You have not lied to men but to God."

[5]When Ananias heard this, he fell down and died. And great fear seized all who heard what had happened. [6]Then the young men came forward, wrapped up his body, and carried him out and buried him.

[7]About three hours later his wife came in, not knowing what had happened. [8]Peter asked her, "Tell me, is this the price you and Ananias got for the land?"

"Yes," she said, "that is the price."

[9]Peter said to her, "How could you agree to test the Spirit of the Lord? Look! The feet of the men who buried your husband are at the door, and they will carry you out also."

[10]At that moment she fell down at his feet and died. Then the young men came in and, finding her dead, carried her out and buried her beside her husband. [11]Great fear seized the whole church and all who heard about these events.

The Apostles Heal Many

[12]The apostles performed many miraculous signs and wonders among the people. And all the believers used to meet together in Solomon's Colonnade. [13]No one else dared join them, even though they were highly regarded by the people.

¹⁴Nevertheless, more and more men and women believed in the Lord and were added to their number. ¹⁵As a result, people brought the sick into the streets and laid them on beds and mats so that at least Peter's shadow might fall on some of them as he passed by. ¹⁶Crowds gathered also from the towns around Jerusalem, bringing their sick and those tormented by evilᵘ spirits, and all of them were healed.

The Apostles Persecuted

¹⁷Then the high priest and all his associates, who were members of the party of the Sadducees, were filled with jealousy. ¹⁸They arrested the apostles and put them in the public jail. ¹⁹But during the night an angel of the Lord opened the doors of the jail and brought them out. ²⁰"Go, stand in the temple courts," he said, "and tell the people the full message of this new life."

²¹At daybreak they entered the temple courts, as they had been told, and began to teach the people.

When the high priest and his associates arrived, they called together the Sanhedrin—the full assembly of the elders of Israel—and sent to the jail for the apostles. ²²But on arriving at the jail, the officers did not find them there. So they went back and reported, ²³"We found the jail securely locked, with the guards standing at the doors; but when we opened them, we found no one inside." ²⁴On hearing this report, the captain of the temple guard and the chief priests were puzzled, wondering what would come of this.

²⁵Then someone came and said, "Look! The men you put in jail are standing in the temple courts teaching the people." ²⁶At that, the captain went with his officers and brought the apostles. They did not use force, because they feared that the people would stone them.

²⁷Having brought the apostles, they made them appear before the Sanhedrin to be questioned by the high priest. ²⁸"We gave you strict orders not to teach in this name," he said. "Yet you have filled Jerusalem with your teaching and are determined to make us guilty of this man's blood."

²⁹Peter and the other apostles replied: "We must obey God rather than men! ³⁰The God of our fathers raised Jesus from the dead—whom you had killed by hanging him on a tree. ³¹God exalted him to his own right hand as Prince and Savior that he might give repentance and forgiveness of sins to Israel. ³²We are witnesses of these things, and so is the Holy Spirit, whom God has given to those who obey him."

³³When they heard this, they were furious and wanted to put them to death. ³⁴But a Pharisee named Gamaliel, a teacher of the law, who was honored by all the people, stood up in the Sanhedrin and ordered that the men be put outside for a little while. ³⁵Then he addressed them: "Men of Israel, consider carefully what you intend to do to these men. ³⁶Some time ago Theudas appeared, claiming to be somebody, and about four hundred men rallied to him. He was killed, all his followers were dis-

OPEN: 1. What has been your experience on either side of jail cell bars? What sights, sounds, and feelings do you associate with jail? **2.** When you leave home or your car unattended do you always lock it? Why or why not?

DIG: 1. How do you account for the jealousy of the Sadducees? **2.** As an apostle, how would you feel during the events of verses 18-21? What would you expect to happen next? **3.** Cast people in your group to be the high priest, an officer (v.22), the captain, and the "someone" of verse 25. Have them play the scene in verses 21-26 (everyone else plays the full assembly). What are the leaders feeling as the events proceed? **4.** Of what do they accuse the apostles in 5:28? How is this different from what bothered them in 4:2? How could they miss the impact of these miracles? **5.** What assertions in Peter's response (vv.29-32) would arouse their fury? Why is Peter being so direct (see 4:1-12; 5:19-20)? **6.** Prior to Jesus, there were many Jewish zealots who led rebellions against Rome. What is Gamaliel's point in recalling two such leaders? Do you think he might be one of the secret believers mentioned in John 12:42? Or a political opportunist not wanting to arouse the public? Why? How do you think Peter's statement in verse 29 (and 4:19) may have influenced Gamaliel? **7.** Flogging sometimes resulted in death. How would you react if you were freed from jail, only to experience a more severe punishment? What does the response of the apostles show about them (vv.41-42)?

REFLECT: 1. What is the ultimate authority in your life? When does this create problems for you? What can you do to overcome these problems? **2.** How do you think you would feel if you were sent to jail for what you believe? How would your family feel? What would this do for you? How does joy in suffering relate to your ultimate authority? **3.** In what way

ᵘ16 Greek *unclean*

OPEN: Which responsibility at home or work would you gladly give up? Never give up?

DIG: 1. Given 2:44-45 and 4:32, how could the widows be neglected? 2. How do the apostles resolve this problem? Why would the church choose Greek-speaking Jews to fill all seven slots? 3. Looking at 6:7, 5:42, 4:32-35, and 2:42-47, how would you sum up what has happened in Acts so far? How does this relate to 1:8?

REFLECT: What secondary issues hinder your church from fulfilling Acts 1:8? What principles here could help you free the church for a wider mission?

OPEN: Are you more likely to "rock-the-boat" or keep quiet for "peace-at-any-price"?

DIG: 1. What do you think Stephen was like? 2. Immigrant Jews often formed their own synagogues in Jerusalem. How is their opposition to Stephen like and unlike the opposition the apostles faced from the Sanhedrin (5:27-28)? 3. What might lie behind these accusations against Stephen (see 5:21-24; Jn 2:13-21)?

REFLECT: What two adjectives best describe your spiritual life? What would be different if you were "full of grace and power"?

has God set you free to honor him more fully? 4. How do you explain why God sometimes delivers you *out of* hardships, but at other times he allows you to go *through* them?

persed, and it all came to nothing. ³⁷After him, Judas the Galilean appeared in the days of the census and led a band of people in revolt. He too was killed, and all his followers were scattered. ³⁸Therefore, in the present case I advise you: Leave these men alone! Let them go! For if their purpose or activity is of human origin, it will fail. ³⁹But if it is from God, you will not be able to stop these men; you will only find yourselves fighting against God."

⁴⁰His speech persuaded them. They called the apostles in and had them flogged. Then they ordered them not to speak in the name of Jesus, and let them go.

⁴¹The apostles left the Sanhedrin, rejoicing because they had been counted worthy of suffering disgrace for the Name. ⁴²Day after day, in the temple courts and from house to house, they never stopped teaching and proclaiming the good news that Jesus is the Christ. [v]

The Choosing of the Seven

6 In those days when the number of disciples was increasing, the Grecian Jews among them complained against the Hebraic Jews because their widows were being overlooked in the daily distribution of food. ²So the Twelve gathered all the disciples together and said, "It would not be right for us to neglect the ministry of the word of God in order to wait on tables. ³Brothers, choose seven men from among you who are known to be full of the Spirit and wisdom. We will turn this responsibility over to them ⁴and will give our attention to prayer and the ministry of the word."

⁵This proposal pleased the whole group. They chose Stephen, a man full of faith and of the Holy Spirit; also Philip, Procorus, Nicanor, Timon, Parmenas, and Nicolas from Antioch, a convert to Judaism. ⁶They presented these men to the apostles, who prayed and laid their hands on them.

⁷So the word of God spread. The number of disciples in Jerusalem increased rapidly, and a large number of priests became obedient to the faith.

Stephen Seized

⁸Now Stephen, a man full of God's grace and power, did great wonders and miraculous signs among the people. ⁹Opposition arose, however, from members of the Synagogue of the Freedmen (as it was called)—Jews of Cyrene and Alexandria as well as the provinces of Cilicia and Asia. These men began to argue with Stephen, ¹⁰but they could not stand up against his wisdom or the Spirit by whom he spoke.

¹¹Then they secretly persuaded some men to say, "We have heard Stephen speak words of blasphemy against Moses and against God."

¹²So they stirred up the people and the elders and the teachers of the law. They seized Stephen and brought him before the Sanhedrin. ¹³They produced false witnesses, who testified, "This fellow never stops speaking against this holy place and

*v*42 Or *Messiah*   *w*3 Gen. 12:1   *x*7 Gen. 15:13,14

against the law. [14]For we have heard him say that this Jesus of Nazareth will destroy this place and change the customs Moses handed down to us."

[15]All who were sitting in the Sanhedrin looked intently at Stephen, and they saw that his face was like the face of an angel.

Stephen's Speech to the Sanhedrin

7 Then the high priest asked him, "Are these charges true?" [2]To this he replied: "Brothers and fathers, listen to me! The God of glory appeared to our father Abraham while he was still in Mesopotamia, before he lived in Haran. [3]'Leave your country and your people,' God said, 'and go to the land I will show you.' [w]

[4]"So he left the land of the Chaldeans and settled in Haran. After the death of his father, God sent him to this land where you are now living. [5]He gave him no inheritance here, not even a foot of ground. But God promised him that he and his descendants after him would possess the land, even though at that time Abraham had no child. [6]God spoke to him in this way: 'Your descendants will be strangers in a country not their own, and they will be enslaved and mistreated four hundred years. [7]But I will punish the nation they serve as slaves,' God said, 'and afterward they will come out of that country and worship me in this place.' [x] [8]Then he gave Abraham the covenant of circumcision. And Abraham became the father of Isaac and circumcised him eight days after his birth. Later Isaac became the father of Jacob, and Jacob became the father of the twelve patriarchs.

[9]"Because the patriarchs were jealous of Joseph, they sold him as a slave into Egypt. But God was with him [10]and rescued him from all his troubles. He gave Joseph wisdom and enabled him to gain the goodwill of Pharaoh king of Egypt; so he made him ruler over Egypt and all his palace.

[11]"Then a famine struck all Egypt and Canaan, bringing great suffering, and our fathers could not find food. [12]When Jacob heard that there was grain in Egypt, he sent our fathers on their first visit. [13]On their second visit, Joseph told his brothers who he was, and Pharaoh learned about Joseph's family. [14]After this, Joseph sent for his father Jacob and his whole family, seventy-five in all. [15]Then Jacob went down to Egypt, where he and our fathers died. [16]Their bodies were brought back to Shechem and placed in the tomb that Abraham had bought from the sons of Hamor at Shechem for a certain sum of money.

[17]"As the time drew near for God to fulfill his promise to Abraham, the number of our people in Egypt greatly increased. [18]Then another king, who knew nothing about Joseph, became ruler of Egypt. [19]He dealt treacherously with our people and oppressed our forefathers by forcing them to throw out their newborn babies so that they would die.

[20]"At that time Moses was born, and he was no ordinary child. [y] For three months he was cared for in his father's house. [21]When he was placed outside, Pharaoh's daughter took him and brought him up as her own son. [22]Moses was educated in all the wisdom of the Egyptians and was powerful in speech and action.

OPEN: 1. As a child, who was the best storyteller you ever heard? What made that person so effective? 2. Where did your ancestors come from? Do you have any heroes or "black sheep" in the family? 3. What's the longest speech you've ever listened to? Was it exciting or boring? Why? 4. In which ways are you "just like your mother (or father)?

DIG: 1. From 6:13-14, how would you write up the formal charges against Stephen? 2. What does Stephen's story telling (in effect a history lesson) reveal about his respect for the Mosaic Law? 3. Why does Stephen spend the bulk of his history lesson talking about Moses? What parallels does he draw between Moses and Jesus? How does this relate to the charges against him in 6:13-14? How does the quote in verse 37 begin to turn the tables on his accusers (regarding who is really rejecting Moses)? 4. From verses 44-50, what is his point about the temple and God's presence? How is he turning the tables against his accusers once again? 5. Look at Deuteronomy 10:16 and 30:4. What does Stephen mean by the phrase "uncircumcised hearts and ears"? In this context, what is Stephen really saying about the Sanhedrin's regard for Moses and the Law? 6. Of what does he accuse them in verses 51-53? How does his charge reveal the reason why he gave them this history lesson? 7. Considering this oppressive situation, what type of person is Stephen?

REFLECT: 1. Since the Sanhedrin knew their history every bit as well as Stephen, how do you account for their radically different response to Jesus? To fully understand Jesus, what is needed in your life besides well-rehearsed knowledge? 2. In what ways do people hold on to religious rituals and heroes today, while missing the whole point of what those ceremonies and people represent? How does this tendency affect you? 3. In what ways could the

y20 Or was fair in the sight of God

charges that Stephen makes against the leaders be made against the leaders? How might you be feeling "stiff-necked" this week? How will you begin to bow to God in that area now? **4.** Would you say that the OT is more like a stranger or a close friend to you? How does this speech show the importance of the OT to the early Christians? What will you do to let its importance grow for you? **5.** When Jesus was brought to trial, he was basically quiet before the Sanhedrin; yet Stephen spoke very boldly here. How do you decide when to speak and when to be quiet before opposition?

[23]"When Moses was forty years old, he decided to visit his fellow Israelites. [24]He saw one of them being mistreated by an Egyptian, so he went to his defense and avenged him by killing the Egyptian. [25]Moses thought that his own people would realize that God was using him to rescue them, but they did not. [26]The next day Moses came upon two Israelites who were fighting. He tried to reconcile them by saying, 'Men, you are brothers; why do you want to hurt each other?'

[27]"But the man who was mistreating the other pushed Moses aside and said, 'Who made you ruler and judge over us? [28]Do you want to kill me as you killed the Egyptian yesterday?' [z] [29]When Moses heard this, he fled to Midian, where he settled as a foreigner and had two sons.

[30]"After forty years had passed, an angel appeared to Moses in the flames of a burning bush in the desert near Mount Sinai. [31]When he saw this, he was amazed at the sight. As he went over to look more closely, he heard the Lord's voice: [32]'I am the God of your fathers, the God of Abraham, Isaac and Jacob.' [a] Moses trembled with fear and did not dare to look.

[33]"Then the Lord said to him, 'Take off your sandals; the place where you are standing is holy ground. [34]I have indeed seen the oppression of my people in Egypt. I have heard their groaning and have come down to set them free. Now come, I will send you back to Egypt.' [b]

[35]"This is the same Moses whom they had rejected with the words, 'Who made you ruler and judge?' He was sent to be their ruler and deliverer by God himself, through the angel who appeared to him in the bush. [36]He led them out of Egypt and did wonders and miraculous signs in Egypt, at the Red Sea [c] and for forty years in the desert.

[37]This is that Moses who told the Israelites, 'God will send you a prophet like me from your own people.' [d] [38]He was in the assembly in the desert, with the angel who spoke to him on Mount Sinai, and with our fathers; and he received living words to pass on to us.

[39]"But our fathers refused to obey him. Instead, they rejected him and in their hearts turned back to Egypt. [40]They told Aaron, 'Make us gods who will go before us. As for this fellow Moses who led us out of Egypt—we don't know what has happened to him!' [e] [41]That was the time they made an idol in the form of a calf. They brought sacrifices to it and held a celebration in honor of what their hands had made. [42]But God turned away and gave them over to the worship of the heavenly bodies. This agrees with what is written in the book of the prophets:

" 'Did you bring me sacrifices and offerings
forty years in the desert, O house of Israel?
[43]You have lifted up the shrine of Molech
and the star of your god Rephan,
the idols you made to worship.
Therefore I will send you into exile' [f] beyond Babylon.

---

[z]*28* Exodus 2:14   [a]*32* Exodus 3:6   [b]*34* Exodus 3:5,7,8,10
[c]*36* That is, Sea of Reeds   [d]*37* Deut. 18:15   [e]*40* Exodus 32:1
[f]*43* Amos 5:25-27

44"Our forefathers had the tabernacle of the Testimony with them in the desert. It had been made as God directed Moses, according to the pattern he had seen. 45Having received the tabernacle, our fathers under Joshua brought it with them when they took the land from the nations God drove out before them. It remained in the land until the time of David, 46who enjoyed God's favor and asked that he might provide a dwelling place for the God of Jacob. g 47But it was Solomon who built the house for him.

48"However, the Most High does not live in houses made by men. As the prophet says:

49" 'Heaven is my throne,
     and the earth is my footstool.
What kind of house will you build for me?

says the Lord.

Or where will my resting place be?
50Has not my hand made all these things?' h

51"You stiff-necked people, with uncircumcised hearts and ears! You are just like your fathers: You always resist the Holy Spirit! 52Was there ever a prophet your fathers did not persecute? They even killed those who predicted the coming of the Righteous One. And now you have betrayed and murdered him— 53you who have received the law that was put into effect through angels but have not obeyed it."

The Stoning of Stephen

54When they heard this, they were furious and gnashed their teeth at him. 55But Stephen, full of the Holy Spirit, looked up to heaven and saw the glory of God, and Jesus standing at the right hand of God. 56"Look," he said, "I see heaven open and the Son of Man standing at the right hand of God."

57At this they covered their ears and, yelling at the top of their voices, they all rushed at him, 58dragged him out of the city and began to stone him. Meanwhile, the witnesses laid their clothes at the feet of a young man named Saul.

59While they were stoning him, Stephen prayed, "Lord Jesus, receive my spirit." 60Then he fell on his knees and cried out, "Lord, do not hold this sin against them." When he had said this, he fell asleep.

8 And Saul was there, giving approval to his death.

The Church Persecuted and Scattered

On that day a great persecution broke out against the church at Jerusalem, and all except the apostles were scattered throughout Judea and Samaria. 2Godly men buried Stephen and mourned deeply for him. 3But Saul began to destroy the church. Going from house to house, he dragged off men and women and put them in prison.

OPEN: On an emotional level, have you ever hated someone so much that you resorted to "sticks and stones"? What did you do (instead)?

DIG: 1. Why are Stephen's listeners so enraged (see Da 7:13-14)? **2.** Stephen's death was illegal (see Jn 18:31). What does that reveal about the desperation of the Sanhedrin? **3.** How is Stephen's death and Saul's mission an example of God using evil to fulfill God's plan (1:8)? **4.** This begins phase two ("Judea and Samaria") of God's plan (see 1:8). How would you sum up the "Jerusalem phase" (ch. 2-7)?

REFLECT: 1. What is one very traumatic, upsetting thing that happened to you in your formative years? Can you see now how God has used it for good? **2.** Peter's speech led to mass conversion (ch.2), while Stephen's led to his death. What does that teach about "success" in one's service to God?

g46 Some early manuscripts *the house of Jacob*   h50 Isaiah 66:1,2

Philip in Samaria

[4]Those who had been scattered preached the word wherever they went. [5]Philip went down to a city in Samaria and proclaimed the Christ[i] there. [6]When the crowds heard Philip and saw the miraculous signs he did, they all paid close attention to what he said. [7]With shrieks, evil[j] spirits came out of many, and many paralytics and cripples were healed. [8]So there was great joy in that city.

Simon the Sorcerer

[9]Now for some time a man named Simon had practiced sorcery in the city and amazed all the people of Samaria. He boasted that he was someone great, [10]and all the people, both high and low, gave him their attention and exclaimed, "This man is the divine power known as the Great Power." [11]They followed him because he had amazed them for a long time with his magic. [12]But when they believed Philip as he preached the good news of the kingdom of God and the name of Jesus Christ, they were baptized, both men and women. [13]Simon himself believed and was baptized. And he followed Philip everywhere, astonished by the great signs and miracles he saw.

[14]When the apostles in Jerusalem heard that Samaria had accepted the word of God, they sent Peter and John to them. [15]When they arrived, they prayed for them that they might receive the Holy Spirit, [16]because the Holy Spirit had not yet come upon any of them; they had simply been baptized into[k] the name of the Lord Jesus. [17]Then Peter and John placed their hands on them, and they received the Holy Spirit.

[18]When Simon saw that the Spirit was given at the laying on of the apostles' hands, he offered them money [19]and said, "Give me also this ability so that everyone on whom I lay my hands may receive the Holy Spirit."

[20]Peter answered: "May your money perish with you, because you thought you could buy the gift of God with money! [21]You have no part or share in this ministry, because your heart is not right before God. [22]Repent of this wickedness and pray to the Lord. Perhaps he will forgive you for having such a thought in your heart. [23]For I see that you are full of bitterness and captive to sin."

[24]Then Simon answered, "Pray to the Lord for me so that nothing you have said may happen to me."

[25]When they had testified and proclaimed the word of the Lord, Peter and John returned to Jerusalem, preaching the gospel in many Samaritan villages.

Philip and the Ethiopian

[26]Now an angel of the Lord said to Philip, "Go south to the road—the desert road—that goes down from Jerusalem to Gaza." [27]So he started out, and on his way he met an Ethiopian[l] eunuch, an important official in charge of all the treasury of Candace, queen of the Ethiopians. This man had gone to Jerusa-

i5 Or *Messiah*   j7 Greek *unclean*   k16 Or *in*   l27 That is, from the upper Nile region lem to worship, [28]and on his way home was sitting in his chariot reading the book of Isaiah the prophet. [29]The Spirit told Philip, "Go to that chariot and stay near it."

[30]Then Philip ran up to the chariot and heard the man reading Isaiah the prophet. "Do you understand what you are reading?" Philip asked.

[31]"How can I," he said, "unless someone explains it to me?" So he invited Philip to come up and sit with him.

[32]The eunuch was reading this passage of Scripture:

"He was led like a sheep to the slaughter,
    and as a lamb before the shearer is silent,
    so he did not open his mouth.
[33]In his humiliation he was deprived of justice.
    Who can speak of his descendants?
    For his life was taken from the earth."[m]

[34]The eunuch asked Philip, "Tell me, please, who is the prophet talking about, himself or someone else?" [35]Then Philip began with that very passage of Scripture and told him the good news about Jesus.

[36]As they traveled along the road, they came to some water and the eunuch said, "Look, here is water. Why shouldn't I be baptized?"[n] [38]And he gave orders to stop the chariot. Then both Philip and the eunuch went down into the water and Philip baptized him. [39]When they came up out of the water, the Spirit of the Lord suddenly took Philip away, and the eunuch did not see him again, but went on his way rejoicing. [40]Philip, however, appeared at Azotus and traveled about, preaching the gospel in all the towns until he reached Caesarea.

Saul's Conversion

9 Meanwhile, Saul was still breathing out murderous threats against the Lord's disciples. He went to the high priest [2]and asked him for letters to the synagogues in Damascus, so that if he found any there who belonged to the Way, whether men or women, he might take them as prisoners to Jerusalem. [3]As he neared Damascus on his journey, suddenly a light from heaven flashed around him. [4]He fell to the ground and heard a voice say to him, "Saul, Saul, why do you persecute me?"

[5]"Who are you, Lord?" Saul asked.

"I am Jesus, whom you are persecuting," he replied. [6]"Now get up and go into the city, and you will be told what you must do."

[7]The men traveling with Saul stood there speechless; they heard the sound but did not see anyone. [8]Saul got up from the ground, but when he opened his eyes he could see nothing. So they led him by the hand into Damascus. [9]For three days he was blind, and did not eat or drink anything.

[10]In Damascus there was a disciple named Ananias. The Lord called to him in a vision, "Ananias!"

"Yes, Lord," he answered.

the gospel? **3.** How did God pave the way for his message? What is the relationship between divine preparation and human initiative in this story? **4.** What is the significance of this story for a church being persecuted in Jerusalem? **5.** So far, what has been the effect of Stephen's death upon Phillip? Upon the church as a whole?

REFLECT: 1. From the way God sets up opportunities to witness (8:26-40; 3:6-16; 2:5-14), how does that free you from fears in evangelism? What do these stories show about the context in which evangelism is to happen? **2.** Deep down, do you think successful VIPs really need the gospel as much as poor beggars do (3:2)? Why or why not? **3.** Would you know the Bible well enough to address the eunuch's questions? How can you grow in faith so you will be prepared for surprise ("serendipitous") opportunities?

OPEN: What is the longest you have been without food or drink: Three days? Three meals? Three hours? What was the net effect?

DIG: 1. Saul traveled 150 miles to Damascus in order to expand what started as a local persecution against believers in Jerusalem (8:1). What does that tell you about him? **2.** Saul's former teacher was Gamaliel (see 22:3). What had Gamaliel advised the Sanhedrin regarding Christians in 5:34-39? How is Saul responding to this advice? What does this show about him? **3.** Describe what happened in verses 3-9 from the viewpoint of one of Saul's companions. **4.** How do you think Saul felt when confronted by Jesus (vv.4-6)? Given his previous activities, what would he be thinking about during those three days of blindness and fasting (v.9)? **5.** How would you feel in Ananias' place? Since Jesus had already appeared to Saul directly, why this time would he

---

[m]33 Isaiah 53:7,8   [n]36 Some late manuscripts *baptized?"* [37]*Philip said, "If you believe with all your heart, you may." The eunuch answered, "I believe that Jesus Christ is the Son of God."*

want a person to go to him? What is significant about the way Ananias addresses Saul? **6.** Saul becomes famous, but we never hear of Ananias again: Why did God involve him at all?

REFLECT: 1. How did the Lord first get your attention? Was it in some dramatic event like this or a quieter, more natural way? **2.** What types of people do you assume are beyond God's reach so that, if God spoke to you about them, you would question him? How does this story challenge those assumptions? **3.** When have you, like Ananias, obeyed the Lord even when you had doubts about it? What happened? **4.** Who has played the role of Ananias in your life? To whom does the Lord want you to play that part?

OPEN: Who do people say you look like? Why?

DIG: 1. What would others have expected Saul to say when he came to the synagogue? When he proceeds to preach about Christ, how do they react? Why? **2.** The events of verses 23-28 probably occurred about 2-3 years after Saul's conversion (see Gal 1:15-18). How has the Lord totally changed things for Saul during this time? **3.** Why would the Jerusalem disciples still fear Saul? What risk is Barnabas taking? **4.** People in Damascus and Jerusalem want to kill Saul. What does that say about him? **5.** How is the story of Saul related to 1:8?

REFLECT: 1. What changes has knowing Jesus brought into your life? How have other people responded? **2.** Who has been a Barnabas to you? How? Whom have you served as a Barnabas?

[11]The Lord told him, "Go to the house of Judas on Straight Street and ask for a man from Tarsus named Saul, for he is praying. [12]In a vision he has seen a man named Ananias come and place his hands on him to restore his sight."

[13]"Lord," Ananias answered, "I have heard many reports about this man and all the harm he has done to your saints in Jerusalem. [14]And he has come here with authority from the chief priests to arrest all who call on your name."

[15]But the Lord said to Ananias, "Go! This man is my chosen instrument to carry my name before the Gentiles and their kings and before the people of Israel. [16]I will show him how much he must suffer for my name."

[17]Then Ananias went to the house and entered it. Placing his hands on Saul, he said, "Brother Saul, the Lord—Jesus, who appeared to you on the road as you were coming here—has sent me so that you may see again and be filled with the Holy Spirit." [18]Immediately, something like scales fell from Saul's eyes, and he could see again. He got up and was baptized, [19]and after taking some food, he regained his strength.

Saul in Damascus and Jerusalem

Saul spent several days with the disciples in Damascus. [20]At once he began to preach in the synagogues that Jesus is the Son of God. [21]All those who heard him were astonished and asked, "Isn't he the man who raised havoc in Jerusalem among those who call on this name? And hasn't he come here to take them as prisoners to the chief priests?" [22]Yet Saul grew more and more powerful and baffled the Jews living in Damascus by proving that Jesus is the Christ.[o]

[23]After many days had gone by, the Jews conspired to kill him, [24]but Saul learned of their plan. Day and night they kept close watch on the city gates in order to kill him. [25]But his followers took him by night and lowered him in a basket through an opening in the wall.

[26]When he came to Jerusalem, he tried to join the disciples, but they were all afraid of him, not believing that he really was a disciple. [27]But Barnabas took him and brought him to the apostles. He told them how Saul on his journey had seen the Lord and that the Lord had spoken to him, and how in Damascus he had preached fearlessly in the name of Jesus. [28]So Saul stayed with them and moved about freely in Jerusalem, speaking boldly in the name of the Lord. [29]He talked and debated with the Grecian Jews, but they tried to kill him. [30]When the brothers learned of this, they took him down to Caesarea and sent him off to Tarsus.

[31]Then the church throughout Judea, Galilee and Samaria enjoyed a time of peace. It was strengthened; and encouraged by the Holy Spirit, it grew in numbers, living in the fear of the Lord.

o22 Or Messiah

Aeneas and Dorcas

³²As Peter traveled about the country, he went to visit the saints in Lydda. ³³There he found a man named Aeneas, a paralytic who had been bedridden for eight years. ³⁴"Aeneas," Peter said to him, "Jesus Christ heals you. Get up and take care of your mat." Immediately Aeneas got up. ³⁵All those who lived in Lydda and Sharon saw him and turned to the Lord.

³⁶In Joppa there was a disciple named Tabitha (which, when translated, is Dorcas*ᵖ*), who was always doing good and helping the poor. ³⁷About that time she became sick and died, and her body was washed and placed in an upstairs room. ³⁸Lydda was near Joppa; so when the disciples heard that Peter was in Lydda, they sent two men to him and urged him, "Please come at once!"

³⁹Peter went with them, and when he arrived he was taken upstairs to the room. All the widows stood around him, crying and showing him the robes and other clothing that Dorcas had made while she was still with them.

⁴⁰Peter sent them all out of the room; then he got down on his knees and prayed. Turning toward the dead woman, he said, "Tabitha, get up." She opened her eyes, and seeing Peter she sat up. ⁴¹He took her by the hand and helped her to her feet. Then he called the believers and the widows and presented her to them alive. ⁴²This became known all over Joppa, and many people believed in the Lord. ⁴³Peter stayed in Joppa for some time with a tanner named Simon.

Cornelius Calls for Peter

10 At Caesarea there was a man named Cornelius, a centurion in what was known as the Italian Regiment. ²He and all his family were devout and God-fearing; he gave generously to those in need and prayed to God regularly. ³One day at about three in the afternoon he had a vision. He distinctly saw an angel of God, who came to him and said, "Cornelius!"

⁴Cornelius stared at him in fear. "What is it, Lord?" he asked.

The angel answered, "Your prayers and gifts to the poor have come up as a memorial offering before God. ⁵Now send men to Joppa to bring back a man named Simon who is called Peter. ⁶He is staying with Simon the tanner, whose house is by the sea."

⁷When the angel who spoke to him had gone, Cornelius called two of his servants and a devout soldier who was one of his attendants. ⁸He told them everything that had happened and sent them to Joppa.

Peter's Vision

⁹About noon the following day as they were on their journey and approaching the city, Peter went up on the roof to pray. ¹⁰He became hungry and wanted something to eat, and while the meal was being prepared, he fell into a trance. ¹¹He saw heaven opened and something like a large sheet being let down to earth by its four corners. ¹²It contained all kinds of four-footed ani-

OPEN: 1. What does it take to get you out of bed in the morning? **2.** For what coveted item would you sprint like a gazelle?

DIG: 1. What is the purpose of these signs and wonders (vv.35, 41-42; see 2:22,43; 4:30; 5:12-14)? **2.** Although Peter had healed many people, he had never raised anyone from death. What might he be feeling as he goes to Tabitha's home? **3.** Which of Jesus' miracles do these two incidents remind you of?

REFLECT: 1. Why is it that Tabitha was raised, but Stephen died, even though Peter was there too (8:2)? How would you explain God's ways to Stephen's widow or mother? How might the results of Stephen's death and Tabitha's resurrection help you to understand God's plans? **2.** How have you experienced God's healing in your life? What resulted from this healing for others?

OPEN: What dream (nightmare) has inspired (or haunted) you?

DIG: 1. What is Cornelius like (vv.1-2)? Since he is part of an occupying army, what is unusual about him? About his encounter with God? **2.** What might the three men talk about along their 30-mile trek to Joppa?

REFLECT: 1. Are you very "God-fearing"? If evaluated by how you treated others this week, what would others say? **2.** What memorial offering does your lifestyle present before God? How does Cornelius' life challenge you?

OPEN: 1. In what sense are you like a pig: Piggy eater? Cute tail? Tough skin? Pig-headed? Room like a pigpen? **2.** As a child, what did you refuse to eat?

DIG: 1. Look at Leviticus 11:4-7, 13-19 and 29-30. With these restrictions, how do you think Peter felt when he heard the voice order him to eat these animals? Why was it repeated three times? What

p36 Both Tabitha (Aramaic) and Dorcas (Greek) mean gazelle.

would the new principle given in verse 15 mean to him? How does it fit with the story of Cornelius? **2.** How might Peter feel when the men sent by Cornelius showed up? **3.** How might the example of Jesus (in Lk 7:1-10) also encourage Peter to listen to these men?

REFLECT: 1. What are some principles or beliefs you have held that have limited your ability to reach out to people "different" from you? How would others around you feel if you moved beyond these limits? **2.** What new relationships has God given you recently? How has he brought these people into your life? How have you influenced each other?

OPEN: 1. Did you grow up isolated from or associated with minorities? What was that like? **2.** Later, what books, movies, or actual experiences shaped your adult understanding of prejudice?

DIG: 1. Given Peter's experience in verses 9-23 and what you see of Cornelius here, how do you think each man was feeling as they greeted one another? **2.** Jews regarded even people like Cornelius as pagans, unless they fully submitted to Jewish practices (see 11:3). Hence, what would verse 28 have meant to Peter? To Cornelius? Why is the story of Cornelius so important in Acts (vv.28, 34-35,43)? **3.** What is the main point in Peter's sermon? How does that compare with his sermons in 2:36-39 and 3:17-23? From these three sermons, what do you see as central to the gospel message? **4.** In light of the astonished reaction of the Jews (v.45), what did it mean that the Gentiles could speak in tongues? How does this reinforce Peter's private vision in 10:9-23?

mals, as well as reptiles of the earth and birds of the air. [13]Then a voice told him, "Get up, Peter. Kill and eat."

[14]"Surely not, Lord!" Peter replied. "I have never eaten anything impure or unclean."

[15]The voice spoke to him a second time, "Do not call anything impure that God has made clean."

[16]This happened three times, and immediately the sheet was taken back to heaven.

[17]While Peter was wondering about the meaning of the vision, the men sent by Cornelius found out where Simon's house was and stopped at the gate. [18]They called out, asking if Simon who was known as Peter was staying there.

[19]While Peter was still thinking about the vision, the Spirit said to him, "Simon, three[q] men are looking for you. [20]So get up and go downstairs. Do not hesitate to go with them, for I have sent them."

[21]Peter went down and said to the men, "I'm the one you're looking for. Why have you come?"

[22]The men replied, "We have come from Cornelius the centurion. He is a righteous and God-fearing man, who is respected by all the Jewish people. A holy angel told him to have you come to his house so that he could hear what you have to say." [23]Then Peter invited the men into the house to be his guests.

Peter at Cornelius' House

The next day Peter started out with them, and some of the brothers from Joppa went along. [24]The following day he arrived in Caesarea. Cornelius was expecting them and had called together his relatives and close friends. [25]As Peter entered the house, Cornelius met him and fell at his feet in reverence. [26]But Peter made him get up. "Stand up," he said, "I am only a man myself."

[27]Talking with him, Peter went inside and found a large gathering of people. [28]He said to them: "You are well aware that it is against our law for a Jew to associate with a Gentile or visit him. But God has shown me that I should not call any man impure or unclean. [29]So when I was sent for, I came without raising any objection. May I ask why you sent for me?"

[30]Cornelius answered: "Four days ago I was in my house praying at this hour, at three in the afternoon. Suddenly a man in shining clothes stood before me [31]and said, 'Cornelius, God has heard your prayer and remembered your gifts to the poor. [32]Send to Joppa for Simon who is called Peter. He is a guest in the home of Simon the tanner, who lives by the sea.' [33]So I sent for you immediately, and it was good of you to come. Now we are all here in the presence of God to listen to everything the Lord has commanded you to tell us."

[34]Then Peter began to speak: "I now realize how true it is that God does not show favoritism [35]but accepts men from every nation who fear him and do what is right. [36]You know the message God sent to the people of Israel, telling the good news of peace through Jesus Christ, who is Lord of all. [37]You know

---

[q]19 One early manuscript *two*; other manuscripts do not have the number.

what has happened throughout Judea, beginning in Galilee after the baptism that John preached— ³⁸how God anointed Jesus of Nazareth with the Holy Spirit and power, and how he went around doing good and healing all who were under the power of the devil, because God was with him.

³⁹"We are witnesses of everything he did in the country of the Jews and in Jerusalem. They killed him by hanging him on a tree, ⁴⁰but God raised him from the dead on the third day and caused him to be seen. ⁴¹He was not seen by all the people, but by witnesses whom God had already chosen—by us who ate and drank with him after he rose from the dead. ⁴²He commanded us to preach to the people and to testify that he is the one whom God appointed as judge of the living and the dead. ⁴³All the prophets testify about him that everyone who believes in him receives forgiveness of sins through his name."

⁴⁴While Peter was still speaking these words, the Holy Spirit came on all who heard the message. ⁴⁵The circumcised believers who had come with Peter were astonished that the gift of the Holy Spirit had been poured out even on the Gentiles. ⁴⁶For they heard them speaking in tongues' and praising God.

Then Peter said, ⁴⁷"Can anyone keep these people from being baptized with water? They have received the Holy Spirit just as we have." ⁴⁸So he ordered that they be baptized in the name of Jesus Christ. Then they asked Peter to stay with them for a few days.

Peter Explains His Actions

11 The apostles and the brothers throughout Judea heard that the Gentiles also had received the word of God. ²So when Peter went up to Jerusalem, the circumcised believers criticized him ³and said, "You went into the house of uncircumcised men and ate with them."

⁴Peter began and explained everything to them precisely as it had happened: ⁵"I was in the city of Joppa praying, and in a trance I saw a vision. I saw something like a large sheet being let down from heaven by its four corners, and it came down to where I was. ⁶I looked into it and saw four-footed animals of the earth, wild beasts, reptiles, and birds of the air. ⁷Then I heard a voice telling me, 'Get up, Peter. Kill and eat.'

⁸"I replied, 'Surely not, Lord! Nothing impure or unclean has ever entered my mouth.'

⁹"The voice spoke from heaven a second time, 'Do not call anything impure that God has made clean.' ¹⁰This happened three times, and then it was all pulled up to heaven again.

¹¹"Right then three men who had been sent to me from Caesarea stopped at the house where I was staying. ¹²The Spirit told me to have no hesitation about going with them. These six brothers also went with me, and we entered the man's house. ¹³He told us how he had seen an angel appear in his house and say, 'Send to Joppa for Simon who is called Peter. ¹⁴He will bring you a message through which you and all your household will be saved.'

REFLECT: 1. Using this story, how would you respond to the question: "Can people who have never heard the gospel be saved"? If your answer is "yes," why then did God send Peter to preach (see also 11:14)? If it is "no," how do you explain verses 34-35? **2.** Toward what groups of people do you feel prejudiced? How has that developed? What evidence is there that the lesson of Peter's vision has broken through to you with respect to these people? **3.** Consider the make-up of your community and of your church (ethnically, socially, politically, age-wise, etc.). Are there some people who would just assume that your church is not for them? Are there some forms or practices you could change to remove those barriers? How would you feel about making those changes?

OPEN: 1. Who was "the wrong crowd" to hang out with when you were in school? Did you anyway? Why? **2.** Do you change your mind very easily? Explain.

DIG: 1. Why did Luke take the time and space to record the events of 10:9-46 all over again? **2.** Of what importance is the gift of the Holy Spirit in Peter's argument? Why would this have such a strong effect on the Jerusalem believers? Why is it misunderstood (see 1:6)? **3.** Why do you think God chose Peter to be the first to go to the Gentiles? Would any other disciple have been as successful in both Caesarea and Jerusalem? Why or why not? **4.** How do you explain the change in attitudes from verse 2 to verse 18? How does this story relate to 1:8?

REFLECT: 1. How can this principle affect the way you treat "unacceptable" people you meet? **2.** How have you been criticized for breaking the religious traditions you grew up with? Why did you do so? What did you feel was at stake? **3.** The lesson of 10:34-35 and 11:18 was not easily learned,

---

ʳ46 Or *other languages*

even by Peter (see Gal 2:11-14). What might have happened if the early church denied the new principle (10:15, 28 and 11:9) which God taught Peter?

OPEN: What is the farthest from home you've been? Why were you there?

DIG: 1. Antioch was the third largest city in the Roman empire. What might the apostles feel as they hear the gospel is taking root there? **2.** Write a character reference for Barnabas based on verses 22-26 (also 4:36-37; 9:27-28). From this profile, why did Barnabus recruit Saul?

REFLECT: 1. With whom do you associate that no minister or priest would normally contact? How can you share the gospel with those people? **2.** Would these people be comfortable in your church as it now is? Why or why not? How should you address this issue? **3.** What would you consider as evidence that the grace of God is at work in your life? In your church?

OPEN: If you were arrested by a dictatorial government for being a Christian, what evidence might they point to as proof of your guilt? What could some "well-meaning" character witnesses point to as proof of your innocence?

DIG: 1. This Herod is the nephew of the Herod who ruled in Jesus' day. What do you learn about his character in verses 1-3? Why would this action please the Jewish leaders? Why do you think Herod, as a Roman official, would now join in the Jewish opposition to the church? **2.** When Rhoda announced who was at the door, what would you have said if you

---

[15]"As I began to speak, the Holy Spirit came on them as he had come on us at the beginning. [16]Then I remembered what the Lord had said: 'John baptized with[s] water, but you will be baptized with the Holy Spirit.' [17]So if God gave them the same gift as he gave us, who believed in the Lord Jesus Christ, who was I to think that I could oppose God?"

[18]When they heard this, they had no further objections and praised God, saying, "So then, God has granted even the Gentiles repentance unto life."

The Church in Antioch

[19]Now those who had been scattered by the persecution in connection with Stephen traveled as far as Phoenicia, Cyprus and Antioch, telling the message only to Jews. [20]Some of them, however, men from Cyprus and Cyrene, went to Antioch and began to speak to Greeks also, telling them the good news about the Lord Jesus. [21]The Lord's hand was with them, and a great number of people believed and turned to the Lord.

[22]News of this reached the ears of the church at Jerusalem, and they sent Barnabas to Antioch. [23]When he arrived and saw the evidence of the grace of God, he was glad and encouraged them all to remain true to the Lord with all their hearts. [24]He was a good man, full of the Holy Spirit and faith, and a great number of people were brought to the Lord.

[25]Then Barnabas went to Tarsus to look for Saul, [26]and when he found him, he brought him to Antioch. So for a whole year Barnabas and Saul met with the church and taught great numbers of people. The disciples were called Christians first at Antioch.

[27]During this time some prophets came down from Jerusalem to Antioch. [28]One of them, named Agabus, stood up and through the Spirit predicted that a severe famine would spread over the entire Roman world. (This happened during the reign of Claudius.) [29]The disciples, each according to his ability, decided to provide help for the brothers living in Judea. [30]This they did, sending their gift to the elders by Barnabas and Saul.

Peter's Miraculous Escape From Prison

12 It was about this time that King Herod arrested some who belonged to the church, intending to persecute them. [2]He had James, the brother of John, put to death with the sword. [3]When he saw that this pleased the Jews, he proceeded to seize Peter also. This happened during the Feast of Unleavened Bread. [4]After arresting him, he put him in prison, handing him over to be guarded by four squads of four soldiers each. Herod intended to bring him out for public trial after the Passover.

[5]So Peter was kept in prison, but the church was earnestly praying to God for him.

[6]The night before Herod was to bring him to trial, Peter was sleeping between two soldiers, bound with two chains, and sentries stood guard at the entrance. [7]Suddenly an angel of the

[s]*16 Or in*

Lord appeared and a light shone in the cell. He struck Peter on the side and woke him up. "Quick, get up!" he said, and the chains fell off Peter's wrists.

⁸Then the angel said to him, "Put on your clothes and sandals." And Peter did so. "Wrap your cloak around you and follow me," the angel told him. ⁹Peter followed him out of the prison, but he had no idea that what the angel was doing was really happening; he thought he was seeing a vision. ¹⁰They passed the first and second guards and came to the iron gate leading to the city. It opened for them by itself, and they went through it. When they had walked the length of one street, suddenly the angel left him.

¹¹Then Peter came to himself and said, "Now I know without a doubt that the Lord sent his angel and rescued me from Herod's clutches and from everything the Jewish people were anticipating."

¹²When this had dawned on him, he went to the house of Mary the mother of John, also called Mark, where many people had gathered and were praying. ¹³Peter knocked at the outer entrance, and a servant girl named Rhoda came to answer the door. ¹⁴When she recognized Peter's voice, she was so overjoyed she ran back without opening it and exclaimed, "Peter is at the door!"

¹⁵"You're out of your mind," they told her. When she kept insisting that it was so, they said, "It must be his angel."

¹⁶But Peter kept on knocking, and when they opened the door and saw him, they were astonished. ¹⁷Peter motioned with his hand for them to be quiet and described how the Lord had brought him out of prison. "Tell James and the brothers about this," he said, and then he left for another place.

¹⁸In the morning, there was no small commotion among the soldiers as to what had become of Peter. ¹⁹After Herod had a thorough search made for him and did not find him, he cross-examined the guards and ordered that they be executed.

Herod's Death

Then Herod went from Judea to Caesarea and stayed there a while. ²⁰He had been quarreling with the people of Tyre and Sidon; they now joined together and sought an audience with him. Having secured the support of Blastus, a trusted personal servant of the king, they asked for peace, because they depended on the king's country for their food supply.

²¹On the appointed day Herod, wearing his royal robes, sat on his throne and delivered a public address to the people. ²²They shouted, "This is the voice of a god, not of a man." ²³Immediately, because Herod did not give praise to God, an angel of the Lord struck him down, and he was eaten by worms and died.

²⁴But the word of God continued to increase and spread.

²⁵When Barnabas and Saul had finished their mission, they returned from ' Jerusalem, taking with them John, also called Mark.

had been there? **3.** How do you feel about the fact that God saved Peter but not James? In light of John 21:18-19, how might Peter respond to this question? **4.** Who is John Mark in verses 12, 25 (see 15:37-39; 2Ti 4:11; and the gospel bearing his name)? **5.** Who is the James of verse 17 (see Gal 1:18-19)? Why do you think he is mentioned? What does this tell you about his importance in the Jerusalem church? **6.** Putting yourself in the place of the soldiers (v.18), what would you say to each other in the morning? **7.** In verses 20-22, what contrasts do you see between Herod's power and God's? **8.** What do you make of Herod's death (vv.21-23)? **9.** In this "Judea and Samaria" phase (ch.8-12) of God's plan (1:8), how has the church fared? What opposition has it faced so far? How far has it expanded?

REFLECT: **1.** Who truly has power here: Herod or the Lord of the church? What does this tell you about how Christians ought to deal with opposition and persecution? What worldly forces seem all-powerful to you? How does this chapter put them in perspective for you? **2.** How are you like the people at the prayer meeting in this story? What are some of your prayers that would surprise you if God answered affirmatively? **3.** Although Peter was miraculously rescued from prison, he went into hiding to avoid Herod. In leaving Jerusalem, do you think Peter acted: (a) With a lack of faith? (b) With common sense? (c) Within God's plan? Explain. **4.** Likewise, where do you see an overlap between God's power and human common sense in the ways things work out for your deliverance?

OPEN: 1. What did you feel the first time you "left home without it"? What was "it" that you missed most? **2.** Ever change your name or gone by a new name? Why?

DIG: 1. What was the scene when the Spirit spoke to the leaders at Antioch? How do you think he may have spoken? How could the Spirit speak in your worship times? **2.** Cyprus is a 150-mile sail from Seleucia, and was Barnabas' home (4:36). What might these two men be thinking and feeling as they go? **3.** Since Gentiles were already welcome in the church (11:18), why would Barnabas and Saul go to the synagogue? **4.** Put yourself in Elymas' place. How (and why) would you oppose these missionaries? If you were Sergius Paulus, what would be your response to the missionaries after the events of verses 9-12?

REFLECT: 1. With what types of people do you feel most comfortable talking about the Lord? Why? **2.** When have people tried to turn you from your faith? What happened? How do you deal with such pressures? **3.** When is it right to *strongly confront* people who oppose the faith?

OPEN: 1. Some great speeches in history are worth committing to memory, at least in part. What famous lines or stanzas can you recall? Spout off. **2.** Are you the kind of person that can commit things (names, birthdates, phone numbers, clothing sizes) to memory very easily? Sample quiz: Who in your group can recall the phone number of a previous residence where you once lived? **3.** What failure of memory is most embarrassing to you?

DIG: 1. From Cyprus to Pisidian Antioch is about 350 miles by sea and land. What does their willingness to travel so far show about Paul and Barnabas? Why do you think John Mark (12:12) may have left them to go back to his home? What consequence will this have for Paul and Barnabus later (see 15:36-41)? **2.** Compare verse 15 with verse 5: Why are they using

Barnabas and Saul Sent Off

13 In the church at Antioch there were prophets and teachers: Barnabas, Simeon called Niger, Lucius of Cyrene, Manaen (who had been brought up with Herod the tetrarch) and Saul. [2]While they were worshiping the Lord and fasting, the Holy Spirit said, "Set apart for me Barnabas and Saul for the work to which I have called them." [3]So after they had fasted and prayed, they placed their hands on them and sent them off.

On Cyprus

[4]The two of them, sent on their way by the Holy Spirit, went down to Seleucia and sailed from there to Cyprus. [5]When they arrived at Salamis, they proclaimed the word of God in the Jewish synagogues. John was with them as their helper.

[6]They traveled through the whole island until they came to Paphos. There they met a Jewish sorcerer and false prophet named Bar-Jesus, [7]who was an attendant of the proconsul, Sergius Paulus. The proconsul, an intelligent man, sent for Barnabas and Saul because he wanted to hear the word of God. [8]But Elymas the sorcerer (for that is what his name means) opposed them and tried to turn the proconsul from the faith. [9]Then Saul, who was also called Paul, filled with the Holy Spirit, looked straight at Elymas and said, [10]"You are a child of the devil and an enemy of everything that is right! You are full of all kinds of deceit and trickery. Will you never stop perverting the right ways of the Lord? [11]Now the hand of the Lord is against you. You are going to be blind, and for a time you will be unable to see the light of the sun."

Immediately mist and darkness came over him, and he groped about, seeking someone to lead him by the hand. [12]When the proconsul saw what had happened, he believed, for he was amazed at the teaching about the Lord.

In Pisidian Antioch

[13]From Paphos, Paul and his companions sailed to Perga in Pamphylia, where John left them to return to Jerusalem. [14]From Perga they went on to Pisidian Antioch. On the Sabbath they entered the synagogue and sat down. [15]After the reading from the Law and the Prophets, the synagogue rulers sent word to them, saying, "Brothers, if you have a message of encouragement for the people, please speak."

[16]Standing up, Paul motioned with his hand and said: "Men of Israel and you Gentiles who worship God, listen to me! [17]The God of the people of Israel chose our fathers; he made the people prosper during their stay in Egypt, with mighty power he led them out of that country, [18]he endured their conduct" for about forty years in the desert, [19]he overthrew seven nations in Canaan and gave their land to his people as their inheritance. [20]All this took about 450 years.

"After this, God gave them judges until the time of Samuel the prophet. [21]Then the people asked for a king, and he gave them Saul son of Kish, of the tribe of Benjamin, who ruled forty

"18 Some manuscripts and cared for them

years. ²²After removing Saul, he made David their king. He testified concerning him: 'I have found David son of Jesse a man after my own heart; he will do everything I want him to do.'

²³"From this man's descendants God has brought to Israel the Savior Jesus, as he promised. ²⁴Before the coming of Jesus, John preached repentance and baptism to all the people of Israel. ²⁵As John was completing his work, he said: 'Who do you think I am? I am not that one. No, but he is coming after me, whose sandals I am not worthy to untie.'

²⁶"Brothers, children of Abraham, and you God-fearing Gentiles, it is to us that this message of salvation has been sent. ²⁷The people of Jerusalem and their rulers did not recognize Jesus, yet in condemning him they fulfilled the words of the prophets that are read every Sabbath. ²⁸Though they found no proper ground for a death sentence, they asked Pilate to have him executed. ²⁹When they had carried out all that was written about him, they took him down from the tree and laid him in a tomb. ³⁰But God raised him from the dead, ³¹and for many days he was seen by those who had traveled with him from Galilee to Jerusalem. They are now his witnesses to our people.

³²"We tell you the good news: What God promised our fathers ³³he has fulfilled for us, their children, by raising up Jesus. As it is written in the second Psalm:

" 'You are my Son;
today I have become your Father. ᵛ ʷ

³⁴The fact that God raised him from the dead, never to decay, is stated in these words:

" 'I will give you the holy and sure blessings promised to David.' ˣ

³⁵So it is stated elsewhere:

" 'You will not let your Holy One see decay.' ʸ

³⁶"For when David had served God's purpose in his own generation, he fell asleep; he was buried with his fathers and his body decayed. ³⁷But the one whom God raised from the dead did not see decay.

³⁸"Therefore, my brothers, I want you to know that through Jesus the forgiveness of sins is proclaimed to you. ³⁹Through him everyone who believes is justified from everything you could not be justified from by the law of Moses. ⁴⁰Take care that what the prophets have said does not happen to you:

⁴¹" 'Look, you scoffers,
wonder and perish,
for I am going to do something in your days
that you would never believe,
even if someone told you.' ᶻ"

⁴²As Paul and Barnabas were leaving the synagogue, the people invited them to speak further about these things on the

this strategy? **3.** What is significant about Paul's audience? **4.** From verses 17-23, list all the things Paul says God has done. How do God's actions prepare the way for Paul to speak about Jesus in verse 23? **5.** Compare verses 22-23 and 36-37 with Romans 1:3 and Acts 2:29-31: What is the connection between David and Jesus? Why is this so important to Paul and Peter? **6.** What things about Jesus is Paul emphasizing by recalling three famous quotes in verses 33, 34, and 35? The resurrection is mentioned four times in verses 30-37. How does the resurrection confirm the meaning of these quotes? **7.** In verses 38-39, what does Paul say is the central meaning of the resurrection for his listeners? Compare verse 39 with Romans 3:20-24 and 8:3-4. From these verses, how would you explain what Paul means by being "justified"? **8.** Why would Paul end his sermon with this OT quote, "a warning of judgment" (v.41)? **9.** What feelings and emotions are created by this sermon in the various groups of people mentioned in verses 42-51? How do you explain such a variety of responses?

REFLECT: **1.** If you were to emphasize one central truth about the gospel, what would it be? Why? **2.** What difference would it make to your faith if there were no Easter to celebrate, but only a Good Friday to remember? **3.** How do you think Paul would respond to a modern-day skeptic who felt Jesus was a noble, but misguided, martyr? What role would the OT play in Paul's answer? How would knowing the OT, even memorizing it, help you to understand and share your faith better? **4.** What kind of opposition have you faced because of your faith? How do you usually respond to opposition? Does it make you stronger? Why? Would it be tougher for you to face opposition from community leaders or from family members? Why?

ᵛ33 Or *have begotten you*   ʷ33 Psalm 2:7   ˣ34 Isaiah 55:3   ʸ35 Psalm 16:10   ᶻ41 Hab. 1:5

next Sabbath. [43]When the congregation was dismissed, many of the Jews and devout converts to Judaism followed Paul and Barnabas, who talked with them and urged them to continue in the grace of God.

[44]On the next Sabbath almost the whole city gathered to hear the word of the Lord. [45]When the Jews saw the crowds, they were filled with jealousy and talked abusively against what Paul was saying.

[46]Then Paul and Barnabas answered them boldly: "We had to speak the word of God to you first. Since you reject it and do not consider yourselves worthy of eternal life, we now turn to the Gentiles. [47]For this is what the Lord has commanded us:

" 'I have made you[a] a light for the Gentiles,
    that you[a] may bring salvation to the ends of the
      earth.'[b]"

[48]When the Gentiles heard this, they were glad and honored the word of the Lord; and all who were appointed for eternal life believed.

[49]The word of the Lord spread through the whole region. [50]But the Jews incited the God-fearing women of high standing and the leading men of the city. They stirred up persecution against Paul and Barnabas, and expelled them from their region. [51]So they shook the dust from their feet in protest against them and went to Iconium. [52]And the disciples were filled with joy and with the Holy Spirit.

In Iconium

14 At Iconium Paul and Barnabas went as usual into the Jewish synagogue. There they spoke so effectively that a great number of Jews and Gentiles believed. [2]But the Jews who refused to believe stirred up the Gentiles and poisoned their minds against the brothers. [3]So Paul and Barnabas spent considerable time there, speaking boldly for the Lord, who confirmed the message of his grace by enabling them to do miraculous signs and wonders. [4]The people of the city were divided; some sided with the Jews, others with the apostles. [5]There was a plot afoot among the Gentiles and Jews, together with their leaders, to mistreat them and stone them. [6]But they found out about it and fled to the Lycaonian cities of Lystra and Derbe and to the surrounding country, [7]where they continued to preach the good news.

In Lystra and Derbe

[8]In Lystra there sat a man crippled in his feet, who was lame from birth and had never walked. [9]He listened to Paul as he was speaking. Paul looked directly at him, saw that he had faith to be healed [10]and called out, "Stand up on your feet!" At that, the man jumped up and began to walk.

[11]When the crowd saw what Paul had done, they shouted in the Lycaonian language, "The gods have come down to us in human form!" [12]Barnabas they called Zeus, and Paul they called

---

OPEN: 1. In your youthful idealism, for what social, political or religious causes were you willing to "go to the mat," if need be? Did you ever have to? **2.** What was it like for you to take your first "1000-miles-from-home" trip?

DIG: 1. How does Paul and Barnabas' experience in Iconium differ from their experience in Antioch? How is it similar? **2.** What is the purpose of signs and wonders here (see also 6:8)? Why are the people divided (v.4)? **3.** What was religious life like in Lystra? **4.** Compare 14:8-13 with 3:1-11. How are the two stories alike and different? What results from each healing? **5.** What does Paul emphasize about God in his speech? How is his speech to this crowd (vv.15-17) different from his previous sermon in the synagogue (see 13:17-41)? Why the difference? **6.** Since Antioch was 100 miles away, what does that tell you about the nature of Paul's opposition? **7.** From verses 19-20, how would you characterize Paul? His supporters? How do you suppose they now feel about John's desertion at Perga (13:14)? **8.** How would you feel if you were one of these new believers (vv.21-25) after you had heard about the

---

[a]47 The Greek is singular.   [b]47 Isaiah 49:6

Hermes because he was the chief speaker. [13]The priest of Zeus, whose temple was just outside the city, brought bulls and wreaths to the city gates because he and the crowd wanted to offer sacrifices to them.

[14]But when the apostles Barnabas and Paul heard of this, they tore their clothes and rushed out into the crowd, shouting: [15]"Men, why are you doing this? We too are only men, human like you. We are bringing you good news, telling you to turn from these worthless things to the living God, who made heaven and earth and sea and everything in them. [16]In the past, he let all nations go their own way. [17]Yet he has not left himself without testimony: He has shown kindness by giving you rain from heaven and crops in their seasons; he provides you with plenty of food and fills your hearts with joy." [18]Even with these words, they had difficulty keeping the crowd from sacrificing to them.

[19]Then some Jews came from Antioch and Iconium and won the crowd over. They stoned Paul and dragged him outside the city, thinking he was dead. [20]But after the disciples had gathered around him, he got up and went back into the city. The next day he and Barnabas left for Derbe.

The Return to Antioch in Syria

[21]They preached the good news in that city and won a large number of disciples. Then they returned to Lystra, Iconium and Antioch, [22]strengthening the disciples and encouraging them to remain true to the faith. "We must go through many hardships to enter the kingdom of God," they said. [23]Paul and Barnabas appointed elders[c] for them in each church and, with prayer and fasting, committed them to the Lord, in whom they had put their trust. [24]After going through Pisidia, they came into Pamphylia, [25]and when they had preached the word in Perga, they went down to Attalia.

[26]From Attalia they sailed back to Antioch, where they had been committed to the grace of God for the work they had now completed. [27]On arriving there, they gathered the church together and reported all that God had done through them and how he had opened the door of faith to the Gentiles. [28]And they stayed there a long time with the disciples.

The Council at Jerusalem

15 Some men came down from Judea to Antioch and were teaching the brothers: "Unless you are circumcised, according to the custom taught by Moses, you cannot be saved." [2]This brought Paul and Barnabas into sharp dispute and debate with them. So Paul and Barnabas were appointed, along with some other believers, to go up to Jerusalem to see the apostles and elders about this question. [3]The church sent them on their way, and as they traveled through Phoenicia and Samaria, they told how the Gentiles had been converted. This news made all the brothers very glad. [4]When they came to Jerusalem, they were welcomed by the church and the apostles and elders, to

treatment Paul and Barnabas had received? **9.** From what they have seen in Paul and Barnabas, what would these new elders realize about their job? **10.** Reviewing this journey of about 1100 miles (13:1-14:26), what do you learn about Paul? About the gospel?

REFLECT: 1. Seeing Paul and Barnabas' courage, faith, and endurance, how are you challenged to serve the Lord more completely? **2.** What does the difference between Paul's sermon (13:17-41) and his speech in verses 15-17 teach you about sharing your faith with various groups of people? **3.** The people Paul and Barnabas encountered along the way interpreted the gospel through their own lenses, even calling them Hermes and Zeus. How do people you know interpret the gospel by their own prejudices and beliefs? **4.** What was one of the biggest misunderstandings about Christianity you had to overcome before you could believe?

OPEN: 1. In the church circles you grew up in, what were some of the extra-biblical rules imposed on you, or what cultural manners and morals were expected of you? **2.** When you first became a Christian (or when you joined the church you're in), what behavioral norms were expected of you?

DIG: 1. What other things would these teachers say are necessary for the Gentiles to do (vv.1, 5; see Mk 2:16, 18, 24; 7:1-5)? **2.** If you were a Gentile hearing that these regulations were required, how would you feel about your

[c]23 Or Barnabas ordained elders; or Barnabas had elders elected

faith? As a strict Jew, why would these things be important to you? **3.** What is the main issue as Paul sees it (v.2; see Gal 2:21; 3:5; 3:10-14)? **4.** How would you describe Peter's struggle with this issue (vv.7-11; see 10:28, 34-35; Gal 2:11-13)? How does Paul's teaching in Galatians 2:15-16 show its influence on Peter here? **5.** Knowing Paul's Pharisaic background (26:5) and Peter's desire to keep the law (10:14), how would their testimony carry the day? **6.** What is James' position in the matter (vv.13-21; also Gal 1:19)? What has led him to change his mind? **7.** What is the significance of the council's decision in light of 1:8? Why were the conditions of verse 20 added (see 1Co 8, where Paul dealt with a similar controversy)?

REFLECT: 1. What roles do experience, theology, and practical considerations play in the decision-making process of this council? What issues, now troubling your church, could be resolved by looking at them with these three realities in mind? **2.** Is there some area of your faith where you feel like Peter—going back and forth because you are not sure of what is right? How could verse 11 relate to this concern? **3.** What "add-ons" to the gospel might a new believer sense in your church? What should you do about that?

OPEN: What experience have you had worshiping where the style is historically different from yours (Catholic-Protestant, black-white, Pentecostal-traditional)?

DIG: 1. Why would a letter *and* representatives from the Jerusalem church be a good way to communicate the apostles' decision? **2.** What is the tone of the letter? Its main points? **3.** How do Judas and Silas personally add to this letter? What else brings unity to the primarily Jewish church in Jerusalem and the primarily Gentile church in Antioch? How would things be different if those in 15:5 had won out?

whom they reported everything God had done through them.

[5]Then some of the believers who belonged to the party of the Pharisees stood up and said, "The Gentiles must be circumcised and required to obey the law of Moses."

[6]The apostles and elders met to consider this question. [7]After much discussion, Peter got up and addressed them: "Brothers, you know that some time ago God made a choice among you that the Gentiles might hear from my lips the message of the gospel and believe. [8]God, who knows the heart, showed that he accepted them by giving the Holy Spirit to them, just as he did to us. [9]He made no distinction between us and them, for he purified their hearts by faith. [10]Now then, why do you try to test God by putting on the necks of the disciples a yoke that neither we nor our fathers have been able to bear? [11]No! We believe it is through the grace of our Lord Jesus that we are saved, just as they are."

[12]The whole assembly became silent as they listened to Barnabas and Paul telling about the miraculous signs and wonders God had done among the Gentiles through them. [13]When they finished, James spoke up: "Brothers, listen to me. [14]Simon[d] has described to us how God at first showed his concern by taking from the Gentiles a people for himself. [15]The words of the prophets are in agreement with this, as it is written:

[16]" 'After this I will return
and rebuild David's fallen tent.
Its ruins I will rebuild,
and I will restore it,
[17]that the remnant of men may seek the Lord,
and all the Gentiles who bear my name,
says the Lord, who does these things'[e]
[18]   that have been known for ages.[f]

[19]"It is my judgment, therefore, that we should not make it difficult for the Gentiles who are turning to God. [20]Instead we should write to them, telling them to abstain from food polluted by idols, from sexual immorality, from the meat of strangled animals and from blood. [21]For Moses has been preached in every city from the earliest times and is read in the synagogues on every Sabbath."

The Council's Letter to Gentile Believers

[22]Then the apostles and elders, with the whole church, decided to choose some of their own men and send them to Antioch with Paul and Barnabas. They chose Judas (called Barsabbas) and Silas, two men who were leaders among the brothers. [23]With them they sent the following letter:

The apostles and elders, your brothers,

To the Gentile believers in Antioch, Syria and Cilicia:

Greetings.

---

[d]14 Greek *Simeon*, a variant of *Simon;* that is, Peter   [e]17 Amos 9:11,12
[f]17,18 Some manuscripts *things'*— / [18]*known to the Lord for ages is his work*

²⁴We have heard that some went out from us without our authorization and disturbed you, troubling your minds by what they said. ²⁵So we all agreed to choose some men and send them to you with our dear friends Barnabas and Paul— ²⁶men who have risked their lives for the name of our Lord Jesus Christ. ²⁷Therefore we are sending Judas and Silas to confirm by word of mouth what we are writing. ²⁸It seemed good to the Holy Spirit and to us not to burden you with anything beyond the following requirements: ²⁹You are to abstain from food sacrificed to idols, from blood, from the meat of strangled animals and from sexual immorality. You will do well to avoid these things.

Farewell.

³⁰The men were sent off and went down to Antioch, where they gathered the church together and delivered the letter. ³¹The people read it and were glad for its encouraging message. ³²Judas and Silas, who themselves were prophets, said much to encourage and strengthen the brothers. ³³After spending some time there, they were sent off by the brothers with the blessing of peace to return to those who had sent them.ᵍ ³⁵But Paul and Barnabas remained in Antioch, where they and many others taught and preached the word of the Lord.

Disagreement Between Paul and Barnabas

³⁶Some time later Paul said to Barnabas, "Let us go back and visit the brothers in all the towns where we preached the word of the Lord and see how they are doing." ³⁷Barnabas wanted to take John, also called Mark, with them, ³⁸but Paul did not think it wise to take him, because he had deserted them in Pamphylia and had not continued with them in the work. ³⁹They had such a sharp disagreement that they parted company. Barnabas took Mark and sailed for Cyprus, ⁴⁰but Paul chose Silas and left, commended by the brothers to the grace of the Lord. ⁴¹He went through Syria and Cilicia, strengthening the churches.

Timothy Joins Paul and Silas

16 He came to Derbe and then to Lystra, where a disciple named Timothy lived, whose mother was a Jewess and a believer, but whose father was a Greek. ²The brothers at Lystra and Iconium spoke well of him. ³Paul wanted to take him along on the journey, so he circumcised him because of the Jews who lived in that area, for they all knew that his father was a Greek. ⁴As they traveled from town to town, they delivered the decisions reached by the apostles and elders in Jerusalem for the people to obey. ⁵So the churches were strengthened in the faith and grew daily in numbers.

REFLECT: 1. From the debate, the resulting letter, and the way in which it was delivered, what do you learn about the way to solve disagreements among Christians? How is your style of handling disagreements like (and unlike) the way the issue was handled in chapter 15? **2.** In your community's churches, what are the ethnic, social, and racial lines of division? What is your relationship like with believers in these different churches? How can verses 30-33 be a model for unity within diversity among these churches? In light of 1:8, how important is it to work for this type of relationship?

OPEN: What "break-up" was hardest for you and why: Moving? Losing your first girl/boy friend? Empty nest? Closing shop?

DIG: 1. Role play how you think Paul and Barnabas split up. With which one would you have sided? Why? **2.** Given the decision to reject the teachings of those in 15:1, why did Paul circumcise Timothy? How could this be justified (see 1Co 9:19-23)?

REFLECT: 1. When have you given up your "rights" in order to better represent Christ to others? How can you do so now? **2.** Are you more *person*-oriented (like Barnabus) or *task*-oriented (like Paul)? What are the pros and cons of your type? What does this show you about God's use of various types of people?

ᵍ33 Some manuscripts them, ³⁴but Silas decided to remain there

OPEN: Where do you buy most of your clothes? Why there? What color do you look best in? Do you try things on first, several options, or buy on sight?

DIG: 1. Note the change from "they" (v.8) to "we" (v.10): How does this relate to Luke 1:3-4? 2. How is this closed door (v.7) pivotal? 3. Compare verse 13 with 14:1 and 17:2. What does the fact that there was no synagogue in Philippi mean with respect to the Jewish community there? How did that affect Paul's strategy for mission? 4. What do you make of Lydia's career and conversion?

REFLECT: 1. How did the Lord open your heart to respond to the gospel? What people did he use as part of the process? 2. Where do you have an "open door" for ministry now: In your home? School? Work? Community? How will you take advantage of it?

OPEN: What type of music lifts your spirits? What music reminds you of the "good ol' days"?

DIG: 1. How would you feel if this servant-girl was following you around making this announcement? What influence might her true statement actually have on these missionaries' effectiveness? 2. Retell verses 17-21 from the perspective of the owners of the girl: What do you feel about her? About your money? About these missionaries? 3. Since there was no synagogue in Philippi (v.13), and since the Gentile missionaries (Luke and Timothy) were not seized, how could racism be a factor in the actions described in verses 19-24? What might be meant by the charge against them? 4. If you were falsely accused, severely beaten, and thrown into a dark jail, would you still trust that God had called you to go to this place (16:9-10)? Why or why not? 5. What does the response of Paul and Silas show about them? If you were the jailer, what would you think of Paul and Silas singing? Escaping? Remaining? 6. In what ways does the jailer express his new faith in Jesus? 7. Given

Paul's Vision of the Man of Macedonia

6Paul and his companions traveled throughout the region of Phrygia and Galatia, having been kept by the Holy Spirit from preaching the word in the province of Asia. 7When they came to the border of Mysia, they tried to enter Bithynia, but the Spirit of Jesus would not allow them to. 8So they passed by Mysia and went down to Troas. 9During the night Paul had a vision of a man of Macedonia standing and begging him, "Come over to Macedonia and help us." 10After Paul had seen the vision, we got ready at once to leave for Macedonia, concluding that God had called us to preach the gospel to them.

Lydia's Conversion in Philippi

11From Troas we put out to sea and sailed straight for Samothrace, and the next day on to Neapolis. 12From there we traveled to Philippi, a Roman colony and the leading city of that district of Macedonia. And we stayed there several days.

13On the Sabbath we went outside the city gate to the river, where we expected to find a place of prayer. We sat down and began to speak to the women who had gathered there. 14One of those listening was a woman named Lydia, a dealer in purple cloth from the city of Thyatira, who was a worshiper of God. The Lord opened her heart to respond to Paul's message. 15When she and the members of her household were baptized, she invited us to her home. "If you consider me a believer in the Lord," she said, "come and stay at my house." And she persuaded us.

Paul and Silas in Prison

16Once when we were going to the place of prayer, we were met by a slave girl who had a spirit by which she predicted the future. She earned a great deal of money for her owners by fortune-telling. 17This girl followed Paul and the rest of us, shouting, "These men are servants of the Most High God, who are telling you the way to be saved." 18She kept this up for many days. Finally Paul became so troubled that he turned around and said to the spirit, "In the name of Jesus Christ I command you to come out of her!" At that moment the spirit left her.

19When the owners of the slave girl realized that their hope of making money was gone, they seized Paul and Silas and dragged them into the marketplace to face the authorities. 20They brought them before the magistrates and said, "These men are Jews, and are throwing our city into an uproar 21by advocating customs unlawful for us Romans to accept or practice."

22The crowd joined in the attack against Paul and Silas, and the magistrates ordered them to be stripped and beaten. 23After they had been severely flogged, they were thrown into prison, and the jailer was commanded to guard them carefully. 24Upon receiving such orders, he put them in the inner cell and fastened their feet in the stocks.

25About midnight Paul and Silas were praying and singing hymns to God, and the other prisoners were listening to them. 26Suddenly there was such a violent earthquake that the foundations of the prison were shaken. At once all the prison doors flew open, and everybody's chains came loose. ²⁷The jailer woke up, and when he saw the prison doors open, he drew his sword and was about to kill himself because he thought the prisoners had escaped. ²⁸But Paul shouted, "Don't harm yourself! We are all here!"

²⁹The jailer called for lights, rushed in and fell trembling before Paul and Silas. ³⁰He then brought them out and asked, "Sirs, what must I do to be saved?"

³¹They replied, "Believe in the Lord Jesus, and you will be saved—you and your household." ³²Then they spoke the word of the Lord to him and to all the others in his house. ³³At that hour of the night the jailer took them and washed their wounds; then immediately he and all his family were baptized. ³⁴The jailer brought them into his house and set a meal before them; he was filled with joy because he had come to believe in God—he and his whole family.

³⁵When it was daylight, the magistrates sent their officers to the jailer with the order: "Release those men." ³⁶The jailer told Paul, "The magistrates have ordered that you and Silas be released. Now you can leave. Go in peace."

³⁷But Paul said to the officers: "They beat us publicly without a trial, even though we are Roman citizens, and threw us into prison. And now do they want to get rid of us quietly? No! Let them come themselves and escort us out."

³⁸The officers reported this to the magistrates, and when they heard that Paul and Silas were Roman citizens, they were alarmed. ³⁹They came to appease them and escorted them from the prison, requesting them to leave the city. ⁴⁰After Paul and Silas came out of the prison, they went to Lydia's house, where they met with the brothers and encouraged them. Then they left.

In Thessalonica

17 When they had passed through Amphipolis and Apollonia, they came to Thessalonica, where there was a Jewish synagogue. ²As his custom was, Paul went into the synagogue, and on three Sabbath days he reasoned with them from the Scriptures, ³explaining and proving that the Christ ʰ had to suffer and rise from the dead. "This Jesus I am proclaiming to you is the Christ, ʰ" he said. ⁴Some of the Jews were persuaded and joined Paul and Silas, as did a large number of God-fearing Greeks and not a few prominent women.

⁵But the Jews were jealous; so they rounded up some bad characters from the marketplace, formed a mob and started a riot in the city. They rushed to Jason's house in search of Paul and Silas in order to bring them out to the crowd. ⁱ ⁶But when they did not find them, they dragged Jason and some other brothers before the city officials, shouting: "These men who have caused trouble all over the world have now come here, ⁷and Jason has welcomed them into his house. They are all defying Caesar's decrees, saying that there is another king, one called

ʰ3 Or *Messiah*   ⁱ5 Or *the assembly of the people*

the charge against them (vv.20-21), why would Paul insist on his rights as a Roman citizen? (Note: Most residents in the Roman empire did not have the privilege of citizenship.) How would this diffuse tensions for the young Philippian church?

REFLECT: 1. The girl's owners rejected the gospel because it cost them financially. What financial concerns keep some people from faith today? Are any of these a factor for you? **2.** About 12 years later, Paul wrote the letter to the Philippians from another prison. How could the events here be the basis for what Paul said in Philippians 4:4-7, 12-13? What can you learn from his example about knowing peace and joy, even in hard times? **3.** If asked, "What must I do to be saved?", how would you answer? **4.** What can you learn from the disciples' experiences that will help you as you encounter difficult times?

OPEN: In your experience of the *marketplace*, have you met more "good characters" (benefactors, role models, mentors) or "bad characters" (mafia, con-artists, shop-lifters)? Explain.

DIG: 1. Thessalonica was a wealthy trading city on a major road from the Adriatic Sea to the Black Sea (see map). How is Paul received (see 1 Th 1:4-10; 3:1-4)? **2.** What accusations has Paul encountered so far (vv.5-7; also 16:20-21)? What lies behind these accusations? **3.** Since his conversion, this is the sixth time Paul has been forced by persecution to leave an area. How would you view your mission if that happened to you? How does your response compare with Paul's (see 1 Th 2:1-6)? **4.** Compared with the Thessalonians (vv.2-4), how do the Bereans receive the gospel (vv.11-12)? **5.** How is Paul's teaching on the diversity of gifts (1 Co 12) illustrated here in the functions of Paul, Silas, and Timothy?

REFLECT: 1. Whether Jesus or Caesar was Lord became a real issue for Christians a few years later. When has your faith in Christ led to conflict with other authorities claiming your loyalty? 2. In terms of time, consistency, and intensity, how would you rate your Bible study? Is it at all like the Bereans?

OPEN: If someone made a statue of you, what pose would be most appropriate? What inscription?

DIG: 1. To be noticed by these Greek philosophers, how extensive must Paul's activity have been? 2. What are these philosophers like (vv.18-21)? Since they thought "Jesus" and "Resurrection" were two gods, what is their prior understanding of Christianity? 3. The Stoics believed "god" was in everything and so everything was "god" (pantheism), while the Epicureans had little or no belief in "god" at all. What does Paul emphasize about God (vv.23-30)? How does Paul use their own culture to help them see the weaknesses in the way they relate to deity? 4. How is this sermon unlike that in 13:16-41? In not using Scripture here, is that a strength or a weakness? Why? How are the sermons alike in terms of what they teach about Jesus? In what they call people to do? 5. How does the response in Athens (17:21,32-34) compare with Berea (17:12) and Thessalonica (17:4)?

REFLECT: 1. What distresses you spiritually about the area in which you live? What specific needs do you see? What do you feel God is calling you to do about them? 2. Who do you know that has very little or no background in the gospel? How would your witness to them be different than to someone out of a church background? 3. Paul uses idols and Greek poetry as points of contact between these people and the gospel. How can

Jesus." [8]When they heard this, the crowd and the city officials were thrown into turmoil. [9]Then they made Jason and the others post bond and let them go.

In Berea

[10]As soon as it was night, the brothers sent Paul and Silas away to Berea. On arriving there, they went to the Jewish synagogue. [11]Now the Bereans were of more noble character than the Thessalonians, for they received the message with great eagerness and examined the Scriptures every day to see if what Paul said was true. [12]Many of the Jews believed, as did also a number of prominent Greek women and many Greek men.

[13]When the Jews in Thessalonica learned that Paul was preaching the word of God at Berea, they went there too, agitating the crowds and stirring them up. [14]The brothers immediately sent Paul to the coast, but Silas and Timothy stayed at Berea. [15]The men who escorted Paul brought him to Athens and then left with instructions for Silas and Timothy to join him as soon as possible.

In Athens

[16]While Paul was waiting for them in Athens, he was greatly distressed to see that the city was full of idols. [17]So he reasoned in the synagogue with the Jews and the God-fearing Greeks, as well as in the marketplace day by day with those who happened to be there. [18]A group of Epicurean and Stoic philosophers began to dispute with him. Some of them asked, "What is this babbler trying to say?" Others remarked, "He seems to be advocating foreign gods." They said this because Paul was preaching the good news about Jesus and the resurrection. [19]Then they took him and brought him to a meeting of the Areopagus, where they said to him, "May we know what this new teaching is that you are presenting? [20]You are bringing some strange ideas to our ears, and we want to know what they mean." [21](All the Athenians and the foreigners who lived there spent their time doing nothing but talking about and listening to the latest ideas.)

[22]Paul then stood up in the meeting of the Areopagus and said: "Men of Athens! I see that in every way you are very religious. [23]For as I walked around and looked carefully at your objects of worship, I even found an altar with this inscription: TO AN UNKNOWN GOD. Now what you worship as something unknown I am going to proclaim to you.

[24]"The God who made the world and everything in it is the Lord of heaven and earth and does not live in temples built by hands. [25]And he is not served by human hands, as if he needed anything, because he himself gives all men life and breath and everything else. [26]From one man he made every nation of men, that they should inhabit the whole earth; and he determined the times set for them and the exact places where they should live. [27]God did this so that men would seek him and perhaps reach out for him and find him, though he is not far from each one of us. [28]'For in him we live and move and have our being.' As some of your own poets have said, 'We are his offspring.'

²⁹"Therefore since we are God's offspring, we should not think that the divine being is like gold or silver or stone—an image made by man's design and skill. ³⁰In the past God overlooked such ignorance, but now he commands all people everywhere to repent. ³¹For he has set a day when he will judge the world with justice by the man he has appointed. He has given proof of this to all men by raising him from the dead."

³²When they heard about the resurrection of the dead, some of them sneered, but others said, "We want to hear you again on this subject." ³³At that, Paul left the Council. ³⁴A few men became followers of Paul and believed. Among them was Dionysius, a member of the Areopagus, also a woman named Damaris, and a number of others.

In Corinth

18 After this, Paul left Athens and went to Corinth. ²There he met a Jew named Aquila a native of Pontus, who had recently come from Italy with his wife Priscilla, because Claudius had ordered all the Jews to leave Rome. Paul went to see them, ³and because he was a tentmaker as they were, he stayed and worked with them. ⁴Every Sabbath he reasoned in the synagogue, trying to persuade Jews and Greeks.

⁵When Silas and Timothy came from Macedonia, Paul devoted himself exclusively to preaching, testifying to the Jews that Jesus was the Christ.ʲ ⁶But when the Jews opposed Paul and became abusive, he shook out his clothes in protest and said to them, "Your blood be on your own heads! I am clear of my responsibility. From now on I will go to the Gentiles."

⁷Then Paul left the synagogue and went next door to the house of Titius Justus, a worshiper of God. ⁸Crispus, the synagogue ruler, and his entire household believed in the Lord; and many of the Corinthians who heard him believed and were baptized.

⁹One night the Lord spoke to Paul in a vision: "Do not be afraid; keep on speaking, do not be silent. ¹⁰For I am with you, and no one is going to attack and harm you, because I have many people in this city." ¹¹So Paul stayed for a year and a half, teaching them the word of God.

¹²While Gallio was proconsul of Achaia, the Jews made a united attack on Paul and brought him into court. ¹³"This man," they charged, "is persuading the people to worship God in ways contrary to the law."

¹⁴Just as Paul was about to speak, Gallio said to the Jews, "If you Jews were making a complaint about some misdemeanor or serious crime, it would be reasonable for me to listen to you. ¹⁵But since it involves questions about words and names and your own law—settle the matter yourselves. I will not be a judge of such things." ¹⁶So he had them ejected from the court. ¹⁷Then they all turned on Sosthenes the synagogue ruler and beat him in front of the court. But Gallio showed no concern whatever.

you use movies, books, TV shows, music, etc., as a way of relating the gospel more effectively to others today?

OPEN: 1. Do you prefer working by yourself or with other people? Why? **2.** What practical manual skill of yours might earn you some money if you did it "full time"?

DIG: 1. Claudius' order (v.2) was given in 50 A.D. after a Jewish riot in Rome over the preaching of Christ there. What else reveals the Roman attitude toward Christianity (vv.12-17)? Would this help or hinder Christian witness? **2.** How did Paul's ministry change after Timothy and Silas came to him (see Php 2:20-22; 4:15-16)? **3.** What happened to Crispus' successor, Sothenes (v.17; see 1Co 1:1)? What effect would these two conversions have on the Jewish community? **4.** How might Paul feel about the beginning of his ministry at Corinth (see 1Co 2:3)? How might the vision from God (vv.9-10) and the gift from the Philippians encourage him?

REFLECT: 1. With what missions or missionaries have you entered into financial partnership? If you were called to the foreign mission field, would you seek such partners, or would you become a "tentmaker"? Why? **2.** How could your present job be "tentmaking" to support your family while you engaged in God's kingdom work?

ʲ5 Or *Messiah;* also in verse 28

OPEN: 1. What do you like best about returning home after a long trip? What do you dread the most? 2. Which of your recent vacation or business spots on the road would be the first you'd return to on your own? Why?

DIG: 1. Verses 18-23 sum up a lot of traveling (see map). How far did Paul travel at this time? 2. What do you make of his companions Priscilla and Aquila? What type of person was Apollos (vv.24-26)? 3. What influence did Apollos have in Achaia, specifically Corinth (vv.27-28; see 1Co 3:4-6)? How effective would he be in the intellectual circles there?

REFLECT: 1. Who was very helpful to you when you were young and enthusiastic about the faith? How did this person help? Who could you be helping now? How? 2. Where do you sense God has equipped you to serve? How can you do so this week? 3. How does your church balance evangelism with the strengthening and equipping of believers?

OPEN: 1. What experiences (reading, meeting, testing) have you had with religious counterfeits (relics, forgeries, hoaxes, cults, and the like)? Any that have really scared you? 2. When and where were you baptized?

DIG: 1. Why do you think Paul headed right to Ephesus on his next trip (see 18:19-21)? 2. Apollos was from Egypt (18:24), and these disciples were about 800 miles from Jerusalem. What does the fact that they were followers of John the Baptist tell you about the extent of his influence? How would their awareness of John be good preparation for them to hear the gospel (see Jn 1:19-34)? 3. Since Paul had to teach these people about Jesus (v.4), they apparently had not heard about him or the Spirit (v.2). From 2:38 and 10:43-44 (as well as this section) what do you learn about the relationship between faith in Jesus and receiving the Spirit? 4. What seems to be the signal throughout Acts for Paul to stop teaching in the synagogues? Why do you

Priscilla, Aquila and Apollos

[18]Paul stayed on in Corinth for some time. Then he left the brothers and sailed for Syria, accompanied by Priscilla and Aquila. Before he sailed, he had his hair cut off at Cenchrea because of a vow he had taken. [19]They arrived at Ephesus, where Paul left Priscilla and Aquila. He himself went into the synagogue and reasoned with the Jews. [20]When they asked him to spend more time with them, he declined. [21]But as he left, he promised, "I will come back if it is God's will." Then he set sail from Ephesus. [22]When he landed at Caesarea, he went up and greeted the church and then went down to Antioch.

[23]After spending some time in Antioch, Paul set out from there and traveled from place to place throughout the region of Galatia and Phrygia, strengthening all the disciples.

[24]Meanwhile a Jew named Apollos, a native of Alexandria, came to Ephesus. He was a learned man, with a thorough knowledge of the Scriptures. [25]He had been instructed in the way of the Lord, and he spoke with great fervor[k] and taught about Jesus accurately, though he knew only the baptism of John. [26]He began to speak boldly in the synagogue. When Priscilla and Aquila heard him, they invited him to their home and explained to him the way of God more adequately.

[27]When Apollos wanted to go to Achaia, the brothers encouraged him and wrote to the disciples there to welcome him. On arriving, he was a great help to those who by grace had believed. [28]For he vigorously refuted the Jews in public debate, proving from the Scriptures that Jesus was the Christ.

Paul in Ephesus

19 While Apollos was at Corinth, Paul took the road through the interior and arrived at Ephesus. There he found some disciples [2]and asked them, "Did you receive the Holy Spirit when[l] you believed?"

They answered, "No, we have not even heard that there is a Holy Spirit."

[3]So Paul asked, "Then what baptism did you receive?"

"John's baptism," they replied.

[4]Paul said, "John's baptism was a baptism of repentance. He told the people to believe in the one coming after him, that is, in Jesus." [5]On hearing this, they were baptized into[m] the name of the Lord Jesus. [6]When Paul placed his hands on them, the Holy Spirit came on them, and they spoke in tongues[n] and prophesied. [7]There were about twelve men in all.

[8]Paul entered the synagogue and spoke boldly there for three months, arguing persuasively about the kingdom of God. [9]But some of them became obstinate; they refused to believe and publicly maligned the Way. So Paul left them. He took the disciples with him and had discussions daily in the lecture hall of Tyrannus. [10]This went on for two years, so that all the Jews and Greeks who lived in the province of Asia heard the word of the Lord.

k25 Or with fervor in the Spirit   *l2 Or after*   *m5 Or in*   *n6 Or other languages*

[11]God did extraordinary miracles through Paul, [12]so that even handkerchiefs and aprons that had touched him were taken to the sick, and their illnesses were cured and the evil spirits left them.

[13]Some Jews who went around driving out evil spirits tried to invoke the name of the Lord Jesus over those who were demon-possessed. They would say, "In the name of Jesus, whom Paul preaches, I command you to come out." [14]Seven sons of Sceva, a Jewish chief priest, were doing this. [15]One day, the evil spirit answered them, "Jesus I know, and I know about Paul, but who are you?" [16]Then the man who had the evil spirit jumped on them and overpowered them all. He gave them such a beating that they ran out of the house naked and bleeding.

[17]When this became known to the Jews and Greeks living in Ephesus, they were all seized with fear, and the name of the Lord Jesus was held in high honor. [18]Many of those who believed now came and openly confessed their evil deeds. [19]A number who had practiced sorcery brought their scrolls together and burned them publicly. When they calculated the value of the scrolls, the total came to fifty thousand drachmas. [o] [20]In this way the word of the Lord spread widely and grew in power.

[21]After all this had happened, Paul decided to go to Jerusalem, passing through Macedonia and Achaia. "After I have been there," he said, "I must visit Rome also." [22]He sent two of his helpers, Timothy and Erastus, to Macedonia, while he stayed in the province of Asia a little longer.

The Riot in Ephesus

[23]About that time there arose a great disturbance about the Way. [24]A silversmith named Demetrius, who made silver shrines of Artemis, brought in no little business for the craftsmen. [25]He called them together, along with the workmen in related trades, and said: "Men, you know we receive a good income from this business. [26]And you see and hear how this fellow Paul has convinced and led astray large numbers of people here in Ephesus and in practically the whole province of Asia. He says that man-made gods are no gods at all. [27]There is danger not only that our trade will lose its good name, but also that the temple of the great goddess Artemis will be discredited, and the goddess herself, who is worshiped throughout the province of Asia and the world, will be robbed of her divine majesty."

[28]When they heard this, they were furious and began shouting: "Great is Artemis of the Ephesians!" [29]Soon the whole city was in an uproar. The people seized Gaius Aristarchus, Paul's traveling companions from Macedonia, and rushed as one man into the theater. [30]Paul wanted to appear before the crowd, but the disciples would not let him. [31]Even some of the officials of the province, friends of Paul, sent him a message begging him not to venture into the theater.

[32]The assembly was in confusion: Some were shouting one thing, some another. Most of the people did not even know why

think this is so? What do these "stop and go" signals teach you about ministry in general? **5.** Compare verses 8-9 with 13-15: How do these two groups of Jews view Jesus differently? If you were one of Sceva's sons, what would you say about Jesus after being jumped by this evil spirit (v.16)? **6.** From the reaction of the crowd in verses 17-19, how would you describe the general response to Jesus prior to verses 13-16? Why would those events change people's ideas so much?

REFLECT: **1.** How do people try to use Jesus for their own purposes today? What is the difference between that and real faith in Christ? **2.** What did you have to change in your lifestyle when you first began to follow Jesus? Are there some things you are reluctant to burn now in order to be really honest with God? What would it cost you to burn them?

OPEN: In your experience, is the *pen* (rational discourse, judicial review, preaching) mightier than the *sword* (mob looting, strong-arm politics, police tactics)? Why?

DIG: **1.** Why would Demetrius rally people against Paul (vv. 25-27; see 17:24-29)? Since this temple was one of the seven wonders of the ancient world, what businesses would Paul be affecting? **2.** Role play a TV interviewer in the crowd (vv.32-34). What do they see and hear? Why are they there? Why are the Jews trying to get a speaker to represent them? Why would he be shouted down? **3.** How do the concerns of the city clerk and Demetrius compare?

REFLECT: **1.** Success, money, and independence are some cultural "idols" (values most people accept without question). What others come to mind? How has your faith affected your relationship to these idols? **2.** Could Demetrius have become a Christian *and* kept his business? Can you think of situations today where someone in a "respectable" trade would be forced to choose between that

[o]19 A drachma was a silver coin worth about a day's wages.

trade and Christ? What pressures would that cause? **3.** Where have you seen religious and patriotic loyalties used as a cover for economic concerns? What does it mean to follow Jesus at these times? **4.** What began as Artemis-*worship* became Artemis-*business*. How can Christians fall into the same trap and make Jesus-worship into Jesus-business?

they were there. ³³The Jews pushed Alexander to the front, and some of the crowd shouted instructions to him. He motioned for silence in order to make a defense before the people. ³⁴But when they realized he was a Jew, they all shouted in unison for about two hours: "Great is Artemis of the Ephesians!"

³⁵The city clerk quieted the crowd and said: "Men of Ephesus, doesn't all the world know that the city of Ephesus is the guardian of the temple of the great Artemis and of her image, which fell from heaven? ³⁶Therefore, since these facts are undeniable, you ought to be quiet and not do anything rash. ³⁷You have brought these men here, though they have neither robbed temples nor blasphemed our goddess. ³⁸If, then, Demetrius and his fellow craftsmen have a grievance against anybody, the courts are open and there are proconsuls. They can press charges. ³⁹If there is anything further you want to bring up, it must be settled in a legal assembly. ⁴⁰As it is, we are in danger of being charged with rioting because of today's events. In that case we would not be able to account for this commotion, since there is no reason for it." ⁴¹After he had said this, he dismissed the assembly.

Through Macedonia and Greece

20 When the uproar had ended, Paul sent for the disciples and, after encouraging them, said good-by and set out for Macedonia. ²He traveled through that area, speaking many words of encouragement to the people, and finally arrived in Greece, ³where he stayed three months. Because the Jews made a plot against him just as he was about to sail for Syria, he decided to go back through Macedonia. ⁴He was accompanied by Sopater son of Pyrrhus from Berea, Aristarchus and Secundus from Thessalonica, Gaius from Derbe, Timothy also, Tychicus and Trophimus from the province of Asia. ⁵These men went on ahead and waited for us at Troas. ⁶But we sailed from Philippi after the Feast of Unleavened Bread, and five days later joined the others at Troas, where we stayed seven days.

Eutychus Raised From the Dead at Troas

OPEN: 1. What do you do best with money: Earn it? Keep it? Lose it? Spend it? Give it away? **2.** When have you taken a spill or "fallen off your rocker," much to your embarrassment?

DIG: 1. One reason for this trip was to collect money for Christians in Judea (see Ro 15:25-29). Why then would Paul want companions for this task (see 2Co 8:16-23; 1Co 16:1-4)? Why else might Paul want these Gentiles along for the presentation in Jerusalem (see ch.15)? **2.** What can you learn about Paul and the church in Troas from this lengthy meeting? **3.** Peter raised a dead person in 9:37. Why does Luke tell a similar story about Paul?

REFLECT: 1. Paul's companions protect him from anyone accusing him of misusing the funds. How could churches and "faith ministries" today be helped by such accountability? How would this enhance outsiders' opinion of Christian integrity? **2.** Are you at all related to Eutychus: Do sermons put you to sleep? Or are you wide awake spiritually? How can you keep from falling flat?

⁷On the first day of the week we came together to break bread. Paul spoke to the people and, because he intended to leave the next day, kept on talking until midnight. ⁸There were many lamps in the upstairs room where we were meeting. ⁹Seated in a window was a young man named Eutychus, who was sinking into a deep sleep as Paul talked on and on. When he was sound asleep, he fell to the ground from the third story and was picked up dead. ¹⁰Paul went down, threw himself on the young man and put his arms around him. "Don't be alarmed," he said. "He's alive!" ¹¹Then he went upstairs again and broke bread and ate. After talking until daylight, he left. ¹²The people took the young man home alive and were greatly comforted.

Paul's Farewell to the Ephesian Elders

¹³We went on ahead to the ship and sailed for Assos, where we were going to take Paul aboard. He had made this arrangement because he was going there on foot. ¹⁴When he met us at Assos, we took him aboard and went on to Mitylene. ¹⁵The next day we set sail from there and arrived off Kios. The day after that we crossed over to Samos, and on the following day arrived at Miletus. ¹⁶Paul had decided to sail past Ephesus to avoid spending time in the province of Asia, for he was in a hurry to reach Jerusalem, if possible, by the day of Pentecost.

¹⁷From Miletus, Paul sent to Ephesus for the elders of the church. ¹⁸When they arrived, he said to them: "You know how I lived the whole time I was with you, from the first day I came into the province of Asia. ¹⁹I served the Lord with great humility and with tears, although I was severely tested by the plots of the Jews. ²⁰You know that I have not hesitated to preach anything that would be helpful to you but have taught you publicly and from house to house. ²¹I have declared to both Jews and Greeks that they must turn to God in repentance and have faith in our Lord Jesus.

²²"And now, compelled by the Spirit, I am going to Jerusalem, not knowing what will happen to me there. ²³I only know that in every city the Holy Spirit warns me that prison and hardships are facing me. ²⁴However, I consider my life worth nothing to me, if only I may finish the race and complete the task the Lord Jesus has given me—the task of testifying to the gospel of God's grace.

²⁵"Now I know that none of you among whom I have gone about preaching the kingdom will ever see me again. ²⁶Therefore, I declare to you today that I am innocent of the blood of all men. ²⁷For I have not hesitated to proclaim to you the whole will of God. ²⁸Keep watch over yourselves and all the flock of which the Holy Spirit has made you overseers.ᵖ Be shepherds of the church of God,ᵠ which he bought with his own blood. ²⁹I know that after I leave, savage wolves will come in among you and will not spare the flock. ³⁰Even from your own number men will arise and distort the truth in order to draw away disciples after them. ³¹So be on your guard! Remember that for three years I never stopped warning each of you night and day with tears.

³²"Now I commit you to God and to the word of his grace, which can build you up and give you an inheritance among all those who are sanctified. ³³I have not coveted anyone's silver or gold or clothing. ³⁴You yourselves know that these hands of mine have supplied my own needs and the needs of my companions. ³⁵In everything I did, I showed you that by this kind of hard work we must help the weak, remembering the words the Lord Jesus himself said: 'It is more blessed to give than to receive.' "

³⁶When he had said this, he knelt down with all of them and

OPEN: 1. Who has served as a spiritual role model for you? What about that person has rubbed off on you? **2.** As "parting is such sweet sorrow," what in your life is "sweet 'n sour" these days?

DIG: 1. Why "sail past" Ephesus to reach Jerusalem for Pentecost (see 2:1)? **2.** What has characterized Paul's ministry so far? Why does he emphasize how he lived among them? **3.** From your reading of Acts, what kinds of hardships has Paul already encountered? How would you explain what motivates Paul to keep on (compare 20:24 with Php 3:7-8)? **4.** What does it mean to "keep watch" (v.28; see 1Ti 4:11-16)? How and why is their appointment as elders divine, humbling, and dangerous (vv. 28-31)? **5.** How does the message of grace (v.32) and the example of Paul (vv.33-35) protect them from these dangers? Some people viewed the office of elder as a way of gaining power and wealth (see 1Ti 5:6-10; 1Pe 5:3). How does Paul oppose that idea here? **6.** What do you suppose the Ephesians will miss most about Paul?

REFLECT: 1. If someone watched you the past year, what would they assume a Christian lifestyle is like? How would you like to change so they can get a more accurate picture? How would you paraphrase Paul's summary of the gospel (v.21) to explain the faith to someone? **2.** Who makes up the "flock" for whom you are responsible? In what specific way can you shepherd them? **3.** How would you complete this sentence: "The one thing I must accomplish at any cost is _____? How does it relate to Paul's goal in verse 24? **4.** In the race of doing God's will, are you in the front of the pack, one of the stragglers, or an onlooker? Why?

---

p28 Traditionally *bishops*　　*q28* Many manuscripts *of the Lord* prayed. [37]They all wept as they embraced him and kissed him. [38]What grieved them most was his statement that they would never see his face again. Then they accompanied him to the ship.

On to Jerusalem

21 After we had torn ourselves away from them, we put out to sea and sailed straight to Cos. The next day we went to Rhodes and from there to Patara. [2]We found a ship crossing over to Phoenicia, went on board and set sail. [3]After sighting Cyprus and passing to the south of it, we sailed on to Syria. We landed at Tyre, where our ship was to unload its cargo. [4]Finding the disciples there, we stayed with them seven days. Through the Spirit they urged Paul not to go on to Jerusalem. [5]But when our time was up, we left and continued on our way. All the disciples and their wives and children accompanied us out of the city, and there on the beach we knelt to pray. [6]After saying good-by to each other, we went aboard the ship, and they returned home.

[7]We continued our voyage from Tyre and landed at Ptolemais, where we greeted the brothers and stayed with them for a day. [8]Leaving the next day, we reached Caesarea and stayed at the house of Philip the evangelist, one of the Seven. [9]He had four unmarried daughters who prophesied.

[10]After we had been there a number of days, a prophet named Agabus came down from Judea. [11]Coming over to us, he took Paul's belt, tied his own hands and feet with it and said, "The Holy Spirit says, 'In this way the Jews of Jerusalem will bind the owner of this belt and will hand him over to the Gentiles.' "

[12]When we heard this, we and the people there pleaded with Paul not to go up to Jerusalem. [13]Then Paul answered, "Why are you weeping and breaking my heart? I am ready not only to be bound, but also to die in Jerusalem for the name of the Lord Jesus." [14]When he would not be dissuaded, we gave up and said, "The Lord's will be done."

[15]After this, we got ready and went up to Jerusalem. [16]Some of the disciples from Caesarea accompanied us and brought us to the home of Mnason, where we were to stay. He was a man from Cyprus and one of the early disciples.

Paul's Arrival at Jerusalem

[17]When we arrived at Jerusalem, the brothers received us warmly. [18]The next day Paul and the rest of us went to see James, and all the elders were present. [19]Paul greeted them and reported in detail what God had done among the Gentiles through his ministry.

[20]When they heard this, they praised God. Then they said to Paul: "You see, brother, how many thousands of Jews have believed, and all of them are zealous for the law. [21]They have been informed that you teach all the Jews who live among the Gentiles to turn away from Moses, telling them not to circumcise their children or live according to our customs. [22]What shall we do? They will certainly hear that you have come, [23]so do what we tell you. There are four men with us who have made a vow. [24]Take these men, join in their purification rites and pay their

---

OPEN: 1. What piece of clothing that you are wearing (belt, hat, shoes, etc.) best represents your lifestyle now? Why? **2.** What place did your parents have to drag you to, because you were scared to go there: Circus? Dentist's? Grandmom's? Somewhere else?

DIG: 1. How is Paul interpreting these warnings differently than his friends do (vv.4,10-13; see 20:22-23)? Why doesn't he listen to their advice? **2.** What else do you know about Agabus (see 11:27-29) that gives more credence to his prophecy? Does Paul strike you as courageous or foolish, given this belt-tightening message? Why? **3.** For Paul, it's "Jerusalem or Bust!" How does that compare with Jesus' determination (see Lk 13:31-33)?

REFLECT: 1. In your eyes, did Paul make the right decision to go to Jerusalem, even though godly people through the Spirit urged him not to go? Why or why not? **2.** When have you made decisions against the wishes of people you admired and trusted? What happened? In retrospect, were your decisions wise ones? Explain.

OPEN: What "rites of passage" have been significant for you in maturing in your faith, and why: Baptism/confirmation? Summer mission project? Ordination? Marriage? Raising a new generation of believers? A "serendipity"?

DIG: 1. What pressure do James and the elders face as Paul comes to Jerusalem? How would Paul's teaching cause strict Jews to be upset? **2.** This issue was supposedly settled at least six years earlier (see ch.15). Why do these tensions still plague Jerusalem believers? **3.** How would James' suggestion to Paul solve the problem for both of them? Why remind Paul's Gentile companions what expenses, so that they can have their heads shaved. Then everybody will know there is no truth in these reports about you, but that you yourself are living in obedience to the law. ²⁵As for the Gentile believers, we have written to them our decision that they should abstain from food sacrificed to idols, from blood, from the meat of strangled animals and from sexual immorality.''

²⁶The next day Paul took the men and purified himself along with them. Then he went to the temple to give notice of the date when the days of purification would end and the offering would be made for each of them.

Paul Arrested

²⁷When the seven days were nearly over, some Jews from the province of Asia saw Paul at the temple. They stirred up the whole crowd and seized him, ²⁸shouting, "Men of Israel, help us! This is the man who teaches all men everywhere against our people and our law and this place. And besides, he has brought Greeks into the temple area and defiled this holy place." ²⁹(They had previously seen Trophimus the Ephesian in the city with Paul and assumed that Paul had brought him into the temple area.)

³⁰The whole city was aroused, and the people came running from all directions. Seizing Paul, they dragged him from the temple, and immediately the gates were shut. ³¹While they were trying to kill him, news reached the commander of the Roman troops that the whole city of Jerusalem was in an uproar. ³²He at once took some officers and soldiers and ran down to the crowd. When the rioters saw the commander and his soldiers, they stopped beating Paul.

³³The commander came up and arrested him and ordered him to be bound with two chains. Then he asked who he was and what he had done. ³⁴Some in the crowd shouted one thing and some another, and since the commander could not get at the truth because of the uproar, he ordered that Paul be taken into the barracks. ³⁵When Paul reached the steps, the violence of the mob was so great he had to be carried by the soldiers. ³⁶The crowd that followed kept shouting, "Away with him!"

Paul Speaks to the Crowd

³⁷As the soldiers were about to take Paul into the barracks, he asked the commander, "May I say something to you?"

"Do you speak Greek?" he replied. ³⁸"Aren't you the Egyptian who started a revolt and led four thousand terrorists out into the desert some time ago?"

³⁹Paul answered, "I am a Jew, from Tarsus in Cilicia, a citizen of no ordinary city. Please let me speak to the people."

⁴⁰Having received the commander's permission, Paul stood on the steps and motioned to the crowd. When they were all **22** silent, he said to them in Aramaicʳ: ¹"Brothers and fathers, listen now to my defense."

²When they heard him speak to them in Aramaic, they became very quiet.

ʳ40 Or possibly *Hebrew;* also in 22:2

to do (see 15:20)? **4.** How does Paul's action in verses 24-26 square with his view of grace and law (see 20:24; 1Co 9:10-20)?

REFLECT: How do you decide when you should bend for the sake of others, and when you should stand for your principles?

_____

OPEN: What was one of the most raucous crowd scenes you have ever been a part of?

DIG: 1. Paul spent more time in Asia than anywhere else (19:8-10). Why would these men be especially upset when they see Paul? Gentiles were forbidden from the temple under penalty of death. How would the accusation of verse 28 fuel the suspicions of James (v.21)? **2.** Compare the reaction against Paul (vv.30-31) with that against Stephen (6:11-13) twenty years earlier. What does this tell you about Christian-Jewish relationships in Jerusalem during this period? **3.** What memories of lynch mobs does Paul have (see 20:23; 21:13)?

REFLECT: In your opinion, what group is the most critical of the church today? What could be done to lessen this animosity? What can you do to help?

_____

OPEN: 1. When have you wished you could understand another language better? How did you do in languages in school? **2.** If you had 4,000 trained terrorists at your disposal, what mission would you design for them?

DIG: 1. From 21:30-36, why would the commander mistake Paul for the Egyptian revolutionary (v.38)? **2.** Under the circumstances, why did Paul think it so important to address this hostile crowd? How would Jewish-Christian relationships erode even further if the charges of 21:28 were left unanswered? **3.** Many foreign-born

Jews did not know Aramaic well. How does Paul's use of this language (along with the content of his speech) force these Jews to listen? 4. This speech (22:1-10) recounts the events of 9:1-18. What points of identification does Paul make with his hostile audience? What is he hoping to achieve by this? 5. Why does Paul's reference to the *Gentiles* (v.21) upset the crowd (v.22), whereas they did not react to his speaking about *Jesus*? What was the real sticking point about the gospel for the Jews? 6. How was Paul's status as a Roman citizen an asset in his ministry to Gentiles (vv.25-29; see also 16:37-38)?

REFLECT: 1. Paul told his own story instead of preaching a sermon to this crowd. When do you find your story most effective and helpful to others? Option: If you have not already done so, share your story with the small group — in three minutes or less. 2. How has your faith in Jesus redirected your life in a surprising way? How do you struggle with that redirection? In what ways have you embraced some of these changes for yourself? 3. What is one of the hardest things you have had to experience because of your faith? 4. How is your citizenship an asset for spreading the gospel? How can you use this asset better?

OPEN: What is the cleverest putdown you have heard recently? (Perhaps you received it, dished it out, overheard your kids squabbling, or read it in the paper.)

DIG: 1. What sparks this exchange of insults (see 21:21 ,28)? 2. Why (and how) does Paul show his respect and zeal for the Jewish law (vv.1-5)? 3. Why does Paul change the focus of attention from whether he has kept the law to his hope in the resurrection? Given

Then Paul said: [3]"I am a Jew, born in Tarsus of Cilicia, but brought up in this city. Under Gamaliel I was thoroughly trained in the law of our fathers and was just as zealous for God as any of you are today. [4]I persecuted the followers of this Way to their death, arresting both men and women and throwing them into prison, [5]as also the high priest and all the Council can testify. I even obtained letters from them to their brothers in Damascus, and went there to bring these people as prisoners to Jerusalem to be punished.

[6]"About noon as I came near Damascus, suddenly a bright light from heaven flashed around me. [7]I fell to the ground and heard a voice say to me, 'Saul! Saul! Why do you persecute me?'

[8]" 'Who are you, Lord?' I asked.

" 'I am Jesus of Nazareth, whom you are persecuting,' he replied. [9]My companions saw the light, but they did not understand the voice of him who was speaking to me.

[10]" 'What shall I do, Lord?' I asked.

" 'Get up,' the Lord said, 'and go into Damascus. There you will be told all that you have been assigned to do.' [11]My companions led me by the hand into Damascus, because the brilliance of the light had blinded me.

[12]"A man named Ananias came to see me. He was a devout observer of the law and highly respected by all the Jews living there. [13]He stood beside me and said, 'Brother Saul, receive your sight!' And at that very moment I was able to see him.

[14]"Then he said: 'The God of our fathers has chosen you to know his will and to see the Righteous One and to hear words from his mouth. [15]You will be his witness to all men of what you have seen and heard. [16]And now what are you waiting for? Get up, be baptized and wash your sins away, calling on his name.'

[17]"When I returned to Jerusalem and was praying at the temple, I fell into a trance [18]and saw the Lord speaking. 'Quick!' he said to me. 'Leave Jerusalem immediately, because they will not accept your testimony about me.'

[19]" 'Lord,' I replied, 'these men know that I went from one synagogue to another to imprison and beat those who believe in you. [20]And when the blood of your martyr[s] Stephen was shed, I stood there giving my approval and guarding the clothes of those who were killing him.'

[21]"Then the Lord said to me, 'Go; I will send you far away to the Gentiles.' "

Paul the Roman Citizen

[22]The crowd listened to Paul until he said this. Then they raised their voices and shouted, "Rid the earth of him! He's not fit to live!"

[23]As they were shouting and throwing off their cloaks and flinging dust into the air, [24]the commander ordered Paul to be taken into the barracks. He directed that he be flogged and questioned in order to find out why the people were shouting at him like this. [25]As they stretched him out to flog him, Paul said to the centurion standing there, "Is it legal for you to flog

[s]20 Or *witness*

a Roman citizen who hasn't even been found guilty?"

²⁶When the centurion heard this, he went to the commander and reported it. "What are you going to do?" he asked. "This man is a Roman citizen."

²⁷The commander went to Paul and asked, "Tell me, are you a Roman citizen?"

"Yes, I am," he answered.

²⁸Then the commander said, "I had to pay a big price for my citizenship."

"But I was born a citizen," Paul replied.

²⁹Those who were about to question him withdrew immediately. The commander himself was alarmed when he realized that he had put Paul, a Roman citizen, in chains.

Before the Sanhedrin

³⁰The next day, since the commander wanted to find out exactly why Paul was being accused by the Jews, he released him and ordered the chief priests and all the Sanhedrin to assemble. Then he brought Paul and had him stand before them.

23 Paul looked straight at the Sanhedrin and said, "My brothers, I have fulfilled my duty to God in all good conscience to this day." ²At this the high priest Ananias ordered those standing near Paul to strike him on the mouth. ³Then Paul said to him, "God will strike you, you whitewashed wall! You sit there to judge me according to the law, yet you yourself violate the law by commanding that I be struck!"

⁴Those who were standing near Paul said, "You dare to insult God's high priest?"

⁵Paul replied, "Brothers, I did not realize that he was the high priest; for it is written: 'Do not speak evil about the ruler of your people.'ᵗ"

⁶Then Paul, knowing that some of them were Sadducees and the others Pharisees, called out in the Sanhedrin, "My brothers, I am a Pharisee, the son of a Pharisee. I stand on trial because of my hope in the resurrection of the dead." ⁷When he said this, a dispute broke out between the Pharisees and the Sadducees, and the assembly was divided. ⁸(The Sadducees say that there is no resurrection, and that there are neither angels nor spirits, but the Pharisees acknowledge them all.)

⁹There was a great uproar, and some of the teachers of the law who were Pharisees stood up and argued vigorously. "We find nothing wrong with this man," they said. "What if a spirit or an angel has spoken to him?" ¹⁰The dispute became so violent that the commander was afraid Paul would be torn to pieces by them. He ordered the troops to go down and take him away from them by force and bring him into the barracks.

¹¹The following night the Lord stood near Paul and said, "Take courage! As you have testified about me in Jerusalem, so you must also testify in Rome."

the tensions on this issue between the Pharisees and Sadducees, describe what you think the next few minutes of the assembly must have been like. **4.** What effect does the split have on Paul's case (vv.7-10)? **5.** We last heard God speak to Paul in 18:9-10, after he had experienced a series of setbacks. How would the Lord's message here (v.11) help Paul again? How would this help Paul remember what the Lord said about him to Ananias in 9:15-16?

REFLECT: 1. When facing death, what duty do you want to have fulfilled before God? How can you pursue that course this week? **2.** How has the Lord encouraged you during hard times? **3.** What could be your "Rome"—the next crucial step in your spiritual journey? Why do you think so?

ᵗ5 Exodus 22:28

OPEN: When you were growing up, who was one of your favorite "uncles"? What incident brought the two of you closer? Do you have a favorite nephew? What bonds the two of you together?

DIG: 1. How do you explain the fierce determination of these men to kill Paul (see Ro 10:2)? Why do they think he is so dangerous? 2. Given verse 11, how would you feel if you were Paul and you heard this news from your nephew (vv.12-16)? 3. By sending his nephew to the commander, is Paul showing a lack of faith in God's promise? Why or why not?

REFLECT: 1. What examples of irrational hatred have you seen or felt? What could be a way to break through that? When is it better just to get away from them? 2. What risks did Paul's nephew take in this story? How might you be called upon this week to risk yourself by standing up for someone that others dislike?

OPEN: What place or person made you feel safe and protected as a child? As an adult, where and when (or with whom) do you feel most secure?

DIG: 1. How does the commander's provision for Paul contrast with the way Pilate dealt with Jesus (see Lk 23:1-25)? Why do you think this is the case? 2. What has the commander decided to do with the "Paul problem"? Why the elaborate security precautions and the constant "passing the buck"? (Or is it passing "the hot potato"?) How does all this relate to 9:15? 3. How would you feel if you were one of the men in 23:12-13, and you found out the next day that Paul was gone?

REFLECT: 1. How do Paul's experiences with Roman authority here shed light on his comments in Romans 13:1-7? How

The Plot to Kill Paul

[12]The next morning the Jews formed a conspiracy and bound themselves with an oath not to eat or drink until they had killed Paul. [13]More than forty men were involved in this plot. [14]They went to the chief priests and elders and said, "We have taken a solemn oath not to eat anything until we have killed Paul. [15]Now then, you and the Sanhedrin petition the commander to bring him before you on the pretext of wanting more accurate information about his case. We are ready to kill him before he gets here."

[16]But when the son of Paul's sister heard of this plot, he went into the barracks and told Paul.

[17]Then Paul called one of the centurions and said, "Take this young man to the commander; he has something to tell him." [18]So he took him to the commander.

The centurion said, "Paul, the prisoner, sent for me and asked me to bring this young man to you because he has something to tell you."

[19]The commander took the young man by the hand, drew him aside and asked, "What is it you want to tell me?"

[20]He said: "The Jews have agreed to ask you to bring Paul before the Sanhedrin tomorrow on the pretext of wanting more accurate information about him. [21]Don't give in to them, because more than forty of them are waiting in ambush for him. They have taken an oath not to eat or drink until they have killed him. They are ready now, waiting for your consent to their request."

[22]The commander dismissed the young man and cautioned him, "Don't tell anyone that you have reported this to me."

Paul Transferred to Caesarea

[23]Then he called two of his centurions and ordered them, "Get ready a detachment of two hundred soldiers, seventy horsemen and two hundred spearmen" to go to Caesarea at nine tonight. [24]Provide mounts for Paul so that he may be taken safely to Governor Felix."

[25]He wrote a letter as follows:

[26]Claudius Lysias,

To His Excellency, Governor Felix:

Greetings.

[27]This man was seized by the Jews and they were about to kill him, but I came with my troops and rescued him, for I had learned that he is a Roman citizen. [28]I wanted to know why they were accusing him, so I brought him to their Sanhedrin. [29]I found that the accusation had to do with questions about their law, but there was no charge against him that deserved death or imprisonment. [30]When I was informed of a plot to be carried out against the man,

---

a23 The meaning of the Greek for this word is uncertain.

I sent him to you at once. I also ordered his accusers to present to you their case against him.

³¹So the soldiers, carrying out their orders, took Paul with them during the night and brought him as far as Antipatris. ³²The next day they let the cavalry go on with him, while they returned to the barracks. ³³When the cavalry arrived in Caesarea, they delivered the letter to the governor and handed Paul over to him. ³⁴The governor read the letter and asked what province he was from. Learning that he was from Cilicia, ³⁵he said, "I will hear your case when your accusers get here." Then he ordered that Paul be kept under guard in Herod's palace.

The Trial Before Felix

24 Five days later the high priest Ananias went down to Caesarea with some of the elders and a lawyer named Tertullus, and they brought their charges against Paul before the governor. ²When Paul was called in, Tertullus presented his case before Felix: "We have enjoyed a long period of peace under you, and your foresight has brought about reforms in this nation. ³Everywhere and in every way, most excellent Felix, we acknowledge this with profound gratitude. ⁴But in order not to weary you further, I would request that you be kind enough to hear us briefly.

⁵"We have found this man to be a troublemaker, stirring up riots among the Jews all over the world. He is a ringleader of the Nazarene sect ⁶and even tried to desecrate the temple; so we seized him. ⁸By^v examining him yourself you will be able to learn the truth about all these charges we are bringing against him."

⁹The Jews joined in the accusation, asserting that these things were true.

¹⁰When the governor motioned for him to speak, Paul replied: "I know that for a number of years you have been a judge over this nation; so I gladly make my defense. ¹¹You can easily verify that no more than twelve days ago I went up to Jerusalem to worship. ¹²My accusers did not find me arguing with anyone at the temple, or stirring up a crowd in the synagogues or anywhere else in the city. ¹³And they cannot prove to you the charges they are now making against me. ¹⁴However, I admit that I worship the God of our fathers as a follower of the Way, which they call a sect. I believe everything that agrees with the Law and that is written in the Prophets, ¹⁵and I have the same hope in God as these men, that there will be a resurrection of both the righteous and the wicked. ¹⁶So I strive always to keep my conscience clear before God and man.

¹⁷"After an absence of several years, I came to Jerusalem to bring my people gifts for the poor and to present offerings. ¹⁸I was ceremonially clean when they found me in the temple courts doing this. There was no crowd with me, nor was I involved in any disturbance. ¹⁹But there are some Jews from the province

v6-8 Some manuscripts him and wanted to judge him according to our law. ⁷But the commander, Lysias, came and with the use of much force snatched him from our hands ⁸and ordered his accusers to come before you. By

does this contrast with Peter's experience with the Jewish authorities in Acts 13:19-20? **2.** What do these two incidents show you about the Christian's relationship with civil authority? Where do you need to show your support of government authority? Where should you be challenging it?

OPEN: 1. Who's your favorite TV lawyer or judge? Why? **2.** If someone were to bribe you to do a favor for them, what's the most effective incentive they could use: A return favor? Your favorite meal? Free babysitting? Hugs and ___? Flattery? Give an example of how bribery has worked with your parents, spouse, or kids.

DIG: 1. Felix had a reputation of violently suppressing rebellions against Rome. How might Tertullus hope that would compensate for the lack of evidence he can offer? **2.** How would all the charges in verses 5-6 seem true to Ananias and Tertullus? What does their reference to Christians as the "Nazarene sect" show about their view of Christianity? **3.** How then does Paul defend himself (vv.11-19)? **4.** Put yourself in the place of Felix. In light of the riot in Jerusalem over Paul (if you only had Lysias' letter 23:26-30), the accusations of the Jews, and Paul's word to go on), what would you do? **5.** Given what happened in Corinth (18:12-16), why would Paul want to shift the focus of the controversy to his belief in the resurrection? **6.** What do you learn about Felix from verses 22-26? Why does he merely put Paul under house arrest? **7.** If Felix had been in Pilate's place, what do you think he would have done with Jesus (compare Lk 23:1-25)? **8.** In light of Acts 23:11, what must Paul be feeling as time wears on and no progress at all is made?

REFLECT: 1. How has your desire to serve Christ been misunderstood by others? How did you feel then? **2.** What's the difference between being "well acquainted with the Way" (v.22) and being a true believer? How long were you well acquainted before you became a believer? **3.** Have you ever felt there was a period in your life that was "dead time"—time when nothing seemed to be happening at all (as seems to be the case with Paul)? Why do you think God allows such times in our lives?

OPEN: When a substitute parent, teacher, or boss came on the scene, how did/do you act?

DIG: 1. Two years has passed since the trial before Felix (24:27). Why hasn't the opposition to Paul by the Jewish leaders dissipated during this time? **2.** Paul has come a long way since the events of 9:1-2. What irony do you see in that? How could 9:1-2 also account in part for their animosity? **3.** How is Paul like a pawn to these Roman officials (v.9; see 24:27)? How might this account for his decision to appeal to Caesar?

REFLECT: 1. What do you do when you feel that no matter what you say, you will not really be heard by another person? **2.** What was one circumstance that threatened to ambush you in your spiritual life? How did you deal with it? **3.** If someone wanted to prove you were a Christian, what evidence from this past week could they use?

of Asia, who ought to be here before you and bring charges if they have anything against me. ²⁰Or these who are here should state what crime they found in me when I stood before the Sanhedrin— ²¹unless it was this one thing I shouted as I stood in their presence: 'It is concerning the resurrection of the dead that I am on trial before you today.' "

²²Then Felix, who was well acquainted with the Way, adjourned the proceedings. "When Lysias the commander comes," he said, "I will decide your case." ²³He ordered the centurion to keep Paul under guard but to give him some freedom and permit his friends to take care of his needs.

²⁴Several days later Felix came with his wife Drusilla, who was a Jewess. He sent for Paul and listened to him as he spoke about faith in Christ Jesus. ²⁵As Paul discoursed on righteousness, self-control and the judgment to come, Felix was afraid and said, "That's enough for now! You may leave. When I find it convenient, I will send for you." ²⁶At the same time he was hoping that Paul would offer him a bribe, so he sent for him frequently and talked with him.

²⁷When two years had passed, Felix was succeeded by Porcius Festus, but because Felix wanted to grant a favor to the Jews, he left Paul in prison.

The Trial Before Festus

25 Three days after arriving in the province, Festus went up from Caesarea to Jerusalem, ²where the chief priests and Jewish leaders appeared before him and presented the charges against Paul. ³They urgently requested Festus, as a favor to them, to have Paul transferred to Jerusalem, for they were preparing an ambush to kill him along the way. ⁴Festus answered, "Paul is being held at Caesarea, and I myself am going there soon. ⁵Let some of your leaders come with me and press charges against the man there, if he has done anything wrong."

⁶After spending eight or ten days with them, he went down to Caesarea, and the next day he convened the court and ordered that Paul be brought before him. ⁷When Paul appeared, the Jews who had come down from Jerusalem stood around him, bringing many serious charges against him, which they could not prove.

⁸Then Paul made his defense: "I have done nothing wrong against the law of the Jews or against the temple or against Caesar."

⁹Festus, wishing to do the Jews a favor, said to Paul, "Are you willing to go up to Jerusalem and stand trial before me there on these charges?"

¹⁰Paul answered: "I am now standing before Caesar's court, where I ought to be tried. I have not done any wrong to the Jews, as you yourself know very well. ¹¹If, however, I am guilty of doing anything deserving death, I do not refuse to die. But if the charges brought against me by these Jews are not true, no one has the right to hand me over to them. I appeal to Caesar!"

¹²After Festus had conferred with his council, he declared: "You have appealed to Caesar. To Caesar you will go!"

Festus Consults King Agrippa

¹³A few days later King Agrippa and Bernice arrived at Caesarea to pay their respects to Festus. ¹⁴Since they were spending many days there, Festus discussed Paul's case with the king. He said: "There is a man here whom Felix left as a prisoner. ¹⁵When I went to Jerusalem, the chief priests and elders of the Jews brought charges against him and asked that he be condemned.

¹⁶"I told them that it is not the Roman custom to hand over any man before he has faced his accusers and has had an opportunity to defend himself against their charges. ¹⁷When they came here with me, I did not delay the case, but convened the court the next day and ordered the man to be brought in. ¹⁸When his accusers got up to speak, they did not charge him with any of the crimes I had expected. ¹⁹Instead, they had some points of dispute with him about their own religion and about a dead man named Jesus who Paul claimed was alive. ²⁰I was at a loss how to investigate such matters; so I asked if he would be willing to go to Jerusalem and stand trial there on these charges. ²¹When Paul made his appeal to be held over for the Emperor's decision, I ordered him held until I could send him to Caesar."

²²Then Agrippa said to Festus, "I would like to hear this man myself."

He replied, "Tomorrow you will hear him."

Paul Before Agrippa

²³The next day Agrippa and Bernice came with great pomp and entered the audience room with the high ranking officers and the leading men of the city. At the command of Festus, Paul was brought in. ²⁴Festus said: "King Agrippa, and all who are present with us, you see this man! The whole Jewish community has petitioned me about him in Jerusalem and here in Caesarea, shouting that he ought not to live any longer. ²⁵I found he had done nothing deserving of death, but because he made his appeal to the Emperor I decided to send him to Rome. ²⁶But I have nothing definite to write to His Majesty about him. Therefore I have brought him before all of you, and especially before you, King Agrippa, so that as a result of this investigation I may have something to write. ²⁷For I think it is unreasonable to send on a prisoner without specifying the charges against him."

26 Then Agrippa said to Paul, "You have permission to speak for yourself."

So Paul motioned with his hand and began his defense: ²"King Agrippa, I consider myself fortunate to stand before you today as I make my defense against all the accusations of the Jews, ³and especially so because you are well acquainted with all the Jewish customs and controversies. Therefore, I beg you to listen to me patiently.

⁴"The Jews all know the way I have lived ever since I was a child, from the beginning of my life in my own country, and also in Jerusalem. ⁵They have known me for a long time and can testify, if they are willing, that according to the strictest sect of our religion, I lived as a Pharisee. ⁶And now it is because of my hope in what God has promised our fathers that I am on trial today. ⁷This is the promise our twelve tribes are hoping to see

OPEN: 1. Who is the first person you turn to when you want good advice? **2.** If you could be king or queen for a day, what new law would you enact?

DIG: 1. How fair is Festus in describing the case? How much does he seem to know about Judaism? About Christianity? How would this have affected any decision he would have made in the case? Do you think he is honestly trying to find the truth in this matter? Why? **2.** This Agrippa was the son of the Herod in 12:1-23. Why would he be especially interested in hearing from Paul?

REFLECT: When you have questions about your faith, to whom do you turn? Why? How else do you seek input?

OPEN: 1. When have you had to publicly appear before an important or powerful person and put your fate in his/her hands: (a) Defending yourself in a tax audit? (b) Asking for a pay raise or an allowance hike? (c) Asking for his daughter's hand in marriage? (d) Defending your thesis?(e) Asking for liability damages? (f) Submitting to the dentist or surgeon? **2.** How did you feel as you thought about what to say beforehand?

DIG: 1. What is the problem Festus faces? Why doesn't he simply let Paul go? How could Agrippa be in a position to help (26:3)? **2.** According to Paul, what issue is the real source of his conflict with the Jewish leaders (see 23:6; 24:21; 26:6-8)? Why do you think his adversaries never directly bring this out (see 18:15)? How does his conviction about the resurrection differ from that of the Pharisees, who in theory believed in a general resurrection as well? **3.** Compare 26:20 with 20:21. How could you tell someone what it means to be a Christian from these two verses? **4.** Would you describe Paul's speech as a *legal defense* or a *personal testimony*? How are the two related? Do you think Paul's primary goal in this speech is to convince Agrippa of his innocence, or of the truth of

Christianity's claims? Why? **5.** From 25:19 and 26:24, how convinced is Festus regarding the resurrection of Jesus? How might Paul's response in verses 25-27 surprise Festus? **6.** If you were in this hall, what impressions would you have of Paul as he concluded his speech? **7.** Up to this point, the Romans considered Christians and Jews as basically one and the same. Within five years, the emperor Nero was aware of enough differences to violently persecute Christians in Rome. From this speech, what can the Romans begin to see as some of the differences?

REFLECT: 1. What difference does it make to you that Jesus truly rose from the dead? What would be different about your faith if that were not the case? **2.** How does verse 18 fit as a description of your spiritual journey? Which other images describe what coming to faith was like for you? **3.** In verse 14, Paul adds a comment not found in his conversion story in chapters 9 or 22. When has God pointed out to you that your struggle has been against *him* all along? How has he redirected you since then? **4.** Paul considered himself a servant and a witness. In what way is God's call to you similar to his call to Paul? Different? **5.** What difference does it make to you that the events in Jesus' life were public knowledge, things "not done in a corner"? How does that fact negate charges some people make today that the disciples made up all those stories about Jesus? **6.** How has Christ brought light into your life? How can you pass on that light to someone else this week?

fulfilled as they earnestly serve God day and night. O king, it is because of this hope that the Jews are accusing me. [8]Why should any of you consider it incredible that God raises the dead?

[9]"I too was convinced that I ought to do all that was possible to oppose the name of Jesus of Nazareth. [10]And that is just what I did in Jerusalem. On the authority of the chief priests I put many of the saints in prison, and when they were put to death, I cast my vote against them. [11]Many a time I went from one synagogue to another to have them punished, and I tried to force them to blaspheme. In my obsession against them, I even went to foreign cities to persecute them.

[12]"On one of these journeys I was going to Damascus with the authority and commission of the chief priests. [13]About noon, O king, as I was on the road, I saw a light from heaven, brighter than the sun, blazing around me and my companions. [14]We all fell to the ground, and I heard a voice saying to me in Aramaic,[w] 'Saul, Saul, why do you persecute me? It is hard for you to kick against the goads.'

[15]"Then I asked, 'Who are you, Lord?'

" 'I am Jesus, whom you are persecuting,' the Lord replied. [16]'Now get up and stand on your feet. I have appeared to you to appoint you as a servant and as a witness of what you have seen of me and what I will show you. [17]I will rescue you from your own people and from the Gentiles. I am sending you to them [18]to open their eyes and turn them from darkness to light, and from the power of Satan to God, so that they may receive forgiveness of sins and a place among those who are sanctified by faith in me.'

[19]"So then, King Agrippa, I was not disobedient to the vision from heaven. [20]First to those in Damascus, then to those in Jerusalem and in all Judea, and to the Gentiles also, I preached that they should repent and turn to God and prove their repentance by their deeds. [21]That is why the Jews seized me in the temple courts and tried to kill me. [22]But I have had God's help to this very day, and so I stand here and testify to small and great alike. I am saying nothing beyond what the prophets and Moses said would happen— [23]that the Christ[x] would suffer and, as the first to rise from the dead, would proclaim light to his own people and to the Gentiles."

[24]At this point Festus interrupted Paul's defense. "You are out of your mind, Paul!" he shouted. "Your great learning is driving you insane."

[25]"I am not insane, most excellent Festus," Paul replied. "What I am saying is true and reasonable. [26]The king is familiar with these things, and I can speak freely to him. I am convinced that none of this has escaped his notice, because it was not done in a corner. [27]King Agrippa, do you believe the prophets? I know you do."

[28]Then Agrippa said to Paul, "Do you think that in such a short time you can persuade me to be a Christian?"

[29]Paul replied, "Short time or long—I pray God that not only

w14 Or Hebrew   *x23 Or Messiah*

you but all who are listening to me today may become what I am, except for these chains."

³⁰The king rose, and with him the governor and Bernice and those sitting with them. ³¹They left the room, and while talking with one another, they said, "This man is not doing anything that deserves death or imprisonment."

³²Agrippa said to Festus, "This man could have been set free if he had not appealed to Caesar."

Paul Sails for Rome

27 When it was decided that we would sail for Italy, Paul and some other prisoners were handed over to a centurion named Julius, who belonged to the Imperial Regiment. ²We boarded a ship from Adramyttium about to sail for ports along the coast of the province of Asia, and we put out to sea. Aristarchus, a Macedonian from Thessalonica, was with us.

³The next day we landed at Sidon; and Julius, in kindness to Paul, allowed him to go to his friends so they might provide for his needs. ⁴From there we put out to sea again and passed to the lee of Cyprus because the winds were against us. ⁵When we had sailed across the open sea off the coast of Cilicia and Pamphylia, we landed at Myra in Lycia. ⁶There the centurion found an Alexandrian ship sailing for Italy and put us on board. ⁷We made slow headway for many days and had difficulty arriving off Cnidus. When the wind did not allow us to hold our course, we sailed to the lee of Crete, opposite Salmone. ⁸We moved along the coast with difficulty and came to a place called Fair Havens, near the town of Lasea.

⁹Much time had been lost, and sailing had already become dangerous because by now it was after the Fast.ʸ So Paul warned them, ¹⁰"Men, I can see that our voyage is going to be disastrous and bring great loss to ship and cargo, and to our own lives also." ¹¹But the centurion, instead of listening to what Paul said, followed the advice of the pilot and of the owner of the ship. ¹²Since the harbor was unsuitable to winter in, the majority decided that we should sail on, hoping to reach Phoenix and winter there. This was a harbor in Crete, facing both southwest and northwest.

The Storm

¹³When a gentle south wind began to blow, they thought they had obtained what they wanted; so they weighed anchor and sailed along the shore of Crete. ¹⁴Before very long, a wind of hurricane force, called the "northeaster," swept down from the island. ¹⁵The ship was caught by the storm and could not head into the wind; so we gave way to it and were driven along. ¹⁶As we passed to the lee of a small island called Cauda, we were hardly able to make the lifeboat secure. ¹⁷When the men had hoisted it aboard, they passed ropes under the ship itself to hold it together. Fearing that they would run aground on the sandbars of Syrtis, they lowered the sea anchor and let the ship be driven along. ¹⁸We took such a violent battering from the storm

OPEN: 1. If you could take a "honeymoon cruise" anywhere, where would you go? Why? **2.** Can you recall a time when you were warned not to do something, but you did it anyway? What happened? **3.** Have you ever been seasick? From what? How did you recover?

DIG: 1. As Paul sets sail for Rome, consult the map at the back of this Bible. What points of interest can you locate along the way from Paul's diary? **2.** From verses 1-3 and 43, what do you know about the centurion in charge? How does his concern for Paul indicate the way Paul used his time while imprisoned in Caesarea? **3.** If you were the ship's owner or pilot, how would you react to Paul's warning about the 50-mile trip they wanted to make (v.10)? Would you have responded any differently than Julius did to Paul's concern? **4.** What in verses 13-20 reveals how severe this storm was? Verse 27 indicates this situation lasted two weeks. How would you be feeling by the end of the first week? What would a page from your ship's diary sound like? **5.** As a sailor on board, how would you feel about Paul's message in verses 21-26? **6.** After being in Caesarea for at least two years, why would Paul need to hear the promise of 23:11 repeated (v.24)? **7.** Compare verse 31 with verse 11. How does the centurion feel about Paul now? About the God Paul serves? **8.** How do Paul's words and his example serve to encourage the others? How would your estimation of Paul change during the two weeks of the storm? **9.** What do you imagine the scene in verses 39-44 was like? What was said? How did people look? Feel? **10.** How do Paul's attitudes and actions compare with those of the sailors? To what would you attribute Paul's ability to remain calm under pressure?

ʸ9 That is, the Day of Atonement (Yom Kippur)

REFLECT: 1. When have you felt caught in a "northeaster," driven along by the wind? What happened? What did you learn from the situation? **2.** In terms of a weather report, how would you describe your life at present? Your life five years ago? **3.** In a crisis, Paul reacted with urgent forewarnings, maintaining hope, counseling, common sense, giving thanks, remaining calm, persevering to the end. In comparison, how do you react to crisis? **4.** What is the greatest pressure situation you're facing now? How can Paul's example and the principles you've learned from this story help you in your situation? What is your part and what is God's part in the resolution of your storm? **5.** When have you been tempted to bail out of a stormy situation, to sneak away in a lifeboat? What happened? What did you learn?

that the next day they began to throw the cargo overboard. [19]On the third day, they threw the ship's tackle overboard with their own hands. [20]When neither sun nor stars appeared for many days and the storm continued raging, we finally gave up all hope of being saved.

[21]After the men had gone a long time without food, Paul stood up before them and said: "Men, you should have taken my advice not to sail from Crete; then you would have spared yourselves this damage and loss. [22]But now I urge you to keep up your courage, because not one of you will be lost; only the ship will be destroyed. [23]Last night an angel of the God whose I am and whom I serve stood beside me [24]and said, 'Do not be afraid, Paul. You must stand trial before Caesar; and God has graciously given you the lives of all who sail with you.' [25]So keep up your courage, men, for I have faith in God that it will happen just as he told me. [26]Nevertheless, we must run aground on some island."

The Shipwreck

[27]On the fourteenth night we were still being driven across the Adriatic[z] Sea, when about midnight the sailors sensed they were approaching land. [28]They took soundings and found that the water was a hundred and twenty feet[a] deep. A short time later they took soundings again and found it was ninety feet[b] deep. [29]Fearing that we would be dashed against the rocks, they dropped four anchors from the stern and prayed for daylight. [30]In an attempt to escape from the ship, the sailors let the lifeboat down into the sea, pretending they were going to lower some anchors from the bow. [31]Then Paul said to the centurion and the soldiers, "Unless these men stay with the ship, you cannot be saved." [32]So the soldiers cut the ropes that held the lifeboat and let it fall away.

[33]Just before dawn Paul urged them all to eat. "For the last fourteen days," he said, "you have been in constant suspense and have gone without food—you haven't eaten anything. [34]Now I urge you to take some food. You need it to survive. Not one of you will lose a single hair from his head." [35]After he said this, he took some bread and gave thanks to God in front of them all. Then he broke it and began to eat. [36]They were all encouraged and ate some food themselves. [37]Altogether there were 276 of us on board. [38]When they had eaten as much as they wanted, they lightened the ship by throwing the grain into the sea.

[39]When daylight came, they did not recognize the land, but they saw a bay with a sandy beach, where they decided to run the ship aground if they could. [40]Cutting loose the anchors, they left them in the sea and at the same time untied the ropes that held the rudders. Then they hoisted the foresail to the wind and made for the beach. [41]But the ship struck a sandbar and ran aground. The bow stuck fast and would not move, and the stern was broken to pieces by the pounding of the surf.

---

[z]27 In ancient times the name referred to an area extending well south of Italy.
[a]28 Greek *twenty orguias* (about 37 meters)   [b]28 Greek *fifteen orguias* (about 27 meters)

⁴²The soldiers planned to kill the prisoners to prevent any of them from swimming away and escaping. ⁴³But the centurion wanted to spare Paul's life and kept them from carrying out their plan. He ordered those who could swim to jump overboard first and get to land. ⁴⁴The rest were to get there on planks or on pieces of the ship. In this way everyone reached land in safety.

Ashore on Malta

28 Once safely on shore, we found out that the island was called Malta. ²The islanders showed us unusual kindness. They built a fire and welcomed us all because it was raining and cold. ³Paul gathered a pile of brushwood and, as he put it on the fire, a viper, driven out by the heat, fastened itself on his hand. ⁴When the islanders saw the snake hanging from his hand, they said to each other, "This man must be a murderer; for though he escaped from the sea, Justice has not allowed him to live." ⁵But Paul shook the snake off into the fire and suffered no ill effects. ⁶The people expected him to swell up or suddenly fall dead, but after waiting a long time and seeing nothing unusual happen to him, they changed their minds and said he was a god.

⁷There was an estate nearby that belonged to Publius, the chief official of the island. He welcomed us to his home and for three days entertained us hospitably. ⁸His father was sick in bed, suffering from fever and dysentery. Paul went in to see him and, after prayer, placed his hands on him and healed him. ⁹When this had happened, the rest of the sick on the island came and were cured. ¹⁰They honored us in many ways and when we were ready to sail, they furnished us with the supplies we needed.

Arrival at Rome

¹¹After three months we put out to sea in a ship that had wintered in the island. It was an Alexandrian ship with the figurehead of the twin gods Castor and Pollux. ¹²We put in at Syracuse and stayed there three days. ¹³From there we set sail and arrived at Rhegium. The next day the south wind came up, and on the following day we reached Puteoli. ¹⁴There we found some brothers who invited us to spend a week with them. And so we came to Rome. ¹⁵The brothers there had heard that we were coming, and they traveled as far as the Forum of Appius and the Three Taverns to meet us. At the sight of these men Paul thanked God and was encouraged. ¹⁶When we got to Rome, Paul was allowed to live by himself, with a soldier to guard him.

Paul Preaches at Rome Under Guard

¹⁷Three days later he called together the leaders of the Jews. When they had assembled, Paul said to them: "My brothers, although I have done nothing against our people or against the customs of our ancestors, I was arrested in Jerusalem and handed over to the Romans. ¹⁸They examined me and wanted to release me, because I was not guilty of any crime deserving death. ¹⁹But when the Jews objected, I was compelled to appeal to Caesar—not that I had any charge to bring against my own people. ²⁰For this reason I have asked to see you and talk with

OPEN: Who would you elect as "Mr. or Mrs. Hospitality" at work? In your neighborhood? In your church?

DIG: 1. In light of the fact God wanted Paul to get to Rome, why do you think he allowed all the events of 27:1-28:9 to happen? What stories would the centurion tell his fellow officers once they arrive? **2.** How could this set the stage for Paul to write about the way his imprisonment at Rome served to advance the gospel (see Php 1:12-13)? **3.** How do you see Acts 1:8 still being carried out?

REFLECT: How has God used a disaster in your life for ministry? What have you learned from this?

OPEN: 1. As a child, whose visit would you be so excited about that you would wait outside (or by the window) until they arrived? Why? **2.** If in jail, what three items would you want most (a file, saw or key is not permitted!)?

DIG: 1. Given the long delay, his shipwreck at sea, and his continuing status as a prisoner, how would Paul feel upon finally arriving in Rome? What must the believers' reunion with Paul have been like (vv.14-15)? **2.** Why might Paul take the initiative to call this meeting with the Jewish leaders in Rome (vv.17-20)? **3.** How do Paul's statements in 23:6, 24:21, 26:8 and 28:20 illustrate what he means by being a "prisoner for the Lord" (see Eph 4:1; Php 1:13-14; Col 4:3; Phm 1)? How does the existence of these prison epistles demonstrate the way Paul made the best of his situation? **4.** In light of all that Paul has been through, how do you think he felt when he heard the Jews' response in verse 21? How is their attitude different from that of the Jews in Jerusalem? How do you account for this difference? Why didn't the

299

Jerusalem Jews pursue the case after it left their area? **5.** How does Isaiah's "hardening ministry" (vv. 25-28) bridge the gap in perception between those who view Christianity as a narrow Jewish sect (v.21) and those who view Christianity as a faith for all peoples (v.28)? How does this thematic bridge relate to 1:8? To 9:15-16? To 26:22-23? **6.** Verse 31 is similar to other summary verses in Acts (see 6:7; 9:31; 12:24; 16:5; 19:20; etc.). What does this ending reveal about Luke's central concern in writing this book?

REFLECT: 1. What bothers your non-Christian friends about the faith? How can you help them overcome those barriers? **2.** When limitations are placed upon you by circumstances beyond your control, how do you react? How can you serve the Lord within these limits? **3.** How does verse 31 set the stage for the way your life could become a continuation of Acts 28? In what way would you like to contribute an "Acts, chapter 29" to this movement of God during the next two years? **4.** Probably within a few years, Paul was killed by the emperor Nero. How would verse 31 serve as a fitting epitaph on Paul's grave? What do you need to build into your life now, so that your faith in Christ will be what people remember about you at death?

you. It is because of the hope of Israel that I am bound with this chain."

[21]They replied, "We have not received any letters from Judea concerning you, and none of the brothers who have come from there has reported or said anything bad about you. [22]But we want to hear what your views are, for we know that people everywhere are talking against this sect."

[23]They arranged to meet Paul on a certain day, and came in even larger numbers to the place where he was staying. From morning till evening he explained and declared to them the kingdom of God and tried to convince them about Jesus from the Law of Moses and from the Prophets. [24]Some were convinced by what he said, but others would not believe. [25]They disagreed among themselves and began to leave after Paul had made this final statement: "The Holy Spirit spoke the truth to your forefathers when he said through Isaiah the prophet:

[26]" 'Go to this people and say,
   "You will be ever hearing but never understanding;
      you will be ever seeing but never perceiving."
[27]For this people's heart has become calloused;
      they hardly hear with their ears,
      and they have closed their eyes.
   Otherwise they might see with their eyes,
      hear with their ears,
      understand with their hearts
   and turn, and I would heal them.'[c]

[28]"Therefore I want you to know that God's salvation has been sent to the Gentiles, and they will listen!"[d]

[30]For two whole years Paul stayed there in his own rented house and welcomed all who came to see him. [31]Boldly and without hindrance he preached the kingdom of God and taught about the Lord Jesus Christ.

[c]27 Isaiah 6:9,10   [d]28 Some manuscripts *listen!"* [29]*After he said this, the Jews left, arguing vigorously among themselves.*

ROMANS

INTRODUCTION

Date and Audience

For nearly ten years Paul had been at work evangelizing the Gentile territories ringing the Aegean Sea. Now that there were established churches throughout the region, he turns his eyes to fresh fields. He would go to Spain, the oldest Roman colony in the West. But first there was unfinished business: He had taken up a collection to aid the poor in Jerusalem—a fine gesture on the part of the newer churches—and now he had to take this to Jerusalem, though he did so with some misgiving (Rom. 15:31).

After Jerusalem, he planned to travel to Spain, stopping enroute to fulfill a long-held dream. He would visit Rome—the capital of the world. In anticipation of that visit, he wrote the Letter to the Romans by way of introduction (the Roman Christians did not know him, though, as chapter 16 reveals, he had friends there). He was also eager to assure the Roman Christians, contrary to false rumors they might have heard, that the gospel he was preaching was, indeed, the gospel of Jesus Christ. Paul wrote his letter during a three-month period spent in Corinth at the home of his friend and convert Gaius (Rom. 16:23). It was winter. The time was probably A.D. 56-57 (though it was certainly sometime between A.D. 54-59).

Paul's plan did not work as he intended. He would visit Rome, but not for three more years, and then he would come not as a tourist but as a prisoner. His misgivings about his Jerusalem trip proved accurate. Once there he was quickly arrested and eventually sent to Rome for trial. Paul remained in Rome under house arrest for at least two years. Ultimately, according to reliable tradition, he was executed at a place just outside Rome. He never went to Spain.

It is not known how the Roman church began. It is not unlikely that some Roman Jews, converted on the Day of Pentecost (Acts 2:10), began the church. The Roman historian Suetonius writes that Jews were expelled from Rome about A.D. 50 for rioting, probably as a result of preaching Jesus in synagogues. As for the Gentile Christians in Rome, it is known that other Christian missionaries besides Paul were active in founding churches.

Characteristics

Romans is Paul's most complete theological statement—carefully written, precise, and painstakingly logical (though its logic is "rabbinic" and somewhat baffling to modern readers). This is not to say, however, that Romans is dull and ponderous. Quite the contrary, it is alive and vital, full of surprises and paradox, colorful, compassionate, and sweeping in scope. In fact, the very magnitude of its themes makes Romans, at times, heavy going. Even the apostle Peter sometimes found Paul's writing hard to understand (2 Peter 3:16)!

Theme

At issue is the question of how God will judge each of us on the final day. Will it be on the basis of how "good" we were, that is, how well we kept the Law? If so, our life would be full of unending tension. Acutely aware of repeated failure, we would never have any assurance of acquittal. The Law would then be a cursed thing to us—a constant reminder of our inadequacy.

But this is not how God intends life to be. Here the great theme of Romans emerges: We can have assurance of right standing before God and hence know we will be given a positive verdict on Judgment Day. Such confidence does not come because of what we have done. It comes because of what God does—thanks to Christ's death in our place, he freely offers us his grace. Salvation is a gift which we cannot earn; we can only receive it by faith with such gratitude that our whole life changes.

Paul sets this theme against the teaching of certain Jewish Christians, legalists who would add circumcision to grace (thus nullifying grace). If we have to do anything to deserve it, salvation is not an unearned gift freely given by God. In the course of his argument, Paul sets up a series of antitheses: faith versus works, Spirit versus flesh, and liberty versus bondage.

In answering the question of how we gain right standing before God, Paul argues first that both pagans and religious people stand condemned before God (1:18-3:20), that right standing comes only by God's grace shown in Christ's sacrificial death and acceptance by faith (3:21-5:21), and that such righteousness leads to a whole new lifestyle (6:1-8:39). He then deals with the question of why Israel rejected Christ (9:1-11:36), ending with practical exhortations for a life of faith (12:1-15:13).

Such a rich and complex piece of writing deserves repeated study. Still the major themes are readily visible and the key words are obvious.

The Importance of Romans

The impact of Romans on the history of the church can hardly be overstated. Many great advances occurred as the result of a fresh reading of this book. In A.D. 386, Augustine was converted by reading Romans 13:13-14. He then went on to write his definitive analysis of human nature and original sin (based on Romans 5 and 7), which shaped Western theology for centuries. By 1516, Martin Luther had grasped the doctrine of justification by faith alone, and so the Protestant Reformation was born. In 1738, John Wesley was converted upon hearing someone read Luther's preface to Romans, and so the evangelical revival in England was launched. In 1918, Karl Barth published his commentary on Romans, which fell like a "bomb on the playground of the theologians" (Karl Adam, quoted in *The Epistle to the Romans*, F. F. Bruce, p. 60), and so the modern period of theology was inaugurated.

Luther wrote: "This Epistle is really the chief part of the New Testament and the very purest Gospel, and is worthy not only that every Christian should know it word for word, by heart, but occupy himself with it everyday, as the bread of the soul" (*Commentary on Romans*, trans. by J. Theodore Mueller, p. xiii). Calvin wrote that "if we understand this Epistle, we have a passage opened to us to the understanding of the whole Scripture" (*The Epistles of Paul the Apostle to the Romans and the Thessalonians*, trans. by R. MacKenzie, p. 2).

Romans

1 Paul, a servant of Christ Jesus, called to be an apostle and set apart for the gospel of God— [2]the gospel he promised beforehand through his prophets in the Holy Scriptures [3]regarding his Son, who as to his human nature was a descendant of David, [4]and who through the Spirit[a] of holiness was declared with power to be the Son of God[b] by his resurrection from the dead: Jesus Christ our Lord. [5]Through him and for his name's sake, we received grace and apostleship to call people from among all the Gentiles to the obedience that comes from faith. [6]And you also are among those who are called to belong to Jesus Christ.

[7]To all in Rome who are loved by God and called to be saints:

Grace and peace to you from God our Father and from the Lord Jesus Christ.

Paul's Longing to Visit Rome

[8]First, I thank my God through Jesus Christ for all of you, because your faith is being reported all over the world. [9]God, whom I serve with my whole heart in preaching the gospel of his Son, is my witness how constantly I remember you [10]in my prayers at all times; and I pray that now at last by God's will the way may be opened for me to come to you.

[11]I long to see you so that I may impart to you some spiritual gift to make you strong— [12]that is, that you and I may be mutually encouraged by each other's faith. [13]I do not want you to be unaware, brothers, that I planned many times to come to you (but have been prevented from doing so until now) in order that I might have a harvest among you, just as I have had among the other Gentiles.

[14]I am obligated both to Greeks and non-Greeks, both to the wise and the foolish. [15]That is why I am so eager to preach the gospel also to you who are at Rome.

[16]I am not ashamed of the gospel, because it is the power of God for the salvation of everyone who believes: first for the Jew, then for the Gentile. [17]For in the gospel a righteousness from God is revealed, a righteousness that is by faith from first to last,[c] just as it is written: "The righteous will live by faith."[d]

God's Wrath Against Mankind

[18]The wrath of God is being revealed from heaven against all the godlessness and wickedness of men who suppress the truth by their wickedness, [19]since what may be known about God is plain to them, because God has made it plain to them. [20]For since the creation of the world God's invisible qualities—his eternal power and divine nature—have been clearly seen, being understood from what has been made, so that men are without excuse.

OPEN: 1. What is one place you have never seen that you'd love to visit? Why? 2. What title best fits you: Parent? Student? Family taxi driver? Couch potato? 3. What sorts of letters do you save? Why?

DIG: 1. What does *servant* and *apostle* reveal about Paul? 2. From the use of "call" and "called" (vv.5-7), what does it mean to be a Christian? What do the terms in verse 7 indicate about the way God views us? 3. Note all the "I" statements. What do these say about Paul? 4. Why would Paul, a highly educated Jew, write verse 14? How would he rewrite that to address your community? 5. What facts can you learn about the gospel from verses 2-4 and 16-17? Pretend someone is "turned off" to religious words: how would you explain verse 17 to her or him?

REFLECT: 1. What in this passage impresses you most about Paul? About the gospel? Why? 2. How did God call you to Christ? How has that call changed your goals? Your sense of obligation to others? To what mission or task do you sense God nudging you? How is that reflected in your prayers? Your actions? 3. What grabs you about verse 17? What questions does it raise that you hope further study will answer?

OPEN: What was the best excuse you ever gave as a kid when your parents caught you doing something wrong? What's the best one you've heard from your own kids?

DIG: 1. If verse 17 is the solution, how do verses 18-21 describe the problem? What is wrong with the people's relationship to God? 2. What can be learned about God

---

[a]4 Or *who as to his spirit*   [b]4 Or *was appointed to be the Son of God with power*   [c]17 Or *is from faith to faith*   [d]17 Hab. 2:4

through nature (vv.19-21; also Ps 8:3-4; 19:1; 139:13-15)? **3.** Why then do people tend to worship creation rather than the Creator (vv.18,21-23,25,28)? How do these attitudes lead to evil acts? **4.** How does God respond to these evil attitudes? How is giving people over to evil (vv.24,26,28) a part of their punishment? **5.** How does their "freedom" (to do as they desire) actually become a trap (that is, an inescapable consequence)?

REFLECT: 1. When in your life have you experienced a "futile mind" or a "darkened heart"? When has the freedom to resist God only ended up hurting you? **2.** How do you explain God's wrath to someone who believes all people are basically good? **3.** In reading through the list of sins in verses 29-32, how do you feel when you see that some of your faults are listed along with the "really awful" sins others commit?

OPEN: When you were young, which of your parents was more strict? Merciful? Consistent?

DIG: 1. Who does Paul address in 2:1 (see 2:17)? The Roman church was a mix of Jewish and Gentile converts. What in this section indicates the possible areas of tension between them? **2.** What "same things" is each group guilty of (v.4): Does this refer to the specific *symptoms* of sin, such as idolatry (1:28) and homosexuality (1:27), which were scandalous to the Jews? Or does "same things" refer to *root causes* of sin (1:18, 21)? **3.** What evidence do you see in verses 5-13 that God's kindness to these people has led to presumption rather than to repentance? How are they in the same boat as those in 1:18-32? **4.** How do you reconcile 1:17 with what Paul says about doing good (2:7) and obeying the law (2:13)? What is Paul's point in each section?

[21]For although they knew God, they neither glorified him as God nor gave thanks to him, but their thinking became futile and their foolish hearts were darkened. [22]Although they claimed to be wise, they became fools [23]and exchanged the glory of the immortal God for images made to look like mortal man and birds and animals and reptiles.

[24]Therefore God gave them over in the sinful desires of their hearts to sexual impurity for the degrading of their bodies with one another. [25]They exchanged the truth of God for a lie, and worshiped and served created things rather than the Creator—who is forever praised. Amen.

[26]Because of this, God gave them over to shameful lusts. Even their women exchanged natural relations for unnatural ones. [27]In the same way the men also abandoned natural relations with women and were inflamed with lust for one another. Men committed indecent acts with other men, and received in themselves the due penalty for their perversion.

[28]Furthermore, since they did not think it worthwhile to retain the knowledge of God, he gave them over to a depraved mind, to do what ought not to be done. [29]They have become filled with every kind of wickedness, evil, greed and depravity. They are full of envy, murder, strife, deceit and malice. They are gossips, [30]slanderers, God-haters, insolent, arrogant and boastful; they invent ways of doing evil; they disobey their parents; [31]they are senseless, faithless, heartless, ruthless. [32]Although they know God's righteous decree that those who do such things deserve death, they not only continue to do these very things but also approve of those who practice them.

God's Righteous Judgment

2 You, therefore, have no excuse, you who pass judgment on someone else, for at whatever point you judge the other, you are condemning yourself, because you who pass judgment do the same things. [2]Now we know that God's judgment against those who do such things is based on truth. [3]So when you, a mere man, pass judgment on them and yet do the same things, do you think you will escape God's judgment? [4]Or do you show contempt for the riches of his kindness, tolerance and patience, not realizing that God's kindness leads you towards repentance?

[5]But because of your stubbornness and your unrepentant heart, you are storing up wrath against yourself for the day of God's wrath, when his righteous judgment will be revealed. [6]God "will give to each person according to what he has done." [7]To those who by persistence in doing good seek glory, honor and immortality, he will give eternal life. [8]But for those who are self-seeking and who reject the truth and follow evil, there will be wrath and anger. [9]There will be trouble and distress for every human being who does evil: first for the Jew, then for the Gentile; [10]but glory, honor and peace for everyone who does good: first for the Jew, then for the Gentile. [11]For God does not show favoritism.

[12]All who sin apart from the law will also perish apart from

[e]6 Psalm 62:12; Prov. 24:12

the law, and all who sin under the law will be judged by the law. [13]For it is not those who hear the law who are righteous in God's sight, but it is those who obey the law who will be declared righteous. [14](Indeed, when Gentiles, who do not have the law, do by nature things required by the law, they are a law for themselves, even though they do not have the law, [15]since they show that the requirements of the law are written on their hearts, their consciences also bearing witness, and their thoughts now accusing, now even defending them.) [16]This will take place on the day when God will judge men's secrets through Jesus Christ, as my gospel declares.

The Jews and the Law

[17]Now you, if you call yourself a Jew; if you rely on the law and brag about your relationship to God; [18]if you know his will and approve of what is superior because you are instructed by the law; [19]if you are convinced that you are a guide for the blind, a light for those who are in the dark, [20]an instructor of the foolish, a teacher of infants, because you have in the law the embodiment of knowledge and truth— [21]you, then, who teach others, do you not teach yourself? You who preach against stealing, do you steal? [22]You who say that people should not commit adultery, do you commit adultery? You who abhor idols, do you rob temples? [23]You who brag about the law, do you dishonor God by breaking the law? [24]As it is written: "God's name is blasphemed among the Gentiles because of you."[f]

[25]Circumcision has value if you observe the law, but if you break the law, you have become as though you had not been circumcised. [26]If those who are not circumcised keep the law's requirements, will they not be regarded as though they were circumcised? [27]The one who is not circumcised physically and yet obeys the law will condemn you who, even though you have the[g] written code and circumcision, are a lawbreaker.

[28]A man is not a Jew if he is only one outwardly, nor is circumcision merely outward and physical. [29]No, a man is a Jew if he is one inwardly; and circumcision is circumcision of the heart, by the Spirit, not by the written code. Such a man's praise is not from men, but from God.

God's Faithfulness

3 What advantage, then, is there in being a Jew, or what value is there in circumcision? [2]Much in every way! First of all, they have been entrusted with the very words of God.

[3]What if some did not have faith? Will their lack of faith nullify God's faithfulness? [4]Not at all! Let God be true, and every man a liar. As it is written:

"So that you may be proved right when you speak
and prevail when you judge."[h]

[5]But if our unrighteousness brings out God's righteousness more clearly, what shall we say? That God is unjust in bringing his wrath on us? (I am using a human argument.) [6]Certainly not!

REFLECT: 1. Has God's kindness led you toward real love for him? Or do you now take the relationship for granted? How so? **2.** Do you see yourself more as a "gross sinner" (1:18-32)? Or as a "respectable sinner" (2:1-16)? Does it matter to God?

OPEN: What do you remember most about your religious training prior to your teen years?

DIG: 1. If you were one of the Jews in verses 17-24, what would you write about yourself on a job application? What type of reference would your Gentile neighbor write? What accounts for the difference? **2.** What was the original intent of the law and of circumcision (see Ge 17:1-14)? How is that being twisted here? **3.** What does Paul mean by "circumcision of the heart" (v.29; see Dt 10:16; 30:6; Jer 4:4; 9:25-26)? What is the real mark of God's family?

REFLECT: 1. The finger pointed at the Jews in verses 17-24 could also be pointed at you. How does that realization affect you? **2.** When did your faith become more than a ritual? What helped that to happen? **3.** What religious rituals and symbols are twisted today like circumcision was then?

OPEN: 1. What were the "perks" of belonging to your family? **2.** As a child, to whom did you compare yourself? Were you better or worse than your point of comparison?

DIG: 1. Have one person take the role of someone protesting Paul's conclusion in 2:28-29. That person reads the questions in verses 1,3,5 and 7. Have another person read Paul's response in verses 2,4,6 and 8. What is the issue in each objection? How do the questions continue the practice of

[f]24 Isaiah 52:5; Ezek. 36:22   [g]27 Or *who, by means of a*   [h]4 Psalm 51:4

misapplying God's teachings? **2.** Although the Jewish Christians in Rome apparently felt superior to the Gentiles (2:1; 3:1), what does Paul say they have in common? **3.** From verses 10-18, list what is said regarding human thought, direction, speech, and action. How does this list make you feel? **4.** How do 3:19 and 1:20 prove Paul's point that the whole world is accountable to God? **5.** From verse 20, would you say that the law is *descriptive* (more like a doctor's thermometer)? Or *prescriptive* (more like medicine to a sick patient)? What is its purpose?

REFLECT: 1. What "positions of privilege" do people claim today with respect to God: (a) "My dad's a minister"? (b) "I go to church every week"? (c) "I was baptized"? (d) "I belong to a Serendipity group"? Have you ever heard yourself appeal to one of these? How do these actually make you more responsible? **2.** Suppose this letter ended with verse 20. How would you feel about yourself? About God? **3.** When did you first truly sense your sin and need for God? **4.** What can you learn about witnessing from Paul's example in chapters 2-3? What kinds of people today may need to be approached like this?

OPEN: Who was your favorite "superstar" as a kid? What made him or her so special?

DIG: 1. Look up "justification," "redemption," and "atonement" in a dictionary. What everyday examples could you use to illustrate each word? **2.** What do each of these words point out about the death of Christ? **3.** How does this section break down barriers between Jew and Gentile?

REFLECT: 1. How does *your* life in Christ illustrate the key words here? **2.** When did the message of God's grace become real to you? What impact is it having on your life right now?

If that were so, how could God judge the world? [7]Someone might argue, "If my falsehood enhances God's truthfulness and so increases his glory, why am I still condemned as a sinner?" [8]Why not say—as we are being slanderously reported as saying and as some claim that we say—"Let us do evil that good may result"? Their condemnation is deserved.

No One Is Righteous

[9]What shall we conclude then? Are we any better[i]? Not at all! We have already made the charge that Jews and Gentiles alike are all under sin. [10]As it is written:

> "There is no one righteous, not even one;
> [11] there is no one who understands,
>   no one who seeks God.
> [12]All have turned away,
>   they have together become worthless;
> there is no one who does good,
>   not even one."[j]
> [13]"Their throats are open graves;
>   their tongues practice deceit."[k]
>   "The poison of vipers is on their lips."[l]
> [14] "Their mouths are full of cursing and bitterness."[m]
> [15]"Their feet are swift to shed blood;
> [16] ruin and misery mark their ways,
> [17]and the way of peace they do not know."[n]
> [18] "There is no fear of God before their eyes."[o]

[19]Now we know that whatever the law says, it says to those who are under the law, so that every mouth may be silenced and the whole world held accountable to God. [20]Therefore no one will be declared righteous in his sight by observing the law; rather, through the law we become conscious of sin.

Righteousness Through Faith

[21]But now a righteousness from God, apart from law, has been made known, to which the Law and the Prophets testify. [22]This righteousness from God comes through faith in Jesus Christ to all who believe. There is no difference, [23]for all have sinned and fall short of the glory of God, [24]and are justified freely by his grace through the redemption that came by Christ Jesus. [25]God presented him as a sacrifice of atonement,[p] through faith in his blood. He did this to demonstrate his justice, because in his forbearance he had left the sins committed beforehand unpunished — [26]he did it to demonstrate his justice at the present time, so as to be just and the one who justifies those who have faith in Jesus.

[27]Where, then, is boasting? It is excluded. On what principle? On that of observing the law? No, but on that of faith. [28]For we maintain that a man is justified by faith apart from observing the law. [29]Is God the God of Jews only? Is he not the God of Gentiles too? Yes, of Gentiles too, [30]since there is only one God, who will

---

i9 Or *worse*   j12 Psalms 14:1-3; 53:1-3; Eccles. 7:20   k13 Psalm 5:9
l13 Psalm 140:3   m14 Psalm 10:7   n17 Isaiah 59:7,8   o18 Psalm 36:1
p25 Or *as the one who would turn aside his wrath, taking away sin*

justify the circumcised by faith and the uncircumcised through that same faith. ³¹Do we, then, nullify the law by this faith? Not at all! Rather, we uphold the law.

Abraham Justified by Faith

4 What then shall we say that Abraham, our forefather, discovered in this matter? ²If, in fact, Abraham was justified by works, he had something to boast about—but not before God. ³What does the Scripture say? "Abraham believed God, and it was credited to him as righteousness."*q*

⁴Now when a man works, his wages are not credited to him as a gift, but as an obligation. ⁵However, to the man who does not work but trusts God who justifies the wicked, his faith is credited as righteousness. ⁶David says the same thing when he speaks of the blessedness of the man to whom God credits righteousness apart from works:

⁷"Blessed are they
  whose transgressions are forgiven,
  whose sins are covered.
⁸Blessed is the man
  whose sin the Lord will never count against him."*r*

⁹Is this blessedness only for the circumcised, or also for the uncircumcised? We have been saying that Abraham's faith was credited to him as righteousness. ¹⁰Under what circumstances was it credited? Was it after he was circumcised, or before? It was not after, but before! ¹¹And he received the sign of circumcision, a seal of the righteousness that he had by faith while he was still uncircumcised. So then, he is the father of all who believe but have not been circumcised, in order that righteousness might be credited to them. ¹²And he is also the father of the circumcised who not only are circumcised but who also walk in the footsteps of the faith that our father Abraham had before he was circumcised.

¹³It was not through law that Abraham and his offspring received the promise that he would be heir of the world, but through the righteousness that comes by faith. ¹⁴For if those who live by law are heirs, faith has no value and the promise is worthless, ¹⁵because law brings wrath. And where there is no law there is no transgression.

¹⁶Therefore, the promise comes by faith, so that it may be by grace and may be guaranteed to all Abraham's offspring—not only to those who are of the law but also to those who are of the faith of Abraham. He is the father of us all. ¹⁷As it is written: "I have made you a father of many nations."*s* He is our father in the sight of God, in whom he believed—the God who gives life to the dead and calls things that are not as though they were.

¹⁸Against all hope, Abraham in hope believed and so became the father of many nations, just as it had been said to him, "So shall your offspring be."*t* ¹⁹Without weakening in his faith, he faced the fact that his body was as good as dead—since he was about a hundred years old—and that Sarah's womb was also

OPEN: 1. What is one unbelievable (even laughable) thing you have been promised on TV, in junk mail, or on the campaign trail? What prompts you to toss it aside instead of trusting in the promised "free lunch"? **2.** How do these gimmicks affect your view of "big" promises in general? Of Bible promises in particular?

DIG: 1. Since some of the Jewish converts believed they were set right with God by the law, why does Paul go back to the examples of Abraham and David? **2.** How does 4:3-8 illustrate what is said in 3:27-28? On what basis, then, is a right relationship with God given or credited to us? **3.** What is Paul's point in stressing that Abraham was counted as right with God *before* he was circumcised? How does 4:9-17 support Paul's statement in 3:29-31 about faith and the law? **4.** What do you learn about faith from the example in verses 18-21? How would you feel in Abraham's place? **5.** What are the key points in Abraham's view of God? How do these truths relate to what Paul calls us to believe in verses 23-25? **6.** How would you sum up the gospel from verses 23-25?

REFLECT: 1. Who are some other biblical characters that you respect as examples of faith? Who are some Christians today that set the pace for you about trusting in God? What is most important about these persons to you? **2.** What does it matter to you—practically or emotionally—whether a right relationship with God is a *gift to be received* or a *prize to be earned*? **3.** Since this right relationship is a gift, how would you use Abraham's example to argue against a presumptuous attitude toward God? **4.** Where are you being stretched in your ability to trust God's promises? What can you learn from Abraham's example to encourage you?

*q*3 Gen. 15:6; also in verse 22   *r*8 Psalm 32:1,2   *s*17 Gen. 17:5   *t*18 Gen. 15:5

dead. [20]Yet he did not waver through unbelief regarding the promise of God, but was strengthened in his faith and gave glory to God, [21]being fully persuaded that God had power to do what he had promised. [22]This is why "it was credited to him as righteousness." [23]The words "it was credited to him" were written not for him alone, [24]but also for us, to whom God will credit righteousness—for us who believe in him who raised Jesus our Lord from the dead. [25]He was delivered over to death for our sins and was raised to life for our justification.

Peace and Joy

5 Therefore, since we have been justified through faith, we[u] have peace with God through our Lord Jesus Christ, [2]through whom we have gained access by faith into this grace in which we now stand. And we[u] rejoice in the hope of the glory of God. [3]Not only so, but we[u] also rejoice in our sufferings, because we know that suffering produces perseverance; [4]perseverance, character; and character, hope. [5]And hope does not disappoint us, because God has poured out his love into our hearts by the Holy Spirit, whom he has given us.

[6]You see, at just the right time, when we were still powerless, Christ died for the ungodly. [7]Very rarely will anyone die for a righteous man, though for a good man someone might possibly dare to die. [8]But God demonstrates his own love for us in this: While we were still sinners, Christ died for us.

[9]Since we have now been justified by his blood, how much more shall we be saved from God's wrath through him! [10]For if, when we were God's enemies, we were reconciled to him through the death of his Son, how much more, having been reconciled, shall we be saved through his life! [11]Not only is this so, but we also rejoice in God through our Lord Jesus Christ, through whom we have now received reconciliation.

Death Through Adam, Life Through Christ

[12]Therefore, just as sin entered the world through one man, and death through sin, and in this way death came to all men, because all sinned— [13]for before the law was given, sin was in the world. But sin is not taken into account when there is no law. [14]Nevertheless, death reigned from the time of Adam to the time of Moses, even over those who did not sin by breaking a command, as did Adam, who was a pattern of the one to come.

[15]But the gift is not like the trespass. For if the many died by the trespass of the one man, how much more did God's grace and the gift that came by the grace of the one man, Jesus Christ, overflow to the many! [16]Again, the gift of God is not like the result of the one man's sin: The judgment followed one sin and brought condemnation, but the gift followed many trespasses and brought justification. [17]For if, by the trespass of the one man, death reigned through that one man, how much more will those who receive God's abundant provision of grace and of the gift of righteousness reign in life through the one man, Jesus Christ.

[u]1,2,3 Or *let us*

OPEN: Who is the "cock-eyed optimist" in your family or group?

DIG: 1. Paraphrase what it means to be "justified through faith" (v.1). What benefits are ours as a result (vv.1-5)? How are suffering, hope, and God's love interrelated? **2.** What words describe what we once were in God's eyes (vv.6,8, 10)? How does the death of Christ change all this? **3.** What tone of voice is Paul using in verses 9-11? Why? **4.** How does the OT sacrificial system illustrate what Christ did on the cross (v.9; see 3:25; Lev 16:3-16; 17:11)?

REFLECT: What three words best describe your life before you were a Christian? How about now? Why the change?

OPEN: What quirks did you inherit from each of your parents? How do you see yourself reflected in your own children (if any)?

DIG: 1. What is the logic behind the "bad news" in verses 12-14? When have you made a decision that affected others in a bad way? How does this help you understand verse 12? **2.** From verses 15-19, list in two columns the comparisons and contrasts between Adam and Jesus. What results from each one? **3.** From 5:1-21, what do you note that God has done through Jesus for us? How does this add to your understanding of God's grace (vv.1,15, 17,20,21)? How does this chapter illustrate why "Grace and peace to you" (1:7) is such an appropriate greeting for Christians?

REFLECT: 1. Does the gospel message excite you as it does Paul? Why or why not? What could help you to experience its life and

[18]Consequently, just as the result of one trespass was condemnation for all men, so also the result of one act of righteousness was justification that brings life for all men. [19]For just as through the disobedience of the one man the many were made sinners, so also through the obedience of the one man the many will be made righteous.

[20]The law was added so that the trespass might increase. But where sin increased, grace increased all the more, [21]so that, just as sin reigned in death, so also grace might reign through righteousness to bring eternal life through Jesus Christ our Lord.

Dead to Sin, Alive in Christ

6 What shall we say, then? Shall we go on sinning so that grace may increase? [2]By no means! We died to sin; how can we live in it any longer? [3]Or don't you know that all of us who were baptized into Christ Jesus were baptized into his death? [4]We were therefore buried with him through baptism into death in order that, just as Christ was raised from the dead through the glory of the Father, we too may live a new life.

[5]If we have been united with him like this in his death, we will certainly also be united with him in his resurrection. [6]For we know that our old self was crucified with him so that the body of sin might be done away with,[v] that we should no longer be slaves to sin— [7]because anyone who has died has been freed from sin.

[8]Now if we died with Christ, we believe that we will also live with him. [9]For we know that since Christ was raised from the dead, he cannot die again; death no longer has mastery over him. [10]The death he died, he died to sin once for all; but the life he lives, he lives to God.

[11]In the same way, count yourselves dead to sin but alive to God in Christ Jesus. [12]Therefore do not let sin reign in your mortal body so that you obey its evil desires. [13]Do not offer the parts of your body to sin, as instruments of wickedness, but rather offer yourselves to God, as those who have been brought from death to life; and offer the parts of your body to him as instruments of righteousness. [14]For sin shall not be your master, because you are not under law, but under grace.

Slaves to Righteousness

[15]What then? Shall we sin because we are not under law but under grace? By no means! [16]Don't you know that when you offer yourselves to someone to obey him as slaves, you are slaves to the one whom you obey—whether you are slaves to sin, which leads to death, or to obedience, which leads to righteousness? [17]But thanks be to God that, though you used to be slaves to sin, you wholeheartedly obeyed the form of teaching to which you were entrusted. [18]You have been set free from sin and have become slaves to righteousness.

[19]I put this in human terms because you are weak in your natural selves. Just as you used to offer the parts of your body in slavery to impurity and to ever-increasing wickedness, so now

[v]6 Or be rendered powerless

---

vitality again? **2.** Write a thank-you letter to Jesus, reflecting on what he has done for you (as described by Paul in this chapter). Read these letters as closing prayers.

OPEN: What do you remember about Easter Sunday when you were a child: Sunrise Services? New clothes? The Easter Bunny? Hunting eggs?

DIG: 1. Some people are misusing God's grace (see 3:8; 5:20-21). How so? What is Paul's response to that here? **2.** The idea of death is mentioned 15 times in this section: How does Christ's death and resurrection tie into our relationship with sin? **3.** What does it mean to practice the teaching in verses 11-13? What is the motivation?

REFLECT: 1. What do you do when you hear voices from your former life (in sin), as do these believers? **2.** What specifically will you do this week to count yourself dead to sin and alive to Christ? If you could bury one thing with Christ forever, what would it be?

OPEN: What boss have you had who seemed most like a "slave driver"? How so?

DIG: 1. How is the question in verse 15 another attempt to misuse Paul's teaching on grace (see v.1)? **2.** Compare Paul's image of death (6:1-14) with this one about slavery. What is similar and different in the points he makes in each case? **3.** What is the "cost and benefit" of each type of slavery here? **4.** Theologically and practically, how is *slavery* to Christ *freedom* from sin?

REFLECT: 1. What modern image (in music, sports, art, etc.) illustrates Paul's point that submission to a good "master" leads to freedom? **2.** If you had seen yourself as God's willing servant this past week, what would have changed in your attitudes and actions? Where do you particularly want to work on this in the coming week?

OPEN: What was so special about your first "steady" boyfriend or girlfriend?

DIG: 1. After "death and life" and "slavery and freedom," what new image is used here? Which of these three images helps you to understand your relationship with Christ? **2.** What did the law produce in those who tried to live by it? How has Jesus changed this?

REFLECT: 1. Do you feel more "married" to the living Christ, or to some religious code? Explain how you experience the difference. **2.** In your life's vineyard, what would "fruit to God" look like? "Fruit for death"?

OPEN: In what way is your "spirit willing" but your "flesh weak": Starting an exercise plan? Getting to work on time? Cutting out junk food? Finishing projects around the house? Other:_____?

DIG: 1. What is the significance of the shift in pronouns from 7:1-6 and this section? How does Paul's example in verses 7-11 illustrate what he meant in verse 5? Give an example of this principle in your life. **2.** How does the law which was supposed to lead to *life* actually lead to *death*? How do verses 14-20 answer this question? **3.** Prior to Paul's conversion, how must he have felt about the inner turmoil described here? How did he try to deal with it then (see Php 3:4-6)? What has he found in Christ? **4.** Why do you think God's law was given for us to follow: (a) Means to follow *in order to be* saved? (b) Guide to follow *once we are* saved by grace? (c) Stumbling block, impossible to follow, which only points the sinner to God's grace? How do verses 10, 12 and 22 support your answer?

REFLECT: 1. In light of your own

---

offer them in slavery to righteousness leading to holiness. [20]When you were slaves to sin, you were free from the control of righteousness. [21]What benefit did you reap at that time from the things you are now ashamed of? Those things result in death! [22]But now that you have been set free from sin and have become slaves to God, the benefit you reap leads to holiness, and the result is eternal life. [23]For the wages of sin is death, but the gift of God is eternal life in [w] Christ Jesus our Lord.

An Illustration From Marriage

7 Do you not know, brothers—for I am speaking to men who know the law—that the law has authority over a man only as long as he lives? [2]For example, by law a married woman is bound to her husband as long as he is alive, but if her husband dies, she is released from the law of marriage. [3]So then, if she marries another man while her husband is still alive, she is called an adulteress. But if her husband dies, she is released from that law and is not an adulteress, even though she marries another man.

[4]So, my brothers, you also died to the law through the body of Christ, that you might belong to another, to him who was raised from the dead, in order that we might bear fruit to God. [5]For when we were controlled by the sinful nature,[x] the sinful passions aroused by the law were at work in our bodies, so that we bore fruit for death. [6]But now, by dying to what once bound us, we have been released from the law so that we serve in the new way of the Spirit, and not in the old way of the written code.

Struggling With Sin

[7]What shall we say, then? Is the law sin? Certainly not! Indeed I would not have known what sin was except through the law. For I would not have known what coveting really was if the law had not said, "Do not covet."[y] [8]But sin, seizing the opportunity afforded by the commandment, produced in me every kind of covetous desire. For apart from law, sin is dead. [9]Once I was alive apart from law; but when the commandment came, sin sprang to life and I died. [10]I found that the very commandment that was intended to bring life actually brought death. [11]For sin, seizing the opportunity afforded by the commandment, deceived me, and through the commandment put me to death. [12]So then, the law is holy, and the commandment is holy, righteous and good.

[13]Did that which is good, then, become death to me? By no means! But in order that sin might be recognized as sin, it produced death in me through what was good, so that through the commandment sin might become utterly sinful.

[14]We know that the law is spiritual; but I am unspiritual, sold as a slave to sin. [15]I do not understand what I do. For what I want to do I do not do, but what I hate I do. [16]And if I do what I do not want to do, I agree that the law is good. [17]As it is, it is no longer I myself who do it, but it is sin living in me. [18]I know that nothing good lives in me, that is, in my sinful nature.[z] For

w23 Or *through*   *x5* Or *the flesh;* also in verse 25   *y7* Exodus 20:17; Deut. 5:21
z18 Or *my flesh*

I have the desire to do what is good, but I cannot carry it out. ¹⁹For what I do is not the good I want to do; no, the evil I do not want to do—this I keep on doing. ²⁰Now if I do what I do not want to do, it is no longer I who do it, but it is sin living in me that does it.

²¹So I find this law at work: When I want to do good, evil is right there with me. ²²For in my inner being I delight in God's law; ²³but I see another law at work in the members of my body, waging war against the law of my mind and making me a prisoner of the law of sin at work within my members. ²⁴What a wretched man I am! Who will rescue me from this body of death? ²⁵Thanks be to God—through Jesus Christ our Lord!

So then, I myself in my mind am a slave to God's law, but in the sinful nature a slave to the law of sin.

Life Through the Spirit

8 Therefore, there is now no condemnation for those who are in Christ Jesus,ᵃ ²because through Christ Jesus the law of the Spirit of life set me free from the law of sin and death. ³For what the law was powerless to do in that it was weakened by the sinful nature,ᵇ God did by sending his own Son in the likeness of sinful man to be a sin offering.ᶜ And so he condemned sin in sinful man,ᵈ ⁴in order that the righteous requirements of the law might be fully met in us, who do not live according to the sinful nature but according to the Spirit.

⁵Those who live according to the sinful nature have their minds set on what that nature desires; but those who live in accordance with the Spirit have their minds set on what the Spirit desires. ⁶The mind of sinful manᵉ is death, but the mind controlled by the Spirit is life and peace; ⁷the sinful mindᶠ is hostile to God. It does not submit to God's law, nor can it do so. ⁸Those controlled by the sinful nature cannot please God.

⁹You, however, are controlled not by the sinful nature but by the Spirit, if the Spirit of God lives in you. And if anyone does not have the Spirit of Christ, he does not belong to Christ. ¹⁰But if Christ is in you, your body is dead because of sin, yet your spirit is alive because of righteousness. ¹¹And if the Spirit of him who raised Jesus from the dead is living in you, he who raised Christ from the dead will also give life to your mortal bodies through his Spirit, who lives in you.

¹²Therefore, brothers, we have an obligation—but it is not to the sinful nature, to live according to it. ¹³For if you live according to the sinful nature, you will die; but if by the Spirit you put to death the misdeeds of the body, you will live, ¹⁴because those who are led by the Spirit of God are sons of God. ¹⁵For you did not receive a spirit that makes you a slave again to fear, but you received the Spirit of sonship.ᵍ And by him we cry, "*Abba,*ʰ Father." ¹⁶The Spirit himself testifies with our spirit that we are God's children. ¹⁷Now if we are children, then we are heirs—heirs of God and co-heirs with Christ, if indeed we share in his sufferings in order that we may also share in his glory.

struggles with sin, how do you feel reading about Paul's conflict? How is this a model for a healthy, realistic self-image? **2.** If you were comparing your spiritual life to a football game, what would the score be? What quarter is it? Are you now on offense or defense? What is your game plan? How does knowing Christ make a difference? **3.** When have you experienced the sense of Jesus rescuing you from sins or situations that were too big for you to handle? How does Jesus help you now?

OPEN: 1. What do you expect to inherit from your parents or grandparents? What do you expect to pass on to your kin? **2.** When your mind wanders, where does it go?

DIG: 1. From 8:1-4, how would you explain the gospel to one who senses he is not "good enough" for God? How is "no condemnation" related to the idea of "justification" (3:24; 5:1)? **2.** Make a list comparing what Paul says about living according to the sinful nature and living according to the Spirit (vv.5-11). What is the relationship of each mindset to the Law of God? **3.** Since we are not set right with God by doing good works, what is the motive for changing our lives? How are we to deal with our sinful nature (vv. 13-14; see 6:13,19)? **4.** What does it mean to be "led by the Spirit" (v.14)? How is that evident?

REFLECT: 1. What truths here can help you to handle feelings of guilt and unworthiness? What does it mean to you that you are not God's slave, but his child? **2.** When unhealthy thoughts enter your mind, what have you found most useful in dealing with them? **3.** Give an example from your life of being dependent on the Spirit as you worked to "put to death" an area of sin.

ᵃ1 Some later manuscripts *Jesus, who do not live according to the sinful nature but according to the Spirit,* ᵇ3 Or *the flesh;* also in verses 4, 5, 8, 9, 12 and 13 ᶜ3 Or *man, for sin* ᵈ3 Or *in the flesh* ᵉ6 Or *mind set on the flesh* ᶠ7 Or *the mind set on the flesh* ᵍ15 Or *adoption* ʰ15 Aramaic for *Father*

OPEN: 1. What have you eagerly expected during this past year or two that did not come off as planned? How did you express your disappointment? **2.** What is one pleasant and one painful memory you have of experiencing or witnessing childbirth?

DIG: 1. From 8:17, what type of suffering does Paul have in view here? What do you think he means by the glory to come? How does this relate to what he says about creation (vv.19-23)? **2.** What would a world like ours be like if there were no decay or death? irit

REFLECT: 1. What frustrates you most about living in a fallen world? How can the hope in verses 22-25 help you during times of trial? **2.** What is the difference between hope and wishful thinking? How has your hope in Christ aided you this week? **3.** When was the last time you did not know how to pray? How did the Holy Spirit help you?

OPEN: On an optimist-pessimist scale, where would you position yourself? Why?

DIG: 1. How does verse 28 relate to the idea of suffering (v.18)? **2.** What do the five verbs that describe God's role in our coming to know him mean (vv.29-30)? How do these support the truth of verse 28? **3.** What are the five questions and their answers in verses 31-35? What is Paul's point in raising them? **4.** How would the forces in verses 38-39 disrupt our trust in God's love? **5.** How does this section sum up Paul's message so far?

REFLECT: 1. How is God putting you through the school of hard knocks now? How do you see God at work in this? **2.** Of the enemies mentioned in verses 38-39, which one is the most real to you? **3.** How could your group pray for you? What helps you most here?

Future Glory

[18]I consider that our present sufferings are not worth comparing with the glory that will be revealed in us. [19]The creation waits in eager expectation for the sons of God to be revealed. [20]For the creation was subjected to frustration, not by its own choice, but by the will of the one who subjected it, in hope [21]that[i] the creation itself will be liberated from its bondage to decay and brought into the glorious freedom of the children of God.

[22]We know that the whole creation has been groaning as in the pains of childbirth right up to the present time. [23]Not only so, but we ourselves, who have the firstfruits of the Spirit, groan inwardly as we wait eagerly for our adoption as sons, the redemption of our bodies. [24]For in this hope we were saved. But hope that is seen is no hope at all. Who hopes for what he already has? [25]But if we hope for what we do not yet have, we wait for it patiently.

[26]In the same way, the Spirit helps us in our weakness. We do not know what we ought to pray for, but the Spirit himself intercedes for us with groans that words cannot express. [27]And he who searches our hearts knows the mind of the Spirit, because the Spirit intercedes for the saints in accordance with God's will.

More Than Conquerors

[28]And we know that in all things God works for the good of those who love him,[j] who[k] have been called according to his purpose. [29]For those God foreknew he also predestined to be conformed to the likeness of his Son, that he might be the firstborn among many brothers. [30]And those he predestined, he also called; those he called, he also justified; those he justified, he also glorified.

[31]What, then, shall we say in response to this? If God is for us, who can be against us? [32]He who did not spare his own Son, but gave him up for us all—how will he not also, along with him, graciously give us all things? [33]Who will bring any charge against those whom God has chosen? It is God who justifies. [34]Who is he that condemns? Christ Jesus, who died—more than that, who was raised to life—is at the right hand of God and is also interceding for us. [35]Who shall separate us from the love of Christ? Shall trouble or hardship or persecution or famine or nakedness or danger or sword? [36]As it is written:

"For your sake we face death all day long;
    we are considered as sheep to be slaughtered."[l]

[37]No, in all these things we are more than conquerors through him who loved us. [38]For I am convinced that neither death nor life, neither angels nor demons,[m] neither the present nor the future, nor any powers, [39]neither height nor depth, nor anything else in all creation, will be able to separate us from the love of God that is in Christ Jesus our Lord.

---

[i]20,21 Or *subjected it in hope.* [21]*For* [j]28 Some manuscripts *And we know that all things work together for good to those who love God* [k]28 Or *works together for those who love him to bring about what is good—with those who heavenly rulers* [l]36 Psalm 44:22 [m]38 Or *nor*

God's Sovereign Choice

9 I speak the truth in Christ—I am not lying, my conscience confirms it in the Holy Spirit— [2]I have great sorrow and unceasing anguish in my heart. [3]For I could wish that I myself were cursed and cut off from Christ for the sake of my brothers, those of my own race, [4]the people of Israel. Theirs is the adoption as sons; theirs the divine glory, the covenants, the receiving of the law, the temple worship and the promises. [5]Theirs are the patriarchs, and from them is traced the human ancestry of Christ, who is God over all, forever praised![n] Amen.

[6]It is not as though God's word had failed. For not all who are descended from Israel are Israel. [7]Nor because they are his descendants are they all Abraham's children. On the contrary, "It is through Isaac that your offspring will be reckoned."[o] [8]In other words, it is not the natural children who are God's children, but it is the children of the promise who are regarded as Abraham's offspring. [9]For this was how the promise was stated: "At the appointed time I will return, and Sarah will have a son."[p]

[10]Not only that, but Rebekah's children had one and the same father, our father Isaac. [11]Yet, before the twins were born or had done anything good or bad—in order that God's purpose in election might stand: [12]not by works but by him who calls—she was told, "The older will serve the younger."[q] [13]Just as it is written: "Jacob I loved, but Esau I hated."[r]

[14]What then shall we say? Is God unjust? Not at all! [15]For he says to Moses,

"I will have mercy on whom I have mercy,
and I will have compassion on whom I have
      compassion."[s]

[16]It does not, therefore, depend on man's desire or effort, but on God's mercy. [17]For the Scripture says to Pharaoh: "I raised you up for this very purpose, that I might display my power in you and that my name might be proclaimed in all the earth."[t] [18]Therefore God has mercy on whom he wants to have mercy, and he hardens whom he wants to harden.

[19]One of you will say to me: "Then why does God still blame us? For who resists his will?" [20]But who are you, O man, to talk back to God? "Shall what is formed say to him who formed it, 'Why did you make me like this?' "[u] [21]Does not the potter have the right to make out of the same lump of clay some pottery for noble purposes and some for common use?

[22]What if God, choosing to show his wrath and make his power known, bore with great patience the objects of his wrath—prepared for destruction? [23]What if he did this to make the riches of his glory known to the objects of his mercy, whom he prepared in advance for glory— [24]even us, whom he also called, not only from the Jews but also from the Gentiles? [25]As he says in Hosea:

OPEN: 1. As a kid, were you ever envious of other families? Did you ever want to trade places, switch parents or adopt someone as your brother or sister? How so? **2.** What was one thing about which your folks used to say, "Wait 'til you're older—you'll understand then"?

DIG: 1. Given Paul's assurance in 8:39, why does he now discuss the problem of widespread Jewish unbelief? What question does unbelief raise for some (v.6)? **2.** How and why does Paul express his concern for his people? **3.** How should each of the benefits he mentions in verses 4-5 have drawn the Jewish people to Christ? How does he account for their unbelief in spite of such advantages (vv.6-9; see 4:11-12)? **4.** How would this link to Abraham help resolve conflicts between Jews and Gentiles? **5.** In light of verses 11-13, how does Paul maintain God's justice? What would be just and fair for each of us to receive from God (see 3:9-20)? On what basis does God relate to us (vv.15-16; see 5:9-10)? **6.** How does Paul respond to further questions about God's fairness in choosing some but not others (v.19)? What is God's overriding purpose? **7.** How do the OT quotes in verses 25-29 relate to Paul's argument here? How would these be effective in solving tensions between Jewish and Gentile Christians?

REFLECT: 1. Of the implied or stated questions (vv.6,14,19), which one expresses your concern about God's plan? If you could ask Paul for clarification, what would you ask him? Why? **2.** In what area are you growing in your understanding of God's will for your life? What questions would you like to ask God about this? **3.** How deeply do you hurt for unbelievers? Why? **4.** Have you ever wondered why God chose you to be part of his plan for the universe? What have you concluded? **5.** Who are some non-Christians God has used to help you toward spiritual maturity? How so? **6.** What are five benefits to your spiritual life that have come to you because of where you live? How might these benefits blind you to aspects of God's saving grace? What will you do to insure that this does not happen? **7.** Suppose salvation did depend on

---

n5 Or *Christ, who is over all. God be forever praised!* Or *Christ. God who is over all be forever praised!*   o7 Gen. 21:12   p9 Gen. 18:10,14   q12 Gen. 25:23
r13 Mal. 1:2,3   s15 Exodus 33:19   t17 Exodus 9:16   u20 Isaiah 29:16; 45:9

313

human desire and effort. What grade would God give you: "E" for effort? "C" for creative? "A" for accomplishment? "F" for failure to follow directions? If God graded on a "curve," would you have a better chance of passing his life-long course? Why or why not? Would "crib sheets" help? How about remedial education? Going back to pre-school? Polishing a few apples and becoming the Teacher's pet?

OPEN: 1. Would you rather raise your children in a pagan society where you have to fight for what you believe, or in a religious society where everyone believes as you do? Why? Likewise, would you prefer to send your child to private/parochial schooling, or to public/secular schooling? **2.** As a child, what was one goal you worked hard to achieve?

DIG: 1. In what characteristic way did Jews seek to be right with God? What was the basic problem in this approach (see 3:20; 7:7-11)? How do you see people taking this same path today? **2.** On the basis of 10:1-2, how would you respond to someone who said, "*What* you believe doesn't matter as long as you are *sincere*"? How can zeal for God sometimes get in the way of knowing him? **3.** How would the attitude of a person coming to God on the basis of his or her performance (v.5) be different from that of someone coming to him by faith in Christ (vv.8-9)? **4.** What does it mean to confess "Jesus is Lord"? How would you illustrate this from earlier chapters in Romans? How does this tie in with belief? **5.** Look at 3:22-23: In that context, how does the phrase, "there is no difference" compare with its use here in 10:12? What hope is given here? **6.** What is the purpose of Paul's series of questions in verses 14-17? How does this

"I will call them 'my people' who are not my people;
    and I will call her 'my loved one' who is not my loved
        one,"[v]

[26]and,

"It will happen that in the very place where it was said
    to them,
'You are not my people,'
they will be called 'sons of the living God.'"[w]

[27]Isaiah cries out concerning Israel:

"Though the number of the Israelites be like the sand
    by the sea,
only the remnant will be saved.
[28]For the Lord will carry out
    his sentence on earth with speed and finality."[x]

[29]It is just as Isaiah said previously:

"Unless the Lord Almighty
    had left us descendants,
we would have become like Sodom,
    we would have been like Gomorrah."[y]

Israel's Unbelief

[30]What then shall we say? That the Gentiles, who did not pursue righteousness, have obtained it, a righteousness that is by faith; [31]but Israel, who pursued a law of righteousness, has not attained it. [32]Why not? Because they pursued it not by faith but as if it were by works. They stumbled over the "stumbling stone." [33]As it is written:

"See, I lay in Zion a stone that causes men to stumble
    and a rock that makes them fall,
and the one who trusts in him will never be put to
    shame."[z]

10 Brothers, my heart's desire and prayer to God for the Israelites is that they may be saved. [2]For I can testify about them that they are zealous for God, but their zeal is not based on knowledge. [3]Since they did not know the righteousness that comes from God and sought to establish their own, they did not submit to God's righteousness. [4]Christ is the end of the law so that there may be righteousness for everyone who believes.

[5]Moses describes in this way the righteousness that is by the law: "The man who does these things will live by them."[a] [6]But the righteousness that is by faith says: "Do not say in your heart, 'Who will ascend into heaven?'[b]" (that is, to bring Christ down) [7]"or 'Who will descend into the deep?'[c]" (that is, to bring Christ up from the dead). [8]But what does it say? "The word is near you; it is in your mouth and in your heart,"[d] that is, the word of faith we are proclaiming: [9]That if you confess with your mouth, "Jesus is Lord," and believe in your heart that God raised him

[v]25 Hosea 2:23   [w]26 Hosea 1:10   [x]28 Isaiah 10:22,23   [y]29 Isaiah 1:9
[z]33 Isaiah 8:14; 28:16   [a]5 Lev. 18:5   [b]6 Deut. 30:12   [c]7 Deut. 30:13
[d]8 Deut. 30:14

from the dead, you will be saved. [10]For it is with your heart that you believe and are justified, and it is with your mouth that you confess and are saved. [11]As the Scripture says, "Anyone who trusts in him will never be put to shame."[e] [12]For there is no difference between Jew and Gentile—the same Lord is Lord of all and richly blesses all who call on him, [13]for, "Everyone who calls on the name of the Lord will be saved."[f]

[14]How, then, can they call on the one they have not believed in? And how can they believe in the one of whom they have not heard? And how can they hear without someone preaching to them? [15]And how can they preach unless they are sent? As it is written, "How beautiful are the feet of those who bring good news!"[g]

[16]But not all the Israelites accepted the good news. For Isaiah says, "Lord, who has believed our message?"[h] [17]Consequently, faith comes from hearing the message, and the message is heard through the word of Christ. [18]But I ask: Did they not hear? Of course they did:

"Their voice has gone out into all the earth,
  their words to the ends of the world."[i]

[19]Again I ask: Did Israel not understand? First, Moses says,

"I will make you envious by those who are not a nation;
  I will make you angry by a nation that has no
    understanding."[j]

[20]And Isaiah boldly says,

"I was found by those who did not seek me;
  I revealed myself to those who did not ask for me."[k]

[21]But concerning Israel he says,

"All day long I have held out my hands
  to a disobedient and obstinate people."[l]

The Remnant of Israel

11 I ask then: Did God reject his people? By no means! I am an Israelite myself, a descendant of Abraham, from the tribe of Benjamin. [2]God did not reject his people, whom he foreknew. Don't you know what the Scripture says in the passage about Elijah—how he appealed to God against Israel: [3]"Lord, they have killed your prophets and torn down your altars; I am the only one left, and they are trying to kill me"[m]? [4]And what was God's answer to him? "I have reserved for myself seven thousand who have not bowed the knee to Baal."[n] [5]So too, at the present time there is a remnant chosen by grace. [6]And if by grace, then it is no longer by works; if it were, grace would no longer be grace.[o]

[7]What then? What Israel sought so earnestly it did not obtain, but the elect did. The others were hardened, [8]as it is written:

underscore the importance of evangelism? **7.** Although Israel *heard* the message, Gentiles *understood* it (vv.18-21). What does this tell you about the severity of the Jew-Gentile division in the Roman church?

REFLECT: 1. If a friend asked you to explain the difference between Christianity and other religions, how would 9:30-31 help you answer? **2.** What is one major way your confession of Christ as Lord has influenced your life? **3.** The central affirmation of the early church was "Jesus is Lord"; everyone else was saying "Caesar is Lord." Who (or what) are some gods that compete with your allegiance to Christ? **4.** What are the stumbling blocks in your walk with God? Has the need to have faith been a stumbling block or a stepping stone for you? **5.** How can you bring the good news into the life of a particular family member or friend this week?

***

OPEN: 1. What experience of rejection do you vividly recall from your teen years: Getting cut from the team? Not being invited to the big party? Turned down for a date? **2.** How did you get over it?

DIG: 1. How might Paul's comments in 9:25 and 10:21 lead someone to ask the question in 11:1? How do the examples given here answer that concern? How does his response illustrate 9:6-7? **2.** On what basis are Paul and others of the remnant chosen? Why would this be so difficult for his fellow Israelites to grasp (see 10:3)? **3.** Are church people today relying more on their performance (of religious rituals or good works) than on God's grace? How so?

[e]11 Isaiah 28:16   [f]13 Joel 2:32   [g]15 Isaiah 52:7   [h]16 Isaiah 53:1
[i]18 Psalm 19:4   [j]19 Deut. 32:21   [k]20 Isaiah 65:1   [l]21 Isaiah 65:2
[m]3 1 Kings 19:10,14   [n]4 1 Kings 19:18   [o]6 Some manuscripts *by grace. But if by works, then it is no longer grace; if it were, work would no longer be work.*

REFLECT: 1. When have you felt like the only one left who seems to care about God? What were the circumstances? How did God respond? **2.** How is it possible for someone to try so hard to please God that they actually resist his love for them? When have you experienced this?

OPEN: 1. As a child, when did your desire to be like one of your heroes help you to change and grow? **2.** Do you like cookie dough as much, less than, or more than the whole batch baked? Which batch is your favorite? **3.** Which fruit or vegetable do you like to eat raw or wild, but never canned, processed, or even cooked?

DIG: 1. How does Paul's question in verse 11 relate to verse 1? What hope does he give in his answer? **2.** In what ways would God's grace toward Gentiles break through the walls of presumption which the Jews had built around God? **3.** Up to now, Paul has been dealing with the Jewish believers' feelings of superiority over Gentiles. How does his image of dough and of an olive tree deal with the other side of the coin (vv.13-24)? **4.** What phrases indicate what the Gentile believers were thinking? What attitude ought they to have about their acceptance by God? What difference, if any, is there between Jew and Gentile before God? **5.** Why does Paul want his Gentile readers to be aware of God's plan (v.25)? Why would pride become a danger for them? **6.** How would you paraphrase God's purpose in verses 25-26 and 30-31? How would this diffuse tensions between the two groups? **7.** What is the ultimate hope for Israel (vv.26-27)? For Gentiles (v.32)? How does this tie in with Paul's teaching in 3:21-24?

REFLECT: 1. How has arrogance between groups of Christians hurt your church experience? When have you shown this attitude to natives and outsiders? **2.** What modern illustration would serve as an equivalent to the grafted olive branch? Where would you fit

"God gave them a spirit of stupor,
   eyes so that they could not see
   and ears so that they could not hear,
to this very day."*p*

⁹And David says:

"May their table become a snare and a trap,
   a stumbling block and a retribution for them.
¹⁰May their eyes be darkened so they cannot see,
   and their backs be bent forever."*q*

Ingrafted Branches

¹¹Again I ask: Did they stumble so as to fall beyond recovery? Not at all! Rather, because of their transgression, salvation has come to the Gentiles to make Israel envious. ¹²But if their transgression means riches for the world, and their loss means riches for the Gentiles, how much greater riches will their fullness bring!

¹³I am talking to you Gentiles. Inasmuch as I am the apostle to the Gentiles, I make much of my ministry ¹⁴in the hope that I may somehow arouse my own people to envy and save some of them. ¹⁵For if their rejection is the reconciliation of the world, what will their acceptance be but life from the dead? ¹⁶If the part of the dough offered as firstfruits is holy, then the whole batch is holy; if the root is holy, so are the branches.

¹⁷If some of the branches have been broken off, and you, though a wild olive shoot, have been grafted in among the others and now share in the nourishing sap from the olive root, ¹⁸do not boast over those branches. If you do, consider this: You do not support the root, but the root supports you. ¹⁹You will say then, "Branches were broken off so that I could be grafted in." ²⁰Granted. But they were broken off because of unbelief, and you stand by faith. Do not be arrogant, but be afraid. ²¹For if God did not spare the natural branches, he will not spare you either.

²²Consider therefore the kindness and sternness of God: sternness to those who fell, but kindness to you, provided that you continue in his kindness. Otherwise, you also will be cut off. ²³And if they do not persist in unbelief, they will be grafted in, for God is able to graft them in again. ²⁴After all, if you were cut out of an olive tree that is wild by nature, and contrary to nature were grafted into a cultivated olive tree, how much more readily will these, the natural branches, be grafted into their own olive tree!

All Israel Will Be Saved

²⁵I do not want you to be ignorant of this mystery, brothers, so that you may not be conceited: Israel has experienced a hardening in part until the full number of the Gentiles has come in. ²⁶And so all Israel will be saved, as it is written:

"The deliverer will come from Zion;
   he will turn godlessness away from Jacob.

---

*p*8 Deut. 29:4; Isaiah 29:10   *q*10 Psalm 69:22,23

[27]And this is[r] my covenant with them
when I take away their sins."[s]

[28]As far as the gospel is concerned, they are enemies on your account; but as far as election is concerned, they are loved on account of the patriarchs, [29]for God's gifts and his call are irrevocable. [30]Just as you who were at one time disobedient to God have now received mercy as a result of their disobedience, [31]so they too have now become disobedient in order that they too may now[t] receive mercy as a result of God's mercy to you. [32]For God has bound all men over to disobedience so that he may have mercy on them all.

Doxology

[33]Oh, the depth of the riches of the wisdom and[u]
knowledge of God!
How unsearchable his judgments,
and his paths beyond tracing out!
[34]"Who has known the mind of the Lord?
Or who has been his counselor?"[v]
[35]"Who has ever given to God,
that God should repay him?"[w]
[36]For from him and through him and to him are all things.
To him be the glory forever! Amen.

Living Sacrifices

12 Therefore, I urge you, brothers, in view of God's mercy, to offer your bodies as living sacrifices, holy and pleasing to God—this is your spiritual[x] act of worship. [2]Do not conform any longer to the pattern of this world, but be transformed by the renewing of your mind. Then you will be able to test and approve what God's will is—his good, pleasing and perfect will.

[3]For by the grace given me I say to every one of you: Do not think of yourself more highly than you ought, but rather think of yourself with sober judgment, in accordance with the measure of faith God has given you. [4]Just as each of us has one body with many members, and these members do not all have the same function, [5]so in Christ we who are many form one body, and each member belongs to all the others. [6]We have different gifts, according to the grace given us. If a man's gift is prophesying, let him use it in proportion to his[y] faith. [7]If it is serving, let him serve; if it is teaching, let him teach; [8]if it is encouraging, let him encourage; if it is contributing to the needs of others, let him give generously; if it is leadership, let him govern diligently; if it is showing mercy, let him do it cheerfully.

Love

[9]Love must be sincere. Hate what is evil; cling to what is good. [10]Be devoted to one another in brotherly love. Honor one another above yourselves. [11]Never be lacking in zeal, but keep your spiritual fervor, serving the Lord. [12]Be joyful in hope,

OPEN: When caught up by the "bigness" of God, are you silent with wonder, or singing with joy?

DIG: 1. How does this song relate to: (a) Paul's argument in verses 25-32? (b) Any questions that may have been raised by chapters 9-11? **2.** Which traits of God does Paul celebrate here? Why these?

REFLECT: Why is this a good place for a doxology—Paul's, yours, and your group's?

OPEN: As a teen, how did peer pressure affect the way you dressed? Where you went? How you acted?

DIG: 1. How does this section relate to 11:30-32? **2.** What does 12:1 add to your understanding of true worship (see also 6:13; 8:13)? **3.** Given the tensions between Jews and Gentiles, why would Paul write about gifts and their interdependence?

REFLECT: 1. How does the world squeeze you into its mold? What pressure points seem strongest to you? **2.** How can you present your body as a living sacrifice in everyday life? How does this relate to using your gifts?

OPEN: What is one of the best practical jokes anyone has pulled on you? How did you try to repay them in kind?

DIG: 1. How does this section disclose what Paul means in verses 1-2? **2.** How does your dedication to God show in your

within this new analogy? **3.** When a prodigal receives God's blessing and grace in their life, does that spur you on to seek God all the more, or does it make you jealous (even upset)? Why?

---

[r]27 Or *will be do not have now.*   [s]27 Isaiah 59:20,21; 27:9; Jer. 31:33,34   [t]31 Some manuscripts
[u]33 Or *riches and the wisdom and the*   [v]34 Isaiah 40:13
[w]35 Job 41:11   [x]1 Or *reasonable*   [y]6 Or *in agreement with the*

relationships with others (the poor, outsiders, your enemies, those suffering)? **3.** How are love (v.9) and peace (v.18) the general rules out of which all the rest of these examples flow?

REFLECT: 1. This week, how can you practice "love" and "peace" with your family? Co-workers? Small group? Church? **2.** Of the commands listed in verses 9-21, which two are easiest for you to keep? Which two are the most difficult? Why? **3.** If you could have three wishes for your church, what would they be? What can you do now to make these wishes come true?

OPEN: When was the last time you got a traffic ticket? How did you feel about the police officer?

DIG: 1. In light of Paul's teaching about freedom in Christ, why would this section be important for the church in Rome? How does government relate to God in terms of its origin? Power? Purpose? How is that different than the world's way of governing? **2.** Compare this passage with Acts 5:27-32. What principles do you find for helping you deal with authority?

REFLECT: What would Paul advise people in modern democracies who face injustice? Those in countries banning Christianity?

OPEN: Do you feel more comfortable in dress clothes, loungewear, PJs, or grubbies? Why?

DIG: 1. How does the law help us know what it means to love? How does this differ from popular notions of love? **2.** What is meant by this light and darkness theme (vv.12-14)? **3.** What does the "clothing" in verse 14 mean to you? How would you use this section to explain holiness?

REFLECT: How would your life be different if you consciously tried to "wear" Jesus Christ? What must change to insure a better fit?

patient in affliction, faithful in prayer. [13]Share with God's people who are in need. Practice hospitality.

[14]Bless those who persecute you; bless and do not curse. [15]Rejoice with those who rejoice; mourn with those who mourn. [16]Live in harmony with one another. Do not be proud, but be willing to associate with people of low position.[z] Do not be conceited.

[17]Do not repay anyone evil for evil. Be careful to do what is right in the eyes of everybody. [18]If it is possible, as far as it depends on you, live at peace with everyone. [19]Do not take revenge, my friends, but leave room for God's wrath, for it is written: "It is mine to avenge; I will repay,"[a] says the Lord. [20]On the contrary:

"If your enemy is hungry, feed him;
　if he is thirsty, give him something to drink.
In doing this, you will heap burning coals on his
　head."[b]

[21]Do not be overcome by evil, but overcome evil with good.

Submission to the Authorities

13 Everyone must submit himself to the governing authorities, for there is no authority except that which God has established. The authorities that exist have been established by God. [2]Consequently, he who rebels against the authority is rebelling against what God has instituted, and those who do so will bring judgment on themselves. [3]For rulers hold no terror for those who do right, but for those who do wrong. Do you want to be free from fear of the one in authority? Then do what is right and he will commend you. [4]For he is God's servant to do you good. But if you do wrong, be afraid, for he does not bear the sword for nothing. He is God's servant, an agent of wrath to bring punishment on the wrongdoer. [5]Therefore, it is necessary to submit to the authorities, not only because of possible punishment but also because of conscience.

[6]This is also why you pay taxes, for the authorities are God's servants, who give their full time to governing. [7]Give everyone what you owe him: If you owe taxes, pay taxes; if revenue, then revenue; if respect, then respect; if honor, then honor.

Love, for the Day Is Near

[8]Let no debt remain outstanding, except the continuing debt to love one another, for he who loves his fellowman has fulfilled the law. [9]The commandments, "Do not commit adultery," "Do not murder," "Do not steal," "Do not covet,"[c] and whatever other commandment there may be, are summed up in this one rule: "Love your neighbor as yourself."[d] [10]Love does no harm to its neighbor. Therefore love is the fulfillment of the law.

[11]And do this, understanding the present time. The hour has come for you to wake up from your slumber, because our salvation is nearer now than when we first believed. [12]The night is nearly over; the day is almost here. So let us put aside the deeds

z16 Or willing to do menial work　　*a19 Deut. 32:35*　　*b20 Prov. 25:21,22*
c9 Exodus 20:13-15,17; Deut. 5:17-19,21　　*d9 Lev. 19:18*

of darkness and put on the armor of light. [13]Let us behave decently, as in the daytime, not in orgies and drunkenness, not in sexual immorality and debauchery, not in dissension and jealousy. [14]Rather, clothe yourselves with the Lord Jesus Christ, and do not think about how to gratify the desires of the sinful nature. [e]

The Weak and the Strong

14 Accept him whose faith is weak, without passing judgment on disputable matters. [2]One man's faith allows him to eat everything, but another man, whose faith is weak, eats only vegetables. [3]The man who eats everything must not look down on him who does not, and the man who does not eat everything must not condemn the man who does, for God has accepted him. [4]Who are you to judge someone else's servant? To his own master he stands or falls. And he will stand, for the Lord is able to make him stand.

[5]One man considers one day more sacred than another; another man considers every day alike. Each one should be fully convinced in his own mind. [6]He who regards one day as special, does so to the Lord. He who eats meat, eats to the Lord, for he gives thanks to God; and he who abstains, does so to the Lord and gives thanks to God. [7]For none of us lives to himself alone and none of us dies to himself alone. [8]If we live, we live to the Lord; and if we die, we die to the Lord. So, whether we live or die, we belong to the Lord.

[9]For this very reason, Christ died and returned to life so that he might be the Lord of both the dead and the living. [10]You, then, why do you judge your brother? Or why do you look down on your brother? For we will all stand before God's judgment seat. [11]It is written:

> " 'As surely as I live,' says the Lord,
> 'every knee will bow before me;
>   every tongue will confess to God.' "[f]

[12]So then, each of us will give an account of himself to God.

[13]Therefore let us stop passing judgment on one another. Instead, make up your mind not to put any stumbling block or obstacle in your brother's way. [14]As one who is in the Lord Jesus, I am fully convinced that no food[g] is unclean in itself. But if anyone regards something as unclean, then for him it is unclean. [15]If your brother is distressed because of what you eat, you are no longer acting in love. Do not by your eating destroy your brother for whom Christ died. [16]Do not allow what you consider good to be spoken of as evil. [17]For the kingdom of God is not a matter of eating and drinking, but of righteousness, peace and joy in the Holy Spirit, [18]because anyone who serves Christ in this way is pleasing to God and approved by men.

[19]Let us therefore make every effort to do what leads to peace and to mutual edification. [20]Do not destroy the work of God for the sake of food. All food is clean, but it is wrong for a man to eat anything that causes someone else to stumble. [21]It is better

e14 Or *the flesh*   *f11* Isaiah 45:23   *g14* Or *that nothing*

OPEN: 1. When you were a child, were you argumentative, appeasing, or compromising in how you settled disputes over "personal space" or "my rights"? Which argument was never-ending? **2.** What vegetable do you still refuse to eat? Why?

DIG: 1. What is causing the disunity in the church at Rome? **2.** What attitudes and motivations do you see here (14:3,7,8,10, 13,19,22; 15:2,7) which guide our relationship toward those with whom we disagree? **3.** From these examples, how would you define what Paul means by "disputable matters" in verse 1? What might be such an issue today? **4.** What principles here should guide us when we are dealing with differences of opinion on matters that do not violate the moral law? **5.** Instead of judging, what should occupy our energy (14:13,17-18; 15:2)? **6.** What does Paul mean by the words "stumble" and "fall" in verses 20-21? **7.** What is the essential motivation for this lifestyle of putting others first (15:3, 7)? **8.** What should characterize the church (14:17; 15:13)? How would obeying Paul's instructions in this passage contribute to this goal?

REFLECT: 1. How weak or strong are you in the faith: Like a lion in a zoo, who looks strong but has never been tested? Or a palm tree, not very strong but having a solid root structure? **2.** Would you be more like the *weak* or the *strong* in this passage? Why? Contemporize the issues which divide the so-called *strong* (libertarians) and *weak* (legalists): Which "gray area" divides your church or fellowship group? **3.** When has your freedom been a stumbling block to someone else? What happened? **4.** As you've matured in the faith, how has your sensitivity to the consciences of other Christians changed? Where do you draw the line on trying to please everyone? **5.** What have you done in the past six months that has led "to peace and to mutual edification" among people in your church?

not to eat meat or drink wine or to do anything else that will cause your brother to fall.

22So whatever you believe about these things keep between yourself and God. Blessed is the man who does not condemn himself by what he approves. 23But the man who has doubts is condemned if he eats, because his eating is not from faith; and everything that does not come from faith is sin.

15 We who are strong ought to bear with the failings of the weak and not to please ourselves. 2Each of us should please his neighbor for his good, to build him up. 3For even Christ did not please himself but, as it is written: "The insults of those who insult you have fallen on me."h 4For everything that was written in the past was written to teach us, so that through endurance and the encouragement of the Scriptures we might have hope.

5May the God who gives endurance and encouragement give you a spirit of unity among yourselves as you follow Christ Jesus, 6so that with one heart and mouth you may glorify the God and Father of our Lord Jesus Christ.

7Accept one another, then, just as Christ accepted you, in order to bring praise to God. 8For I tell you that Christ has become a servant of the Jewsi on behalf of God's truth, to confirm the promises made to the patriarchs 9so that the Gentiles may glorify God for his mercy, as it is written:

"Therefore I will praise you among the Gentiles;
I will sing hymns to your name."j

10Again, it says,

"Rejoice, O Gentiles, with his people."k

11And again,

"Praise the Lord, all you Gentiles,
and sing praises to him, all you peoples."l

12And again, Isaiah says,

"The Root of Jesse will spring up,
one who will arise to rule over the nations;
the Gentiles will hope in him."m

13May the God of hope fill you with all joy and peace as you trust in him, so that you may overflow with hope by the power of the Holy Spirit.

Paul the Minister to the Gentiles

14I myself am convinced, my brothers, that you yourselves are full of goodness, complete in knowledge and competent to instruct one another. 15I have written you quite boldly on some points, as if to remind you of them again, because of the grace God gave me 16to be a minister of Christ Jesus to the Gentiles with the priestly duty of proclaiming the gospel of God, so that the Gentiles might become an offering acceptable to God, sanctified by the Holy Spirit.

OPEN: 1. As a child, what do you remember about the first time you went away from home without a parent? **2.** To what "hot spot" would you gladly accept a round-trip ticket for two? Why?

DIG: 1. Why would Paul feel the need for an encouraging word at this point (vv.14-15)? From reading Romans, what are some of the major points Paul has

h3 Psalm 69:9   i8 Greek *circumcision*   j9 2 Samuel 22:50; Psalm 18:49
k10 Deut. 32:43   l11 Psalm 117:1   m12 Isaiah 11:10

[17]Therefore I glory in Christ Jesus in my service to God. [18]I will not venture to speak of anything except what Christ has accomplished through me in leading the Gentiles to obey God by what I have said and done— [19]by the power of signs and miracles, through the power of the Spirit. So from Jerusalem all the way around to Illyricum, I have fully proclaimed the gospel of Christ. [20]It has always been my ambition to preach the gospel where Christ was not known, so that I would not be building on someone else's foundation. [21]Rather, as it is written:

"Those who were not told about him will see,
and those who have not heard will understand." [n]

[22]This is why I have often been hindered from coming to you.

Paul's Plan to Visit Rome

[23]But now that there is no more place for me to work in these regions, and since I have been longing for many years to see you, [24]I plan to do so when I go to Spain. I hope to visit you while passing through and to have you assist me on my journey there, after I have enjoyed your company for a while. [25]Now, however, I am on my way to Jerusalem in the service of the saints there. [26]For Macedonia and Achaia were pleased to make a contribution for the poor among the saints in Jerusalem. [27]They were pleased to do it, and indeed they owe it to them. For if the Gentiles have shared in the Jews' spiritual blessings, they owe it to the Jews to share with them their material blessings. [28]So after I have completed this task and have made sure that they have received this fruit, I will go to Spain and visit you on the way. [29]I know that when I come to you, I will come in the full measure of the blessing of Christ.

[30]I urge you, brothers, by our Lord Jesus Christ and by the love of the Spirit, to join me in my struggle by praying to God for me. [31]Pray that I may be rescued from the unbelievers in Judea and that my service in Jerusalem may be acceptable to the saints there, [32]so that by God's will I may come to you with joy and together with you be refreshed. [33]The God of peace be with you all. Amen.

Personal Greetings

16 I commend to you our sister Phoebe, a servant[o] of the church in Cenchrea. [2]I ask you to receive her in the Lord in a way worthy of the saints and to give her any help she may need from you, for she has been a great help to many people, including me.

[3]Greet Priscilla[p] and Aquila, my fellow workers in Christ Jesus. [4]They risked their lives for me. Not only I but all the churches of the Gentiles are grateful to them. [5]Greet also the church that meets at their house.

Greet my dear friend Epenetus, who was the first convert to Christ in the province of Asia.
[6]Greet Mary, who worked very hard for you.
[7]Greet Andronicus and Junias, my relatives who have been in

stressed? **2.** How does Paul define his ministry and motivation (vv.16-22)? **3.** Illyricum (v.19) is in present-day Yugoslavia: How far is that from Jerusalem? Likewise, how far away is Spain (v.29)? What does this tell you about Paul? **4.** Why was this collection so important to Paul (see also 2Co 8:1-15)? Why should it be important to his Gentile readers who are living in tension with Jewish believers? **5.** Why ask them to pray as he does (v.30; also Ac 20:22-24)?

REFLECT: 1. Looking over your schedule and priorities this past month, what would you say is your ambition in life? Is that what you want it to be? How do your ambitions compare with Paul's in terms of clarity? Value? Concern for God's kingdom? **2.** What in Paul's life and mission do you want to see most in your life? What could you begin to work on to make that happen? **3.** What has helped you to become more aware of the world's needs? Of world missions? How are you involved in acting on that awareness?

OPEN: Who is one person in your past toward whom you feel a special debt of gratitude? Why?

DIG: 1. Go through verses 1-16, listing all the things for which Paul commends these people. What does this show about the way we ought to measure a person's success in life? **2.** If you received this letter, how would you treat Phoebe when she arrived? How many other women are named here? (In v.7, "Junias" is most likely "Junia," a woman's name.) What roles do these women have in the church? **3.** Although Paul had never been to Rome, what does this greeting show about his perception of this church? **4.** What divisions and obstacles are the people to keep away from (vv.17-20; see 3:8; 6:1,15; 7:7; 9:14; also Gal 5:2-6)? How are these false teachers contradicting Paul's main point about serving Christ? What is the purpose and plan of God throughout history (vv.25-27)?

REFLECT: 1. What does it mean to you that in these final chapters, God is described as the "God of hope" (15:13) and the "God of peace" (15:33; 16:20)? Summarize how we can know God in this way, especially since Paul began the letter by revealing the God of wrath. 2. What are some of the teachings that divide the church today? How do you work for a balance between the desire for unity and the desire to maintain truth? 3. Who are some people you know whom you consider real servants of Christ? What impresses you about them? 4. What can your group do to increase your participation in God's plan to lead all nations to believe and obey him? Do you view this task more as a grim duty, or as a tremendous privilege? What does this show about your heart attitude toward the gospel?

prison with me. They are outstanding among the apostles, and they were in Christ before I was.

⁸Greet Ampliatus, whom I love in the Lord.

⁹Greet Urbanus, our fellow worker in Christ, and my dear friend Stachys.

¹⁰Greet Apelles, tested and approved in Christ.

Greet those who belong to the household of Aristobulus.

¹¹Greet Herodion, my relative.

Greet those in the household of Narcissus who are in the Lord.

¹²Greet Tryphena and Tryphosa, those women who work hard in the Lord.

Greet my dear friend Persis, another woman who has worked very hard in the Lord.

¹³Greet Rufus, chosen in the Lord, and his mother, who has been a mother to me, too.

¹⁴Greet Asyncritus, Phlegon, Hermes, Patrobas, Hermas and the brothers with them.

¹⁵Greet Philologus, Julia, Nereus and his sister, and Olympas and all the saints with them.

¹⁶Greet one another with a holy kiss.

All the churches of Christ send greetings.

¹⁷I urge you, brothers, to watch out for those who cause divisions and put obstacles in your way that are contrary to the teaching you have learned. Keep away from them. ¹⁸For such people are not serving our Lord Christ, but their own appetites. By smooth talk and flattery they deceive the minds of naive people. ¹⁹Everyone has heard about your obedience, so I am full of joy over you; but I want you to be wise about what is good, and innocent about what is evil.

²⁰The God of peace will soon crush Satan under your feet. The grace of our Lord Jesus be with you.

²¹Timothy, my fellow worker, sends his greetings to you, as do Lucius, Jason and Sosipater, my relatives.

²²I, Tertius, who wrote down this letter, greet you in the Lord.

²³Gaius, whose hospitality I and the whole church here enjoy, sends you his greetings.

Erastus, who is the city's director of public works, and our brother Quartus send you their greetings.^q

²⁵Now to him who is able to establish you by my gospel and the proclamation of Jesus Christ, according to the revelation of the mystery hidden for long ages past, ²⁶but now revealed and made known through the prophetic writings by the command of the eternal God, so that all nations might believe and obey him— ²⁷to the only wise God be glory forever through Jesus Christ! Amen.

---

q23 Some manuscripts their greetings. ²⁴May the grace of our Lord Jesus Christ be with all of you. Amen.

1 CORINTHIANS

INTRODUCTION

Audience

Corinth the City

Corinth was an unusual city. After its capture by the Roman legions in 146 B.C., the city was leveled. It lay in waste for nearly a hundred years until Julius Caesar rebuilt it in 44 B.C. Then it grew rapidly, thanks largely to its unique geographical location. Because it lay at the neck of a narrow isthmus connecting the Peloponnesus with central Greece, it controlled all north-south land traffic. To the east and the west of the city were two fine harbors. Both goods and ships were hauled across the four-mile-wide Isthmus of Corinth. Thus Corinth also controlled most east-west sea routes. This strategic location commanded wealth and influence. By the time of Paul's visit some one hundred years after its rebuilding, Corinth had become the capital of the province of Achaia and the third most important city in the Roman Empire, after Rome and Alexandria.

In this wealthy young city, excess seemed to be the norm. The city was stocked with art purchased from around the Roman Empire. It became a center of philosophy, though apparently few citizens were seriously interested in studying philosophy, preferring rather to listen to stirring orations on faddish topics delivered by the city's numerous itinerant philosophers. Even in religion, this excess was obvious. The Greek author Pausanias describes twenty-six pagan shrines and temples including the great temples of Apollo and Aphrodite. In Old Corinth, a thousand temple prostitutes had served Aphrodite, the goddess of love, and New Corinth continued this tradition of sexual worship practices. The city developed a worldwide reputation for vice and debauchery.

Luxury was the hallmark of Corinth. Because storms in the Aegean Sea were frequent and treacherous, sailors preferred to put into one of the harbors and transship to the other, despite the exorbitant prices charged by the Corinthians. Consequently, goods from around the world passed through Corinthian ports, and some 400,000 slaves were kept in the city to provide the labor for this arduous job.

Into Corinth flowed people from around the Roman Empire. There were "Greek adventurers and Roman bourgeois, with a tainting infusion of Phoenicians, a mass of Jews, ex-soldiers, philosophers, merchants, sailors, freed men, slaves, tradespeople, hucksters and agents of every form of vice" (Farrar, quoted by William Barclay, *The Letters to the Corinthians,* p. 4.). Rootless, proud, independent, egalitarian, individualistic, rich—together the Corinthians shaped their new city into the cosmopolitan capital that it was in Paul's day. Not surprisingly, it was in Corinth that Paul had to fight this battle to prevent Christianity from succumbing to debilitating enticements offered by paganism.

Paul and the Corinthians

Paul visited Corinth during his second missionary journey, probably in A.D. 50. Having been in some peril in Macedonia, he fled by ship to Athens (Acts 17:5-15). Not meeting with great success there (Acts 17:16-34), he then journeyed the short distance to Corinth where he met Priscilla and Aquila (Acts 18:1-3). At first he preached in the synagogue with some success (even the ruler of the synagogue was won to Christ). But then the Jews forced him to leave, so he moved next door into the home of a Gentile. Hoping to silence him, the Jews eventually hauled Paul before the governor Gallio, but Gallio threw the case out of court as having no merit. After some eighteen months (his longest stay anywhere except Ephesus), Paul left and continued his missionary work in Syria.

Two events sparked the writing of 1 Corinthians some three or four years later. First, Paul heard that a divisive spirit was loose in the church (1 Cor. 1:11). Second, he received a letter in which the Corinthians asked him questions about marriage and other matters (1 Cor. 7:1). In addition, a delegation from Corinth completed his knowledge of the problems there (1 Cor. 16:15-17). Being unable to visit Corinth personally, Paul sought to deal with the issues by letter. Thus the Corinthian correspondence was begun.

Theme

First Corinthians is a practical, issue-oriented letter in which Paul tells his readers what they ought or ought not to do. Paul's typical pattern in other letters is to begin with a strong theological statement and then to follow up by applying this insight to daily life. But this is not the case in 1 Corinthians. Here we find little direct theological teaching. Rather Paul discusses, in turn, a number of behavioral issues.

The problem was that these proud, materialistic, independent ex-pagans were having a most difficult time learning how to live as Christians. It was at this level of lifestyle that paganism directed its attack on the newly emerging Christian faith. *Christian behavior was the underlying issue.* Where were the lines to be drawn? How much of one's culture had to be abandoned to become a Christian? Residual paganism was mounting a frontal attack on Christianity. If Christianity lost in Corinth, its existence would be threatened throughout the Roman Empire. So just as he did in Galatians, when residual Judaism attacked Christianity over the issue of the Law, here in 1 Corinthians Paul struck back decisively and directly.

The Structure of 1 Corinthians

The problem in understanding 1 Corinthians is that we only have Paul's responses. We don't know with certainty what questions and problems he is addressing. These have to be deduced. Still, it is clear that there are two major divisions in the letter. In chapters 1-6, Paul responds to four problems of which he has become aware. Then in chapters 7-15, he responds to a series of specific questions raised in a letter the Corinthians have sent him.

Outline

An outline of 1 Corinthians looks like this:
1. Problems Reported to Paul (1:10-6:20)
    A. Divisions in the Church (1:10-4:21)
    B. Incest (5:1-13)
    C. Lawsuits among Believers (6:1-11)
    D. Sexual Immorality (6:12-20)
2. Questions asked of Paul (7:1-15:58)
    A. Marriage (7:1-24)
    B. Virgins (7:25-40)
    C. Food Sacrificed to Idols (8:1-11:1)
    D. Propriety in Worship (11:2-16)
    E. The Lord's Supper (11:17-34)
    F. Spiritual Gifts (12:1-14:40)
    G. The Resurrection (15:1-58)
In 1:1-9, Paul begins this letter in usual fashion; in chapter 16, he writes a concluding note.

1 Corinthians

1 Paul, called to be an apostle of Christ Jesus by the will of God, and our brother Sosthenes,

²To the church of God in Corinth, to those sanctified in Christ Jesus and called to be holy, together with all those everywhere who call on the name of our Lord Jesus Christ—their Lord and ours:

³Grace and peace to you from God our Father and the Lord Jesus Christ.

Thanksgiving

⁴I always thank God for you because of his grace given you in Christ Jesus. ⁵For in him you have been enriched in every way—in all your speaking and in all your knowledge— ⁶because our testimony about Christ was confirmed in you. ⁷Therefore you do not lack any spiritual gift as you eagerly wait for our Lord Jesus Christ to be revealed. ⁸He will keep you strong to the end, so that you will be blameless on the day of our Lord Jesus Christ. ⁹God, who has called you into fellowship with his Son Jesus Christ our Lord, is faithful.

Divisions in the Church

¹⁰I appeal to you, brothers, in the name of our Lord Jesus Christ, that all of you agree with one another so that there may be no divisions among you and that you may be perfectly united in mind and thought. ¹¹My brothers, some from Chloe's household have informed me that there are quarrels among you. ¹²What I mean is this: One of you says, "I follow Paul"; another, "I follow Apollos"; another, "I follow Cephas*"; still another, "I follow Christ."

¹³Is Christ divided? Was Paul crucified for you? Were you baptized into*ᵇ* the name of Paul? ¹⁴I am thankful that I did not baptize any of you except Crispus and Gaius, ¹⁵so no one can say that you were baptized into my name. ¹⁶(Yes, I also baptized the household of Stephanas; beyond that, I don't remember if I baptized anyone else.) ¹⁷For Christ did not send me to baptize, but to preach the gospel—not with words of human wisdom, lest the cross of Christ be emptied of its power.

Christ the Wisdom and Power of God

¹⁸For the message of the cross is foolishness to those who are perishing, but to us who are being saved it is the power of God. ¹⁹For it is written:

"I will destroy the wisdom of the wise;
  the intelligence of the intelligent I will frustrate."ᶜ

²⁰Where is the wise man? Where is the scholar? Where is the philosopher of this age? Has not God made foolish the wisdom of the world? ²¹For since in the wisdom of God the world

a12 That is, Peter   *b13* Or *in;* also in verse 15   *c19* Isaiah 29:14

rejecting education itself, or some related and prideful assumptions? Explain. **4.** In 1:30, Paul uses four terms to describe what Christ is for those who trust him. How would you define each one: Wisdom (see also Col 2:2, 8-10)? Righteousness (see Ro 3:22)? Holiness (see Gal 2:20)? Redemption (see 1 Pe 1:18-19)?

REFLECT: 1. What pictures come to mind when you think about powerful, successful people? How do those images sometimes conflict with following Christ? **2.** How do people today confuse the world's power with God's power? How does that affect you? **3.** What situations can you think of where God uses the weak, lowly, and despised to build his kingdom in our day?

OPEN: 1. What is one thing you recall your parents telling you, "You'll have to wait 'til you're older"? How did you feel then? **2.** In what area are you a specialist? How did you achieve this status?

DIG: 1. From the references to "wisdom" in this passage, what differences do you see between human wisdom and God's? **2.** What point is Paul making by his quote from the OT in verse 9 (see also v.7)? **3.** Philosophers were respected as people who could search out deep truths; in contrast, how does Paul say the truth of the gospel is discovered (vv.10-13)? Why is that significant for the Corinthians' unity? **4.** How does the condition for receiving spiritual wisdom differ from those necessary to gain the world's wisdom (vv.9, 14-16)? Why is that significant for their unity?

REFLECT: The Corinthians were measuring "truth and success" by how powerful, influential, and articulate someone was. How is that idea communicated today? How does it square with the gospel?

through its wisdom did not know him, God was pleased through the foolishness of what was preached to save those who believe. [22]Jews demand miraculous signs and Greeks look for wisdom, [23]but we preach Christ crucified: a stumbling block to Jews and foolishness to Gentiles, [24]but to those whom God has called, both Jews and Greeks, Christ the power of God and the wisdom of God. [25]For the foolishness of God is wiser than man's wisdom, and the weakness of God is stronger than man's strength.

[26]Brothers, think of what you were when you were called. Not many of you were wise by human standards; not many were influential; not many were of noble birth. [27]But God chose the foolish things of the world to shame the wise; God chose the weak things of the world to shame the strong. [28]He chose the lowly things of this world and the despised things—and the things that are not—to nullify the things that are, [29]so that no one may boast before him. [30]It is because of him that you are in Christ Jesus, who has become for us wisdom from God—that is, our righteousness, holiness and redemption. [31]Therefore, as it is written: "Let him who boasts boast in the Lord."[d]

2 When I came to you, brothers, I did not come with eloquence or superior wisdom as I proclaimed to you the testimony about God.[e] [2]For I resolved to know nothing while I was with you except Jesus Christ and him crucified. [3]I came to you in weakness and fear, and with much trembling. [4]My message and my preaching were not with wise and persuasive words, but with a demonstration of the Spirit's power, [5]so that your faith might not rest on men's wisdom, but on God's power.

Wisdom From the Spirit

[6]We do, however, speak a message of wisdom among the mature, but not the wisdom of this age or of the rulers of this age, who are coming to nothing. [7]No, we speak of God's secret wisdom, a wisdom that has been hidden and that God destined for our glory before time began. [8]None of the rulers of this age understood it, for if they had, they would not have crucified the Lord of glory. [9]However, as it is written:

> "No eye has seen,
>   no ear has heard,
> no mind has conceived
>   what God has prepared for those who love him"[f]—

[10]but God has revealed it to us by his Spirit.

The Spirit searches all things, even the deep things of God. [11]For who among men knows the thoughts of a man except the man's spirit within him? In the same way no one knows the thoughts of God except the Spirit of God. [12]We have not received the spirit of the world but the Spirit who is from God, that we may understand what God has freely given us. [13]This is what we speak, not in words taught us by human wisdom but in words taught by the Spirit, expressing spiritual truths in spiritual words.[g] [14]The man without the Spirit does not accept

---

d31 Jer. 9:24   e1 Some manuscripts *as I proclaimed to you God's mystery*
f9 Isaiah 64:4   g13 Or *Spirit, interpreting spiritual truths to spiritual men*

the things that come from the Spirit of God, for they are foolishness to him, and he cannot understand them, because they are spiritually discerned. [15]The spiritual man makes judgments about all things, but he himself is not subject to any man's judgment:

[16]"For who has known the mind of the Lord
  that he may instruct him?"[h]

But we have the mind of Christ.

On Divisions in the Church

3 Brothers, I could not address you as spiritual but as worldly—mere infants in Christ. [2]I gave you milk, not solid food, for you were not yet ready for it. Indeed, you are still not ready. [3]You are still worldly. For since there is jealousy and quarreling among you, are you not worldly? Are you not acting like mere men? [4]For when one says, "I follow Paul," and another, "I follow Apollos," are you not mere men?

[5]What, after all, is Apollos? And what is Paul? Only servants, through whom you came to believe—as the Lord has assigned to each his task. [6]I planted the seed, Apollos watered it, but God made it grow. [7]So neither he who plants nor he who waters is anything, but only God, who makes things grow. [8]The man who plants and the man who waters have one purpose, and each will be rewarded according to his own labor. [9]For we are God's fellow workers; you are God's field, God's building.

[10]By the grace God has given me, I laid a foundation as an expert builder, and someone else is building on it. But each one should be careful how he builds. [11]For no one can lay any foundation other than the one already laid, which is Jesus Christ. [12]If any man builds on this foundation using gold, silver, costly stones, wood, hay or straw, [13]his work will be shown for what it is, because the Day will bring it to light. It will be revealed with fire, and the fire will test the quality of each man's work. [14]If what he has built survives, he will receive his reward. [15]If it is burned up, he will suffer loss; he himself will be saved, but only as one escaping through the flames.

[16]Don't you know that you yourselves are God's temple and that God's Spirit lives in you? [17]If anyone destroys God's temple, God will destroy him; for God's temple is sacred, and you are that temple.

[18]Do not deceive yourselves. If any one of you thinks he is wise by the standards of this age, he should become a "fool" so that he may become wise. [19]For the wisdom of this world is foolishness in God's sight. As it is written: "He catches the wise in their craftiness"[i]; [20]and again, "The Lord knows that the thoughts of the wise are futile."[j] [21]So then, no more boasting about men! All things are yours, [22]whether Paul or Apollos or Cephas[k] or the world or life or death or the present or the future—all are yours, [23]and you are of Christ, and Christ is of God.

OPEN: How would you describe yourself in terms of a building (skyscraper, grass shack, bomb shelter, greenhouse, etc.)? Why?

DIG: 1. Since each faction at Corinth thought it was more spiritual than the others, how would they react to verses 1-4? What does Paul mean by "infants"? "Milk"? "Solid food"? **2.** How are "worldly" versus "spiritual" people defined here? **3.** In choosing between Paul and Apollos, how well did they understand the work of either one? **4.** What is the point of Paul's extended metaphor in verses 5-9? In verses 10-15? **5.** How is Jesus the foundation? Who are the building materials? How is each person's work tested? **6.** The "you" in verses 16-18 is plural, referring to the community as a whole. How would you explain to someone what Paul means by this picture (v.16)? This warning (v.17)? Becoming a "fool" (v.18)? **7.** In what sense does he mean that "all things are yours" (v.22)? Why then fight over which leader to follow?

REFLECT: 1. What is the difference between respecting a Christian leader, and the problem Paul deals with here? **2.** How is Paul's use of the term "worldly" different than its common use today? **3.** Given the clues about what makes for good "building materials," what is one "concrete" way you could help build God's temple in your community?

[h]16 Isaiah 40:13   [i]19 Job 5:13   [j]20 Psalm 94:11   [k]22 That is, Peter

OPEN: 1. What significant symbol of trust were you given early on, which later resulted in something funny happening: (a) Babysitting? (b) Housesitting? (c) Keys to Dad's car? (d) Preparing the Sunday meal? (e) Caring for your pet? **2.** What mess did you once make while entrusted with this duty?

DIG: 1. What was going on in this church (v.1)? **2.** Although faithfulness is required in a leader, how do some people view Paul (vv.3-5)? How does Paul deal with this suspicion? What is the distinction between a "clear conscience" and being "innocent"? **3.** Corinthian factions judged one another by the reputation of the leader they followed. What then does Paul mean by the proverb in verse 6? How should they apply it? **4.** Was their pride based in their leaders or in themselves? Explain. **5.** In this church, what "attitude problem" provokes Paul's ironic statements in verses 8 and 10 (also v.18)? **6.** In contrast to the self-centered, "power-oriented" message some Corinthians believed, what does Paul's life exemplify (vv.9, 10-13)? **7.** Paul tells them to imitate his way of life. How does this square with not following one leader or another?

REFLECT: 1. Who do you admire for putting their faith on the line: Archbishop Desmond Tutu? Mother Teresa? Billy Graham? Some "lesser-known" believer who is faithful in hard times? What in their life do you want to imitate? **2.** How would Paul respond to the idea, popular today, that "God wants you to be happy, rich, and successful"? **3.** If Paul were to come to your group, would he come "with a whip, in love, or with a gentle spirit"? Why?

Apostles of Christ

4 So then, men ought to regard us as servants of Christ and as those entrusted with the secret things of God. ²Now it is required that those who have been given a trust must prove faithful. ³I care very little if I am judged by you or by any human court; indeed, I do not even judge myself. ⁴My conscience is clear, but that does not make me innocent. It is the Lord who judges me. ⁵Therefore judge nothing before the appointed time; wait till the Lord comes. He will bring to light what is hidden in darkness and will expose the motives of men's hearts. At that time each will receive his praise from God.

⁶Now, brothers, I have applied these things to myself and Apollos for your benefit, so that you may learn from us the meaning of the saying, "Do not go beyond what is written." Then you will not take pride in one man over against another. ⁷For who makes you different from anyone else? What do you have that you did not receive? And if you did receive it, why do you boast as though you did not?

⁸Already you have all you want! Already you have become rich! You have become kings—and that without us! How I wish that you really had become kings so that we might be kings with you! ⁹For it seems to me that God has put us apostles on display at the end of the procession, like men condemned to die in the arena. We have been made a spectacle to the whole universe, to angels as well as to men. ¹⁰We are fools for Christ, but you are so wise in Christ! We are weak, but you are strong! You are honored, we are dishonored! ¹¹To this very hour we go hungry and thirsty, we are in rags, we are brutally treated, we are homeless. ¹²We work hard with our own hands. When we are cursed, we bless; when we are persecuted, we endure it; ¹³when we are slandered, we answer kindly. Up to this moment we have become the scum of the earth, the refuse of the world.

¹⁴I am not writing this to shame you, but to warn you, as my dear children. ¹⁵Even though you have ten thousand guardians in Christ, you do not have many fathers, for in Christ Jesus I became your father through the gospel. ¹⁶Therefore I urge you to imitate me. ¹⁷For this reason I am sending to you Timothy, my son whom I love, who is faithful in the Lord. He will remind you of my way of life in Christ Jesus, which agrees with what I teach everywhere in every church.

¹⁸Some of you have become arrogant, as if I were not coming to you. ¹⁹But I will come to you very soon, if the Lord is willing, and then I will find out not only how these arrogant people are talking, but what power they have. ²⁰For the kingdom of God is not a matter of talk but of power. ²¹What do you prefer? Shall I come to you with a whip, or in love and with a gentle spirit?

ˡ5 Or *that his body*; or *that the flesh*   ᵐ13 Deut. 17:7; 19:19; 21:21; 22:21,24; 24:7

Expel the Immoral Brother!

5 It is actually reported that there is sexual immorality among you, and of a kind that does not occur even among pagans: A man has his father's wife. [2]And you are proud! Shouldn't you rather have been filled with grief and have put out of your fellowship the man who did this? [3]Even though I am not physically present, I am with you in spirit. And I have already passed judgment on the one who did this, just as if I were present. [4]When you are assembled in the name of our Lord Jesus and I am with you in spirit, and the power of our Lord Jesus is present, [5]hand this man over to Satan, so that the sinful nature[l] may be destroyed and his spirit saved on the day of the Lord.

[6]Your boasting is not good. Don't you know that a little yeast works through the whole batch of dough? [7]Get rid of the old yeast that you may be a new batch without yeast—as you really are. For Christ, our Passover lamb, has been sacrificed. [8]Therefore let us keep the Festival, not with the old yeast, the yeast of malice and wickedness, but with bread without yeast, the bread of sincerity and truth.

[9]I have written you in my letter not to associate with sexually immoral people— [10]not at all meaning the people of this world who are immoral, or the greedy and swindlers, or idolaters. In that case you would have to leave this world. [11]But now I am writing you that you must not associate with anyone who calls himself a brother but is sexually immoral or greedy, an idolater or a slanderer, a drunkard or a swindler. With such a man do not even eat.

[12]What business is it of mine to judge those outside the church? Are you not to judge those inside? [13]God will judge those outside. "Expel the wicked man from among you."[m]

Lawsuits Among Believers

6 If any of you has a dispute with another, dare he take it before the ungodly for judgment instead of before the saints? [2]Do you not know that the saints will judge the world? And if you are to judge the world, are you not competent to judge trivial cases? [3]Do you not know that we will judge angels? How much more the things of this life! [4]Therefore, if you have disputes about such matters, appoint as judges even men of little account in the church![n] [5]I say this to shame you. Is it possible that there is nobody among you wise enough to judge a dispute between believers? [6]But instead, one brother goes to law against another—and this in front of unbelievers!

[7]The very fact that you have lawsuits among you means you have been completely defeated already. Why not rather be wronged? Why not rather be cheated? [8]Instead, you yourselves cheat and do wrong, and you do this to your brothers.

[9]Do you not know that the wicked will not inherit the kingdom of God? Do not be deceived: Neither the sexually immoral nor idolaters nor adulterers nor male prostitutes nor homosexual offenders [10]nor thieves nor the greedy nor drunkards nor slanderers nor swindlers will inherit the kingdom of God. [11]And that

---

OPEN: How openly did your parents or youth group leaders talk with you about sex: Freely? Only negatively? What sex talk?

DIG: 1. How does Paul's view of this situation differ from that at Corinth (vv.2,6)? **2.** How would you paraphrase what Paul tells them to do (vv.3-5)? **3.** If you were a Corinthian church member, how would you explain to your pagan neighbor why this man had been expelled (v.5)? **4.** From the yeast imagery (vv.6-8), what is Paul's concern if this situation is allowed to go on without discipline? How is this consistent with the "new bread" they have become (vv.7-8)? **5.** Why is there a difference between the way Christians relate to those outside the faith and the way they relate to believers (vv.9-11)? **6.** How do you reconcile Paul's teaching here with that in 4:3-5? What is the point of each?

REFLECT: In matters of discipline, are you overly judgmental? Too permissive? Inconsistent? Helpful? Explain.

OPEN: With your attitude, what type of judge would you be: Hanging judge? Pushover? One known for creative sentencing? Why?

DIG: 1. What is going on here (vv. 2-6)? **2.** What is the real problem (vv.7-8)? Why do lawsuits cast a shadow over the Church? **3.** In the kingdom, are certain people excluded, or will their sin be removed before entering (vv.9-10)? **4.** How does verse 11 fit the rest of this passage?

REFLECT: 1. What attitudes underlying this situation do you see in yourself: (a) Insistence on "my rights"? (b) Desire for revenge? (c) Desire to make things right? (d) Willingness to "bend the rules"? (e) Preferring my old way of life rather than following Christ? **2.** How can the group help you change these attitudes?

---

n4 Or matters, do you appoint as judges men of little account in the church?

is what some of you were. But you were washed, you were sanctified, you were justified in the name of the Lord Jesus Christ and by the Spirit of our God.

Sexual Immorality

[12]"Everything is permissible for me"—but not everything is beneficial. "Everything is permissible for me"—but I will not be mastered by anything. [13]"Food for the stomach and the stomach for food"—but God will destroy them both. The body is not meant for sexual immorality, but for the Lord, and the Lord for the body. [14]By his power God raised the Lord from the dead, and he will raise us also. [15]Do you not know that your bodies are members of Christ himself? Shall I then take the members of Christ and unite them with a prostitute? Never! [16]Do you not know that he who unites himself with a prostitute is one with her in body? For it is said, "The two will become one flesh."*o* [17]But he who unites himself with the Lord is one with him in spirit.

[18]Flee from sexual immorality. All other sins a man commits are outside his body, but he who sins sexually sins against his own body. [19]Do you not know that your body is a temple of the Holy Spirit, who is in you, whom you have received from God? You are not your own; [20]you were bought at a price. Therefore honor God with your body.

Marriage

7 Now for the matters you wrote about: It is good for a man not to marry.*p* [2]But since there is so much immorality, each man should have his own wife, and each woman her own husband. [3]The husband should fulfill his marital duty to his wife, and likewise the wife to her husband. [4]The wife's body does not belong to her alone but also to her husband. In the same way, the husband's body does not belong to him alone but also to his wife. [5]Do not deprive each other except by mutual consent and for a time, so that you may devote yourselves to prayer. Then come together again so that Satan will not tempt you because of your lack of self-control. [6]I say this as a concession, not as a command. [7]I wish that all men were as I am. But each man has his own gift from God; one has this gift, another has that.

[8]Now to the unmarried and the widows I say: It is good for them to stay unmarried, as I am. [9]But if they cannot control themselves, they should marry, for it is better to marry than to burn with passion.

[10]To the married I give this command (not I, but the Lord): A wife must not separate from her husband. [11]But if she does, she must remain unmarried or else be reconciled to her husband. And a husband must not divorce his wife.

[12]To the rest I say this (I, not the Lord): If any brother has a wife who is not a believer and she is willing to live with him, he must not divorce her. [13]And if a woman has a husband who is not a believer and he is willing to live with her, she must not divorce him. [14]For the unbelieving husband has been sanctified

o16 Gen. 2:24   *p1* Or "*It is good for a man not to have sexual relations with a woman.*"

through his wife, and the unbelieving wife has been sanctified through her believing husband. Otherwise your children would be unclean, but as it is, they are holy.

¹⁵But if the unbeliever leaves, let him do so. A believing man or woman is not bound in such circumstances; God has called us to live in peace. ¹⁶How do you know, wife, whether you will save your husband? Or, how do you know, husband, whether you will save your wife?

¹⁷Nevertheless, each one should retain the place in life that the Lord assigned to him and to which God has called him. This is the rule I lay down in all the churches. ¹⁸Was a man already circumcised when he was called? He should not become uncircumcised. Was a man uncircumcised when he was called? He should not be circumcised. ¹⁹Circumcision is nothing and uncircumcision is nothing. Keeping God's commands is what counts. ²⁰Each one should remain in the situation which he was in when God called him. ²¹Were you a slave when you were called? Don't let it trouble you—although if you can gain your freedom, do so. ²²For he who was a slave when he was called by the Lord is the Lord's freedman; similarly, he who was a free man when he was called is Christ's slave. ²³You were bought at a price; do not become slaves of men. ²⁴Brothers, each man, as responsible to God, should remain in the situation God called him to.

²⁵Now about virgins: I have no command from the Lord, but I give a judgment as one who by the Lord's mercy is trustworthy. ²⁶Because of the present crisis, I think that it is good for you to remain as you are. ²⁷Are you married? Do not seek a divorce. Are you unmarried? Do not look for a wife. ²⁸But if you do marry, you have not sinned; and if a virgin marries, she has not sinned. But those who marry will face many troubles in this life, and I want to spare you this.

²⁹What I mean, brothers, is that the time is short. From now on those who have wives should live as if they had none; ³⁰those who mourn, as if they did not; those who are happy, as if they were not; those who buy something, as if it were not theirs to keep; ³¹those who use the things of the world, as if not engrossed in them. For this world in its present form is passing away.

³²I would like you to be free from concern. An unmarried man is concerned about the Lord's affairs—how he can please the Lord. ³³But a married man is concerned about the affairs of this world—how he can please his wife— ³⁴and his interests are divided. An unmarried woman or virgin is concerned about the Lord's affairs: Her aim is to be devoted to the Lord in both body and spirit. But a married woman is concerned about the affairs of this world—how she can please her husband. ³⁵I am saying this for your own good, not to restrict you, but that you may live in a right way in undivided devotion to the Lord.

³⁶If anyone thinks he is acting improperly toward the virgin he is engaged to, and if she is getting along in years and he feels he ought to marry, he should do as he wants. He is not sinning. They should get married. ³⁷But the man who has settled the matter in his own mind, who is under no compulsion but has control over his own will, and who has made up his mind not to marry the virgin—this man also does the right thing. ³⁸So

20 and 24? **6.** In verses 25-28, how does Paul apply this general rule specifically to those engaged to be married (the word for "unmarried" and "divorce" in v.27 is the same)? **7.** What does he mean by his suggestions about how to live in view of the "present crisis" (vv. 29-31)? (Note: What the "crisis" was is unclear. It might mean persecution against Christians, as in Ac 18:1-17, or the expected second coming of Christ.) **8.** How does his advice to the married in this context (v.29) relate to his teaching in Ephesians 5:21-32? What is his point in each passage? **9.** Verses 36-40 suggest that singleness is an option they ought to consider. What reasons does he give for that (vv.28b, 32-34)? **10.** Whether people marry or not, what is the overriding issue?

REFLECT: **1.** Have you seen new Christians (perhaps yourself) make crazy changes in their lives based on new-found "freedom" in Christ? What problems did that cause you, which could have been avoided by applying Paul's principle? When is pursuing a change in circumstances appropriate? **2.** Paul's teaching about divorce here primarily relates to the false idea that to be spiritual meant to forego sex (7:1). What principles might he suggest to a person considering divorce for other reasons (e.g., cruelty, neglect, emotional exhaustion)? **3.** How has your marital status (single or married) helped you to serve Christ more effectively? How has it hindered your service? **4.** By his general principle, what is Paul really saying: (a) Change is usually misguided? (b) Think before you act? (c) Bloom where you are planted? How does his principle work in truly unjust situations? **5.** Whether you have never been married, are currently married, divorced, or widowed, what is one way you can show your "undivided devotion" to the Lord this week?

then, he who marries the virgin does right, but he who does not marry her does even better. *q*

[39] A woman is bound to her husband as long as he lives. But if her husband dies, she is free to marry anyone she wishes, but he must belong to the Lord. [40] In my judgment, she is happier if she stays as she is—and I think that I too have the Spirit of God.

Food Sacrificed to Idols

8 Now about food sacrificed to idols: We know that we all possess knowledge. *r* Knowledge puffs up, but love builds up. [2] The man who thinks he knows something does not yet know as he ought to know. [3] But the man who loves God is known by God.

[4] So then, about eating food sacrificed to idols: We know that an idol is nothing at all in the world and that there is no God but one. [5] For even if there are so-called gods, whether in heaven or on earth (as indeed there are many "gods" and many "lords"), [6] yet for us there is but one God, the Father, from whom all things came and for whom we live; and there is but one Lord, Jesus Christ, through whom all things came and through whom we live.

[7] But not everyone knows this. Some people are still so accustomed to idols that when they eat such food they think of it as having been sacrificed to an idol, and since their conscience is weak, it is defiled. [8] But food does not bring us near to God; we are no worse if we do not eat, and no better if we do.

[9] Be careful, however, that the exercise of your freedom does not become a stumbling block to the weak. [10] For if anyone with a weak conscience sees you who have this knowledge eating in an idol's temple, won't he be emboldened to eat what has been sacrificed to idols? [11] So this weak brother, for whom Christ died, is destroyed by your knowledge. [12] When you sin against your brothers in this way and wound their weak conscience, you sin against Christ. [13] Therefore, if what I eat causes my brother to fall into sin, I will never eat meat again, so that I will not cause him to fall.

The Rights of an Apostle

9 Am I not free? Am I not an apostle? Have I not seen Jesus our Lord? Are you not the result of my work in the Lord? [2] Even though I may not be an apostle to others, surely I am to you! For you are the seal of my apostleship in the Lord.

[3] This is my defense to those who sit in judgment on me. [4] Don't we have the right to food and drink? [5] Don't we have the right to take a believing wife along with us, as do the other apostles and the Lord's brothers and Cephas *s*? [6] Or is it only I and Barnabas who must work for a living?

OPEN: In settling disputes with a parent, child, or spouse, do you: (a) Dig in your heels until you win? (b) Seek out a compromise? (c) Give in to the other? How do you feel about your "fighting style"?

DIG: 1. From verses 1,4,7 and 10, what side of the argument is each group taking? **2.** What "knowledge" do the people claim to have (v.1,4-6)? **3.** Although Paul does not dispute that knowledge, what does he mean by contrasting it with love (v.1b)? What else does he want these people to realize is involved (vv.7-8,9,12)? **4.** What is meant by "weak brother" (vv.9-13)? **5.** How is it that what is not sin for one group is sin for another? What general principle is Paul applying here?

REFLECT: 1. Where in your life is one person's "freedom" another's "stumbling block": To drink or not to drink? To wear certain styles of clothes? To listen to "New Age" music or not? To pursue a certain standard of living? To be involved in certain political causes? **2.** Of the issues where you have been on the "weak" side, how did you feel toward those who ignored your concerns?

OPEN: 1. What "race" (gunny sack, track meet, back roads dare, etc.) is still vivid in your memory? Did you win, lose, fall down, or crack up? Why would or wouldn't you do it again? **2.** What kind of work around the house do you like to do best? Least? Why?

DIG: 1. Why does Paul make such a big deal about being an apostle? What is the implied answer to each of the questions in verse 1? How does this argumentative attitude square with his teaching in 8:9? **2.** What rights does he have as an apostle? How does he illustrate his right to financial gain (vv.7-12)? Why didn't he claim

---

q36-38 Or [36]If anyone thinks he is not treating his daughter properly, and if she is getting along in years, and he feels she ought to marry, he should do as he wants. He is not sinning. He should let her get married. [37]But the man who has settled the matter in his own mind, who is under no compulsion but has control over his own will, and who has made up his mind to keep the virgin unmarried—this man also does the right thing. [38]So then, he who gives his virgin in marriage does right, but he who does not give her in marriage does even better.   r1 Or "We all possess knowledge," as you say   s5 That is, Peter

7Who serves as a soldier at his own expense? Who plants a vineyard and does not eat of its grapes? Who tends a flock and does not drink of the milk? 8Do I say this merely from a human point of view? Doesn't the Law say the same thing? 9For it is written in the Law of Moses: "Do not muzzle an ox while it is treading out the grain."ᶠ Is it about oxen that God is concerned? 10Surely he says this for us, doesn't he? Yes, this was written for us, because when the plowman plows and the thresher threshes, they ought to do so in the hope of sharing in the harvest. 11If we have sown spiritual seed among you, is it too much if we reap a material harvest from you? 12If others have this right of support from you, shouldn't we have it all the more?

But we did not use this right. On the contrary, we put up with anything rather than hinder the gospel of Christ. 13Don't you know that those who work in the temple get their food from the temple, and those who serve at the altar share in what is offered on the altar? 14In the same way, the Lord has commanded that those who preach the gospel should receive their living from the gospel.

15But I have not used any of these rights. And I am not writing this in the hope that you will do such things for me. I would rather die than have anyone deprive me of this boast. 16Yet when I preach the gospel, I cannot boast, for I am compelled to preach. Woe to me if I do not preach the gospel! 17If I preach voluntarily, I have a reward; if not voluntarily, I am simply discharging the trust committed to me. 18What then is my reward? Just this: that in preaching the gospel I may offer it free of charge, and so not make use of my rights in preaching it.

19Though I am free and belong to no man, I make myself a slave to everyone, to win as many as possible. 20To the Jews I became like a Jew, to win the Jews. To those under the law I became like one under the law (though I myself am not under the law), so as to win those under the law. 21To those not having the law I became like one not having the law (though I am not free from God's law but am under Christ's law), so as to win those not having the law. 22To the weak I became weak, to win the weak. I have become all things to all men so that by all possible means I might save some. 23I do all this for the sake of the gospel, that I may share in its blessings.

24Do you not know that in a race all the runners run, but only one gets the prize? Run in such a way as to get the prize. 25Everyone who competes in the games goes into strict training. They do it to get a crown that will not last; but we do it to get a crown that will last forever. 26Therefore I do not run like a man running aimlessly; I do not fight like a man beating the air. 27No, I beat my body and make it my slave so that after I have preached to others, I myself will not be disqualified for the prize.

this right (vv. 12-18)? **3.** What compels Paul to preach? **4.** How has Paul used his freedom in Christ (vv. 19-23)? How does this relate to the principle he told the Corinthians to follow in 8:13? **5.** What is his motivation for shaping his life around the needs and concerns of others (vv. 19, 22, 23)? **6.** What point is Paul making by comparing the Christian life to a race (vv. 24-27)? **7.** Why then was Paul being criticized by the Corinthians?

REFLECT: 1. What groups of people in your community are not being ministered to: The poor? Unwed mothers? The gays? The Yuppies? An ethnic group? Students? The elderly? What would it mean for you to apply the principle of verses 19-23 in order to communicate the gospel to them? What "baggage" in your lifestyle would be a barrier between them and you? What would it cost you to get rid of that in order to reach them? **2.** In the Christian race, how are you doing: (a) "Fresh because I'm just starting"? (b) "Feeling tired and achy, thinking of dropping out for awhile"? (c) "Going great, I've got my second wind"? (d) "Where in the world is the finish line"? (e) "I thought this was a sprint, not a marathon"? **3.** From this passage, what are the obligations of a church to its pastors and leaders? What is a fair way of determining appropriate compensation for them?

ᶠ9 Deut. 25:4

OPEN: What family holiday tradition is your favorite? Why?

DIG: 1. After reminding them of the discipline needed to "run the race" (9:24-27), Paul cites this example of Israel's past (10:1-5; see Ex 13-17). Why were these reminders necessary? **2.** To what "sacraments" is he pointing by the example of Israel? What point is Paul making by showing that these "sacraments" failed to protect Israel from God's anger? **3.** How do the four examples from Israel's past relate to the Corinthian situation? **4.** What is the moral of this teaching (vv.12-13)?

REFLECT: 1. What is a contemporary parallel of the way these examples and warnings apply to you? **2.** What temptations do you most consistently have to face? Hence, does verse 13 encourage or frustrate you? How so?

OPEN: 1. Were you raised in a permissive environment, or in a strict, but forgiving one? Give an example. **2.** With your boss (or parent) do you find it easier to get *permission* (ahead of time), or to get *forgiveness* (later if it turns out badly)? Give an example.

DIG: 1. What is meant by drinking the cup and eating the bread? How is that a "participation" in Christ's blood and body (see also Lk 22:19-20; Jn 6:53-57)? **2.** Why mention eating the OT sacrifices (v.18) in this context? **3.** How do these two illustrations relate to Paul's instruction to avoid participation in the feasts at pagan temples (vv.14,20)? Why should they flee from these activities (v.20; see 8:10)? **4.** How is Paul's argument against idolatry and immorality similar (v.23; see 6:12)? **5.** In what sense is a Christian "free" (v.24; see 8:1b,13)? How does this freedom apply to eating sacrificial meat sold in public meat markets (vv.25-27)? However, when is it proper to abstain from eating this meat (vv.28-29)? What makes it all right (in general) to eat this sacrificial meat in private, but not at the temple feasts?

Warnings From Israel's History

10 For I do not want you to be ignorant of the fact, brothers, that our forefathers were all under the cloud and that they all passed through the sea. [2]They were all baptized into Moses in the cloud and in the sea. [3]They all ate the same spiritual food [4]and drank the same spiritual drink; for they drank from the spiritual rock that accompanied them, and that rock was Christ. [5]Nevertheless, God was not pleased with most of them; their bodies were scattered over the desert.

[6]Now these things occurred as examples[u] to keep us from setting our hearts on evil things as they did. [7]Do not be idolaters, as some of them were; as it is written: "The people sat down to eat and drink and got up to indulge in pagan revelry."[v] [8]We should not commit sexual immorality, as some of them did—and in one day twenty-three thousand of them died. [9]We should not test the Lord, as some of them did—and were killed by snakes. [10]And do not grumble, as some of them did—and were killed by the destroying angel.

[11]These things happened to them as examples and were written down as warnings for us, on whom the fulfillment of the ages has come. [12]So, if you think you are standing firm, be careful that you don't fall! [13]No temptation has seized you except what is common to man. And God is faithful; he will not let you be tempted beyond what you can bear. But when you are tempted, he will also provide a way out so that you can stand up under it.

Idol Feasts and the Lord's Supper

[14]Therefore, my dear friends, flee from idolatry. [15]I speak to sensible people; judge for yourselves what I say. [16]Is not the cup of thanksgiving for which we give thanks a participation in the blood of Christ? And is not the bread that we break a participation in the body of Christ? [17]Because there is one loaf, we, who are many, are one body, for we all partake of the one loaf.

[18]Consider the people of Israel: Do not those who eat the sacrifices participate in the altar? [19]Do I mean then that a sacrifice offered to an idol is anything, or that an idol is anything? [20]No, but the sacrifices of pagans are offered to demons, not to God, and I do not want you to be participants with demons. [21]You cannot drink the cup of the Lord and the cup of demons too; you cannot have a part in both the Lord's table and the table of demons. [22]Are we trying to arouse the Lord's jealousy? Are we stronger than he?

The Believer's Freedom

[23]"Everything is permissible"—but not everything is beneficial. "Everything is permissible"—but not everything is constructive. [24]Nobody should seek his own good, but the good of others.

[25]Eat anything sold in the meat market without raising questions of conscience, [26]for, "The earth is the Lord's, and everything in it."[w]

---

[u]6 Or *types*; also in verse 11   [v]7 Exodus 32:6   [w]26 Psalm 24:1

[27]If some unbeliever invites you to a meal and you want to go, eat whatever is put before you without raising questions of conscience. [28]But if anyone says to you, "This has been offered in sacrifice," then do not eat it, both for the sake of the man who told you and for conscience' sake[x]— [29]the other man's conscience, I mean, not yours. For why should my freedom be judged by another's conscience? [30]If I take part in the meal with thankfulness, why am I denounced because of something I thank God for?

[31]So whether you eat or drink or whatever you do, do it all for the glory of God. [32]Do not cause anyone to stumble, whether Jews, Greeks or the church of God— [33]even as I try to please everybody in every way. For I am not seeking my own good but

11 the good of many, so that they may be saved. [1]Follow my example, as I follow the example of Christ.

Propriety in Worship

[2]I praise you for remembering me in everything and for holding to the teachings,[y] just as I passed them on to you.

[3]Now I want you to realize that the head of every man is Christ, and the head of the woman is man, and the head of Christ is God. [4]Every man who prays or prophesies with his head covered dishonors his head. [5]And every woman who prays or prophesies with her head uncovered dishonors her head—it is just as though her head were shaved. [6]If a woman does not cover her head, she should have her hair cut off; and if it is a disgrace for a woman to have her hair cut or shaved off, she should cover her head. [7]A man ought not to cover his head,[z] since he is the image and glory of God; but the woman is the glory of man. [8]For man did not come from woman, but woman from man; [9]neither was man created for woman, but woman for man. [10]For this reason, and because of the angels, the woman ought to have a sign of authority on her head.

[11]In the Lord, however, woman is not independent of man, nor is man independent of woman. [12]For as woman came from man, so also man is born of woman. But everything comes from God. [13]Judge for yourselves: Is it proper for a woman to pray to God with her head uncovered? [14]Does not the very nature of things teach you that if a man has long hair, it is a disgrace to him, [15]but that if a woman has long hair, it is her glory? For long hair is given to her as a covering. [16]If anyone wants to be contentious about this, we have no other practice—nor do the churches of God.

REFLECT: 1. Idolatry can take many forms. What are two "idols" you see that are "worshiped" by people around you? When do you find yourself attracted to this idol? How can you guard against that? **2.** As for making judgment calls in *grey areas*, what principles have you found most helpful?

OPEN: How did you wear your hair 15 years ago?

DIG: 1. This passage is difficult because of uncertainty about a) the text, b) whether Paul is quoting (and then refuting) their arguments, and c) the standards of propriety for women. What do the Corinthians seem to be doing wrong? **2.** What theological arguments does Paul use? What cultural ones? What questions does this raise for you? **3.** "Head" (v.3) means *source*, not *ruler*. Does this make a difference in your interpretation? **4.** Is a head-covering a permanent need for women? Why?

REFLECT: Concern for the glory of God, the interdependence of men and women, and sensitivity to the culture are three principles here. Given the discussions about the role of women in the Church, how do these principles apply in your circles?

---

[x]28 Some manuscripts *conscience' sake, for "the earth is the Lord's and everything in it"*
[y]2 Or *traditions*   [z]4-7 Or [4]*Every man who prays or prophesies with long hair dishonors his head.* [5]*And every woman who prays or prophesies with no covering of hair, on her head dishonors her head—she is just like one of the "shorn women."* [6]*If a woman has no covering, let her be for now with short hair, but since it is a disgrace for a woman to have her hair shorn or shaved, she should grow it again.* [7]*A man ought not to have long hair*

OPEN: During your teen years, what was dinner time like: Who sat where? Who did what? Who ate like a pig (indiscriminately)? Like a bird (very little)? Like a cat (very finicky)? Who cleaned up?

DIG: 1. Had you been there, what would you have seen, heard, and felt as the Corinthians observed the Lord's Supper (vv.17-22)? **2.** How was the Lord's Supper being distorted (see also 10:17)? **3.** Why then does Paul repeat the account of the Lord's Supper (vv.23-25; compare Lk 22:19-20)? **4.** What does Paul mean by eating and drinking in "an unworthy manner" (v.27)? By "not recognizing the body of the Lord" (v. 29)? By self-examination (v.28)? By judging oneself (v.31)? **5.** What is the alternative to this self-evaluation (vv.32,34)?

REFLECT: 1. Remembrance (vv. 24,25), proclamation (v.26), and participation (10:16) are three realities of the Lord's Supper. How would you explain to a non-believer how the Lord's Supper accomplishes each of these? **2.** What are some ways modern Christians fail to "recognize the body of the Lord" by creating distinctions between types of Christians? (E.g., the unwritten "dress code" of some churches excludes those who can't afford that style.) **3.** How could your service be more inclusive of the types of people where you live?

OPEN: 1. What was the best gift you ever received or gave? What was the occasion? **2.** How many different kinds of service or work situations have you had since you finished school?

DIG: 1. What do you imagine was happening in the Corinthian worship services (vv.1-3; see 10:19-20)? Therefore, why is the content (rather than the experience) of the speech most important (v.3)? **2.** How is the diversity of the gifts related to the unity of the Father, Son, and Spirit? **3.** Since the Corinthians were proud of their spirituality (1:12; 4:8; 5:2), how might verses 7 and 11 surprise them? **4.** In verses 12-13, in what ways does Paul stress the unity of the believers? What other points does this body image convey (vv.14-20)? **5.** How does Paul counter

The Lord's Supper

[17]In the following directives I have no praise for you, for your meetings do more harm than good. [18]In the first place, I hear that when you come together as a church, there are divisions among you, and to some extent I believe it. [19]No doubt there have to be differences among you to show which of you have God's approval. [20]When you come together, it is not the Lord's Supper you eat, [21]for as you eat, each of you goes ahead without waiting for anybody else. One remains hungry, another gets drunk. [22]Don't you have homes to eat and drink in? Or do you despise the church of God and humiliate those who have nothing? What shall I say to you? Shall I praise you for this? Certainly not!

[23]For I received from the Lord what I also passed on to you: The Lord Jesus, on the night he was betrayed, took bread, [24]and when he had given thanks, he broke it and said, "This is my body, which is for you; do this in remembrance of me." [25]In the same way, after supper he took the cup, saying, "This cup is the new covenant in my blood; do this, whenever you drink it, in remembrance of me." [26]For whenever you eat this bread and drink this cup, you proclaim the Lord's death until he comes.

[27]Therefore, whoever eats the bread or drinks the cup of the Lord in an unworthy manner will be guilty of sinning against the body and blood of the Lord. [28]A man ought to examine himself before he eats of the bread and drinks of the cup. [29]For anyone who eats and drinks without recognizing the body of the Lord eats and drinks judgment on himself. [30]That is why many among you are weak and sick, and a number of you have fallen asleep. [31]But if we judged ourselves, we would not come under judgment. [32]When we are judged by the Lord, we are being disciplined so that we will not be condemned with the world.

[33]So then, my brothers, when you come together to eat, wait for each other. [34]If anyone is hungry, he should eat at home, so that when you meet together it may not result in judgment. And when I come I will give further directions.

Spiritual Gifts

12 Now about spiritual gifts, brothers, I do not want you to be ignorant. [2]You know that when you were pagans, somehow or other you were influenced and led astray to mute idols. [3]Therefore I tell you that no one who is speaking by the Spirit of God says, "Jesus be cursed," and no one can say, "Jesus is Lord," except by the Holy Spirit.

[4]There are different kinds of gifts, but the same Spirit. [5]There are different kinds of service, but the same Lord. [6]There are different kinds of working, but the same God works all of them in all men.

[7]Now to each one the manifestation of the Spirit is given for the common good. [8]To one there is given through the Spirit the message of wisdom, to another the message of knowledge by means of the same Spirit, [9]to another faith by the same Spirit, to another gifts of healing by that one Spirit, [10]to another miraculous powers, to another prophecy, to another distinguishing between spirits, to another speaking in different kinds of

tongues,^{a} and to still another the interpretation of tongues.^{a} ^{11}All these are the work of one and the same Spirit, and he gives them to each one, just as he determines.

One Body, Many Parts

^{12}The body is a unit, though it is made up of many parts; and though all its parts are many, they form one body. So it is with Christ. ^{13}For we were all baptized by^b one Spirit into one body— whether Jews or Greeks, slave or free—and we were all given the one Spirit to drink.

^{14}Now the body is not made up of one part but of many. ^{15}If the foot should say, "Because I am not a hand, I do not belong to the body," it would not for that reason cease to be part of the body. ^{16}And if the ear should say, "Because I am not an eye, I do not belong to the body," it would not for that reason cease to be part of the body. ^{17}If the whole body were an eye, where would the sense of hearing be? If the whole body were an ear, where would the sense of smell be? ^{18}But in fact God has arranged the parts in the body, every one of them, just as he wanted them to be. ^{19}If they were all one part, where would the body be? ^{20}As it is, there are many parts, but one body.

^{21}The eye cannot say to the hand, "I don't need you!" And the head cannot say to the feet, "I don't need you!" ^{22}On the contrary, those parts of the body that seem to be weaker are indispensable, ^{23}and the parts that we think are less honorable we treat with special honor. And the parts that are unpresentable are treated with special modesty, ^{24}while our presentable parts need no special treatment. But God has combined the members of the body and has given greater honor to the parts that lacked it, ^{25}so that there should be no division in the body, but that its parts should have equal concern for each other. ^{26}If one part suffers, every part suffers with it; if one part is honored, every part rejoices with it.

^{27}Now you are the body of Christ, and each one of you is a part of it. ^{28}And in the church God has appointed first of all apostles, second prophets, third teachers, then workers of miracles, also those having gifts of healing, those able to help others, those with gifts of administration, and those speaking in different kinds of tongues. ^{29}Are all apostles? Are all prophets? Are all teachers? Do all work miracles? ^{30}Do all have gifts of healing? Do all speak in tongues^c? Do all interpret? ^{31}But eagerly desire^d the greater gifts.

Love

And now I will show you the most excellent way.

13 If I speak in the tongues^e of men and of angels, but have not love, I am only a resounding gong or a clanging cymbal. ^{2}If I have the gift of prophecy and can fathom all mysteries and all knowledge, and if I have a faith that can move mountains, but have not love, I am nothing. ^{3}If I give all I possess to the poor and surrender my body to the flames,^{f} but have not love, I gain nothing.

$^a10$ Or *languages*; also in verse 28 $^b13$ Or *with*; or *in* $^c30$ Or *other languages* $^d31$ Or *But you are eagerly desiring* $^e1$ Or *languages* $^f3$ Some early manuscripts *body that I may boast*

their spiritual pride in verses 21-26? How could you illustrate the truth of verse 26 from your own body? From your church? **6.** What categories of gifts do you find in the lists in verses 8-10? In verses 28-30? Which ones do you want more information about? **7.** Do you think either list is meant to be exhaustive or all-inclusive? Why? Is there any significance in his ordering them as "first," "second," etc.? If so, what? **8.** From his rhetorical questions in verse 29-30, what is another problem in this church?

REFLECT: 1. Regardless of your church's official doctrinal position, what attitudes toward spiritual gifts dominate: (a) For pastors only? (b) For all believers? (c) For the good of others? (d) For the first-century church only? (e) For believers who have a post-conversion experience? (f) More spiritual gifts for the more spiritually mature? **2.** How do such attitudes affect the church at large? The church where you worship? **3.** Of the gifts listed here, do any have your name on it? How so? **4.** Take time to go around the group affirming the strengths and gifts you see in one another. Take turns having one person sit in silence while the others affirm his or her strengths.

OPEN: 1. Sing (or recite) a line of your favorite love song as a teenager. **2.** If I wanted to test your patience, what could I do to see how short a fuse you had?

DIG: 1. Given the Corinthians' quest for spiritual gifts and power, what is Paul's point in verses 1-3? **2.** What is love? List the seven characteristics of what love is, and the eight that it is not (vv.4-7). **3.** What is the significance of the contrast he makes between gifts, perfection, and love (vv.8-13)? Why will spiritual gifts cease to be relevant? What will endure? Why?

REFLECT: Have group members rewrite each of the "love is..." qualities to show what love should look like in their specific situation at home, work, political views, church, etc. Which one do you need to work on this week?

OPEN: 1. If you were a musical instrument, what would you be: "Brassy"? Finely-tuned? Off-beat? "Down-home"? Explain. 2. What foreign languages have you studied? Do you still use them? When have you dearly wished you knew a certain language?

DIG: 1. How does Paul's emphasis on the use of "tongues" reveal what is going on in the church? 2. Given the Corinthian's spiritual pride, why are the commands in verse 1 important? 3. How does Paul contrast the gifts of prophecy and tongues? What are the values and limits of tongues (vv.4, 9, 13-19)? How does he illustrate his point? 4. In what way is the Corinthian obsession with tongues another mark of their spiritual immaturity (v.20; see also 3:1-4)? 5. What does it mean "in regard to evil, be infants" (v.20)? Likewise, "in your thinking be adults"? 6. In verses 21-25, why does Paul caution the use of tongues in public worship? Verse 21 quotes Isaiah 28:11-12, where God says that since the people will not listen to his prophets, he will send foreigners among them to conquer them. Their "strange tongues" will be a sign of God's judgment. In that context, why does Paul prefer to have the Corinthians exercise intelligible gifts like preaching and prophecy in their public meetings?

REFLECT: 1. Things that were flashy, exciting, and powerful attracted the Corinthians (they knew the "love of power" more than the "power of love"). In what ways do

4Love is patient, love is kind. It does not envy, it does not boast, it is not proud. 5It is not rude, it is not self-seeking, it is not easily angered, it keeps no record of wrongs. 6Love does not delight in evil but rejoices with the truth. 7It always protects, always trusts, always hopes, always perseveres.

8Love never fails. But where there are prophecies, they will cease; where there are tongues, they will be stilled; where there is knowledge, it will pass away. 9For we know in part and we prophesy in part, 10but when perfection comes, the imperfect disappears. 11When I was a child, I talked like a child, I thought like a child, I reasoned like a child. When I became a man, I put childish ways behind me. 12Now we see but a poor reflection as in a mirror; then we shall see face to face. Now I know in part; then I shall know fully, even as I am fully known.

13And now these three remain: faith, hope and love. But the greatest of these is love.

Gifts of Prophecy and Tongues

14 Follow the way of love and eagerly desire spiritual gifts, especially the gift of prophecy. 2For anyone who speaks in a tongue*g* does not speak to men but to God. Indeed, no one understands him; he utters mysteries with his spirit.*h* 3But everyone who prophesies speaks to men for their strengthening, encouragement and comfort. 4He who speaks in a tongue edifies himself, but he who prophesies edifies the church. 5I would like every one of you to speak in tongues,*i* but I would rather have you prophesy. He who prophesies is greater than one who speaks in tongues,*i* unless he interprets, so that the church may be edified.

6Now, brothers, if I come to you and speak in tongues, what good will I be to you, unless I bring you some revelation or knowledge or prophecy or word of instruction? 7Even in the case of lifeless things that make sounds, such as the flute or harp, how will anyone know what tune is being played unless there is a distinction in the notes? 8Again, if the trumpet does not sound a clear call, who will get ready for battle? 9So it is with you. Unless you speak intelligible words with your tongue, how will anyone know what you are saying? You will just be speaking into the air. 10Undoubtedly there are all sorts of languages in the world, yet none of them is without meaning. 11If then I do not grasp the meaning of what someone is saying, I am a foreigner to the speaker, and he is a foreigner to me. 12So it is with you. Since you are eager to have spiritual gifts, try to excel in gifts that build up the church.

13For this reason anyone who speaks in a tongue should pray that he may interpret what he says. 14For if I pray in a tongue, my spirit prays, but my mind is unfruitful. 15So what shall I do? I will pray with my spirit, but I will also pray with my mind; I will sing with my spirit, but I will also sing with my mind. 16If you are praising God with your spirit, how can one who finds himself among those who do not understand*j* say "Amen" to

g2 Or another language; also in verses 4, 13, 14, 19, 26 and 27   h2 Or by the Spirit
i5 Or other languages; also in verses 6, 18, 22, 23 and 39   j16 Or among the inquirers

your thanksgiving, since he does not know what you are saying? [17]You may be giving thanks well enough, but the other man is not edified.

[18]I thank God that I speak in tongues more than all of you. [19]But in the church I would rather speak five intelligible words to instruct others than ten thousand words in a tongue.

[20]Brothers, stop thinking like children. In regard to evil be infants, but in your thinking be adults. [21]In the Law it is written:

> "Through men of strange tongues
> and through the lips of foreigners
> I will speak to this people,
> but even then they will not listen to me,"[k]

says the Lord.

[22]Tongues, then, are a sign, not for believers but for unbelievers; prophecy, however, is for believers, not for unbelievers. [23]So if the whole church comes together and everyone speaks in tongues, and some who do not understand[l] or some unbelievers come in, will they not say that you are out of your mind? [24]But if an unbeliever or someone who does not understand[m] comes in while everybody is prophesying, he will be convinced by all that he is a sinner and will be judged by all, [25]and the secrets of his heart will be laid bare. So he will fall down and worship God, exclaiming, "God is really among you!"

Orderly Worship

[26]What then shall we say, brothers? When you come together, everyone has a hymn, or a word of instruction, a revelation, a tongue or an interpretation. All of these must be done for the strengthening of the church. [27]If anyone speaks in a tongue, two—or at the most three—should speak, one at a time, and someone must interpret. [28]If there is no interpreter, the speaker should keep quiet in the church and speak to himself and God.

[29]Two or three prophets should speak, and the others should weigh carefully what is said. [30]And if a revelation comes to someone who is sitting down, the first speaker should stop [31]For you can all prophesy in turn so that everyone may be instructed and encouraged. [32]The spirits of prophets are subject to the control of prophets. [33]For God is not a God of disorder but of peace.

As in all the congregations of the saints, [34]women should remain silent in the churches. They are not allowed to speak, but must be in submission, as the Law says. [35]If they want to inquire about something, they should ask their own husbands at home; for it is disgraceful for a woman to speak in the church.

[36]Did the word of God originate with you? Or are you the only people it has reached? [37]If anybody thinks he is a prophet or spiritually gifted, let him acknowledge that what I am writing to you is the Lord's command. [38]If he ignores this, he himself will be ignored.[n]

you see that tendency in yourself? Your church? (Example: "That beautiful singer is more important than I am.") **2.** In the context of your spiritual gifts, what is one way you want to "follow the way of love" this week? **3.** Whether or not your church practices the gifts of tongues and prophecy, what principles for church life do you find here that need to be exercised more fully in your church? **4.** What has been your experience with the gift of tongues? What has been its value? Its limits?

OPEN: Have each person take a turn singing a few measures of a favorite childhood Sunday school or camp song. Do hand motions too if they are part of the song! How did you feel after doing this?

DIG: 1. What would you have felt, seen, and heard in a Corinthian worship service? What is wrong with that? **2.** What is the purpose of Paul's directives about tongues and prophecy (vv.26-33,39-40)? **3.** In light of 11:5, verses 34-35 are difficult to understand. What type of talk, contributing to the general disorder of their services, might be in view here?

REFLECT: 1. Although Paul did not want the Corinthian worship services to be like the frenzied services at the pagan temples, what positive qualities about public worship could you and your church learn from their extremism? **2.** What was the most helpful aspect of the last worship service you attended? **3.** What is one new way the public worship in your church could help newcomers feel the peace of God rather than feeling strange and out of place?

---

[k]21 Isaiah 28:11,12   [l]23 Or some inquirers   [m]24 Or or some inquirer
[n]38 Some manuscripts If he is ignorant of this, let him be ignorant

[39]Therefore, my brothers, be eager to prophesy, and do not forbid speaking in tongues. [40]But everything should be done in a fitting and orderly way.

The Resurrection of Christ

15 Now, brothers, I want to remind you of the gospel I preached to you, which you received and on which you have taken your stand. [2]By this gospel you are saved, if you hold firmly to the word I preached to you. Otherwise, you have believed in vain.

[3]For what I received I passed on to you as of first importance[o]: that Christ died for our sins according to the Scriptures, [4]that he was buried, that he was raised on the third day according to the Scriptures, [5]and that he appeared to Peter,[p] and then to the Twelve. [6]After that, he appeared to more than five hundred of the brothers at the same time, most of whom are still living, though some have fallen asleep. [7]Then he appeared to James, then to all the apostles, [8]and last of all he appeared to me also, as to one abnormally born.

[9]For I am the least of the apostles and do not even deserve to be called an apostle, because I persecuted the church of God. [10]But by the grace of God I am what I am, and his grace to me was not without effect. No, I worked harder than all of them— yet not I, but the grace of God that was with me. [11]Whether, then, it was I or they, this is what we preach, and this is what you believed.

The Resurrection of the Dead

[12]But if it is preached that Christ has been raised from the dead, how can some of you say that there is no resurrection of the dead? [13]If there is no resurrection of the dead, then not even Christ has been raised. [14]And if Christ has not been raised, our preaching is useless and so is your faith. [15]More than that, we are then found to be false witnesses about God, for we have testified about God that he raised Christ from the dead. But he did not raise him if in fact the dead are not raised. [16]For if the dead are not raised, then Christ has not been raised either. [17]And if Christ has not been raised, your faith is futile; you are still in your sins. [18]Then those also who have fallen asleep in Christ are lost. [19]If only for this life we have hope in Christ, we are to be pitied more than all men.

[20]But Christ has indeed been raised from the dead, the firstfruits of those who have fallen asleep. [21]For since death came through a man, the resurrection of the dead comes also through a man. [22]For as in Adam all die, so in Christ all will be made alive. [23]But each in his own turn: Christ, the firstfruits; then, when he comes, those who belong to him. [24]Then the end will come, when he hands over the kingdom to God the Father after he has destroyed all dominion, authority and power. [25]For he must reign until he has put all his enemies under his feet. [26]The last enemy to be destroyed is death. [27]For he "has put everything under his feet."[q] Now when it says that "everything" has been

o3 Or you at the first   p5 Greek Cephas   q27 Psalm 8:6 put under him, it is clear that this does not include God himself, who put everything under Christ. 28When he has done this, then the Son himself will be made subject to him who put everything under him, so that God may be all in all.

29Now if there is no resurrection, what will those do who are baptized for the dead? If the dead are not raised at all, why are people baptized for them? 30And as for us, why do we endanger ourselves every hour? 31I die every day—I mean that, brothers—just as surely as I glory over you in Christ Jesus our Lord. 32If I fought wild beasts in Ephesus for merely human reasons, what have I gained? If the dead are not raised,

> "Let us eat and drink,
>   for tomorrow we die."r

33Do not be misled: "Bad company corrupts good character." 34Come back to your senses as you ought, and stop sinning; for there are some who are ignorant of God—I say this to your shame.

The Resurrection Body

35But someone may ask, "How are the dead raised? With what kind of body will they come?" 36How foolish! What you sow does not come to life unless it dies. 37When you sow, you do not plant the body that will be, but just a seed, perhaps of wheat or of something else. 38But God gives it a body as he has determined, and to each kind of seed he gives its own body. 39All flesh is not the same: Men have one kind of flesh, animals have another, birds another and fish another. 40There are also heavenly bodies and there are earthly bodies; but the splendor of the heavenly bodies is one kind, and the splendor of the earthly bodies is another. 41The sun has one kind of splendor, the moon another and the stars another; and star differs from star in splendor.

42So will it be with the resurrection of the dead. The body that is sown is perishable, it is raised imperishable; 43it is sown in dishonor, it is raised in glory; it is sown in weakness, it is raised in power; 44it is sown a natural body, it is raised a spiritual body.

If there is a natural body, there is also a spiritual body. 45So it is written: "The first man Adam became a living being"s; the last Adam, a life-giving spirit. 46The spiritual did not come first, but the natural, and after that the spiritual. 47The first man was of the dust of the earth, the second man from heaven. 48As was the earthly man, so are those who are of the earth; and as is the man from heaven, so also are those who are of heaven. 49And just as we have borne the likeness of the earthly man, so shall wet bear the likeness of the man from heaven.

50I declare to you, brothers, that flesh and blood cannot inherit the kingdom of God, nor does the perishable inherit the imperishable. 51Listen, I tell you a mystery: We will not all sleep, but we will all be changed— 52in a flash, in the twinkling of an eye, at the last trumpet. For the trumpet will sound, the dead will be raised imperishable, and we will be changed. 53For

REFLECT: 1. When did you connect the resurrection of Christ with your own victory over death? What difference has that made to you in terms of hope and courage? What new sense of purpose does this give you? 2. When have you felt that life was futile? How do you go on when those feelings come? 3. What arguments have you found helpful in showing unbelieving friends that Christ did rise from the dead?

OPEN: As a teen, what did you like least about your body? What did you try to do to change that? As an older person, what do you fear about your changing body?

DIG: 1. What practical problem undercuts belief in the resurrection for some of these people (v.35)? 2. How does Paul's analogy with the seed deal with this objection (vv.36-38,42-44)? What does this teach you about the resurrected body? 3. How does the analogy of the different types of bodies (vv.39-41) relate to the initial objection? 4. What is the point of the comparison between Adam and Christ (vv.45-49; also vv.21-22)? 5. What is meant by "we shall bear the likeness of the man from heaven" (v.49)? 6. What is the significance of the events Paul discusses in verses 50-53? Of the quote in verses 54-55? What is the relation between sin and death? Between the Law and Christ's victory? 7. What practical difference is the hope of resurrection to have in the lives of believers (v.58)?

REFLECT: 1. What is the most comforting thing here for you as you consider the reality of your own death? What here is hardest for you to understand? 2. Whose death was the toughest for you to experience? What did you learn through it? 3. What motivates you to push on with the Christian life: The hope of resurrection? The fear of judgment? The knowledge

r32 Isaiah 22:13   s45 Gen. 2:7   t49 Some early manuscripts *so let us*

God will reward faithfulness? Explain. **4.** Write out a prayer of thanks to the Lord for what the hope of the resurrection means to you. Read these prayers as way of closing your meeting.

the perishable must clothe itself with the imperishable, and the mortal with immortality. [54]When the perishable has been clothed with the imperishable, and the mortal with immortality, then the saying that is written will come true: "Death has been swallowed up in victory."[u]

[55]"Where, O death, is your victory?
　　Where, O death, is your sting?"[v]

[56]The sting of death is sin, and the power of sin is the law. [57]But thanks be to God! He gives us the victory through our Lord Jesus Christ.

[58]Therefore, my dear brothers, stand firm. Let nothing move you. Always give yourselves fully to the work of the Lord, because you know that your labor in the Lord is not in vain.

The Collection for God's People

16 Now about the collection for God's people: Do what I told the Galatian churches to do. [2]On the first day of every week, each one of you should set aside a sum of money in keeping with his income, saving it up, so that when I come no collections will have to be made. [3]Then, when I arrive, I will give letters of introduction to the men you approve and send them with your gift to Jerusalem. [4]If it seems advisable for me to go also, they will accompany me.

Personal Requests

OPEN: 1. When, if ever, have you received a surprise gift of money? **2.** When you travel, do you like to plan things thoroughly, or just take off and see what happens?

DIG: 1. What exactly is this collection Paul was receiving from the Greek churches (vv.1-4; see Ac 11:30; 24:17; Ro 15:25-28; 2Co 8:13-14)? **2.** How would you explain to a friend Paul's principle about how much to give (v.2)? **3.** What is significant about the ones who will have the responsibility over this gift (vv.3-4)? **4.** Although Paul wants to come, he will delay for a while (vv.5-9). As Timothy and Apollos plan to come soon, what fears or hesitations might they have (see also 1:12; 3:5)? **5.** What should the Corinthians imitate regarding Stephanas and the others (vv.15-18)? **6.** Given all the hard things Paul wrote to this church, how do you account for the warmth of verses 19-24? How does this compare with how he began the letter (1:1-9)?

REFLECT: 1. Which of Paul's concluding exhortations in verses 13-14 do you want to apply at this time: (a) "Be on your guard"? (b) "Stand firm in your faith"? (c) "Have courage"? (d) "Be strong"? (e) "Do everything in love"? How will you apply *a, b, c, d,* or *e* to your life right now? **2.** What have you learned about setting priorities for how much you will give, and to whom? Is your giving more planned or more spontaneous? What are the strengths and weaknesses of each way of giving? **3.** If you had been a member of the Corinthian church at odds with Paul, which part of this letter would you find most helpful? Most challenging?

[5]After I go through Macedonia, I will come to you—for I will be going through Macedonia. [6]Perhaps I will stay with you awhile, or even spend the winter, so that you can help me on my journey, wherever I go. [7]I do not want to see you now and make only a passing visit; I hope to spend some time with you, if the Lord permits. [8]But I will stay on at Ephesus until Pentecost, [9]because a great door for effective work has opened to me, and there are many who oppose me.

[10]If Timothy comes, see to it that he has nothing to fear while he is with you, for he is carrying on the work of the Lord, just as I am. [11]No one, then, should refuse to accept him. Send him on his way in peace so that he may return to me. I am expecting him along with the brothers.

[12]Now about our brother Apollos: I strongly urged him to go to you with the brothers. He was quite unwilling to go now, but he will go when he has the opportunity.

[13]Be on your guard; stand firm in the faith; be men of courage; be strong. [14]Do everything in love.

[15]You know that the household of Stephanas were the first converts in Achaia, and they have devoted themselves to the service of the saints. I urge you, brothers, [16]to submit to such as these and to everyone who joins in the work, and labors at it. [17]I was glad when Stephanas, Fortunatus and Achaicus arrived, because they have supplied what was lacking from you. [18]For they refreshed my spirit and yours also. Such men deserve recognition.

u54 Isaiah 25:8　　*v55* Hosea 13:14

Final Greetings

[19]The churches in the province of Asia send you greetings. Aquila and Priscilla[w] greet you warmly in the Lord, and so does the church that meets at their house. [20]All the brothers here send you greetings. Greet one another with a holy kiss.

[21]I, Paul, write this greeting in my own hand.

[22]If anyone does not love the Lord—a curse be on him. Come, O Lord[x]!

[23]The grace of the Lord Jesus be with you.

[24]My love to all of you in Christ Jesus. Amen.[y]

4. As a member of your church and of your small group, what in this letter has helped you? Challenged you? In what way would you like to grow from here?

---

[w]19 Greek *Prisca*, a variant of *Priscilla*   [x]22 In Aramaic the expression *Come, O Lord* is *Marana tha*.   [y]24 Some manuscripts do not have *Amen*.

2 CORINTHIANS

INTRODUCTION

Audience

See the introductory notes to 1 Corinthians.

The Occasion

C. K. Barrett says that 2 Corinthians is "surely the most difficult book in the New Testament" (*The Second Epistle to the Corinthians: Harper New Testament Commentaries*). Part of its difficulty is that one cannot understand the epistle without understanding what happened during the period between the writing of 1 and 2 Corinthians, since much of the epistle is devoted to Paul's explanation of his actions then. Unfortunately, no one really knows what happened. What follows is a "best guess" based on the work of Barrett and Fee (Gordon D. Fee, *Corinthians: A Study Guide*).

Paul's visits to Corinth

Paul's first visit to Corinth took place during his second missionary journey. It was then that he founded the Corinthian church. In 2 Corinthians 13:1, Paul proposes a third visit to the city. It seems that his second visit was the cause of much trouble and the reason he wrote 2 Corinthians.

This second visit had been promised in 1 Corinthians 16:1-9. Paul wrote that he would leave Ephesus, journey to Macedonia, and then come down to Corinth en route to Jerusalem with the collection. (See map, Plan A.) As the time drew near to the trip, Paul changed to Plan B, in which he went straight to Corinth, intending to go from there up to Macedonia and then back to Corinth once again. (See map, Plan B.) He thought this would bring the Christians in Corinth great pleasure, since he would be with them twice instead of just once (1:15-16). Instead his unexpected visit proved so painful (because of a conflict with false apostles), he cancelled his return trip from Macedonia. Instead he went back to Ephesus, then north again to Troas, and finally back once more to Macedonia. (See map, Actual Trip.) At Macedonia, he wrote 2 Corinthians to prepare them for a third visit.

Paul's letters to the Corinthians

Reconstructing the events surrounding the writing of 2 Corinthians is further complicated because Paul wrote at least two other letters to the Corinthians that have not been preserved (see 1 Cor. 5:9; 2 Cor. 2:3-4, 9; 7:8-13). Paul wrote one of these letters prior to 1 Corinthians and another (the "sorrowful" letter) in between 1 and 2 Corinthians, probably to explain why he was not returning to Corinth from Macedonia (1:23; 2:4).

Second Corinthians may itself be not one but two letters: The fierce tone of chapters 10-13 stands in sharp contrast to the gentle, reconciling tone of chapters 1-9. According to this conjecture, the first nine chapters (Paul's fourth letter) seem to be based on the report of Titus (7:6-16) that the situation in Corinth had been rectified. But when Titus returned to Corinth with Chapters 1-9, he found to his horror that the "super-apostles" were back in charge, so he beat a hasty retreat back to Macedonia. Reacting to the new situation, Paul penned chapters 10-13 (his fifth letter). The fourth and fifth letters were later copied together, since they were so closely related in subject matter, and they became what we know as 2 Corinthians.

Paul's new opponents

Who, then, opposed Paul with such vigor during his second "painful" visit? The best guess (and it is only that) is that the troublemakers were not from the Corinthian church itself. Rather, they were a band of outside "apostles" (called cynically by Paul "super-apostles" in 11:5 and 12:11), probably Jewish Christians from Palestine who sought to conform the Corinthian church to Jewish law. In any case, they attacked Paul vigorously, calling him two-faced (10:1-11); they questioned his credentials as an apostle; and they criticized him for drawing no financial support from the Corinthians (the way a real apostle would). Apparently Paul's real pain came because the Corinthians did not rally to his support in this conflict. They remained on the sidelines, supporting neither party.

Paul's pain

In many ways, 2 Corinthians is Paul's most personal letter. He reveals his pain and his joy, his outrage and his suffering, his love and his convictions. 2 Corinthians is filled with profound feeling. As C. K. Barrett said: "Writing 2 Corinthians must have come near to breaking Paul, and . . . a church that is prepared to read it with him and understand it, may find itself broken too" (*The Second Epistle to the Corinthians: Harper New Testament Commentaries*).

But not only is Paul's pain evident in this letter; but also his toughness. He was willing to fight tooth and nail to wrest the Corinthians from the corrupting influence of the false apostles. "It would have been natural for Paul simply to give up the ungrateful, unruly, unloving, unintelligent Corinthians and leave them to their destiny. There is no indication that this thought ever crossed his mind" (Barrett, *The Second Epistle*, pp. 32-33). The reason for his tenacity is found in the strength of his calling. He was an apostle — called by God to bring men and women into the kingdom. No band of petty pretenders was going to defeat him in that God-given purpose. He was an apostle and so, of course, he had to write as he did.

Structure

2 Corinthians can be divided into three major sections:
1. Paul's travel plans (chapters 1-7), with a long digression on the nature of ministry (2:14-7:3).
2. The Corinthian collection (chapters 8-9).
3. Paul's defense of his apostleship and exposure of the false apostles (chapters 10-13).

2 Corinthians

OPEN: 1. When sick or hurt as a child, what expression of TLC did you find most comforting? **2.** When have you been in a real "pressure cooker" situation? What happened? What relieved it?

DIG: 1. Do you think "grace and peace" would serve as a good bumper sticker to describe what the gospel is all about? Why? **2.** What's the relationship between God's ability to comfort us and our ability to comfort others? **3.** How are Christ's and Paul's sufferings related to the Corinthians? What pressures do you suppose Paul is facing that would cause him to despair even of life (see 7:5-7 and Ac 19:23-41)? **4.** What response is Paul trying to solicit from the Corinthians (vv.6-7,10-11)?

REFLECT: 1. Paul found that intense pressures led him to depend on God all the more (v.9). How do you respond to pressures that seem beyond your ability to handle? **2.** Whom do you know that is under intense pressure now? How would Paul have you pray for them this week?

OPEN: 1. What was one accomplishment as a teenager of which you felt proud? If you were permitted to brag a little about your kids or grandkids (if any) what would you boast about? **2.** From which parent could you bank on a "no" reply? A "yes" reply? Which one waffled? Why was that?

DIG: 1. In what does Paul boast? What is the basis for his integrity? **2.** How does a leader who uses his authority according to "worldly wisdom" differ from one who does so by "God's grace" (v.12)? **3.** From 1:15-17, of what may Paul have been accused? How does he account for his change of plans (1:23-2:2)? **4.** What does it mean that Jesus is the "Yes" of God's promise to us? How does this relate to Paul's argument? **5.** Corinth was the commercial center of the empire: What do the three trading metaphors in 1:22 indicate that Jesus has done for us?

1 Paul, an apostle of Christ Jesus by the will of God, and Timothy our brother,

To the church of God in Corinth, together with all the saints throughout Achaia:

[2]Grace and peace to you from God our Father and the Lord Jesus Christ.

The God of All Comfort

[3]Praise be to the God and Father of our Lord Jesus Christ, the Father of compassion and the God of all comfort, [4]who comforts us in all our troubles, so that we can comfort those in any trouble with the comfort we ourselves have received from God. [5]For just as the sufferings of Christ flow over into our lives, so also through Christ our comfort overflows. [6]If we are distressed, it is for your comfort and salvation; if we are comforted, it is for your comfort, which produces in you patient endurance of the same sufferings we suffer. [7]And our hope for you is firm, because we know that just as you share in our sufferings, so also you share in our comfort.

[8]We do not want you to be uninformed, brothers, about the hardships we suffered in the province of Asia. We were under great pressure, far beyond our ability to endure, so that we despaired even of life. [9]Indeed, in our hearts we felt the sentence of death. But this happened that we might not rely on ourselves but on God, who raises the dead. [10]He has delivered us from such a deadly peril, and he will deliver us. On him we have set our hope that he will continue to deliver us, [11]as you help us by your prayers. Then many will give thanks on our[a] behalf for the gracious favor granted us in answer to the prayers of many.

Paul's Change of Plans

[12]Now this is our boast: Our conscience testifies that we have conducted ourselves in the world, and especially in our relations with you, in the holiness and sincerity that are from God. We have done so not according to worldly wisdom but according to God's grace. [13]For we do not write you anything you cannot read or understand. And I hope that, [14]as you have understood us in part, you will come to understand fully that you can boast of us just as we will boast of you in the day of the Lord Jesus.

[15]Because I was confident of this, I planned to visit you first so that you might benefit twice. [16]I planned to visit you on my way to Macedonia and to come back to you from Macedonia, and then to have you send me on my way to Judea. [17]When I planned this, did I do it lightly? Or do I make my plans in a worldly manner so that in the same breath I say, "Yes, yes" and "No, no"?

[18]But as surely as God is faithful, our message to you is not "Yes" and "No." [19]For the Son of God, Jesus Christ, who was

[a]11 Many manuscripts *your*

preached among you by me and Silas[b] and Timothy, was not "Yes" and "No," but in him it has always been "Yes." [20]For no matter how many promises God has made, they are "Yes" in Christ. And so through him the "Amen" is spoken by us to the glory of God. [21]Now it is God who makes both us and you stand firm in Christ. He anointed us, [22]set his seal of ownership on us, and put his Spirit in our hearts as a deposit, guaranteeing what is to come.

[23]I call God as my witness that it was in order to spare you that I did not return to Corinth. [24]Not that we lord it over your faith, but we work with you for your joy, because it is by faith you stand firm. [1]So I made up my mind that I would not make another painful visit to you. [2]For if I grieve you, who is left to make me glad but you whom I have grieved? [3]I wrote as I did so that when I came I should not be distressed by those who ought to make me rejoice. I had confidence in all of you, that you would all share my joy. [4]For I wrote you out of great distress and anguish of heart and with many tears, not to grieve you but to let you know the depth of my love for you.

Forgiveness for the Sinner

[5]If anyone has caused grief, he has not so much grieved me as he has grieved all of you, to some extent—not to put it too severely. [6]The punishment inflicted on him by the majority is sufficient for him. [7]Now instead, you ought to forgive and comfort him, so that he will not be overwhelmed by excessive sorrow. [8]I urge you, therefore, to reaffirm your love for him. [9]The reason I wrote you was to see if you would stand the test and be obedient in everything. [10]If you forgive anyone, I also forgive him. And what I have forgiven—if there was anything to forgive—I have forgiven in the sight of Christ for your sake, [11]in order that Satan might not outwit us. For we are not unaware of his schemes.

Ministers of the New Covenant

[12]Now when I went to Troas to preach the gospel of Christ and found that the Lord had opened a door for me, [13]I still had no peace of mind, because I did not find my brother Titus there. So I said good-by to them and went on to Macedonia.

[14]But thanks be to God, who always leads us in triumphal procession in Christ and through us spreads everywhere the fragrance of the knowledge of him. [15]For we are to God the aroma of Christ among those who are being saved and those who are perishing. [16]To the one we are the smell of death; to the other, the fragrance of life. And who is equal to such a task? [17]Unlike so many, we do not peddle the word of God for profit. On the contrary, in Christ we speak before God with sincerity, like men sent from God.

Are we beginning to commend ourselves again? Or do we need, like some people, letters of recommendation to you or from you? [2]You yourselves are our letter, written on our hearts, known and read by everybody. [3]You show that you are a letter from Christ, the result of our ministry, written not with

[b]19 Greek *Silvanus*, a variant of *Silas*

6. What are the causes of joy and grief for Paul and the Corinthians (1:23-2:5)? 7. What must Paul's grievous letter have been about (see 2:3-9; 7:8-12)? 8. What has happened since the letter was received (2:6-8)? How might their continuation of punishment be a scheme of Satan (vv.10-11)?

REFLECT: 1. What does Paul's example mean for you in terms of how you relate to others? 2. Paraphrase the "business deal" of 1:22 in modern terms. How have you experienced this spiritual "new deal"? 3. How does this passage apply to church discipline and restoration of fallen leaders today? Is there someone you need to forgive and comfort (no names)? Why not now?

OPEN: As a child, what did you like best about parades?

DIG: 1. Until Titus returns with "good news" (see 7:6-13), Paul has "no peace of mind" (2:13): What does that say about Paul's concern for this church? 2. How can the same gospel be either the smell of death or the fragrance of life? 3. What might be happening in Corinth (2:17-3:1)? Although preachers often had letters of recommendation when they traveled to new areas (3Jn 5-8), why does Paul need no such letter? 4. Why should the Corinthians listen to Paul (1:1-3:6)?

REFLECT: 1. How can you spread the aroma of Christ in the environment of your home? Your work place? What effects could that scent have on others? 2. If you were the only "Bible" someone else had to read, how much of the gospel would they grasp?

ink but with the Spirit of the living God, not on tablets of stone but on tablets of human hearts.

[4]Such confidence as this is ours through Christ before God. [5]Not that we are competent in ourselves to claim anything for ourselves, but our competence comes from God. [6]He has made us competent as ministers of a new covenant—not of the letter but of the Spirit; for the letter kills, but the Spirit gives life.

The Glory of the New Covenant

[7]Now if the ministry that brought death, which was engraved in letters on stone, came with glory, so that the Israelites could not look steadily at the face of Moses because of its glory, fading though it was, [8]will not the ministry of the Spirit be even more glorious? [9]If the ministry that condemns men is glorious, how much more glorious is the ministry that brings righteousness! [10]For what was glorious has no glory now in comparison with the surpassing glory. [11]And if what was fading away came with glory, how much greater is the glory of that which lasts!

[12]Therefore, since we have such a hope, we are very bold. [13]We are not like Moses, who would put a veil over his face to keep the Israelites from gazing at it while the radiance was fading away. [14]But their minds were made dull, for to this day the same veil remains when the old covenant is read. It has not been removed, because only in Christ is it taken away. [15]Even to this day when Moses is read, a veil covers their hearts. [16]But whenever anyone turns to the Lord, the veil is taken away. [17]Now the Lord is the Spirit, and where the Spirit of the Lord is, there is freedom. [18]And we, who with unveiled faces all reflect[c] the Lord's glory, are being transformed into his likeness with ever-increasing glory, which comes from the Lord, who is the Spirit.

Treasures in Jars of Clay

4 Therefore, since through God's mercy we have this ministry, we do not lose heart. [2]Rather, we have renounced secret and shameful ways; we do not use deception, nor do we distort the word of God. On the contrary, by setting forth the truth plainly we commend ourselves to every man's conscience in the sight of God. [3]And even if our gospel is veiled, it is veiled to those who are perishing. [4]The god of this age has blinded the minds of unbelievers, so that they cannot see the light of the gospel of the glory of Christ, who is the image of God. [5]For we do not preach ourselves, but Jesus Christ as Lord, and ourselves as your servants for Jesus' sake. [6]For God, who said, "Let light shine out of darkness,"[d] made his light shine in our hearts to give us the light of the knowledge of the glory of God in the face of Christ.

[7]But we have this treasure in jars of clay to show that this all-surpassing power is from God and not from us. [8]We are hard pressed on every side, but not crushed; perplexed, but not in despair; [9]persecuted, but not abandoned; struck down, but not destroyed. [10]We always carry around in our body the death of

[c]18 Or *contemplate*   [d]6 Gen. 1:3

Jesus, so that the life of Jesus may also be revealed in our body. [11]For we who are alive are always being given over to death for Jesus' sake, so that his life may be revealed in our mortal body. [12]So then, death is at work in us, but life is at work in you.

[13]It is written: "I believed; therefore I have spoken."[e] With that same spirit of faith we also believe and therefore speak, [14]because we know that the one who raised the Lord Jesus from the dead will also raise us with Jesus and present us with you in his presence. [15]All this is for your benefit, so that the grace that is reaching more and more people may cause thanksgiving to overflow to the glory of God.

[16]Therefore we do not lose heart. Though outwardly we are wasting away, yet inwardly we are being renewed day by day. [17]For our light and momentary troubles are achieving for us an eternal glory that far outweighs them all. [18]So we fix our eyes not on what is seen, but on what is unseen. For what is seen is temporary, but what is unseen is eternal.

Our Heavenly Dwelling

5 Now we know that if the earthly tent we live in is destroyed, we have a building from God, an eternal house in heaven, not built by human hands. [2]Meanwhile we groan, longing to be clothed with our heavenly dwelling, [3]because when we are clothed, we will not be found naked. [4]For while we are in this tent, we groan and are burdened, because we do not wish to be unclothed but to be clothed with our heavenly dwelling, so that what is mortal may be swallowed up by life. [5]Now it is God who has made us for this very purpose and has given us the Spirit as a deposit, guaranteeing what is to come.

[6]Therefore we are always confident and know that as long as we are at home in the body we are away from the Lord. [7]We live by faith, not by sight. [8]We are confident, I say, and would prefer to be away from the body and at home with the Lord. [9]So we make it our goal to please him, whether we are at home in the body or away from it. [10]For we must all appear before the judgment seat of Christ, that each one may receive what is due him for the things done while in the body, whether good or bad.

The Ministry of Reconciliation

[11]Since, then, we know what it is to fear the Lord, we try to persuade men. What we are is plain to God, and I hope it is also plain to your conscience. [12]We are not trying to commend ourselves to you again, but are giving you an opportunity to take pride in us, so that you can answer those who take pride in what is seen rather than in what is in the heart. [13]If we are out of our mind, it is for the sake of God; if we are in our right mind, it is for you. [14]For Christ's love compels us, because we are convinced that one died for all, and therefore all died. [15]And he died for all, that those who live should no longer live for themselves but for him who died for them and was raised again.

[16]So from now on we regard no one from a worldly point of view. Though we once regarded Christ in this way, we do so no

REFLECT: 1. How did the light of Christ first break through to you? **2.** Why is being a servant to others essential for sharing the gospel? What is one way you could be more of a servant to someone you are concerned about now? **3.** How do verses 7-12 and 16-18 help you cope with your present difficulties and anxieties? **4.** How does this section challenge common ideas of what makes a person a "success"?

OPEN: 1. If time or money were no object, what room of your house would you begin to re-model? **2.** Complete this sentence: "Home is where..."

DIG: 1. How does Paul's confidence in his future relate to 4:16-18? To John 14:1-3? What role does faith play in this? How does Paul's "home" affect his daily living (vv.6-10)? **2.** What is this "heavenly dwelling" like? **3.** Is Paul motivated more by the desire to be with Christ, or by fear of judgment? Which motivates you?

REFLECT: 1. How does God's purpose (v.5) apply to a current crisis of yours? **2.** How can knowing the location of your ultimate "home" encourage you to be more hospitable to others now?

OPEN: If you were appointed as an ambassador for your country, where would you like to be sent?

DIG: 1. What is Paul's motive for evangelism in verses 10-11? In verse 14? How do they fit together? How would someone motivated by these values stand in contrast to someone motivated by those mentioned in 2:17 and 5:12? **2.** What does Paul mean by what he says about Christ and our response to him (vv.15-17; see also Ro 6:5-13)? **3.** What does "reconciliation" mean? What story from your life illustrates this? **4.** What does God do through Christ (v.18)? Through us (v.20)? For us (vv.17-18)?

e13 Psalm 116:10

REFLECT: 1. What motivates you to share your faith? If you rarely do so, what inhibits you? 2. How can you grow in your awe of God and love for Christ this week? 3. Knowing what it is like to be alienated and reconciled in other relationships, how is it going with God: Still a family feud, a truce, or have you made up?

DIG: 1. How does Paul defend the authenticity of his ministry here? How does this differ from the ways those who are challenging him assert their authority (see 3:1; 4:2; 5:12; 11:23-29)? By appealing to these things instead of his supernatural conversion or miracles (Ac 9:3-5; 19:11-12), what is he saying the real test of faith is? 2. What is Paul asking the Corinthians (and us) to do in verses 11-13 (see 3:2-3; 4:15)?

REFLECT: 1. By what standards do you gauge a successful ministry? Why? How do they compare with verses 4-10? Would Paul be a success by your standards? Would you? 2. What, from Paul's example, do you want to incorporate into your life?

OPEN: If you and yours were to appear on the "Newlywed Game," what would each of you say was the reason you were first attracted to the other?

DIG: 1. What is a yoke? How is unequal yoking an apt metaphor in this context? 2. To what do the opposites contrasted in verses 14-16 refer? 3. Check out verses 16-18 in their OT contexts. What do these imply about having God as our Father?

REFLECT: 1. Of the different relationships Paul has in view here, which one(s) apply to you? 2. What does it mean that you are

longer. [17]Therefore, if anyone is in Christ, he is a new creation; the old has gone, the new has come! [18]All this is from God, who reconciled us to himself through Christ and gave us the ministry of reconciliation: [19]that God was reconciling the world to himself in Christ, not counting men's sins against them. And he has committed to us the message of reconciliation. [20]We are therefore Christ's ambassadors, as though God were making his appeal through us. We implore you on Christ's behalf: Be reconciled to God. [21]God made him who had no sin to be sin[f] for us, so that in him we might become the righteousness of God.

[6] As God's fellow workers we urge you not to receive God's grace in vain. [2]For he says,

"In the time of my favor I heard you,
and in the day of salvation I helped you."[g]

I tell you, now is the time of God's favor, now is the day of salvation.

Paul's Hardships

[3]We put no stumbling block in anyone's path, so that our ministry will not be discredited. [4]Rather, as servants of God we commend ourselves in every way: in great endurance; in troubles, hardships and distresses; [5]in beatings, imprisonments and riots; in hard work, sleepless nights and hunger; [6]in purity, understanding, patience and kindness; in the Holy Spirit and in sincere love; [7]in truthful speech and in the power of God; with weapons of righteousness in the right hand and in the left; [8]through glory and dishonor, bad report and good report; genuine, yet regarded as impostors; [9]known, yet regarded as unknown; dying, and yet we live on; beaten, and yet not killed; [10]sorrowful, yet always rejoicing; poor, yet making many rich; having nothing, and yet possessing everything.

[11]We have spoken freely to you, Corinthians, and opened wide our hearts to you. [12]We are not withholding our affection from you, but you are withholding yours from us. [13]As a fair exchange—I speak as to my children—open wide your hearts also.

Do Not Be Yoked With Unbelievers

[14]Do not be yoked together with unbelievers. For what do righteousness and wickedness have in common? Or what fellowship can light have with darkness? [15]What harmony is there between Christ and Belial[h]? What does a believer have in common with an unbeliever? [16]What agreement is there between the temple of God and idols? For we are the temple of the living God. As God has said: "I will live with them and walk among them, and I will be their God, and they will be my people."[i]

[17]"Therefore come out from them
and be separate,

says the Lord.

---

[f]21 Or be a sin offering   [g]2 Isaiah 49:8   [h]15 Greek Beliar, a variant of Belial
[i]16 Lev. 26:12; Jer. 32:38; Ezek. 37:27

Touch no unclean thing,
and I will receive you." [j]
18"I will be a Father to you,
and you will be my sons and daughters,
says the Lord Almighty." [k]

7 Since we have these promises, dear friends, let us purify ourselves from everything that contaminates body and spirit, perfecting holiness out of reverence for God.

Paul's Joy

2Make room for us in your hearts. We have wronged no one, we have corrupted no one, we have exploited no one. 3I do not say this to condemn you; I have said before that you have such a place in our hearts that we would live or die with you. 4I have great confidence in you; I take great pride in you. I am greatly encouraged; in all our troubles my joy knows no bounds.

5For when we came into Macedonia, this body of ours had no rest, but we were harassed at every turn—conflicts on the outside, fears within. 6But God, who comforts the downcast, comforted us by the coming of Titus, 7and not only by his coming but also by the comfort you had given him. He told us about your longing for me, your deep sorrow, your ardent concern for me, so that my joy was greater than ever.

8Even if I caused you sorrow by my letter, I do not regret it. Though I did regret it—I see that my letter hurt you, but only for a little while— 9yet now I am happy, not because you were made sorry, but because your sorrow led you to repentance. For you became sorrowful as God intended and so were not harmed in any way by us. 10Godly sorrow brings repentance that leads to salvation and leaves no regret, but worldly sorrow brings death. 11See what this godly sorrow has produced in you: what earnestness, what eagerness to clear yourselves, what indignation, what alarm, what longing, what concern, what readiness to see justice done. At every point you have proved yourselves to be innocent in this matter. 12So even though I wrote to you, it was not on account of the one who did the wrong or of the injured party, but rather that before God you could see for yourselves how devoted to us you are. 13By all this we are encouraged.

In addition to our own encouragement, we were especially delighted to see how happy Titus was, because his spirit has been refreshed by all of you. 14I had boasted to him about you, and you have not embarrassed me. But just as everything we said to you was true, so our boasting about you to Titus has proved to be true as well. 15And his affection for you is all the greater when he remembers that you were all obedient, receiving him with fear and trembling. 16I am glad I can have complete confidence in you.

the dwelling place of God? What contaminants can affect your body? Your spirit? Is there something contaminating you now from which you should separate?

OPEN: 1. What does "homecoming" mean to you? **2.** What finally gets your attention: Tough talk? Slammed door? Tears? Letter? Walkout? Give a recent example.

DIG: 1. Why does Paul want this church to open up to him (vv.2-4; see 6:11-13)? Hence, do you think Titus' report (v.7) was entirely positive? Why or why not? **2.** In 7:5, Paul picks up the account of his travels (which he left off in 2:12-13). How does his account in 7:5-7 illustrate why he began this letter with thanks to God for his comfort (1:3-7)? **3.** What was the result of Paul's previous letter to them (vv.8-13; see also 2:3-4)? What intentions does Paul clarify here? Practically, how does *godly* sorrow differ from *worldly* sorrow? **4.** What tone of voice do you hear in verse 16? In light of his previous hurtful letter, why would he underscore his present joy and confidence? If you were the first to read this, how would you feel?

REFLECT: 1. Have you ever been confronted with a wrong you have done by someone who loves you? How did you feel about that person at the time? **2.** When is it more loving to confront someone with their sin than to ignore it? What attitudes are needed to keep loving confrontation from becoming judgmental? How do you see those attitudes in Paul? **3.** Would you share a time when godly sorrow motivated you to make a real change in your life? How do you feel about that change now?

---

j17 Isaiah 52:11; Ezek. 20:34,41   *k18* 2 Samuel 7:14; 7:8

OPEN: 1. With what are you generous: Your money? Time? Talents? Toys? With what are you stingy? Why the difference? **2.** What were you doing last year at this time which still needs to be completed?

DIG: 1. From 1 Corinthians 16:1-4 (written about a year earlier) and Romans 15:25-27 (written either during or shortly after Paul had revisited Corinth), what is this collection all about? **2.** What do you learn about the Macedonians from their giving? In light of the struggles in Corinth, why would Paul draw their attention to the Macedonian example? What would this test of generosity reveal? **3.** What principles about giving do you observe?

REFLECT: 1. If you were to evaluate your zeal for God in light of your checkbook, what grade would you give yourself? What from Jesus' example (v.9) prompts you to be generous with your money, time, and energy? What inhibits you? **2.** How can the equality principle (vv.13-15) help you decide which needs your immediate attention?

OPEN: 1. Whom do you trust with money: (a) Your kids? (b) Bank? (c) Broker? (d) Government? (e) No one but God? (f) What money, I'm broke? Why is that? **2.** Who is "Mr. Enthusiasm" in your life?

DIG: 1. Why is this gift for the Jerusalem church so important? What dangers or suspicions accompany Paul? How does Paul attempt to diminish these criticisms? **2.** What commends Titus for his role of ensuring fiscal accountability in this mission relief work? **3.** Does Paul expect Titus and the others to be well-received (see 3:16-24)? Why or why not? **4.** Why does Paul expect the Corinthians to be generous (9:1-5)? In what ways?

REFLECT: 1. How do the groups you contribute to practice Paul's principle in verses 20-21? Why is

Generosity Encouraged

8 And now, brothers, we want you to know about the grace that God has given the Macedonian churches. [2]Out of the most severe trial, their overflowing joy and their extreme poverty welled up in rich generosity. [3]For I testify that they gave as much as they were able, and even beyond their ability. Entirely on their own, [4]they urgently pleaded with us for the privilege of sharing in this service to the saints. [5]And they did not do as we expected, but they gave themselves first to the Lord and then to us in keeping with God's will. [6]So we urged Titus, since he had earlier made a beginning, to bring also to completion this act of grace on your part. [7]But just as you excel in everything—in faith, in speech, in knowledge, in complete earnestness and in your love for us[l]—see that you also excel in this grace of giving.

[8]I am not commanding you, but I want to test the sincerity of your love by comparing it with the earnestness of others. [9]For you know the grace of our Lord Jesus Christ, that though he was rich, yet for your sakes he became poor, so that you through his poverty might become rich.

[10]And here is my advice about what is best for you in this matter: Last year you were the first not only to give but also to have the desire to do so. [11]Now finish the work, so that your eager willingness to do it may be matched by your completion of it, according to your means. [12]For if the willingness is there, the gift is acceptable according to what one has, not according to what he does not have.

[13]Our desire is not that others might be relieved while you are hard pressed, but that there might be equality. [14]At the present time your plenty will supply what they need, so that in turn their plenty will supply what you need. Then there will be equality, [15]as it is written: "He who gathered much did not have too much, and he who gathered little did not have too little."[m]

Titus Sent to Corinth

[16]I thank God, who put into the heart of Titus the same concern I have for you. [17]For Titus not only welcomed our appeal, but he is coming to you with much enthusiasm and on his own initiative. [18]And we are sending along with him the brother who is praised by all the churches for his service to the gospel. [19]What is more, he was chosen by the churches to accompany us as we carry the offering, which we administer in order to honor the Lord himself and to show our eagerness to help. [20]We want to avoid any criticism of the way we administer this liberal gift. [21]For we are taking pains to do what is right, not only in the eyes of the Lord but also in the eyes of men.

[22]In addition, we are sending with them our brother who has often proved to us in many ways that he is zealous, and now even more so because of his great confidence in you. [23]As for Titus, he is my partner and fellow worker among you; as for our brothers, they are representatives of the churches and an honor to Christ. [24]Therefore show these men the proof of your love and the reason for our pride in you, so that the churches can see it.

l7 Some manuscripts *in our love for you*   *m15* Exodus 16:18

9 There is no need for me to write to you about this service to the saints. [2]For I know your eagerness to help, and I have been boasting about it to the Macedonians, telling them that since last year you in Achaia were ready to give; and your enthusiasm has stirred most of them to action. [3]But I am sending the brothers in order that our boasting about you in this matter should not prove hollow, but that you may be ready, as I said you would be. [4]For if any Macedonians come with me and find you unprepared, we—not to say anything about you—would be ashamed of having been so confident. [5]So I thought it necessary to urge the brothers to visit you in advance and finish the arrangements for the generous gift you had promised. Then it will be ready as a generous gift, not as one grudgingly given.

Sowing Generously

[6]Remember this: Whoever sows sparingly will also reap sparingly, and whoever sows generously will also reap generously. [7]Each man should give what he has decided in his heart to give, not reluctantly or under compulsion, for God loves a cheerful giver. [8]And God is able to make all grace abound to you, so that in all things at all times, having all that you need, you will abound in every good work. [9]As it is written:

"He has scattered abroad his gifts to the poor;
his righteousness endures forever." [n]

[10]Now he who supplies seed to the sower and bread for food will also supply and increase your store of seed and will enlarge the harvest of your righteousness. [11]You will be made rich in every way so that you can be generous on every occasion, and through us your generosity will result in thanksgiving to God.

[12]This service that you perform is not only supplying the needs of God's people but is also overflowing in many expressions of thanks to God. [13]Because of the service by which you have proved yourselves, men will praise God for the obedience that accompanies your confession of the gospel of Christ, and for your generosity in sharing with them and with everyone else. [14]And in their prayers for you their hearts will go out to you, because of the surpassing grace God has given you. [15]Thanks be to God for his indescribable gift!

Paul's Defense of His Ministry

10 By the meekness and gentleness of Christ, I appeal to you—I, Paul, who am "timid" when face to face with you, but "bold" when away! [2]I beg you that when I come I may not have to be as bold as I expect to be toward some people who think that we live by the standards of this world. [3]For though we live in the world, we do not wage war as the world does. [4]The weapons we fight with are not the weapons of the world. On the contrary, they have divine power to demolish strongholds. [5]We demolish arguments and every pretension that sets itself up against the knowledge of God, and we take captive every thought to make it obedient to Christ. [6]And we will be ready to

[n]9 Psalm 112:9

OPEN: What is one lesson about money you can recall learning from your parents?

DIG: 1. By "sowing and reaping" imagery, is Paul saying that if you give $100 you will get $1,000? Why or why not? **2.** How is giving money away a source of cheer for the giver? **3.** What do you make of the "allness" in verse 8? **4.** For what purpose will God materially bless these people? How does generosity effect righteousness, and the ever-widening circles of people giving thanks to God? **5.** How is giving contagious? How does it reflect God's grace?

REFLECT: 1. How have you reaped by being generous to others in need? **2.** How can God's promise (v.8) enable you to be more generous? **3.** Try writing thank-you notes to God for his "indescribable gift" to you.

OPEN: Is "authority" more of a positive or a negative word to you? How so? Why is that?

DIG: 1. Things have improved in Corinth since Paul wrote his last letter (7:8-16), but not altogether. How is Paul discredited (vv.1-2,9-11)? How is Paul's gentleness and meekness being misunderstood? Where have you seen Paul's strength and concern for others? **2.** How is Paul's exercise of authority (vv.3-8) different than his usurpers, the so-called "super-apostles" (see 11:5, 20)? How and why does he play upon their boastful attitude? **3.** What must

this especially critical for Christian organizations? **2.** If Macedonians came to visit you, would they find your generosity lacking or overflowing? With what else besides money are you generous? **3.** To become more generous, what would have to change: Your job, time priorities, spending habits, mission vision, or what?

change before Paul comes to visit again (vv.5-7,11)? If you were the Corinthians, who would you listen to at this point, and why?

REFLECT: 1. From Paul's example here, what is supposed to be the "normal" way Christians exercise leadership over one another? On a scale from 1-10, how well do you demonstrate Christ's gentleness and meekness in leading others? **2.** What will you work on this week that demonstrates your interest in building others up? **3.** When is it right to show "tough love" by demanding that someone change? What risks does this involve? **4.** As an act of "tough love," what worldly, anti-God thoughts prevail in your circle of friends, which you can "take captive" and "make obedient to Christ" (v.5)?

OPEN: What springs to mind when you hear the word "Satan"?

DIG: 1. What upsets Paul about these "super-apostles"? How does this relate to 6:14? **2.** Why do you think Paul refused to be supported by the Corinthians, yet accepted help from the Macedonian churches? How is Paul's servant-attitude being distorted by the false apostles? How do their motives compare with his? **3.** What is Paul's final conclusion about these teachers (vv.13-15)? What tensions would you feel as a Corinthian Christian when you read this accusation?

REFLECT: 1. Spiritually, you have been promised to one husband who is Christ (v.2). How are you getting ready for that upcoming wedding? **2.** What "different gospel" has at one point or another pulled you away from Jesus? How did you become aware of its deceitfulness? **3.** Sin rarely approaches us as evil, but as "virtue in disguise." From verses 2-4, how can you guard yourself against this satanic strategy?

punish every act of disobedience, once your obedience is complete.

[7]You are looking only on the surface of things. [o] If anyone is confident that he belongs to Christ, he should consider again that we belong to Christ just as much as he. [8]For even if I boast somewhat freely about the authority the Lord gave us for building you up rather than pulling you down, I will not be ashamed of it. [9]I do not want to seem to be trying to frighten you with my letters. [10]For some say, "His letters are weighty and forceful, but in person he is unimpressive and his speaking amounts to nothing." [11]Such people should realize that what we are in our letters when we are absent, we will be in our actions when we are present.

[12]We do not dare to classify or compare ourselves with some who commend themselves. When they measure themselves by themselves and compare themselves with themselves, they are not wise. [13]We, however, will not boast beyond proper limits, but will confine our boasting to the field God has assigned to us, a field that reaches even to you. [14]We are not going too far in our boasting, as would be the case if we had not come to you, for we did get as far as you with the gospel of Christ. [15]Neither do we go beyond our limits by boasting of work done by others. [p] Our hope is that, as your faith continues to grow, our area of activity among you will greatly expand, [16]so that we can preach the gospel in the regions beyond you. For we do not want to boast about work already done in another man's territory. [17]But, "Let him who boasts boast in the Lord." [q] [18]For it is not the one who commends himself who is approved, but the one whom the Lord commends.

Paul and the False Apostles

11 I hope you will put up with a little of my foolishness; but you are already doing that. [2]I am jealous for you with a godly jealousy. I promised you to one husband, to Christ, so that I might present you as a pure virgin to him. [3]But I am afraid that just as Eve was deceived by the serpent's cunning, your minds may somehow be led astray from your sincere and pure devotion to Christ. [4]For if someone comes to you and preaches a Jesus other than the Jesus we preached, or if you receive a different spirit from the one you received, or a different gospel from the one you accepted, you put up with it easily enough. [5]But I do not think I am in the least inferior to those "super-apostles." [6]I may not be a trained speaker, but I do have knowledge. We have made this perfectly clear to you in every way.

[7]Was it a sin for me to lower myself in order to elevate you

---

[o]7 Or *Look at the obvious facts*   [p]13-15 Or [13]*We, however, will not boast about things that cannot be measured, but we will boast according to the standard of measurement that the God of measure has assigned us—a measurement that relates even to you.* [14] . . . . [15]*Neither do we boast about things that cannot be measured in regard to the work done by others.*   [q]17 Jer. 9:24

by preaching the gospel of God to you free of charge? [8]I robbed other churches by receiving support from them so as to serve you. [9]And when I was with you and needed something, I was not a burden to anyone, for the brothers who came from Macedonia supplied what I needed. I have kept myself from being a burden to you in any way, and will continue to do so. [10]As surely as the truth of Christ is in me, nobody in the regions of Achaia will stop this boasting of mine. [11]Why? Because I do not love you? God knows I do! [12]And I will keep on doing what I am doing in order to cut the ground from under those who want an opportunity to be considered equal with us in the things they boast about.

[13]For such men are false apostles, deceitful workmen, masquerading as apostles of Christ. [14]And no wonder, for Satan himself masquerades as an angel of light. [15]It is not surprising, then, if his servants masquerade as servants of righteousness. Their end will be what their actions deserve.

Paul Boasts About His Sufferings

[16]I repeat: Let no one take me for a fool. But if you do, then receive me just as you would a fool, so that I may do a little boasting. [17]In this self-confident boasting I am not talking as the Lord would, but as a fool. [18]Since many are boasting in the way the world does, I too will boast. [19]You gladly put up with fools since you are so wise! [20]In fact, you even put up with anyone who enslaves you or exploits you or takes advantage of you or pushes himself forward or slaps you in the face. [21]To my shame I admit that we were too weak for that!

What anyone else dares to boast about—I am speaking as a fool—I also dare to boast about. [22]Are they Hebrews? So am I. Are they Israelites? So am I. Are they Abraham's descendants? So am I. [23]Are they servants of Christ? (I am out of my mind to talk like this.) I am more. I have worked much harder, been in prison more frequently, been flogged more severely, and been exposed to death again and again. [24]Five times I received from the Jews the forty lashes minus one. [25]Three times I was beaten with rods, once I was stoned, three times I was shipwrecked, I spent a night and a day in the open sea, [26]I have been constantly on the move. I have been in danger from rivers, in danger from bandits, in danger from my own countrymen, in danger from Gentiles; in danger in the city, in danger in the country, in danger at sea; and in danger from false brothers. [27]I have labored and toiled and have often gone without sleep; I have known hunger and thirst and have often gone without food; I have been cold and naked. [28]Besides everything else, I face daily the pressure of my concern for all the churches. [29]Who is weak, and I do not feel weak? Who is led into sin, and I do not inwardly burn?

[30]If I must boast, I will boast of the things that show my weakness. [31]The God and Father of the Lord Jesus, who is to be praised forever, knows that I am not lying. [32]In Damascus the governor under King Aretas had the city of the Damascenes guarded in order to arrest me. [33]But I was lowered in a basket from a window in the wall and slipped through his hands.

REFLECT: 1. What dampens your enthusiasm and pulls you away from your first love to Christ? What are some of the things or people who deceive you? How do you deal with these factors? **2.** When have you been maligned by people you were trying to help? What happened? How did you feel? How did Christ minister to you in that situation? **3.** What are a couple of things you can boast in the Lord?

OPEN: Where was the last place you felt you were really in danger of being hurt? Would you put yourself in that position again?

DIG: 1. In 10:1, Paul made it clear how he would like to appeal to them, so why does he sarcastically resort to "boasting," as the false apostles are doing? What is the irony that galls Paul (see also 12:11-13)? **2.** What has Paul already boasted about (see 1:12; 9:2; 10:8; 11:10)? How does this differ from the boasting of the false teachers? **3.** The false teachers were apparently Palestinian Jews (11:22), preaching a distorted gospel (11:4). How does Paul validate his claim to serve Christ more than they? How is his suffering a more eloquent witness to his authority than fine speech (11:6)? **4.** How would you regard a minister coming to your church who had been through these experiences (vv.23-33)? Would you feel grateful, guilty, or what?

REFLECT: 1. Both Jesus' and Paul's gentleness was mis- understood as weakness. How has that resulted in blessing (see Mt 5:5)? In what area do you need to embrace their example right now? **2.** Would Paul have been more popular if he had pushed his weight around? How would that have misrepresented the gospel? **3.** In your witness, where are you caught "between a rock and a hard place"?

Paul's Vision and His Thorn

12 I must go on boasting. Although there is nothing to be gained, I will go on to visions and revelations from the Lord. [2]I know a man in Christ who fourteen years ago was caught up to the third heaven. Whether it was in the body or out of the body I do not know—God knows. [3]And I know that this man—whether in the body or apart from the body I do not know, but God knows— [4]was caught up to paradise. He heard inexpressible things, things that man is not permitted to tell. [5]I will boast about a man like that, but I will not boast about myself, except about my weaknesses. [6]Even if I should choose to boast, I would not be a fool, because I would be speaking the truth. But I refrain, so no one will think more of me than is warranted by what I do or say.

[7]To keep me from becoming conceited because of these surpassingly great revelations, there was given me a thorn in my flesh, a messenger of Satan, to torment me. [8]Three times I pleaded with the Lord to take it away from me. [9]But he said to me, "My grace is sufficient for you, for my power is made perfect in weakness." Therefore I will boast all the more gladly about my weaknesses, so that Christ's power may rest on me. [10]That is why, for Christ's sake, I delight in weaknesses, in insults, in hardships, in persecutions, in difficulties. For when I am weak, then I am strong.

Paul's Concern for the Corinthians

[11]I have made a fool of myself, but you drove me to it. I ought to have been commended by you, for I am not in the least inferior to the "super-apostles," even though I am nothing. [12]The things that mark an apostle—signs, wonders and miracles—were done among you with great perseverance. [13]How were you inferior to the other churches, except that I was never a burden to you? Forgive me this wrong!

[14]Now I am ready to visit you for the third time, and I will not be a burden to you, because what I want is not your possessions but you. After all, children should not have to save up for their parents, but parents for their children. [15]So I will very gladly spend for you everything I have and expend myself as well. If I love you more, will you love me less? [16]Be that as it may, I have not been a burden to you. Yet, crafty fellow that I am, I caught you by trickery! [17]Did I exploit you through any of the men I sent you? [18]I urged Titus to go to you and I sent our brother with him. Titus did not exploit you, did he? Did we not act in the same spirit and follow the same course?

[19]Have you been thinking all along that we have been defending ourselves to you? We have been speaking in the sight of God as those in Christ; and everything we do, dear friends, is for your strengthening. [20]For I am afraid that when I come I may not find you as I want you to be, and you may not find me as you want me to be. I fear that there may be quarreling, jealousy, outbursts of anger, factions, slander, gossip, arrogance and disorder. [21]I am afraid that when I come again my God will humble me before you, and I will be grieved over many who have sinned earlier

and have not repented of the impurity, sexual sin and debauchery in which they have indulged.

Final Warnings

13 This will be my third visit to you. "Every matter must be established by the testimony of two or three witnesses."[r] [2]I already gave you a warning when I was with you the second time. I now repeat it while absent: On my return I will not spare those who sinned earlier or any of the others, [3]since you are demanding proof that Christ is speaking through me. He is not weak in dealing with you, but is powerful among you. [4]For to be sure, he was crucified in weakness, yet he lives by God's power. Likewise, we are weak in him, yet by God's power we will live with him to serve you.

[5]Examine yourselves to see whether you are in the faith; test yourselves. Do you not realize that Christ Jesus is in you—unless, of course, you fail the test? [6]And I trust that you will discover that we have not failed the test. [7]Now we pray to God that you will not do anything wrong. Not that people will see that we have stood the test but that you will do what is right even though we may seem to have failed. [8]For we cannot do anything against the truth, but only for the truth. [9]We are glad whenever we are weak but you are strong; and our prayer is for your perfection. [10]This is why I write these things when I am absent, that when I come I may not have to be harsh in my use of authority—the authority the Lord gave me for building you up, not for tearing you down.

Final Greetings

[11]Finally, brothers, good-by. Aim for perfection, listen to my appeal, be of one mind, live in peace. And the God of love and peace will be with you.

[12]Greet one another with a holy kiss. [13]All the saints send their greetings.

[14]May the grace of the Lord Jesus Christ, and the love of God, and the fellowship of the Holy Spirit be with you all.

OPEN: In high school or college, what did you do to prepare yourself for big exams?

DIG: 1. Acts 18 records Paul's first visit to Corinth, and Acts 20: 2-3 alludes to what must have been his third visit. Given that he stayed there three months, what do you think happened as a result of this letter? **2.** Paul prefers to come to them in "the gentleness and meekness of Christ" (10:1), and as a loving parent (12:14-15). How will he come, instead, if repentance has not occurred? How does this relate to the ministry of Jesus? **3.** While they have been critical of Paul's "credentials" as an apostle all along, what does he tell them to do in verse 5? Whether or not they approve of him, what does he pray for them in verses 7-9? **4.** What does he hope for as he considers his upcoming visit (vv. 10-11)? **5.** Considering the problems of this church, how would his benediction in verse 14 be appropriate?

REFLECT: 1. Misunderstanding gentleness and compassion as negative traits was a real problem in Corinth. How is that same problem true in your community? In your church? **2.** If you were searching for a new pastor or new small group leaders, what leadership profile (modelled by Paul) would you look for? How do you fit that profile? **3.** In which area of your spiritual life will you aim for "perfection" (13:9) this week? In which area will you be content with "weakness" (12:9-10)? How can others pray for and encourage you? **4.** As you leave this last study, give a "benediction" to each other, praying specifically for one another's needs.

GALATIANS

INTRODUCTION

Audience

Paul tells us he is writing "to the churches in Galatia" (1:2). But where are these churches located? This is a problem because in 25 B.C. the Romans created a new imperial province that they named Galatia. This new province was made up of the original kingdom of Galatia plus a new region to the south forged out of territory originally belonging to six other regions. So when a first-century writer speaks of Galatia, it is not always clear whether he is referring to the original territory in the north or the new province extending southward. In these notes, though scholarly opinion is divided at this point, the view is taken that Paul was writing to the churches he planted in South Galatia (Pisidian Antioch, Iconium, Lystra, and Derbe) during his first missionary journey described in Acts 13-14.

Date

The date of Paul's Epistle depends on whether he was writing to churches in North or South Galatia. If Paul had been writing to congregations in North Galatia, the letter could not have been written before his third missionary expedition after the journey mentioned in Acts 16:6 and 18:23, around A.D. 55. On the other hand, if Paul were writing to the churches in the southern region, as we are assuming, the Epistle to the Galatians is his earliest letter written in A.D. 48 or 49, possibly while he was in Syrian Antioch just prior to the Council in Jerusalem (Acts 15:6-21).

Theme

The Issue

Paul was furious and he didn't care who knew it. "You foolish Galatians!" he cried, "who has bewitched you?" (3:1). He felt so strongly because the issue he was addressing in this letter was not a minor matter of church policy. It struck right to the heart of the gospel.

Apparently some legalistic Jewish-Christians (Judaizers) had been stirring up trouble. They had twisted the gospel into something Jesus never intended, and then they had cast aspersions on Paul. "Who is that fellow, anyway. He wasn't one of the Twelve. He is a self-appointed apostle. No wonder he left out some crucial parts of the message. Let us set you straight. . . ." And the Galatians were taken in, so it seems. Paul wrote, "I am astonished that you are so quickly deserting the one who called you by the grace of Christ and are turning to a different gospel" (1:6).

What were the Judaizers saying? At first glance, they seemed to be adding only a little to the message. "Believe in Christ," they were saying (they were Christians), "but also be circumcised" (6:12). Now to be circumcised was not such a high requirement, but Paul saw the implications. If the Galatians let themselves be circumcised, it would be but the first step back to keeping the whole Law (5:3). This is slavery (4:9). This is bondage (5:1). This is not the gospel. The gospel is that salvation is a free gift, by grace. If you add anything else to grace, salvation is no longer free. It then becomes a matter of doing the "other thing."

The core issue in Galatians is justification. How does a person gain right standing before God? The Judaizers said that Christ (grace) plus circumcision (law keeping) equals right standing. Paul's equation was different: Christ (grace) plus *nothing else* equals right standing. Works are excluded from Paul's equation. "Know that a man is not justified by observing the law, but by faith in Jesus Christ. So we, too, have put our faith in Christ Jesus that we may be justified by faith in Christ and not by observing the law, because by observing the law no one will be justified" (2:16). This key verse sums up Paul's argument.

The Implications

To the modern reader, it may seem, at times, as if Paul is getting worked up over a relatively small issue. After all, the important thing is to believe in Jesus, and all the parties agreed to that. But in fact, as history demonstrated, this issue was profound. Paul's concerns were more than validated. The underlying issue related to the universality of Christianity. Was Christianity for all people in all cultures (as Paul was arguing), or was it only a Jewish sect? To be a Christian, did you first have to become a Jew (which is the implication of the Judaizers' argument)? Did you have to accept Jewish customs, live a Jewish lifestyle, and submit to Jewish laws? If so, if the Judaizers had won, Christianity would probably have died out in the first century.

As we know, Christianity did not disappear along with all the Palestinian sects. Rather, the church was able to expand into the Graeco-Roman world because the gospel was truly universal. It was not tied to temple sacrifice and the law of Moses, about which most pagans neither knew nor cared. The Judaizers wanted a Christianity circumscribed by Jewish exclusiveness, taboos, and customs — in which, perforce, Gentile believers would always be second-class citizens. Paul fought this with vehemence and passion, as had other believers from Stephen onward; so Christianity became the transcultural world religion Christ intended (Matt. 28:19-20).

The Relationship between Galatians and Romans

It is obvious that there is a close thematic connection between Galatians and Romans. Galatians appears to be Paul's first attempt at wrestling with the issue of justification by faith alone. Paul does so in the context of having to deal with a local problem. Romans, on the other hand, is a more studied consideration of the same issue. It is an eloquent, carefully stated, logical argument, which stands as one of the finest pieces of theological writing ever penned. Paul lifts the core of his argument from Galatians and shapes and refines it into a theological whole in Romans. As J. B. Lightfoot wrote: "The Epistle to the Galatians stands in relation to the Roman letter, as the rough model to the finished statue" (*St. Paul's Epistle to the Galatians*, p. 49).

Structure

After a terse greeting (1:1-5) and pronouncement of anathema against the troublemaker (1:6-10), Paul launches into his first major theme: his *personal defense* in which he deals with the charge that he is not a real apostle (1:11-2:21). This is followed by a *doctrinal defense* in which he shows that Christianity lived under the law is inferior to Christianity lived by faith (3:1-4:31). On the basis of these two arguments, he then shows what true Christian freedom is (5:1-6:10), ending with an unusual conclusion written in his own hand (6:11-18).

Galatians

[Handwritten top margin:] Apostle — Met Jesus personally — Happened on Damascus Road. Totally unexpected — Thought impossible AS Dramatic as OJ Simpson Confessing —

OPEN: 1. Who contributed to your spiritual beginnings? How so? **2.** How do you respond to anger?

[Handwritten left margin:] Undeserved Generosity / Every good thing from God —

DIG: 1. How does Paul assert his authority (v.1)? Why does he do so (v.6)? What is happening to these churches which Paul himself had started (Ac 13-14)? **2.** Which elements of the gospel does Paul stress? Why? Otherwise, what might happen due to the distorted gospel (see 4:8-11, 17; 6:12-13)? **3.** What accusation is Paul refuting in verse 10? Why would some see him as a "people-pleaser"? **4.** Compared to other introductions to Paul's letters, do you find this one to be "quite chilly" or "red-hot"? How so?

REFLECT: What "distorted gospel" upsets you? Why? How can Galatians help you to refute it?

[Handwritten:] Not serving men but God — He made a mistake first time C Persecution.

[Handwritten left margin:] FREE — Not Earned, special Prosecutor Law, Persecution, God's Plan, Personally Chosen, Even though He chose another way, and thought he was RIGHTEOUS

OPEN: At age 18, where was "home" for you? What career were you preparing for then? Now? Back then, how long were you in the "cocoon" stage before you were ready to fly?

DIG: 1. Why does Paul stress the origin of his message (vv.11-12)? **2.** What do Paul's comments here add to his conversion story (compare with Ac 9:1-31 and Php 3:4-6)? Why do the Galatians need to understand that he is not just passing on second-hand information to them? How does this validate Paul's claim to be an apostle (v.1)? **3.** Paul preached extensively without formal approval by the apostles in Jerusalem. How does that independence relate to Paul's major point here?

REFLECT: 1. If you had to argue for the reality of the gospel by giving one example of how faith in Christ has changed you, what would you share? In what way is your experience of Christ an important part of your witness to others? **2.** Whom do you know who was once very hostile to Christ, but is now his follower? What brought about that change?

1 Paul, an apostle—sent not from men nor by man, but by Jesus Christ and God the Father, who raised him from the dead— 2and all the brothers with me,

[Handwritten right margin:] Some years later

To the churches in Galatia:

3Grace and peace to you from God our Father and the Lord Jesus Christ, 4who gave himself for our sins to rescue us from the present evil age, according to the will of our God and Father, 5to whom be glory for ever and ever. Amen.

No Other Gospel

6I am astonished that you are so quickly deserting the one who called you by the grace of Christ and are turning to a different gospel— 7which is really no gospel at all. Evidently some people are throwing you into confusion and are trying to pervert the gospel of Christ. 8But even if we or an angel from heaven should preach a gospel other than the one we preached to you, let him be eternally condemned! 9As we have already said, so now I say again: If anybody is preaching to you a gospel other than what you accepted, let him be eternally condemned!

[Handwritten right margin:] Jude to b mus beco Jew ever

10Am I now trying to win the approval of men, or of God? Or am I trying to please men? If I were still trying to please men, I would not be a servant of Christ. *[Handwritten:] I would still be a prosecutor*

Paul Called by God

11I want you to know, brothers, that the gospel I preached is not something that man made up. 12I did not receive it from any man, nor was I taught it; rather, I received it by revelation from Jesus Christ.

[Handwritten right margin:] Dam Com + hs

13For you have heard of my previous way of life in Judaism, how intensely I persecuted the church of God and tried to destroy it. 14I was advancing in Judaism beyond many Jews of my own age and was extremely zealous for the traditions of my fathers. 15But when God, who set me apart from birth[a] and called me by his grace, was pleased 16to reveal his Son in me so that I might preach him among the Gentiles, I did not consult any man, 17nor did I go up to Jerusalem to see those who were apostles before I was, but I went immediately into Arabia and later returned to Damascus.

[Handwritten right margin:] Alon Conversion P Victi

18Then after three years, I went up to Jerusalem to get acquainted with Peter[b] and stayed with him fifteen days. 19I saw none of the other apostles—only James, the Lord's brother. 20I assure you before God that what I am writing you is no lie. 21Later I went to Syria and Cilicia. 22I was personally unknown to the churches of Judea that are in Christ. 23They only heard the report: "The man who formerly persecuted us is now preaching the faith he once tried to destroy." 24And they praised God because of me.

[Handwritten right margin:] Bir Pla

[Handwritten bottom:] Believers — Saw him as a MIRACLE MAN. [Ken Starr supporting Clinton]

[a] 15 Or from my mother's womb   [b] 18 Greek Cephas

360

[handwritten: Jerusalem Questions + complaints are Over — Now he has Apostle Status from Big 3 —]

Paul Accepted by the Apostles

2 Fourteen years later I went up again to Jerusalem, this time with Barnabas. I took Titus along also. ²I went in response to a revelation and set before them the gospel that I preach among the Gentiles. But I did this privately to those who seemed to be leaders, for fear that I was running or had run my race in vain. ³Yet not even Titus, who was with me, was compelled to be circumcised, even though he was a Greek. ⁴This matter arose, because some false brothers had infiltrated our ranks to spy on the freedom we have in Christ Jesus and to make us slaves. ⁵We did not give in to them for a moment, so that the truth of the gospel might remain with you.

⁶As for those who seemed to be important—whatever they were makes no difference to me; God does not judge by external appearance—those men added nothing to my message. ⁷On the contrary, they saw that I had been entrusted with the task of preaching the gospel to the Gentiles,[c] just as Peter had been to the Jews.[d] ⁸For God, who was at work in the ministry of Peter as an apostle to the Jews, was also at work in my ministry as an apostle to the Gentiles. ⁹James, Peter[e] and John, those reputed to be pillars, gave me and Barnabas the right hand of fellowship when they recognized the grace given to me. They agreed that we should go to the Gentiles, and they to the Jews. ¹⁰All they asked was that we should continue to remember the poor, the very thing I was eager to do.

[handwritten: Big 3 but change of Order James is now BOSS —]

Paul Opposes Peter

¹¹When Peter came to Antioch, I opposed him to his face, because he was clearly in the wrong. ¹²Before certain men came from James, he used to eat with the Gentiles. But when they arrived, he began to draw back and separate himself from the Gentiles because he was afraid of those who belonged to the circumcision group. ¹³The other Jews joined him in his hypocrisy, so that by their hypocrisy even Barnabas was led astray.

¹⁴When I saw that they were not acting in line with the truth of the gospel, I said to Peter in front of them all, "You are a Jew, yet you live like a Gentile and not like a Jew. How is it, then, that you force Gentiles to follow Jewish customs?

¹⁵"We who are Jews by birth and not 'Gentile sinners' ¹⁶know that a man is not justified by observing the law, but by faith in Jesus Christ. So we, too, have put our faith in Christ Jesus that we may be justified by faith in Christ and not by observing the law, because by observing the law no one will be justified.

¹⁷"If, while we seek to be justified in Christ, it becomes evident that we ourselves are sinners, does that mean that Christ promotes sin? Absolutely not! ¹⁸If I rebuild what I destroyed, I prove that I am a lawbreaker. ¹⁹For through the law I died to the law so that I might live for God. ²⁰I have been crucified with Christ and I no longer live, but Christ lives in me. The life I live in the body, I live by faith in the Son of God, who loved me and

[handwritten bottom: Temptations - Earn God's favor - make comparisons]

c7 Greek *uncircumcised*   d7 Greek *circumcised*; also in verses 8 and 9   e9 Greek *Cephas*; also in verses 11 and 14

OPEN: What group (in-crowd, fraternity, club, guild) did you want to join so much that you'd do almost anything they asked?

DIG: 1. How does Paul confront "spies" who believe Gentiles had to first become Jewish before accepting Christ? **2.** How did the decision about Titus confirm Paul's message? Given the charges (1:10), why was this a critical issue for Paul? **3.** Given the position of Peter, James, and John, how would their approval of Paul's message validate his claim in 1:11-12? **4.** How does caring for the poor relate to preaching the gospel (v.10; see Ac 11:25-30)?

REFLECT: How do you feel when your beliefs are contrary to popular opinion? What would you have done in Paul's place? Would it matter to you if Paul's argument had failed? Why or why not?

OPEN: If God was like Santa Claus, checking his list twice to see "who's naughty or nice," would you get "your heart's desire" or a "lump of coal" for this week? Why?

DIG: 1. Read Acts 11:1-18. In light of this experience, how do you account for Peter's actions here when he comes to Antioch? **2.** How is the word "justified" commonly used today? How does Paul use the term as compared with his opponents (vv.15-16)? Why do these differences matter so much? Comparing verses 15-16 with Paul's preaching in Acts 13:38-39, how would you sum up what the gospel is all about? **3.** What is "justification by faith": (a) Legal fiction? (b) An excuse to keep on sinning? (c) New reality that leads us away from sin? Explain. **4.** How does Paul turn the tables on his rule-keeping opponents (v.21)?

REFLECT: 1. What difference would it make to you if you had to earn your way to God by keeping the Jewish laws? Conversely, if you are a self-made person who likes to see everyone "pay their own way" or "earn their fair share," how does this gospel of unmerited favor strike you? **2.** What "additions" to faith might outsiders

[handwritten right margin: Peter changes his mind / Trying to please Everyone / Doesn't Work]

sense in your Christian circles, regarding what they should do to be approved?

OPEN: What "family ties" (rituals, inherited traits, blessings, curses) encourage you to repeat the past?

DIG: 1. How does Paul's appeal in verses 1-5 validate what he argued for in 2:15-16? **2.** How does Paul's appeal to their suffering (v.4), their experience (vv.2-5), and Christ's death (2:21) expose the foolishness and futility of human effort? **3.** How does the example of Abraham (vv.6-9) support Paul's argument? How is our faith in Christ a fulfillment of God's promise to Abraham? **4.** How does each OT quote (vv.10-13) expose the problem of trying to be right with God by trusting in one's ability to keep his law? **5.** How does Jesus solve this problem for us (vv.13-14)?

REFLECT: 1. What "Christian" rules seem to be important in your circles? Why? **2.** How would you explain the promised "righteousness" (v.6), "blessing" (vv.8-9, 14), "curse" (v.10), and Spirit (v.14) to a prospective convert?

OPEN: When your parents had to leave, who was "in charge" around the house? How did you feel about that?

DIG: 1. What is the distinction here between seeds and Seed? What is the parallel point Paul emphasizes regarding the types of covenants (wills) people make, and the covenant-promise (3:8) God made to Abraham? **2.** Since the law was not to take the place of the promise, how do verses 19 and 23 explain what the law's purpose actually is (see also Ro 3:20)? **3.** How is relating to God by the law like being kept in prison, or scolded by a harsh disciplinarian (vv.22-25)? How does Christ change all this? Why then would anyone go back to the law?

REFLECT: 1. Paul's logic may seem obscure or irrelevant today. How would you clarify Paul's argument for someone who could

gave himself for me. 21I do not set aside the grace of God, for if righteousness could be gained through the law, Christ died for nothing!"*f*

Faith or Observance of the Law

3 You foolish Galatians! Who has bewitched you? Before your very eyes Jesus Christ was clearly portrayed as crucified. 2I would like to learn just one thing from you: Did you receive the Spirit by observing the law, or by believing what you heard? 3Are you so foolish? After beginning with the Spirit, are you now trying to attain your goal by human effort? 4Have you suffered so much for nothing—if it really was for nothing? 5Does God give you his Spirit and work miracles among you because you observe the law, or because you believe what you heard?

6Consider Abraham: "He believed God, and it was credited to him as righteousness."*g* 7Understand, then, that those who believe are children of Abraham. 8The Scripture foresaw that God would justify the Gentiles by faith, and announced the gospel in advance to Abraham: "All nations will be blessed through you."*h* 9So those who have faith are blessed along with Abraham, the man of faith.

10All who rely on observing the law are under a curse, for it is written: "Cursed is everyone who does not continue to do everything written in the Book of the Law."*i* 11Clearly no one is justified before God by the law, because, "The righteous will live by faith."*j* 12The law is not based on faith; on the contrary, "The man who does these things will live by them."*k* 13Christ redeemed us from the curse of the law by becoming a curse for us, for it is written: "Cursed is everyone who is hung on a tree."*l* 14He redeemed us in order that the blessing given to Abraham might come to the Gentiles through Christ Jesus, so that by faith we might receive the promise of the Spirit.

The Law and the Promise

15Brothers, let me take an example from everyday life. Just as no one can set aside or add to a human covenant that has been duly established, so it is in this case. 16The promises were spoken to Abraham and to his seed. The Scripture does not say "and to seeds," meaning many people, but "and to your seed,"*m* meaning one person, who is Christ. 17What I mean is this: The law, introduced 430 years later, does not set aside the covenant previously established by God and thus do away with the promise. 18For if the inheritance depends on the law, then it no longer depends on a promise; but God in his grace gave it to Abraham through a promise.

19What, then, was the purpose of the law? It was added because of transgressions until the Seed to whom the promise referred had come. The law was put into effect through angels by a mediator. 20A mediator, however, does not represent just one party; but God is one.

21Is the law, therefore, opposed to the promises of God?

---

f21 Some interpreters end the quotation after verse 14.   *g6* Gen. 15:6
h8 Gen. 12:3; 18:18; 22:18   *i10* Deut. 27:26   *j11* Hab. 2:4   *k12* Lev. 18:5
l13 Deut. 21:23   *m16* Gen. 12:7; 13:15; 24:7

Absolutely not! For if a law had been given that could impart life, then righteousness would certainly have come by the law. [22]But the Scripture declares that the whole world is a prisoner of sin, so that what was promised, being given through faith in Jesus Christ, might be given to those who believe.

[23]Before this faith came, we were held prisoners by the law, locked up until faith should be revealed. [24]So the law was put in charge to lead us to Christ[n] that we might be justified by faith. [25]Now that faith has come, we are no longer under the supervision of the law.

Sons of God

[26]You are all sons of God through faith in Christ Jesus, [27]for all of you who were baptized into Christ have clothed yourselves with Christ. [28]There is neither Jew nor Greek, slave nor free, male nor female, for you are all one in Christ Jesus. [29]If you belong to Christ, then you are Abraham's seed, and heirs according to the promise.

4 What I am saying is that as long as the heir is a child, he is no different from a slave, although he owns the whole estate. [2]He is subject to guardians and trustees until the time set by his father. [3]So also, when we were children, we were in slavery under the basic principles of the world. [4]But when the time had fully come, God sent his Son, born of a woman, born under law, [5]to redeem those under law, that we might receive the full rights of sons. [6]Because you are sons, God sent the Spirit of his Son into our hearts, the Spirit who calls out, "*Abba*,[o] Father." [7]So you are no longer a slave, but a son; and since you are a son, God has made you also an heir.

Paul's Concern for the Galatians

[8]Formerly, when you did not know God, you were slaves to those who by nature are not gods. [9]But now that you know God—or rather are known by God—how is it that you are turning back to those weak and miserable principles? Do you wish to be enslaved by them all over again? [10]You are observing special days and months and seasons and years! [11]I fear for you, that somehow I have wasted my efforts on you.

[12]I plead with you, brothers, become like me, for I became like you. You have done me no wrong. [13]As you know, it was because of an illness that I first preached the gospel to you. [14]Even though my illness was a trial to you, you did not treat me with contempt or scorn. Instead, you welcomed me as if I were an angel of God, as if I were Christ Jesus himself. [15]What has happened to all your joy? I can testify that, if you could have done so, you would have torn out your eyes and given them to me. [16]Have I now become your enemy by telling you the truth?

[17]Those people are zealous to win you over, but for no good. What they want is to alienate you ,from us,, so that you may be zealous for them. [18]It is fine to be zealous, provided the purpose is good, and to be so always and not just when I am with you. [19]My dear children, for whom I am again in the pains of child-

care less about such fine distinctions? How would you use this passage with someone who thinks that keeping the Golden Rule or the Ten Commandments is enough to get right with God? **2.** What experience showed you that keeping rules was not the way to obtain God's mercy?

OPEN: If you could send yourself into the past and influence history, where would you go? Why?

DIG: 1. How does being "clothed with Christ" (v.27) eliminate major cultural barriers (v.28)? **2.** How is being under the Law like being an heir who is still a minor (vv.1-3)? How has Jesus changed all that?

REFLECT: 1. What are some contemporary cultural barriers between people? What does 3:28 mean to you in that context? **2.** What does being a "child of God" and "clothed with Christ" say to you about living the Christian life?

OPEN: What is one of your more compulsive habits? How do you try to break it?

DIG: 1. Prior to their conversion, the Galatians followed the customs of honoring the Greek gods. How are they now doing the same with Jewish festivals (v.10)? **2.** What is the difference between celebrating religious holidays (Christmas or Easter) and what the Galatians were doing? **3.** What are the differences in attitudes and goals between Paul (vv.11, 18-20) and the other teachers (v.17)? Why is Paul so perplexed?

REFLECT: 1. How has your relationship with God changed from being one based on love and trust to one based on keeping the rules? Why does that happen? **2.** What difference has knowing God, and being known by him, made in your life?

---

[n]*24 Or charge until Christ came*   [o]*6 Aramaic for Father*

birth until Christ is formed in you, [20]how I wish I could be with you now and change my tone, because I am perplexed about you!

Hagar and Sarah

[21]Tell me, you who want to be under the law, are you not aware of what the law says? [22]For it is written that Abraham had two sons, one by the slave woman and the other by the free woman. [23]His son by the slave woman was born in the ordinary way; but his son by the free woman was born as the result of a promise.

[24]These things may be taken figuratively, for the women represent two covenants. One covenant is from Mount Sinai and bears children who are to be slaves: This is Hagar. [25]Now Hagar stands for Mount Sinai in Arabia and corresponds to the present city of Jerusalem, because she is in slavery with her children. [26]But the Jerusalem that is above is free, and she is our mother. [27]For it is written:

> "Be glad, O barren woman,
>   who bears no children;
> break forth and cry aloud,
>   you who have no labor pains;
> because more are the children of the desolate woman
>   than of her who has a husband."[p]

[28]Now you, brothers, like Isaac, are children of promise. [29]At that time the son born in the ordinary way persecuted the son born by the power of the Spirit. It is the same now. [30]But what does the Scripture say? "Get rid of the slave woman and her son, for the slave woman's son will never share in the inheritance with the free woman's son."[q] [31]Therefore, brothers, we are not children of the slave woman, but of the free woman.

Freedom in Christ   Jewish + Greek Religion OBLIGATORY!

5 It is for freedom that Christ has set us free. Stand firm, then, and do not let yourselves be burdened again by a yoke of slavery.

[2]Mark my words! I, Paul, tell you that if you let yourselves be circumcised, Christ will be of no value to you at all. [3]Again I declare to every man who lets himself be circumcised that he is obligated to obey the whole law. [4]You who are trying to be justified by law have been alienated from Christ; you have fallen away from grace. [5]But by faith we eagerly await through the Spirit the righteousness for which we hope. [6]For in Christ Jesus neither circumcision nor uncircumcision has any value. The only thing that counts is faith expressing itself through love.

[7]You were running a good race. Who cut in on you and kept you from obeying the truth? [8]That kind of persuasion does not come from the one who calls you. [9]"A little yeast works through the whole batch of dough." [10]I am confident in the Lord that you will take no other view. The one who is throwing you into confusion will pay the penalty, whoever he may be. [11]Brothers,

---

OPEN: 1. What story do your parents tell about your birth? 2. How would you like to be married to two women or be the wife of a man with two wives?

DIG: 1. Read Genesis 16:1-4; 18:10-14; 21:1-10. What is the birth story for these two sons of Abraham? How does this story relate to Paul's argument in 3:7 and 4:7? 2. Normally, the Jews would regard Sarah as their spiritual mother and Hagar as the spiritual mother of Gentiles. Why does Paul reverse the picture? How are the spiritual descendants of Sarah distinguished from the other line of descent?

REFLECT: 1. Has your experience as a Christian been more of a growing into freedom or a coming under rules? Why? 2. Has your joy in Christ ever been crushed by someone's belief that you were breaking traditions or rules? Have you imposed standards on others, limiting their freedom? How so? 3. What difference will the fact of justification and the fullness of the Spirit make in your life?

OPEN: What do you do when others "cut in on you" (lunch, traffic, shopping, speaking)?

DIG: 1. What's at stake here (vv.1-4)? What does Paul mean by "yoke of slavery"? 2. Since rule-keeping isn't the way to God, what is (v.6)? How are we to show our dependency on Christ? 3. What is Paul's tone (vv.7-12)? Why does this issue move him so strongly? 4. In verses 13-15, how does Paul navigate between the dangers of legalism and total license? 5. Paul says: (a) we are not under the law anymore, and (b) we are to fulfill it. What's the difference between (a) and (b)?

REFLECT: 1. What "spiritual yardstick" does your church use to see who measures up? How does it compare to verse 6? 2. How have you seen Christian

---

p27 Isaiah 54:1   *q30* Gen. 21:10

if I am still preaching circumcision, why am I still being persecuted? In that case the offense of the cross has been abolished. [12]As for those agitators, I wish they would go the whole way and emasculate themselves!

[13]You, my brothers, were called to be free. But do not use your freedom to indulge the sinful nature'; rather, serve one another in love. [14]The entire law is summed up in a single command: "Love your neighbor as yourself."' [15]If you keep on biting and devouring each other, watch out or you will be destroyed by each other.

Life by the Spirit

[16]So I say, live by the Spirit, and you will not gratify the desires of the sinful nature. [17]For the sinful nature desires what is contrary to the Spirit, and the Spirit what is contrary to the sinful nature. They are in conflict with each other, so that you do not do what you want. [18]But if you are led by the Spirit, you are not under law.

[19]The acts of the sinful nature are obvious: sexual immorality, impurity and debauchery; [20]idolatry and witchcraft; hatred, discord, jealousy, fits of rage, selfish ambition, dissensions, factions [21]and envy; drunkenness, orgies, and the like. I warn you, as I did before, that those who live like this will not inherit the kingdom of God.

[22]But the fruit of the Spirit is love, joy, peace, patience, kindness, goodness, faithfulness, [23]gentleness and self-control. Against such things there is no law. [24]Those who belong to Christ Jesus have crucified the sinful nature its passions and desires. [25]Since we live by the Spirit, let us keep in step with the Spirit. [26]Let us not become conceited, provoking and envying each other.

Doing Good to All

6 Brothers, if someone is caught in a sin, you who are spiritual should restore him gently. But watch yourself, or you also may be tempted. [2]Carry each other's burdens, and in this way you will fulfill the law of Christ. [3]If anyone thinks he is something when he is nothing, he deceives himself. [4]Each one should test his own actions. Then he can take pride in himself, without comparing himself to somebody else, [5]for each one should carry his own load.

[6]Anyone who receives instruction in the word must share all good things with his instructor.

[7]Do not be deceived: God cannot be mocked. A man reaps what he sows. [8]The one who sows to please his sinful nature, from that nature' will reap destruction; the one who sows to please the Spirit, from the Spirit will reap eternal life. [9]Let us not become weary in doing good, for at the proper time we will reap a harvest if we do not give up. [10]Therefore, as we have opportunity, let us do good to all people, especially to those who belong to the family of believers.

freedom abused? How is verse 6 an antidote to those who think their freedom in Christ gives them license to do anything they wish?

OPEN: What grows in your garden without help? With your help?

DIG: 1. What does Paul mean by "living in…" and "keeping in step with the Spirit" (vv.16,18,25; also 5:13-14)? If we are made alive by the Spirit, why do we still struggle with sin? **2.** Since we are not under the law, what is wrong with indulging our sinful nature once in a while? **3.** How then do you grow spiritual fruit (vv.22-23) and live out what Paul means by "Christ formed in you" (4:19)? **4.** Illustrate practically what it means to "crucify" the sinful nature (v.24).

REFLECT: 1. Which spiritual fruit are "blossoming" for you? Which are in the "bud" stage? **2.** Which sinful acts are "dead and buried"? Which are "mortally wounded"? "Alive and well"? **3.** How can you and the Spirit grow the one and

OPEN: 1. As a child, were you ever caught "red-handed" by your parents for doing something you knew they didn't want you to do? What happened? **2.** What is one good deed you've done recently that you'd love to boast about if the group let you?

DIG: 1. How do verses 1-2 illustrate ways of helping someone "keep in step with the Spirit" (5:25)? What is the "law of Christ" (see 5:14)? **2.** How can you restore a brother caught in sin and avoid feeling superior to him or being victimized by it yourself? **3.** How do verses 5-6 relate to verse 2? What is the gist of Paul's teaching on the Spirit-filled life (vv.7-10)? **4.** How does Paul sum up the motives of the false teachers (vv.12-13)? His own motives (v.11)? **5.** Ultimately, why is keeping the Jewish rules irrelevant? From elsewhere in Galatians, how

---

'13 Or the flesh; also in verses 16, 17, 19 and 24   '14 Lev. 19:18   '8 Or his flesh, from the flesh

365

would you describe what this "new creation" is all about? **6.** Why does Paul call these Gentile Galatians the "Israel of God" (see 3:6-9)? How is that a final rebuke to those who would compel these believers to obey Jewish rules first? **7.** What does Paul mean by bearing on his body the marks of Jesus and boasting only in cross of Jesus (vv.14,17; see 2Co 11:23-30)? Why would Paul's willingness to suffer be a further rebuke to the false teachers?

REFLECT: 1. How can you help a friend of yours with a specific burden he or she has? **2.** As you reflect on what you have "sown" this year, what "harvest" are you expecting: Weeds? A bumper crop? Pretty spindly plants? Why? What can you do this week to "sow to the Spirit"? **3.** In what ways do people today tamper with the gospel of the cross to make it less "offensive" to others? Have you been tempted to do so? How? **4.** How has coming to Christ changed your attitudes toward the common values and ideas of the world? Where do you find worldly things still pressuring you? What can the group do to help?

Not Circumcision but a New Creation

[11]See what large letters I use as I write to you with my own hand!

[12]Those who want to make a good impression outwardly are trying to compel you to be circumcised. The only reason they do this is to avoid being persecuted for the cross of Christ. [13]Not even those who are circumcised obey the law, yet they want you to be circumcised that they may boast about your flesh. [14]May I never boast except in the cross of our Lord Jesus Christ, through which " the world has been crucified to me, and I to the world. [15]Neither circumcision nor uncircumcision means anything; what counts is a new creation. [16]Peace and mercy to all who follow this rule, even to the Israel of God.

[17]Finally, let no one cause me trouble, for I bear on my body the marks of Jesus.

[18]The grace of our Lord Jesus Christ be with your spirit, brothers. Amen.

u14 Or whom

EPHESIANS

INTRODUCTION

Characteristics

William Barclay called Ephesians "The Queen of the Epistles" (*The Letters to the Galatians and Ephesians,* p. 83). Samuel Taylor Coleridge, the English poet, said it was "the divinest composition of man" (Barclay, p. 71). Indeed, there is a breathtaking grandeur about Paul's letter to the Ephesians as it sketches the reconciling work of God in Christ—making one of all peoples of the earth, subduing the hostile cosmic powers, and creating a new humanity and a new society. It is with not a little awe that one approaches Ephesians, the "greatest" and "the most relevant of all Paul's works" (John Mackay, *God's Order: The Ephesian Letter and This Present Time,* pp. 9-10).

The Captivity Letters

Paul is in prison once again, and Epaphras has come to visit him bearing disturbing news about the church at Colossae. Since Paul is about to send back the runaway slave Onesimus (now converted) to his owner Philemon, a member of the Colossian Church, he takes this opportunity to send along a letter in which he addresses the Colossian heresy. He also writes two more letters: one to Philemon and one to a neighboring area, the Letter to the Ephesians. These three epistles form the core of what we now know as the Prison Epistles or the Captivity Letters. The fourth Prison Epistle, Philippians, was written in prison on another occasion.

Ephesians and Colossians are more similar in language and content than any other two letters in the New Testament. Seventy-five of the 155 verses in Ephesians are found in parallel form in Colossians. It seems that Paul first developed those themes in Colossians while dealing with a local problem, and then expanded them, explained them, and cast them into a universal setting in Ephesians.

Place and Date of Writing

It is unclear from which city Paul wrote. It seems that he spent time in prisons throughout the Roman Empire (see 2 Cor. 11:23). While Caesarea (Acts 24) and Ephesus have been suggested as possible sites, the most likely place was Rome (Acts 28). In that case, the letter to the Ephesians was written in the early sixties, some thirty years after Jesus' crucifixion and only a few years before Paul's death.

Structure

Between an introductory greeting (1:1-2) and a concluding salutation (6:21-24)—both typical of letters written in Paul's day—the material falls easily into two parts. Part 1 (chaps. 1-3) concerns *doctrine*, while part 2 (chaps. 4-6) is about *ethics*. In part 1, Paul preaches about the new life and the new society God has brought into being through Jesus Christ. In part 2, he teaches about the new standards and new relationships expected of believers. In other words, he moves from theory to practice, from the indicative ("This is the way things are") to the imperative ("Therefore, do this"). Throughout, the emphasis is on *unity*. In part 1, Paul extols the great reconciling work of Christ who through the Cross overcame the demonic powers (chap. 1), thus breaking down the wall between God and the human race (2:1-10) and the walls between people themselves (2:11-22). In part 2, the imperatives are largely exhortations for unity in relationships.

Ephesians

OPEN: What is the best medicine when you get down in the dumps?

DIG: 1. What is Paul's tone of voice as he invokes this blessing? **2.** In your words, describe the "blessings in Christ" (vv.3-9). How do they relate to praising God? **3.** What activities and descriptive words relate to the Father, Jesus, and the Holy Spirit (vv.3-14)? What does this show you about the triune God? **4.** How does being chosen by God (v.4) relate to our believing (v.13)? Who are the *we* and the *you* mentioned here? **5.** What phrases from 1:1-14 define *your reason to live*? What does each phrase mean?

REFLECT: 1. What excites you most about God's relationship to you? **2.** How do you know if you are "chosen"? Knowing you are adopted, how will you view yourself and God differently? **3.** What changes in your lifestyle would help you live more effectively for the praise of God's glory this week?

OPEN: What do you remember about Thanksgiving Day when you were a child? What is most meaningful about that day now?

DIG: 1. What motivated Paul to pray for these people? **2.** What is this wisdom, hope, and power for which Paul prays (vv.17-19)? To what end are these resources applied? **3.** What does Paul mean by our inheritance and spiritual power (vv.18-19)? **4.** If the church is Christ's "body" (vv.22-23), what does this imply for us? **5.** How does Jesus give hope and power?

REFLECT: 1. How would you change if your group prayed verses 17-19 every week for each other? Try it and see. **2.** In light of the power available to Christians (v.19), what is your favorite excuse for "operating on one or two cylinders"?

1 Paul, an apostle of Christ Jesus by the will of God,

To the saints in Ephesus,*a* the faithful*b* in Christ Jesus:

²Grace and peace to you from God our Father and the Lord Jesus Christ.

Spiritual Blessings in Christ

³Praise be to the God and Father of our Lord Jesus Christ, who has blessed us in the heavenly realms with every spiritual blessing in Christ. ⁴For he chose us in him before the creation of the world to be holy and blameless in his sight. In love ⁵he*c* predestined us to be adopted as his sons through Jesus Christ, in accordance with his pleasure and will— ⁶to the praise of his glorious grace, which he has freely given us in the One he loves. ⁷In him we have redemption through his blood, the forgiveness of sins, in accordance with the riches of God's grace ⁸that he lavished on us with all wisdom and understanding. ⁹And he*d* made known to us the mystery of his will according to his good pleasure, which he purposed in Christ, ¹⁰to be put into effect when the times will have reached their fulfillment—to bring all things in heaven and on earth together under one head, even Christ.

¹¹In him we were also chosen,*e* having been predestined according to the plan of him who works out everything in conformity with the purpose of his will, ¹²in order that we, who were the first to hope in Christ, might be for the praise of his glory. ¹³And you also were included in Christ when you heard the word of truth, the gospel of your salvation. Having believed, you were marked in him with a seal, the promised Holy Spirit, ¹⁴who is a deposit guaranteeing our inheritance until the redemption of those who are God's possession—to the praise of his glory.

Thanksgiving and Prayer

¹⁵For this reason, ever since I heard about your faith in the Lord Jesus and your love for all the saints, ¹⁶I have not stopped giving thanks for you, remembering you in my prayers. ¹⁷I keep asking that the God of our Lord Jesus Christ, the glorious Father, may give you the Spirit*f* of wisdom and revelation, so that you may know him better. ¹⁸I pray also that the eyes of your heart may be enlightened in order that you may know the hope to which he has called you, the riches of his glorious inheritance in the saints, ¹⁹and his incomparably great power for us who believe. That power is like the working of his mighty strength, ²⁰which he exerted in Christ when he raised him from the dead and seated him at his right hand in the heavenly realms, ²¹far above all rule and authority, power and dominion, and every title that can be given, not only in the present age but also in

---

*a*1 Some early manuscripts do not have *in Ephesus.*   *b*1 Or *believers who are*
*c*4,5 Or *sight in love.* ⁵*He*   *d*8,9 Or *us. With all wisdom and understanding,* ⁹*he*
*e*11 Or *were made heirs*   *f*17 Or *a spirit*

the one to come. [22]And God placed all things under his feet and appointed him to be head over everything for the church, [23]which is his body, the fullness of him who fills everything in every way.

Made Alive in Christ

2 As for you, you were dead in your transgressions and sins, [2]in which you used to live when you followed the ways of this world and of the ruler of the kingdom of the air, the spirit who is now at work in those who are disobedient. [3]All of us also lived among them at one time, gratifying the cravings of our sinful nature[g] and following its desires and thoughts. Like the rest, we were by nature objects of wrath. [4]But because of his great love for us, God, who is rich in mercy, [5]made us alive with Christ even when we were dead in transgressions—it is by grace you have been saved. [6]And God raised us up with Christ and seated us with him in the heavenly realms in Christ Jesus, [7]in order that in the coming ages he might show the incomparable riches of his grace, expressed in his kindness to us in Christ Jesus. [8]For it is by grace you have been saved, through faith— and this not from yourselves, it is the gift of God— [9]not by works, so that no one can boast. [10]For we are God's workmanship, created in Christ Jesus to do good works, which God prepared in advance for us to do.

One in Christ

[11]Therefore, remember that formerly you who are Gentiles by birth and called "uncircumcised" by those who call themselves "the circumcision" (that done in the body by the hands of men)— [12]remember that at that time you were separate from Christ, excluded from citizenship in Israel and foreigners to the covenants of the promise, without hope and without God in the world. [13]But now in Christ Jesus you who once were far away have been brought near through the blood of Christ.

[14]For he himself is our peace, who has made the two one and has destroyed the barrier, the dividing wall of hostility, [15]by abolishing in his flesh the law with its commandments and regulations. His purpose was to create in himself one new man out of the two, thus making peace, [16]and in this one body to reconcile both of them to God through the cross, by which he put to death their hostility. [17]He came and preached peace to you who were far away and peace to those who were near. [18]For through him we both have access to the Father by one Spirit.

[19]Consequently, you are no longer foreigners and aliens, but fellow citizens with God's people and members of God's household, [20]built on the foundation of the apostles and prophets, with Christ Jesus himself as the chief cornerstone. [21]In him the whole building is joined together and rises to become a holy temple in the Lord. [22]And in him you too are being built together to become a dwelling in which God lives by his Spirit.

OPEN: What was one of the best gifts you received as a child? What made it so special for you?

DIG: 1. What does it mean to be "dead in sin"? What caused this? **2.** Why must God take the initiative to give life? How does Christ's experience (1:20-23) compare to ours (vv.5-7)? **3.** What is the relation between *wrath* and *love* (vv.3-4)? Between *grace* and *works* (vv.8-10)? How would you illustrate what each key word means?

REFLECT: 1. Spiritually, do you feel more dead or alive now? Why? **2.** What has God prepared for you to be and to do?

OPEN: From where did your ancestors emigrate? What did their new citizenship mean to them? What does yours mean to you?

DIG: 1. Before Christ, what problems did the Gentiles face? What results from being "in Christ"? **2.** What is the bomb that Jesus dropped on the religious "class system" of his day? What impact would verses 14-18 have on the divisions between Jews and Gentiles? **3.** How is the reconciling work of Christ (vv.19-22) like new citizenship? Like a new family? A new temple?

REFLECT: 1. What relationship in your life still has walls to be knocked down? How will that happen? **2.** Although God's grace is personal (2:8), what social barriers should it be affecting in your community? Your church? What is your role in that process?

g3 Or our flesh

OPEN: 1. What would you do with a "time out" from your weekly routine? 2. What was your secret hiding place when you were a child?

DIG: 1. What is Paul's train of thought (v.1; see 2:11-20; 3:14-30)? What breaks in here? 2. Paul uses his "time out" in prison to fathom the "mystery of Christ" and write letters. What is that mystery (vv.3-4,6,9)? 3. In unveiling this mystery, what part is played by grace? By the Church? By Paul? 4. How would you explain the way one can know God (2:18; 3:12)?

REFLECT: 1. Paul's intense desire was to make Christ known. How does this relate to what drives you in life? 2. What kinds of people would feel awkward in your church? What can you do to break down those barriers? Why is it important to do so? 3. Where does the unifying gospel (v.6) challenge you: e.g., issues of racism? Sexism? Missions? Concern for the poor and elderly?

OPEN: At age 12, what did you want to be when you grew up?

DIG: 1. Considering 2:19-22, why does Paul pray as he does? What are his underlying views of God? 2. What is the nature of the spiritual power, love, and fullness for which he prays? 3. How would you express this prayer in your own words?

REFLECT: How do you expect to change as you become more confident of Christ's love?

OPEN: Who among your peers do you regard as "most mature"? As "most infantile"? Why do you think so? On the road to maturity, which of the two are you like?

DIG: 1. Reading between the lines, what problems do you think Paul was concerned about in Ephesus? 2. What qualities ought to characterize "a life worthy of the calling"? What happens when believers live out these qualities? How does each quality promote

Paul the Preacher to the Gentiles

3 For this reason I, Paul, the prisoner of Christ Jesus for the sake of you Gentiles—

[2]Surely you have heard about the administration of God's grace that was given to me for you, [3]that is, the mystery made known to me by revelation, as I have already written briefly. [4]In reading this, then, you will be able to understand my insight into the mystery of Christ, [5]which was not made known to men in other generations as it has now been revealed by the Spirit to God's holy apostles and prophets. [6]This mystery is that through the gospel the Gentiles are heirs together with Israel, members together of one body, and sharers together in the promise in Christ Jesus.

[7]I became a servant of this gospel by the gift of God's grace given me through the working of his power. [8]Although I am less than the least of all God's people, this grace was given me: to preach to the Gentiles the unsearchable riches of Christ, [9]and to make plain to everyone the administration of this mystery, which for ages past was kept hidden in God, who created all things. [10]His intent was that now, through the church, the manifold wisdom of God should be made known to the rulers and authorities in the heavenly realms, [11]according to his eternal purpose which he accomplished in Christ Jesus our Lord. [12]In him and through faith in him we may approach God with freedom and confidence. [13]I ask you, therefore, not to be discouraged because of my sufferings for you, which are your glory.

A Prayer for the Ephesians

[14]For this reason I kneel before the Father, [15]from whom his whole family[h] in heaven and on earth derives its name. [16]I pray that out of his glorious riches he may strengthen you with power through his Spirit in your inner being, [17]so that Christ may dwell in your hearts through faith. And I pray that you, being rooted and established in love, [18]may have power, together with all the saints, to grasp how wide and long and high and deep is the love of Christ, [19]and to know this love that surpasses knowledge— that you may be filled to the measure of all the fullness of God.

[20]Now to him who is able to do immeasurably more than all we ask or imagine, according to his power that is at work within us, [21]to him be glory in the church and in Christ Jesus throughout all generations, for ever and ever! Amen.

Unity in the Body of Christ

4 As a prisoner for the Lord, then, I urge you to live a life worthy of the calling you have received. [2]Be completely humble and gentle; be patient, bearing with one another in love. [3]Make every effort to keep the unity of the Spirit through the bond of peace. [4]There is one body and one Spirit— just as you were called to one hope when you were called— [5]one Lord, one faith, one baptism; [6]one God and Father of all, who is over all and through all and in all.

h15 Or whom all fatherhood

[7]But to each one of us grace has been given as Christ apportioned it. [8]This is why it[i] says:

"When he ascended on high,
he led captives in his train
and gave gifts to men."[j]

[9](What does "he ascended" mean except that he also descended to the lower, earthly regions[k]? [10]He who descended is the very one who ascended higher than all the heavens, in order to fill the whole universe.) [11]It was he who gave some to be apostles, some to be prophets, some to be evangelists, and some to be pastors and teachers, [12]to prepare God's people for works of service, so that the body of Christ may be built up [13]until we all reach unity in the faith and in the knowledge of the Son of God and become mature, attaining to the whole measure of the fullness of Christ.

[14]Then we will no longer be infants, tossed back and forth by the waves, and blown here and there by every wind of teaching and by the cunning and craftiness of men in their deceitful scheming. [15]Instead, speaking the truth in love, we will in all things grow up into him who is the Head, that is, Christ. [16]From him the whole body, joined and held together by every supporting ligament, grows and builds itself up in love, as each part does its work.

Living as Children of Light

[17]So I tell you this, and insist on it in the Lord, that you must no longer live as the Gentiles do, in the futility of their thinking. [18]They are darkened in their understanding and separated from the life of God because of the ignorance that is in them due to the hardening of their hearts. [19]Having lost all sensitivity, they have given themselves over to sensuality so as to indulge in every kind of impurity, with a continual lust for more.

[20]You, however, did not come to know Christ that way. [21]Surely you heard of him and were taught in him in accordance with the truth that is in Jesus. [22]You were taught, with regard to your former way of life, to put off your old self, which is being corrupted by its deceitful desires; [23]to be made new in the attitude of your minds; [24]and to put on the new self, created to be like God in true righteousness and holiness.

[25]Therefore each of you must put off falsehood and speak truthfully to his neighbor, for we are all members of one body. [26]"In your anger do not sin"[l]: Do not let the sun go down while you are still angry, [27]and do not give the devil a foothold. [28]He who has been stealing must steal no longer, but must work, doing something useful with his own hands, that he may have something to share with those in need.

[29]Do not let any unwholesome talk come out of your mouths, but only what is helpful for building others up according to their needs, that it may benefit those who listen. [30]And do not grieve the Holy Spirit of God, with whom you were sealed for the day of redemption. [31]Get rid of all bitterness, rage and anger, brawl-

unity? How does viewing God as Father (not just as Creator or Judge) add to our unity? **3.** What is the purpose of the various gifts (vv.8-13)? **4.** What are the differences between the unity that already exists (vv.3-6) and that which is yet to come (vv.13-16)? **5.** What is the climactic point of this whole passage? How will this happen?

REFLECT: **1.** Of the five qualities listed in verse 2, which one needs to be developed most in your life? What relationship will profit from developing that quality now? **2.** What does it mean to "speak the truth in love", as opposed to love without truth or truth without love? **3.** From this passage, what is the problem with living the Christian life apart from the church? In what way do you need others? What strength can you give others? **4.** How can your group help you discover, develop, and use your gifts?

OPEN: **1.** At what age did Mom let you start choosing your own clothes to wear, or does she still know what looks best on you? **2.** What "New Year's Resolution" haven't you been able to keep?

DIG: **1.** According to verses 17-19, how do the mind, heart, and conscience influence the actions of non-believers? How are Christians to deal with these realities? **2.** What does "put on...put off" entail (vv.22-24)? When does this action take place? **3.** Is it possible to change conduct without a transformation of the heart (v.18)? Likewise, can the heart be changed without a resulting change of conduct? Why is that? **4.** According to Paul, what specific actions distinguish the Christian lifestyle from the pagan lifestyle (4:25-5:4)? **5.** In 4:1, Paul urges us to model our lives in accordance with our high calling as God's people. In 5:1, what is the model he holds up for us? How about in 5:8? In 5:15? What incentives does he give in 5:2-21 to live according to these models? **6.** What is the difference between "foolish talk or course joking" (5:4) and a good belly-laugh story or clean joke? Between "the fruitless deeds of darkness" (5:11)

---

[i]8 Or *God*   [j]8 Psalm 68:18   [k]9 Or *the depths of the earth*   [l]26 Psalm 4:4

and good clean fun? **7.** What contrasts does he draw between the old and new life in 5:15-21? What does it mean, practically, to "always give thanks...for everything" (v.20)? **8.** In sum, what sights, sounds, feelings, attitudes, and actions define one who lives out this new life?

REFLECT: 1. What is one way you have seen the contrast of the "old" and the "new" in your life? What piece of "old life" clothing seems to be skin-tight and hard to remove now? **2.** What are the positive and/or negative motivations which prompt you to live a Christian life? Where do you feel you are making progress in your Christian life at the moment? **3.** Of the different pictures of what it means to live as a Christian, which means the most to you, and why: (a) Putting off? (b) Putting on? (c) Imitating God as his "dearly beloved children" (5:1)? (d) Being light instead of darkness? **4.** Compare Paul's view of a Spirit-filled life with your own life. In comparison, how full have you been with the Spirit this week? What do you want to work on, so that he may fill you more?

OPEN: Which of these TV families reflects the way everyone gets along in your family: The Bradys? Cleavers? Nelsons? Waltons? Keatons? Cosbys? Kate & Allie?

DIG: 1. What is unusual about the way Paul applies the general principle of verse 21 specifically to wives (vv.23-24)? **2.** How and why does he address husbands the way he does (vv.25-33)? Christ's love led him to *die* for us: what would it mean for a husband to *live* with his wife with this type of love? **3.** In your own words, how would you express the goal of Christian marriage (v.31)? **4.** What qualities would characterize a home where the children and parents applied 6:1-4 consistently? What four reasons are

ing and slander, along with every form of malice. [32]Be kind and compassionate to one another, forgiving each other, just as in Christ God forgave you.

5 Be imitators of God, therefore, as dearly loved children [2]and live a life of love, just as Christ loved us and gave himself up for us as a fragrant offering and sacrifice to God.

[3]But among you there must not be even a hint of sexual immorality, or of any kind of impurity, or of greed, because these are improper for God's holy people. [4]Nor should there be obscenity, foolish talk or coarse joking, which are out of place, but rather thanksgiving. [5]For of this you can be sure: No immoral, impure or greedy person—such a man is an idolater—has any inheritance in the kingdom of Christ and of God. [m][6]Let no one deceive you with empty words, for because of such things God's wrath comes on those who are disobedient. [7]Therefore do not be partners with them.

[8]For you were once darkness, but now you are light in the Lord. Live as children of light [9](for the fruit of the light consists in all goodness, righteousness and truth) [10]and find out what pleases the Lord. [11]Have nothing to do with the fruitless deeds of darkness, but rather expose them. [12]For it is shameful even to mention what the disobedient do in secret. [13]But everything exposed by the light becomes visible, [14]for it is light that makes everything visible. This is why it is said:

> "Wake up, O sleeper,
>   rise from the dead,
>   and Christ will shine on you."

[15]Be very careful, then, how you live—not as unwise but as wise, [16]making the most of every opportunity, because the days are evil. [17]Therefore do not be foolish, but understand what the Lord's will is. [18]Do not get drunk on wine, which leads to debauchery. Instead, be filled with the Spirit. [19]Speak to one another with psalms, hymns and spiritual songs. Sing and make music in your heart to the Lord, [20]always giving thanks to God the Father for everything, in the name of our Lord Jesus Christ.

[21]Submit to one another out of reverence for Christ.

Wives and Husbands

[22]Wives, submit to your husbands as to the Lord. [23]For the husband is the head of the wife as Christ is the head of the church, his body, of which he is the Savior. [24]Now as the church submits to Christ, so also wives should submit to their husbands in everything.

[25]Husbands, love your wives, just as Christ loved the church and gave himself up for her [26]to make her holy, cleansing[n] her by the washing with water through the word, [27]and to present her to himself as a radiant church, without stain or wrinkle or any other blemish, but holy and blameless. [28]In this same way, husbands ought to love their wives as their own bodies. He who loves his wife loves himself. [29]After all, no one ever hated his

[m]5 Or *kingdom of the Christ and God*   [n]26 Or *having cleansed*

own body, but he feeds and cares for it, just as Christ does the church— ³⁰for we are members of his body. ³¹"For this reason a man will leave his father and mother and be united to his wife, and the two will become one flesh."ᵒ ³²This is a profound mystery—but I am talking about Christ and the church. ³³However, each one of you also must love his wife as he loves himself, and the wife must respect her husband.

Children and Parents

6 Children, obey your parents in the Lord, for this is right. ²"Honor your father and mother"—which is the first commandment with a promise— ³"that it may go well with you and that you may enjoy long life on the earth."ᵖ

⁴Fathers, do not exasperate your children; instead, bring them up in the training and instruction of the Lord.

Slaves and Masters

⁵Slaves, obey your earthly masters with respect and fear, and with sincerity of heart, just as you would obey Christ. ⁶Obey them not only to win their favor when their eye is on you, but like slaves of Christ, doing the will of God from your heart. ⁷Serve wholeheartedly, as if you were serving the Lord, not men, ⁸because you know that the Lord will reward everyone for whatever good he does, whether he is slave or free.

⁹And masters, treat your slaves in the same way. Do not threaten them, since you know that he who is both their Master and yours is in heaven, and there is no favoritism with him.

The Armor of God

¹⁰Finally, be strong in the Lord and in his mighty power. ¹¹Put on the full armor of God so that you can take your stand against the devil's schemes. ¹²For our struggle is not against flesh and blood, but against the rulers, against the authorities, against the powers of this dark world and against the spiritual forces of evil in the heavenly realms. ¹³Therefore put on the full armor of God, so that when the day of evil comes, you may be able to stand your ground, and after you have done everything, to stand. ¹⁴Stand firm then, with the belt of truth buckled around your waist, with the breastplate of righteousness in place, ¹⁵and with your feet fitted with the readiness that comes from the gospel of peace. ¹⁶In addition to all this, take up the shield of faith, with which you can extinguish all the flaming arrows of the evil one. ¹⁷Take the helmet of salvation and the sword of the Spirit, which is the word of God. ¹⁸And pray in the Spirit on all occasions with all kinds of prayers and requests. With this in mind, be alert and always keep on praying for all the saints.

¹⁹Pray also for me, that whenever I open my mouth, words may be given me so that I will fearlessly make known the mystery of the gospel, ²⁰for which I am an ambassador in chains. Pray that I may declare it fearlessly, as I should.

ᵒ31 Gen. 2:24   ᵖ3 Deut. 5:16

given for children to obey their parents? **5.** How is the slave/master relationship affected by Christ? **6.** In sum, how does 5:21 apply to all the relationships here? How could Paul's instructions be misused apart from that context?

REFLECT: 1. What counter-cultural principles from Paul can you work on to help you be a better spouse (or potential spouse)? **2.** What does it mean for you to honor your parents? How can this help improve relationships with them? **3.** Applying Paul's teaching in 6:5-9 to your work environment, what will you do differently this week?

OPEN: For yourself (or for your kids), what were some of your favorite Halloween or dress-up costumes? Why those?

DIG: 1. From 1:19-21, where is Christ now? How powerful is he? How does this instill hope in Christians as we encounter the evil forces described here? **2.** From what you have read so far (2:1-3, 14; 4:14,17-19,26-27; 5:3-18), in what ways can these forces operate in our lives? In light of the reasons for Paul's imprisonment, how can these forces also infect social, political, and religious structures? **3.** With what attitudes should we face these forces? How does prayer fit into this battle? **4.** What does Paul mean by each of the six pieces of armor (vv.14-17)? What is the purpose of each? Which are defensive? Which are offensive? **5.** How do the words *peace*, *love*, *faith*, and *grace* (vv. 23-24) sum up Paul's teaching in this letter?

REFLECT: 1. As you consider your armor, what parts are in good shape? What is moldy and rusty? What do you need to do to get ready for battle? What is at stake if you don't? **2.** Paul was on the front lines of the battle (v.20). What evidence do you see of the battle in your life? Your church? Your community? Your nation? The world? What would it mean for you "to stand" in these particular battlefields? **3.** What can you learn from Paul's prayers (1:16-18; 3:14-19; 6:19-20) about your prayers for others in your small group? For missionaries? **4.** Of the four key words in verses 23-24 (peace, love, faith, and grace), which means the most to you now? Why?

Final Greetings

[21]Tychicus, the dear brother and faithful servant in the Lord, will tell you everything, so that you also may know how I am and what I am doing. [22]I am sending him to you for this very purpose, that you may know how we are, and that he may encourage you.

[23]Peace to the brothers, and love with faith from God the Father and the Lord Jesus Christ. [24]Grace to all who love our Lord Jesus Christ with an undying love.

PHILIPPIANS

INTRODUCTION

Audience

Setting

Located in the Roman province of Macedonia (a territory corresponding to northern Greece and parts of several other Balkan countries), Philippi was a historic city. Founded by Alexander the Great's father in 360 B.C. so he could mine its gold to pay for his army, Philippi eventually came to prominence as the result of two battles. In 42 B.C. on the plains of Philippi, the Caesarean forces of Anthony and Octavian defeated the Republican forces led by the assassins of Julius Caesar — Brutus and Cassius. Then in 31 B.C., Octavian (who later became the Emperor Caesar Augustus) became sole ruler by defeating his former colleague Anthony, who was in alliance with the Egyptian Queen Cleopatra. Veterans from these conflicts were given land in Philippi, and Octavian declared it to be a Roman colony with all the rights, tax breaks, and privileges thereof. To be in Philippi was to be in a miniature Rome.

Paul and the Philippian Church

Philippi was certainly one of Paul's favorite churches. There was such a warm feeling of mutual care and concern that Paul called the Philippians his "joy and crown" (4:1).

Paul had founded the church around A.D. 50 as the result of a night vision in which a "man of Macedonia" beckoned him to "come over . . . and help us" (Acts 16:9). He sailed immediately from Asia, thus launching Christianity in Europe. Paul's stay at Philippi was marked by joy and trial. On the positive side was the conversion of Lydia, the dealer in purple cloth, as well as the conversion of the jailer and his family after an earthquake unexpectedly released Paul from prison. On the negative side, in Philippi the first recorded conflict between Christians and Gentiles occurred, and Paul was thrown in jail for casting out a demon from a fortuneteller's slave girl.

This letter to the largely Gentile church was written some twelve or thirteen years later, probably around A.D. 63 or 64.

Theme

Paul is in prison (probably in Rome) when Epaphroditus, an old friend from Philippi, arrives bearing yet another gift from the church. Unfortunately, Epaphroditus falls gravely ill. His home church hears about it and is grieved. In due course he recovers, and Paul is anxious for him to return home and relieve their fears. This affords Paul an opportunity to send along a letter.

So he writes these old friends in the warmest and most personal of his epistles. There is no need for him to assert his apostolity, as he usually does when beginning a letter. There is no formality in his outline either. Paul puts down ideas as they occur to him, often with strong declarations of emotion.

Basically, Philippians is a letter of thanksgiving (1:3-11 and 4:14-20) and a report on his imprisonment (1:12-26; 2:19-30; 4:10-13). Still, Paul has two concerns: a tendency in the church toward disunity (1:27-2:18 and 4:2-3) and potential dangers from Judaizers (3:2-16) and false teachers (3:17-21).

Philippians

OPEN: When you care for someone, are you more likely to send a funny card or a touching one?

DIG: 1. Paul often greets with "grace and peace." What does that say about the gospel? What in your life illustrates what "grace" or "peace" feels like (e.g., a baby's smile, a friend's call, the sun poking out after days of rain)? **2.** What are Paul's feelings for this church? What does that show about his leadership style? **3.** What qualities are important in a fellowship (vv.5-6,9-11)? Why?

REFLECT: 1. Would "Grace and Peace" or "Guilt and Pressure" better describe your experience with Christ now? Why? **2.** Take five minutes to put Paul's prayer into your own words, applying it to your group, to be read as prayers.

OPEN: 1. When you are feeling down, what helps you get "on top of it" again? **2.** What kind of "laugher" are you: The quiet-smile type? One who guffaws? A twitterer? A nasal type?

DIG: 1. How does Paul decide if an event (like his jailing) is good or bad? How would his example encourage others? **2.** What possible motives do these various people have for preaching (vv.15-17)? **3.** What is Paul's main concern in all this (v.21)? What does he mean by that? **4.** What conduct is worthy of the gospel (v.27)? Why is this so important to Paul? Why should it matter whether Paul comes to them? **5.** Why is suffering a benefit granted by God? How does this relate to Paul's joy in difficult circumstances? What does this tell you about the nature of the Christian life?

REFLECT: 1. "For me to live is _____." Given your priorities and schedule this week, how would you honestly fill in the blank? What things would change if you filled it in with "Christ"? How would this new reason for living affect your daily life, or any hardship you're facing? **2.** Since churches often

1 Paul and Timothy, servants of Christ Jesus,

To all the saints in Christ Jesus at Philippi, together with the overseers[a] and deacons:

[2]Grace and peace to you from God our Father and the Lord Jesus Christ.

Thanksgiving and Prayer

[3]I thank my God every time I remember you. [4]In all my prayers for all of you, I always pray with joy [5]because of your partnership in the gospel from the first day until now, [6]being confident of this, that he who began a good work in you will carry it on to completion until the day of Christ Jesus.

[7]It is right for me to feel this way about all of you, since I have you in my heart; for whether I am in chains or defending and confirming the gospel, all of you share in God's grace with me. [8]God can testify how I long for all of you with the affection of Christ Jesus.

[9]And this is my prayer: that your love may abound more and more in knowledge and depth of insight, [10]so that you may be able to discern what is best and may be pure and blameless until the day of Christ, [11]filled with the fruit of righteousness that comes through Jesus Christ—to the glory and praise of God.

Paul's Chains Advance the Gospel

[12]Now I want you to know, brothers, that what has happened to me has really served to advance the gospel. [13]As a result, it has become clear throughout the whole palace guard[b] and to everyone else that I am in chains for Christ. [14]Because of my chains, most of the brothers in the Lord have been encouraged to speak the word of God more courageously and fearlessly.

[15]It is true that some preach Christ out of envy and rivalry, but others out of good will. [16]The latter do so in love, knowing that I am put here for the defense of the gospel. [17]The former preach Christ out of selfish ambition, not sincerely, supposing that they can stir up trouble for me while I am in chains.[c] [18]But what does it matter? The important thing is that in every way, whether from false motives or true, Christ is preached. And because of this I rejoice.

Yes, and I will continue to rejoice, [19]for I know that through your prayers and the help given by the Spirit of Jesus Christ, what has happened to me will turn out for my deliverance.[d] [20]I eagerly expect and hope that I will in no way be ashamed, but will have sufficient courage so that now as always Christ will be exalted in my body, whether by life or by death. [21]For to me, to live is Christ and to die is gain. [22]If I am to go on living in the body, this will mean fruitful labor for me. Yet what shall I choose? I do not know! [23]I am torn between the two: I desire to depart and be with Christ, which is better by far; [24]but it is

---

[a]1 Traditionally *bishops*   [b]13 Or *whole palace*   [c]16,17 Some late manuscripts have verses 16 and 17 in reverse order.   [d]19 Or *salvation*

376

more necessary for you that I remain in the body. ²⁵Convinced of this, I know that I will remain, and I will continue with all of you for your progress and joy in the faith, ²⁶so that through my being with you again your joy in Christ Jesus will overflow on account of me.

²⁷Whatever happens, conduct yourselves in a manner worthy of the gospel of Christ. Then, whether I come and see you or only hear about you in my absence, I will know that you stand firm in one spirit, contending as one man for the faith of the gospel ²⁸without being frightened in any way by those who oppose you. This is a sign to them that they will be destroyed, but that you will be saved—and that by God. ²⁹For it has been granted to you on behalf of Christ not only to believe on him, but also to suffer for him, ³⁰since you are going through the same struggle you saw I had, and now hear that I still have.

Imitating Christ's Humility

2 If you have any encouragement from being united with Christ, if any comfort from his love, if any fellowship with the Spirit, if any tenderness and compassion, ²then make my joy complete by being like-minded, having the same love, being one in spirit and purpose. ³Do nothing out of selfish ambition or vain conceit, but in humility consider others better than yourselves. ⁴Each of you should look not only to your own interests, but also to the interests of others.

⁵Your attitude should be the same as that of Christ Jesus:

⁶Who, being in very nature*ᵉ* God,
did not consider equality with God something to be grasped,
⁷but made himself nothing,
taking the very nature*ᶠ* of a servant,
being made in human likeness.
⁸And being found in appearance as a man,
he humbled himself
and became obedient to death—
even death on a cross!
⁹Therefore God exalted him to the highest place
and gave him the name that is above every name,
¹⁰that at the name of Jesus every knee should bow,
in heaven and on earth and under the earth,
¹¹and every tongue confess that Jesus Christ is Lord,
to the glory of God the Father.

Shining as Stars

¹²Therefore, my dear friends, as you have always obeyed—not only in my presence, but now much more in my absence—continue to work out your salvation with fear and trembling, ¹³for it is God who works in you to will and to act according to his good purpose.

¹⁴Do everything without complaining or arguing, ¹⁵so that you may become blameless and pure, children of God without fault in a crooked and depraved generation, in which you shine

ᵉ6 Or in the form of   ᶠ7 Or the form

OPEN: 1. Who in your family hogs the bathroom or tracks the most mud? Who cleans it up? **2.** What verse or slogan (either sung or posted) keeps your spirits up?

DIG: 1. Reading between the lines, what was wrong with the church in Philippi? **2.** What are four motives for living in unity? How is this unity related to humility? **3.** How does Jesus exemplify this humility? (What stories from the Gospels come to mind?) **4.** What else stands out about Jesus from this early church hymn (vv.6-11; Isa 45:23)?

REFLECT: 1. How would things change if verses 3-8 marked your family life? Church life? Work life? **2.** How does *humility* (using your strength for the good of others) differ from *being a doormat*?

OPEN: Who are you more like in the morning: Big Bird or Oscar the Grouch? Odie or Garfield?

DIG: 1. In light of 2:1-4, what does it mean to "work out *your* (plural) salvation"? What part is up to God? Up to you? **2.** What makes God's people "shine like stars"?

REFLECT: As a star, is your fellowship a "twinkle, twinkle"? A nova? Burned out? Why? How can you help it burn brightly?

divide along denominational, cultural, theological, and social lines, what would it mean to apply verse 27 in your community in concrete ways? What would have to change in you to make such unity possible?

like stars in the universe [16]as you hold out[g] the word of life—in order that I may boast on the day of Christ that I did not run or labor for nothing. [17]But even if I am being poured out like a drink offering on the sacrifice and service coming from your faith, I am glad and rejoice with all of you. [18]So you too should be glad and rejoice with me.

Timothy and Epaphroditus

[19]I hope in the Lord Jesus to send Timothy to you soon, that I also may be cheered when I receive news about you. [20]I have no one else like him, who takes a genuine interest in your welfare. [21]For everyone looks out for his own interests, not those of Jesus Christ. [22]But you know that Timothy has proved himself, because as a son with his father he has served with me in the work of the gospel. [23]I hope, therefore, to send him as soon as I see how things go with me. [24]And I am confident in the Lord that I myself will come soon.

[25]But I think it is necessary to send back to you Epaphroditus, my brother, fellow worker and fellow soldier, who is also your messenger, whom you sent to take care of my needs. [26]For he longs for all of you and is distressed because you heard he was ill. [27]Indeed he was ill, and almost died. But God had mercy on him, and not on him only but also on me, to spare me sorrow upon sorrow. [28]Therefore I am all the more eager to send him, so that when you see him again you may be glad and I may have less anxiety. [29]Welcome him in the Lord with great joy, and honor men like him, [30]because he almost died for the work of Christ, risking his life to make up for the help you could not give me.

No Confidence in the Flesh

3 Finally, my brothers, rejoice in the Lord! It is no trouble for me to write the same things to you again, and it is a safeguard for you.

[2]Watch out for those dogs, those men who do evil, those mutilators of the flesh. [3]For it is we who are the circumcision, we who worship by the Spirit of God, who glory in Christ Jesus, and who put no confidence in the flesh— [4]though I myself have reasons for such confidence.

If anyone else thinks he has reasons to put confidence in the flesh, I have more: [5]circumcised on the eighth day, of the people of Israel, of the tribe of Benjamin, a Hebrew of Hebrews; in regard to the law, a Pharisee; [6]as for zeal, persecuting the church; as for legalistic righteousness, faultless.

[7]But whatever was to my profit I now consider loss for the sake of Christ. [8]What is more, I consider everything a loss compared to the surpassing greatness of knowing Christ Jesus my Lord, for whose sake I have lost all things. I consider them rubbish, that I may gain Christ [9]and be found in him, not having a righteousness of my own that comes from the law, but that which is through faith in Christ—the righteousness that comes from God and is by faith. [10]I want to know Christ and the power

---

OPEN: 1. If you had to turn over your business affairs or life's belongings to someone outside the family, who would you choose? **2.** Would you like to take over Dad's or Mom's business? Why (not)?

DIG: 1. If you had to give a character reference for Timothy or Epaphroditus, what would you say? How do they illustrate 2:1-4? **2.** Which of the Philippians' problems (1:17; 2:3; 3:2 and 4:3) would they be best suited to deal with?

REFLECT: 1. If these two came to your church to solve problems, how would you deploy them? **2.** Who are the models of humility and service you can look up to today, as Paul looks to Timothy and Epaphroditus? How do they challenge you to grow?

OPEN: If you had to brag about what you can do better than others, what would it be?

DIG: 1. What accounts for Paul's change: (a) In *tone* from verse 1 to 2? (b) In *status*, from basing his confidence before God in performance and privilege to Christ's grace (vv.4-6)? **2.** If this problem with the circumcision party had gone unchallenged, how would have this hurt the gospel? **3.** What were the costs to Paul and to Christ to recalculate Paul's "net worth statement"? Who profited from the new deal? Who lost?

REFLECT: 1. How much merit would you assign to each "confidence in the flesh": Good looks? Good works? Reputation? Religious traditions? **2.** From 3:1-11, how can a person *know* he/she is "found in Christ"?

---

g16 Or hold on to

of his resurrection and the fellowship of sharing in his sufferings, becoming like him in his death, [11]and so, somehow, to attain to the resurrection from the dead.

Pressing on Toward the Goal

[12]Not that I have already obtained all this, or have already been made perfect, but I press on to take hold of that for which Christ Jesus took hold of me. [13]Brothers, I do not consider myself yet to have taken hold of it. But one thing I do: Forgetting what is behind and straining toward what is ahead, [14]I press on toward the goal to win the prize for which God has called me heavenward in Christ Jesus.

[15]All of us who are mature should take such a view of things. And if on some point you think differently, that too God will make clear to you. [16]Only let us live up to what we have already attained.

[17]Join with others in following my example, brothers, and take note of those who live according to the pattern we gave you. [18]For, as I have often told you before and now say again even with tears, many live as enemies of the cross of Christ. [19]Their destiny is destruction, their god is their stomach, and their glory is in their shame. Their mind is on earthly things. [20]But our citizenship is in heaven. And we eagerly await a Savior from there, the Lord Jesus Christ, [21]who, by the power that enables him to bring everything under his control, will transform our lowly bodies so that they will be like his glorious body.

4 Therefore, my brothers, you whom I love and long for, my joy and crown, that is how you should stand firm in the Lord, dear friends!

Exhortations

[2]I plead with Euodia and I plead with Syntyche to agree with each other in the Lord. [3]Yes, and I ask you, loyal yokefellow,[h] help these women who have contended at my side in the cause of the gospel, along with Clement and the rest of my fellow workers, whose names are in the book of life.

[4]Rejoice in the Lord always. I will say it again: Rejoice! [5]Let your gentleness be evident to all. The Lord is near. [6]Do not be anxious about anything, but in everything, by prayer and petition, with thanksgiving, present your requests to God. [7]And the peace of God, which transcends all understanding, will guard your hearts and your minds in Christ Jesus.

[8]Finally, brothers, whatever is true, whatever is noble, whatever is right, whatever is pure, whatever is lovely, whatever is admirable—if anything is excellent or praiseworthy—think about such things. [9]Whatever you have learned or received or heard from me, or seen in me—put it into practice. And the God of peace will be with you.

OPEN: In your dream of the ideal lifestyle, are you more like the *pioneer* (always pushing on) or the *settler* (fixin' to settle down)?

DIG: 1. Using the imagery of a track race, where does Paul picture himself in his spiritual life? What prize is he after? How is he going to reach his goal? **2.** If the Philippians imitated this attitude, how would that contribute to their unity? **3.** Whereas Jewish legalism was one source of opposition to Christ (vv.2-3), what kind of opposition is in view here (vv.18-19)? In contrast, what is to characterize the "citizens of heaven"?

REFLECT: 1. Comparing your spiritual life to a race, are you sitting it out due to lack of practice, an injury, or no warm-up? Are you at the starting blocks? Going full-tilt? Ready to give up? Why? What "hurdles" seem especially high to jump? **2.** How do you see the opposition of verses 18-19 at work today? How would you "stand firm" against them?

OPEN: Who makes peace in your family? How does he or she do it?

DIG: 1. What attitudes of these women harm the church? How can others help? **2.** What would someone marked by verses 4-6 look like? How do these qualities relate to Paul's peace objectives (vv.2-3,7,9)? **3.** What comes to mind in verse 8 for Paul? For you?

REFLECT: On a scale of 1 ("I'm going nuts!") to 10 ("I could lead a stress management seminar"), what is your anxiety level now? Why? What in this passage could help relieve it?

Thanks for Their Gifts

[10]I rejoice greatly in the Lord that at last you have renewed your concern for me. Indeed, you have been concerned, but you had no opportunity to show it. [11]I am not saying this because I am in need, for I have learned to be content whatever the circumstances. [12]I know what it is to be in need, and I know what it is to have plenty. I have learned the secret of being content in any and every situation, whether well fed or hungry, whether living in plenty or in want. [13]I can do everything through him who gives me strength.

[14]Yet it was good of you to share in my troubles. [15]Moreover, as you Philippians know, in the early days of your acquaintance with the gospel, when I set out from Macedonia, not one church shared with me in the matter of giving and receiving, except you only; [16]for even when I was in Thessalonica, you sent me aid again and again when I was in need. [17]Not that I am looking for a gift, but I am looking for what may be credited to your account. [18]I have received full payment and even more; I am amply supplied, now that I have received from Epaphroditus the gifts you sent. They are a fragrant offering, an acceptable sacrifice, pleasing to God. [19]And my God will meet all your needs according to his glorious riches in Christ Jesus.

[20]To our God and Father be glory for ever and ever. Amen.

Final Greetings

[21]Greet all the saints in Christ Jesus. The brothers who are with me send greetings. [22]All the saints send you greetings, especially those who belong to Caesar's household.

[23]The grace of the Lord Jesus Christ be with your spirit. Amen. [i]

---

[i]23 Some manuscripts do not have *Amen*.

COLOSSIANS

INTRODUCTION

Date

Tradition has it that Paul wrote Colossians, Ephesians, and Philemon during his imprisonment in Rome. This would mean these letters were written in the early sixties. However, other sites including Caesarea and Ephesus have been proposed as the place of Paul's confinement, so that neither date nor place is certain.

Audience

The City of Colossae

About a hundred miles west of Ephesus in the Lycus River valley stood the city of Colossae. In Paul's time, it was located in the Roman province of Asia (in what today is Turkey). It was one of three major population centers that had flourished in the region. Hierapolis and Laodicea (4:13) stood on opposite sides of the River Lycus, about six miles apart, while Colossae straddled the river some twelve miles upstream.

Since it was located on a major trade route from Ephesus, Colossae was considered a great city in the days of Xerxes, the Persian general (fifth century B.C.). A hundred years later, it had developed into a prosperous commerical center on account of its weaving industry. In fact, Colossian came to mean a certain color of dyed wool.

By the time of Paul, however, Colossae's prominence had diminished, though its sister cities, Laodicea and Hierapolis, were still prospering. Laodicea had become the seat of Roman government in the region, and Heirapolis was famous for its healing waters. But Colossae, when Paul wrote, was no longer even a city. In fact, as Lightfoot notes, Colossae was the least important town to which Paul ever wrote (*St. Paul's Epistles to the Colossians and Philemon,* p. 16).

The Church of Colossae

Paul did not found this church, at least not directly. It was probably established as a result of his ministry in Ephesus, since during Paul's two or three years in Ephesus the whole province of Asia was evangelized (Acts 19:10). Paul, however, never visited the churches at Colossae or Laodicea (2:1).

Epaphras probably founded the Colossian church. A native of Colossae (4:12), he worked hard on behalf of the church there (4:13). In fact, in 1:6-7 Paul says: "All over the world this gospel is producing fruit and growing . . . You learned it from Epaphras. . . ." Paul then commends Epaphras as his dear friend and a faithful minister of Christ. In fact, because of their friendship, Epaphras stayed with Paul during his imprisonment (Philem. 23) and so was unable to deliver the letter to the Colossians personally.

We meet the church at Colossae in another of Paul's letters. Paul wrote to one of its members, Philemon, asking that he accept back the runaway slave Onesimus converted through Paul's ministry.

The church at Colossae was probably mainly Gentile in composition. In 1:21 Paul speaks of the Colossian Christians as having once been "alienated from God" and "enemies in your minds"—phrases he uses elsewhere to describe those who are not part of God's covenant with Israel. Then in 1:27, he talks about making the mystery of God clear to the Gentiles; the reference is obviously to the Colossians. Finally in 3:5-7, Paul lists their past sins that are characteristic of Gentiles rather than Jews.

Religion in Colossae

A large number of Jews had lived in the region of Colossae, ever since the second century B.C. when Antiochus III brought two thousand Jews from Mesopotamia and Babylon to settle there. By Paul's time there may have been as many as fifty thousand Jews living in the region and practicing their religion. However, their synagogues had a "reputation for laxity and openness to speculation drifting in from the hellenistic world" (Ralph P. Martin, *Colossians and Philemon: New Century Bible Commentary*, p. 18)

But freethinking Judaism was not the major religious force in the Lycus valley. The Greek religions also flourished there. The cult of Cybele, for example, was highly popular. This was a fertility cult characterized by ecstasy and excessive enthusiasm, though it also had an ascetic side. Throughout the Roman Empire, the worship of Isis, Apollo, Dionysus, Asclepius, and other gods was widespread. In particular, the cult of Mithras, a mystery religion based on astrology and sacrifice, abounded in Colossae.

The church at Colossae, therefore, grew up in an atmosphere that blended a variety of religious traditions that may have been sources of heresy within the church. "In the Colossian church we appear to be in touch with a meeting-place where the freethinking Judaism of the dispersion and the speculative ideas of Greek mystery-religion are in close contact. Out of this interchange and fusion comes a syncretism, which is theologically novel (bringing Christ into a hierarchy and a system) and ethically conditioned (advocating a rigorous discipline and an ecstatic visionary reward). On both counts, in Paul's eyes, it is a deadly danger to the incipient church" (Martin, *Colossians and Philemon*, pp. 18-19).

The Colossian Heresy

Something was wrong in the church. Although Epaphras had good news to report to Paul (1:4-8; 2:5), Paul knew there was also a problem of some sort. Apparently the young church had been exposed to an attractive but heretical teaching which threatened its growth and existence. We do not know exactly what this heresy was. Nowhere does Paul define the problem. It is only by inferences from his arguments against the heresy that we begin to piece together its character.

Apparently it had something to do with astrology. Paul talks about the *stoicheia* or "basic principles of this world" (2:8, 20), understood by Greeks as "immortal lords of creation, existing in their own right, and as astrological tyrants who laid claim to control men's lives as the playthings of fate" (Martin). These star-deities were kept at bay by ascetic practices. In fact, a life of abstinence and self-punishment was thought to lead to salvation (Paul probably refers to such ascetic practices in 2:20-23).

In contrast, Paul insists that Jesus alone is Lord of the universe (1:15-18; 2:9-10) and that rules and regulations are not the path to salvation (2:20, 23).

Theme

As Paul does so often, he begins his letter with a strong doctrinal statement and concludes it by drawing out the behavioral implications of the doctrine. Here his doctrinal emphasis is on the cosmic nature of Jesus Christ. Jesus is the divine Lord of the universe who reconciles all things to himself through his death. Paul sets this strong statement of Christ's deity (1:13-2:7) over against the speculative, ritual-oriented, ascetic faith of the false teachers (2:8-23). Once the truth about Christ is stated, Paul turns to the implications of Christ's cosmic lordship and describes how those in union with him ought to live (3:1-4:6). As Barclay has written: "It remains a strange and wonderful fact that Paul wrote the letter which contains the highest reach of his thought to so unimportant a town as Colossae then was. But in doing so he checked a tendency, which, if it had been allowed to develop, would have wrecked Asian Christianity, and which might well have done irreparable damage to the faith of the whole Church" (*The Letters to the Philippians, Colossians, and Thessalonians*, p. 122).

The Epistle to the Colossians begins, like most of Paul's letters, with a lengthy introduction (1:1-12). In the first major division on doctrine, Paul establishes the preeminence of Christ (1:13-2:23). He follows this with an exhortation to the Colossians to live in union with Christ (3:1-4:6). He concludes with personal greetings (4:7-18).

Colossians

1 Paul, an apostle of Christ Jesus by the will of God, and Timothy our brother,

²To the holy and faithful*ᵃ* brothers in Christ at Colosse:

Grace and peace to you from God our Father.*ᵇ*

Thanksgiving and Prayer

³We always thank God, the Father of our Lord Jesus Christ, when we pray for you, ⁴because we have heard of your faith in Christ Jesus and of the love you have for all the saints— ⁵the faith and love that spring from the hope that is stored up for you in heaven and that you have already heard about in the word of truth, the gospel ⁶that has come to you. All over the world this gospel is bearing fruit and growing, just as it has been doing among you since the day you heard it and understood God's grace in all its truth. ⁷You learned it from Epaphras, our dear fellow servant, who is a faithful minister of Christ on our*ᶜ* behalf, ⁸and who also told us of your love in the Spirit.

⁹For this reason, since the day we heard about you, we have not stopped praying for you and asking God to fill you with the knowledge of his will through all spiritual wisdom and understanding. ¹⁰And we pray this in order that you may live a life worthy of the Lord and may please him in every way: bearing fruit in every good work, growing in the knowledge of God, ¹¹being strengthened with all power according to his glorious might so that you may have great endurance and patience, and joyfully ¹²giving thanks to the Father, who has qualified you*ᵈ* to share in the inheritance of the saints in the kingdom of light. ¹³For he has rescued us from the dominion of darkness and brought us into the kingdom of the Son he loves, ¹⁴in whom we have redemption,*ᵉ* the forgiveness of sins.

The Supremacy of Christ

¹⁵He is the image of the invisible God, the firstborn over all creation. ¹⁶For by him all things were created: things in heaven and on earth, visible and invisible, whether thrones or powers or rulers or authorities; all things were created by him and for him. ¹⁷He is before all things, and in him all things hold together. ¹⁸And he is the head of the body, the church; he is the beginning and the firstborn from among the dead, so that in everything he might have the supremacy. ¹⁹For God was pleased to have all his fullness dwell in him, ²⁰and through him to reconcile to himself all things, whether things on earth or things in heaven, by making peace through his blood, shed on the cross.

OPEN: What attracts you to certain strangers? Concerning the members of your study group, what have you heard that prepares you to like them?

DIG: 1. Paul hasn't met these believers (2:1), yet he is attracted to them. Why? What qualities of this church would attract you the most? **2.** If faith, hope, and love are the fruit of the gospel (vv.5-6), then what does this fruit look like? Feel like? **3.** What does it mean to tell the whole truth about God's grace (v.6)? Conversely, how does one betray grace? What truth about grace do you see in verses 12-14? **4.** How does what Paul prays for (vv.9-12) compare with what he thanks God for?

REFLECT: 1. How does your intercessory prayer compare with Paul's: (a) In intensity? (b) In thankfulness? (c) In clarity? (d) In faithfulness? **2.** How is the fruit of faith, love, and hope growing in your life: Developing well? Suffering from drought? Destroyed by the last storm? Budding? How will you help this "crop" develop?

OPEN: As a kid, what "superhuman" character (on TV or in real life) did you look up to? Why?

DIG: 1. The "firstborn" has the rights of an heir. What rights does Jesus have (vv.15-18)? What is his relationship to "all things"? Why stress this? **2.** What is his relationship to God and the church? What does "fullness" imply? **3.** How would you define "reconciliation" in ordinary terms? How was this achieved by Jesus? **4.** What *before* and *after* story do you see in verses 21-23?

ᵃ2 Or *believing*   *ᵇ2* Some manuscripts *Father and the Lord Jesus Christ*
ᶜ7 Some manuscripts *your*   *ᵈ12* Some manuscripts *us*   *ᵉ14* A few late manuscripts *redemption through his blood*

REFLECT: 1. From this passage, what would you say to someone who asked you, "How can I get to know God?" 2. At times, what people (or forces) seem to be more powerful that Jesus? Why? How do you respond to the fact that even these things are under Christ's authority?

OPEN: What memories do you have as a child hunting for "buried treasure" or Easter eggs?

DIG: 1. In what sense are Paul's sufferings a continuation of Jesus' sufferings? Why would this lead him to rejoice (see 2Co 12:9-10)? 2. In verses 3-4, Paul contrasts clever speech and true wisdom. What does this indicate about the false teaching infecting the church?

REFLECT: 1. Is Paul's stated purpose (1:28; 2:2) a reality in your life? Or are you still somewhere along the way? How far along the way are you? 2. What "fine sounding arguments" hinder you in following Jesus? How does Paul's argument speak to your concerns? 3. How has finding Christ been like uncovering buried treasure for you?

OPEN: 1. As a kid, what did you think a "religious" person was like? How did you feel about that type of person? 2. Do you consider your parents "permissive" or "strict"? Why? (Did they have a lot of rules for you, or just a few? Which one was the biggie?)

DIG: 1. What does "living in Christ" (v.6) entail (see 1:10-12)? What does the phrase "rooted and built up" imply to you? 2. What are "the basic principles of this world" (vv.8, 20) and the "powers and authorities" (vv.10,15)? How did Christ give the Colossians victory over these things? 3. What kind of circumcision is done by Christ (v.11)? How did he do it (vv.12-15)? 4. What experiences does the believer share with Christ (vv.9-13)? What implications are drawn from this (vv.13,16-17,20-23)? 5. What is the result of trying

[21]Once you were alienated from God and were enemies in your minds because of[f] your evil behavior. [22]But now he has reconciled you by Christ's physical body through death to present you holy in his sight, without blemish and free from accusation— [23]if you continue in your faith, established and firm, not moved from the hope held out in the gospel. This is the gospel that you heard and that has been proclaimed to every creature under heaven, and of which I, Paul, have become a servant.

Paul's Labor for the Church

[24]Now I rejoice in what was suffered for you, and I fill up in my flesh what is still lacking in regard to Christ's afflictions, for the sake of his body, which is the church. [25]I have become its servant by the commission God gave me to present to you the word of God in its fullness— [26]the mystery that has been kept hidden for ages and generations, but is now disclosed to the saints. [27]To them God has chosen to make known among the Gentiles the glorious riches of this mystery, which is Christ in you, the hope of glory.

[28]We proclaim him, admonishing and teaching everyone with all wisdom, so that we may present everyone perfect in Christ. [29]To this end I labor, struggling with all his energy, which so powerfully works in me.

2 I want you to know how much I am struggling for you and for those at Laodicea, and for all who have not met me personally. [2]My purpose is that they may be encouraged in heart and united in love, so that they may have the full riches of complete understanding, in order that they may know the mystery of God, namely, Christ, [3]in whom are hidden all the treasures of wisdom and knowledge. [4]I tell you this so that no one may deceive you by fine-sounding arguments. [5]For though I am absent from you in body, I am present with you in spirit and delight to see how orderly you are and how firm your faith in Christ is.

Freedom From Human Regulations Through Life With Christ

[6]So then, just as you received Christ Jesus as Lord, continue to live in him, [7]rooted and built up in him, strengthened in the faith as you were taught, and overflowing with thankfulness.

[8]See to it that no one takes you captive through hollow and deceptive philosophy, which depends on human tradition and the basic principles of this world rather than on Christ.

[9]For in Christ all the fullness of the Deity lives in bodily form, [10]and you have been given fullness in Christ, who is the head over every power and authority. [11]In him you were also circumcised, in the putting off of the sinful nature,[g] not with a circumcision done by the hands of men but with the circumcision done by Christ, [12]having been buried with him in baptism and raised with him through your faith in the power of God, who raised him from the dead.

---

f21 Or minds, as shown by   *g11 Or the flesh*

[13]When you were dead in your sins and in the uncircumcision of your sinful nature,[h] God made you[i] alive with Christ. He forgave us all our sins, [14]having canceled the written code, with its regulations, that was against us and that stood opposed to us; he took it away, nailing it to the cross. [15]And having disarmed the powers and authorities, he made a public spectacle of them, triumphing over them by the cross.[j]

[16]Therefore do not let anyone judge you by what you eat or drink, or with regard to a religious festival, a New Moon celebration or a Sabbath day. [17]These are a shadow of the things that were to come; the reality, however, is found in Christ. [18]Do not let anyone who delights in false humility and the worship of angels disqualify you for the prize. Such a person goes into great detail about what he has seen, and his unspiritual mind puffs him up with idle notions. [19]He has lost connection with the Head, from whom the whole body, supported and held together by its ligaments and sinews, grows as God causes it to grow.

[20]Since you died with Christ to the basic principles of this world, why, as though you still belonged to it, do you submit to its rules: [21]"Do not handle! Do not taste! Do not touch!"? [22]These are all destined to perish with use, because they are based on human commands and teachings. [23]Such regulations indeed have an appearance of wisdom, with their self-imposed worship, their false humility and their harsh treatment of the body, but they lack any value in restraining sensual indulgence.

Rules for Holy Living

3 Since, then, you have been raised with Christ, set your hearts on things above, where Christ is seated at the right hand of God. [2]Set your minds on things above, not on earthly things. [3]For you died, and your life is now hidden with Christ in God. [4]When Christ, who is your[k] life, appears, then you also will appear with him in glory.

[5]Put to death, therefore, whatever belongs to your earthly nature: sexual immorality, impurity, lust, evil desires and greed, which is idolatry. [6]Because of these, the wrath of God is coming.[l] [7]You used to walk in these ways, in the life you once lived. [8]But now you must rid yourselves of all such things as these: anger, rage, malice, slander, and filthy language from your lips. [9]Do not lie to each other, since you have taken off your old self with its practices [10]and have put on the new self, which is being renewed in knowledge in the image of its Creator. [11]Here there is no Greek or Jew, circumcised or uncircumcised, barbarian, Scythian, slave or free, but Christ is all, and is in all.

[12]Therefore, as God's chosen people, holy and dearly loved, clothe yourselves with compassion, kindness, humility, gentleness and patience. [13]Bear with each other and forgive whatever grievances you may have against one another. Forgive as the Lord forgave you. [14]And over all these virtues put on love, which binds them all together in perfect unity.

to base one's relationship with God on rule-keeping or on private visions, as the false teachers were doing?

REFLECT: 1. When have you felt like the "roots" of your faith in Christ were barely below the surface? What helps you to sink those roots deeper? **2.** What additions to the faith have you encountered from people who try to encourage you to be "more spiritual"? **3.** What convinced you that trying to live up to religious rules couldn't change you on the inside? In what area do you want to apply Paul's solution this week?

OPEN: 1. When you need to feel like a "new person," what outfit do you like to wear? **2.** In buying clothes, are you a name-brand buyer? A bargain hunter? Style conscious? Spouse conscious? Quality conscious? Tailored to fit your clients? (Or could you care less what others think?—Really?)

DIG: 1. What is the way to spiritual life (vv.1-4)? How does that contrast with the things that don't lead to growth (see 2:16-23)? How is setting your mind and heart on Christ related to what he *has already done* for us (v.1)? To what he *will do* for us (v.4)? **2.** What contrasts do you see between the "clothes" of the "earthly nature" (vv.5-11) and those of "God's chosen people" (vv.12-17)? **3.** What does all this "putting off" and "putting on" actually involve: A quick-change act? A disguise? A burial service? A shopping spree? **4.** What practical difference does this "new clothing" make in the relationship between wives and husbands? Between parents and children? Slaves and masters? **5.** What confirms that all these relationships are to be built around Christ?

---

[h]13 Or *your flesh*   [i]13 Some manuscripts *us*   [j]15 Or *them in him*   [k]4 Some manuscripts *our*   [l]6 Some early manuscripts *coming on those who are disobedient*

REFLECT: 1. We get all too used to "earthly nature" clothing. Which aspect of your old nature feels like a comfortable old T-shirt to you now? Why is it difficult to shed or remove? **2.** With what piece of Christ's wardrobe would you like to replace it? Which aspect of Christ's character do you need to clothe yourself with, in relation to your husband or wife? Your parents or children? Your employer or employees? **3.** How can your small group help with your clothing selection?

[15]Let the peace of Christ rule in your hearts, since as members of one body you were called to peace. And be thankful. [16]Let the word of Christ dwell in you richly as you teach and admonish one another with all wisdom, and as you sing psalms, hymns and spiritual songs with gratitude in your hearts to God. [17]And whatever you do, whether in word or deed, do it all in the name of the Lord Jesus, giving thanks to God the Father through him.

Rules for Christian Households

[18]Wives, submit to your husbands, as is fitting in the Lord. [19]Husbands, love your wives and do not be harsh with them. [20]Children, obey your parents in everything, for this pleases the Lord. [21]Fathers, do not embitter your children, or they will become discouraged. [22]Slaves, obey your earthly masters in everything; and do it, not only when their eye is on you and to win their favor, but with sincerity of heart and reverence for the Lord. [23]Whatever you do, work at it with all your heart, as working for the Lord, not for men, [24]since you know that you will receive an inheritance from the Lord as a reward. It is the Lord Christ you are serving. [25]Anyone who does wrong will be repaid for his wrong, and there is no favoritism.

4 Masters, provide your slaves with what is right and fair, because you know that you also have a Master in heaven.

Further Instructions

[2]Devote yourselves to prayer, being watchful and thankful. [3]And pray for us, too, that God may open a door for our message, so that we may proclaim the mystery of Christ, for which I am in chains. [4]Pray that I may proclaim it clearly, as I should. [5]Be wise in the way you act toward outsiders; make the most of every opportunity. [6]Let your conversation be always full of grace, seasoned with salt, so that you may know how to answer everyone.

Final Greetings

OPEN: In high school, who were two of your best friends? What was one quality about them that stands out to you?

DIG: 1. In advancing the gospel (vv.2-6), what role is played by prayer? By watchfulness? Thankfulness? Open doors? Closed doors or chains? Wise actions? Opportunism? Graceful talk? Salty talk? **2.** Why is thankfulness such a key ingredient in a Christian's life (see 2:6; 3:15,17)? **3.** What type of friend is Tychicus (vv.7-8; see Ac 20:4; Eph 6:21; 2Ti 4:12; Tit 3:12)? **4.** Likewise, what do you know about Onesimus (v.9; see Phm 10-16)? Which of Paul's rules, instructions, and greetings would be appropriate in preparing to receive this runaway slave from Colossae? How might the Colossians feel about him? **5.** Aristarchus (Ac 19:29; 27:2; Phm 24), Mark (Ac 12:12; 13:5,13; 15:36-40 and the author of Mark), Luke (the author of Luke-Acts), and Demas (Phm 24; 2Ti 4:10) were all with Paul at various times. Why would he include them in his greetings to the church? **6.** In light of the influence of the false teachers, why would Paul's commendation of Epaphras be especially important (1:7; 4:12-13)?

[7]Tychicus will tell you all the news about me. He is a dear brother, a faithful minister and fellow servant in the Lord. [8]I am sending him to you for the express purpose that you may know about our[m] circumstances and that he may encourage your hearts. [9]He is coming with Onesimus, our faithful and dear brother, who is one of you. They will tell you everything that is happening here.

[10]My fellow prisoner Aristarchus sends you his greetings, as does Mark, the cousin of Barnabas. (You have received instructions about him; if he comes to you, welcome him.) [11]Jesus, who is called Justus, also sends greetings. These are the only Jews among my fellow workers for the kingdom of God, and they

[m]8 Some manuscripts *that he may know about your*

have proved a comfort to me. [12]Epaphras, who is one of you and a servant of Christ Jesus, sends greetings. He is always wrestling in prayer for you, that you may stand firm in all the will of God, mature and fully assured. [13]I vouch for him that he is working hard for you and for those at Laodicea and Hierapolis. [14]Our dear friend Luke, the doctor, and Demas send greetings. [15]Give my greetings to the brothers at Laodicea, and to Nympha and the church in her house.

[16]After this letter has been read to you, see that it is also read in the church of the Laodiceans and that you in turn read the letter from Laodicea.

[17]Tell Archippus: "See to it that you complete the work you have received in the Lord."

[18]I, Paul, write this greeting in my own hand. Remember my chains. Grace be with you.

REFLECT: 1. What has helped you to grow the most in your prayer life? What obstacles to prayer do you feel now? **2.** From verses 5-6, what principles do you want to build into your life as you relate to non-believers? **3.** Seeing how Paul operated with a team of fellow Christians, what does that imply for you? For your small group? **4.** Of the qualities used to describe these people, which one would you like others to say about you in five years? How do 2:6-7 and 3:1-2 suggest you can get moving in that direction? **5.** How has your respect and love for Christ grown through this study? What from this book has helped you to develop a more thankful heart?

1 THESSALONIANS

INTRODUCTION

Date

First Thessalonians may well be the first document in what eventually became the New Testament. Many scholars believe that it is Paul's earliest letter, although a few say that Galatians has that honor. In any case, it is generally agreed that 1 Thessalonians was written about A.D. 50, during Paul's second missionary journey not long after the founding of the church in Thessalonica. Paul probably wrote from Corinth, where he went after he left Athens. Timothy had returned with news from Thessalonica, and this letter was Paul's response to his report.

Audience

The City of Thessalonica

Thessalonica was a great city. Originally named Therme, its famous harbor became the base for the Persian fleet during Xerxes' invasion of Europe. In 315 B.C., Cassander, the Macedonian king, renamed the city Thessalonica after his wife, the half-sister of Alexander the Great. In 146 B.C. after Rome had taken over Greece, Thessalonica was made the capital of the Roman province of Macedonia. In 42 B.C., Rome granted it the status of a free city, which gave Thessalonica a high degree of autonomy.

The key to its importance was Thessalonica's location astride the famous *Via Egnatia* – the great Roman military road across northern Greece, which stretched from the Adriatic Sea on the west to Constantinople in the east. Hence trade between Rome and Asia Minor and points farther east flowed through Thessalonica, making it very wealthy. This was a crucial site for a church if Christianity were to spread throughout the world.

The Church

When Paul crossed over into Macedonia in A.D. 50, a new era began for Christianity. Now the gospel had spread to Europe and only in a matter of time would it flow west, through Greece, into Italy, on to Spain and the limits of the Roman Empire. After the night vision that sent Paul across the Aegean Sea to Philippi, in due course he came to Thessalonica, which turned out to be a key stop in his pioneering work in Europe.

His stay in Thessalonica was brief and stormy. After he had preached in the synagogue for three Sabbaths, the Jews were so jealous of his success that they organized a mob by rounding up "some bad characters from the marketplace" (Acts 17:5). The mob then rushed around looking for Paul and Silas. Failing to find them, they dragged Jason (at whose home Paul was staying) and a few other Christians before the city officials. They claimed that these men were cohorts of Paul who was preaching that Jesus, not Caesar, was king. That night after Jason and the others were released on bail, Paul and Silas slipped away to Berea.

The Concerns

Could three weeks of ministry produce a viable church at Thessalonica? Apparently this question troubled Paul. After ministering in Berea, Paul had gone on to Athens. He attempted to return to Thessalonica, but his efforts were frustrated (2:17-18). In his place he sent Timothy to see how they were doing and to give them what help he could (2:17-3:5).

What Timothy found was twofold. Generally the news was good. The converts were standing fast in their faith despite persecution and Paul's hasty departure from the city. In fact, they were even doing evangelistic work on their own. On the other hand, there were (not unexpectedly) some problems. Some of the converts had not fully understood the ethical implications of the gospel. In particular, there was laxity in sexual matters (4:3-8). Some felt it unnecessary to work and had become a burden to the others (4:11-12; 5:14). There was also misunderstanding about the Second Coming. They knew Christ would return again and rescue them from the "coming wrath" (1:1-10; 5:9-10). But some worried about those Christians who died prior to the Lord's return (4:13-14). Quite possibly Paul and the others had departed from Thessalonica before their teaching on this subject was complete. So Paul assures them that the dead in Christ were at no disadvantage. In fact, the first event of the Second Coming would be the resurrection of the dead (4:16).

In his letter to them, Paul expresses his relief and joy at their good progress in the gospel. They have become, he says "a model to all the believers in Macedonia and Achaia" (1:7). Paul goes on to explain why he never returned to them. He ends his letter with further instruction about the life of holiness they ought to be leading and about the Second Coming.

The Converts

Who were these believers? Luke says (in Acts 17) that the church had its roots in the Jewish community. Some members of the synagogue, where Paul preached along with a large number of God-fearing Greeks — Gentiles who worshiped at the synagogue — and several prominent women, had become convinced that Jesus was the Messiah and so became Christians. These included Jason who opened his home to Paul and his companions, and Aristarchus who was later Paul's traveling companion and prison mate (Col. 4:10; Philem. 24; Acts 19:29; 20:4, 27:2).

In fact, throughout Paul's ministry in Macedonia, many prominent women were converted. Lydia, the businesswoman, was his first convert in Philippi (Acts 16:14). Many "prominent Greek women" were converted in Berea (Acts 17:12). Unlike most other women in the first century, the women in Macedonia had been noted for their competence and for the active role they played in society. As it turns out, they were crucial to the growth of the church in Europe.

The greater part of the church, however, seems to have been made up of converted pagans, as Paul's comment in 1:9 indicates: "You turned to God from idols."

1 Thessalonians

OPEN: What teams did you belong to (or aspire to) as a kid? Of which team were you most proud?

DIG: 1. What do you know about the Thessalonian church from Paul's experiences in Acts 17:1-9? **2.** What convinced Paul that the Thessalonians were indeed chosen by God? **3.** How did they first become imitators of, and then models for, the faith (vv.6-10)? What does this tell you about their growth in Christ? **4.** In an age without mass media, how do you suppose their faith became so legendary?

REFLECT: 1. What kind of "model" are you in matters of faith: Still on the drawing board? A work in progress? Secured in a private collection? On display at the National Museum? **2.** Which of the qualities in verse 3 do you most wish to see developed in your life now? How can the group help?

OPEN: What was one of your most memorable failures in junior or senior high school?

DIG: 1. What rumors about Paul have been spread by his opposition (vv.1-6)? Does Paul sound reassuring to you? Why or why not? What concerns might linger? **2.** From verses 1-11, what does *ethical* evangelism look like? What would its opposite look like? What do the images of being a mother (v.7) and father (v.11) add to this picture? **3.** What difficulties were the Thessalonians facing (vv.14-15)? How would Paul's example of perseverance in the face of persecution encourage them? **4.** How does Paul know that the wrath of God has come upon his opponents (v.16)?

REFLECT: 1. List all the characteristics of a faithful Christian worker given in this passage. Of these, which do you possess? Which do you want to develop? **2.** Who has been a positive influence on you for godly living? How

1 Paul, Silas[a] and Timothy,

To the church of the Thessalonians in God the Father and the Lord Jesus Christ:

Grace and peace to you. [b]

Thanksgiving for the Thessalonians' Faith

[2]We always thank God for all of you, mentioning you in our prayers. [3]We continually remember before our God and Father your work produced by faith, your labor prompted by love, and your endurance inspired by hope in our Lord Jesus Christ.

[4]For we know, brothers loved by God, that he has chosen you, [5]because our gospel came to you not simply with words, but also with power, with the Holy Spirit and with deep conviction. You know how we lived among you for your sake. [6]You became imitators of us and of the Lord; in spite of severe suffering, you welcomed the message with the joy given by the Holy Spirit. [7]And so you became a model to all the believers in Macedonia and Achaia. [8]The Lord's message rang out from you not only in Macedonia and Achaia—your faith in God has become known everywhere. Therefore we do not need to say anything about it, [9]for they themselves report what kind of reception you gave us. They tell how you turned to God from idols to serve the living and true God, [10]and to wait for his Son from heaven, whom he raised from the dead—Jesus, who rescues us from the coming wrath.

Paul's Ministry in Thessalonica

2 You know, brothers, that our visit to you was not a failure. [2]We had previously suffered and been insulted in Philippi, as you know, but with the help of our God we dared to tell you his gospel in spite of strong opposition. [3]For the appeal we make does not spring from error or impure motives, nor are we trying to trick you. [4]On the contrary, we speak as men approved by God to be entrusted with the gospel. We are not trying to please men but God, who tests our hearts. [5]You know we never used flattery, nor did we put on a mask to cover up greed—God is our witness. [6]We were not looking for praise from men, not from you or anyone else.

As apostles of Christ we could have been a burden to you, [7]but we were gentle among you, like a mother caring for her little children. [8]We loved you so much that we were delighted to share with you not only the gospel of God but our lives as well, because you had become so dear to us. [9]Surely you remember, brothers, our toil and hardship; we worked night and day in order not to be a burden to anyone while we preached the gospel of God to you.

---

[a]1 Greek *Silvanus*, a variant of *Silas*   [b]1 Some early manuscripts *you from God our Father and the Lord Jesus Christ*

[10]You are witnesses, and so is God, of how holy, righteous and blameless we were among you who believed. [11]For you know that we dealt with each of you as a father deals with his own children, [12]encouraging, comforting and urging you to live lives worthy of God, who calls you into his kingdom and glory.

[13]And we also thank God continually because, when you received the word of God, which you heard from us, you accepted it not as the word of men, but as it actually is, the word of God, which is at work in you who believe. [14]For you, brothers, became imitators of God's churches in Judea, which are in Christ Jesus: You suffered from your own countrymen the same things those churches suffered from the Jews, [15]who killed the Lord Jesus and the prophets and also drove us out. They displease God and are hostile to all men [16]in their effort to keep us from speaking to the Gentiles so that they may be saved. In this way they always heap up their sins to the limit. The wrath of God has come upon them at last.[c]

Paul's Longing to See the Thessalonians

[17]But, brothers, when we were torn away from you for a short time (in person, not in thought), out of our intense longing we made every effort to see you. [18]For we wanted to come to you—certainly I, Paul, did, again and again—but Satan stopped us. [19]For what is our hope, our joy, or the crown in which we will glory in the presence of our Lord Jesus when he comes? Is it not you? [20]Indeed, you are our glory and joy.

3 So when we could stand it no longer, we thought it best to be left by ourselves in Athens. [2]We sent Timothy, who is our brother and God's fellow worker[d] in spreading the gospel of Christ, to strengthen and encourage you in your faith, [3]so that no one would be unsettled by these trials. You know quite well that we were destined for them. [4]In fact, when we were with you, we kept telling you that we would be persecuted. And it turned out that way, as you well know. [5]For this reason, when I could stand it no longer, I sent to find out about your faith. I was afraid that in some way the tempter might have tempted you and our efforts might have been useless.

Timothy's Encouraging Report

[6]But Timothy has just now come to us from you and has brought good news about your faith and love. He has told us that you always have pleasant memories of us and that you long to see us, just as we also long to see you. [7]Therefore, brothers, in all our distress and persecution we were encouraged about you because of your faith. [8]For now we really live, since you are standing firm in the Lord. [9]How can we thank God enough for you in return for all the joy we have in the presence of our God because of you? [10]Night and day we pray most earnestly that we may see you again and supply what is lacking in your faith.

[11]Now may our God and Father himself and our Lord Jesus clear the way for us to come to you. [12]May the Lord make your

so? How can you be more like that person for someone else this week? **3.** What really turns you off about the way some people present the gospel? How are you attempting to avoid these mistakes, and yet still maintain a strong witness? **4.** What opposition to your faith are you facing? What encourages you to persevere?

OPEN: 1. As a kid, when and where did homesickness strike hard? What did you do about it? **2.** What room in your childhood home fills you with warm memories? What happened there?

DIG: 1. Why do you think Paul called the Thessalonian church his "hope," "joy," and "crown"? **2.** If Paul promised them trials and persecution when he was with them (v.4), why is he writing to them about it now? **3.** What in Timothy's report particularly encourages Paul? What does this tell you about Paul's desires and concerns for the Thessalonians? **4.** What guidelines can you find in Paul's desires, concerns, and prayers for those who disciple new Christians today?

REFLECT: 1. If someone were to tell you that God promises a trouble-free life to those who are true Christians, how would you respond? What are you struggling with most right now? **2.** In what specific ways have you been encouraged by someone else's faith? Have you told them about it? **3.** Which of Paul's prayer requests would you want someone to pray for you? Do likewise for someone else in your small group.

---

[c]16 Or *them fully*   [d]2 Some manuscripts *brother and fellow worker;* other manuscripts *brother and God's servant*

love increase and overflow for each other and for everyone else, just as ours does for you. [13]May he strengthen your hearts so that you will be blameless and holy in the presence of our God and Father when our Lord Jesus comes with all his holy ones.

Living to Please God

4 Finally, brothers, we instructed you how to live in order to please God, as in fact you are living. Now we ask you and urge you in the Lord Jesus to do this more and more. [2]For you know what instructions we gave you by the authority of the Lord Jesus.

[3]It is God's will that you should be sanctified: that you should avoid sexual immorality; [4]that each of you should learn to control his own body[e] in a way that is holy and honorable, [5]not in passionate lust like the heathen, who do not know God; [6]and that in this matter no one should wrong his brother or take advantage of him. The Lord will punish men for all such sins, as we have already told you and warned you. [7]For God did not call us to be impure, but to live a holy life. [8]Therefore, he who rejects this instruction does not reject man but God, who gives you his Holy Spirit.

[9]Now about brotherly love we do not need to write to you, yourselves have been taught by God to love each other. [10]And in fact, you do love all the brothers throughout Macedonia. Yet we urge you, brothers, to do so more and more.

[11]Make it your ambition to lead a quiet life, to mind your own business and to work with your hands, just as we told you, [12]so that your daily life may win the respect of outsiders and so that you will not be dependent on anybody.

The Coming of the Lord

[13]Brothers, we do not want you to be ignorant about those who fall asleep, or to grieve like the rest of men, who have no hope. [14]We believe that Jesus died and rose again and so we believe that God will bring with Jesus those who have fallen asleep in him. [15]According to the Lord's own word, we tell you that we who are still alive, who are left till the coming of the Lord, will certainly not precede those who have fallen asleep. [16]For the Lord himself will come down from heaven, with a loud command, with the voice of the archangel and with the trumpet call of God, and the dead in Christ will rise first. [17]After that, we who are still alive and are left will be caught up together with them in the clouds to meet the Lord in the air. And so we will be with the Lord forever. [18]Therefore encourage each other with these words.

5 Now, brothers, about times and dates we do not need to write to you, [2]for you know very well that the day of the Lord will come like a thief in the night. [3]While people are saying, "Peace and safety," destruction will come on them suddenly, as labor pains on a pregnant woman, and they will not escape.

OPEN: What was the last thing you made from scratch with your own two hands?

DIG: 1. What three areas of life-style, discussed here, most affect a Christian's ministry? How so? **2.** What "behavioral psychology" is Paul using here? What is the guiding principle behind Paul's injunctions and warnings? **3.** When urged to love "more and more" (v.10), how do you suppose the Thessalonians felt? Why?

REFLECT: 1. In what ways will a lifestyle that bears witness to God affect human sexuality? Work relationships? Small group dynamics? **2.** What do you say to someone who believes you can do anything you want, as long as you mind your own business (v.11) and no one gets hurt (v.6)? Would you say anything different to a Christian who believed the same thing about sexual freedom? If so, what?

OPEN: Who was the first family member you recall dying? Who have you been closest to through their dying days? What effect did their death have on you? What else has shaped your view of death and dying?

DIG: 1. How would the Thessalonians have felt if they had remained ignorant of the Christian's resurrection and of Christ's return? How would Paul's words here encourage them? **2.** Does Paul's word about Christ coming as "a thief in the night" (at an unknown time) calm, or stir up, fear? How does Paul's analogy of night and day speak to this fear? **3.** How do *faith*, *love*, and *hope* sum up what it means to "belong to the day" (5:8; see 1:3)?

REFLECT: 1. Of all the places you live (at home, work, school, or church), where do you feel the need for more faith, more hope, or more love? How can the group

---

[e]4 Or *learn to live with his own wife*; or *learn to acquire a wife*

[4]But you, brothers, are not in darkness so that this day should surprise you like a thief. [5]You are all sons of the light and sons of the day. We do not belong to the night or to the darkness. [6]So then, let us not be like others, who are asleep, but let us be alert and self-controlled. [7]For those who sleep, sleep at night, and those who get drunk, get drunk at night. [8]But since we belong to the day, let us be self-controlled, putting on faith and love as a breastplate, and the hope of salvation as a helmet. [9]For God did not appoint us to suffer wrath but to receive salvation through our Lord Jesus Christ. [10]He died for us so that, whether we are awake or asleep, we may live together with him. [11]Therefore encourage one another and build each other up, just as in fact you are doing.

Final Instructions

[12]Now we ask you, brothers, to respect those who work hard among you, who are over you in the Lord and who admonish you. [13]Hold them in the highest regard in love because of their work. Live in peace with each other. [14]And we urge you, brothers, warn those who are idle, encourage the timid, help the weak, be patient with everyone. [15]Make sure that nobody pays back wrong for wrong, but always try to be kind to each other and to everyone else.

[16]Be joyful always; [17]pray continually; [18]give thanks in all circumstances, for this is God's will for you in Christ Jesus.

[19]Do not put out the Spirit's fire; [20]do not treat prophecies with contempt. [21]Test everything. Hold on to the good. [22]Avoid every kind of evil.

[23]May God himself, the God of peace, sanctify you through and through. May your whole spirit, soul and body be kept blameless at the coming of our Lord Jesus Christ. [24]The one who calls you is faithful and he will do it.

[25]Brothers, pray for us. [26]Greet all the brothers with a holy kiss. [27]I charge you before the Lord to have this letter read to all the brothers.

[28]The grace of our Lord Jesus Christ be with you.

help you "put it on"? **2.** Does the reality of Christ's return encourage or threaten you? How so? How can you be better prepared for that time? **3.** How does this passage help you as you consider your own death?

OPEN: What causes you to "blow a gasket": Traffic jams? Christmas shopping? Bickering children? Burned dinners? Or what?

DIG: 1. From this passage, what kinds of people make up the Christian community? **2.** What attitudes underlie Paul's various commands here? What impressions of the Christian life do these commands give you? **3.** How would you summarize the goal and hope of the Christian life (vv.23-24) in your own words? **4.** How do the many commands in verses 12-22 relate to the multi-dimensional blessing of verse 23? To the promise of verse 24? To the requests of verses 25-27? To the benediction of verse 28?

REFLECT: 1. Of the various commands, which ones are most relevant to your church? Your small group? You? Which ones do you feel you are practicing pretty well? Which one will you work on this week? Why? How? **2.** What encouragement do you receive from the God of peace, sanctification, and grace to fulfill these commands? How has the small group been a help to you in this regard?

2 THESSALONIANS

INTRODUCTION

Characteristics

Why a Second Letter?

First and Second Thessalonians are very much alike. In fact, 2 Thessalonians covers almost the same ground as 1 Thessalonians, although in a more perfunctory fashion. There is thanksgiving for the faith and love of the Thessalonians, encouragement to them in the midst of their persecution, teaching about the Second Coming, and a warning against idleness. Furthermore, 2 Thessalonians was probably written within months, if not weeks, of 1 Thessalonians. Why was it necessary?

The answer may well be that Paul's first letter to these young, untaught Christians produced a serious misunderstanding that necessitated a second, clarifying letter. Specifically, his teaching that "the day of the Lord will come like a thief in the night" (1 Thess. 5:2) may have encouraged people to abandon normal pursuits to prepare for the Second Coming. Thus, he wrote 2 Thessalonians 2:1-12, outlining the events that must take place *prior to* the return of Christ. "The Second Coming is imminent," he seems to be saying, "but not so imminent that you have to stop everything else." Then he goes on to reiterate what he said in his earlier letter: Stand firm and do not be idle.

Amplifying a Theme

In fact, 1 and 2 Thessalonians compliment one another concerning the Second Coming. Paul's teaching in 1 Thessalonians "is mainly on a personal level: It is given in response to questions about the lot of believers who have died before the *Parousia*. This is followed by a brief reference to the Day of the Lord as it affects men and women in general: It will take the ungodly by surprise, but believers, being children of light, will be awake and prepared for it. In 2 Thessalonians believers are told further how they may be prepared for the great day. They will recognize the events which signal its approach" (F. F. Bruce, *1 and 2 Thessalonians: Word Biblical Commentary* Vol. 45 p. xliii).

"The Secret Power of Lawlessness"

Paul was not unaware of what was happening around him. To this point, the peaceful conditions in the Roman Empire had been of great value to the spread of Christianity. But "there were disquieting straws in the wind. There was mounting unrest in Judea, and this unrest had repercussions elsewhere, he and his colleagues learned in Thessalonica, where they were branded as men who had 'subverted the world.' By the time they had arrived in Corinth, they had heard of the expulsion of Jews from Rome. The troubles which had driven him from one Macedonian city after another were fresh in Paul's mind when 2 Thessalonians was written. Probably Gallio's encouraging judgment at Corinth had not yet been given. Roman law and order were still in control, but it was only too clear that the 'hidden power of lawlessness' was already at work, and it would probably continue to work until it erupted violently and swept all before it. When the Thessalonians were told that the Day of the Lord cannot arrive until the great rebellion has broken out, the Day is not being postponed to the indefinite future: the great rebellion might well break out within a few years. If they paid heed to what they were being told, they would be ready—well informed as well as morally alert" (Bruce, *1 and 2 Thessalonians,* p. xliii).

The Audience

See the notes on 1 Thessalonians for further details about this church.

2 Thessalonians

1 Paul, Silas[a] and Timothy,

To the church of the Thessalonians in God our Father and the Lord Jesus Christ:

²Grace and peace to you from God the Father and the Lord Jesus Christ.

Thanksgiving and Prayer

³We ought always to thank God for you, brothers, and rightly so, because your faith is growing more and more, and the love every one of you has for each other is increasing. ⁴Therefore, among God's churches we boast about your perseverance and faith in all the persecutions and trials you are enduring.

⁵All this is evidence that God's judgment is right, and as a result you will be counted worthy of the kingdom of God, for which you are suffering. ⁶God is just: He will pay back trouble to those who trouble you ⁷and give relief to you who are troubled, and to us as well. This will happen when the Lord Jesus is revealed from heaven in blazing fire with his powerful angels. ⁸He will punish those who do not know God and do not obey the gospel of our Lord Jesus. ⁹They will be punished with everlasting destruction and shut out from the presence of the Lord and from the majesty of his power ¹⁰on the day he comes to be glorified in his holy people and to be marveled at among all those who have believed. This includes you, because you believed our testimony to you.

¹¹With this in mind, we constantly pray for you, that our God may count you worthy of his calling, and that by his power he may fulfill every good purpose of yours and every act prompted by your faith. ¹²We pray this so that the name of our Lord Jesus may be glorified in you, and you in him, according to the grace of our God and the Lord Jesus Christ.[b]

The Man of Lawlessness

2 Concerning the coming of our Lord Jesus Christ and our being gathered to him, we ask you, brothers, ²not to become easily unsettled or alarmed by some prophecy, report or letter supposed to have come from us, saying that the day of the Lord has already come. ³Don't let anyone deceive you in any way, for that day will not come until the rebellion occurs and the man of lawlessness[c] is revealed, the man doomed to destruction. ⁴He will oppose and will exalt himself over everything that is called God or is worshiped, so that he sets himself up in God's temple, proclaiming himself to be God.

⁵Don't you remember that when I was with you I used to tell you these things? ⁶And now you know what is holding him back, so that he may be revealed at the proper time. ⁷For the secret

---

OPEN: What did your parents do right in raising you? What rewards and punishments worked best?

DIG: 1. What has happened since Paul wrote 1 Thessalonians? How has persecution affected this church? **2.** What is the evidence that they are "worthy" of God's kingdom? **3.** Who is on trial here? Who is on the witness stand? In the judge's chambers? **4.** Why is God waiting until the Second Coming to punish these persecutors? Who benefits from this delayed justice? How so? **5.** What quality do you think Paul admires most in these Christians? **6.** What do you see as the net effect of Paul's thanksgiving and prayer?

REFLECT: 1. How will you exercise faith and love this week in some specific way or relationship? **2.** Which of your current struggles are a result of being a Christian? How so? **3.** How do you feel about the punishment mentioned in verses 8-9? How might you feel if you were being severely oppressed? **4.** Put Paul's prayer (vv. 11-12) in your own words and pray it for one another this week.

OPEN: At what stage in life were you "rebellious"? What memory (painful or humorous) is associated with those times of conflict?

DIG: 1. What must have been happening in Thessalonica to lead Paul to write this? **2.** How much time was Paul able to spend with the Thessalonians (see Ac 17:2)? How would this affect their willingness to believe rumors about Christ's return (v.2)? **3.** Who do you think is the restrainer of this lawless one? How do you think this "restraining order" is enforced? **4.** What is God's ultimate purpose in allowing the "man of lawlessness" to deceive people? What signs mark his appearing? **5.** How will those who refuse Christ respond to this "man"? How does the "powerful delusion" sent by God differ from the deceptive evil

---

a] Greek *Silvanus*, a variant of *Silas*   *b12* Or *God and Lord, Jesus Christ*
c3 Some manuscripts *sin*

of this "man" (vv.10-12)? **6.** How and why will God save his people (vv.13-14)? In response to God's initiative and Paul's ministry, what are the people to do?

REFLECT: 1. In contrast to verse 10, what do you think would be the result of choosing to "love the truth"? **2.** What do we need to do today to be morally alert? **3.** What encouragement do verses 13-14 give you as you face hard times? Where do you need encouragement and strength from God now? **4.** Put this prayer (vv.16-17) in your own words and pray it for one another this week.

OPEN: 1. What is one prayer you were taught to memorize? **2.** What was your first paid job? How long or hard did you work at it? What did you do with your money? **3.** What rule did your family have about eating? What happened if you broke it?

DIG: 1. Paul has twice prayed for these people (1:11-12; 2:16-17). How does he want them to pray for him and his companions? How would the encouragements in verses 3-5 help them in their trials? **2.** How might a misunderstanding of Paul's earlier teaching (1Th 5:1-3) have led to the problem of idleness? Why would Paul see that as a serious problem *then* (see 1Th 4:11-12) and *now* (see 2:13-17)? What model does Paul leave for the others to follow (vv.7-13)? **3.** Why does Paul call attention to his handwriting (v.17)? How else is the close of the letter similar to its beginning? Why do you think he emphasizes grace and peace? What does it say about God's will?

REFLECT: 1. On a scale from 1 ("blissfully peaceful") to 10 ("high anxiety"), where would you rate

power of lawlessness is already at work; but the one who now holds it back will continue to do so till he is taken out of the way. [8]And then the lawless one will be revealed, whom the Lord Jesus will overthrow with the breath of his mouth and destroy by the splendor of his coming. [9]The coming of the lawless one will be in accordance with the work of Satan displayed in all kinds of counterfeit miracles, signs and wonders, [10]and in every sort of evil that deceives those who are perishing. They perish because they refused to love the truth and so be saved. [11]For this reason God sends them a powerful delusion so that they will believe the lie [12]and so that all will be condemned who have not believed the truth but have delighted in wickedness.

Stand Firm

[13]But we ought always to thank God for you, brothers loved by the Lord, because from the beginning God chose you[d] to be saved through the sanctifying work of the Spirit and through belief in the truth. [14]He called you to this through our gospel, that you might share in the glory of our Lord Jesus Christ. [15]So then, brothers, stand firm and hold to the teachings[e] we passed on to you, whether by word of mouth or by letter.

[16]May our Lord Jesus Christ himself and God our Father, who loved us and by his grace gave us eternal encouragement and good hope, [17]encourage your hearts and strengthen you in every good deed and word.

Request for Prayer

3 Finally, brothers, pray for us that the message of the Lord may spread rapidly and be honored, just as it was with you. [2]And pray that we may be delivered from wicked and evil men, for not everyone has faith. [3]But the Lord is faithful, and he will strengthen and protect you from the evil one. [4]We have confidence in the Lord that you are doing and will continue to do the things we command. [5]May the Lord direct your hearts into God's love and Christ's perseverance.

Warning Against Idleness

[6]In the name of the Lord Jesus Christ, we command you, brothers, to keep away from every brother who is idle and does not live according to the teaching[f] you received from us. [7]For you yourselves know how you ought to follow our example. We were not idle when we were with you, [8]nor did we eat anyone's food without paying for it. On the contrary, we worked night and day, laboring and toiling so that we would not be a burden to any of you. [9]We did this, not because we do not have the right to such help, but in order to make ourselves a model for you to follow. [10]For even when we were with you, we gave you this rule: "If a man will not work, he shall not eat."

[11]We hear that some among you are idle. They are not busy; they are busybodies. [12]Such people we command and urge in the Lord Jesus Christ to settle down and earn the bread they eat.

---

d13 Some manuscripts *because God chose you as his firstfruits*   *e15* Or *traditions*   *f6* Or *tradition*

[13]And as for you, brothers, never tire of doing what is right.

[14]If anyone does not obey our instruction in this letter, take special note of him. Do not associate with him, in order that he may feel ashamed. [15]Yet do not regard him as an enemy, but warn him as a brother.

Final Greetings

[16]Now may the Lord of peace himself give you peace at all times and in every way. The Lord be with all of you.

[17]I, Paul, write this greeting in my own hand, which is the distinguishing mark in all my letters. This is how I write.

[18]The grace of our Lord Jesus Christ be with you all.

your sense of God's peace now? Where in particular do you need group prayer and support? **2.** How are God's love and Christ's perseverance needed in your life now? **3.** What have you found helpful in encouraging you to pray for missionaries? For whom do you regularly pray? What types of pressures may he or she face in that part of the world? **4.** Are you idle, a busybody, a worrywart, or a workaholic? What is God's word to you here?

1 TIMOTHY

INTRODUCTION

The Pastoral Letters

In 1726, Paul Anton of Halle gave a series of lectures about 1 and 2 Timothy and Titus that he entitled "The Pastoral Epistles." Ever since, this name has stuck to these three books — with unfortunate results. Because of the title, these books have come to be viewed, in Anton's words, as consisting "mostly of advice to younger ministers." They are understood to be church manuals in which one finds instructions on church organization and guidelines for ministry.

There are real problems with this view, not the least of which is that denominations as diverse as Roman Catholics, Plymouth Brethren, and Presbyterians all claim to have found their organizational guidelines within the Pastoral Epistles (Gordon Fee, *1 and 2 Timothy, Titus: A Good News Commentary*, p. xxxii). The dramatically different structures in these three denominations proves that whatever the Pastoral Epistles might be, they are not primarily guides to church order.

"First Timothy is not intended to *establish* church order, but to *respond* in a very *ad hoc* way to the Ephesian situation with its straying elders. To put it another way: What we learn about church order in 1 Timothy is not so much organizational as reformational. We see *reflections* of church structure, not organizational charts; paradigms, not imperatives; qualifications, not duties; the correcting of error and abuse, not a 'How to' manual on church organization" (Gordon Fee, "The Sticky Wicket: Intentionality and Particularity/Externality," an unpublished paper, pp. 8-9)

The Audience

Timothy—Paul's Friend and Colleague

When Paul first met Timothy, he was living at Lystra in the Roman province of Galatia (modern Turkey). Timothy was the child of a mixed marriage. His father was a Gentile and his mother was Jewish (Acts 16:1). Timothy, along with his mother Eunice and his grandmother Lois, was probably converted during Paul's first missionary journey (Acts 14:8-25; compare 2 Tim. 3:10-11). By the time of Paul's second visit to the area a year or two later, Timothy had matured so much as a Christian that the local church recommended Timothy to Paul as a traveling companion (Acts 16:2). However, Paul decided that Timothy must be circumcised first to legitimize him in the eyes of Paul's Jewish critics. Without circumcision, they would have considered him a Gentile (because of his Greek father), even though he had been brought up in his mother's religion.

From this point on, Timothy seems to be associated with Paul's ministry in one way or another. He was a co-worker with Paul (Rom. 16:21; 1 Thess. 3:2; 1 Cor. 16:10; Phil. 2:22). He collaborated in the writing of six of Paul's letters (1 and 2 Thess., 2 Cor., Phil., Col., and Philem.). He was Paul's trusted representative on three missions before this one in Ephesus (to Thessalonica around A.D. 50; to Corinth between A.D. 53 and 54; and to Philippi around A.D. 60-62).

Timothy was not just a colleague of Paul's; he was a beloved friend. Paul called him "my son whom I love, who is faithful in the Lord" (1 Cor. 4:17). In Philippians 2:20-22, the aging apostle says: "I have no one else like him . . . Timothy has proved himself, because as a son with his father he has served with me in the work of the gospel."

A Personal Letter

The three so-called Pastoral Epistles (plus Philemon) are set apart from the other letters written by Paul; they are addressed to persons, not churches. In the case of 1 Timothy, however, it seems that Paul intended to write his instructions directly to the church but was unable to do so, since the local leadership was itself the problem. Consequently, he wrote to the church via his envoy, Timothy. There are few personal remarks in 1 Timothy, and all of these are directed toward Timothy's commission to restore proper order in the church (see 1:18-19; 4:6-16; 6:11-21).

Theme

Paul tells us why he wrote 1 Timothy:

> As I urged you when I went into Macedonia, stay there in Ephesus so that you may command certain men not to teach false doctrines any longer. . . . (1:3).

> Although I hope to come to you soon, I am writing you these instructions so that, if I am delayed, you will know how people ought to conduct themselves in God's household, which is the church of the living God, the pillar and foundation of the truth (3:14-15).

Timothy had been left in Ephesus for one purpose: to prevent those who had "shipwrecked their [own] faith" (1:19) from corrupting the rest of the church (see 2 Tim. 2:17-18). He was Paul's apostolic delegate, taking temporary charge of the Ephesian church during the crises it was facing.

The False Teachers

Who were these false teachers who had so upset the Ephesian church? Were they outsiders who had infiltrated the church? Were they philosophers unaffiliated with the church, but whose ideas were being listened to nevertheless? Or were these false teachers members of the church itself?

The best guess is that these troubling teachers were *elders* of the Ephesian church! A careful reading of 1 Timothy seems to indicate this. First of all, it is clear that the teaching in Ephesians was done by the elders (3:2; 5:17). Furthermore, Paul devotes considerable space to outlining the qualifications for leaders in the church. These qualifications contrast sharply with what he says about the false teachers. For example, the false teachers "forbid people to marry" (4:3). Paul says that an overseer (elder), in contrast, "must be . . . the husband of but one wife" and "must manage his own family well" (3:2, 4-5; see also 3:12). The false teachers "think that godliness is a means to financial gain" (6:5); whereas an elder must "not [be] a lover of money" (3:3). In other words, Paul is saying: "Here is what true elders are like, in contrast to your erring elders." Finally in 5:17-25, he outlines the process of selection and discipline of elders "who sin" (v. 20).

Paul had a sense that this might happen in Ephesus. In his farewell address he said, "Even from your own number men will arise and distort the truth in order to draw away disciples after them" (Acts 20:30).

Two further notes: From various references (2:9-15; 5:11-15; 2 Tim. 3:6-7), it appears that these false teachers were listened to, supported, and encouraged by some of the women in the church, especially younger widows. Second, it is likely that the church in Ephesus was not a single large body that met together on Sunday. Rather, it consisted of a number of house churches some of which had been taken over by the false teachers.

The Nature of the False Teaching

As is often the case, since we have only Paul's response to the problem and not a clear exposition of it, we are forced to deduce the nature of the heresy. From the text, it seems that the false teachers were involved in esoteric speculation rather than the exposition of accepted Christian teaching. Furthermore, the teachers were proud, arrogant, disputatious, and greedy. They used religion to make money and gain power. Their false teaching was connected with the Old Testament, but it also had an ascetic component and a strong Greek element. It appears to be much like the false teaching in the Lycus valley churches (see the introduction to Colossians).

1 Timothy

OPEN: 1. What chores were you assigned at home? **2.** How did your folks settle sibling disputes over who got (or had) to do what?

DIG: 1. What problems are plaguing this church (vv.3-7; see 4:1-3; 6:3-5)? **2.** Knowing the conflicts here, what assignment is Timothy given? How does the goal he is to work for differ from that of the false teachers? **3.** Reading between the lines, how are these false teachers misusing the law (vv.7-10; see Gal 2:15-16)? For what audience and what purpose is the law intended (see Ro 3:20)?

REFLECT: 1. This past week, what was more important to you than love: The desire to be "on top"? To be right? In control? To look good? What else? **2.** In your church, what seems to be lacking: Sound doctrine, clear conscience, pure heart, or sincere faith? **3.** Which of these do you lack? Why?

OPEN: Who holds the record in your group for the most speeding tickets? The most days of playing hooky from school?

DIG: 1. How does Paul establish both his authority and humility (vv.12-16)? **2.** How has Christ changed Paul? How would Paul's example (v.16) affect others? How does his situation compare with Hymenaeus and Alexander (v. 20)? **3.** What does Paul teach about the Lord in this section? (Note the nouns, verbs, and adjectives.) How can these truths keep Timothy on the right course in the face of opposition from false teachers?

REFLECT: 1. What word would you use to describe your life before you became a Christian? Since then? What does that show you about the Lord's patience? **2.** Should our response to those who act in "ignorance and unbelief" (v.13) be different from those who "have shipwrecked their faith" (v.19)? Why? How so? Illustrate without naming names.

1 Paul, an apostle of Christ Jesus by the command of God our Savior and of Christ Jesus our hope,

[2]To Timothy my true son in the faith:

Grace, mercy and peace from God the Father and Christ Jesus our Lord.

Warning Against False Teachers of the Law

[3]As I urged you when I went into Macedonia, stay there in Ephesus so that you may command certain men not to teach false doctrines any longer [4]nor to devote themselves to myths and endless genealogies. These promote controversies rather than God's work—which is by faith. [5]The goal of this command is love, which comes from a pure heart and a good conscience and a sincere faith. [6]Some have wandered away from these and turned to meaningless talk. [7]They want to be teachers of the law, but they do not know what they are talking about or what they so confidently affirm.

[8]We know that the law is good if one uses it properly. [9]We also know that law[a] is made not for the righteous but for lawbreakers and rebels, the ungodly and sinful, the unholy and irreligious; for those who kill their fathers or mothers, for murderers, [10]for adulterers and perverts, for slave traders and liars and perjurers—and for whatever else is contrary to the sound doctrine [11]that conforms to the glorious gospel of the blessed God, which he entrusted to me.

The Lord's Grace to Paul

[12]I thank Christ Jesus our Lord, who has given me strength, that he considered me faithful, appointing me to his service. [13]Even though I was once a blasphemer and a persecutor and a violent man, I was shown mercy because I acted in ignorance and unbelief. [14]The grace of our Lord was poured out on me abundantly, along with the faith and love that are in Christ Jesus.

[15]Here is a trustworthy saying that deserves full acceptance: Christ Jesus came into the world to save sinners—of whom I am the worst. [16]But for that very reason I was shown mercy so that in me, the worst of sinners, Christ Jesus might display his unlimited patience as an example for those who would believe on him and receive eternal life. [17]Now to the King eternal, immortal, invisible, the only God, be honor and glory for ever and ever. Amen.

[18]Timothy, my son, I give you this instruction in keeping with the prophecies once made about you, so that by following them you may fight the good fight, [19]holding on to faith and a good conscience. Some have rejected these and so have shipwrecked their faith. [20]Among them are Hymenaeus and Alexander, whom I have handed over to Satan to be taught not to blaspheme.

---

a9 Or that the law

Instructions on Worship

2 I urge, then, first of all, that requests, prayers, intercession and thanksgiving be made for everyone— ²for kings and all those in authority, that we may live peaceful and quiet lives in all godliness and holiness. ³This is good, and pleases God our Savior, ⁴who wants all men to be saved and to come to a knowledge of the truth. ⁵For there is one God and one mediator between God and men, the man Christ Jesus, ⁶who gave himself as a ransom for all men—the testimony given in its proper time. ⁷And for this purpose I was appointed a herald and an apostle—I am telling the truth, I am not lying—and a teacher of the true faith to the Gentiles.

⁸I want men everywhere to lift up holy hands in prayer, without anger or disputing.

⁹I also want women to dress modestly, with decency and propriety, not with braided hair or gold or pearls or expensive clothes, ¹⁰but with good deeds, appropriate for women who profess to worship God.

¹¹A woman should learn in quietness and full submission. ¹²I do not permit a woman to teach or to have authority over a man; she must be silent. ¹³For Adam was formed first, then Eve. ¹⁴And Adam was not the one deceived; it was the woman who was deceived and became a sinner. ¹⁵But women ᵇ will be saved ᶜ through childbearing—if they continue in faith, love and holiness with propriety.

Overseers and Deacons

3 Here is a trustworthy saying: If anyone sets his heart on being an overseer,ᵈ he desires a noble task. ²Now the overseer must be above reproach, the husband of but one wife, temperate, self-controlled, respectable, hospitable, able to teach, ³not given to drunkenness, not violent but gentle, not quarrelsome, not a lover of money. ⁴He must manage his own family well and see that his children obey him with proper respect. ⁵(If anyone does not know how to manage his own family, how can he take care of God's church?) ⁶He must not be a recent convert, or he may become conceited and fall under the same judgment as the devil. ⁷He must also have a good reputation with outsiders, so that he will not fall into disgrace and into the devil's trap.

⁸Deacons, likewise, are to be men worthy of respect, sincere, not indulging in much wine, and not pursuing dishonest gain. ⁹They must keep hold of the deep truths of the faith with a clear conscience. ¹⁰They must first be tested; and then if there is nothing against them, let them serve as deacons.

¹¹In the same way, their wivesᵉ are to be women worthy of respect, not malicious talkers but temperate and trustworthy in everything.

¹²A deacon must be the husband of but one wife and must manage his children and his household well. ¹³Those who have served well gain an excellent standing and great assurance in their faith in Christ Jesus.

ᵇ15 Greek *she*   ᶜ15 Or *restored*   ᵈ1 Traditionally *bishop*; also in verse 2
ᵉ11 Or *way*, *deaconesses*

OPEN: Where did you go to church when you were a kid? Was anything special done to make church and Sunday feel "holy"?

DIG: 1. For whom are prayers for salvation specifically requested (vv.1,4,6,7)? How might the false teachers (1:7), who want people to obey Jewish rules, feel about this request? **2.** What do verses 8-10 imply about proper attitudes toward worship? **3.** Do you think verses 11-15 are meant to be applied at all times and places, or was Paul just dealing with a special problem at Ephesus (see 1:3-4; 2Ti 3:6-7)? What reasons support your answer?

REFLECT: 1. What attitudes for worship mentioned here are yours to cultivate? **2.** When church and society treat people unequally, how do you feel or act?

OPEN: 1. When you were young, what did you want to be when you grew up? **2.** Were you a "little angel" or a "big brat" when left with a new baby-sitter? Why?

DIG: 1. Given the struggle with the false teachers (1:7), why is Timothy given this list of qualifications for leadership? Why a list of *qualifications* only, and not *duties* also? What, if anything, is distinctly Christian about these qualifications? Why are all these qualifications *outward*, not *inward*, in orientation? What is Paul's main concern? **2.** How do you interpret "the husband of one wife"? Does that mean the overseer must not be single? Nor divorced? Widowed? Remarried? A polygamist? Or does it demand sexual fidelity if married (see also 5:9)? **3.** What kind of "test" do you suppose the deacons were given? Why? **4.** What is Paul's main purpose for writing these instructions to Timothy? **5.** What central facts about Jesus are summed up in the hymn (v.16)?

REFLECT: 1. Although applied specifically to leaders here, why are these qualities important for

all Christians? **2.** Of these qualities, what are two or three you
have made progress with in this
past year? In which area do you
want to grow now? How can the
group help you in that process?

OPEN: 1. What dumb rule was
once imposed on you by school
authorities? Why didn't you like
it? **2.** What do you do to keep in
shape physically? How faithful are
you in carrying out your plan?

DIG: 1. What was really behind
Paul's concern about false teachers (vv.1-2)? Why is it hypocritical
to preach abstinence from marriage and certain foods (vv.3-5;
see Mk 7:18-19)? **2.** What does
Paul mean by "training to be godly"
(vv. 7,11-16)? How is this lifestyle
to differ from the teaching of as-
ceticism? How would this counteract their influence? **3.** What would
these Ephesians find most convincing about young Timothy?

REFLECT: 1. What were you
raised to believe a Christian can
and cannot do? If a friend was
being swayed by these teachings
today, what would you say? Do?
2. If you were to design a spiritual
fitness training program comparable to the one you use to keep
physically fit, what would it consist of? Why? **3.** What "rites of
passage" would you set up for a
young Christian aspiring to lead?

OPEN: 1. When you were growing up, what proverb best described the way your family used
money: (a) "Waste not, want not"?
(b) "Eat, drink, and be merry"? (c)
"You can't take it with you"? (d) "A
penny saved is a penny earned"?
(e) "Penny wise, pound foolish"?
2. What memorable story lies
behind your proverb?

---

[14]Although I hope to come to you soon, I am writing you these
instructions so that, [15]if I am delayed, you will know how people
ought to conduct themselves in God's household, which is the
church of the living God, the pillar and foundation of the truth.
[16]Beyond all question, the mystery of godliness is great:

> He*f* appeared in a body,*g*
> was vindicated by the Spirit,
> was seen by angels,
> was preached among the nations,
> was believed on in the world,
> was taken up in glory.

New age stuff

Instructions to Timothy

4 The Spirit clearly says that in later times some will abandon
the faith and follow deceiving spirits and things taught by
demons. [2]Such teachings come through hypocritical liars, whose
consciences have been seared as with a hot iron. [3]They forbid
people to marry and order them to abstain from certain foods,
which God created to be received with thanksgiving by those
who believe and who know the truth. [4]For everything God
created is good, and nothing is to be rejected if it is received with
thanksgiving, [5]because it is consecrated by the word of God and
prayer.

[6]If you point these things out to the brothers, you will be a
good minister of Christ Jesus, brought up in the truths of the
faith and of the good teaching that you have followed. [7]Have
nothing to do with godless myths and old wives' tales; rather,
train yourself to be godly. [8]For physical training is of some
value, but godliness has value for all things, holding promise for
both the present life and the life to come.

[9]This is a trustworthy saying that deserves full acceptance
[10](and for this we labor and strive), that we have put our hope
in the living God, who is the Savior of all men, and especially
of those who believe.

[11]Command and teach these things. [12]Don't let anyone look
down on you because you are young, but set an example for the
believers in speech, in life, in love, in faith and in purity. [13]Until
I come, devote yourself to the public reading of Scripture, to
preaching and to teaching. [14]Do not neglect your gift, which was
given you through a prophetic message when the body of elders
laid their hands on you.

[15]Be diligent in these matters; give yourself wholly to them,
so that everyone may see your progress. [16]Watch your life and
doctrine closely. Persevere in them, because if you do, you will
save both yourself and your hearers.

Advice About Widows, Elders and Slaves

5 Do not rebuke an older man harshly, but exhort him as if
he were your father. Treat younger men as brothers, [2]older
women as mothers, and younger women as sisters, with absolute
purity.

[3]Give proper recognition to those widows who are really in

f16 Some manuscripts God   *g16 Or in the flesh*

need. [4]But if a widow has children or grandchildren, these should learn first of all to put their religion into practice by caring for their own family and so repaying their parents and grandparents, for this is pleasing to God. [5]The widow who is really in need and left all alone puts her hope in God and continues night and day to pray and to ask God for help. [6]But the widow who lives for pleasure is dead even while she lives. [7]Give the people these instructions, too, so that no one may be open to blame. [8]If anyone does not provide for his relatives, and especially for his immediate family, he has denied the faith and is worse than an unbeliever.

[9]No widow may be put on the list of widows unless she is over sixty, has been faithful to her husband,[h] [10]and is well known for her good deeds, such as bringing up children, showing hospitality, washing the feet of the saints, helping those in trouble and devoting herself to all kinds of good deeds.

[11]As for younger widows, do not put them on such a list. For when their sensual desires overcome their dedication to Christ, they want to marry. [12]Thus they bring judgment on themselves, because they have broken their first pledge. [13]Besides, they get into the habit of being idle and going about from house to house. And not only do they become idlers, but also gossips and busybodies, saying things they ought not to. [14]So I counsel younger widows to marry, to have children, to manage their homes and to give the enemy no opportunity for slander. [15]Some have in fact already turned away to follow Satan.

[16]If any woman who is a believer has widows in her family, she should help them and not let the church be burdened with them, so that the church can help those widows who are really in need.

[17]The elders who direct the affairs of the church well are worthy of double honor, especially those whose work is preaching and teaching. [18]For the Scripture says, "Do not muzzle the ox while it is treading out the grain,"[i] and "The worker deserves his wages."[j] [19]Do not entertain an accusation against an elder unless it is brought by two or three witnesses. [20]Those who sin are to be rebuked publicly, so that the others may take warning.

[21]I charge you, in the sight of God and Christ Jesus and the elect angels, to keep these instructions without partiality, and to do nothing out of favoritism.

[22]Do not be hasty in the laying on of hands, and do not share in the sins of others. Keep yourself pure.

[23]Stop drinking only water, and use a little wine because of your stomach and your frequent illnesses.

[24]The sins of some men are obvious, reaching the place of judgment ahead of them; the sins of others trail behind them. [25]In the same way, good deeds are obvious, and even those that are not cannot be hidden.

6 All who are under the yoke of slavery should consider their masters worthy of full respect, so that God's name and our teaching may not be slandered. [2]Those who have believing masters are not to show less respect for them because they are

DIG: 1. From what you read between the lines, what was the problem concerning widows in this church? What distinguishes the various kinds of widows? How is the church to respond differently to each kind (see also Ac 6:1-6)? **2.** What possible abuses of this care for the needy does Paul anticipate in verses 4-8? Verses 9-10? Verses 11-15? How does Paul's teaching prevent those abuses? **3.** Why are church elders in general to receive "double honor"? Why do some deserve public rebuke? **4.** How would the early church protect a leader from a frivolous or malicious charge (vv.19-20)? Why should "favoritism" not be shown some elders who have clout, contrary to what is often done today? **5.** Why might a Christian slave's lack of respect for his master result in slandering God's name and Christian teaching? What should be done about that?

REFLECT: 1. How many widows are there in your extended family? At present, how are their needs met? **2.** When (if ever) have you suddenly become single? What was that time like? **3.** How would you evaluate what your church is doing for those in need? Who, besides widows, are people in your church that need some help the church can provide? What is your church doing, specifically, to target help for widowers? Single parents? Divorcees? The unemployed? The chronically ill? **4.** Of the various instructions in chapter 5, which one has your name on it? Why?

---

[h]9 Or *has had but one husband*   [i]18 Deut. 25:4   [j]18 Luke 10:7

OPEN: Which Beatles' song expresses your attitude towards money: "Money (That's What I Want)" or "Money Can't Buy Me Love"?

DIG: 1. What motivations does Paul see in these false teachers? With what results? **2.** What is the "great gain" in "godliness with contentment" (v.6)?

REFLECT: As for loving God or money, how can you tell which is "number 1" in your life? How is the "love of money" tugging on your heartstrings now?

OPEN: 1. When you were growing up, did your parents tend to over-protect you, or push you beyond your limits? **2.** With your kids, what are you going to do differently when it comes to risk-taking versus playing it safe?

DIG: 1. What is Timothy to flee? To pursue? What does it mean to pursue these qualities? **2.** Do you think the challenge in verses 12-16 would intimidate or encourage Timothy? Why? **3.** What does Paul's "fight" imagery tell you about the nature of the Christian life? **4.** What is Paul saying about the wealthy: That their wealth is sinful? That it's a temptation? A great responsibility to help others? A great means to attain heavenly riches for oneself? **5.** Given Paul's lengthy stay and comprehensive teaching at Ephesus, why is that church so open to false teaching and irrelevancies (see 1:3-4; 4:1-3; 6:3,21)?

REFLECT: 1. Are you wandering spiritually, or are you in hot pursuit of the qualities in verse 11? Why? Which quality do you especially want to develop in your life? What "witnesses" (v.12) could help keep you accountable? **2.** Who was a "Paul," who served as a spiritual coach in your life and gave you strong advice when you needed it? **3.** Who is a "Timothy" in your life, for whom you can be a "Paul"?

brothers. Instead, they are to serve them even better, because those who benefit from their service are believers, and dear to them. These are the things you are to teach and urge on them.

Love of Money

[3]If anyone teaches false doctrines and does not agree to the sound instruction of our Lord Jesus Christ and to godly teaching, [4]he is conceited and understands nothing. He has an unhealthy interest in controversies and quarrels about words that result in envy, strife, malicious talk, evil suspicions [5]and constant friction between men of corrupt mind, who have been robbed of the truth and who think that godliness is a means to financial gain.

[6]But godliness with contentment is great gain. [7]For we brought nothing into the world, and we can take nothing out of it. [8]But if we have food and clothing, we will be content with that. [9]People who want to get rich fall into temptation and a trap and into many foolish and harmful desires that plunge men into ruin and destruction. [10]For the love of money is a root of all kinds of evil. Some people, eager for money, have wandered from the faith and pierced themselves with many griefs.

Paul's Charge to Timothy

[11]But you, man of God, flee from all this, and pursue righteousness, godliness, faith, love, endurance and gentleness. [12]Fight the good fight of the faith. Take hold of the eternal life to which you were called when you made your good confession in the presence of many witnesses. [13]In the sight of God, who gives life to everything, and of Christ Jesus, who while testifying before Pontius Pilate made the good confession, I charge you [14]to keep this command without spot or blame until the appearing of our Lord Jesus Christ, [15]which God will bring about in his own time—God, the blessed and only Ruler, the King of kings and Lord of lords, [16]who alone is immortal and who lives in unapproachable light, whom no one has seen or can see. To him be honor and might forever. Amen.

[17]Command those who are rich in this present world not to be arrogant nor to put their hope in wealth, which is so uncertain, but to put their hope in God, who richly provides us with everything for our enjoyment. [18]Command them to do good, to be rich in good deeds, and to be generous and willing to share. [19]In this way they will lay up treasure for themselves as a firm foundation for the coming age, so that they may take hold of the life that is truly life.

[20]Timothy, guard what has been entrusted to your care. Turn away from godless chatter and the opposing ideas of what is falsely called knowledge, [21]which some have professed and in so doing have wandered from the faith.

Grace be with you.

2 TIMOTHY

INTRODUCTION

The Last Letter

Second Timothy is probably the last epistle Paul ever wrote. He is an old man now, in prison once again, deserted by most all of his friends, and facing the likely prospect of death. "For I am already being poured out like a drink offering, and the time has come for my departure. I have fought the good fight, I have finished the race, I have kept the faith. Now there is in store for me the crown of righteousness" (4:6-8). Bishop Handley Moule once said that he found it difficult to read 2 Timothy "without finding something like a mist gathering in the eyes" (*The Second Epistle to Timothy: The Devotional Commentary*, p. 16).

Audience

Timothy's Time

Indeed, 2 Timothy is deeply moving as Paul writes the younger man, imploring him to come and be with him in the waning days of his life. In 2 Timothy, the urgency of the problem in Ephesus is the background. Paul's more pressing need is to have Timothy at his side once again. Even more than personal comfort, Paul wants to pass on the torch of his ministry to Timothy.

Timothy was the logical choice for this new responsibility. He had been Paul's trusted colleague for over fifteen years, and he really cared for the welfare of the churches (Phil. 2:20-22). This was a crucial time for the churches in Europe and Asia. They seemed fragile in the face of the forces pressing against them. For one thing, Rome had turned against Christianity. Nero seemed bent on destroying the church. Furthermore, in Asia there had been widespread apostasy (1:15). Only a generation after Christ's resurrection, "Christianity . . . trembled, humanly speaking, on the verge of annihilation" (Moule, *The Second Epistle to Timothy*, p. 18). But Paul's ministry was over. No longer could he travel through the Roman Empire putting out fires, correcting errors, establishing order. Now it was up to Timothy and the others.

To lay this responsibility on Timothy was not easy. In many ways he was an unlikely leader. He was relatively young by Roman standards, in his mid-thirties (1 Tim. 4:12; 2 Tim. 2:22). He was prone to illness (1 Tim. 5:23). And he was, apparently, somewhat shy and in need of encouragement (2 Tim. 1:7-8; 2:1, 3; 3:12-14; 4:15); to his credit, Timothy overcame his natural inclination and tackled risky assignments for Paul (e.g., in Corinth).

If Timothy did not make it to Rome in time, these instructions in 2 Timothy would have to suffice. Paul's last letter was a crucial one.

Paul's Situation

It is difficult to trace Paul's movements during the period when he wrote the Pastoral Epistles. The best guess is that after being released from the house arrest in Rome (described at the end of Acts), Paul went on another preaching tour taking with him Timothy and Titus. In the course of their travels, they came to Crete. When it came time to move on, Paul left Titus behind to appoint proper leaders for the new church there. Paul and Timothy went to Macedonia via Ephesus. At Ephesus, Paul discovered that heresy was rotting away the church. So he excommunicated Hymenaeus and Alexander, two of the erring leaders (1 Tim. 1:19-20), and he left Timothy behind to help the church through its difficulties (1 Tim. 1:3-4). Paul himself went on to Macedonia. Once there he wrote both 1 Timothy and Titus (hence the similarity between the two letters).

Paul wintered in the Adriatic seacoast town of Nicopolis where he was (presumably) joined by Titus. In the spring, Paul started back to Ephesus, only to be arrested along the way —

probably at Troas at the instigation of Alexander the metalworker (2 Tim. 4:13-15).

Paul was eventually taken back to Rome and thrown into prison. This time he was not allowed the relative comfort of a rented house with twenty-four-hour-a-day guards, as was the case during his first imprisonment. Instead he was chained and thrown into a dark, damp dungeon (1:16), "like a criminal" (2:9). Onesiphorus was able to find Paul only after a long search (1:17). Paul was cold ("bring the cloak," 4:13), bored ("bring . . . my scrolls, especially the parchments," 4:13), and lonely ("only Luke is with me," 4:11). He had already had a preliminary hearing (4:16-17). His full trial was yet to come, and he did not expect to be acquitted. Nero's insane persecution of the Christians was at its height.

So Paul wrote Timothy to come to him in Rome. He sent this letter (2 Timothy) via Tychicus, who was to replace Timothy in Ephesus. (See also Fee, *1 and 2 Timothy, Titus,* p. xix.)

Characteristics

Although 2 Timothy is similar in content and focus to both 1 Timothy and Titus, there are some marked differences. Second Timothy is far more personal than 1 Timothy. First Timothy has the feel of a business letter containing important instructions to be heeded by the local congregation. But in 2 Timothy, Paul is writing to Timothy and not to the church, and he reminisces about the work he and Timothy did together. His primary purpose is not combating heresy (although that is a background concern), but to call Timothy to join him in Rome.

In fact, it is Paul's altered situation that gives 2 Timothy its distinct flavor. There is an urgency to his writing. His ministry is over. He tells Timothy to "fan into flame the gift of God, which is in you" (1:6). Timothy must "not be ashamed to testify about our Lord" (1:8). He must "guard the good deposit that was entrusted" to him (1:14). "Preach the Word" (4:2), Paul says, "in season and out of season." So Paul instructs his heir apparent.

Second Timothy is also characterized, somewhat surprisingly, by a note of triumph. Paul knows that despite all the difficulties he is facing, despite the pressure on the church, the gospel will prevail. It cannot be chained even if he is chained (2:9). Nor will the church ultimately be hampered. It, too, will prevail (2:11-13; 4:8). Therefore, Paul writes to Timothy to carry on the work of the gospel despite persecution, despite Paul's death, because God's kingdom will prevail (3:10-4:8).

2 Timothy

1 Paul, an apostle of Christ Jesus by the will of God, according to the promise of life that is in Christ Jesus,

²To Timothy, my dear son:

Grace, mercy and peace from God the Father and Christ Jesus our Lord.

Encouragement to Be Faithful

³I thank God, whom I serve, as my forefathers did, with a clear conscience, as night and day I constantly remember you in my prayers. ⁴Recalling your tears, I long to see you, so that I may be filled with joy. ⁵I have been reminded of your sincere faith, which first lived in your grandmother Lois and in your mother Eunice and, I am persuaded, now lives in you also. ⁶For this reason I remind you to fan into flame the gift of God, which is in you through the laying on of my hands. ⁷For God did not give us a spirit of timidity, but a spirit of power, of love and of self-discipline.

⁸So do not be ashamed to testify about our Lord, or ashamed of me his prisoner. But join with me in suffering for the gospel, by the power of God, ⁹who has saved us and called us to a holy life—not because of anything we have done but because of his own purpose and grace. This grace was given us in Christ Jesus before the beginning of time, ¹⁰but it has now been revealed through the appearing of our Savior, Christ Jesus, who has destroyed death and has brought life and immortality to light through the gospel. ¹¹And of this gospel I was appointed a herald and an apostle and a teacher. ¹²That is why I am suffering as I am. Yet I am not ashamed, because I know whom I have believed, and am convinced that he is able to guard what I have entrusted to him for that day.

¹³What you heard from me, keep as the pattern of sound teaching, with faith and love in Christ Jesus. ¹⁴Guard the good deposit that was entrusted to you—guard it with the help of the Holy Spirit who lives in us.

¹⁵You know that everyone in the province of Asia has deserted me, including Phygelus and Hermogenes.

¹⁶May the Lord show mercy to the household of Onesiphorus, because he often refreshed me and was not ashamed of my chains. ¹⁷On the contrary, when he was in Rome, he searched hard for me until he found me. ¹⁸May the Lord grant that he will find mercy from the Lord on that day! You know very well in how many ways he helped me in Ephesus.

2 You then, my son, be strong in the grace that is in Christ Jesus. ²And the things you have heard me say in the presence of many witnesses entrust to reliable men who will also be qualified to teach others. ³Endure hardship with us like a good soldier of Christ Jesus. ⁴No one serving as a soldier gets involved in civilian affairs—he wants to please his commanding officer. ⁵Similarly, if anyone competes as an athlete, he does not receive the victor's crown unless he competes according to the rules.

out your faith, what do you have in common with a soldier? An athlete? A farmer? What don't you have in common with them?

[6]The hardworking farmer should be the first to receive a share of the crops. [7]Reflect on what I am saying, for the Lord will give you insight into all this.

[8]Remember Jesus Christ, raised from the dead, descended from David. This is my gospel, [9]for which I am suffering even to the point of being chained like a criminal. But God's word is not chained. [10]Therefore I endure everything for the sake of the elect, that they too may obtain the salvation that is in Christ Jesus, with eternal glory.

[11]Here is a trustworthy saying:

If we died with him,
  we will also live with him;
[12]if we endure,
  we will also reign with him.
If we disown him,
  he will also disown us;
[13]if we are faithless,
  he will remain faithful,
  for he cannot disown himself.

A Workman Approved by God

[14]Keep reminding them of these things. Warn them before God against quarreling about words; it is of no value, and only ruins those who listen. [15]Do your best to present yourself to God as one approved, a workman who does not need to be ashamed and who correctly handles the word of truth. [16]Avoid godless chatter, because those who indulge in it will become more and more ungodly. [17]Their teaching will spread like gangrene. Among them are Hymenaeus and Philetus, [18]who have wandered away from the truth. They say that the resurrection has already taken place, and they destroy the faith of some. [19]Nevertheless, God's solid foundation stands firm, sealed with this inscription: "The Lord knows those who are his,"[a] and, "Everyone who confesses the name of the Lord must turn away from wickedness."

[20]In a large house there are articles not only of gold and silver, but also of wood and clay; some are for noble purposes and some for ignoble. [21]If a man cleanses himself from the latter, he will be an instrument for noble purposes, made holy, useful to the Master and prepared to do any good work.

[22]Flee the evil desires of youth, and pursue righteousness, faith, love and peace, along with those who call on the Lord out of a pure heart. [23]Don't have anything to do with foolish and stupid arguments, because you know they produce quarrels. [24]And the Lord's servant must not quarrel; instead, he must be kind to everyone, able to teach, not resentful. [25]Those who oppose him he must gently instruct, in the hope that God will grant them repentance leading them to a knowledge of the truth, [26]and that they will come to their senses and escape from the trap of the devil, who has taken them captive to do his will.

_a19_ Num. 16:5 (see Septuagint)

Godlessness in the Last Days

3 But mark this: There will be terrible times in the last days. [2]People will be lovers of themselves, lovers of money, boastful, proud, abusive, disobedient to their parents, ungrateful, unholy, [3]without love, unforgiving, slanderous, without self-control, brutal, not lovers of the good, [4]treacherous, rash, conceited, lovers of pleasure rather than lovers of God— [5]having a form of godliness but denying its power. Have nothing to do with them.

[6]They are the kind who worm their way into homes and gain control over weak-willed women, who are loaded down with sins and are swayed by all kinds of evil desires, [7]always learning but never able to acknowledge the truth. [8]Just as Jannes and Jambres opposed Moses, so also these men oppose the truth—men of depraved minds, who, as far as the faith is concerned, are rejected. [9]But they will not get very far because, as in the case of those men, their folly will be clear to everyone.

Paul's Charge to Timothy

[10]You, however, know all about my teaching, my way of life, my purpose, faith, patience, love, endurance, [11]persecutions, sufferings—what kinds of things happened to me in Antioch, Iconium and Lystra, the persecutions I endured. Yet the Lord rescued me from all of them. [12]In fact, everyone who wants to live a godly life in Christ Jesus will be persecuted, [13]while evil men and impostors will go from bad to worse, deceiving and being deceived. [14]But as for you, continue in what you have learned and have become convinced of, because you know those from whom you learned it, [15]and how from infancy you have known the holy Scriptures, which are able to make you wise for salvation through faith in Christ Jesus. [16]All Scripture is God-breathed and is useful for teaching, rebuking, correcting and training in righteousness, [17]so that the man of God may be thoroughly equipped for every good work.

4 In the presence of God and of Christ Jesus, who will judge the living and the dead, and in view of his appearing and his kingdom, I give you this charge: [2]Preach the Word; be prepared in season and out of season; correct, rebuke and encourage—with great patience and careful instruction. [3]For the time will come when men will not put up with sound doctrine. Instead, to suit their own desires, they will gather around them a great number of teachers to say what their itching ears want to hear. [4]They will turn their ears away from the truth and turn aside to myths. [5]But you, keep your head in all situations, endure hardship, do the work of an evangelist, discharge all the duties of your ministry.

[6]For I am already being poured out like a drink offering, and the time has come for my departure. [7]I have fought the good fight, I have finished the race, I have kept the faith. [8]Now there is in store for me the crown of righteousness, which the Lord, the righteous Judge, will award to me on that day—and not only to me, but also to all who have longed for his appearing.

OPEN: What do you do when a movie gets scary and you've run out of popcorn and fingernails?

DIG: 1. Given the catalog of vices, what "form of godliness" (v.5) could these people possibly exhibit? **2.** Jannes and Jambres were Pharoah's magicians (see Ex 7:11,22; 8:7,18). How do they reveal what Paul means by a "form of godliness"? Why are they so dangerous?

REFLECT: 1. Has an external show of religion taken priority over your heart's condition? How so? How can you nurture the proper heart condition? **2.** How do you reconcile 2:25-26 with 3:5 in dealing with those who oppose you?

OPEN: Who was the best teacher you ever had? What did you like about him or her? How have you tried to be like him or her?

DIG: 1. Why does Paul emphasize his character and suffering? By contrast, what is happening to the "evil men and imposters" (v.13)? **2.** Is persecution necessarily a result of godliness? Why or why not? **3.** What does Paul say about the origin and purpose of Scripture that is especially relevant to Timothy's case? **4.** Why would the temptation to tell people what they *want* to hear (rather than what they *need* to hear) be especially strong in Timothy's situation? Instead, what is Timothy supposed to do (4:2-5)? Why? **5.** What incentives are provided here to do this very tough work (3:10,14; 4:1,6-8)?

REFLECT: 1. What barriers to faithful living do you encounter? How does Paul's example and charge encourage you in those situations? **2.** What "myths" about Jesus are people buying into these "last days"? How will you counteract that? **3.** Since the Bible is central to Christian living, how will you build it into your life?

OPEN: If you left home without anything, what would be the first thing you'd ask someone to send to you? Why?

DIG: 1. What do verses 9-16 reveal about the circumstances in which Paul wrote this letter? What is he feeling as he writes? **2.** What (and who) is he missing? Why is that significant (see Ac 13:13; 15:36-41)? **3.** What is Paul's hope in the midst of this hardship and loneliness? **4.** How does Paul echo Jesus in Gethsemane? On the cross? Why be so forgiving?

REFLECT: 1. What do you find in Paul's sense of hope (in spite of his suffering) that is a particular inspiration to you? Is there a theme verse which summarizes that point for you? Memorize it this week. **2.** How do you intend to guard the gospel that has been entrusted to you? What will you pass along—to whom, in what manner, and by when? **3.** What else will you apply from this study?

Personal Remarks

⁹Do your best to come to me quickly, ¹⁰for Demas, because he loved this world, has deserted me and has gone to Thessalonica. Crescens has gone to Galatia, and Titus to Dalmatia. ¹¹Only Luke is with me. Get Mark and bring him with you, because he is helpful to me in my ministry. ¹²I sent Tychicus to Ephesus. ¹³When you come, bring the cloak that I left with Carpus at Troas, and my scrolls, especially the parchments.

¹⁴Alexander the metalworker did me a great deal of harm. The Lord will repay him for what he has done. ¹⁵You too should be on your guard against him, because he strongly opposed our message.

¹⁶At my first defense, no one came to my support, but everyone deserted me. May it not be held against them. ¹⁷But the Lord stood at my side and gave me strength, so that through me the message might be fully proclaimed and all the Gentiles might hear it. And I was delivered from the lion's mouth. ¹⁸The Lord will rescue me from every evil attack and will bring me safely to his heavenly kingdom. To him be glory for ever and ever. Amen.

Final Greetings

¹⁹Greet Priscilla[b] and Aquila and the household of Onesiphorus. ²⁰Erastus stayed in Corinth, and I left Trophimus sick in Miletus. ²¹Do your best to get here before winter. Eubulus greets you, and so do Pudens, Linus, Claudia and all the brothers.

²²The Lord be with your spirit. Grace be with you.

---

b19 Greek *Prisca*, a variant of *Priscilla*

TITUS

INTRODUCTION

Audience
The Church on Crete

Paul and Titus, along with Timothy, went to Crete as part of a preaching tour following Paul's release from his first imprisonment in Rome. When Paul and Timothy left for Macedonia, Titus stayed behind to establish firmly the new church on Crete. When Paul reached Macedonia he wrote two letters — one to Timothy who had remained in Ephesus and the other to Titus.

In his letter to Titus, Paul reminds the younger man of his role: to appoint good leaders who will guide the church wisely. He also urges Titus to combat the false teachers found on the island. Finally, he tells him that either Artemas or Tychicus will come to relieve him (3:12), after which he is to join Paul for the winter. (See details of Paul's itinerary during this period in the introduction to 2 Timothy.)

Crete

Crete is a large island in the Mediterranean, southeast of Greece. The Minoan civilization flourished there before the time of Christ. A Jewish colony existed on the island. On the Day of Pentecost, Jews from Crete were in Jerusalem and witnessed the coming of the Holy Spirit (Acts 2:11). During his voyage to Rome, the ship on which Paul sailed skimmed the coast of Crete before being caught by a storm and driven to Malta (Acts 27:7-21).

Titus

Titus was a Greek (Gal. 2:3) who was probably converted through Paul's ministry. He accompanied Paul on his crucial second visit to Jerusalem when the inflammatory question was raised about whether Gentiles had to become Jews before they could become Christians (Gal. 2:1-10). Paul used Titus as a test case, refusing to allow him to be circumcised despite the insistence of the Judaizers.

Titus was a trusted colleague of Paul's and one of his special envoys sent on difficult assignments. For example, when the conflict between Paul and the Corinthian church had reached a breaking point, it was Titus who delivered Paul's "harsh" letter and restored order in that community. After reporting back to Paul that he had succeeded in this mission (2 Cor. 7:5-7), Titus was sent back to Corinth. This time he carried with him the letter known as 2 Corinthians (2 Cor. 8:6). On the second trip he was also charged with arranging for the collection to be given to the poor in Jerusalem.

Titus (presumably) left Crete when his replacement Artemas arrived, and he spent the winter with Paul at Nicopolis. In the spring, Paul left for Ephesus, was arrested and then sent to prison in Rome. At some point, Titus was sent to Dalmatia (modern Yugoslavia) for yet another mission.

In short, Titus was a valued friend and a trusted colleague of Paul's, one whom he called "my true son in our common faith" (1:4).

Characteristics

Titus is strikingly similar to 1 Timothy. Apart from the greeting and two pieces of theological writing in 2:11-14 and 3:3-7 (which appear to be creeds), all the material is parallel to 1 Timothy.

Still, the differences are notable. The main difference is found in the contrasting situation of Titus and Timothy. Timothy had been left to straighten out a mess in an already established church. Titus, on the other hand, had the job of appointing elders in a new church. As a result, there is less intensity in Titus. There are few imperatives ("Do this"); there is no mention of endurance (as one finds in 1 Timothy); and there are no appeals to "keep the faith." Establishing order in a new church was quite different from restoring order to an established church.

Titus

OPEN: 1. If a friend was introducing you to her (or his) parents, which of your credentials would she (he) mention? **2.** If your local newspaper wanted to interview a Christian for a feature article, who would you recommend? Why?

DIG: 1. What does Paul say here about his relationship to God? To Titus? The goal of his ministry? **2.** Why is Titus given a list of leadership qualifications, where the emphasis is mostly on "being" and not on "doing"? How do you account for the similarities between this list and the one in 1 Timothy 3:2-7? How do you account for the differences? **3.** How do you interpret "the husband of but one wife" (v.6)? Does this exclude bachelors or remarried widowers? **4.** What should disqualify someone from church leadership? **5.** What's going on at Crete that Titus would nee to appoint such elders? What is Paul's main purpose for instructing Titus in this?

REFLECT: 1. If you were on a search committee at church, responsible for finding people who meet these qualifications, would you fit the criteria? Why or why not? **2.** Of the qualities in verses 8-9, which do you desire to develop in yourself? How can your group help you to develop them?

1 Paul, a servant of God and an apostle of Jesus Christ for the faith of God's elect and the knowledge of the truth that leads to godliness— [2]a faith and knowledge resting on the hope of eternal life, which God, who does not lie, promised before the beginning of time, [3]and at his appointed season he brought his word to light through the preaching entrusted to me by the command of God our Savior,

[4]To Titus, my true son in our common faith:

Grace and peace from God the Father and Christ Jesus our Savior.

Titus' Task on Crete

[5]The reason I left you in Crete was that you might straighten out what was left unfinished and appoint[a] elders in every town, as I directed you. [6]An elder must be blameless, the husband of but one wife, a man whose children believe and are not open to the charge of being wild and disobedient. [7]Since an overseer[b] is entrusted with God's work, he must be blameless—not overbearing, not quick-tempered, not given to drunkenness, not violent, not pursuing dishonest gain. [8]Rather he must be hospitable, one who loves what is good, who is self-controlled, upright, holy and disciplined. [9]He must hold firmly to the trustworthy message as it has been taught, so that he can encourage others by sound doctrine and refute those who oppose it.

[10]For there are many rebellious people, mere talkers and deceivers, especially those of the circumcision group. [11]They must be silenced, because they are ruining whole households by teaching things they ought not to teach—and that for the sake of dishonest gain. [12]Even one of their own prophets has said, "Cretans are always liars, evil brutes, lazy gluttons." [13]This testimony is true. Therefore, rebuke them sharply, so that they will be sound in the faith [14]and will pay no attention to Jewish myths or to the commands of those who reject the truth. [15]To the pure, all things are pure, but to those who are corrupted and do not believe, nothing is pure. In fact, both their minds and consciences are corrupted. [16]They claim to know God, but by their actions they deny him. They are detestable, disobedient and unfit for doing anything good.

What Must Be Taught to Various Groups

2 You must teach what is in accord with sound doctrine. [2]Teach the older men to be temperate, worthy of respect, self-controlled, and sound in faith, in love and in endurance.

[3]Likewise, teach the older women to be reverent in the way they live, not to be slanderers or addicted to much wine, but to teach what is good. [4]Then they can train the younger women to love their husbands and children, [5]to be self-controlled and

OPEN: 1. As a teenager or college freshmen, how did you decorate your room or living space so that it was really "you"? **2.** What is the "no-no" that you have trouble just saying "no" to? Why?

DIG: 1. What qualities is Titus to teach to various groups? What methods might he use to instill these attitudes and actions (vv.7-8)? **2.** Why the chain of mentors?

a5 Or ordain   b7 Traditionally bishop

pure, to be busy at home, to be kind, and to be subject to their husbands, so that no one will malign the word of God.

[6]Similarly, encourage the young men to be self-controlled. [7]In everything set them an example by doing what is good. In your teaching show integrity, seriousness [8]and soundness of speech that cannot be condemned, so that those who oppose you may be ashamed because they have nothing bad to say about us.

[9]Teach slaves to be subject to their masters in everything, to try to please them, not to talk back to them, [10]and not to steal from them, but to show that they can be fully trusted, so that in every way they will make the teaching about God our Savior attractive.

[11]For the grace of God that brings salvation has appeared to all men. [12]It teaches us to say "No" to ungodliness and worldly passions, and to live self-controlled, upright and godly lives in this present age, [13]while we wait for the blessed hope—the glorious appearing of our great God and Savior, Jesus Christ, [14]who gave himself for us to redeem us from all wickedness and to purify for himself a people that are his very own, eager to do what is good.

[15]These, then, are the things you should teach. Encourage and rebuke with all authority. Do not let anyone despise you.

Doing What Is Good

3 Remind the people to be subject to rulers and authorities, to be obedient, to be ready to do whatever is good, [2]to slander no one, to be peaceable and considerate, and to show true humility toward all men.

[3]At one time we too were foolish, disobedient, deceived and enslaved by all kinds of passions and pleasures. We lived in malice and envy, being hated and hating one another. [4]But when the kindness and love of God our Savior appeared, [5]he saved us, not because of righteous things we had done, but because of his mercy. He saved us through the washing of rebirth and renewal by the Holy Spirit, [6]whom he poured out on us generously through Jesus Christ our Savior, [7]so that, having been justified by his grace, we might become heirs having the hope of eternal life. [8]This is a trustworthy saying. And I want you to stress these things, so that those who have trusted in God may be careful to devote themselves to doing what is good. These things are excellent and profitable for everyone.

[9]But avoid foolish controversies and genealogies and arguments and quarrels about the law, because these are unprofitable and useless. [10]Warn a divisive person once, and then warn him a second time. After that, have nothing to do with him. [11]You may be sure that such a man is warped and sinful; he is self-condemned.

Final Remarks

[12]As soon as I send Artemas or Tychicus to you, do your best to come to me at Nicopolis, because I have decided to winter there. [13]Do everything you can to help Zenas the lawyer and Apollos on their way and see that they have everything they need. [14]Our people must learn to devote themselves to doing

Why emphasize "self-control" (1:6, 10;2:2,5,6,12;3:3) and doing "what is good" (2:3,6,14;3:1,8)? **3.** What does salvation mean for our behavior in the "present age" (v.12)? What conflicts does this verse imply Christians will face? **4.** How does this new lifestyle relate to Jesus' death (v.14)? To his return (v.13)?

REFLECT: **1.** Who has taught you in practical ways what it means to be a Christian? How has that mentor helped you? Who could you help now? **2.** What could you do this week to "make the teaching about God our Savior" (v.10) more attractive to your family? Among your friends? At work? **3.** How can the group help you say "no" to a current temptation?

OPEN: In what situation do you least exhibit your faith: In a checkout line? In a fender bender? After a tough exam? At the company picnic? In athletics? Other:____?

DIG: **1.** In this context, why do you suppose Paul again stresses "doing what is good" (vv.1, 8, 14)? What is it about human nature that makes such reminders necessary (v.3)? **2.** From verses 4-7, what can you learn about God's character? His work in us? His purposes for us? **3.** How do these truths promote humility? Gratitude? A life of service? **4.** What is the problem with the people mentioned in verses 9-11? How does this relate to Paul's other teachings on this matter (see 2Ti 2:25-26; 3:5)?

REFLECT: **1.** What were you like before God showed you his mercy? What were you like soon thereafter? If there's no dramatic "before and after" story to tell, what memories do you have about what happened "back then"? **2.** In doing what is good, which are you motivated by: (a) Call of duty? (b) Fear of Judgment? (c) Hope of Christ's return? (d) Gratitude for what God has done for you? (e) Desire to make peace in your relationships? (f) Needs of others? **3.** What "good" are you around your home? Around church? In

413

your city, state, or nation? (Or are you "up to no good"?) **4.** Over the past year, where do you sense growth in leading a "productive" life for God?

what is good, in order that they may provide for daily necessities and not live unproductive lives.

[15]Everyone with me sends you greetings. Greet those who love us in the faith.

Grace be with you all.

PHILEMON

INTRODUCTION

Characteristics

Philemon is the shortest of Paul's New Testament letters and it is his only private letter preserved in Scripture. All his other letters, whether to churches or to co-workers, relate to Paul's ministry. But Philemon is a personal note written to a friend about a private matter — the fate of Onesimus, the runaway slave. As such, it gives us a valuable glimpse into Paul's personality. He is deeply sympathetic to the plight of Onesimus, so much so that he is willing to deprive himself of Onesimus' help and to pay Philemon for any loss Onesimus has caused him (v. 19). This is certainly Christian compassion in action.

Slaves in the Roman Empire

We cannot understand the Epistle to Philemon without understanding something about the status of slaves in the first-century Roman world. First, slaves were considered property, not people. Therefore, they were under the absolute control of their master or mistress. A slave owner could beat or even kill a slave if he or she chose, although, in all fairness, many slaves fared quite well. Pliny, a Roman official, tells that Vedius Pollio ordered that a slave who had dropped a crystal goblet be thrown into the fishpond. There he was torn to pieces by lamprey (William Barclay, *Letters to Timothy, Titus, Philemon,* p. 316).

Onesimus had run away from his owner, Philemon. As a fugitive, he was subject to severe punishment or even death if caught. For Paul to send him back was an inconsiderable risk. Philemon had every right to brand Onesimus with the Letter F on his forehead (for *fugitivus* or runaway) or do even worse.

We often wonder why Paul does not simply condemn slavery on this occasion. This would have been a fine time to do so. Yet, as Lightfoot says, "The word 'emancipation' seems to be trembling on his lips, and yet he does not once utter it" (*Saint Paul and Epistles to the Colossians and to Philemon,* p. 321). The reason is partly clear: social conditions were not yet right for such a massive upheaval. There were sixty million slaves in the Roman Empire when Paul wrote. The social and economic structure of Rome was built around them. The Romans would never have voluntarily freed their slaves, and any revolt would have been crushed savagely. Emancipation did eventually come, spearheaded by Christian effort, but it was hundreds of years away.

In the meantime, Paul struck the first blow in that direction by declaring to the church at Colossae in his companion letter that "there is no Greek or Jew, circumcised or uncircumcised, barbarian, Scythian, slave or free, but Christ is all, and is in all" (Col. 3:11). In this private letter to Philemon, he said that Onesimus was returning "no longer as a slave, but better than a slave, as a dear brother" (v. 16).

Thus the master-slave relationship was transformed, and so the seeds were sown that led eventually to the abolition of slavery.

Onesimus

He was a slave. He may well have been a thief ("if he has done you any wrong or owes you anything, charge it to me," v. 18). He was certainly a fugitive. But he had become a Christian. Somehow he had met up with Paul. Perhaps he had gone to Rome to try to escape notice in that vast city, and his path had crossed Paul's. Or perhaps he had been caught and imprisoned alongside Paul. In any case, he was now a new man — living proof of Christ's power about which Paul writes to the Colossians.

The outcome of this story is never told. We do not know whether Paul's letter had the impact he hoped. But a curious piece of historical information might shed light on what happened. Some fifty years after Paul wrote Philemon, Ignatius, the bishop of Antioch, was being taken to Rome to be executed. Along the way at Smyrna, he wrote a letter to the church at Ephesus. In this letter he extolled their wonderful bishop, whose name was Onesimus! He referred to this man exactly as Paul did by making a pun on his name. Onesimus means "useful" or "profitable." "Formerly he was useless to you, but now he has become useful," Paul said (v. 11). Ignatius commented that "he is Onesimus by name and Onesimus by nature, the profitable one to Christ. It may well be that Onesimus, the runaway slave, had become with the passing years none other than Onesimus, the great bishop of Ephesus" (Barclay, *Letters to Timothy, Titus, Philemon,* p. 316).

If this was the case, it would explain how the letter to Philemon got into the New Testament. Many scholars feel that the first collection of Paul's letters was made at Ephesus at about the time Onesimus was bishop. He may have included this note as a vivid demonstration of how the great Christ can change and use even a fugitive slave like himself.

Philemon

[1]Paul, a prisoner of Christ Jesus, and Timothy our brother,

To Philemon our dear friend and fellow worker, [2]to Apphia our sister, to Archippus our fellow soldier and to the church that meets in your home:

[3]Grace to you and peace from God our Father and the Lord Jesus Christ.

Thanksgiving and Prayer

[4]I always thank my God as I remember you in my prayers, [5]because I hear about your faith in the Lord Jesus and your love for all the saints. [6]I pray that you may be active in sharing your faith, so that you will have a full understanding of every good thing we have in Christ. [7]Your love has given me great joy and encouragement, because you, brother, have refreshed the hearts of the saints.

Paul's Plea for Onesimus

[8]Therefore, although in Christ I could be bold and order you to do what you ought to do, [9]yet I appeal to you on the basis of love. I then, as Paul—an old man and now also a prisoner of Christ Jesus— [10]I appeal to you for my son Onesimus,[a] who became my son while I was in chains. [11]Formerly he was useless to you, but now he has become useful both to you and to me.

[12]I am sending him—who is my very heart—back to you. [13]I would have liked to keep him with me so that he could take your place in helping me while I am in chains for the gospel. [14]But I did not want to do anything without your consent, so that any favor you do will be spontaneous and not forced. [15]Perhaps the reason he was separated from you for a little while was that you might have him back for good— [16]no longer as a slave, but better than a slave, as a dear brother. He is very dear to me but even dearer to you, both as a man and as a brother in the Lord.

[17]So if you consider me a partner, welcome him as you would welcome me. [18]If he has done you any wrong or owes you anything, charge it to me. [19]I, Paul, am writing this with my own hand. I will pay it back—not to mention that you owe me your very self. [20]I do wish, brother, that I may have some benefit from you in the Lord; refresh my heart in Christ. [21]Confident of your obedience, I write to you, knowing that you will do even more than I ask.

[22]And one thing more: Prepare a guest room for me, because I hope to be restored to you in answer to your prayers.

[23]Epaphras, my fellow prisoner in Christ Jesus, sends you greetings. [24]And so do Mark, Aristarchus, Demas and Luke, my fellow workers.

[25]The grace of the Lord Jesus Christ be with your spirit.

OPEN: What name were you given at birth? What nicknames have you been given since? What do they mean? How are you living up to their meaning?

DIG: 1. What qualities in Philemon does Paul commend (vv.1-7)? How does this prepare the way for Paul's plea in verse 8? **2.** Given the seriousness of the crime committed by Onesimus (see Invitation page), what impact will Onesimus' return have on Philemon's household? On Paul's relationship with Philemon? On Onesimus himself? **3.** Does the fact that Onesimus has become a Christian lessen the seriousness of his crime? Why or why not? **4.** What is radical about Paul's view of Onesimus (vv.10-18)? **5.** Given Paul's concern and need for Onesimus, why does Paul return Onesimus to Philemon, anyway? Why doesn't Paul exert his apostolic authority, declare Onesimus free, and keep him as a partner in the gospel? **6.** What do you think the chances are that Philemon will do what Paul asks? In what way would Philemon be right to refuse Paul?

REFLECT: 1. Which of the qualities in Philemon (vv.4-7) do you wish to develop for yourself? How could doing so cause you to grow in new areas? **2.** Like Onesimus, do you have something you need to return to and make right? Do you have someone like Paul who can help you do that? **3.** When do you feel obligated to forgive someone: When they confess their sin? When they later change their behavior? When someone else intercedes for the offending party? **4.** For whom might you serve as a "Paul" in bringing about reconciliation?

---

[a]10 Onesimus means useful.

417

HEBREWS

INTRODUCTION

Author

No one knows who wrote the Epistle to the Hebrews. The author is nowhere named within it, nor is there any strong external evidence pointing to one particular person. These facts have not deterred speculation, however. At least eight good candidates for the role of author have been proposed.

A favorite choice has been Paul, probably because the King James translation wrongly lists him as author, even though such a designation is found in none of the ancient manuscripts. It is unlikely that Paul wrote Hebrews. The style and language of this epistle is quite unlike Paul's, although this fact is more evident in the Greek original than in the English translation. The Epistle to the Hebrews is a polished piece of writing. Its transitions are neatly in place and its argument carefully spelled out. This is in sharp contrast to Paul's more ragged style. He had the habit of losing the thread of his argument because he would become excited about some new piece of God's revelation before he had drawn to a logical conclusion the case he originally started to build.

Other suggested authors include Barnabas, Luke, Priscilla, Silvanus (1 Peter 5:12), Apollos, and Clement of Rome. Origen, a third-century Christian scholar, had the last word on this issue: He wrote that as to the identity of the author "only God knows certainly" (recorded in Eusebius, *Historia Ecclesiastica*).

Audience

The title "To the Hebrews" can be traced back to manuscripts of the late second century. Even though it was not a part of the original document, it seems an accurate designation given the very Jewish flavor of the epistle. This letter was probably written to a particular assembly of Jewish-Christian believers (perhaps a house church) that was part of a larger community, quite possibly in Rome.

Whoever these people were, it is clear that they had suffered great persecution (10:32-34) and that they were being tempted to abandon Christianity. What is less clear is the nature of the pressures weighing against them. Perhaps the constant indignities they suffered as Christians were beginning to take their toll. Or perhaps they were facing the prospect of severe persecution in the near future. Or the problem may have been internal. Maybe they were being enticed away from Christ by false teaching that seemed to offer relief from their struggles. They might have been considering a return to a form of Judaism as one way to bring community acceptance and thus lessen tensions.

In any case, the temptation to apostasy or reversion was severe enough that the letter to the Hebrews had to be written to encourage these beleaguered Christians to "hold on" (3:6), to "persevere" (10:36), and to "hold unswervingly to the hope we profess" (10:23) lest they compromise Christ and lose all the enormous blessings of the New Covenant.

Date

As with so much else about this epistle, it is difficult to be certain about its date of composition. If the persecution referred to is that of Nero, then Hebrews was written after A.D. 64. Some hold that it must have been written prior to the fall of Jerusalem and the destruction of the temple in A.D. 70, for such an unprecedented event would probably have been mentioned by the book's author as the sure sign of the end of the sacrificial system. Others argue for a later date. If the fall of Jerusalem were recent, they reason, it would be so gigantic and so fresh in the minds of the readers that it need not be mentioned. In that case, the book could have been written prior to the persecution by Emperor Domitian in A.D. 85, probably somewhere around A.D. 80.

Characteristics

To many modern readers, Hebrews is a strange book filled with references to ancient practices, with the presuppositions of a wholly different culture, and with images that evoke no recognition in the twentieth century. It is true that to understand Hebrews, the reader must understand the Old Testament. Yet for all its strangeness, the book of Hebrews continues to fascinate modern readers because of its vivid images, its relentless argument that refuses to detour from the main point, its stirring remembrances of the heroes of the faith, and most of all its almost breathtaking portrait of Jesus — the ultimate priest who, for ourselves for a time, was made a little lower than the angels. This Jesus captivates the mind and imagination of the twentieth-century person — this Jesus who not only gave strength to those enduring persecution two thousand years ago, but who still today gives strength to those facing the possibility of nuclear annihilation.

Themes

How does one write to suffering Christians and tell them to stay faithful despite the price they are paying? The author wisely begins not by considering their difficult circumstances nor by simply telling them, "This is the right thing to do, so do it." Instead, he points them to Jesus, the only one who is worth such costly allegiance. As a result, in the Book of Hebrews, we get a marvelous portrait of Christ — the prophet, priest, and king whose New Covenant is so superior to the Old Covenant that to fall away from him should be unthinkable. The central theme of Hebrews, therefore, is the superiority of Christ. He is superior to the great religious leaders of the past such as Moses, Joshua, and Aaron. He is superior to the great supernatural powers like angels. The New Covenant he established and the new order he inaugurated are superior to the old beliefs and practices of the Jewish religion.

Structure

This particular New Testament book has been called an epistle but in fact, it lacks several key features of a true letter. It has no introductory greeting, nor does it name either the sender or the recipients. Its ending is typical of a letter, however, with personal greetings and a standard conclusion.

If Hebrews is not a true letter, then what is it? Some have suggested that Hebrews is a written sermon. Certainly the book frequently has the feel of a sermon (e.g., 11:32), and it is written in the style of a sermon. Its method of argument is sermonic in nature. Structurally, its closest New Testament parallel is 1 John, which also seems to be a sermon.

Outline

Given its theme of Christ's superiority contrasted with warnings not to depart from him, the Book of Hebrews may be outlined as follows (adapted from Philip Edgcumbe Hughes, *A Commentary on the Epistle to the Hebrews*, pp. ix-x):
   1. Christ is superior to the prophets (1:1-3)
   2. Christ is superior to angels (1:4-2:18)
      (Warning 1: 2:1-4)
   3. Christ is superior to Moses (3:1-4:13)
      (Warning 2: 3:7-4:2)
   4. Christ is superior to the old priesthood (4:14-10:18)
      (Warning 3: 5:11-6:8)
   5. Christ is superior as the new and living way (10:19-13:25)
      (Warning 4: 10:26-31)
      (Warning 5: 12:14-17)
      (Warning 6: 12:25-29)

Hebrews

OPEN: 1. How are you like your mother or father: In artistic talent? Mechanical ability? Athletic ability? Forgetfulness? Distinctive features? **2.** What does your father do? Would you like to take over his business? Why (not)?

DIG: 1. To what (or whom) is Jesus compared here? **2.** What was the function of the OT prophets (v.1)? In what ways was Jesus' function similar? How was it different (vv.2-3)? How is Jesus superior to the prophets? What is the difference between "the past" (v.1) and "these last days" (v.2)? **3.** How does Jesus compare with God in terms of activity, authority, and relationship (vv.1-3)? **4.** In verses 5-14, what new facts does the author add to his portrait of Jesus? Which of these OT quotes, first said of the Lord God, is now applied to the Son Jesus? What does that imply? **5.** What do you suppose these readers thought of angels and of prophets that caused the author to write as he does? What counterpoint is the author trying to make about each?

REFLECT: 1. When did Jesus Christ become more than just a name to you? **2.** Of all the qualities of Jesus mentioned in verses 2-4, which one are you beginning to appreciate more and more? **3.** Of what help is it for the Christian that God has indeed spoken "at many times and in various ways"? Why not in just one way? Which seems to be God's chosen way of speaking especially to you? **4.** Does this passage imply that Jesus is God's *final* revelation? Most *authoritative* revelation? Most *complete* revelation? Only *self*-revelation? In each instance, tell why you think so.

The Son Superior to Angels

1 In the past God spoke to our forefathers through the prophets at many times and in various ways, [2]but in these last days he has spoken to us by his Son, whom he appointed heir of all things, and through whom he made the universe. [3]The Son is the radiance of God's glory and the exact representation of his being, sustaining all things by his powerful word. After he had provided purification for sins, he sat down at the right hand of the Majesty in heaven. [4]So he became as much superior to the angels as the name he has inherited is superior to theirs.

[5]For to which of the angels did God ever say,

> "You are my Son;
>   today I have become your Father[a]"[b]?

Or again,

> "I will be his Father,
>   and he will be my Son"[c]?

[6]And again, when God brings his firstborn into the world, he says,

> "Let all God's angels worship him."[d]

[7]In speaking of the angels he says,

> "He makes his angels winds,
>   his servants flames of fire."[e]

[8]But about the Son he says,

> "Your throne, O God, will last for ever and ever,
>   and righteousness will be the scepter of your
>   kingdom.
> [9]You have loved righteousness and hated wickedness;
>   therefore God, your God, has set you above your
>   companions
>   by anointing you with the oil of joy."[f]

[10]He also says,

> "In the beginning, O Lord, you laid the foundations of
>   the earth,
>   and the heavens are the work of your hands.
> [11]They will perish, but you remain;
>   they will all wear out like a garment.
> [12]You will roll them up like a robe;
>   like a garment they will be changed.
> But you remain the same,
>   and your years will never end."[g]

[13]To which of the angels did God ever say,

a5 Or *have begotten you*   *b5* Psalm 2:7   *c5* 2 Samuel 7:14; 1 Chron. 17:13
d6 Deut. 32:43 (see Dead Sea Scrolls and Septuagint)   *e7* Psalm 104:4
f9 Psalm 45:6,7   *g12* Psalm 102:25-27

420

"Sit at my right hand
until I make your enemies
a footstool for your feet"[h]?

[14]Are not all angels ministering spirits sent to serve those who will inherit salvation?

Warning to Pay Attention

2 We must pay more careful attention, therefore, to what we have heard, so that we do not drift away. [2]For if the message spoken by angels was binding, and every violation and disobedience received its just punishment, [3]how shall we escape if we ignore such a great salvation? This salvation, which was first announced by the Lord, was confirmed to us by those who heard him. [4]God also testified to it by signs, wonders and various miracles, and gifts of the Holy Spirit distributed according to his will.

Jesus Made Like His Brothers

[5]It is not to angels that he has subjected the world to come, about which we are speaking. [6]But there is a place where someone has testified:

"What is man that you are mindful of him,
the son of man that you care for him?
[7]You made him a little[i] lower than the angels;
you crowned him with glory and honor
[8] and put everything under his feet."[j]

In putting everything under him, God left nothing that is not subject to him. Yet at present we do not see everything subject to him. [9]But we see Jesus, who was made a little lower than the angels, now crowned with glory and honor because he suffered death, so that by the grace of God he might taste death for everyone.

[10]In bringing many sons to glory, it was fitting that God, for whom and through whom everything exists, should make the author of their salvation perfect through suffering. [11]Both the one who makes men holy and those who are made holy are of the same family. So Jesus is not ashamed to call them brothers. [12]He says,

"I will declare your name to my brothers;
in the presence of the congregation I will sing your praises."[k]

[13]And again,

"I will put my trust in him."[l]

And again he says,

"Here am I, and the children God has given me."[m]

[14]Since the children have flesh and blood, he too shared in their humanity so that by his death he might destroy him who holds the power of death—that is, the devil— [15]and free those

OPEN: 1. Back in school, what subject matter were you least attentive to? Why? **2.** When your parents went away, who were you "subject to" as a kid? How did you look upon this person or the rules imposed on you?

DIG: 1. What danger faces these people? What does it mean to "drift away"? **2.** What is the answer to the rhetorical question in verse 3? **3.** In contrast to the popular expectation of that day (v.5), to whom does God subject the world (vv.6-8a)? Why is this rule not yet complete nor universal? Who rules instead? **4.** In comparing people and angels (vv.5-8), how are we both lower and higher? What is the ultimate destiny of humanity? **5.** To what does the phrase "the world to come" refer (v.5)? How can the kingdom of God be *both present* (in Jesus, in history) *and future* (yet to come in history, or at end of time)? **6.** In what respects was Jesus "made lower than the angels" (v.9)? What elevated him above them? What does Jesus share in common with humanity (vv.7,9)? In which respect is Jesus unique? **7.** Why did we need someone with flesh and blood like us—not an angel—to die in our place (vv.14-18)? What did Jesus accomplish by his death as one of us? What is the goal of our salvation (vv.10-11)? What does it mean that Jesus *authors* salvation? **8.** What is the difference between the way Jesus made atonement (v.17) and the way the priests mediate atonement?

REFLECT: 1. When (if ever) did you drift away from the faith? Why? What "evidences for faith" helped bring you back? **2.** At what points might you be tempted to "bag the faith": After a big loss? When you seem to be making it very well on your own? When away from fellowship? When things are not going your way? When Christianity is mocked on TV talk shows? **3.** How do the achievements and example of

---

[h]13 Psalm 110:1   [i]7 Or *him for a little while;* also in verse 9   [j]8 Psalm 8:4-6
[k]12 Psalm 22:22   [l]13 Isaiah 8:17   [m]13 Isaiah 8:18

Jesus described here encourage you at such times? **4.** Of Jesus' three titles (brother, author of salvation, high priest), which one means most to you now? Why?

OPEN: 1. When lost on a trip, what do you do: Stop and ask directions? Check the map? Drive around until you find the way? **2.** Are you usually early or late getting to places, even to this Bible study? Why?

DIG: 1. What is the significance of "therefore" (v.1)? What are the practical implications of what has been written about Jesus in chapters 1 and 2? How is Jesus like an apostle? **2.** In what ways are Jesus and Moses similar? In what ways is Jesus greater? Why is that important? **3.** What new warning is given (vv.8,12)? How does this compare with 3:6 and 2:1-4? **4.** To what incident does the quotation from Psalms refer (vv.7-11; see Nu 14)? How did the people of Israel harden their hearts? With what results (vv.10-11)? What does it mean to turn away from the living God (v.12)? **5.** What role does the Christian community play in keeping us true to God (v.13)? What will be the outcome of faithfulness (vv.14-18)? **6.** What does it mean to "enter God's rest" (vv.11,18-19; see 4:1-11; Mt 11:28-30)?

REFLECT: 1. What are some practical ways that your church or small group could put verse 13 into practice? How can that help you? What apprehensions does it cause? **2.** What was one of the most rebellious times in your spiritual life? What resulted from it? Who (or what) helped to bring you back? **3.** How would you describe your heart now: Soft? Hard? Cold? Warm? Why is that?

who all their lives were held in slavery by their fear of death. [16]For surely it is not angels he helps, but Abraham's descendants. [17]For this reason he had to be made like his brothers in every way, in order that he might become a merciful and faithful high priest in service to God, and that he might make atonement for[n] the sins of the people. [18]Because he himself suffered when he was tempted, he is able to help those who are being tempted.

Jesus Greater Than Moses

3 Therefore, holy brothers, who share in the heavenly calling, fix your thoughts on Jesus, the apostle and high priest whom we confess. [2]He was faithful to the one who appointed him, just as Moses was faithful in all God's house. [3]Jesus has been found worthy of greater honor than Moses, just as the builder of a house has greater honor than the house itself. [4]For every house is built by someone, but God is the builder of everything. [5]Moses was faithful as a servant in all God's house, testifying to what would be said in the future. [6]But Christ is faithful as a son over God's house. And we are his house, if we hold on to our courage and the hope of which we boast.

Warning Against Unbelief

[7]So, as the Holy Spirit says:

"Today, if you hear his voice,
[8] do not harden your hearts
 as you did in the rebellion,
   during the time of testing in the desert,
[9]where your fathers tested and tried me
  and for forty years saw what I did.
[10]That is why I was angry with that generation,
  and I said, 'Their hearts are always going astray,
  and they have not known my ways.'
[11]So I declared on oath in my anger,
  'They shall never enter my rest.' "[o]

[12]See to it, brothers, that none of you has a sinful, unbelieving heart that turns away from the living God. [13]But encourage one another daily, as long as it is called Today, so that none of you may be hardened by sin's deceitfulness. [14]We have come to share in Christ if we hold firmly till the end the confidence we had at first. [15]As has just been said:

"Today, if you hear his voice,
  do not harden your hearts
  as you did in the rebellion."[p]

[16]Who were they who heard and rebelled? Were they not all those Moses led out of Egypt? [17]And with whom was he angry for forty years? Was it not with those who sinned, whose bodies fell in the desert? [18]And to whom did God swear that they would never enter his rest if not to those who disobeyed[q]? [19]So we see that they were not able to enter, because of their unbelief.

---

[n]17 Or *and that he might turn aside God's wrath, taking away*   [o]11 Psalm 95:7-11
[p]15 Psalm 95:7,8   [q]18 Or *disbelieved*

A Sabbath-Rest for the People of God

4 Therefore, since the promise of entering his rest still stands, let us be careful that none of you be found to have fallen short of it. ²For we also have had the gospel preached to us, just as they did; but the message they heard was of no value to them, because those who heard did not combine it with faith.ʳ ³Now we who have believed enter that rest, just as God has said,

"So I declared on oath in my anger,
'They shall never enter my rest.' "ˢ

And yet his work has been finished since the creation of the world. ⁴For somewhere he has spoken about the seventh day in these words: "And on the seventh day God rested from all his work."ᵗ ⁵And again in the passage above he says, "They shall never enter my rest."

⁶It still remains that some will enter that rest, and those who formerly had the gospel preached to them did not go in, because of their disobedience. ⁷Therefore God again set a certain day, calling it Today, when a long time later he spoke through David, as was said before:

"Today, if you hear his voice,
do not harden your hearts."ᵘ

⁸For if Joshua had given them rest, God would not have spoken later about another day. ⁹There remains, then, a Sabbath-rest for the people of God; ¹⁰for anyone who enters God's rest also rests from his own work, just as God did from his. ¹¹Let us, therefore, make every effort to enter that rest, so that no one will fall by following their example of disobedience.

¹²For the word of God is living and active. Sharper than any double-edged sword, it penetrates even to dividing soul and spirit, joints and marrow; it judges the thoughts and attitudes of the heart. ¹³Nothing in all creation is hidden from God's sight Everything is uncovered and laid bare before the eyes of him to whom we must give account.

Jesus the Great High Priest

¹⁴Therefore, since we have a great high priest who has gone through the heavens,ᵛ Jesus the Son of God, let us hold firmly to the faith we profess. ¹⁵For we do not have a high priest who is unable to sympathize with our weaknesses, but we have one who has been tempted in every way, just as we are—yet was without sin. ¹⁶Let us then approach the throne of grace with confidence, so that we may receive mercy and find grace to help us in our time of need.

5 Every high priest is selected from among men and is appointed to represent them in matters related to God, to offer gifts and sacrifices for sins. ²He is able to deal gently with those who are ignorant and are going astray, since he himself is subject to weakness. ³This is why he has to offer sacrifices for his own sins, as well as for the sins of the people.

---

r2 Many manuscripts *because they did not share in the faith of those who obeyed*
s3 Psalm 95:11; also in verse 5   t4 Gen. 2:2   u7 Psalm 95:7,8   v14 Or *gone into heaven*

OPEN: What is your favorite way to spend a restful Sunday afternoon?

DIG: 1. What is the author warning his readers about from the story of Israel's rebellion? What "message" (v.2) was given each community (see Ex 3:7; Nu 14:7-9)? With what reception and results? Why is hearing not enough? **2.** What is this "rest" promised by God: The promised land? Sunday off? Heaven? God's presence? How do verses 3b-10 support your answer? **3.** What is the proper response to the warning in verses 1 and 11? What does it mean that God's Word is living? Active? That it penetrates? How has the author used the "Word of God" thus far?

REFLECT: 1. How would you explain the promised rest to someone who is not a Christian? What situations today would make this type of exhortation necessary? **2.** What efforts (v.11) can help you enter into God's rest (see Mt 11:28-30; Jn 6:27-29)? **3.** What evidence do you have that the Word of God is living and active in your group study?

OPEN: 1. When you "blew it" as a kid, how did you feel about the mistake? About yourself? About others involved? **2.** From whom did you then draw comfort: A parent? Sibling? Friend? Your dog?

DIG: 1. What about Jesus' priesthood is most encouraging (vv.14-15; see 2:17; 3:1)? **2.** How does the role of the Jewish high priest compare to Jesus' role in terms of: (a) How each is chosen? (b) How each relates to sinners? (c) How each relates to God? **3.** What two qualities of Jesus allows the comparison to Melchizedek (vv. 6,10; see ch. 7)? **4.** What is the significance for our eternal salvation and current situation that Jesus was *fully human*? That Jesus was also *without sin*?

[4]No one takes this honor upon himself; he must be called by God, just as Aaron was. [5]So Christ also did not take upon himself the glory of becoming a high priest. But God said to him,

> "You are my Son;
>   today I have become your Father. [w] [x]

[6]And he says in another place,

> "You are a priest forever,
>   in the order of Melchizedek." [y]

[7]During the days of Jesus' life on earth, he offered up prayers and petitions with loud cries and tears to the one who could save him from death, and he was heard because of his reverent submission. [8]Although he was a son, he learned obedience from what he suffered [9]and, once made perfect, he became the source of eternal salvation for all who obey him [10]and was designated by God to be high priest in the order of Melchizedek.

Warning Against Falling Away

[11]We have much to say about this, but it is hard to explain because you are slow to learn. [12]In fact, though by this time you ought to be teachers, you need someone to teach you the elementary truths of God's word all over again. You need milk, not solid food! [13]Anyone who lives on milk, being still an infant, is not acquainted with the teaching about righteousness. [14]But solid food is for the mature, who by constant use have trained themselves to distinguish good from evil.

6 Therefore let us leave the elementary teachings about Christ and go on to maturity, not laying again the foundation of repentance from acts that lead to death, [z] and of faith in God, [2]instruction about baptisms, the laying on of hands, the resurrection of the dead, and eternal judgment. [3]And God permitting, we will do so.

[4]It is impossible for those who have once been enlightened, who have tasted the heavenly gift, who have shared in the Holy Spirit, [5]who have tasted the goodness of the word of God and the powers of the coming age, [6]if they fall away, to be brought back to repentance, because [a] to their loss they are crucifying the Son of God all over again and subjecting him to public disgrace.

[7]Land that drinks in the rain often falling on it and that produces a crop useful to those for whom it is farmed receives the blessing of God. [8]But land that produces thorns and thistles is worthless and is in danger of being cursed. In the end it will be burned.

[9]Even though we speak like this, dear friends, we are confident of better things in your case—things that accompany salvation. [10]God is not unjust; he will not forget your work and the love you have shown him as you have helped his people and continue to help them. [11]We want each of you to show this same diligence to the very end, in order to make your hope sure. [12]We do not want you to become lazy, but to imitate those who through faith and patience inherit what has been promised.

[w]5 Or *have begotten you*   [x]5 Psalm 2:7   [y]6 Psalm 110:4   [z]1 Or *from useless rituals*   [a]6 Or *repentance while*

The Certainty of God's Promise

[13]When God made his promise to Abraham, since there was no one greater for him to swear by, he swore by himself, [14]saying, "I will surely bless you and give you many descendants."[b] [15]And so after waiting patiently, Abraham received what was promised.

[16]Men swear by someone greater than themselves, and the oath confirms what is said and puts an end to all argument. [17]Because God wanted to make the unchanging nature of his purpose very clear to the heirs of what was promised, he confirmed it with an oath. [18]God did this so that, by two unchangeable things in which it is impossible for God to lie, we who have fled to take hold of the hope offered to us may be greatly encouraged. [19]We have this hope as an anchor for the soul, firm and secure. It enters the inner sanctuary behind the curtain, [20]where Jesus, who went before us, has entered on our behalf. He has become a high priest forever, in the order of Melchizedek.

Melchizedek the Priest

7 This Melchizedek was king of Salem and priest of God Most High. He met Abraham returning from the defeat of the kings and blessed him, [2]and Abraham gave him a tenth of everything. First, his name means "king of righteousness"; then also, "king of Salem" means "king of peace." [3]Without father or mother, without genealogy, without beginning of days or end of life, like the Son of God he remains a priest forever.

[4]Just think how great he was: Even the patriarch Abraham gave him a tenth of the plunder! [5]Now the law requires the descendants of Levi who become priests to collect a tenth from the people—that is, their brothers—even though their brothers are descended from Abraham. [6]This man, however, did not trace his descent from Levi, yet he collected a tenth from Abraham and blessed him who had the promises. [7]And without doubt the lesser person is blessed by the greater. [8]In the one case, the tenth is collected by men who die; but in the other case, by him who is declared to be living. [9]One might even say that Levi, who collects the tenth, paid the tenth through Abraham, [10]because when Melchizedek met Abraham, Levi was still in the body of his ancestor.

Jesus Like Melchizedek

[11]If perfection could have been attained through the Levitical priesthood (for on the basis of it the law was given to the people), why was there still need for another priest to come—one in the order of Melchizedek, not in the order of Aaron? [12]For when there is a change of the priesthood, there must also be a change of the law. [13]He of whom these things are said belonged to a different tribe, and no one from that tribe has ever served at the altar. [14]For it is clear that our Lord descended from Judah, and in regard to that tribe Moses said nothing about priests. [15]And what we have said is even more clear if another priest like

b14 Gen. 22:17

OPEN: Which tries your patience more: Slow elevators? Slow food service? Traffic jams? Christmas sales lines? Dad's homecoming?

DIG: 1. How would Abraham's example help these people (see 3:12; 6:6)? **2.** What effect did God's promise and oath have on Abraham's heir? How is this to affect Christians now?

REFLECT: 1. Where in your life does trust in God come hardest? Easiest? Why? **2.** What promises of God are your anchor?

OPEN: 1. As a child, who was your favorite super-hero? What could he or she do that you wished you could: Fly? Display super-strength? Always win? Talk his way out of anything? **2.** If you could live to be 100, but could retain either the *body* or the *mind* of a 30-year old, which would you choose to retain? Why?

DIG: 1. Chapter 7 picks up where 5:10 left off. From 7:1-10, what do we know about Melchizedek (see also Ge 14:17-20)? How did Abraham regard him? **2.** What is the main point in the comparison between Melchizedek and Abraham? How does Abraham's tithe and the blessing of Melchizedek demonstrate the greatness of Melchizedek? How is his priesthood superior to that which descended from Levi and Aaron (v.11)? Why is another type of priesthood needed? **3.** In what ways is Jesus like the Melchizedek portrayed here (vv.12-17)? **4.** Why was the law set aside (vv.18-19)? In what sense had it failed? How does the argument in verse 18 parallel that in verse 11? What are the two features of the Jewish religious system that have been superseded? **5.** In what ways is Jesus a better priest than those under the Jewish system (vv.20-28)? What is the relationship between the law and the oath? Why is the oath better?

REFLECT: 1. The author was showing Jesus' superiority over the priests to Jews who were tempted to go back to their old ways. What are some of the "old ways" that tempt you to turn from Jesus? How is Jesus superior to those old ways in your life? **2.** What difference does Jesus' "once-for-all" sacrifice make to you in terms of your security with God? Your self-image? Your desire to follow Christ?

Melchizedek appears, [16]one who has become a priest not on the basis of a regulation as to his ancestry but on the basis of the power of an indestructible life. [17]For it is declared:

> "You are a priest forever,
>   in the order of Melchizedek."[c]

[18]The former regulation is set aside because it was weak and useless [19](for the law made nothing perfect), and a better hope is introduced, by which we draw near to God.

[20]And it was not without an oath! Others became priests without any oath, [21]but he became a priest with an oath when God said to him:

> "The Lord has sworn
>   and will not change his mind:
> 'You are a priest forever.' "[c]

[22]Because of this oath, Jesus has become the guarantee of a better covenant.

[23]Now there have been many of those priests, since death prevented them from continuing in office; [24]but because Jesus lives forever, he has a permanent priesthood. [25]Therefore he is able to save completely[d] those who come to God through him, because he always lives to intercede for them.

[26]Such a high priest meets our need—one who is holy, blameless, pure, set apart from sinners, exalted above the heavens. [27]Unlike the other high priests, he does not need to offer sacrifices day after day, first for his own sins, and then for the sins of the people. He sacrificed for their sins once for all when he offered himself. [28]For the law appoints as high priests men who are weak; but the oath, which came after the law, appointed the Son, who has been made perfect forever.

The High Priest of a New Covenant

8 The point of what we are saying is this: We do have such a high priest, who sat down at the right hand of the throne of the Majesty in heaven, [2]and who serves in the sanctuary, the true tabernacle set up by the Lord, not by man.

[3]Every high priest is appointed to offer both gifts and sacrifices, and so it was necessary for this one also to have something to offer. [4]If he were on earth, he would not be a priest, for there are already men who offer the gifts prescribed by the law. [5]They serve at a sanctuary that is a copy and shadow of what is in heaven. This is why Moses was warned when he was about to build the tabernacle: "See to it that you make everything according to the pattern shown you on the mountain."[e] [6]But the ministry Jesus has received is as superior to theirs as the covenant of which he is mediator is superior to the old one, and it is founded on better promises.

[7]For if there had been nothing wrong with that first covenant, no place would have been sought for another. [8]But God found fault with the people and said[f]:

OPEN: 1. What are you best at forgetting: Names? Chores? Birthdays? Scripture references? **2.** If your car develops chronic problems, are you the type to keep fixing it up, or to buy a new one? How do you decide "it's got to go"?

DIG: 1. What's the point of the previous argument (vv.1-2)? How would this offer a strong incentive not to turn away from Christianity, as some were considering? **2.** Contrast the location, nature, and function of the two priesthoods (vv.1-5; see 5:14-15; 6:19-20; 7:23-28). How does an OT priest pre-figure what Jesus would really do? **3.** What is a covenant? What is the significance of the fact that God initiates and guarantees it? What is a mediator? Why is one needed? **4.** From Exodus 19:5-6, 20:1-17 and 29:35-41, what characterized the old covenant administered by the priests?

c17,21 Psalm 110:4   d25 Or forever   e5 Exodus 25:40   f8 Some manuscripts may be translated fault and said to the people.

"The time is coming, declares the Lord,
　when I will make a new covenant
with the house of Israel
　and with the house of Judah.
⁹It will not be like the covenant
　I made with their forefathers
when I took them by the hand
　to lead them out of Egypt,
because they did not remain faithful to my covenant,
　and I turned away from them,
　　　　　　　　　　　　　　declares the Lord.
¹⁰This is the covenant I will make with the house of Israel
　after that time, declares the Lord.
I will put my laws in their minds
　and write them on their hearts.
I will be their God,
　and they will be my people.
¹¹No longer will a man teach his neighbor,
　or a man his brother, saying, 'Know the Lord,'
because they will all know me,
　from the least of them to the greatest.
¹²For I will forgive their wickedness
　and will remember their sins no more." ᵍ

¹³By calling this covenant "new," he has made the first one obsolete; and what is obsolete and aging will soon disappear.

Worship in the Earthly Tabernacle

9 Now the first covenant had regulations for worship and also an earthly sanctuary. ²A tabernacle was set up. In its first room were the lampstand, the table and the consecrated bread; this was called the Holy Place. ³Behind the second curtain was a room called the Most Holy Place, ⁴which had the golden altar of incense and the gold-covered ark of the covenant. This ark contained the gold jar of manna, Aaron's staff that had budded, and the stone tablets of the covenant. ⁵Above the ark were the cherubim of the Glory, overshadowing the atonement cover. ʰ But we cannot discuss these things in detail now.

⁶When everything had been arranged like this, the priests entered regularly into the outer room to carry on their ministry. ⁷But only the high priest entered the inner room, and that only once a year, and never without blood, which he offered for himself and for the sins the people had committed in ignorance. ⁸The Holy Spirit was showing by this that the way into the Most Holy Place had not yet been disclosed as long as the first tabernacle was still standing. ⁹This is an illustration for the present time, indicating that the gifts and sacrifices being offered were not able to clear the conscience of the worshiper. ¹⁰They are only a matter of food and drink and various ceremonial washings—external regulations applying until the time of the new order.

How does the new covenant mediated by Jesus differ (vv.10-12)? What four promises does this new covenant involve? **5.** Why was a new covenant needed (vv.7-9,13)?

REFLECT: 1. Which aspect of the new covenant brings great joy to you now, and why: (a) Having God's law on your heart? (b) Being one of God's people? (c) Knowing God? (d) Having your sins forgiven? **2.** Which aspect of the covenant do you wish to experience more? Why? **3.** Has your experience of these promises been sudden and dramatic, a gradual awareness, or both? **4.** The old covenant ended up focusing on the people's ability (or inability) to measure up to God's demands. How do you still try to come to God on that basis? What happens? What does it mean to you that the new covenant is based on God's actions in Christ, and not on your efforts?

OPEN: In your childhood home, what place was off limits, or what thing were you told, "Don't touch"?

DIG: 1. How do you picture the earthly sanctuary described in verses 1-5? What is the significance of each item in the Holy Place? In the Most Holy Place? If your group wants to "discuss these things in detail now" (v.5), read Exodus 25-31 and 35-40. **2.** What goes on in the outer room (vv.6-10)? In the inner room (see Lev 16:14-16)? **3.** What did *not* happen here at this time (vv. 8-9)? Why were their gifts and sacrifices not sufficient to clear their consciences?

REFLECT: 1. Does "church" ever feel like a labyrinth to you? Why? **2.** When you feel guilty, how do you try to clear your conscience?

ᵍ12 Jer. 31:31-34　ʰ5 Traditionally *the mercy seat*

OPEN: 1. What event have you gone through once, but have since vowed "never again"? **2.** Have you ever seen a "blood and gore" movie? Which one? How did you feel about it?

DIG: 1. Jesus' priesthood is exercised here in what setting? By what right (v.12)? How often? **2.** How is the priesthood of Christ distinguished from the old system (vv.12-14)? What types of cleansing did the two sacrificial systems bring about? Why does Christ's sacrifice have the more significant, everlasting result? **3.** How is Christ's mediation like a "ransom" (v.15): Who are the hostages? Hostage to what? What is the ransom price? Are those who lived and died before Christ somehow covered by this ransom, too (see Ro 3:25)? **4.** How is Christ's death like a "will" made good (vv.16-18): Who are the beneficiaries? What is their inheritance? What puts the will in force? **5.** Why the emphasis on shed blood (vv.19-22): Whose blood? What for? How extensive is the application? How effective? **6.** What are the "copies" in this next analogy (vv. 23-24)? What is the real thing? What makes that reality "better" (vv.24-26)? **7.** In the last analogy here (vv.27-28), how is the once-and-for-allness of Christ's death illustrated?

REFLECT: 1. The author used OT analogies to explain the meaning of Christ's death to religious Jews. What analogies might clarify this with *non*-religious people today? **2.** In telling others that Christ died to take away their sins, what responses do you get: Lazy indifference? Sincere gratitude? Zealous devotion? What would help your message to have more impact?

OPEN: What repetitious activity do you dislike most: (a) Cleaning the bathroom? (b) Mowing the lawn? (c) Shaving? (d) Driving to and from work? (e) Doing the dishes? (f) Getting out of bed? Why? What daily rituals do you enjoy most?

The Blood of Christ

[11]When Christ came as high priest of the good things that are already here,[i] he went through the greater and more perfect tabernacle that is not man-made, that is to say, not a part of this creation. [12]He did not enter by means of the blood of goats and calves; but he entered the Most Holy Place once for all by his own blood, having obtained eternal redemption. [13]The blood of goats and bulls and the ashes of a heifer sprinkled on those who are ceremonially unclean sanctify them so that they are outwardly clean. [14]How much more, then, will the blood of Christ, who through the eternal Spirit offered himself unblemished to God, cleanse our consciences from acts that lead to death,[j] so that we may serve the living God!

[15]For this reason Christ is the mediator of a new covenant, that those who are called may receive the promised eternal inheritance—now that he has died as a ransom to set them free from the sins committed under the first covenant.

[16]In the case of a will,[k] it is necessary to prove the death of the one who made it, [17]because a will is in force only when somebody has died; it never takes effect while the one who made it is living. [18]This is why even the first covenant was not put into effect without blood. [19]When Moses had proclaimed every commandment of the law to all the people, he took the blood of calves, together with water, scarlet wool and branches of hyssop, and sprinkled the scroll and all the people. [20]He said, "This is the blood of the covenant, which God has commanded you to keep."[l] [21]In the same way, he sprinkled with the blood both the tabernacle and everything used in its ceremonies. [22]In fact, the law requires that nearly everything be cleansed with blood, and without the shedding of blood there is no forgiveness.

[23]It was necessary, then, for the copies of the heavenly things to be purified with these sacrifices, but the heavenly things themselves with better sacrifices than these. [24]For Christ did not enter a man-made sanctuary that was only a copy of the true one; he entered heaven itself, now to appear for us in God's presence. [25]Nor did he enter heaven to offer himself again and again, the way the high priest enters the Most Holy Place every year with blood that is not his own. [26]Then Christ would have had to suffer many times since the creation of the world. But now he has appeared once for all at the end of the ages to do away with sin by the sacrifice of himself. [27]Just as man is destined to die once, and after that to face judgment, [28]so Christ was sacrificed once to take away the sins of many people; and he will appear a second time, not to bear sin, but to bring salvation to those who are waiting for him.

Christ's Sacrifice Once for All

10 The law is only a shadow of the good things that are coming—not the realities themselves. For this reason it can never, by the same sacrifices repeated endlessly year after year, make perfect those who draw near to worship. [2]If it could, would they not have stopped being offered? For the worshipers

[i]11 Some early manuscripts *are to come*   [j]14 Or *from useless rituals*
[k]16 Same Greek word as *covenant*; also in verse 17   [l]20 Exodus 24:8

would have been cleansed once for all, and would no longer have felt guilty for their sins. ³But those sacrifices are an annual reminder of sins, ⁴because it is impossible for the blood of bulls and goats to take away sins.

⁵Therefore, when Christ came into the world, he said:

"Sacrifice and offering you did not desire,
but a body you prepared for me;
⁶with burnt offerings and sin offerings
you were not pleased.
⁷Then I said, 'Here I am—it is written about me in the
scroll—
I have come to do your will, O God.' " ᵐ

⁸First he said, "Sacrifices and offerings, burnt offerings and sin offerings you did not desire, nor were you pleased with them" (although the law required them to be made). ⁹Then he said, "Here I am, I have come to do your will." He sets aside the first to establish the second. ¹⁰And by that will, we have been made holy through the sacrifice of the body of Jesus Christ once for all.

¹¹Day after day every priest stands and performs his religious duties; again and again he offers the same sacrifices, which can never take away sins. ¹²But when this priest had offered for all time one sacrifice for sins, he sat down at the right hand of God. ¹³Since that time he waits for his enemies to be made his footstool, ¹⁴because by one sacrifice he has made perfect forever those who are being made holy.

¹⁵The Holy Spirit also testifies to us about this. First he says:

¹⁶"This is the covenant I will make with them
after that time, says the Lord.
I will put my laws in their hearts,
and I will write them on their minds." ⁿ

¹⁷Then he adds:

"Their sins and lawless acts
I will remember no more." ᵒ

¹⁸And where these have been forgiven, there is no longer any sacrifice for sin.

A Call to Persevere

¹⁹Therefore, brothers, since we have confidence to enter the Most Holy Place by the blood of Jesus, ²⁰by a new and living way opened for us through the curtain, that is, his body, ²¹and since we have a great priest over the house of God, ²²let us draw near to God with a sincere heart in full assurance of faith, having our hearts sprinkled to cleanse us from a guilty conscience and having our bodies washed with pure water. ²³Let us hold unswervingly to the hope we profess, for he who promised is faithful. ²⁴And let us consider how we may spur one another on toward love and good deeds. ²⁵Let us not give up meeting together, as some are in the habit of doing, but let us encourage one another—and all the more as you see the Day approaching.

ᵐ7 Psalm 40:6-8 (see Septuagint)   ⁿ16 Jer. 31:33   ᵒ17 Jer. 31:34

DIG: 1. Why is the law insufficient? Knowing how a shadow is produced, how then is the law a "shadow" of reality? Where is true reality? **2.** What is one positive function of the annual animal sacrifice? **3.** In what ways does Christ replace the inadequate sacrifices of the law? How does Jesus' obedience relate to our holiness? **4.** What is the significance of the contrasts between the old sacrificial system and the new (vv.11-13)? How did Jesus' once-and-for-all sacrifice make future sacrifices unnecessary? **5.** In the context of verse 14, in what sense are Christians *already* made perfect (or holy), while *still in the process* of being made holy (or perfect)?

REFLECT: 1. How much of your time is spent with a gnawing and vague sense of guilt: (a) All the time? (b) Most of the time? (c) Some of the time? (d) A fraction of the time? Why is that? **2.** Do you live your life as if you were being made holy (v.14)? Why or why not? In what way is God calling you to practice greater holiness? **3.** If you were asked to memorize one verse from this section, which would you choose, and why?

OPEN: How did you meet your spouse or "friend"? What was your first date with him or her?

DIG: 1. Based on Christ's sacrifice (vv.19-20; 9:1–10:18) and priesthood (v.21; 7:1–8:13), what attitudes and actions follow? Note the four "let us" statements in verses 22-25. What does each one mean? What incentives are given? **2.** How do verses 19-25 parallel 4:14-16? Why does the author need to stress this to these readers? **3.** If they habitually reject Christ in favor of sin, what do they forfeit (v.26; also 3:14; 6:4-6)? What can they expect instead (vv.27, 30-31)? Why is this fate not so unexpected (vv.28-29; also Dt 17:2-6)? **4.** In rejecting Christ, of what three grievous sins would they be guilty? With what consequence (v.31)? What false security would make such a warning necessary (see 4:12-13; 6:8)? **5.** After such a dire warning, how does the author appeal to previous testing, present action, and future events—all to encourage the Hebrews (vv.32-39)? Which appeal do you find persuasive?

REFLECT: 1. In what specific ways can you spur another Christian on toward love and good deeds? How have you been spurred on by others in your group? Whose exhortation, example, or encouragement means the most to you? **2.** How have you seen the difference between someone *assured* of their salvation (vv.19-25) and someone *presumptuous* about it (vv.26-31)? How can you develop confidence without presumption? **3.** How does the Second Coming help you to "keep on keeping on"?

<hr />

OPEN: As you consider the people in your small group, what's one positive adjective you would use to describe each person?

DIG: 1. What are the connections between 10:35-39 and the themes of chapter 11? **2.** In the definition and focus of faith in verses 1 and 6, what verbs describe faith? What is the object of these verbs? Is our faith directed toward the future, toward the present, or toward both? Toward God alone, or people as well? Why do you conclude this? Write your own expanded definition of faith as you try to capture the meaning of verse 1. **3.** How does verse 3 illustrate this understanding of faith? **4.** Why is Abel's sacrifice regarded as better than Cain's (see Ge 4:1-12)? How did Abel's sacrifice prefigure Christ's ultimate sacrifice in a way Cain's did not (recall ch. 9-10)? **5.** What aspect of faith (v.1) is demonstrated by Enoch (v.5; Ge 5: 21-24)? By Noah (v.7; Ge 6:5-22;

²⁶If we deliberately keep on sinning after we have received the knowledge of the truth, no sacrifice for sins is left, ²⁷but only a fearful expectation of judgment and of raging fire that will consume the enemies of God. ²⁸Anyone who rejected the law of Moses died without mercy on the testimony of two or three witnesses. ²⁹How much more severely do you think a man deserves to be punished who has trampled the Son of God under foot, who has treated as an unholy thing the blood of the covenant that sanctified him, and who has insulted the Spirit of grace? ³⁰For we know him who said, "It is mine to avenge; I will repay,"[p] and again, "The Lord will judge his people."[q] ³¹It is a dreadful thing to fall into the hands of the living God.

³²Remember those earlier days after you had received the light, when you stood your ground in a great contest in the face of suffering. ³³Sometimes you were publicly exposed to insult and persecution; at other times you stood side by side with those who were so treated. ³⁴You sympathized with those in prison and joyfully accepted the confiscation of your property, because you knew that you yourselves had better and lasting possessions.

³⁵So do not throw away your confidence; it will be richly rewarded. ³⁶You need to persevere so that when you have done the will of God, you will receive what he has promised. ³⁷For in just a very little while,

"He who is coming will come and will not delay.
³⁸   But my righteous one[r] will live by faith.
And if he shrinks back,
   I will not be pleased with him."[s]

³⁹But we are not of those who shrink back and are destroyed, but of those who believe and are saved.

By Faith

11 Now faith is being sure of what we hope for and certain of what we do not see. ²This is what the ancients were commended for.

³By faith we understand that the universe was formed at God's command, so that what is seen was not made out of what was visible.

⁴By faith Abel offered God a better sacrifice than Cain did. By faith he was commended as a righteous man, when God spoke well of his offerings. And by faith he still speaks, even though he is dead.

⁵By faith Enoch was taken from this life, so that he did not experience death; he could not be found, because God had taken him away. For before he was taken, he was commended as one who pleased God. ⁶And without faith it is impossible to please God, because anyone who comes to him must believe that he exists and that he rewards those who earnestly seek him.

⁷By faith Noah, when warned about things not yet seen, in holy fear built an ark to save his family. By his faith he condemned the world and became heir of the righteousness that comes by faith.

---

p30 Deut. 32:35   *q30* Deut. 32:36; Psalm 135:14   *r38* One early manuscript
But the righteous   *s38* Hab. 2:3,4

⁸By faith Abraham, when called to go to a place he would later receive as his inheritance, obeyed and went, even though he did not know where he was going. ⁹By faith he made his home in the promised land like a stranger in a foreign country; he lived in tents, as did Isaac and Jacob, who were heirs with him of the same promise. ¹⁰For he was looking forward to the city with foundations, whose architect and builder is God.

¹¹By faith Abraham, even though he was past age—and Sarah herself was barren—was enabled to become a father because he ' considered him faithful who had made the promise. ¹²And so from this one man, and he as good as dead, came descendants as numerous as the stars in the sky and as countless as the sand on the seashore.

¹³All these people were still living by faith when they died. They did not receive the things promised; they only saw them and welcomed them from a distance. And they admitted that they were aliens and strangers on earth. ¹⁴People who say such things show that they are looking for a country of their own. ¹⁵If they had been thinking of the country they had left, they would have had opportunity to return. ¹⁶Instead, they were longing for a better country—a heavenly one. Therefore God is not ashamed to be called their God, for he has prepared a city for them.

¹⁷By faith Abraham, when God tested him, offered Isaac as a sacrifice. He who had received the promises was about to sacrifice his one and only son, ¹⁸even though God had said to him, "It is through Isaac that your offspring ᵘ will be reckoned." ᵛ ¹⁹Abraham reasoned that God could raise the dead, and figuratively speaking, he did receive Isaac back from death.

²⁰By faith Isaac blessed Jacob and Esau in regard to their future.

²¹By faith Jacob, when he was dying, blessed each of Joseph's sons, and worshiped as he leaned on the top of his staff.

²²By faith Joseph, when his end was near, spoke about the exodus of the Israelites from Egypt and gave instructions about his bones.

²³By faith Moses' parents hid him for three months after he was born, because they saw he was no ordinary child, and they were not afraid of the king's edict.

²⁴By faith Moses, when he had grown up, refused to be known as the son of Pharaoh's daughter. ²⁵He chose to be mistreated along with the people of God rather than to enjoy the pleasures of sin for a short time. ²⁶He regarded disgrace for the sake of Christ as of greater value than the treasures of Egypt, because he was looking ahead to his reward. ²⁷By faith he left Egypt, not fearing the king's anger; he persevered because he saw him who is invisible. ²⁸By faith he kept the Passover and the sprinkling of blood, so that the destroyer of the firstborn would not touch the firstborn of Israel.

²⁹By faith the people passed through the Red Sea ʷ as on dry land; but when the Egyptians tried to do so, they were drowned.

³⁰By faith the walls of Jericho fell, after the people had marched around them for seven days.

7:11-12)? **6.** How is faith demonstrated or explained in each of the three examples from Abraham's life (vv.8-10, 11-12, 17-19)? What obstacles had to be overcome? What changed for him? For his family? **7.** What group of people does the author use next to illustrate faith (vv.17-31)? Recall each Old Testament story which is referred to: What do the stories in verses 17-22 have in common? **8.** What do you learn about faith from the example of Moses (vv.24-28)? **9.** In verses 29-38, what great achievements were accomplished as a result of faith? What price was paid? What came of such faith (vv.39-40)?

REFLECT: **1.** What are some verbs that describe your present level of faith? Why these? **2.** Of the people mentioned in this section, with whom do you feel you have the most in common? Why? With whom do you have the least in common? Why? Which situation would have been the most difficult for you to face? Why? What does it mean to you that not all these people of faith met with "success"? **3.** How has your life changed as a result of your faith in God? What has your faith cost you? How has your faith affected your neighbors? **4.** What does it mean to you to be an alien and a stranger on earth? In what ways do you feel like a stranger in this world? **5.** Who are some contemporary "heroes of faith" that spur you on today?

---

11 Or *By faith even Sarah, who was past age, was enabled to bear children because she* ᵘ*18* Greek *seed* ᵛ*18* Gen. 21:12 ʷ*29* That is, Sea of Reeds

[31]By faith the prostitute Rahab, because she welcomed the spies, was not killed with those who were disobedient. [x]

[32]And what more shall I say? I do not have time to tell about Gideon, Barak, Samson, Jephthah, David, Samuel and the prophets, [33]who through faith conquered kingdoms, administered justice, and gained what was promised; who shut the mouths of lions, [34]quenched the fury of the flames, and escaped the edge of the sword; whose weakness was turned to strength; and who became powerful in battle and routed foreign armies. [35]Women received back their dead, raised to life again. Others were tortured and refused to be released, so that they might gain a better resurrection. [36]Some faced jeers and flogging, while still others were chained and put in prison. [37]They were stoned[y]; they were sawed in two; they were put to death by the sword. They went about in sheepskins and goatskins, destitute, persecuted and mistreated— [38]the world was not worthy of them. They wandered in deserts and mountains, and in caves and holes in the ground.

[39]These were all commended for their faith, yet none of them received what had been promised. [40]God had planned something better for us so that only together with us would they be made perfect.

God Disciplines His Sons

12 Therefore, since we are surrounded by such a great cloud of witnesses, let us throw off everything that hinders and the sin that so easily entangles, and let us run with perseverance the race marked out for us. [2]Let us fix our eyes on Jesus, the author and perfecter of our faith, who for the joy set before him endured the cross, scorning its shame, and sat down at the right hand of the throne of God. [3]Consider him who endured such opposition from sinful men, so that you will not grow weary and lose heart.

[4]In your struggle against sin, you have not yet resisted to the point of shedding your blood. [5]And you have forgotten that word of encouragement that addresses you as sons:

"My son, do not make light of the Lord's discipline,
    and do not lose heart when he rebukes you,
[6]because the Lord disciplines those he loves,
    and he punishes everyone he accepts as a son." [z]

[7]Endure hardship as discipline; God is treating you as sons. For what son is not disciplined by his father? [8]If you are not disciplined (and everyone undergoes discipline), then you are illegitimate children and not true sons. [9]Moreover, we have all had human fathers who disciplined us and we respected them for it. How much more should we submit to the Father of our spirits and live! [10]Our fathers disciplined us for a little while as they thought best; but God disciplines us for our good, that we may share in his holiness. [11]No discipline seems pleasant at the time, but painful. Later on, however, it produces a harvest of righteousness and peace for those who have been trained by it.

OPEN: 1. What discipline did you sometimes resent as a child that you appreciate now: Practicing piano? Having a place for everything and everything in its place? Getting work in on time? Not overspending your allowance? **2.** Do you perform better before a crowd or in private? Why is that?

DIG: 1. How shall Christians run the race? What does it mean to throw off sin and hindrances? To run with perseverance? To fix our eyes on Jesus? **2.** What does hardship demonstrate about a person's relationship to God? How should a person respond to God when disciplined? How does Christ's discipline differ from human discipline? What benefits does discipline bring?

REFLECT: 1. What comfort do you get from knowing that a cloud of witnesses is watching you run the Christian race? **2.** What are two obstacles that hinder and entangle you in your race? Why? **3.** What have you discovered that helps you keep your eyes fixed on Jesus? **4.** How has God disciplined you in the past? How did his discipline lead to peace for you? **5.** What's the hardest thing you're going through right now? How is God using this in your life?

x31 Or *unbelieving*   y37 Some early manuscripts *stoned; they were put to the test;*
z6 Prov. 3:11,12

[12]Therefore, strengthen your feeble arms and weak knees. [13]"Make level paths for your feet,"[a] so that the lame may not be disabled, but rather healed.

Warning Against Refusing God

[14]Make every effort to live in peace with all men and to be holy; without holiness no one will see the Lord. [15]See to it that no one misses the grace of God and that no bitter root grows up to cause trouble and defile many. [16]See that no one is sexually immoral, or is godless like Esau, who for a single meal sold his inheritance rights as the oldest son. [17]Afterward, as you know, when he wanted to inherit this blessing, he was rejected. He could bring about no change of mind, though he sought the blessing with tears.

[18]You have not come to a mountain that can be touched and that is burning with fire; to darkness, gloom and storm; [19]to a trumpet blast or to such a voice speaking words that those who heard it begged that no further word be spoken to them, [20]because they could not bear what was commanded: "If even an animal touches the mountain, it must be stoned."[b] [21]The sight was so terrifying that Moses said, "I am trembling with fear."[c]

[22]But you have come to Mount Zion, to the heavenly Jerusalem, the city of the living God. You have come to thousands upon thousands of angels in joyful assembly, [23]to the church of the firstborn, whose names are written in heaven. You have come to God, the judge of all men, to the spirits of righteous men made perfect, [24]to Jesus the mediator of a new covenant, and to the sprinkled blood that speaks a better word than the blood of Abel.

[25]See to it that you do not refuse him who speaks. If they did not escape when they refused him who warned them on earth, how much less will we, if we turn away from him who warns us from heaven? [26]At that time his voice shook the earth, but now he has promised, "Once more I will shake not only the earth but also the heavens."[d] [27]The words "once more" indicate the removing of what can be shaken—that is, created things—so that what cannot be shaken may remain.

[28]Therefore, since we are receiving a kingdom that cannot be shaken, let us be thankful, and so worship God acceptably with reverence and awe, [29]for our "God is a consuming fire."[e]

Concluding Exhortations

13 Keep on loving each other as brothers. [2]Do not forget to entertain strangers, for by so doing some people have entertained angels without knowing it. [3]Remember those in prison as if you were their fellow prisoners, and those who are mistreated as if you yourselves were suffering.

[4]Marriage should be honored by all, and the marriage bed kept pure, for God will judge the adulterer and all the sexually immoral. [5]Keep your lives free from the love of money and be content with what you have, because God has said,

[a]13 Prov. 4:26   [b]20 Exodus 19:12,13   [c]21 Deut. 9:19   [d]26 Haggai 2:6
[e]29 Deut. 4:24

OPEN: If you could choose any major city to move to with the right job, by what criteria would you choose the city: Friends or family? Climate? Housing? Cultural or athletic pursuits? Skyline?

DIG: 1. How do the instructions and Esau's example given here (vv.14-17; see Ge 25:29-34) relate to disciplining your weaker members (vv.12-13)? **2.** What is the point of the comparison between are Mt. Sinai (vv.18-21) and Mt. Zion (vv.22-24)? **3.** What is the "better word" (v.24) in contrast to "no further word" (v.19)? What do the words "once more" convey (vv.26-27)? **4.** How does this play on words sum up the author's argument throughout the book? What happens to any who refuse God's voice (vv.18-21,25-29)? To those who heed his call?

REFLECT: 1. What efforts have you made to "live in peace with all"? **2.** In relationships that fail, do you believe it is because one or both parties didn't try hard enough? What can be done to see that people who are torn apart, despite their best efforts, do not also miss the grace of God? **2.** What in this passage comforts you? What makes you uneasy? What thrills you most about the city of the living God?

OPEN: 1. In one or two words, how would you describe the relationship you had with your brothers and sisters when you were growing up? **2.** Who has been as close to you as a brother?

DIG: 1. In what areas should "brotherly love" define Christians (vv.1-7)? What consequences are spelled out here for those who do? For those who don't? What help is offered for those who struggle (vv.6,8)? **2.** How are we to regard our leaders (vv.7,11,17), and why? How does this reflect our regard for the changeless

Christ? **3.** What "strange teaching" was a particular temptation to Hebrew Christians (vv.9-10)? What rituals, mores, and other forms of legalism tempt believers of any age? Why? **4.** What is the point of the argument in verses 9-14? Based on his argument, what types of "sacrifices" is God concerned with (vv.15-16)? **5.** Why does the author desire their prayers (vv.18-19)? How would you paraphrase his prayer for them (vv.20-21)? **6.** From verses 1-19, how would you sum up the Christian lifestyle?

REFLECT: 1. In which of these six areas have you made the most progress this year: (a) Loving one another as brothers? (b) Providing hospitality? (c) Caring for those suffering for their faith? (d) Keeping your marriage strong? (e) Staying free from the love of money? (f) Submitting to leaders in authority? Which do you need the most work on? **2.** In which of these six areas is your church the strongest? The weakest? Would you say "an obedient congregation prays for its leaders"? Or would you say "a praying congregation obeys its leaders"? What's the difference? **3.** Considering all you have seen about Jesus in this book, write out a "sacrifice of praise" to him now reflecting on all he has done for us. What sacrifice of "doing good and sharing" can you offer this week? **4.** What's been the most significant thing you've learned from studying Hebrews? How has this affected your life?

"Never will I leave you;
  never will I forsake you."*f*

⁶So we say with confidence,

"The Lord is my helper; I will not be afraid.
  What can man do to me?"*g*

⁷Remember your leaders, who spoke the word of God to you. Consider the outcome of their way of life and imitate their faith. ⁸Jesus Christ is the same yesterday and today and forever.

⁹Do not be carried away by all kinds of strange teachings. It is good for our hearts to be strengthened by grace, not by ceremonial foods, which are of no value to those who eat them. ¹⁰We have an altar from which those who minister at the tabernacle have no right to eat.

¹¹The high priest carries the blood of animals into the Most Holy Place as a sin offering, but the bodies are burned outside the camp. ¹²And so Jesus also suffered outside the city gate to make the people holy through his own blood. ¹³Let us, then, go to him outside the camp, bearing the disgrace he bore. ¹⁴For here we do not have an enduring city, but we are looking for the city that is to come.

¹⁵Through Jesus, therefore, let us continually offer to God a sacrifice of praise—the fruit of lips that confess his name. ¹⁶And do not forget to do good and to share with others, for with such sacrifices God is pleased.

¹⁷Obey your leaders and submit to their authority. They keep watch over you as men who must give an account. Obey them so that their work will be a joy, not a burden, for that would be of no advantage to you.

¹⁸Pray for us. We are sure that we have a clear conscience and desire to live honorably in every way. ¹⁹I particularly urge you to pray so that I may be restored to you soon.

²⁰May the God of peace, who through the blood of the eternal covenant brought back from the dead our Lord Jesus, that great Shepherd of the sheep, ²¹equip you with everything good for doing his will, and may he work in us what is pleasing to him, through Jesus Christ, to whom be glory for ever and ever. Amen.

²²Brothers, I urge you to bear with my word of exhortation, for I have written you only a short letter.

²³I want you to know that our brother Timothy has been released. If he arrives soon, I will come with him to see you.

²⁴Greet all your leaders and all God's people. Those from Italy send you their greetings.

²⁵Grace be with you all.

*f*5 Deut. 31:6 *g*6 Psalm 118:6,7

JAMES

INTRODUCTION

Authorship

In the New Testament there are apparently five men by the name of James, but only two who might conceivably have written this epistle — either James the apostle, or James the brother of Jesus. Since it is almost certain that the apostle James (the son of Zebedee) was killed by Herod in A.D. 44 (before the epistle could have been written), traditionally the author has been assumed to be James, the leader of the church in Jerusalem and the brother of Jesus (Mark 6:3).

The pilgrimage of James to faith is fascinating. At first Jesus' family was hostile to his ministry (John 7:5) and, in fact, tried to stop it at one point (Mark 3:21). Yet after Jesus' ascension, Jesus' mother and brothers are listed among the early believers (Acts 1:14). For James, this coming to faith may have resulted from Jesus' postresurrection appearance to him (1 Cor. 15:7).

Apart from the fact that they were closely related, James' relationship to Jesus is not totally clear. Some maintained that they were cousins (the New Testament word for "brother" is looser in meaning than the modern equivalent). Some suggest he was a half-brother to Jesus, a son of Mary and Joseph. Others say that James might have been an older stepbrother of Jesus by a (conjectural) marriage of Joseph previous to his marriage to Mary. The latter view, which excludes any blood relationship to Jesus, might better explain the failure of Jesus' brother to believe in Him during His lifetime (Mark 3:21, John 7:2-8); and James' lack of concern for Mary because she was only their stepmother might also explain why Jesus, from the cross, committed His mother to the apostle John (John 19:25-27). But the reason may have been that Mary's discipleship alienated her from her other children, who still did not believe in Jesus (Robert H. Gundrey, *A Survey of the New Testament,* p. 324).

A Church Leader

In any case, James emerged as the leader of the church in Jerusalem. It was to James that Peter reported after his miraculous escape from Herod's prison (Acts 12:17). James presided over the first Jerusalem Council which decided the important question of whether to admit Gentiles to the church (Acts 15, especially vv. 13-21). James was consulted by Paul during his first trip to Jerusalem after his conversion (Gal. 1:19), and then James joined in the official recognition of Paul's call as Apostle to the Gentiles (Gal. 2:8-10). It is to James that Paul later brought the collection for the poor (Acts 21:17-25).

A Jew

We also know that James was a strict Jew who adhered to the Mosaic Law (Gal. 2:12), yet unlike the Judaizers, he supported Paul's ministry to the Gentiles (Acts 21:17-26). Later accounts indicate that James was martyred in A.D. 62.

The question of who wrote the book of James is, however, still somewhat of a puzzle primarily because Jesus and his saving work is mentioned so little — a curious omission if the author was Jesus' brother. This question baffled even the ancient church. Both the Latin Father Jerome and the church historian Eusebius (as well as others) observe that not all accept James as having been written by our Lord's brother.

Audience

James is one of the Catholic (general) Epistles (along with 1 and 2 Peter, John's epistles, and Jude), so called because it has no single destination. Thus, it is not clear to whom James

435

is addressing his comments. At first glance, it appears that he is writing to Jewish Christians dispersed around the Greek world: "to the twelve tribes scattered among the nations" (1:1). But since Peter uses the same sort of inscription (1 Peter 1:1-2) when he is clearly addressing Gentile Christians who consider themselves the New Israel, James' destination remains unclear. In fact, a strong case can be made (see Sophie Laws, *The Epistle of James: Harper New Testament Commentaries,* pp. 32-38) that James was writing for a community of "God-fearers," that is, Gentiles who had been deeply attracted to Judaism. That such folk were then drawn to Christianity is clear from examples in Acts, such as Cornelius (Acts 10:2, 22), Lydia (Acts 16:14), Titius Justus (Acts 18:7), and others. This would help to explain the convergence of Jewish, Greek, and Christian elements in the book of James.

Date

It is difficult to date the Book of James. Some place it very early, around A.D. 45, making it the first New Testament book. Others date it quite late.

Characteristics

Among the New Testament books, James is an oddity. It is written in quite a different style from the others, more like the Book of Proverbs than Paul's epistles. But even more than its style, its contents set James apart. It does not treat many of those themes we have come to expect in the New Testament.

Its Omissions

There is no mention of the Holy Spirit and no reference to the redemptive work or resurrection of Christ. In fact, it contains only two references to the name Jesus Christ (1:1 and 2:1). Furthermore, when examples are given, they are drawn from the lives of Old Testament prophets, not from the experiences of Jesus. Although the title *Lord* appears eleven times, it generally refers to the name of God (in Old Testament fashion) and not to the kingly authority of Jesus. Indeed, it is God the Father who is the focus of the Book of James.

Thus, Martin Luther wrote in his preface to the New Testament that "St. John's Gospel and his first epistle, St. Paul's epistles, especially Romans, Galatians, and Ephesians, and St. Peter's first epistle are the books that show you Christ and teach you all that is necessary and salvatory for you to know, even if you were never to see or hear any other book or doctrine. Therefore St. James' epistle is really an epistle of straw, compared to these others, for it has nothing of the nature of the gospel about it."

Its Contributions

Luther notwithstanding, James is clearly a Christian piece of writing. Full of wisdom, it is based solidly on the teaching of Jesus and is a genuine product of first-century Christianity. To be sure, it is not as directly theological as many other New Testament Epistles, but then James' concern is not doctrinal (which he seems to assume) but rather ethical — how the Christian faith is to be lived on a day-by-day basis. As Johann Gottfrieds Herder wrote, "If the Epistle is of straw, then there is within that straw a very hearty, firm, nourishing . . . grain" (*Briefe Zweener Brüder Jesu in unserem Kanon,* in *Herders sömmtliche Werke* ed. Bernard Suphan, Vol 7, p. 500, n. 2).

Background

James draws his language, images, and ideas from three worlds: Judaism, Greek culture, and early Christianity. From Christianity, he uses the language of eschatology (5:7-9), common patterns of Christian ethical instruction, which parallel those in 1 Peter (1:2-4, 21; 4:7-10), and especially, the teachings of Jesus (1:5, 17; 2:5, 8, 19; 4:3; 5:12). From Judaism, he draws his insistence on the unity of God, concern for keeping law, and quotations from Jewish Scriptures (2:8, 11, 21-25; 4:6; 5:11, 17-18) along with his use of Jewish terms (e.g., the word translated "hell" in 3:6 is the Hebrew Gehenna). Christianity and Judaism shared his concern for the poor and oppressed. From the Greek-speaking world — "the shared culture of the eastern Mediterranean area within the Roman Empire that resulted from the conquests of Alexander the Great" (Laws, *The Epistle of James*, p. 5), he takes the language (which he uses with skill), the source of his Old Testament quotations (he uses the Greek Old Testament, not the Hebrew version), Greek forms of composition, and metaphors drawn from Greek and Latin sources (e.g., the horse and the ship in 3:3-4).

Structure

Written in epistle (letter) form, James is loosely structured and rambling in style. It seems to jump from one idea to another without any overall plan, apart from that of providing a manual of Christian conduct. In fact, the Book of James shares many characteristics of the sermonic style of both Greek philosophers and Jewish rabbis. As in Greek sermons, James carries on a conversation with a hypothetical opponent (2:18-26; 5:13-16), switches subjects by means of a question (2:14; 4:1), uses many commands (60 of the 108 verses in James are imperatives), relies on vivid images from everyday life (3:3-6; 5:7), illustrates points by reference to famous people (2:21-23, 25; 5:11, 17), uses vivid antitheses in which the right way is set alongside the wrong way (2:13, 26), begins the sermon with a striking paradox that captures the hearers' attention (1:2, "consider it pure joy . . . whenever you face trials"), is quite stern (2:20; 4:4), and clinches a point by means of a quotation (1:11, 17; 4:6; 5:11, 20) (Ropes and Barclay). It should be noted, as William Barclay writes:

> The main aim of these ancient preachers, it must be remembered, was not to investigate new truth; it was to awaken sinners to the error of their ways, and to compel them to see truths which they knew but deliberately neglected or had forgotten (*The Letters of James and Peter*, pp. 33-34).

Jewish sermons had many of the same characteristics. But rabbis also had the habit, as did James, of constructing sermons that were deliberately disconnected — a series of moral truths and exhortations strung together like beads.

Theme

While James clearly stands in the tradition of other Christian writers, he has some special concerns. The relationship between rich and poor crops up at various points (1:9-11; 5:1-4) — an issue of special significance to the modern affluent West. He is concerned about the use and abuse of speech (1:19, 22-24, 26; 2:12; 3:3-12; 5:12). He gives instruction on prayer (1:5-8; 4:2-3; 5:13-18). Above all, he is concerned with ethical behavior. How believers act, he says, has eschatological significance; future reward or punishment depends on it. In this regard, James bemoans the inconsistence of human behavior (1:6-8, 22-24; 2:14-17; 4:1, 3). Human beings are "double-minded" (1:8; 4:8) in sharp contrast to God, who is one (2:19).

James has been incorrectly understood by some to be contradicting Paul's doctrine of justification by faith (2:14-26). In fact if James had Paul in mind at all, he was addressing himself to those who had perverted Paul's message — insisting that it doesn't matter what you do, as long as you have faith. James responded by asserting that works are the outward evidence of inner faith. Works make faith visible to others. In contrast, Paul was concerned with our standing before God. As is evident from Romans 12-15, Paul certainly agreed with James that faith in Christ has direct implications for how believers live.

James

OPEN: 1. Are you more likely to write a letter or call? **2.** When the mail arrives, what do you open and read first? **3.** As you look back on the "good ol' days" in your life, were they more likely to be the hard times or the easy times?

DIG: 1. What three themes are introduced here? How are they related to each other? **2.** Does James view hardships as an idealist or realist? Why? **3.** What wisdom is needed in those times? In receiving wisdom, is doubt ever to be expressed? Why (not)? How so? **4.** Who are these poor and rich? What's there to take pride in? What is "low" about a rich person's position? **5.** What is the practical difference between *trials* and *temptations*? How would you illustrate the process in verses 14-15? How is this related to the gifts from God (vv.16-18)?

REFLECT: 1. Concerning a trial you have experienced, what pressures did it bring on your faith? What wisdom did you gain through it? **2.** With so much wealth in society, what do verses 9-11 mean to you? What then should you "take pride in"? **3.** What are the warning signs that you are being enticed by your evil desires? What helps you break the spell? **4.** What is a "good and perfect gift" for which you are thankful?

1 James, a servant of God and of the Lord Jesus Christ,

To the twelve tribes scattered among the nations:

Greetings.

Trials and Temptations

[2]Consider it pure joy, my brothers, whenever you face trials of many kinds, [3]because you know that the testing of your faith develops perseverance. [4]Perseverance must finish its work so that you may be mature and complete, not lacking anything. [5]If any of you lacks wisdom, he should ask God, who gives generously to all without finding fault, and it will be given to him. [6]But when he asks, he must believe and not doubt, because he who doubts is like a wave of the sea, blown and tossed by the wind. [7]That man should not think he will receive anything from the Lord; [8]he is a double-minded man, unstable in all he does.

[9]The brother in humble circumstances ought to take pride in his high position. [10]But the one who is rich should take pride in his low position, because he will pass away like a wild flower. [11]For the sun rises with scorching heat and withers the plant; its blossom falls and its beauty is destroyed. In the same way, the rich man will fade away even while he goes about his business.

[12]Blessed is the man who perseveres under trial, because when he has stood the test, he will receive the crown of life that God has promised to those who love him.

[13]When tempted, no one should say, "God is tempting me." For God cannot be tempted by evil, nor does he tempt anyone; [14]but each one is tempted when, by his own evil desire, he is dragged away and enticed. [15]Then, after desire has conceived, it gives birth to sin; and sin, when it is full-grown, gives birth to death.

[16]Don't be deceived, my dear brothers. [17]Every good and perfect gift is from above, coming down from the Father of the heavenly lights, who does not change like shifting shadows. [18]He chose to give us birth through the word of truth, that we might be a kind of firstfruits of all he created.

Listening and Doing

[19]My dear brothers, take note of this: Everyone should be quick to listen, slow to speak and slow to become angry, [20]for man's anger does not bring about the righteous life that God desires. [21]Therefore, get rid of all moral filth and the evil that is so prevalent and humbly accept the word planted in you, which can save you.

[22]Do not merely listen to the word, and so deceive yourselves. Do what it says. [23]Anyone who listens to the word but does not do what it says is like a man who looks at his face in a mirror [24]and, after looking at himself, goes away and immediately forgets what he looks like. [25]But the man who looks intently into the perfect law that gives freedom, and continues to do this, not

OPEN: 1. Which best describes your temper: Short fuse, big bomb? Long fuse, little fizz? Long fuse, H-bomb? Explain. **2.** For what things are you sure to check a mirror before leaving the house?

DIG: 1. What exactly is the "righteous life that God desires" (vv.20, 27)? How is it produced? What is its opposite? **2.** What's the point of the mirror image? How is this point reflected in both worthless and pure religion (vv.26-27)?

forgetting what he has heard, but doing it—he will be blessed in what he does.

²⁶If anyone considers himself religious and yet does not keep a tight rein on his tongue, he deceives himself and his religion is worthless. ²⁷Religion that God our Father accepts as pure and faultless is this: to look after orphans and widows in their distress and to keep oneself from being polluted by the world.

Favoritism Forbidden

2 My brothers, as believers in our glorious Lord Jesus Christ, don't show favoritism. ²Suppose a man comes into your meeting wearing a gold ring and fine clothes, and a poor man in shabby clothes also comes in. ³If you show special attention to the man wearing fine clothes and say, "Here's a good seat for you," but say to the poor man, "You stand there" or "Sit on the floor by my feet," ⁴have you not discriminated among yourselves and become judges with evil thoughts?

⁵Listen, my dear brothers: Has not God chosen those who are poor in the eyes of the world to be rich in faith and to inherit the kingdom he promised those who love him? ⁶But you have insulted the poor. Is it not the rich who are exploiting you? Are they not the ones who are dragging you into court? ⁷Are they not the ones who are slandering the noble name of him to whom you belong?

⁸If you really keep the royal law found in Scripture, "Love your neighbor as yourself,"ᵃ you are doing right. ⁹But if you show favoritism, you sin and are convicted by the law as lawbreakers. ¹⁰For whoever keeps the whole law and yet stumbles at just one point is guilty of breaking all of it. ¹¹For he who said, "Do not commit adultery,"ᵇ also said, "Do not murder."ᶜ If you do not commit adultery but do commit murder, you have become a lawbreaker.

¹²Speak and act as those who are going to be judged by the law that gives freedom, ¹³because judgment without mercy will be shown to anyone who has not been merciful. Mercy triumphs over judgment!

Faith and Deeds

¹⁴What good is it, my brothers, if a man claims to have faith but has no deeds? Can such faith save him? ¹⁵Suppose a brother or sister is without clothes and daily food. ¹⁶If one of you says to him, "Go, I wish you well; keep warm and well fed," but does nothing about his physical needs, what good is it? ¹⁷In the same way, faith by itself, if it is not accompanied by action, is dead.

¹⁸But someone will say, "You have faith; I have deeds."

Show me your faith without deeds, and I will show you my faith by what I do. ¹⁹You believe that there is one God. Good! Even the demons believe that—and shudder.

²⁰You foolish man, do you want evidence that faith without deeds is uselessᵈ? ²¹Was not our ancestor Abraham considered righteous for what he did when he offered his son Isaac on the

---

REFLECT: 1. Think of one failed and one successful relationship you have. What would (or did) change if (when) verses 19-20 were applied with each regularly? **2.** What from God's Word here will you put into action this week?

OPEN: 1. For what event would you buy the "best seats": World Series? Carnegie Hall? Child's school play? **2.** Contrast any two branches of your family tree in terms of what they've got and what they lack. Put yourself on a limb.

DIG: 1. James is writing to an economically depressed community. Why would favoritism be a problem in this setting? **2.** For what reasons does James oppose favoritism (vv.4-13)? **3.** What is the "law" (vv.8-12; see 1:25)? Its purpose? Its consequences?

REFLECT: 1. To you, who are people with "gold rings": The rich? Powerful? Athletic? Mr. Right? **2.** Who are today's "poor": Orphans? School dropouts? Refugees? Single parents? What would change if the "royal law" and "God's favoritism" were applied to them? **3.** How has favoritism in Christian circles affected you and yours?

OPEN: Are you a doer or a thinker? Are you more likely to act without thinking, or think without acting? Give an example.

DIG: 1. Pretend the scene in verses 15-17 happened in your church this Sunday. Role play how "faith without works" differs from "faith with works." What is the underlying problem here? The solution? **2.** How do Abraham (Ge 22) and Rahab (Jos 2) prove James' point? **3.** How does Paul's argument in Romans 3:28 differ from James' point in 2:24? What kind of faith is each criticizing?

ᵃ8 Lev. 19:18   ᵇ11 Exodus 20:14; Deut. 5:18   ᶜ11 Exodus 20:13; Deut. 5:17
ᵈ20 Some early manuscripts *dead*

altar? ²²You see that his faith and his actions were working together, and his faith was made complete by what he did. ²³And the scripture was fulfilled that says, "Abraham believed God, and it was credited to him as righteousness,"ᵉ and he was called God's friend. ²⁴You see that a person is justified by what he does and not by faith alone.

²⁵In the same way, was not even Rahab the prostitute considered righteous for what she did when she gave lodging to the spies and sent them off in a different direction? ²⁶As the body without the spirit is dead, so faith without deeds is dead.

Taming the Tongue

3 Not many of you should presume to be teachers, my brothers, because you know that we who teach will be judged more strictly. ²We all stumble in many ways. If anyone is never at fault in what he says, he is a perfect man, able to keep his whole body in check.

³When we put bits into the mouths of horses to make them obey us, we can turn the whole animal. ⁴Or take ships as an example. Although they are so large and are driven by strong winds, they are steered by a very small rudder wherever the pilot wants to go. ⁵Likewise the tongue is a small part of the body, but it makes great boasts. Consider what a great forest is set on fire by a small spark. ⁶The tongue also is a fire, a world of evil among the parts of the body. It corrupts the whole person, sets the whole course of his life on fire, and is itself set on fire by hell.

⁷All kinds of animals, birds, reptiles and creatures of the sea are being tamed and have been tamed by man, ⁸but no man can tame the tongue. It is a restless evil, full of deadly poison.

⁹With the tongue we praise our Lord and Father, and with it we curse men, who have been made in God's likeness. ¹⁰Out of the same mouth come praise and cursing. My brothers, this should not be. ¹¹Can both fresh water and saltᶠ water flow from the same spring? ¹²My brothers, can a fig tree bear olives, or a grapevine bear figs? Neither can a salt spring produce fresh water.

Two Kinds of Wisdom

¹³Who is wise and understanding among you? Let him show it by his good life, by deeds done in the humility that comes from wisdom. ¹⁴But if you harbor bitter envy and selfish ambition in your hearts, do not boast about it or deny the truth. ¹⁵Such "wisdom" does not come down from heaven but is earthly, unspiritual, of the devil. ¹⁶For where you have envy and selfish ambition, there you find disorder and every evil practice.

¹⁷But the wisdom that comes from heaven is first of all pure; then peace-loving, considerate, submissive, full of mercy and good fruit, impartial and sincere. ¹⁸Peacemakers who sow in peace raise a harvest of righteousness.

ᵉ23 Gen. 15:6   ᶠ11 Greek bitter (see also verse 14)

Submit Yourselves to God

4 What causes fights and quarrels among you? Don't they come from your desires that battle within you? [2]You want something but don't get it. You kill and covet, but you cannot have what you want. You quarrel and fight. You do not have, because you do not ask God. [3]When you ask, you do not receive, because you ask with wrong motives, that you may spend what you get on your pleasures.

[4]You adulterous people, don't you know that friendship with the world is hatred toward God? Anyone who chooses to be a friend of the world becomes an enemy of God. [5]Or do you think Scripture says without reason that the spirit he caused to live in us envies intensely?[g] [6]But he gives us more grace. That is why Scripture says:

"God opposes the proud
  but gives grace to the humble."[h]

[7]Submit yourselves, then, to God. Resist the devil, and he will flee from you. [8]Come near to God and he will come near to you. Wash your hands, you sinners, and purify your hearts, you double-minded. [9]Grieve, mourn and wail. Change your laughter to mourning and your joy to gloom. [10]Humble yourselves before the Lord, and he will lift you up.

[11]Brothers, do not slander one another. Anyone who speaks against his brother or judges him speaks against the law and judges it. When you judge the law, you are not keeping it, but sitting in judgment on it. [12]There is only one Lawgiver and Judge, the one who is able to save and destroy. But you—who are you to judge your neighbor?

Boasting About Tomorrow

[13]Now listen, you who say, "Today or tomorrow we will go to this or that city, spend a year there, carry on business and make money." [14]Why, you do not even know what will happen tomorrow. What is your life? You are a mist that appears for a little while and then vanishes. [15]Instead, you ought to say, "If it is the Lord's will, we will live and do this or that." [16]As it is, you boast and brag. All such boasting is evil. [17]Anyone, then, who knows the good he ought to do and doesn't do it, sins.

Warning to Rich Oppressors

5 Now listen, you rich people, weep and wail because of the misery that is coming upon you. [2]Your wealth has rotted, and moths have eaten your clothes. [3]Your gold and silver are corroded. Their corrosion will testify against you and eat your flesh like fire. You have hoarded wealth in the last days. [4]Look! The wages you failed to pay the workmen who mowed your fields are crying out against you. The cries of the harvesters have reached the ears of the Lord Almighty. [5]You have lived on earth

OPEN: 1. Over what and with whom did you quarrel most when you were a kid? **2.** What purchase is highest on your "wish list" now?

DIG: 1. From what does this strife (vv.1,11) come: Persecution? Possessiveness? Private pleasures? Misguided prayer? Frustrated desire (see 1:14)? **2.** How is James' ten-fold prescription (vv.7-10) an effective antidote? Why the switch to the imperative voice ("Do this, do that")? How does this cure fit the other themes in James? **3.** What is meant by "adulterous people" (v.4), "friendship with the world" (v.4), and submission to God (vv.7-10)? Give examples. **4.** What are some outward signs of this inner submission to God? **5.** Is the law in verse 11 the same as that in 1:25? 2:8? 2:12? Why or why not? How does grace (v.6) relate to this law?

REFLECT: 1. What is your usual response when your desires are frustrated? **2.** How is the "world" trying to get you to be its "friend" now? How is that related to your faithfulness to God? **3.** How is James' cure (vv.7-10) applicable to you as you struggle with the world's seduction?

OPEN: 1. Are you a long-range planner, or do you take one day at a time? Illustrate. **2.** If you won the lottery, how would you use your first $100,000?

DIG: 1. Regarding *tomorrow*, what's wrong with the type of planning here? Likewise, with "boasting"? With profit-making? **2.** What might be going on behind the scenes with these wealthy people (4:13-14; 5:1-6)? How are they violating the "royal law" (2:8)? **3.** What will happen to their wealth? What is the lesson in that?

REFLECT: 1. How does James relate to your plans for the future? Ever omit God in your planning? How do you specifically involve him? **2.** What does James imply about using wealth or power?

g5 Or that God jealously longs for the spirit that he made to live in us; or that the Spirit he caused to live in us longs jealously   h6 Prov. 3:34 in luxury and self-indulgence. You have fattened yourselves in the day of slaughter.[i] [6]You have condemned and murdered innocent men, who were not opposing you.

Patience in Suffering

[7]Be patient, then, brothers, until the Lord's coming. See how the farmer waits for the land to yield its valuable crop and how patient he is for the autumn and spring rains. [8]You too, be patient and stand firm, because the Lord's coming is near. [9]Don't grumble against each other, brothers, or you will be judged. The Judge is standing at the door!

[10]Brothers, as an example of patience in the face of suffering, take the prophets who spoke in the name of the Lord. [11]As you know, we consider blessed those who have persevered. You have heard of Job's perseverance and have seen what the Lord finally brought about. The Lord is full of compassion and mercy.

[12]Above all, my brothers, do not swear—not by heaven or by earth or by anything else. Let your "Yes" be yes, and your "No," no, or you will be condemned.

The Prayer of Faith

[13]Is any one of you in trouble? He should pray. Is anyone happy? Let him sing songs of praise. [14]Is any one of you sick? He should call the elders of the church to pray over him and anoint him with oil in the name of the Lord. [15]And the prayer offered in faith will make the sick person well; the Lord will raise him up. If he has sinned, he will be forgiven. [16]Therefore confess your sins to each other and pray for each other so that you may be healed. The prayer of a righteous man is powerful and effective.

[17]Elijah was a man just like us. He prayed earnestly that it would not rain, and it did not rain on the land for three and a half years. [18]Again he prayed, and the heavens gave rain, and the earth produced its crops.

[19]My brothers, if one of you should wander from the truth and someone should bring him back, [20]remember this: Whoever turns a sinner from the error of his way will save him from death and cover over a multitude of sins.

OPEN: 1. When have you and your community experienced the effects of a lack of rain? Of too much rain? 2. As a child, what did you pray before going to sleep?

DIG: 1. Instead of seeking retaliation or vengeance, what are the poor to do? Why? 2. What lessons are provided by the farmer? By the returning Judge? By the prophets? By Job? By the call to integrity (v.12)? 3. What lessons about prayer is James highlighting in verses 13-18? How is the example of Elijah meant as an encouragement to those addressed in verses 13-16? 4. From this book, what are some ways "wandering from the faith" has been demonstrated in this community? What has James done to try to bring them back?

REFLECT: 1. When you experience hardship, what enables you to be patient and wait for God? What has really tested that? 2. When have you come the closest to wandering from the faith? What (or who) helped bring you back? How does that demonstrate the healing ministry of the body of Christ? How would you help someone else come back to the faith? 3. The book of James can polarize those who grapple with it. Which way do you find yourself leaning: Guilty or inspired? Resistant or repentant? Passing the buck to the rich, or passing out bucks to the poor? 4. How can you be a "doer" of the truth you have heard in James?

---

[i]5 Or yourselves as in a day of feasting

1 PETER

INTRODUCTION

The General Epistles

The so-called Catholic or General Epistles consist of 1 and 2 Peter, Jude, James, and 1, 2, and 3 John. These documents were given this title because they seemed to be universal in scope. They were written to all churches and not just to one particular church or person, as were Paul's letters. This designation is not completely accurate, however. James and 1 Peter are written to specific, albeit widely scattered groups of Christians, while 2 and 3 John have a specific audience.

Audience

Its Location

First Peter is a circular letter to Christians living in the northwest section of Asia Minor (in what is now modern Turkey). Pontus, Galatia, Cappadocia, Asia, and Bithynia (1:1) are all Roman provinces. This area had a large population, and the fact that Christians were living throughout the region testifies to the success of early Christian missionaries.

That these Christians were mainly Gentiles is clear from the way Peter describes their preconversion life; he uses categories and phrases typically applied to pagans but not to Jews (1:14; 2:9-10; 4:3-4). Peter also uses the Greek form of his name, Cephas, in this letter, and not Simon, his Jewish name.

Its Need

On July 19 A.D. 64, Rome caught fire. For three days and three nights the fire blazed out of control. Ancient temples and landmarks were swept away. Homes were destroyed. Ten of the fourteen city wards suffered damage; three wards were reduced to rubble. The people of Rome were distraught and angry, especially because it was widely believed that if Emperor Nero had not actually set the fire, he certainly had done nothing to contain it. In fact, certain of Nero's chamberlains were caught with firebrands trying to rekindle the waning fire. Many felt that Nero's passion for building caused him to want the city destroyed so he might rebuild it. No matter what Nero did to refute this rumor — and he aided the homeless extensively — nothing allayed the suspicion that the fire was his doing. Clearly he needed a scapegoat on which to blame the fire.

The Christians were nominated for this dubious honor. Up to this time, they were thought to be simply a Jewish sect and were hardly noticed by Roman authorities. In fact, the Roman courts protected Christians against the wrath of the synagogue and others. But now all this changed. Nero introduced the church to martyrdom. What began in Rome would soon wash across the Roman Empire.

Under Roman law there were two types of religious systems: those that were legal, such as Judaism, and those that were forbidden. Anyone who practiced a forbidden religion was considered a criminal and was subject to harsh penalties. After the great fire, Christianity was judged to be distinct from Judaism, and it was quickly prohibited. This meant that throughout the Roman Empire, Christians were now technically outlaws and thus subject to persecution. Just such persecution was taking place in Asia Minor among the Christians to whom Peter writes (4:12).

Theme

In the midst of the "painful trial" (4:12) they are suffering, Peter writes to comfort and encourage. "Rejoice that you participate in the sufferings of Christ" (4:13), he says. How can they rejoice at such a difficult time? Because of the great *hope* they have as Christians. Hope is the theme of Peter's letter to these suffering believers.

Author

Peter was one of the first disciples called by Jesus. From Galilee, he was by trade a fisherman. His father was Jonah. His brother was Andrew the apostle. He was married, and his wife accompanied him on some of his preaching tours. Peter quickly became one of the leaders among the twelve apostles; later, he was a leader of the church in Jerusalem. He was the Apostle to the Jews, yet because of his response to a vision, the first Gentile convert, Cornelius, was admitted to the church (Acts 10).

Tradition says that Peter perished in Rome, around A.D. 68, by crucifixion upside down.

Characteristics

Sources

When reading 1 Peter, one keeps hearing echoes from other parts of the Bible. Certainly the Old Testament is present. Peter quotes a number of passages, particularly from Isaiah. For example in 1:24-25, he quotes Isaiah 40:6-8; in 2:6, Isaiah 28:16; in 2:8, Isaiah 8:14; and in 2:22, Isaiah 53:9. Furthermore, he frequently alludes to Old Testament ideas and stories.

Peter is also familiar with Paul's writings. This letter contains parallels to Romans and, in particular, Ephesians. For example, compare 1:3 with Ephesians 1:3 and 1:20 with Ephesians 1:4. Note also similarity between Peter and Paul in their instructions to family members and slaves (1 Peter 1:18-3:7; Eph. 5:21-6:9; Col. 3:18-25). In addition, there are parallels to Hebrews, James, and not surprisingly, to Peter's own sermons in Acts.

Of course, this does not necessarily mean that Peter was consciously quoting from New Testament documents. It may simply be that there was a common pattern of teaching in the early church and that Peter is tapping into this as did other New Testament writers.

Style

First Peter is written in excellent Greek, so much so that some have questioned whether a Galilean fisherman like Peter could have had such a sophisticated command of the language. First Peter contains some of the best Greek in the New Testament. Its style is smoother even than Paul's with his years of training; its rhythmic structure is not unlike that of the Greek masters.

The answer to this question is found in 5:12: "With the help of Silas . . . I have written to you." The Greek here indicates that Silas was more than just a stenographer. In fact, he could well be the source of the excellent style as he helped Peter draft the letter and polish up the language.

1 Peter

1 Peter, an apostle of Jesus Christ,

To God's elect, strangers in the world, scattered throughout Pontus, Galatia, Cappadocia, Asia and Bithynia, ²who have been chosen according to the foreknowledge of God the Father, through the sanctifying work of the Spirit, for obedience to Jesus Christ and sprinkling by his blood:

Grace and peace be yours in abundance.

Praise to God for a Living Hope

³Praise be to the God and Father of our Lord Jesus Christ! In his great mercy he has given us new birth into a living hope through the resurrection of Jesus Christ from the dead, ⁴and into an inheritance that can never perish, spoil or fade—kept in heaven for you, ⁵who through faith are shielded by God's power until the coming of the salvation that is ready to be revealed in the last time. ⁶In this you greatly rejoice, though now for a little while you may have had to suffer grief in all kinds of trials. ⁷These have come so that your faith—of greater worth than gold, which perishes even though refined by fire—may be proved genuine and may result in praise, glory and honor when Jesus Christ is revealed. ⁸Though you have not seen him, you love him; and even though you do not see him now, you believe in him and are filled with an inexpressible and glorious joy, ⁹for you are receiving the goal of your faith, the salvation of your souls.

¹⁰Concerning this salvation, the prophets, who spoke of the grace that was to come to you, searched intently and with the greatest care, ¹¹trying to find out the time and circumstances to which the Spirit of Christ in them was pointing when he predicted the sufferings of Christ and the glories that would follow. ¹²It was revealed to them that they were not serving themselves but you, when they spoke of the things that have now been told you by those who have preached the gospel to you by the Holy Spirit sent from heaven. Even angels long to look into these things.

Be Holy

¹³Therefore, prepare your minds for action; be self-controlled; set your hope fully on the grace to be given you when Jesus Christ is revealed. ¹⁴As obedient children, do not conform to the evil desires you had when you lived in ignorance. ¹⁵But just as he who called you is holy, so be holy in all you do; ¹⁶for it is written: "Be holy, because I am holy."ᵃ

¹⁷Since you call on a Father who judges each man's work impartially, live your lives as strangers here in reverent fear. ¹⁸For you know that it was not with perishable things such as silver or gold that you were redeemed from the empty way of life handed down to you from your forefathers, ¹⁹but with the precious blood of Christ, a lamb without blemish or defect. ²⁰He

ᵃ16 Lev. 11:44,45; 19:2; 20:7

OPEN: 1. How dispersed is your extended family? How often do you bring everyone together? **2.** What from your grandparents did (or would) you enjoy inheriting?

DIG: 1. What circumstances do you think these people faced that would cause Peter to write like this? How do you account for Peter's tone? **2.** What work is each person of the Trinity doing in our lives? **3.** What basis does Peter give his readers for a living hope? **4.** What items here would you list under "already available" to a Christian? What would you list under "not yet, but glad it's coming"? How do the ones on the "not yet" support the "already" list? Are some on both lists? Why? **5.** How does this salvation become ours (vv.8-12)?

REFLECT: 1. Imagining your faith as a mountain climb, what situations in your life would be cliffhangers? Easy trails? Great views? Just walking up the path? What would you pull out of your "1 Peter pack" in these situations? **2.** What aspect of your faith are you, like the prophets, struggling to know more? **3.** Under what fiery circumstances has your faith become more genuine, by melting it down to essentials?

OPEN: 1. What did you do as a child that got you into real trouble? **2.** What toy or game did you enjoy the most when you were 12 or younger? What happened to it? Would you play with it now if you had it? Be honest!

DIG: 1. From the five commands Peter gives in verses 13-15, how would you define "holy"? **2.** What reasons does Peter give for his commands (vv.17-21)? How can those reasons move us to obey? **3.** What does the OT imagery teach you about Jesus (vv.18-21)? **4.** Now that these people have put their faith in Jesus, what difference will that make in the way they think and act (1:22–2:2)?

445

REFLECT: 1. Are you more like a pilgrim, an explorer, or a landowner on this earth? Why? **2.** How does Peter's call to holiness challenge you at home? Work? Community? Church? **3.** In terms of time, effort, and money spent, which comes first for you: perishables or "forever" items? How can you rectify (or verify) that? **4.** Under stress, what helps you to "set your hope fully on the grace of God," rather than to rely on your own wits to solve the problem?

OPEN: What is your "dream house" like? Where would it be?

DIG: 1. What similarities does Peter show between Christ's experience and that of these people? **2.** How is Christ a cornerstone? Why would people stumble over the stone rather than build their lives on it? **3.** How could you reword in practical terms) what Peter meant by his pictures in verses 5 and 9? In what ways would it be difficult for Peter's readers to think of themselves in these terms? **4.** How is their new status with God to influence the way they live (vv.11-12)?

REFLECT: 1. If you were a war correspondent reporting from the front, how would you describe the war going on within yourself (v.11)? **2.** In what dark rooms of your life has God turned on a light? **3.** How does it make you feel to be chosen, royalty, and God's possession? When is it most difficult to remember what God has made you? **4.** If you were to build a spiritual house from the living stones in your group, where would each member be positioned (walls, roof, telephone line, etc.) to realize his or her gifts? How does this fit who you are in Christ?

was chosen before the creation of the world, but was revealed in these last times for your sake. [21]Through him you believe in God, who raised him from the dead and glorified him, and so your faith and hope are in God.

[22]Now that you have purified yourselves by obeying the truth so that you have sincere love for your brothers, love one another deeply, from the heart. [b] [23]For you have been born again, not of perishable seed, but of imperishable, through the living and enduring word of God. [24]For,

"All men are like grass,
    and all their glory is like the flowers of the field;
the grass withers and the flowers fall,
[25]   but the word of the Lord stands forever." [c]

And this is the word that was preached to you.

2 Therefore, rid yourselves of all malice and all deceit, hypocrisy, envy, and slander of every kind. [2]Like newborn babies, crave pure spiritual milk, so that by it you may grow up in your salvation, [3]now that you have tasted that the Lord is good.

The Living Stone and a Chosen People

[4]As you come to him, the living Stone—rejected by men but chosen by God and precious to him— [5]you also, like living stones, are being built into a spiritual house to be a holy priesthood, offering spiritual sacrifices acceptable to God through Jesus Christ. [6]For in Scripture it says:

"See, I lay a stone in Zion,
    a chosen and precious cornerstone,
and the one who trusts in him
    will never be put to shame." [d]

[7]Now to you who believe, this stone is precious. But to those who do not believe,

"The stone the builders rejected
    has become the capstone, [e]" [f]

[8]and,

"A stone that causes men to stumble
    and a rock that makes them fall." [g]

They stumble because they disobey the message—which is also what they were destined for.

[9]But you are a chosen people, a royal priesthood, a holy nation, a people belonging to God, that you may declare the praises of him who called you out of darkness into his wonderful light. [10]Once you were not a people, but now you are the people of God; once you had not received mercy, but now you have received mercy.

[11]Dear friends, I urge you, as aliens and strangers in the world, to abstain from sinful desires, which war against your

[b]22 Some early manuscripts *from a pure heart*   [c]25 Isaiah 40:6-8   [d]6 Isaiah 28:16
[e]7 Or *cornerstone*   [f]7 Psalm 118:22   [g]8 Isaiah 8:14

soul. ¹²Live such good lives among the pagans that, though they accuse you of doing wrong, they may see your good deeds and glorify God on the day he visits us.

Submission to Rulers and Masters

¹³Submit yourselves for the Lord's sake to every authority instituted among men: whether to the king, as the supreme authority, ¹⁴or to governors, who are sent by him to punish those who do wrong and to commend those who do right. ¹⁵For it is God's will that by doing good you should silence the ignorant talk of foolish men. ¹⁶Live as free men, but do not use your freedom as a cover-up for evil; live as servants of God. ¹⁷Show proper respect to everyone: Love the brotherhood of believers, fear God, honor the king.

¹⁸Slaves, submit yourselves to your masters with all respect, not only to those who are good and considerate, but also to those who are harsh. ¹⁹For it is commendable if a man bears up under the pain of unjust suffering because he is conscious of God. ²⁰But how is it to your credit if you receive a beating for doing wrong and endure it? But if you suffer for doing good and you endure it, this is commendable before God. ²¹To this you were called, because Christ suffered for you, leaving you an example, that you should follow in his steps.

²²"He committed no sin,
and no deceit was found in his mouth."ʰ

²³When they hurled their insults at him, he did not retaliate; when he suffered, he made no threats. Instead, he entrusted himself to him who judges justly. ²⁴He himself bore our sins in his body on the tree, so that we might die to sins and live for righteousness; by his wounds you have been healed. ²⁵For you were like sheep going astray, but now you have returned to the Shepherd and Overseer of your souls.

Wives and Husbands

3 Wives, in the same way be submissive to your husbands so that, if any of them do not believe the word, they may be won over without words by the behavior of their wives, ²when they see the purity and reverence of your lives. ³Your beauty should not come from outward adornment, such as braided hair and the wearing of gold jewelry and fine clothes. ⁴Instead, it should be that of your inner self, the unfading beauty of a gentle and quiet spirit, which is of great worth in God's sight. ⁵For this is the way the holy women of the past who put their hope in God used to make themselves beautiful. They were submissive to their own husbands, ⁶like Sarah, who obeyed Abraham and called him her master. You are her daughters if you do what is right and do not give way to fear.

⁷Husbands, in the same way be considerate as you live with your wives, and treat them with respect as the weaker partner and as heirs with you of the gracious gift of life, so that nothing will hinder your prayers.

ʰ22 Isaiah 53:9

OPEN: When you were growing up, what authority figure was hard for you to respect? Why?

DIG: 1. With government persecution, why is submission to authority a concern for Peter (vv.12-14)? **2.** What does Peter mean by "submit" in this context? What equivalent verbs do you see here? **3.** How does their relationship with God influence their regard for human authority? **4.** How can the suffering Christ (vv.21-25) help in situations far beyond our control? From 5:21-25, how would you explain Christ's death to one unfamiliar with the Atonement?

REFLECT: 1. What "authorities" are over you? How do you apply verses 16-17 in those relationships? **2.** Peter wrote to a people who had no civil or employee rights. How would his advice be different to people in a country (or position) where their legal rights were being violated by authority gone bad (see Ac 16:35-37)? **3.** How could Jesus' example help when you face hardships you can't change? How do you know when to submit and when to resist?

OPEN: As a child, how did you picture the man or woman of your dreams?

DIG: 1. How is the submission here similar in purpose to that in 2:13-15? What qualities are singled out? What does Sarah's example add? **2.** In what way are husbands to treat their wives?

REFLECT: 1. Married or not, what qualities here would you like to build into your friendships with the opposite sex? **2.** What would a marriage built on mutual submission actually look like? **3.** Is Peter advocating that spouses stay in cruel situations? Why or why not?

OPEN: How did you prepare for exams in high school: Regular study? All-night cramming? "What, me worry"? Wing it on "prayer"?

DIG: 1. How does the quote from Psalm 34 sum up all Peter has said in 2:11-3:9? What does he mean by setting apart Christ as Lord (v.15)? How will this affect their fears and hopes? **2.** What reasons for hope has Peter already given? **3.** What hope does the Flood story add to this hard-to-interpret passage (vv.20-21)? **4.** What hope does Christ's life and death provide? How does the example of Christ encourage those who suffer?

REFLECT: 1. Is your fellowship or church "in harmony" or "out of tune"? Why? What can you do to strengthen the harmony? How does your church exemplify the qualities of verse 8? **2.** What fears motivate people today? How does following Jesus as Lord free you from these fears? How would that free you to live differently? **3.** How does *hope* change your everyday behavior and cause people to ask about it? What situation seemed hopeless to you until God brought hope? **4.** Choose one difficult relationship in which you are currently involved. How could you *bless* (v.9) that person this week? What would you need to do?

OPEN: Are you more of a doer, thinker, lover, prayer, or sleeper?

DIG: 1. Imagine a specific, compromising situation that Peter's readers (and you) may be encountering: What accusations are being made? What should be the focus of the readers' attention, instead? **2.** How are the realities of judgment (vv.5-7) and Christ's glory (v.11) to influence our daily behavior? **3.** What does this redemptive love look like in action (vv.8-11)? How would this benefit suffering people?

Suffering for Doing Good

[8]Finally, all of you, live in harmony with one another; be sympathetic, love as brothers, be compassionate and humble. [9]Do not repay evil with evil or insult with insult, but with blessing, because to this you were called so that you may inherit a blessing. [10]For,

"Whoever would love life
    and see good days
must keep his tongue from evil
    and his lips from deceitful speech.
[11]He must turn from evil and do good;
    he must seek peace and pursue it.
[12]For the eyes of the Lord are on the righteous
    and his ears are attentive to their prayer,
but the face of the Lord is against those who do evil."[i]

[13]Who is going to harm you if you are eager to do good? [14]But even if you should suffer for what is right, you are blessed. "Do not fear what they fear[j]; do not be frightened."[k] [15]But in your hearts set apart Christ as Lord. Always be prepared to give an answer to everyone who asks you to give the reason for the hope that you have. But do this with gentleness and respect, [16]keeping a clear conscience, so that those who speak maliciously against your good behavior in Christ may be ashamed of their slander. [17]It is better, if it is God's will, to suffer for doing good than for doing evil. [18]For Christ died for sins once for all, the righteous for the unrighteous, to bring you to God. He was put to death in the body but made alive by the Spirit, [19]through whom[l] also he went and preached to the spirits in prison [20]who disobeyed long ago when God waited patiently in the days of Noah while the ark was being built. In it only a few people, eight in all, were saved through water, [21]and this water symbolizes baptism that now saves you also—not the removal of dirt from the body but the pledge[m] of a good conscience toward God. It saves you by the resurrection of Jesus Christ, [22]who has gone into heaven and is at God's right hand—with angels, authorities and powers in submission to him.

Living for God

4 Therefore, since Christ suffered in his body, arm yourselves also with the same attitude, because he who has suffered in his body is done with sin. [2]As a result, he does not live the rest of his earthly life for evil human desires, but rather for the will of God. [3]For you have spent enough time in the past doing what pagans choose to do—living in debauchery, lust, drunkenness, orgies, carousing and detestable idolatry. [4]They think it strange that you do not plunge with them into the same flood of dissipation, and they heap abuse on you. [5]But they will have to give account to him who is ready to judge the living and the dead. [6]For this is the reason the gospel was preached even to those who

---

[i]12 Psalm 34:12-16   [j]14 Or *not fear their threats*   [k]14 Isaiah 8:12
[l]18,19 Or *alive in the spirit,* [19]*through which*   [m]21 Or *response*

are now dead, so that they might be judged according to men in regard to the body, but live according to God in regard to the spirit.

[7]The end of all things is near. Therefore be clear minded and self-controlled so that you can pray. [8]Above all, love each other deeply, because love covers over a multitude of sins. [9]Offer hospitality to one another without grumbling. [10]Each one should use whatever gift he has received to serve others, faithfully administering God's grace in its various forms. [11]If anyone speaks, he should do it as one speaking the very words of God. If anyone serves, he should do it with the strength God provides, so that in all things God may be praised through Jesus Christ. To him be the glory and the power for ever and ever. Amen.

Suffering for Being a Christian

[12]Dear friends, do not be surprised at the painful trial you are suffering, as though something strange were happening to you. [13]But rejoice that you participate in the sufferings of Christ, so that you may be overjoyed when his glory is revealed. [14]If you are insulted because of the name of Christ, you are blessed, for the Spirit of glory and of God rests on you. [15]If you suffer, it should not be as a murderer or thief or any other kind of criminal, or even as a meddler. [16]However, if you suffer as a Christian, do not be ashamed, but praise God that you bear that name. [17]For it is time for judgment to begin with the family of God; and if it begins with us, what will the outcome be for those who do not obey the gospel of God? [18]And,

> "If it is hard for the righteous to be saved,
>   what will become of the ungodly and the sinner?"[n]

[19]So then, those who suffer according to God's will should commit themselves to their faithful Creator and continue to do good.

To Elders and Young Men

5 To the elders among you, I appeal as a fellow elder, a witness of Christ's sufferings and one who also will share in the glory to be revealed: [2]Be shepherds of God's flock that is under your care, serving as overseers—not because you must, but because you are willing, as God wants you to be; not greedy for money, but eager to serve; [3]not lording it over those entrusted to you, but being examples to the flock. [4]And when the Chief Shepherd appears, you will receive the crown of glory that will never fade away.

[5]Young men, in the same way be submissive to those who are older. All of you, clothe yourselves with humility toward one another, because,

> "God opposes the proud
>   but gives grace to the humble."[o]

REFLECT: 1. What thinking hinders your prayer life? Conversely, what helps? **2.** Which commands in verses 7-11 do you need to pay special attention to this week? **3.** What is one gift you think each group member has? How could that gift be used to show love?

DIG: 1. In what sense is the Christian's suffering part of Christ's suffering? Why should the Christian find joy in this? **2.** When Peter tells them to continue to do good (v.19), what reasons does he give for continuing?

REFLECT: 1. When you feel like giving up, what keeps you going? **2.** If you were asked to tell a group of new believers what to expect in the Christian life, what are some things (from 1 Peter) you would tell them? Why? **3.** We Christians are not persecuted a great deal by our government. What form, then, does our suffering for Christ take? Has such suffering purified, changed, molded, or matured you? How?

OPEN: What is one of the most unruly groups you have had to "shepherd": Junior high kids on a school field trip? The church nursery during a long sermon? A small group that wouldn't cooperate? A meeting of professionals vying for recognition? Other: _____?

DIG: 1. What good and bad motives does Peter give for being in leadership? What qualities does he encourage elders to cultivate? Why would these qualities and proper motivation be important in times of persecution? **2.** What connections do you see between submissiveness, humility, and anxiety? What anxieties do these people face? What would replace their fears as they followed verses

---

[n]18 Prov. 11:31   [o]5 Prov. 3:34

6-7? **3.** What sources of opposition to the Christians has Peter spoken of already (2:12,13-14,18; 3:1,16; 4:3-4)? How do these relate to verse 8 here? What is the Christian's defense in this battle? The Christian's hope? **4.** Given that Babylon was one of the main enemies of Israel in the OT and that Peter is writing from Rome, what does he mean by verse 13? **5.** How do verses 10-13 sum up the pressures these believers were facing, as well as Peter's advice on this matter?

REFLECT: 1. What area of your life would you like God to restore and make you strong, firm and steadfast? **2.** What leadership responsibilities do you have? (We all have some!) How do you score on Peter's leadership test? How can you improve your score? **3.** In your life, where is the "lion" (v.8): (a) Just looking for you? (b) Nibbling at your heels? (c) Chewing you up? How can your group help you resist him? What in this letter has helped? **4.** What pictures of Christ has Peter drawn in this letter? How do those pictures bring peace (5:14) to you?

[6]Humble yourselves, therefore, under God's mighty hand, that he may lift you up in due time. [7]Cast all your anxiety on him because he cares for you.

[8]Be self-controlled and alert. Your enemy the devil prowls around like a roaring lion looking for someone to devour. [9]Resist him, standing firm in the faith, because you know that your brothers throughout the world are undergoing the same kind of sufferings.

[10]And the God of all grace, who called you to his eternal glory in Christ, after you have suffered a little while, will himself restore you and make you strong, firm and steadfast. [11]To him be the power for ever and ever. Amen.

Final Greetings

[12]With the help of Silas,[p] whom I regard as a faithful brother, I have written to you briefly, encouraging you and testifying that this is the true grace of God. Stand fast in it.

[13]She who is in Babylon, chosen together with you, sends you her greetings, and so does my son Mark. [14]Greet one another with a kiss of love.

Peace to all of you who are in Christ.

---

[p]12 Greek *Silvanus*, a variant of *Silas*

2 PETER

INTRODUCTION

The Neglected Book

In contrast to 1 Peter, which is "the best known and loved, the most read" of the General Epistles; 2 Peter "is one of the neglected books of the New Testament" (Barclay, *The Letters of James and Peter*, p. 335). Few people seem to have read and studied it. One commentator has called 2 Peter "the least valuable of the New Testament writings" (E. F. Scott in Barclay, *The Letters of James and Peter*, p. 335). Several others have called for it to be deleted from the New Testament. Why is this? What is the problem with 2 Peter?

Second Peter's difficulties are not new. In fact, it almost did not make it into the New Testament. Luther calls it second-class Scripture; Calvin had doubts about it; and Erasmus rejected it altogether.

Author

The problem is that a lot of people question whether Peter actually wrote this particular letter. It was not uncommon in the first century to attribute pieces of writing to famous people. In fact, Peter's name is attached to several other books that clearly were not written by him (e.g., the Gospel of Peter, the Preaching of Peter, and the Apocalypse of Peter).

So questions arise when the language and thought of 1 and 2 Peter are compared. In their original Greek form, these two books are strikingly different. Could the same man have written both? This difference in style, of course, may simply be the result of Peter's use of two different secretaries. Peter indicates in his first letter that Silas helped him write it (1 Peter 5:12), and it is known that Peter had other secretaries (e.g., Mark and Glaucias). As Michael Green has shown, the case against Peter's authorship is not nearly as conclusive as might be supposed (*The Second Epistle of Peter and the Epistles of Jude: Tyndale New Testament Commentaries*). In any case, 2 Peter is a part of the New Testament, and it has a valuable message for the twentieth century which is important to recover.

Theme

Second Peter is a very important book for the twentieth century because it deals with the very issues confronting the modern church: laxity of lifestyle based on defective doctrine. Some church members in Peter's time were arguing that the doctrine of the Second Coming had to be reconsidered. "The plain fact is that Christ has not returned yet," they said, "and he probably won't" (see 3:4, 9). In fact, they suggested that this doctrine may have been invented by the apostles rather than revealed by God (1:16), perhaps to keep Christians in line. The doctrine of the Second Coming was sort of a moral club used to inhibit one's lifestyle. In contrast, the false teachers were saying that behavior does not matter. "Freedom" was their catchword, and evidently they felt free to indulge in sexual immorality, drunkenness, and sensual excesses generally (2:2, 10, 13-14, 18) (Richard Bauckham, *Jude, 2 Peter: Word Biblical Commentary*, p. 155).

"Not so!" roars Peter in this letter. And it is his "not so" that we need to hear in this day of speculative theology and hedonistic lifestyles. We, too, need to remain firmly established within the truth we received from the prophets and from our Lord (chap. 1). We, too, need to be warned against those who would lead people away from that truth (chap. 2). And we, too, need to be reminded (in a passage that is chillingly real in this nuclear age) that the world will one day end when the Lord returns (chap. 3).

Audience

On the basis of 1:1 it appears that there were no specific recipients of the letter. It seems to be for all Christians everywhere (hence its description as a General Epistle). However, in the body of the letter it becomes clear that 2 Peter was sent to a church or group of churches that had received 1 Peter (3:1). This would make the recipients Gentile Christians in Asia Minor. Furthermore, the tone of the letter makes it clear that a specific problem and specific false teachers are in view. All of this indicates that this is a letter to particular people living in a particular area.

Structure

Second Peter is a letter like other New Testament letters. It calls itself a letter (3:1). It begins like a typical first-century letter (1:1-2) by identifying sender and recipients and offering a Christian greeting. And then, in typical fashion, it announces its theme (1:3-11) and tells the occasion of writing (1:12-15). The only thing 2 Peter lacks is personal greetings at the end, but these were not characteristic of all first-century letters.

Second Peter is also a farewell speech or a testament. It sounds like the last words of a great leader. There are many examples of this form of literature in the first century. In the New Testament, Paul's farewell speech to the Ephesian elders had this character (Acts 20:17-35), as does the Book of 2 Timothy.

In 1:12-15, Peter says that his death is soon to take place, and the way he writes his letter is typical of testament literature in general. The letter contains ethical instructions in which the author summarizes his views, and then he makes predictions about the future (Bauckham, *Jude, 2 Peter*).

2 Peter

1 Simon Peter, a servant and apostle of Jesus Christ,

To those who through the righteousness of our God and Savior Jesus Christ have received a faith as precious as ours:

²Grace and peace be yours in abundance through the knowledge of God and of Jesus our Lord.

Making One's Calling and Election Sure

³His divine power has given us everything we need for life and godliness through our knowledge of him who called us by his own glory and goodness. ⁴Through these he has given us his very great and precious promises, so that through them you may participate in the divine nature and escape the corruption in the world caused by evil desires.

⁵For this very reason, make every effort to add to your faith goodness; and to goodness, knowledge; ⁶and to knowledge, self-control; and to self-control, perseverance; and to perseverance, godliness; ⁷and to godliness, brotherly kindness; and to brotherly kindness, love. ⁸For if you possess these qualities in increasing measure, they will keep you from being ineffective and unproductive in your knowledge of our Lord Jesus Christ. ⁹But if anyone does not have them, he is nearsighted and blind, and has forgotten that he has been cleansed from his past sins.

¹⁰Therefore, my brothers, be all the more eager to make your calling and election sure. For if you do these things, you will never fall, ¹¹and you will receive a rich welcome into the eternal kingdom of our Lord and Savior Jesus Christ.

Prophecy of Scripture

¹²So I will always remind you of these things, even though you know them and are firmly established in the truth you now have. ¹³I think it is right to refresh your memory as long as I live in the tent of this body, ¹⁴because I know that I will soon put it aside, as our Lord Jesus Christ has made clear to me. ¹⁵And I will make every effort to see that after my departure you will always be able to remember these things.

¹⁶We did not follow cleverly invented stories when we told you about the power and coming of our Lord Jesus Christ, but we were eyewitnesses of his majesty. ¹⁷For he received honor and glory from God the Father when the voice came to him from the Majestic Glory, saying, "This is my Son, whom I love; with him I am well pleased."[a] ¹⁸We ourselves heard this voice that came from heaven when we were with him on the sacred mountain.

¹⁹And we have the word of the prophets made more certain, and you will do well to pay attention to it, as to a light shining in a dark place, until the day dawns and the morning star rises in your hearts. ²⁰Above all, you must understand that no proph-

---

a17 Matt. 17:5; Mark 9:7; Luke 9:35

OPEN: 1. As a teenager, what did you desire to do most: Career-wise? Sports-wise? Relationship-wise? **2.** How have your desires changed since then?

DIG: 1. From verses 1-4, what is "everything we need for life"? **2.** With *everything* given to us, why must we "*add* to our faith"? And with what effort (vv.5,10)? **3.** What seven qualities are we to zealously desire? How does each fit with the one mentioned before it? **4.** Why is this moral progress and productive knowledge (v.8) so desirable for believers (vv.4,10-11)?

REFLECT: 1. If this step-by-step, moral progression is a ladder, what is the building it is leaning against? Do you feel like climbing, painting, or getting off? Which building is your spiritual ladder leaning against? **2.** Of the seven qualities in verses 5-7, which two do you possess in the greatest measure? How can you grow in one of the other qualities? How can the group help?

OPEN: How is your life like a tent: Always pulling up stakes, moving on? Resistant to winds of change? Cozy with some, cold to others?

DIG: 1. What event of Jesus' life does Peter recall (vv.16-18)? If you were Peter, what other powerful stories of Jesus would come to mind? **2.** Why (and how) does Peter establish his own authority? Likewise, why does Peter defend the authority and inspiration of the prophets? What problem does this imply his readers may have had (vv.20-21)? **3.** If so much prophecy has already been fulfilled in Christ's first coming, how then are we to regard prophecy yet to be fulfilled?

REFLECT: 1. If you could have been with Jesus at one event in his life, which would you choose? Why? **2.** If a non-Christian asked you to "prove" the Scriptures are God's Word, on what would you base your answer? **3.** How does that answer affect your Bible study habits? Your witness? Your lifestyle?

ecy of Scripture came about by the prophet's own interpretation. ²¹For prophecy never had its origin in the will of man, but men spoke from God as they were carried along by the Holy Spirit.

False Teachers and Their Destruction

2 But there were also false prophets among the people, just as there will be false teachers among you. They will secretly introduce destructive heresies, even denying the sovereign Lord who bought them—bringing swift destruction on themselves. ²Many will follow their shameful ways and will bring the way of truth into disrepute. ³In their greed these teachers will exploit you with stories they have made up. Their condemnation has long been hanging over them, and their destruction has not been sleeping.

⁴For if God did not spare angels when they sinned, but sent them to hell,^b putting them into gloomy dungeons^c to be held for judgment; ⁵if he did not spare the ancient world when he brought the flood on its ungodly people, but protected Noah, a preacher of righteousness, and seven others; ⁶if he condemned the cities of Sodom and Gomorrah by burning them to ashes, and made them an example of what is going to happen to the ungodly; ⁷and if he rescued Lot, a righteous man, who was distressed by the filthy lives of lawless men ⁸(for that righteous man, living among them day after day, was tormented in his righteous soul by the lawless deeds he saw and heard)— ⁹if this is so, then the Lord knows how to rescue godly men from trials and to hold the unrighteous for the day of judgment, while continuing their punishment.^d ¹⁰This is especially true of those who follow the corrupt desire of the sinful nature^e and despise authority.

Bold and arrogant, these men are not afraid to slander celestial beings; ¹¹yet even angels, although they are stronger and more powerful, do not bring slanderous accusations against such beings in the presence of the Lord. ¹²But these men blaspheme in matters they do not understand. They are like brute beasts, creatures of instinct, born only to be caught and destroyed, and like beasts they too will perish.

¹³They will be paid back with harm for the harm they have done. Their idea of pleasure is to carouse in broad daylight. They are blots and blemishes, reveling in their pleasures while they feast with you.^f ¹⁴With eyes full of adultery, they never stop sinning; they seduce the unstable; they are experts in greed—an accursed brood! ¹⁵They have left the straight way and wandered off to follow the way of Balaam son of Beor, who loved the wages of wickedness. ¹⁶But he was rebuked for his wrongdoing by a donkey—a beast without speech—who spoke with a man's voice and restrained the prophet's madness.

¹⁷These men are springs without water and mists driven by a storm. Blackest darkness is reserved for them. ¹⁸For they

---

OPEN: 1. If people have pets that are like them in some way, what could one learn about you from your choice of pet? **2.** What "beasts" and other "things which go bump in the night" are you afraid of? Why?

DIG: 1. Having just commended true prophets (1:12-21), who does Peter now condemn? Why? **2.** If it is so plain that judgment awaits these false teachers, why does anyone follow them (vv.2-3, 14,18-19)? If they are so evil, why do you think God allows them to teach in his church? Isn't God's goodness or greatness brought into question by delaying their judgment? **3.** In response to that implied question, Peter recites God's track record in dealing with evil: What examples are cited in verses 4-9? **4.** If neither angels, the ancient world, nor Sodom and Gomorrah were spared from God's wrath against sin, who *does* God protect from judgment? Why? How is that a particular comfort to Peter's audience? **5.** Who are the gross sinners in verses 13-16? What are they like? On what basis is Peter assured they will be paid back in kind? **6.** What other imagery does Peter use to further denounce the false prophets (vv.17-19)? **7.** What "freedom" do they promise: Freedom from sin? From laws? From judgment? From ethical obligations to others and to Christ? All of the above? How is their idea of freedom different from true Christian freedom? **8.** What do verses 20-22 imply about a person's salvation? Can one lose it? Or were these people never converted? Why do you think so?

REFLECT: 1. How do you know when a preacher is "exploiting you with stories they have made up," or feeding you empty promises as "springs without water"? How could the dangers mentioned by Peter affect you now? **2.** Do such false teachers upset you as much as Peter? Why or why not? Which preacher do you trust more than others? Why? **3.** Amidst all this bad news, what good news is

---

^b4 Greek *Tartarus* ^c4 Some manuscripts *into chains of darkness*
^d9 Or *unrighteous for punishment until the day of judgment* ^e10 Or *the flesh*
^f13 Some manuscripts *in their love feasts*

mouth empty, boastful words and, by appealing to the lustful desires of sinful human nature, they entice people who are just escaping from those who live in error. [19]They promise them freedom, while they themselves are slaves of depravity—for a man is a slave to whatever has mastered him. [20]If they have escaped the corruption of the world by knowing our Lord and Savior Jesus Christ and are again entangled in it and overcome, they are worse off at the end than they were at the beginning. [21]It would have been better for them not to have known the way of righteousness, than to have known it and then to turn their backs on the sacred command that was passed on to them. [22]Of them the proverbs are true: "A dog returns to its vomit,"[g] and, "A sow that is washed goes back to her wallowing in the mud."

The Day of the Lord

3 Dear friends, this is now my second letter to you. I have written both of them as reminders to stimulate you to wholesome thinking. [2]I want you to recall the words spoken in the past by the holy prophets and the command given by our Lord and Savior through your apostles.

[3]First of all, you must understand that in the last days scoffers will come, scoffing and following their own evil desires. [4]They will say, "Where is this 'coming' he promised? Ever since our fathers died, everything goes on as it has since the beginning of creation." [5]But they deliberately forget that long ago by God's word the heavens existed and the earth was formed out of water and by water. [6]By these waters also the world of that time was deluged and destroyed. [7]By the same word the present heavens and earth are reserved for fire, being kept for the day of judgment and destruction of ungodly men.

[8]But do not forget this one thing, dear friends: With the Lord a day is like a thousand years, and a thousand years are like a day. [9]The Lord is not slow in keeping his promise, as some understand slowness. He is patient with you, not wanting anyone to perish, but everyone to come to repentance.

[10]But the day of the Lord will come like a thief. The heavens will disappear with a roar; the elements will be destroyed by fire, and the earth and everything in it will be laid bare.[h]

[11]Since everything will be destroyed in this way, what kind of people ought you to be? You ought to live holy and godly lives [12]as you look forward to the day of God and speed its coming.[i] That day will bring about the destruction of the heavens by fire, and the elements will melt in the heat. [13]But in keeping with his promise we are looking forward to a new heaven and a new earth, the home of righteousness.

[14]So then, dear friends, since you are looking forward to this, make every effort to be found spotless, blameless and at peace with him. [15]Bear in mind that our Lord's patience means salvation, just as our dear brother Paul also wrote you with the wisdom that God gave him. [16]He writes the same way in all his

there? Would it be truly good news if there were no judgment? **4.** In your experience, does grace ever come through *perverse channels* (such as the heretics and wicked men depicted here), or only through pure vessels: Always? Sometimes? Never? Why is that?

OPEN: 1. When did your dad promise a fishing trip, a ball game, or a graduation present, and then fail to deliver? How did that make you feel? **2.** When told, "Wait until your birthday," or "Christmas isn't here yet," and "You'd better be good until then," how did that affect your behavior in the meantime?

DIG: 1. Following the digression of chapter 2, to what themes does Peter now return? **2.** What "must" the readers first understand (see also 1:20-21)? **3.** Why does God's creation of the earth support Peter's contention that he will also destroy the earth? Why is that so difficult for people to believe? What does this tell you about their perception of God? **4.** What frustrations does God's patience produce? How is God's patience a benefit (vv.9,15)? **5.** How does God's view of time differ from the readers' view? In this context (vv.10-16), is Peter addressing the certainty, the timing, or the manner of Christ's coming? How is that an effective inducement to godly living now? **6.** How does Peter's reference to Paul also encourage his readers in right behavior? **7.** What is Peter's final antidote to the false teachers of his day (vv.17-18)?

REFLECT: 1. If you were in charge of the world's clock, would you slow it down or speed it up? Why? **2.** If you were in charge of creating, destroying, and redeeming the world, which of these would you take more "time" doing? Why? **3.** In football strategy "the best defense is a good offense," meaning if the other team never gets the ball they can't score against

---

[g]22 Prov. 26:11   [h]10 Some manuscripts *be burned up*   [i]12 Or *as you wait eagerly for the day of God to come*

you. How is Peter's strategy like that in his defense against those who would lead us away from the truth? What can you do to "grow in the grace and knowledge of our Lord"?

letters, speaking in them of these matters. His letters contain some things that are hard to understand, which ignorant and unstable people distort, as they do the other Scriptures, to their own destruction.

[17]Therefore, dear friends, since you already know this, be on your guard so that you may not be carried away by the error of lawless men and fall from your secure position. [18]But grow in the grace and knowledge of our Lord and Savior Jesus Christ. To him be glory both now and forever! Amen.

1 JOHN

INTRODUCTION

Author

Despite the fact that the author is nowhere named in the epistle, it is highly probable that he is none other than the beloved apostle John, now an old man living in Asia Minor and pastoring the churches in and around Ephesus. There are a number of reasons for attributing this anonymous epistle to John, including the following:

1. A strong tradition dating back to the early days of the church holds that John is the author.
2. There are many similarities in style and content between the Gospel of John and this epistle. The same sharp contrasts appear in both—light and darkness, truth and falsehood, love and hate. The differences between them can be traced to differences in purpose and to the length of time that elapsed between the composition of each.
3. The internal information in the epistle points to John. For example, the author tells us that he was one of the original eyewitnesses of Jesus (1:1-2). Also, the author writes with the air of authority that would be expected of an apostle (4:6).

Date

There is little clear evidence by which to date this letter accurately. Although it can be dated as early as A.D. 60, it was probably written toward the end of the New Testament era (A.D. 90-95), by which time the gnosticlike heresy had flourished.

Characteristics

First John is written in the simplest Greek of all the New Testament. (It is usually the first book seminary students learn to translate.) Although 5,437 different Greek words appear in the New Testament, only 303 are used in the three Johannine epistles—less than six percent of the total. This is not to say, however, that 1 John is a superficial book. On the contrary, here the apostle John, now an old man, is writing a distillation of all he has learned. "This is what Christianity is all about," he is saying. "This is what it all boils down to: God is light (1:5); God is love (4:16); Jesus is the Messiah (2:22); the Son of God (4:15), who has come in the flesh (4:2), and we are to be his children (3:1). As such we have eternal life (2:25). We do not continue in sin (2:1), but we love one another (3:11). I repeat we are to love one another (4:7-12)."

A story is told by Jerome of "blessed John the evangelist," an extremely old man, "being carried into the congregation at Ephesus, unable to say anything except 'Little children, love one another.' Having heard this same thing so often, they ask 'Master, why do you always say this?' 'Because,' he replied, 'it is the Lord's command, and if this only is done, it is enough.'" (J. R. W. Stott, *The Epistles of John*, p. 49).

Luther wrote: "I have never read a book written in simpler words than this one, and yet the words are inexpressible" (*Luther's Werke*, 28, 183).

Theme

The problem was heresy. Apparently a group of Christians got involved in false teaching, split off from the church (2:19), and were now hassling their former friends, probably trying to convince them to espouse their new and "advanced" views (2:26). This deeply troubled the church and thus John, as pastor, wrote to assure the Christians in and around Ephesus that they were, indeed, true Christians with the assurance of eternal life.

The nature of the heresy is not completely clear. John wasted no time defining the false position. The recipients of his letter knew well enough what was being taught. Still, by the nature of John's defense of orthodox Christianity, certain features of the heresy emerge.

Deficient Doctrine

For one thing, the false teacher's doctrine was seriously deficient. In particular, they had a low view of Jesus. They did not believe he was the Messiah (2:22, 5:1). They did not believe he was the Son of God (5:5). They denied that Jesus had come in the flesh (4:2). They apparently claimed they did not need Jesus because they already knew God (2:4) and had fellowship with him (1:6). They did not believe that sin separated a person from God (1:6, 8, 10), and thus they had no need of Jesus' atoning death (5:6) to provide forgiveness and a way back to God. It is not by accident that John calls them "antichrists." (2:22).

Spiritual Elitism

This group had come to think of themselves as some sort of spiritual elite, claiming that they had a "deeper" understanding of Christianity, probably by direct revelation (4:1-6). As an antidote to such spiritual pride, John reminded his readers over and over that Christians are called to love one another, not to look down on their brothers and sisters who do not measure up to their own supposed, superior insight.

It is not clear what labels to affix to this group of false teachers. They were probably related to what later became Gnosticism — a philosophy in which matter (including the body) was impure and spirit was all that counted. Therefore, these false teachers denied that Christ was fully human. They kept his deity, but at the expense of his humanity. To them, salvation came by illumination. Thus, esoteric "knowledge" was eagerly sought, often at the expense of apostolic doctrine.

Discerning Authenticity

John's central concerns are quite clear. He wants to define the marks of a true Christian against the claims of the false teachers. He wants his congregation to have assurance that they have eternal life (5:13). He wants them to know the characteristics of a true Christian: right belief (the doctrinal test), righteousness (the moral test), and love (the social test).

Structure

It is very difficult to outline John's first epistle, to trace the flow of his thought and put it into neat categories (as one can do with Romans, for example). Rather, it seems that John (much like James) would write a paragraph and then be reminded of a related topic that he would then deal with in the next paragraph. This, in turn, would spark a further consideration. The ideas are focused and related; they hang together, but not with a Western style of logic. The structure is almost *spiral*, "for the development of a theme often brings us back almost to the starting point; almost but not quite, for there is a slight shift which provides a tranisition to a fresh theme; or it may be to a theme which had apparently been dismissed at an earlier point and now comes up for consideration from a slightly different angle" (C. H. Dodd, *The Johannine Epistles: The Moffatt New Testament Commentaries*, p. xxi).

First John is not an epistle like 2 and 3 John or most of Paul's writings. It lacks identification of writer and recipients, a salutation, and a final greeting. Still, it is not a generalized document written to all Christians. John has a specific audience in mind, probably the churches in his charge in Asia Minor. Despite the lack of usual greetings, he writes in personal terms. Many see 1 John as a tract, perhaps intended to be read as a sermon, in which John deals with a specific problem.

1 John

The Word of Life

1 That which was from the beginning, which we have heard, which we have seen with our eyes, which we have looked at and our hands have touched—this we proclaim concerning the Word of life. [2]The life appeared; we have seen it and testify to it, and we proclaim to you the eternal life, which was with the Father and has appeared to us. [3]We proclaim to you what we have seen and heard, so that you also may have fellowship with us. And our fellowship is with the Father and with his Son, Jesus Christ. [4]We write this to make our[a] joy complete.

Walking in the Light

[5]This is the message we have heard from him and declare to you: God is light; in him there is no darkness at all. [6]If we claim to have fellowship with him yet walk in the darkness, we lie and do not live by the truth. [7]But if we walk in the light, as he is in the light, we have fellowship with one another, and the blood of Jesus, his Son, purifies us from all[b] sin.

[8]If we claim to be without sin, we deceive ourselves and the truth is not in us. [9]If we confess our sins, he is faithful and just and will forgive us our sins and purify us from all unrighteousness. [10]If we claim we have not sinned, we make him out to be a liar and his word has no place in our lives.

2 My dear children, I write this to you so that you will not sin. But if anybody does sin, we have one who speaks to the Father in our defense—Jesus Christ, the Righteous One. [2]He is the atoning sacrifice for our sins, and not only for ours but also for[c] the sins of the whole world.

[3]We know that we have come to know him if we obey his commands. [4]The man who says, "I know him," but does not do what he commands is a liar, and the truth is not in him. [5]But if anyone obeys his word, God's love[d] is truly made complete in him. This is how we know we are in him: [6]Whoever claims to live in him must walk as Jesus did.

[7]Dear friends, I am not writing you a new command but an old one, which you have had since the beginning. This old command is the message you have heard. [8]Yet I am writing you a new command; its truth is seen in him and you, because the darkness is passing and the true light is already shining.

[9]Anyone who claims to be in the light but hates his brother is still in the darkness. [10]Whoever loves his brother lives in the light, and there is nothing in him[e] to make him stumble. [11]But whoever hates his brother is in the darkness and walks around in the darkness; he does not know where he is going, because the darkness has blinded him.

OPEN: 1. As a child, were you afraid of the dark? What "monsters" were in it that scared you? **2.** What was your parents' standard line when you went out for an evening: (a) "Be home on time"? (b) "Drive carefully"? (c) "I love you"? (d) "Don't forget ____"?

DIG: 1. Why does John emphasize the way he experienced "the Word" (vv.1-4)? What does that reveal about Jesus? About John? About his audience? **2.** What does John mean by his statement "God is light" (v.5)? **3.** What three erroneous views (about God, sin, forgiveness) is he exposing by this assertion, and by the "if/then" clauses (1:6,8,10) which follow? What truths about each of these subjects does John then affirm (1:7,9; 2:1b)? **4.** Practically, what does it mean to "walk in the light" and not "in darkness"? If light and love are linked with darkness and hate (1:6; 2:9-11), what does that imply about relating to God? About growing spiritually? **5.** What hope does John give when people fail to live in light of God's love (1:9; 2:1-2)? Explain in your own words what it means that Jesus is the advocate, the righteous one, and the atoning sacrifice. **6.** What additional false claims does John refute by his "old command" made "new" (2:7-8; see Jn 15:12,17; Lev 19:18; Dt 6:5)? In the Gospels, what are some ways that Jesus made the "old" command "new"? **7.** What marks each stage of maturity described in verses 12-14?

REFLECT: 1. Measure your walk with God last week in terms of a spiritual weather report and the "tests" of faith in 1:6, 2:3, 6 and 10. What does your report sound like: (a) Dark and stormy night? (b) Bright and cloudless sky? (c) Partly cloudy? (d) Dull, slate-grey overcast day? Why? What is one specific way these verses challenge you to improve your relationship with God? With others? How will you try to do so this week? **2.** What hope do 1:9 and 2:1-2 give as you face the dark side? As a result, what counsel

---

_a_4 Some manuscripts *your*   _b_7 Or *every*   _c_2 Or *He is the one who turns aside God's wrath, taking away our sins, and not only ours but also*   _d_5 Or *word, love for God*   _e_10 Or *it* would you give to someone who says, "It doesn't matter how I live since God will forgive me anyway"? **3.** Have your friends lost sight of Jesus' deity, or his humanity? With what results? **4.** In your spiritual life, how are you like a "child," just beginning to catch on? A "young man" at the peak of strength? A "father" or seasoned veteran?

OPEN: What do you crave that is "illegal, immoral, or fattening"? If you *could* have it all, *would* you?

DIG: 1. What does John mean by "the world" (vv.15-16)? Do human desires contradict God's will: Always? Never? How so? **2.** How would you recognize and resist an "antichrist" if you met one (vv.18-22; see also 4:3)? **3.** What is the "anointing from the Holy One" (v.20; see Jn 14:17; 15:26; 16: 13)? How is this related to knowing truth "from the beginning" (vv.20-24)? **4.** What does John mean by "acknowledging the Son" (v.23; see 1:3,7; 2:1-7,22; 4:2,15)? Why are there only two options? **5.** What is primary for the *orthodox* Christian: the fellowship of other believers, apostolic doctrine, or the Heavenly Teacher (vv. 19,24, 27)? Why? Conversely, what is primary for an *unorthodox* Christian? Which are you?

REFLECT: 1. Where does love for the world compete with love for God in your life (money, time, priorities, relationships, ambition)? **2.** How can you tell if a "new truth" will bring insight to living, or will undermine the faith?

¹²I write to you, dear children,
  because your sins have been forgiven on account of
    his name.
¹³I write to you, fathers,
  because you have known him who is from the
    beginning.
 I write to you, young men,
  because you have overcome the evil one.
 I write to you, dear children,
  because you have known the Father.
¹⁴I write to you, fathers,
  because you have known him who is from the
    beginning.
 I write to you, young men,
  because you are strong,
  and the word of God lives in you,
  and you have overcome the evil one.

Do Not Love the World

¹⁵Do not love the world or anything in the world. If anyone loves the world, the love of the Father is not in him. ¹⁶For everything in the world—the cravings of sinful man, the lust of his eyes and the boasting of what he has and does—comes not from the Father but from the world. ¹⁷The world and its desires pass away, but the man who does the will of God lives forever.

Warning Against Antichrists

¹⁸Dear children, this is the last hour; and as you have heard that the antichrist is coming, even now many antichrists have come. This is how we know it is the last hour. ¹⁹They went out from us, but they did not really belong to us. For if they had belonged to us, they would have remained with us; but their going showed that none of them belonged to us.

²⁰But you have an anointing from the Holy One, and all of you know the truth.ᶠ ²¹I do not write to you because you do not know the truth, but because you do know it and because no lie comes from the truth. ²²Who is the liar? It is the man who denies that Jesus is the Christ. Such a man is the antichrist—he denies the Father and the Son. ²³No one who denies the Son has the Father; whoever acknowledges the Son has the Father also.

²⁴See that what you have heard from the beginning remains in you. If it does, you also will remain in the Son and in the Father. ²⁵And this is what he promised us—even eternal life.

²⁶I am writing these things to you about those who are trying to lead you astray. ²⁷As for you, the anointing you received from him remains in you, and you do not need anyone to teach you. But as his anointing teaches you about all things and as that anointing is real, not counterfeit—just as it has taught you, remain in him.

f20 Some manuscripts and you know all things

Children of God

[28]And now, dear children, continue in him, so that when he appears we may be confident and unashamed before him at his coming.

[29]If you know that he is righteous, you know that everyone who does what is right has been born of him.

3 How great is the love the Father has lavished on us, that we should be called children of God! And that is what we are! The reason the world does not know us is that it did not know him. [2]Dear friends, now we are children of God, and what we will be has not yet been made known. But we know that when he appears,[g] we shall be like him, for we shall see him as he is. [3]Everyone who has this hope in him purifies himself, just as he is pure.

[4]Everyone who sins breaks the law; in fact, sin is lawlessness. [5]But you know that he appeared so that he might take away our sins. And in him is no sin. [6]No one who lives in him keeps on sinning. No one who continues to sin has either seen him or known him.

[7]Dear children, do not let anyone lead you astray. He who does what is right is righteous, just as he is righteous. [8]He who does what is sinful is of the devil, because the devil has been sinning from the beginning. The reason the Son of God appeared was to destroy the devil's work. [9]No one who is born of God will continue to sin, because God's seed remains in him; he cannot go on sinning, because he has been born of God. [10]This is how we know who the children of God are and who the children of the devil are: Anyone who does not do what is right is not a child of God; nor is anyone who does not love his brother.

Love One Another

[11]This is the message you heard from the beginning: We should love one another. [12]Do not be like Cain, who belonged to the evil one and murdered his brother. And why did he murder him? Because his own actions were evil and his brother's were righteous. [13]Do not be surprised, my brothers, if the world hates you. [14]We know that we have passed from death to life, because we love our brothers. Anyone who does not love remains in death. [15]Anyone who hates his brother is a murderer, and you know that no murderer has eternal life in him.

[16]This is how we know what love is: Jesus Christ laid down his life for us. And we ought to lay down our lives for our brothers. [17]If anyone has material possessions and sees his brother in need but has no pity on him, how can the love of God be in him? [18]Dear children, let us not love with words or tongue but with actions and in truth. [19]This then is how we know that we belong to the truth, and how we set our hearts at rest in his presence [20]whenever our hearts condemn us. For God is greater than our hearts, and he knows everything.

[21]Dear friends, if our hearts do not condemn us, we have confidence before God [22]and receive from him anything we ask,

OPEN: Whose coming would motivate you to clean your house?

DIG: 1. What motives for living a holy life does John give (2:28,29; 3:1-3,6,9)? **2.** What telltale signs mark a person "born of God" (2:29; 3:1,3,6, 7,9,10)? **3.** What implications would John have us draw from 3:1 about God? About our self-image? **4.** Does John mean here that a Christian cannot sin either *absolutely*, or *habitually*, or *deliberately*? Is John condemning such sinners? Or is he providing a gauge to evaluate false teaching about sin? Why? **5.** What are the sources of tension between the world and Christians (3:1,6,9-10; compare 1:6; 2:9-11). What does this say about real spirituality?

REFLECT: 1. Of the motives given here, which one spurs you on to live for God? Why? **2.** As you get older, do you find it harder or easier to resist sinful desires? Why? **3.** When you blow it, what have you found helpful in making it right and getting on with life?

OPEN: What was your first or "most romantic moment"?

DIG: 1. How do Cain and Abel (Ge 4:1-8) illustrate the meaning of "love one another"? How does the cross of Christ illustrate this as well (v.16)? **2.** How does this revealing test compare with John's other "tests" (2:3-6; 2:7-11; 2:19-25 and 3:10)? **3.** What stands out to you about this love (vv.16-18)? How does this differ from your "most romantic moment"? **4.** How does loving others affect our assurance and our prayers? **5.** What links *obedience* to *love* to *belief*?

REFLECT: 1. Where do you see "Cain-like" attitudes in yourself? **2.** If you were to consciously practice "Jesus-like" love this week for a particular "brother," how would you show it in your family? Church? Work? Community? Politics? Toward those you don't like?

*g*2 Or *when it is made known*

OPEN: What big test made you very nervous?

DIG: 1. How do people motivated by God's Spirit differ from false teachers in their attitude toward Christ? To other Christians? To the world? **2.** What power enables you to discern and overcome?

REFLECT: What helps you avoid both: (a) being close-minded to new insights, and (b) being so open-minded your brains fall out? Give an example of (a) and (b).

OPEN: What characteristics or strengths did you get from your father? Your mother?

DIG: 1. "Love" is mentioned 27 times in this passage. What can you learn about: Its origin? Its connection with spiritual reality and knowledge? Its relationship to God? **2.** What models of love (its effect, its motive, its action) do you see here? How love can be suppressed? How it can be made complete or perfect? **3.** From verses 8-15, what can you learn about the relationship between the Father, Son, and Spirit? About their relationship to us? **4.** How does the fact that "God is love" (vv.8,16) relate to the fact that "God is light" (1:5)?

REFLECT: 1. In your life, when has perfect fear cast out love? When has God's love cast out fear? **2.** How will you want put this sacrificial love into action this week: At home? Work? In a difficult relationship? In planning your time? Your budget? In the activities you support? Your political views and involvement?

because we obey his commands and do what pleases him. [23]And this is his command: to believe in the name of his Son, Jesus Christ, and to love one another as he commanded us. [24]Those who obey his commands live in him, and he in them. And this is how we know that he lives in us: We know it by the Spirit he gave us.

Test the Spirits

4 Dear friends, do not believe every spirit, but test the spirits to see whether they are from God, because many false prophets have gone out into the world. [2]This is how you can recognize the Spirit of God: Every spirit that acknowledges that Jesus Christ has come in the flesh is from God, [3]but every spirit that does not acknowledge Jesus is not from God. This is the spirit of the antichrist, which you have heard is coming and even now is already in the world.

[4]You, dear children, are from God and have overcome them, because the one who is in you is greater than the one who is in the world. [5]They are from the world and therefore speak from the viewpoint of the world, and the world listens to them. [6]We are from God, and whoever knows God listens to us; but whoever is not from God does not listen to us. This is how we recognize the Spirit[h] of truth and the spirit of falsehood.

God's Love and Ours

[7]Dear friends, let us love one another, for love comes from God. Everyone who loves has been born of God and knows God. [8]Whoever does not love does not know God, because God is love. [9]This is how God showed his love among us: He sent his one and only Son[i] into the world that we might live through him. [10]This is love: not that we loved God, but that he loved us and sent his Son as an atoning sacrifice for[j] our sins. [11]Dear friends, since God so loved us, we also ought to love one another. [12]No one has ever seen God; but if we love one another, God lives in us and his love is made complete in us.

[13]We know that we live in him and he in us, because he has given us of his Spirit. [14]And we have seen and testify that the Father has sent his Son to be the Savior of the world. [15]If anyone acknowledges that Jesus is the Son of God, God lives in him and he in God. [16]And so we know and rely on the love God has for us.

God is love. Whoever lives in love lives in God, and God in him. [17]In this way, love is made complete among us so that we will have confidence on the day of judgment, because in this world we are like him. [18]There is no fear in love. But perfect love drives out fear, because fear has to do with punishment. The one who fears is not made perfect in love.

[19]We love because he first loved us. [20]If anyone says, "I love God," yet hates his brother, he is a liar. For anyone who does not love his brother, whom he has seen, cannot love God, whom he has not seen. [21]And he has given us this command: Whoever loves God must also love his brother.

[h]6 Or spirit   [i]9 Or his only begotten Son   [j]10 Or as the one who would turn aside his wrath, taking away

Faith in the Son of God

5 Everyone who believes that Jesus is the Christ is born of God, and everyone who loves the father loves his child as well. ²This is how we know that we love the children of God: by loving God and carrying out his commands. ³This is love for God: to obey his commands. And his commands are not burdensome, ⁴for everyone born of God overcomes the world. This is the victory that has overcome the world, even our faith. ⁵Who is it that overcomes the world? Only he who believes that Jesus is the Son of God.

⁶This is the one who came by water and blood—Jesus Christ. He did not come by water only, but by water and blood. And it is the Spirit who testifies, because the Spirit is the truth. ⁷For there are three that testify: ⁸the *k* Spirit, the water and the blood; and the three are in agreement. ⁹We accept man's testimony, but God's testimony is greater because it is the testimony of God, which he has given about his Son. ¹⁰Anyone who believes in the Son of God has this testimony in his heart. Anyone who does not believe God has made him out to be a liar, because he has not believed the testimony God has given about his Son. ¹¹And this is the testimony: God has given us eternal life, and this life is in his Son. ¹²He who has the Son has life; he who does not have the Son of God does not have life.

Concluding Remarks

¹³I write these things to you who believe in the name of the Son of God so that you may know that you have eternal life. ¹⁴This is the confidence we have in approaching God: that if we ask anything according to his will, he hears us. ¹⁵And if we know that he hears us—whatever we ask—we know that we have what we asked of him.

¹⁶If anyone sees his brother commit a sin that does not lead to death, he should pray and God will give him life. I refer to those whose sin does not lead to death. There is a sin that leads to death. I am not saying that he should pray about that. ¹⁷All wrongdoing is sin, and there is sin that does not lead to death.

¹⁸We know that anyone born of God does not continue to sin; the one who was born of God keeps him safe, and the evil one cannot harm him. ¹⁹We know that we are children of God, and that the whole world is under the control of the evil one. ²⁰We know also that the Son of God has come and has given us understanding, so that we may know him who is true. And we are in him who is true—even in his Son Jesus Christ. He is the true God and eternal life.

²¹Dear children, keep yourselves from idols.

OPEN: 1. In the Aesop's fable, are you more like the steady, persistent tortoise, or the fast-starting, easily distracted hare? How so? **2.** Who put you to bed at night and heard your prayers as a child?

DIG: 1. What parallel themes do you see between this concluding section and the prologue (1:1-4)? **2.** How are belief, love, obedience, and life interconnected in this section? Using these four key concepts, how would you explain to someone what being a Christian is all about? **3.** Why the repeated emphasis on right doctrine, holiness, and love? What is John combating? **4.** From what John says about "the world" elsewhere (2:16; 3:13; 5:19), whose is "the victory" that has overcome the world (v.4)? **5.** How has God given witness to Jesus by his baptism ("water"—Jn 1:29-30)? By his death ("blood"—Jn 12:23-33)? By his Spirit (Jn 14:26; 15:26)? How do these three confirm that life is indeed found in Jesus (vv.6-8)? **6.** How is the assurance of eternal life (v.13) the key to: (a) Answered prayer (vv.14-15)? (b) Forgiveness of sin (vv.16-17)? (c) Deliverance from sin and evil (v.18-19)? (d) Avoidance of idols (v.21)? **7.** What might be a "sin that leads to death" (v.16; see Jesus' comments on the Pharisees' refusal to consider his teaching—Mk 3:22-30.)

REFLECT: 1. Using the "love test" of verse 1 (to love God is to show love to his children), how are you doing at loving God? Using the test from verses 2-3 (to love others means to obey God's commands), how are you doing at loving others? **2.** What has convinced you that true life is found in Jesus? What further "proof" do you need? **3.** What "idols" of the world today tempt you away from steadily following Jesus? What is one thing you can do to "keep away" from that idol? **4.** What is one major thing you have decided to work on in your life as a result of studying this letter?

*k*7,8 Late manuscripts of the Vulgate *testify in heaven: the Father, the Word and the Holy Spirit, and these three are one.* ⁸*And there are three that testify on earth: the* (not found in any Greek manuscript before the sixteenth century)

2 JOHN
3 JOHN

INTRODUCTION

Characteristics

Second and Third John are the shortest letters in the New Testament; so short, in fact, that virtually everyone concedes that they are genuine. (Who would bother to fake such brief and unassuming documents?) Their length is determined by the size of a standard papyrus sheet (8 x 10 inches). Each letter would fit exactly on one sheet.

Author

There is much similarity of style and content between 2 and 3 John. (For example, compare 2 John 1 and 3 John 1; 2 John 4 and 3 John 4; 2 John 12 and 3 John 13-14). Undoubtedly both were written by the same person. There is also a close connection between 1 John and these two shorter letters (compare, for example, 1 John 4:3 and 2 John 7). All three epistles seem to deal with the same situation. Therefore, it seems very likely that the "elder" who wrote 2 and 3 John is, indeed, the apostle John.

Theme

The issue addressed by 2 and 3 John is that of wandering missionaries. In a time when Roman inns were notorious for being dirty and flea-infested, visiting Christian teachers would turn to the local church for hospitality. The problem was that some of the people seeking room and board were false teachers, expounding erroneous doctrines; others were phony, pretending to be true prophets to get free hospitality. Even a pagan Greek author like Lucian noticed this sort of abuse. In his satirical work *Peregrinus,* he wrote about a religious charlatan who lived off the generosity of the church simply as a way to avoid working. In an attempt to cope with this problem, the *Didache,* an early church manual, laid down a series of regulations guiding the reception of itinerant ministers. It said, for example, that true prophets were indeed to be entertained — for a day or two. But if a prophet stayed three days, this was a sign that he was false. Likewise, if a prophet under the inspiration of the Spirit asked for money, he was a false prophet.

These concerns are found in 2 and 3 John. In 2 John, the author worries about false prophets who are teaching erroneous doctrine. "Do not welcome such," he says (2 John 10). But in 3 John, he addresses the opposite problem: Christians who failed to provide hospitality for genuine teachers.

2 John

¹The elder,

To the chosen lady and her children, whom I love in the truth—and not I only, but also all who know the truth— ²because of the truth, which lives in us and will be with us forever:

³Grace, mercy and peace from God the Father and from Jesus Christ, the Father's Son, will be with us in truth and love.

⁴It has given me great joy to find some of your children walking in the truth, just as the Father commanded us. ⁵And now, dear lady, I am not writing you a new command but one we have had from the beginning. I ask that we love one another. ⁶And this is love: that we walk in obedience to his commands. As you have heard from the beginning, his command is that you walk in love.

⁷Many deceivers, who do not acknowledge Jesus Christ as coming in the flesh, have gone out into the world. Any such person is the deceiver and the antichrist. ⁸Watch out that you do not lose what you have worked for, but that you may be rewarded fully. ⁹Anyone who runs ahead and does not continue in the teaching of Christ does not have God; whoever continues in the teaching has both the Father and the Son. ¹⁰If anyone comes to you and does not bring this teaching, do not take him into your house or welcome him. ¹¹Anyone who welcomes him shares in his wicked work.

¹²I have much to write to you, but I do not want to use paper and ink. Instead, I hope to visit you and talk with you face to face, so that our joy may be complete.

¹³The children of your chosen sister send their greetings.

3 John

OPEN: 1. Did you ever run out of money when you were away from home? What did you do? **2.** Who extended loving hospitality to you when you needed it most?

DIG: 1. What conflicts were going on in the church that prompted John to write this letter? What personality issues are involved? What type of character sketch would you draw for Gaius? Diotrephes? Demetrius? **2.** In what ways does this letter tackle the hospitality issue differently than 2 John? Why is John urging that these teachers be cared for in their travels? Why would this be so important at this time?

REFLECT: 1. How can you reflect Gaius' desire to be of help to itinerant Christian workers? **2.** Has suspicion about the false motives or messages of some pastors/teachers soured you against them all? What needs to change so you will not hinder the work of God by failing to encourage his true servants? **3.** Do you find opening up your home (or your small group) to new people easy or difficult? Why is that? **4.** In picking close friends (like Gaius was to John), what do you look for? How can you be that kind of friend to others?

[1]The elder,

To my dear friend Gaius, whom I love in the truth.

[2]Dear friend, I pray that you may enjoy good health and that all may go well with you, even as your soul is getting along well. [3]It gave me great joy to have some brothers come and tell about your faithfulness to the truth and how you continue to walk in the truth. [4]I have no greater joy than to hear that my children are walking in the truth.

[5]Dear friend, you are faithful in what you are doing for the brothers, even though they are strangers to you. [6]They have told the church about your love. You will do well to send them on their way in a manner worthy of God. [7]It was for the sake of the Name that they went out, receiving no help from the pagans. [8]We ought therefore to show hospitality to such men so that we may work together for the truth.

[9]I wrote to the church, but Diotrephes, who loves to be first, will have nothing to do with us. [10]So if I come, I will call attention to what he is doing, gossiping maliciously about us. Not satisfied with that, he refuses to welcome the brothers. He also stops those who want to do so and puts them out of the church.

[11]Dear friend, do not imitate what is evil but what is good. Anyone who does what is good is from God. Anyone who does what is evil has not seen God. [12]Demetrius is well spoken of by everyone—and even by the truth itself. We also speak well of him, and you know that our testimony is true.

[13]I have much to write you, but I do not want to do so with pen and ink. [14]I hope to see you soon, and we will talk face to face.

Peace to you. The friends here send their greetings. Greet the friends there by name.

JUDE

INTRODUCTION

Author

In the New Testament there are five people by the name of Jude or Judas (Mark 6:3; Luke 6:16; John 14:22; Acts 9:11; 15:22, 27, 32), but only one is a serious candidate as author: Jude, the brother of Jesus.

Little is known about Jude. He was one of four brothers (Matt. 13:55; Mark 6:3). He was probably not a follower of Jesus during the years of his brother's ministry (Mark 3:21, 31-35; John 7:5). It was only after the Resurrection that Jude became a believer (Acts 1:14).

The brothers of Jesus eventually became itinerant missionaries (1 Cor. 9:5). Tradition has it that they spread the gospel throughout Palestine. Jude's brother, James the Just, was leader of the church in Jerusalem.

So in the book of Jude, a reader comes in touch with "those original Palestinian Christian circles in which Jesus' own blood relatives were leaders" (Richard Bauckham, *Jude, 2 Peter: Word Biblical Commentary*, p. xi).

Characteristics

Another Neglected Book

Most people know Jude only because of its benediction (vv. 24-25):

Now unto him that is able to keep you from falling, and to present you faultless before the presence of his glory with exceeding joy, to the only wise God our Saviour, be glory and majesty, dominion and power, both now and ever. Amen. (KJV)

Like 2 Peter, Jude is widely unread because of doubts about its pedigree and because of its frequent unfamiliar images. To its first readers, however, Jude was anything but obscure. It was heard as a fiery call to defend the faith against the heretics who had wormed their way into the church (v. 4).

The Texts Jude Expounds

This is a sermon, and in true sermonic fashion, Jude quotes (or alludes to) various texts and then explains them. What sets Jude's sermon apart from contemporary Christian sermons is his choice of texts. His first references are to Old Testament stories (vv. 5-7, 11), and his concluding reference is to "what the apostles of our Lord Jesus Christ foretold" (v. 17). This is familiar material. But in between, Jude quotes *1 Enoch* (vv. 14-15), a Jewish apocryphal book, and alludes to the *Assumption of Moses* in verse 9, probably to the *Testament of Naphtali* (v. 7) and to the *Testament of Asher* (v. 8).

The Apocryphal books Jude quotes were written during the time between the Old and New Testament. They were not accepted as orthodox and so never became part of the Bible itself.

Certain of the church fathers concluded (wrongly) that any book that used apocryphal literature as Jude did could not be genuine. But this view says more about the presuppositions of those theologians than it does about what can and cannot be included within Scripture.

Certainly other New Testament authors used nonbiblical Jewish writing in 1 Corinthians 10:4 and 2 Timothy 3:8. Paul quotes the heathen poets in Acts 17:28; 1 Corinthians 15:32-33; and Titus 1:12. The author of Hebrews echoes the works of Philo; James makes reference to nonbiblical sources. The issue is not where the specific words came from but how the New Testament writer used these words to reveal God's truth.

Relationship to 2 Peter

It is clear that Jude and 2 Peter are somehow related. Of the twenty-five verses in Jude, fifteen appear in whole or in part in 2 Peter. The question is: What is the nature of the relationship between Jude and 2 Peter? Did Jude quote from 2 Peter? Or was the reverse true? Or did they both quote from the same outside source? The answer to this question is by no means certain.

Theme

Jude gives an overview of his book in verses 3-4. He makes two points. First, Christians are "to contend for the faith"; second, they are to do so against false Christians who "have secretly slipped in among [them]." The rest of the book develops these two points. In verses 5-19, the nature of the false teachers is explained. Jude makes it exceedingly clear that this is not a new problem and furthermore, their condemnation is sure. In verses 20-23, Jude gets to his main point: He appeals to the Christians to hold on to the Christian faith despite false teachers.

The False Teachers

Jude's opponents are a band of smooth-talking teachers who go from church to church, receiving hospitality in return for their instruction. Such itinerant teachers were often a source of trouble in the early church (Matt. 7:15; 2 Cor. 10-11; 1 John 4:1; 2 John 10). In this case, the teachers were *antinomians,* that is, they rejected all moral standards (since they misunderstood grace) and indulged in all manner of immoral behavior, particularly of a sexual sort. Their teaching was derived largely from individual ecstatic experience ("God told me"), and they considered themselves the sole judge of their own actions.

Structure

Jude is a genuine letter. It has a standard opening (vv. 1-2), and in verses 3-4 the theme and occasion of the epistle are defined — again typical of a letter. But Jude is also a short sermon. The bulk of the book (vv. 5-25) consists of an exposition of certain texts as related to a particular problem facing the church. Thus, Jude is a sermon sent by mail to be read before the congregation(s).

The Book of Jude is a painstakingly crafted document. Jude packs a lot of content into a few words by carefully choosing his words and images. Verses 11-13 are particularly vivid in imagery, evoking a wide range of associations in remarkably few words.

Jude

¹Jude, a servant of Jesus Christ and a brother of James,

To those who have been called, who are loved by God the Father and kept by*a* Jesus Christ:

²Mercy, peace and love be yours in abundance.

The Sin and Doom of Godless Men

³Dear friends, although I was very eager to write to you about the salvation we share, I felt I had to write and urge you to contend for the faith that was once for all entrusted to the saints. ⁴For certain men whose condemnation was written about*b* long ago have secretly slipped in among you. They are godless men, who change the grace of our God into a license for immorality and deny Jesus Christ our only Sovereign and Lord.

⁵Though you already know all this, I want to remind you that the Lord*c* delivered his people out of Egypt, but later destroyed those who did not believe. ⁶And the angels who did not keep their positions of authority but abandoned their own home— these he has kept in darkness, bound with everlasting chains for judgment on the great Day. ⁷In a similar way, Sodom and Gomorrah and the surrounding towns gave themselves up to sexual immorality and perversion. They serve as an example of those who suffer the punishment of eternal fire.

⁸In the very same way, these dreamers pollute their own bodies, reject authority and slander celestial beings. ⁹But even the archangel Michael, when he was disputing with the devil about the body of Moses, did not dare to bring a slanderous accusation against him, but said, "The Lord rebuke you!" ¹⁰Yet these men speak abusively against whatever they do not understand; and what things they do understand by instinct, like unreasoning animals—these are the very things that destroy them.

¹¹Woe to them! They have taken the way of Cain; they have rushed for profit into Balaam's error; they have been destroyed in Korah's rebellion.

¹²These men are blemishes at your love feasts, eating with you without the slightest qualm—shepherds who feed only themselves. They are clouds without rain, blown along by the wind; autumn trees, without fruit and uprooted—twice dead. ¹³They are wild waves of the sea, foaming up their shame; wandering stars, for whom blackest darkness has been reserved forever.

¹⁴Enoch, the seventh from Adam, prophesied about these men: "See, the Lord is coming with thousands upon thousands of his holy ones ¹⁵to judge everyone, and to convict all the ungodly of all the ungodly acts they have done in the ungodly way, and of all the harsh words ungodly sinners have spoken against him." ¹⁶These men are grumblers and faultfinders; they follow their own evil desires; they boast about themselves and flatter others for their own advantage.

---

a1 Or *for; or in*   *b4* Or *men who were marked out for condemnation*
c5 Some early manuscripts *Jesus*

and work? **5.** What has caused you to doubt your faith at times? Who helped you then? How? **6.** In light of the warnings in Jude, what hope do you find in verses 24-25? How does that help as you struggle with evil?

A Call to Persevere

[17]But, dear friends, remember what the apostles of our Lord Jesus Christ foretold. [18]They said to you, "In the last times there will be scoffers who will follow their own ungodly desires." [19]These are the men who divide you, who follow mere natural instincts and do not have the Spirit.

[20]But you, dear friends, build yourselves up in your most holy faith and pray in the Holy Spirit. [21]Keep yourselves in God's love as you wait for the mercy of our Lord Jesus Christ to bring you to eternal life.

[22]Be merciful to those who doubt; [23]snatch others from the fire and save them; to others show mercy, mixed with fear—hating even the clothing stained by corrupted flesh.

Doxology

[24]To him who is able to keep you from falling and to present you before his glorious presence without fault and with great joy— [25]to the only God our Savior be glory, majesty, power and authority, through Jesus Christ our Lord, before all ages, now and forevermore! Amen.

REVELATION

INTRODUCTION

Apocalyptic Literature

The Book of Revelation is unique. It is the only apocalyptic book in the New Testament. What makes this so unusual is that while the New Testament books were written, apocalyptic literature flourished. In fact, during the period between the Old and New Testaments, apocalyptic literature was the most common type of Jewish religious writing.

At the heart of apocalyptic literature was *hope*—hope that God would right wrongs and rescue the righteous. The Jews knew that they were God's chosen people, yet they had been subject to ungodly rules for so long. As a result, they longed for that great day when God would intervene in history and bring about what he promised. They gave shape to these longings in the so-called apocalyptic writings (*apocalypse* is a Greek word meaning an "unveiling" or "uncovering" of future events or hidden realms, like heaven).

Apocalyptic literature dealt with the details of God's return: how he would burst into history, whom he would destroy, how he would set up his kingdom. These books were, of necessity, the products of dreams and visions. Consequently, they were filled with swirling images and vivid pictures of death, supernatural places and creatures, destruction and redemption, and so on. Since the events described were unlike anything that had ever happened, they could only be alluded to, often in cryptic language. The resulting mystery surrounding such writing was further compounded by the need for secrecy. Were these books to fall into the hands of the rulers (the ones singled out for destruction), they would be considered seditious and would land their authors in jail or worse. So the books were written in code. They could be understood only by those on the writer's side who had the key to the code. Outsiders, such as the police, would find them unintelligible. Of course, this is why we have a problem today in deciphering apocalyptic literature. In many cases, we have lost the key.

The Apocalyptic World View

Underlying both Jewish and Christian apocalyptic literature was the view that history is divided into two ages. The present age is evil and corrupt and it will be destroyed. The age-to-come is characterized by goodness and by God's presence and power. The central turning point in history, on which apocalyptic writers often focused, is the Day of the Lord, when the present age will give way to the new age.

Christian writers understood this to be the day of Christ's return—the Second Coming. He had come once, as a baby in Bethlehem, and by his first coming had set in motion the events that would draw the present age to a close. When he came again, it would not be as an infant but as a king before whom the whole creation would bow. For the moment, however, Christians live in the in-between time. Christ's ultimate victory was secured at the Cross; Satan was defeated. But the victory had yet to be claimed in its fullness. Satan still pretended that he was in charge and would do so until the Second Coming.

What is striking is how similar the pattern is in Christian and Jewish apocalyptic literature. Beyond the obvious difference over the role of Christ, the same outline is found in Jewish literature as in Revelation. Specifically:

1. The Messiah will be the central figure in the Day of the Lord.
2. The coming of the new age will be preceded by a terrible time in history filled with war, famine, and calamity of all sorts. In fact, the elements themselves will disintegrate, and hatred and anger will prevail in human affairs.
3. The Day of the Lord will be the time when judgment is rendered.

4. Following judgment, there will be a time of great peace and joy. The New Jerusalem will descend. The dead will rise and the Messiah will reign.

Characteristics

Not only is Revelation strange; it is also difficult. The world of the Book of Revelation is so remote from the modern world that one hardly knows where to begin in trying to understand it. It is a world filled with weird beasts who have ten horns and seven heads; a world of seals and trumpets and bowls that bring disaster; a world populated with angels and demons, with lions and lambs, with horses and dragons. Who can make sense out of all this?

As a result, we often either ignore Revelation or distort it. Barclay calls Revelation "the playground of religious eccentrics" (*The Revelation of John: Daily Study Bible,* Vol. 1, p. 1). Indeed some wild notions have been extracted from Revelation and claimed to have divine sanction. On the other hand, as Philip Carrington has said:

> In the case of the *Revelation* we are dealing with an artist greater than Stevenson or Coleridge or Bach. St. John has a better sense of the right word than Stevenson; he has a greater command of unearthly supernatural loveliness than Coleridge; he has a richer sense of melody and rhythm and composition than Bach . . . It is the only masterpiece of pure art in the New Testament (*The Meaning of Revelation,* pp. xvii, xix).

The Book of Revelation is well worth reading, but it must be approached with humility and caution. To pin one's whole theology on details in the Book of Revelation is dangerous indeed. With prayer and patience, the reader needs to work at understanding the text.

Revelation is written in the worst Greek of any book of the New Testament. There are mistakes in grammar and stylistic errors such as a schoolboy would make. Yet R. H. Charles, an expert on apocalyptic literature, considers the bad grammar deliberate. According to Charles, John wrote this way for emphasis. His clumsy Greek style reflects his attempt to translate Old Testament passages—the author was thinking in Hebrew but writing in Greek. Furthermore, a vision such as John had can never be adequately captured by mere words. John had to push language to its limits even to approximate what he had seen. The poor Greek may also have resulted from John's imprisonment on Patmos, where he probably had no secretary to smooth out his style. (*A Critical Exegetical Commentary on the Revelation of St. John: International Critical Commentary,* pp. x-xi).

Author

Although the author only refers to himself as "John" (1:4), it has traditionally been assumed that he was none other than John the apostle. In fact, this simple designation "John" is strong proof in itself that the apostle was the writer. Typically apocalyptic literature claimed to be authored by famous heroes of the past (e.g., Abraham, Ezra, Enoch, and Baruch). But John writes in his own name, and only a person of the stature of an apostle could expect to have such a work received as authoritative. Furthermore, when Revelation is compared to the Gospel of John and the three letters of John, there are striking similarities in ideas, theology, and language.

John wrote from the island of Patmos, a rocky, barren island in the Aegean Sea (ten miles long and five miles wide), where he had been exiled because of his Christian witness. Tradition says that he was eventually released from Patmos and spent the remaining years of his long life in Ephesus.

Date

Most scholars feel that the Book of Revelation was written toward the end of the reign of Domitian, that is, around A.D. 90-95. This is what Irenaeus, a second-century bishop, claimed. Still, this dating is not conclusive. Evidence has been offered that it might have been written during the last years of Nero's reign (between A.D. 65 and 68) or when Vespasian was emperor (A.D. 69-79).

Audience

The Book of Revelation was addressed to seven churches in the western part of the Roman province of Asia (see map). The order in which these churches are addressed is the order in which a messenger from Patmos would come to each church if he followed the great circular Roman road connecting the cities.

Theme

Rome is a central and consistently negative image in the Book of Revelation. This view of the Roman government stands in sharp contrast to the rest of the New Testament, where Rome is seen as the protector of Christianity. In the early days of missionary activity, Roman judges protected Christians from Jewish mobs (Acts 18:1-17; 19:13-41). It was Roman justice to which Paul turned in his time of need (Acts 23:12-35; 25:10-11). As a result, the apostles urged submission to Rome (Rom. 13:1-7; 1 Peter 2:13-17). But in Revelation, the attitude is quite different. Rome is seen as a whore, drunk with the blood of Christians (17:5-6), deserving nothing but destruction.

This shift in attitude is due to one thing—Caesar worship. Although Roman rulers were long considered divine, their centrality in Roman civil religion was not enforced until the end of the first century. Then it became obligatory for citizens all across the Roman Empire to appear once a year before a magistrate to burn a pinch of incense and declare, "Caesar is Lord." This was more an act of loyalty to Rome than a religious statement, but Christians simply could not bring themselves to declare that anyone except Jesus was Lord. As a result, they were hounded mercilessly by civil authorities. This is the situation to which Revelation speaks. It attempts to encourage Christians by giving them the long view. They may suffer now while Caesar pretends to be Lord, but ahead lies unimaginable glory when Jesus, the true Lord, comes in power. This kind of vision would give harassed Christians the strength to endure.

Structure

John begins with a description of the vision from which the Book of Revelation came (chap. 1). Chapters 2 and 3 contain specific messages to seven churches in Asia Minor. Chapters 4 and 5 describe a vision of God and of Christ. Then in chapters 6-19 various plagues of judgment are described. The book is concluded (chaps. 20-22) by a description of the coming kingdom.

While the overall structure is clear, how it all fits together varies with the reader's interpretive posture.

Interpretation

There are widely varying ways to interpret Revelation. Some limit its meaning to the first-century struggle between the church and Rome. Others see Revelation as a collection of symbols that predict future events (e.g., the locusts from the bottomless pit represent the invasion of Europe by Islam). In fact, the Book of Revelation probably speaks both to the immediate first-century struggle of Christians and to the future when the Lord will return.

Revelation

OPEN: 1. What kind of book are you: Mystery? Sports? Technical? Adventure? Poetry? Unreadable? Sealed book? X-Rated? Explain. **2.** Around the house, are you king, priest, or a servant? What would your spouse, parent, or friend say is your typical role?

DIG: 1. What is *revelation*? In this case, who is revealed? By whom? To whom? For what purpose? **2.** Who is John? Who are the recipient churches (vv.4,11; see map)? **3.** What is significant about the references to God in verses 4 and 8? **4.** What are the meanings of the titles given to Jesus (vv.5-6)? What three things does Christ do for us? **5.** What theme of the book of Revelation is foreshadowed in verse 7? Why is the phrase "every eye will see him" significant?

REFLECT: 1. If asked to share three facts about Jesus that are especially significant to you, what would you say? Why are these facts so important to you? **2.** How will you personalize and pass along the blessing of verse 3?

OPEN: 1. What bizarre dream can you still recall, and why? **2.** What religious pictures or statues adorn the walls of your house (or mind)?

DIG: 1. Why was John on Patmos? What do you know about his assignment there? **2.** What's significant about his spiritual condition and the day when he received this vision? **3.** What do the images in verses 12-18 suggest about Christ? **4.** What is the meaning of the seven stars? The seven lampstands? What does it mean for a church to be a light? **5.** Close your eyes and have someone read verses 12-18 slowly, several times if necessary. Meditate on it. What do you see? Feel?

Prologue

1 The revelation of Jesus Christ, which God gave him to show his servants what must soon take place. He made it known by sending his angel to his servant John, ²who testifies to everything he saw—that is, the word of God and the testimony of Jesus Christ. ³Blessed is the one who reads the words of this prophecy, and blessed are those who hear it and take to heart what is written in it, because the time is near.

Greetings and Doxology

⁴John,

To the seven churches in the province of Asia:

Grace and peace to you from him who is, and who was, and who is to come, and from the seven spirits *a* before his throne, ⁵and from Jesus Christ, who is the faithful witness, the firstborn from the dead, and the ruler of the kings of the earth.

To him who loves us and has freed us from our sins by his blood, ⁶and has made us to be a kingdom and priests to serve his God and Father—to him be glory and power for ever and ever! Amen.

⁷Look, he is coming with the clouds,
    and every eye will see him,
  even those who pierced him;
    and all the peoples of the earth will mourn because of
        him.

So shall it be! Amen.

⁸"I am the Alpha and the Omega," says the Lord God, "who is, and who was, and who is to come, the Almighty."

One Like a Son of Man

⁹I, John, your brother and companion in the suffering and kingdom and patient endurance that are ours in Jesus, was on the island of Patmos because of the word of God and the testimony of Jesus. ¹⁰On the Lord's Day I was in the Spirit, and I heard behind me a loud voice like a trumpet, ¹¹which said: "Write on a scroll what you see and send it to the seven churches: to Ephesus, Smyrna, Pergamum, Thyatira, Sardis, Philadelphia and Laodicea."

¹²I turned around to see the voice that was speaking to me. And when I turned I saw seven golden lampstands, ¹³and among the lampstands was someone "like a son of man," *b* dressed in a robe reaching down to his feet and with a golden sash around his chest. ¹⁴His head and hair were white like wool, as white as snow, and his eyes were like blazing fire. ¹⁵His feet were like

---

a4 Or *the sevenfold Spirit*   *b13* Daniel 7:13

bronze glowing in a furnace, and his voice was like the sound of rushing waters. [16]In his right hand he held seven stars, and out of his mouth came a sharp double-edged sword. His face was like the sun shining in all its brilliance.

[17]When I saw him, I fell at his feet as though dead. Then he placed his right hand on me and said: "Do not be afraid. I am the First and the Last. [18]I am the Living One; I was dead, and behold I am alive for ever and ever! And I hold the keys of death and Hades.

[19]"Write, therefore, what you have seen, what is now and what will take place later. [20]The mystery of the seven stars that you saw in my right hand and of the seven golden lampstands is this: The seven stars are the angels of the seven churches, and the seven lampstands are the seven churches.

To the Church in Ephesus

2 "To the angel[d] of the church in Ephesus write:

These are the words of him who holds the seven stars in his right hand and walks among the seven golden lampstands: [2]I know your deeds, your hard work and your perseverance. I know that you cannot tolerate wicked men, that you have tested those who claim to be apostles but are not, and have found them false. [3]You have persevered and have endured hardships for my name, and have not grown weary.

[4]Yet I hold this against you: You have forsaken your first love. [5]Remember the height from which you have fallen! Repent and do the things you did at first. If you do not repent, I will come to you and remove your lampstand from its place. [6]But you have this in your favor: You hate the practices of the Nicolaitans, which I also hate.

[7]He who has an ear, let him hear what the Spirit says to the churches. To him who overcomes, I will give the right to eat from the tree of life, which is in the paradise of God.

To the Church in Smyrna

[8]"To the angel of the church in Smyrna write:

These are the words of him who is the First and the Last, who died and came to life again. [9]I know your afflictions and your poverty—yet you are rich! I know the slander of those who say they are Jews and are not, but are a synagogue of Satan. [10]Do not be afraid of what you are about to suffer. I tell you, the devil will put some of you in prison to test you, and you will suffer persecution for ten days. Be faithful, even to the point of death, and I will give you the crown of life.

[11]He who has an ear, let him hear what the Spirit says to the churches. He who overcomes will not be hurt at all by the second death.

REFLECT: 1. Using the analogy of a lighting fixture to describe the spiritual condition of your church, what kind fits your situation (a chandelier, a night-light, etc.)? In what condition is it? **2.** Are you right now "on Patmos" (suffering) or "in the Spirit" (reigning)? Why? Can both happen at once?

OPEN: What was your "first love" in elementary school like?

DIG: 1. What do you know about the church at Ephesus (see Acts 19)? **2.** What good things characterize this church? How might its strengths have been the cause of its failure? What do you think their Sunday worship was like? **3.** What is repentance? Why is that necessary for the Ephesian church?

REFLECT: 1. Of the positive qualities mentioned about this group, which best describes you? Your church? Why? **2.** In what ways have you lost your first love for Christ? What has helped you to keep that love alive?

OPEN: If you were rich, what would you like to do?

DIG: 1. What problems is this church facing? How can they be both poor and rich? **2.** Why is Jesus known as the First and Last? **3.** What does this passage teach about suffering?

REFLECT: 1. Has it been harder to live out your faith when you've been poor, or when you've had enough money? Why? **2.** In what ways do you feel spiritually rich?

---

c20 Or *messengers*   d1 Or '*messenger;* also in verses 8, 12 and 18

OPEN: As a kid, where was the local "haunted house" in your town? Did you ever dare to go in?

DIG: 1. What pressures are the Christians in Pergamum facing? At what point are they strong? Where are they tempted? Which do you think is easier to endure: Persecution by enemies or seduction by the culture? Why? **2.** Why is the title by which Christ reveals himself so appropriate to these Christians? **3.** What is the significance of the sword (v.16)? Of the manna and stone (v.17)?

REFLECT: 1. What cultural influences distract you from your relationship with Christ? How subtle are these influences in your life? How direct? **2.** What weapons has God given you to do battle with? Which has proved very helpful?

OPEN: As a teenager, what person or group influenced you the most? How?

DIG: 1. What are the strengths of this church? Its weaknesses? **2.** What does the symbolic name "Jezebel" reveal about the woman in this church? **3.** How does Jesus describe himself? How do you interpret this description? What is he saying about himself? Why is this appropriate for the church at Thyatira? **4.** How is the nature and source of the temptation in Thyatira like (and unlike) that in Pergamum? **5.** What do you think Jesus' promise in verses 26-27 means?

REFLECT: 1. Which of the qualities in verse 19 apply to you this week? Why? **2.** Who or what has played a role similar to Jezebel in your life (names aren't necessary)? How? How did the Lord free you from that influence? **3.** What do you appreciate most about the promise to overcomers in this section? Why?

To the Church in Pergamum

12"To the angel of the church in Pergamum write:

These are the words of him who has the sharp, double-edged sword. 13I know where you live—where Satan has his throne. Yet you remain true to my name. You did not renounce your faith in me, even in the days of Antipas, my faithful witness, who was put to death in your city—where Satan lives.

14Nevertheless, I have a few things against you: You have people there who hold to the teaching of Balaam, who taught Balak to entice the Israelites to sin by eating food sacrificed to idols and by committing sexual immorality. 15Likewise you also have those who hold to the teaching of the Nicolaitans. 16Repent therefore! Otherwise, I will soon come to you and will fight against them with the sword of my mouth.

17He who has an ear, let him hear what the Spirit says to the churches. To him who overcomes, I will give some of the hidden manna. I will also give him a white stone with a new name written on it, known only to him who receives it.

To the Church in Thyatira

18"To the angel of the church in Thyatira write:

These are the words of the Son of God, whose eyes are like blazing fire and whose feet are like burnished bronze. 19I know your deeds, your love and faith, your service and perseverance, and that you are now doing more than you did at first.

20Nevertheless, I have this against you: You tolerate that woman Jezebel, who calls herself a prophetess. By her teaching she misleads my servants into sexual immorality and the eating of food sacrificed to idols. 21I have given her time to repent of her immorality, but she is unwilling. 22So I will cast her on a bed of suffering, and I will make those who commit adultery with her suffer intensely, unless they repent of her ways. 23I will strike her children dead. Then all the churches will know that I am he who searches hearts and minds, and I will repay each of you according to your deeds. 24Now I say to the rest of you in Thyatira, to you who do not hold to her teaching and have not learned Satan's so-called deep secrets (I will not impose any other burden on you): 25Only hold on to what you have until I come.

26To him who overcomes and does my will to the end, I will give authority over the nations—

27'He will rule them with an iron scepter;
    he will dash them to pieces like pottery'ᶜ—

just as I have received authority from my Father. 28I will also give him the morning star. 29He who has an ear, let him hear what the Spirit says to the churches.

ᶜ27 Psalm 2:9

To the Church in Sardis

3 "To the angel*f* of the church in Sardis write:

These are the words of him who holds the seven spirits*g* of God and the seven stars. I know your deeds; you have a reputation of being alive, but you are dead. ²Wake up! Strengthen what remains and is about to die, for I have not found your deeds complete in the sight of my God. ³Remember, therefore, what you have received and heard; obey it, and repent. But if you do not wake up, I will come like a thief, and you will not know at what time I will come to you.

⁴Yet you have a few people in Sardis who have not soiled their clothes. They will walk with me, dressed in white, for they are worthy. ⁵He who overcomes will, like them, be dressed in white. I will never blot out his name from the book of life, but will acknowledge his name before my Father and his angels. ⁶He who has an ear, let him hear what the Spirit says to the churches.

To the Church in Philadelphia

⁷"To the angel of the church in Philadelphia write:

These are the words of him who is holy and true, who holds the key of David. What he opens no one can shut, and what he shuts no one can open. ⁸I know your deeds. See, I have placed before you an open door that no one can shut. I know that you have little strength, yet you have kept my word and have not denied my name. ⁹I will make those who are of the synagogue of Satan, who claim to be Jews though they are not, but are liars—I will make them come and fall down at your feet and acknowledge that I have loved you. ¹⁰Since you have kept my command to endure patiently, I will also keep you from the hour of trial that is going to come upon the whole world to test those who live on the earth.

¹¹I am coming soon. Hold on to what you have, so that no one will take your crown. ¹²Him who overcomes I will make a pillar in the temple of my God. Never again will he leave it. I will write on him the name of my God and the name of the city of my God, the new Jerusalem, which is coming down out of heaven from my God; and I will also write on him my new name. ¹³He who has an ear, let him hear what the Spirit says to the churches.

To the Church in Laodicea

¹⁴"To the angel of the church in Laodicea write:

These are the words of the Amen, the faithful and true witness, the ruler of God's creation. ¹⁵I know your deeds, that you are neither cold nor hot. I wish you were either one or the other! ¹⁶So, because you are lukewarm—neither hot nor cold—I am about to spit you out of my mouth. ¹⁷You say, 'I am rich; I have acquired wealth and do not need a

f1 Or messenger; also in verses 7 and 14   g1 Or the sevenfold Spirit

OPEN: What group of yours had a reputation far better than its performance?

DIG: 1. What is the contrast between reputation and reality in Sardis? What dangers exist for Christians who rely on an image instead of nurturing a genuine spiritual life? **2.** What is the only hope for the survival of the church in Sardis?

REFLECT: 1. If Jesus addressed this "wake-up call" to you, what would he want you to strengthen? **2.** Right now, would Jesus need a fire alarm to wake you up, or would a quiet call do it? Why?

OPEN: When have you been "locked out"?

DIG: 1. What does the "key of David" open (vv.7-8; see Isa 22:20-24; Mt 16:19; 1Co 16:9; Rev 3:20; 4:1)? **2.** How is this church able to persevere? Describe their enemies. How does their reward (v.12) fit their faithfulness?

REFLECT: 1. What open doors has Christ placed before you? How have you taken advantage of the pathways he's made available to you? **2.** What are some closed doors he's placed in your career? In your social life? In your schooling? How have you responded to each of these closed doors? **3.** In what ways are you like the Christians in Philadelphia? Unlike them? Why? **4.** What is the Spirit saying to you now?

OPEN: 1. What is your favorite cold cereal? Hot cereal? Your favorite drink? **2.** If you could invite any famous person for dinner, whom would you ask? Why?

DIG: 1. What does the "faithful and true witness" see when he looks at the Laodicean church? How does the church view itself? Why the contrast? **2.** What does Jesus tell them to do in verse 18? Why? What does this say about

477

true wealth? **3.** How would you describe Christ, based on what you have read so far in this book? How does this expand the picture of Jesus in the Gospels?

REFLECT: 1. If Jesus took your spiritual temperature today, what would he find? Why? **2.** What is Jesus waiting for at the door of your life? Why not let him in?

OPEN: What is the most memorable storm you have ever been in? What happened?

DIG: 1. Where does this scene actually take place: In the afterlife? In some perfect order of things after this world has passed away? Or on the level of spiritual reality here and now (as in Eph 2:6), where good and evil are unmasked to be seen for what they really are? **2.** Who is the figure on the throne? What is he like? What are the 24 elders like? (Note: 24 seems to represent all of God's people, coming from the 12 tribes before Christ and the 12 apostles after Christ; see 21:12-14.) **3.** What does the scene around the throne include? Note its many OT images (Ge 9:12-17; Ex 19:16-19; 25:31-40; 2 Chr 4:2-6; Eze 1). **4.** How does John envision the four living creatures, throbbing with the eternal power of God? What response does the central figure elicit? Why? **5.** What does this say about who God is and how he relates to his creation?

REFLECT: 1. Imagine yourself in this scene. What do you see? Hear? Feel? What impresses you about God? **2.** What aspect of creation best demonstrates God's glory and power to you? Why? **3.** How might this vision of God enhance your worship life? Your everyday life?

thing.' But you do not realize that you are wretched, pitiful, poor, blind and naked. [18]I counsel you to buy from me gold refined in the fire, so you can become rich; and white clothes to wear, so you can cover your shameful nakedness; and salve to put on your eyes, so you can see.

[19]Those whom I love I rebuke and discipline. So be earnest, and repent. [20]Here I am! I stand at the door and knock. If anyone hears my voice and opens the door, I will come in and eat with him, and he with me.

[21]To him who overcomes, I will give the right to sit with me on my throne, just as I overcame and sat down with my Father on his throne. [22]He who has an ear, let him hear what the Spirit says to the churches."

The Throne in Heaven

4 After this I looked, and there before me was a door standing open in heaven. And the voice I had first heard speaking to me like a trumpet said, "Come up here, and I will show you what must take place after this." [2]At once I was in the Spirit, and there before me was a throne in heaven with someone sitting on it. [3]And the one who sat there had the appearance of jasper and carnelian. A rainbow, resembling an emerald, encircled the throne. [4]Surrounding the throne were twenty-four other thrones, and seated on them were twenty-four elders. They were dressed in white and had crowns of gold on their heads. [5]From the throne came flashes of lightning, rumblings and peals of thunder. Before the throne, seven lamps were blazing. These are the seven spirits[h] of God. [6]Also before the throne there was what looked like a sea of glass, clear as crystal.

In the center, around the throne, were four living creatures, and they were covered with eyes, in front and in back. [7]The first living creature was like a lion, the second was like an ox, the third had a face like a man, the fourth was like a flying eagle. [8]Each of the four living creatures had six wings and was covered with eyes all around, even under his wings. Day and night they never stop saying:

> "Holy, holy, holy
> is the Lord God Almighty,
> who was, and is, and is to come."

[9]Whenever the living creatures give glory, honor and thanks to him who sits on the throne and who lives for ever and ever, [10]the twenty-four elders fall down before him who sits on the throne, and worship him who lives for ever and ever. They lay their crowns before the throne and say:

> [11]"You are worthy, our Lord and God,
> to receive glory and honor and power,
> for you created all things,
> and by your will they were created
> and have their being."

---

h5 Or the sevenfold Spirit

The Scroll and the Lamb

5 Then I saw in the right hand of him who sat on the throne a scroll with writing on both sides and sealed with seven seals. ²And I saw a mighty angel proclaiming in a loud voice, "Who is worthy to break the seals and open the scroll?" ³But no one in heaven or on earth or under the earth could open the scroll or even look inside it. ⁴I wept and wept because no one was found who was worthy to open the scroll or look inside. ⁵Then one of the elders said to me, "Do not weep! See, the Lion of the tribe of Judah, the Root of David, has triumphed. He is able to open the scroll and its seven seals."

⁶Then I saw a Lamb, looking as if it had been slain, standing in the center of the throne, encircled by the four living creatures and the elders. He had seven horns and seven eyes, which are the seven spirits[i] of God sent out into all the earth. ⁷He came and took the scroll from the right hand of him who sat on the throne. ⁸And when he had taken it, the four living creatures and the twenty-four elders fell down before the Lamb. Each one had a harp and they were holding golden bowls full of incense, which are the prayers of the saints. ⁹And they sang a new song:

> "You are worthy to take the scroll
>   and to open its seals,
> because you were slain,
>   and with your blood you purchased men for God
>   from every tribe and language and people and nation.
> ¹⁰You have made them to be a kingdom and priests to
>   serve our God,
>   and they will reign on the earth."

¹¹Then I looked and heard the voice of many angels, numbering thousands upon thousands, and ten thousand times ten thousand. They encircled the throne and the living creatures and the elders. ¹²In a loud voice they sang:

> "Worthy is the Lamb, who was slain,
> to receive power and wealth and wisdom and strength
> and honor and glory and praise!"

¹³Then I heard every creature in heaven and on earth and under the earth and on the sea, and all that is in them, singing:

> "To him who sits on the throne and to the Lamb
> be praise and honor and glory and power,
>   for ever and ever!"

¹⁴The four living creatures said, "Amen," and the elders fell down and worshiped.

The Seals

6 I watched as the Lamb opened the first of the seven seals. Then I heard one of the four living creatures say in a voice like thunder, "Come!" ²I looked, and there before me was a white horse! Its rider held a bow, and he was given a crown, and he rode out as a conqueror bent on conquest.

i6 Or *the sevenfold Spirit*

³When the Lamb opened the second seal, I heard the second living creature say, "Come!" ⁴Then another horse came out, a fiery red one. Its rider was given power to take peace from the earth and to make men slay each other. To him was given a large sword.

⁵When the Lamb opened the third seal, I heard the third living creature say, "Come!" I looked, and there before me was a black horse! Its rider was holding a pair of scales in his hand. ⁶Then I heard what sounded like a voice among the four living creatures, saying, "A quart*ʲ* of wheat for a day's wages,*ᵏ* and three quarts of barley for a day's wages,*ᵏ* and do not damage the oil and the wine!"

⁷When the Lamb opened the fourth seal, I heard the voice of the fourth living creature say, "Come!" ⁸I looked, and there before me was a pale horse! Its rider was named Death, and Hades was following close behind him. They were given power over a fourth of the earth to kill by sword, famine and plague, and by the wild beasts of the earth.

⁹When he opened the fifth seal, I saw under the altar the souls of those who had been slain because of the word of God and the testimony they had maintained. ¹⁰They called out in a loud voice, "How long, Sovereign Lord, holy and true, until you judge the inhabitants of the earth and avenge our blood?" ¹¹Then each of them was given a white robe, and they were told to wait a little longer, until the number of their fellow servants and brothers who were to be killed as they had been was completed.

¹²I watched as he opened the sixth seal. There was a great earthquake. The sun turned black like sackcloth made of goat hair, the whole moon turned blood red, ¹³and the stars in the sky fell to earth, as late figs drop from a fig tree when shaken by a strong wind. ¹⁴The sky receded like a scroll, rolling up, and every mountain and island was removed from its place.

¹⁵Then the kings of the earth, the princes, the generals, the rich, the mighty, and every slave and every free man hid in caves and among the rocks of the mountains. ¹⁶They called to the mountains and the rocks, "Fall on us and hide us from the face of him who sits on the throne and from the wrath of the Lamb! ¹⁷For the great day of their wrath has come, and who can stand?"

144,000 Sealed

7 After this I saw four angels standing at the four corners of the earth, holding back the four winds of the earth to prevent any wind from blowing on the land or on the sea or on any tree. ²Then I saw another angel coming up from the east, having the seal of the living God. He called out in a loud voice to the four angels who had been given power to harm the land and the sea: ³"Do not harm the land or the sea or the trees until we put a seal on the foreheads of the servants of our God." ⁴Then I heard the number of those who were sealed: 144,000 from all the tribes of Israel.

ʲ6 Greek *a choinix* (probably about a liter)   *ᵏ6* Greek *a denarius*

⁵From the tribe of Judah 12,000 were sealed,
from the tribe of Reuben 12,000,
from the tribe of Gad 12,000,
⁶from the tribe of Asher 12,000,
from the tribe of Naphtali 12,000,
from the tribe of Manasseh 12,000,
⁷from the tribe of Simeon 12,000,
from the tribe of Levi 12,000,
from the tribe of Issachar 12,000,
⁸from the tribe of Zebulun 12,000,
from the tribe of Joseph 12,000,
from the tribe of Benjamin 12,000.

The Great Multitude in White Robes

⁹After this I looked and there before me was a great multitude that no one could count, from every nation, tribe, people and language, standing before the throne and in front of the Lamb. They were wearing white robes and were holding palm branches in their hands. ¹⁰And they cried out in a loud voice:

"Salvation belongs to our God,
who sits on the throne,
and to the Lamb."

¹¹All the angels were standing around the throne and around the elders and the four living creatures. They fell down on their faces before the throne and worshiped God, ¹²saying:

"Amen!
Praise and glory
and wisdom and thanks and honor
and power and strength
be to our God for ever and ever.
Amen!"

¹³Then one of the elders asked me, "These in white robes—who are they, and where did they come from?"

¹⁴I answered, "Sir, you know."

And he said, "These are they who have come out of the great tribulation; they have washed their robes and made them white in the blood of the Lamb. ¹⁵Therefore,

"they are before the throne of God
and serve him day and night in his temple;
and he who sits on the throne will spread his tent over
them.
¹⁶Never again will they hunger;
never again will they thirst.
The sun will not beat upon them,
nor any scorching heat.
¹⁷For the Lamb at the center of the throne will be their
shepherd;
he will lead them to springs of living water.
And God will wipe away every tear from their eyes."

it mean (see Ge 4:15; Eze 9:4-6; Eph 1:13-14)? **3.** Is this "144,000" a symbol or a statistic? Why (see 7:9; 14:1-5)?

REFLECT: 1. How have you sensed God's protection in the last six months? **2.** What sort of seal has God placed on your life? How is this seal evident to others?

OPEN: What piece of clothing (bathrobe, tennis togs, toga, 3-piece suit, jeans, etc.) do you feel expresses your personality best? How do you feel when wearing it?

DIG: 1. What does John see next? How does he describe the size of the crowd? Is this multitude the same as the 144,000 (v.4)? Why or why not? What are they doing? Wearing? Carrying? **2.** What's the significance of the white robes, the palm branches, and the washing? When the multitude cries out, how do the angels, elders, and the four living creatures respond? What does all this say about God's kingdom and Christ's sacrifice? **3.** What qualifies this white-robed crowd to stand before God? What is their new role? What is "the great tribulation"—is it a particular event or a general experience? **4.** Is the safety, security, and service of these Christians a *present* life experience for them, or only a promise to be realized in some vague and distant *future*? Or both?

REFLECT: 1. Have each group member take one of the words ascribed to God to meditate on and to praise him for as part of your group's devotion to God. **2.** What is your greatest tribulation or persecution? How difficult does that seem next to the majesty of God pictured here? How will you incorporate this glimpse of heavenly worship into your earthly walk?

OPEN: When home alone, do you like silence, or do you have to have some noise going on? Why?

DIG: 1. Amid seals and trumpets, why this silence? Why the golden censer? **2.** What do altars and incense teach about prayer (vv.3-5; see 5:8; 6:9-10; 9:13)?

REFLECT: Does this imagery seem far removed to you? When was the last time you tried silent meditation or cried for justice? What happened?

_____

OPEN: 1. What is one of the most excruciating pains you've ever experienced? What happened? **2.** What color would you use to describe your past week? Why? To describe your past year? Why?

DIG: 1. What events follow the sounding of each of the first four trumpets? What do the trumpets signify: Triumph or doom? Life or death? Or what? **2.** How do these trumpeted events compare with the events inaugurated by the first six seals? **3.** Likewise, how do these events compare with the plagues in Exodus 7-10 and Joel 2:1-11? **4.** What parallels or repeated patterns do you see between the opening of the seals and sounding of the trumpets, which suggest that these two scenes are in reality two sides of the same coin? (Note how the trumpets focus on what will happen to the unbelieving world, whereas the seals focus on what will happen to the church.) **5.** Do these seals and trumpets refer to datable, sequential events or to aspects of the world condition, which may be true at any point in history? Why? **6.** What happens when the fifth trumpet sounds? Who can the fallen star be (see Lk 10:18; Isa 14:12)? What power do the locusts have? Describe them. **7.** What events are inaugurated by the sixth trumpet? What response should this woe elicit from the unbelieving world? Why? Why do you suppose this woe failed to bring the majority to repentance, as intended?

REFLECT: 1. What do you think of Christians who pray for trouble to strike the unbelieving world? And what do you think of God's

The Seventh Seal and the Golden Censer

8 When he opened the seventh seal, there was silence in heaven for about half an hour.

²And I saw the seven angels who stand before God, and to them were given seven trumpets.

³Another angel, who had a golden censer, came and stood at the altar. He was given much incense to offer, with the prayers of all the saints, on the golden altar before the throne. ⁴The smoke of the incense, together with the prayers of the saints, went up before God from the angel's hand. ⁵Then the angel took the censer, filled it with fire from the altar, and hurled it on the earth; and there came peals of thunder, rumblings, flashes of lightning and an earthquake.

The Trumpets

⁶Then the seven angels who had the seven trumpets prepared to sound them.

⁷The first angel sounded his trumpet, and there came hail and fire mixed with blood, and it was hurled down upon the earth. A third of the earth was burned up, a third of the trees were burned up, and all the green grass was burned up.

⁸The second angel sounded his trumpet, and something like a huge mountain, all ablaze, was thrown into the sea. A third of the sea turned into blood, ⁹a third of the living creatures in the sea died, and a third of the ships were destroyed.

¹⁰The third angel sounded his trumpet, and a great star, blazing like a torch, fell from the sky on a third of the rivers and on the springs of water— ¹¹the name of the star is Wormwood.[1] A third of the waters turned bitter, and many people died from the waters that had become bitter.

¹²The fourth angel sounded his trumpet, and a third of the sun was struck, a third of the moon, and a third of the stars, so that a third of them turned dark. A third of the day was without light, and also a third of the night.

¹³As I watched, I heard an eagle that was flying in midair call out in a loud voice: "Woe! Woe! Woe to the inhabitants of the earth, because of the trumpet blasts about to be sounded by the other three angels!"

9 The fifth angel sounded his trumpet, and I saw a star that had fallen from the sky to the earth. The star was given the key to the shaft of the Abyss. ²When he opened the Abyss, smoke rose from it like the smoke from a gigantic furnace. The sun and sky were darkened by the smoke from the Abyss. ³And out of the smoke locusts came down upon the earth and were given power like that of scorpions of the earth. ⁴They were told not to harm the grass of the earth or any plant or tree, but only those people who did not have the seal of God on their foreheads. ⁵They were not given power to kill them, but only to torture them for five months. And the agony they suffered was like that of the sting of a scorpion when it strikes a man. ⁶During those days men will seek death, but will not find it; they will long to die, but death will elude them.

[1]11 That is, Bitterness

[7]The locusts looked like horses prepared for battle. On their heads they wore something like crowns of gold, and their faces resembled human faces. [8]Their hair was like women's hair, and their teeth were like lions' teeth. [9]They had breastplates like breastplates of iron, and the sound of their wings was like the thundering of many horses and chariots rushing into battle. [10]They had tails and stings like scorpions, and in their tails they had power to torment people for five months. [11]They had as king over them the angel of the Abyss, whose name in Hebrew is Abaddon, and in Greek, Apollyon. [m]

[12]The first woe is past; two other woes are yet to come.

[13]The sixth angel sounded his trumpet, and I heard a voice coming from the horns [n] of the golden altar that is before God. [14]It said to the sixth angel who had the trumpet, "Release the four angels who are bound at the great river Euphrates." [15]And the four angels who had been kept ready for this very hour and day and month and year were released to kill a third of mankind. [16]The number of the mounted troops was two hundred million. I heard their number.

[17]The horses and riders I saw in my vision looked like this: Their breastplates were fiery red, dark blue, and yellow as sulfur. The heads of the horses resembled the heads of lions, and out of their mouths came fire, smoke and sulfur. [18]A third of mankind was killed by the three plagues of fire, smoke and sulfur that came out of their mouths. [19]The power of the horses was in their mouths and in their tails; for their tails were like snakes, having heads with which they inflict injury.

[20]The rest of mankind that were not killed by these plagues still did not repent of the work of their hands; they did not stop worshiping demons, and idols of gold, silver, bronze, stone and wood—idols that cannot see or hear or walk. [21]Nor did they repent of their murders, their magic arts, their sexual immorality or their thefts.

The Angel and the Little Scroll

10 Then I saw another mighty angel coming down from heaven. He was robed in a cloud, with a rainbow above his head; his face was like the sun, and his legs were like fiery pillars. [2]He was holding a little scroll, which lay open in his hand. He planted his right foot on the sea and his left foot on the land, [3]and he gave a loud shout like the roar of a lion. When he shouted, the voices of the seven thunders spoke. [4]And when the seven thunders spoke, I was about to write; but I heard a voice from heaven say, "Seal up what the seven thunders have said and do not write it down."

[5]Then the angel I had seen standing on the sea and on the land raised his right hand to heaven. [6]And he swore by him who lives for ever and ever, who created the heavens and all that is in them, the earth and all that is in it, and the sea and all that is in it, and said, "There will be no more delay! [7]But in the days when the seventh angel is about to sound his trumpet, the mystery of God will be accomplished, just as he announced to his servants the prophets."

answer to such prayers? What modern-day realities does the imagery of these plagues bring to mind for you? How might they have applied equally well in John's day? **2.** How do you feel when you read this account of stranger-than-fiction events? What is the "who" and "why" behind all these events? **3.** How has the star named "Wormwood" or "Bitterness" affected your life? How has your bitterness affected others? What have you discovered as an antidote to bitterness? **4.** What do you have in common with the people mentioned in 9:20-21? What will you do about this today?

OPEN: Who was one of your fictional heroes when you were a child: Buck Rogers? The Lone Ranger? The Roadrunner? Why?

DIG: 1. Describe the angel who announces the coming of the seventh trumpet? In what ways does this picture contrast with the traditional view of angels? Why would John be forbidden to record the words of the seven thunders (see 2Co 12:4)? **2.** What purposes have the disasters of the first six trumpets served? What do you anticipate the seventh trumpet will bring forth? What is the "mystery of God" (v.7; see Ro 11:25-36; 16:25-27; Eph 1:9-14)? **3.** What happens to the small scroll? How can a revelation from God be both sweet and bitter?

---

m11 Abaddon and *Apollyon* mean *Destroyer.*   *n13* That is, projections

[8]Then the voice that I had heard from heaven spoke to me once more: "Go, take the scroll that lies open in the hand of the angel who is standing on the sea and on the land."

[9]So I went to the angel and asked him to give me the little scroll. He said to me, "Take it and eat it. It will turn your stomach sour, but in your mouth it will be as sweet as honey." [10]I took the little scroll from the angel's hand and ate it. It tasted as sweet as honey in my mouth, but when I had eaten it, my stomach turned sour. [11]Then I was told, "You must prophesy again about many peoples, nations, languages and kings."

The Two Witnesses

11 I was given a reed like a measuring rod and was told, "Go and measure the temple of God and the altar, and count the worshipers there. [2]But exclude the outer court; do not measure it, because it has been given to the Gentiles. They will trample on the holy city for 42 months. [3]And I will give power to my two witnesses, and they will prophesy for 1,260 days, clothed in sackcloth." [4]These are the two olive trees and the two lampstands that stand before the Lord of the earth. [5]If anyone tries to harm them, fire comes from their mouths and devours their enemies. This is how anyone who wants to harm them must die. [6]These men have power to shut up the sky so that it will not rain during the time they are prophesying; and they have power to turn the waters into blood and to strike the earth with every kind of plague as often as they want.

[7]Now when they have finished their testimony, the beast that comes up from the Abyss will attack them, and overpower and kill them. [8]Their bodies will lie in the street of the great city, which is figuratively called Sodom and Egypt, where also their Lord was crucified. [9]For three and a half days men from every people, tribe, language and nation will gaze on their bodies and refuse them burial. [10]The inhabitants of the earth will gloat over them and will celebrate by sending each other gifts, because these two prophets had tormented those who live on the earth.

[11]But after the three and a half days a breath of life from God entered them, and they stood on their feet, and terror struck those who saw them. [12]Then they heard a loud voice from heaven saying to them, "Come up here." And they went up to heaven in a cloud, while their enemies looked on.

[13]At that very hour there was a severe earthquake and a tenth of the city collapsed. Seven thousand people were killed in the earthquake, and the survivors were terrified and gave glory to the God of heaven.

[14]The second woe has passed; the third woe is coming soon.

The Seventh Trumpet

[15]The seventh angel sounded his trumpet, and there were loud voices in heaven, which said:

"The kingdom of the world has become the kingdom of
   our Lord and of his Christ,
   and he will reign for ever and ever."

[16]And the twenty-four elders, who were seated on their thrones

before God, fell on their faces and worshiped God, [17]saying:

"We give thanks to you, Lord God Almighty,
  the One who is and who was,
because you have taken your great power
  and have begun to reign.
[18]The nations were angry;
  and your wrath has come.
The time has come for judging the dead,
  and for rewarding your servants the prophets
and your saints and those who reverence your name,
  both small and great—
and for destroying those who destroy the earth."

[19]Then God's temple in heaven was opened, and within his temple was seen the ark of his covenant. And there came flashes of lightning, rumblings, peals of thunder, an earthquake and a great hailstorm.

The Woman and the Dragon

12 A great and wondrous sign appeared in heaven: a woman clothed with the sun, with the moon under her feet and a crown of twelve stars on her head. [2]She was pregnant and cried out in pain as she was about to give birth. [3]Then another sign appeared in heaven: an enormous red dragon with seven heads and ten horns and seven crowns on his heads. [4]His tail swept a third of the stars out of the sky and flung them to the earth. The dragon stood in front of the woman who was about to give birth, so that he might devour her child the moment it was born. [5]She gave birth to a son, a male child, who will rule all the nations with an iron scepter. And her child was snatched up to God and to his throne. [6]The woman fled into the desert to a place prepared for her by God, where she might be taken care of for 1,260 days.

[7]And there was war in heaven. Michael and his angels fought against the dragon, and the dragon and his angels fought back. [8]But he was not strong enough, and they lost their place in heaven. [9]The great dragon was hurled down—that ancient serpent called the devil or Satan, who leads the whole world astray. He was hurled to the earth, and his angels with him.

[10]Then I heard a loud voice in heaven say:

"Now have come the salvation and the power and the
    kingdom of our God,
  and the authority of his Christ.
For the accuser of our brothers,
  who accuses them before our God day and night,
  has been hurled down.
[11]They overcame him
  by the blood of the Lamb
  and by the word of their testimony;
they did not love their lives so much
  as to shrink from death.
[12]Therefore rejoice, you heavens
  and you who dwell in them!
But woe to the earth and the sea,

REFLECT: 1. How do you react to God's power over unbelieving people: to *hurt* them (trumpet 5 or 1st woe), to *kill* them (trumpet 6 or 2nd woe), or to *damn* them (trumpet 7 or 3rd woe)? Why? **2.** As God displays this power in response to prayers (8:4), how do you respond to what he has called you to do? What will you pray? Why?

OPEN: When you were a child, who was the most important woman in your life besides your mother? Why?

DIG: 1. Where, in the thematic development of Revelation, does the unveiling of God's heavenly temple and ark of the covenant fit best? (Note: Some or all of the phenomena occurring in 11:19 also occur in 4:5 and 8:5). **2.** Describe the woman, the dragon, and the child. Who does the woman represent? The dragon? The child? **3.** Where does the next conflict occur? Who are the protagonists? What the outcome of this conflict? What is the significance of this outcome for the earth? For Christians? What Old Testament and New Testament events are parallel to this passage? **4.** When do you see this heavenly battle occurring: (a) At some particular time and place in history? (b) Pre-history? (c) Post-history? (d) Any time and any place during the ongoing heavenly battle between the kingdom of God and the kingdom of Satan (that is, in the spiritual realm which is behind *all* of this world's history)? Why do you think so?

REFLECT: 1. What do you learn here about conflict between the Christian church and demonic evil? **2.** When has Satan seemed very real to you? Why? How do you overcome Satan (see v.11)? How could you apply these tactics in your own life? What do you need to do to become stronger for spiritual battle? **3.** How can your Christian friends pray for you in battles you are facing? Likewise, how can you pray for them? Do this in your group.

because the devil has gone down to you!
He is filled with fury,
because he knows that his time is short."

¹³When the dragon saw that he had been hurled to the earth, he pursued the woman who had given birth to the male child. ¹⁴The woman was given the two wings of a great eagle, so that she might fly to the place prepared for her in the desert, where she would be taken care of for a time, times and half a time, out of the serpent's reach. ¹⁵Then from his mouth the serpent spewed water like a river, to overtake the woman and sweep her away with the torrent. ¹⁶But the earth helped the woman by opening its mouth and swallowing the river that the dragon had spewed out of his mouth. ¹⁷Then the dragon was enraged at the woman and went off to make war against the rest of her offspring—those who obey God's commandments and hold to the testimony of Jesus. ¹And the dragon° stood on the shore of the sea.

13

The Beast out of the Sea

And I saw a beast coming out of the sea. He had ten horns and seven heads, with ten crowns on his horns, and on each head a blasphemous name. ²The beast I saw resembled a leopard, but had feet like those of a bear and a mouth like that of a lion. The dragon gave the beast his power and his throne and great authority. ³One of the heads of the beast seemed to have had a fatal wound, but the fatal wound had been healed. The whole world was astonished and followed the beast. ⁴Men worshiped the dragon because he had given authority to the beast, and they also worshiped the beast and asked, "Who is like the beast? Who can make war against him?"

⁵The beast was given a mouth to utter proud words and blasphemies and to exercise his authority for forty-two months. ⁶He opened his mouth to blaspheme God, and to slander his name and his dwelling place and those who live in heaven. ⁷He was given power to make war against the saints and to conquer them. And he was given authority over every tribe, people, language and nation. ⁸All inhabitants of the earth will worship the beast—all whose names have not been written in the book of life belonging to the Lamb that was slain from the creation of the world.ᵖ

⁹He who has an ear, let him hear.

¹⁰If anyone is to go into captivity,
  into captivity he will go.
If anyone is to be killedᵠ with the sword,
  with the sword he will be killed.

This calls for patient endurance and faithfulness on the part of the saints.

OPEN: 1. Who do you think is one of the most charismatic leaders living today? How has charisma helped him or her to lead? **2.** When you were growing up, who was the most patient person in your family? What impressed you about his or her patience?

DIG: 1. What is this beast from the sea like? What is the source of its power? How does it use its power? What is the extent of its power? What is the relationship between the beast and the dragon? **2.** Who worships the beast? **3.** Who do you think the first-century Christians would have identified as this beast (see Da 7 and Ro 13:1)? **4.** What impact will this beast have on the Christians? How ought they to respond? Why?

REFLECT: 1. Who are some of the beasts or idols in your life (people, forces, institutions, etc.) that test your allegiance to Christ? How have you been swayed from your allegiance to Christ by talk of "patriotism" and "tradition"? How is God helping you deal with that? **2.** Is your name written in the Book of Life? How do you know? **3.** What kind of grade would you give yourself on patient endurance and faithfulness? Why?

°1 Some late manuscripts *And I*   ᵖ8 Or *written from the creation of the world in the book of life belonging to the Lamb that was slain*   ᵠ10 Some manuscripts *anyone kills*

The Beast out of the Earth

[11]Then I saw another beast, coming out of the earth. He had two horns like a lamb, but he spoke like a dragon. [12]He exercised all the authority of the first beast on his behalf, and made the earth and its inhabitants worship the first beast, whose fatal wound had been healed. [13]And he performed great and miraculous signs, even causing fire to come down from heaven to earth in full view of men. [14]Because of the signs he was given power to do on behalf of the first beast, he deceived the inhabitants of the earth. He ordered them to set up an image in honor of the beast who was wounded by the sword and yet lived. [15]He was given power to give breath to the image of the first beast, so that it could speak and cause all who refused to worship the image to be killed. [16]He also forced everyone, small and great, rich and poor, free and slave, to receive a mark on his right hand or on his forehead, [17]so that no one could buy or sell unless he had the mark, which is the name of the beast or the number of his name.

[18]This calls for wisdom. If anyone has insight, let him calculate the number of the beast, for it is man's number. His number is 666.

OPEN: What Halloween costume best hid your identity as a child?

DIG: 1. What is this beast from the earth like? **2.** If the first beast exercises political power, what authority does this second beast exercise? How are true government and religion connected (and mimicked) by these two beasts? **3.** Since "7" is the number of completeness in Revelation, what might "666" mean? **4.** Compare the view of the Roman Empire here with that in Romans 13:1-7. How had Rome changed since Paul's day?

REFLECT: How can we discern between false religion and governments?

The Lamb and the 144,000

14 Then I looked, and there before me was the Lamb, standing on Mount Zion, and with him 144,000 who had his name and his Father's name written on their foreheads. [2]And I heard a sound from heaven like the roar of rushing waters and like a loud peal of thunder. The sound I heard was like that of harpists playing their harps. [3]And they sang a new song before the throne and before the four living creatures and the elders. No one could learn the song except the 144,000 who had been redeemed from the earth. [4]These are those who did not defile themselves with women, for they kept themselves pure. They follow the Lamb wherever he goes. They were purchased from among men and offered as firstfruits to God and the Lamb. [5]No lie was found in their mouths; they are blameless.

OPEN: What kind of singer are you: Off-Broadway? Off-key?

DIG: 1. Given the chaos described in chapters 12-13, what comfort do you find in this passage? What sights? Sounds? Feelings? **2.** Who is the Lamb? What has he done? Why are the people following him?

REFLECT: How are you like (and unlike) the 144,000? Why do you follow the Lamb?

The Three Angels

[6]Then I saw another angel flying in midair, and he had the eternal gospel to proclaim to those who live on the earth—to every nation, tribe, language and people. [7]He said in a loud voice, "Fear God and give him glory, because the hour of his judgment has come. Worship him who made the heavens, the earth, the sea and the springs of water."

[8]A second angel followed and said, "Fallen! Fallen is Babylon the Great, which made all the nations drink the maddening wine of her adulteries."

[9]A third angel followed them and said in a loud voice: "If anyone worships the beast and his image and receives his mark on the forehead or on the hand, [10]he, too, will drink of the wine of God's fury, which has been poured full strength into the cup of his wrath. He will be tormented with burning sulfur in the presence of the holy angels and of the Lamb. [11]And the smoke of their torment rises for ever and ever. There is no rest day or night for those who worship the beast and his image, or for

OPEN: Heard any good news lately? Any "good news/bad news" jokes? Tell one. (One with the best news or joke gets to lead the study—that's the bad news.)

DIG: 1. What is the essence of the "eternal gospel" proclaimed by the angel of grace? Who will hear it? Has this vision yet been fulfilled? What response to the gospel is called for? **2.** By contrast, what message does the angel of doom spread? Who is the fallen Babylon? Who has been infected by the spirit of Babylon? **3.** How does Satan's system (13:2-10) differ from God's church (14:1-5)? How does Satan's ideology (13:11-18) differ from God's truth (14:6-13)?

REFLECT: 1. What have you done to help proclaim the gospel to every nation, tribe, language, and people? **2.** How do you look upon death: As a rest? A reward? A new phase in the journey? **3.** What would you like to be doing when God calls you home?

OPEN: Ever harvest anything? How hard did you work? Did you enjoy it? Why or why not?

DIG: **1.** Identify the four supernatural beings in this fifth vision. What is the role of each? **2.** What are the differences between the two parts of the vision (vv.14-16 and 17-20)? What is the nature of the judgment that will occur (see Mt 13:30,39)? **3.** Who might the first figure be (see Da 7:13)?

REFLECT: How ripe do you think the world is now? Do you feel that the end of the world is close at hand? Why or why not? How does this affect your lifestyle?

OPEN: If you could have a bowl full of anything right now, what would you want? Why?

DIG: **1.** How does John describe this new sign? Why does he say these are the last plagues? **2.** What picture does he paint in verse 2? Compare Moses' song of deliverance from Egypt (Ex 15:1-18) with the song sung by those delivered from the beast. What praise is given to God? By whom? **3.** What does John see next? How does the angels' attire contrast with what they are given to do? **4.** What does the temple in heaven mean: A haven of rest and a place to play harps for those who die? Or time to reckon with God's holiness and wrath unveiled in that very temple? Why?

REFLECT: **1.** How does this passage make you feel? Why? What does it make you want to do? Why? **2.** What great and mighty deeds has God done in your life for which you will praise him today? How appropriate is the song in this passage to your experience with God? Why?

anyone who receives the mark of his name." [12]This calls for patient endurance on the part of the saints who obey God's commandments and remain faithful to Jesus.

[13]Then I heard a voice from heaven say, "Write: Blessed are the dead who die in the Lord from now on."

"Yes," says the Spirit, "they will rest from their labor, for their deeds will follow them."

The Harvest of the Earth

[14]I looked, and there before me was a white cloud, and seated on the cloud was one "like a son of man"[r] with a crown of gold on his head and a sharp sickle in his hand. [15]Then another angel came out of the temple and called in a loud voice to him who was sitting on the cloud, "Take your sickle and reap, because the time to reap has come, for the harvest of the earth is ripe." [16]So he who was seated on the cloud swung his sickle over the earth, and the earth was harvested.

[17]Another angel came out of the temple in heaven, and he too had a sharp sickle. [18]Still another angel, who had charge of the fire, came from the altar and called in a loud voice to him who had the sharp sickle, "Take your sharp sickle and gather the clusters of grapes from the earth's vine, because its grapes are ripe." [19]The angel swung his sickle on the earth, gathered its grapes and threw them into the great winepress of God's wrath. [20]They were trampled in the winepress outside the city, and blood flowed out of the press, rising as high as the horses' bridles for a distance of 1,600 stadia.[s]

Seven Angels With Seven Plagues

15 I saw in heaven another great and marvelous sign: seven angels with the seven last plagues—last, because with them God's wrath is completed. [2]And I saw what looked like a sea of glass mixed with fire and, standing beside the sea, those who had been victorious over the beast and his image and over the number of his name. They held harps given them by God [3]and sang the song of Moses the servant of God and the song of the Lamb:

"Great and marvelous are your deeds,
  Lord God Almighty.
Just and true are your ways,
  King of the ages.
[4]Who will not fear you, O Lord,
  and bring glory to your name?
For you alone are holy.
All nations will come
  and worship before you,
for your righteous acts have been revealed."

[5]After this I looked and in heaven the temple, that is, the tabernacle of the Testimony, was opened. [6]Out of the temple came the seven angels with the seven plagues. They were

---

[r]14 Daniel 7:13   [s]20 That is, about 180 miles (about 300 kilometers)

dressed in clean, shining linen and wore golden sashes around their chests. ⁷Then one of the four living creatures gave to the seven angels seven golden bowls filled with the wrath of God, who lives for ever and ever. ⁸And the temple was filled with smoke from the glory of God and from his power, and no one could enter the temple until the seven plagues of the seven angels were completed.

The Seven Bowls of God's Wrath

16 Then I heard a loud voice from the temple saying to the seven angels, "Go, pour out the seven bowls of God's wrath on the earth."

²The first angel went and poured out his bowl on the land, and ugly and painful sores broke out on the people who had the mark of the beast and worshiped his image.

³The second angel poured out his bowl on the sea, and it turned into blood like that of a dead man, and every living thing in the sea died.

⁴The third angel poured out his bowl on the rivers and springs of water, and they became blood. ⁵Then I heard the angel in charge of the waters say:

"You are just in these judgments,
　　you who are and who were, the Holy One,
　　because you have so judged;
⁶for they have shed the blood of your saints and
　　prophets,
　　and you have given them blood to drink as they
　　deserve."

⁷And I heard the altar respond:

"Yes, Lord God Almighty,
　　true and just are your judgments."

⁸The fourth angel poured out his bowl on the sun, and the sun was given power to scorch people with fire. ⁹They were seared by the intense heat and they cursed the name of God, who had control over these plagues, but they refused to repent and glorify him.

¹⁰The fifth angel poured out his bowl on the throne of the beast, and his kingdom was plunged into darkness. Men gnawed their tongues in agony ¹¹and cursed the God of heaven because of their pains and their sores, but they refused to repent of what they had done.

¹²The sixth angel poured out his bowl on the great river Euphrates, and its water was dried up to prepare the way for the kings from the East. ¹³Then I saw three evil' spirits that looked like frogs; they came out of the mouth of the dragon, out of the mouth of the beast and out of the mouth of the false prophet. ¹⁴They are spirits of demons performing miraculous signs, and they go out to the kings of the whole world, to gather them for the battle on the great day of God Almighty.

OPEN: 1. What firsthand experience have you had with a natural disaster? What happened? What are your most vivid memories about it? **2.** What would be the worst plague for you to experience: Sores all over your body? Intense heat without air conditioning? Total darkness? Or great thirst with very little water? Why?

DIG: 1. What contents are in each bowl of wrath? Why are these plagues worse than those ushered in by the trumpets (contrast, for example, 8:8 with 16:3)? What was the function of the trumpet plagues? What is the function of the plagues in this passage? **2.** Why does the angel (speaking on behalf of nature) react to the outpouring of God's wrath, not with pain or sorrow, but with recognition of divine justice? **3.** What is described in the interlude (vv.13-16) between the sixth and seventh bowls? What function did the frogs perform? **4.** How will the just purposes of God and the evil purposes of Satan finally and awfully converge at Armageddon (or "hill of Megiddo," an historic crossroads of the Middle East)? With what result (vv.17-21)? **5.** Compare the seven seals, seven trumpets, and seven bowls to each other and to the ten plagues of Egypt (Ex 7-10). What examples of contrast (e.g., "not only... but...") can you find in each section? **6.** What is the connection between the three scenes (of seals, trumpets, and bowls)? Is it chronological or logical, or what? Why? How would these seals, trumpets, and bowls comfort John's original readers?

REFLECT: 1. What has God done in your life to help you repent? How receptive are you to admitting your guilt and repenting when you sin? **2.** If "war is hell" (says Hawkeye on M*A*S*H), could John be envisioning that "hell is war"? What does this passage tell you about God's judgment? **3.** What are the "frogs" that are battling with you? How is the battle

¹13 Greek unclean

going? **4.** How is the book of Revelation making you feel? Why? What has surprised you about God or about this book? How would you explain the necessity of these plagues to someone who is not a Christian?

OPEN: 1. If you could be famous for one hour, for what would you like to be known? Why? **2.** What bumper sticker or sign sums up your life now? Why?

DIG: 1. Who is the central figure in the next scene? Who appears to be "off-stage"? In what sense is she influential? Evil? Attractive? Repulsive? Who is she (see also 14:8 and 16:19)? How is the woman and this beast like the first and second beasts of chapter 13? **2.** What here is the ultimate sin? Why? **3.** What does the angel say about the origin of the beast? Its history? Its future? What response does the beast elicit? Why? **4.** Geographically, historically, and spiritually, what do you think the beast's seven heads and ten horns represent (see also Da 7:15-28)? Why do the kings and the beast join forces? With what result? How can evil turn on itself, Satan (in effect) casting out Satan? How does God's greater purpose triumph in all this? **5.** How are the readers of Revelation comforted by the various "definitions" of the symbols? How do these many symbols draw attention to a single object from different angles?

REFLECT: 1. In this passage how does Babylon symbolize what is wrong in society today? For example, what institutions have been overthrown by revolution, only to be replaced by new regimes which surrender to the same godless ideology? **2.** Of society's wrongs, which ones have entrapped you from time to time? How has God

[15]"Behold, I come like a thief! Blessed is he who stays awake and keeps his clothes with him, so that he may not go naked and be shamefully exposed."

[16]Then they gathered the kings together to the place that in Hebrew is called Armageddon.

[17]The seventh angel poured out his bowl into the air, and out of the temple came a loud voice from the throne, saying, "It is done!" [18]Then there came flashes of lightning, rumblings, peals of thunder and a severe earthquake. No earthquake like it has ever occurred since man has been on earth, so tremendous was the quake. [19]The great city split into three parts, and the cities of the nations collapsed. God remembered Babylon the Great and gave her the cup filled with the wine of the fury of his wrath. [20]Every island fled away and the mountains could not be found. [21]From the sky huge hailstones of about a hundred pounds each fell upon men. And they cursed God on account of the plague of hail, because the plague was so terrible.

The Woman on the Beast

17 One of the seven angels who had the seven bowls came and said to me, "Come, I will show you the punishment of the great prostitute, who sits on many waters. [2]With her the kings of the earth committed adultery and the inhabitants of the earth were intoxicated with the wine of her adulteries."

[3]Then the angel carried me away in the Spirit into a desert. There I saw a woman sitting on a scarlet beast that was covered with blasphemous names and had seven heads and ten horns. [4]The woman was dressed in purple and scarlet, and was glittering with gold, precious stones and pearls. She held a golden cup in her hand, filled with abominable things and the filth of her adulteries. [5]This title was written on her forehead:

MYSTERY

BABYLON THE GREAT

THE MOTHER OF PROSTITUTES

AND OF THE ABOMINATIONS OF THE EARTH.

[6]I saw that the woman was drunk with the blood of the saints, the blood of those who bore testimony to Jesus.

When I saw her, I was greatly astonished. [7]Then the angel said to me: "Why are you astonished? I will explain to you the mystery of the woman and of the beast she rides, which has the seven heads and ten horns. [8]The beast, which you saw, once was, now is not, and will come up out of the Abyss and go to his destruction. The inhabitants of the earth whose names have not been written in the book of life from the creation of the world will be astonished when they see the beast, because he once was, now is not, and yet will come.

[9]"This calls for a mind with wisdom. The seven heads are seven hills on which the woman sits. [10]They are also seven kings. Five have fallen, one is, the other has not yet come; but when he does come, he must remain for a little while. [11]The beast who once was, and now is not, is an eighth king. He belongs to the seven and is going to his destruction.

12"The ten horns you saw are ten kings who have not yet received a kingdom, but who for one hour will receive authority as kings along with the beast. 13They have one purpose and will give their power and authority to the beast. 14They will make war against the Lamb, but the Lamb will overcome them because he is Lord of lords and King of kings—and with him will be his called, chosen and faithful followers."

15Then the angel said to me, "The waters you saw, where the prostitute sits, are peoples, multitudes, nations and languages. 16The beast and the ten horns you saw will hate the prostitute. They will bring her to ruin and leave her naked; they will eat her flesh and burn her with fire. 17For God has put it into their hearts to accomplish his purpose by agreeing to give the beast their power to rule, until God's words are fulfilled. 18The woman you saw is the great city that rules over the kings of the earth."

The Fall of Babylon

18 After this I saw another angel coming down from heaven. He had great authority, and the earth was illuminated by his splendor. 2With a mighty voice he shouted:

"Fallen! Fallen is Babylon the Great!
She has become a home for demons
and a haunt for every evil^u spirit,
a haunt for every unclean and detestable bird.
3For all the nations have drunk
the maddening wine of her adulteries.
The kings of the earth committed adultery with her,
and the merchants of the earth grew rich from her
excessive luxuries."

4Then I heard another voice from heaven say:

"Come out of her, my people,
so that you will not share in her sins,
so that you will not receive any of her plagues;
5for her sins are piled up to heaven,
and God has remembered her crimes.
6Give back to her as she has given;
pay her back double for what she has done.
Mix her a double portion from her own cup.
7Give her as much torture and grief
as the glory and luxury she gave herself.
In her heart she boasts,
'I sit as queen; I am not a widow,
and I will never mourn.'
8Therefore in one day her plagues will overtake her:
death, mourning and famine.
She will be consumed by fire,
for mighty is the Lord God who judges her.

enabled you to avoid the snares of "the great prostitute"? **3.** Surely by now you are "calling for a mind with wisdom" (v.9). What wisdom do you want in the next few weeks? What wisdom do you need in understanding the message of Revelation? **4.** If you have not grasped the full meaning of the various beasts, have you at least been frightened by the power of evil? How will you translate that fear into action or hope?

OPEN: 1. If you were a piece of merchandise, would you be made of precious stones, fine linens, or costly woods? Why? **2.** Remember as a child when you built a tower of dominoes or blocks, only to have it all fall down—what did you like best about it? Least? Why? **3.** If you could be captain of any kind of ship, what kind would you want? Why?

DIG: 1. As compelling as the power of evil is, a more compelling authority shouts an overriding double-edged message: one edge cutting Babylon and her followers, the other exhorting God's people. What are the two voices, the two messages, and the two responses from the two audiences? How does God's perspective on Babylon (vv.2-6) differ from Babylon's self-understanding (v.7)? **2.** How do the voices from the world greet the fall of Babylon (vv.9-20)? Contemporize each of their laments—make them your own. Why do they mourn? Why would you mourn if you were in their situation? **3.** Compare this passage with the following OT prophecies about the fall of the cities of Sodom and Gomorrah (Ge 19), Babylon (Isa 13, 47), and Tyre (Eze 27-28). How is each an historical example of the fall of this spiritual Babylon? **4.** What conclusions do you draw concerning the destruction of Babylon from this comparison? What do you learn about God?

u2 Greek unclean

REFLECT: 1. If you were going to describe your life in terms of a city, what would you say? What kinds of cargoes are coming into it? What activities occur within its walls? How does it compare with Babylon? What would be a fitting name for your city? Why that name? What do you do to keep the evils listed in this passage out of your city or life? **2.** When has an important part of your life collapsed? What did other individuals say about this demise? What perspective did God bring to your fallen situation? **3.** What is the most important lesson you have learned from this passage? What actions will you take today based on this insight?

9"When the kings of the earth who committed adultery with her and shared her luxury see the smoke of her burning, they will weep and mourn over her. 10Terrified at her torment, they will stand far off and cry:

" 'Woe! Woe, O great city,
O Babylon, city of power!
In one hour your doom has come!'

11"The merchants of the earth will weep and mourn over her because no one buys their cargoes any more— 12cargoes of gold, silver, precious stones and pearls; fine linen, purple, silk and scarlet cloth; every sort of citron wood, and articles of every kind made of ivory, costly wood, bronze, iron and marble; 13cargoes of cinnamon and spice, of incense, myrrh and frankincense, of wine and olive oil, of fine flour and wheat; cattle and sheep; horses and carriages; and bodies and souls of men.

14"They will say, 'The fruit you longed for is gone from you. All your riches and splendor have vanished, never to be recovered.' 15The merchants who sold these things and gained their wealth from her will stand far off, terrified at her torment. They will weep and mourn 16and cry out:

" 'Woe! Woe, O great city,
dressed in fine linen, purple and scarlet,
and glittering with gold, precious stones and pearls!
17In one hour such great wealth has been brought to
ruin!'

"Every sea captain, and all who travel by ship, the sailors, and all who earn their living from the sea, will stand far off. 18When they see the smoke of her burning, they will exclaim, 'Was there ever a city like this great city?' 19They will throw dust on their heads, and with weeping and mourning cry out:

" 'Woe! Woe, O great city,
where all who had ships on the sea
became rich through her wealth!
In one hour she has been brought to ruin!
20Rejoice over her, O heaven!
Rejoice, saints and apostles and prophets!
God has judged her for the way she treated you.' "

21Then a mighty angel picked up a boulder the size of a large millstone and threw it into the sea, and said:

"With such violence
the great city of Babylon will be thrown down,
never to be found again.
22The music of harpists and musicians, flute players and
trumpeters,
will never be heard in you again.
No workman of any trade
will ever be found in you again.
The sound of a millstone
will never be heard in you again.

²³The light of a lamp
will never shine in you again.
The voice of bridegroom and bride
will never be heard in you again.
Your merchants were the world's great men.
By your magic spell all the nations were led astray.
²⁴In her was found the blood of prophets and of the
saints,
and of all who have been killed on the earth."

Hallelujah!

19 After this I heard what sounded like the roar of a great multitude in heaven shouting:

"Hallelujah!
Salvation and glory and power belong to our God,
² for true and just are his judgments.
He has condemned the great prostitute
who corrupted the earth by her adulteries.
He has avenged on her the blood of his servants."

³And again they shouted:

"Hallelujah!
The smoke from her goes up for ever and ever."

⁴The twenty-four elders and the four living creatures fell down and worshiped God, who was seated on the throne. And they cried:

"Amen, Hallelujah!"

⁵Then a voice came from the throne, saying:

"Praise our God,
all you his servants,
you who fear him,
both small and great!"

⁶Then I heard what sounded like a great multitude, like the roar of rushing waters and like loud peals of thunder, shouting:

"Hallelujah!
For our Lord God Almighty reigns.
⁷Let us rejoice and be glad
and give him glory!
For the wedding of the Lamb has come,
and his bride has made herself ready.
⁸Fine linen, bright and clean,
was given her to wear."

(Fine linen stands for the righteous acts of the saints.)

⁹Then the angel said to me, "Write: 'Blessed are those who are invited to the wedding supper of the Lamb!'" And he added, "These are the true words of God."

¹⁰At this I fell at his feet to worship him. But he said to me, "Do not do it! I am a fellow servant with you and with your brothers who hold to the testimony of Jesus. Worship God! For the testimony of Jesus is the spirit of prophecy."

OPEN: 1. When was the last time your favorite ball team finally won it all? Tell the group about any ticker-tape parades and other local celebrations you may have witnessed. **2.** What was the most festive wedding and reception you ever attended? **3.** What funeral have you attended where the eulogy was memorable for its praise of God's salvation?

DIG: 1. In contrast to the silence that comes with the fall of Babylon (18:22), what characterizes the new scene in heaven? Who participates in this praise? **2.** Compare and contrast the five songs of praise. What is the most frequent refrain? What do you learn about God's character? **3.** Contrast the prostitute of chapters 17 and 18 with the bride of verses 6-9 (see also Eph 5:25-27). What do you find interesting about this contrast? Why? **4.** How is John (and how might we be) tempted to worship the angel or messenger of the good news? **5.** How is the witness of Jesus related to prophecy?

REFLECT: 1. What are four things for which you are extremely grateful to God? How do you usually express your gratitude to him about these things? **2.** How has your interest in worshiping God increased or decreased in the last year? Since beginning your study of Revelation? Why? **3.** What sounds of worship do you really appreciate? Why? How will you use them this week to worship God? **4.** How does the defeat and condemnation of Babylon and the triumph and glory of the Lord God affect your overall view of your problems here and now? What is one problem you hope to manage more confidently and joyfully as a result of your study of Revelation?

OPEN: When you were young, how much did you want a horse? Why? Who was your favorite fictional or real horse? Why?

DIG: 1. What regarding the horse, the rider, and the setting commands your attention? What description, titles, and names from the rest of Revelation help you to identify the rider? 2. Who is following Christ: The church *militant* (still on earth)? Or the church *triumphant* (now in heaven)? Why? 3. What weapon does the rider wield? 4. How does this supper (vv.17-18) compare with the wedding supper (19:9)? 5. Who are the combatants in this war (vv.19-21)? Who wins? What happens to the enemy leaders? To the army? 6. How does this "last battle" compare to "previous" ones (16:12-16; 17:14-16) and a "later" one (20:7-10)? Do you think these are different accounts of the same battle? Why?

REFLECT: What hopes and fears does this triumphant picture bring out in you? Why? How has Jesus been your deliverer this year?

OPEN: 1. When did you last "lose your head"? What happened? 2. Have you read any good books lately? How do you judge a book?

DIG: 1. Why is Satan bound? By whom? How? 2. Where and when will this 1000-year reign begin: On earth or in heaven? Beginning when Christ first came? Or when he comes again? Why? 3. What will life be like without Satan deceiving the nations, but with the church reigning instead? In what sense is that *already* true? And *not yet* true? 4. What is the first resurrection? The second death (see also 20:11-15)? What do these mean to Christians? To the rest of the dead? 5. Why do you think Satan will again try to deceive the nations? Why do you suppose God released him and let him out of the Abyss? 6. Describe this version of the last battle, comparing it to the other versions in Revelation and to Ezekiel 38-39. What is the final fate of the

The Rider on the White Horse

[11]I saw heaven standing open and there before me was a white horse, whose rider is called Faithful and True. With justice he judges and makes war. [12]His eyes are like blazing fire, and on his head are many crowns. He has a name written on him that no one knows but he himself. [13]He is dressed in a robe dipped in blood, and his name is the Word of God. [14]The armies of heaven were following him, riding on white horses and dressed in fine linen, white and clean. [15]Out of his mouth comes a sharp sword with which to strike down the nations. "He will rule them with an iron scepter."[v] He treads the winepress of the fury of the wrath of God Almighty. [16]On his robe and on his thigh he has this name written:

KING OF KINGS AND LORD OF LORDS.

[17]And I saw an angel standing in the sun, who cried in a loud voice to all the birds flying in midair, "Come, gather together for the great supper of God, [18]so that you may eat the flesh of kings, generals, and mighty men, of horses and their riders, and the flesh of all people, free and slave, small and great."

[19]Then I saw the beast and the kings of the earth and their armies gathered together to make war against the rider on the horse and his army. [20]But the beast was captured, and with him the false prophet who had performed the miraculous signs on his behalf. With these signs he had deluded those who had received the mark of the beast and worshiped his image. The two of them were thrown alive into the fiery lake of burning sulfur. [21]The rest of them were killed with the sword that came out of the mouth of the rider on the horse, and all the birds gorged themselves on their flesh.

The Thousand Years

20 And I saw an angel coming down out of heaven, having the key to the Abyss and holding in his hand a great chain. [2]He seized the dragon, that ancient serpent, who is the devil, or Satan, and bound him for a thousand years. [3]He threw him into the Abyss, and locked and sealed it over him, to keep him from deceiving the nations anymore until the thousand years were ended. After that, he must be set free for a short time.

[4]I saw thrones on which were seated those who had been given authority to judge. And I saw the souls of those who had been beheaded because of their testimony for Jesus and because of the word of God. They had not worshiped the beast or his image and had not received his mark on their foreheads or their hands. They came to life and reigned with Christ a thousand years. [5](The rest of the dead did not come to life until the thousand years were ended.) This is the first resurrection. [6]Blessed and holy are those who have part in the first resurrection. The second death has no power over them, but they will be priests of God and of Christ and will reign with him for a thousand years.

[v]15 Psalm 2:9

Satan's Doom

[7]When the thousand years are over, Satan will be released from his prison [8]and will go out to deceive the nations in the four corners of the earth—Gog and Magog—to gather them for battle. In number they are like the sand on the seashore. [9]They marched across the breadth of the earth and surrounded the camp of God's people, the city he loves. But fire came down from heaven and devoured them. [10]And the devil, who deceived them, was thrown into the lake of burning sulfur, where the beast and the false prophet had been thrown. They will be tormented day and night for ever and ever.

The Dead Are Judged

[11]Then I saw a great white throne and him who was seated on it. Earth and sky fled from his presence, and there was no place for them. [12]And I saw the dead, great and small, standing before the throne, and books were opened. Another book was opened, which is the book of life. The dead were judged according to what they had done as recorded in the books. [13]The sea gave up the dead that were in it, and death and Hades gave up the dead that were in them, and each person was judged according to what he had done. [14]Then death and Hades were thrown into the lake of fire. The lake of fire is the second death. [15]If anyone's name was not found written in the book of life, he was thrown into the lake of fire.

The New Jerusalem

21 Then I saw a new heaven and a new earth, for the first heaven and the first earth had passed away, and there was no longer any sea. [2]I saw the Holy City, the new Jerusalem, coming down out of heaven from God, prepared as a bride beautifully dressed for her husband. [3]And I heard a loud voice from the throne saying, "Now the dwelling of God is with men, and he will live with them. They will be his people, and God himself will be with them and be their God. [4]He will wipe every tear from their eyes. There will be no more death or mourning or crying or pain, for the old order of things has passed away."

[5]He who was seated on the throne said, "I am making everything new!" Then he said, "Write this down, for these words are trustworthy and true."

[6]He said to me: "It is done. I am the Alpha and the Omega, the Beginning and the End. To him who is thirsty I will give to drink without cost from the spring of the water of life. [7]He who overcomes will inherit all this, and I will be his God and he will be my son. [8]But the cowardly, the unbelieving, the vile, the murderers, the sexually immoral, those who practice magic arts, the idolaters and all liars—their place will be in the fiery lake of burning sulfur. This is the second death."

[9]One of the seven angels who had the seven bowls full of the seven last plagues came and said to me, "Come, I will show you the bride, the wife of the Lamb." [10]And he carried me away in the Spirit to a mountain great and high, and showed me the Holy City, Jerusalem, coming down out of heaven from God. [11]It shone with the glory of God, and its brilliance was like that of

beast and the false prophet? **7.** Who is exempted and who is exhumed at the great white throne judgment? On what basis?

REFLECT: 1. What do you find comforting in this chapter? What disturbs you? Why? **2.** What is your biggest spiritual battle today? What is the outcome so far? What is the hope in this passage for you? **3.** Imagine a book made of your life, with every thought and deed recorded, then read by all. How would you feel? If Christ edited that book by substituting his works for yours, how would you feel then? How will you then live today?

OPEN: 1. Where is one of the most beautiful places you have ever been? What impressed you about that place? **2.** What was one of the most beautiful spots in your hometown when you were growing up? **3.** How do you think your city would be different if God were the mayor?

DIG: 1. Where will the new age be lived out—on earth or in heaven? Why do you think so? **2.** Who will be the "residents" of the New Jerusalem and the "wife" of the Lamb? Whose presence is the vision caught up with? What's missing from this picture? Why? **3.** What do you think it will be like living without fear, pain, or death and with the continual and direct presence of God? Will this new world to come be recognizable? How so? **4.** What is the significance of the names ascribed to God, especially for those who "overcome" and those who do not? **5.** What is it about the city that John and his readers are meant to notice in particular? Why? What impresses you the most about the city and its central figure? Why? **6.** Compare John's vision of reality here with the related visions in Ezekiel 40-48 and Isaiah 60-66. Accordingly, what was the function of the temple in

495

the old Jerusalem? Why is there no need for a temple in the New Jerusalem? What is more "real": The spiritual things visualized here in the New Jerusalem? Or the physical objects of the Old Jerusalem? **7.** What features will be found in the New Jerusalem (22:1-6)? Where else do we see these same features (see Ge 1-3; Eze 47:1-2; Joel 3:18; Zec 14:8)? **8.** Trace the origin of the river and tree of life from its source to its fruit. What does this comparison suggest about the unity of Scripture? The completeness of God's salvation?

REFLECT: 1. Imagine yourself at the wedding feast with Christ: Are you the happy bride, or a lady-in-waiting? A direct participant, or a distant spectator? Why? **2.** How do you feel about knowing that the Holy City will be your hometown? How do you feel about the fact that this is what Jesus has prepared you for? **3.** What has caused you mourning, crying, and pain in the past year? What does it mean to you to know that this will pass away? **4.** How must the early Christians have greeted this vision of what was in store for them? How do you respond to this same hope? **5.** Create your own worship service based on Revelation 21:1–22:6. **6.** What difficulties of comprehension does this eternal city, the river of life, and the immediacy of these events pose for you? What bearing, if any, do these realities have on your present life? Why?

a very precious jewel, like a jasper, clear as crystal. [12]It had a great, high wall with twelve gates, and with twelve angels at the gates. On the gates were written the names of the twelve tribes of Israel. [13]There were three gates on the east, three on the north, three on the south and three on the west. [14]The wall of the city had twelve foundations, and on them were the names of the twelve apostles of the Lamb.

[15]The angel who talked with me had a measuring rod of gold to measure the city, its gates and its walls. [16]The city was laid out like a square, as long as it was wide. He measured the city with the rod and found it to be 12,000 stadia[w] in length, and as wide and high as it is long. [17]He measured its wall and it was 144 cubits[x] thick,[y] by man's measurement, which the angel was using. [18]The wall was made of jasper, and the city of pure gold, as pure as glass. [19]The foundations of the city walls were decorated with every kind of precious stone. The first foundation was jasper, the second sapphire, the third chalcedony, the fourth emerald, [20]the fifth sardonyx, the sixth carnelian, the seventh chrysolite, the eighth beryl, the ninth topaz, the tenth chrysoprase, the eleventh jacinth, and the twelfth amethyst.[z] [21]The twelve gates were twelve pearls, each gate made of a single pearl. The great street of the city was of pure gold, like transparent glass.

[22]I did not see a temple in the city, because the Lord God Almighty and the Lamb are its temple. [23]The city does not need the sun or the moon to shine on it, for the glory of God gives it light, and the Lamb is its lamp. [24]The nations will walk by its light, and the kings of the earth will bring their splendor into it. [25]On no day will its gates ever be shut, for there will be no night there. [26]The glory and honor of the nations will be brought into it. [27]Nothing impure will ever enter it, nor will anyone who does what is shameful or deceitful, but only those whose names are written in the Lamb's book of life.

The River of Life

22 Then the angel showed me the river of the water of life, as clear as crystal, flowing from the throne of God and of the Lamb [2]down the middle of the great street of the city. On each side of the river stood the tree of life, bearing twelve crops of fruit, yielding its fruit every month. And the leaves of the tree are for the healing of the nations. [3]No longer will there be any curse. The throne of God and of the Lamb will be in the city, and his servants will serve him. [4]They will see his face, and his name will be on their foreheads. [5]There will be no more night. They will not need the light of a lamp or the light of the sun, for the Lord God will give them light. And they will reign for ever and ever.

[6]The angel said to me, "These words are trustworthy and true. The Lord, the God of the spirits of the prophets, sent his angel to show his servants the things that must soon take place."

---

[w]16 That is, about 1,400 miles (about 2,200 kilometers)   [x]17 That is, about 200 feet (about 65 meters)   [y]17 Or *high*   [z]20 The precise identification of some of these precious stones is uncertain.

Jesus Is Coming

7"Behold, I am coming soon! Blessed is he who keeps the words of the prophecy in this book."

8I, John, am the one who heard and saw these things. And when I had heard and seen them, I fell down to worship at the feet of the angel who had been showing them to me. 9But he said to me, "Do not do it! I am a fellow servant with you and with your brothers the prophets and of all who keep the words of this book. Worship God!"

10Then he told me, "Do not seal up the words of the prophecy of this book, because the time is near. 11Let him who does wrong continue to do wrong; let him who is vile continue to be vile; let him who does right continue to do right; and let him who is holy continue to be holy."

12"Behold, I am coming soon! My reward is with me, and I will give to everyone according to what he has done. 13I am the Alpha and the Omega, the First and the Last, the Beginning and the End.

14"Blessed are those who wash their robes, that they may have the right to the tree of life and may go through the gates into the city. 15Outside are the dogs, those who practice magic arts, the sexually immoral, the murderers, the idolaters and everyone who loves and practices falsehood.

16"I, Jesus, have sent my angel to give you*a* this testimony for the churches. I am the Root and the Offspring of David, and the bright Morning Star."

17The Spirit and the bride say, "Come!" And let him who hears say, "Come!" Whoever is thirsty, let him come; and whoever wishes, let him take the free gift of the water of life.

18I warn everyone who hears the words of the prophecy of this book: If anyone adds anything to them, God will add to him the plagues described in this book. 19And if anyone takes words away from this book of prophecy, God will take away from him his share in the tree of life and in the holy city, which are described in this book.

20He who testifies to these things says, "Yes, I am coming soon."

Amen. Come, Lord Jesus.

21The grace of the Lord Jesus be with God's people. Amen.

OPEN: If you could give yourself a new name, symbolizing the legacy your family gave you, the God-given potential you have, or some hidden aspiration you have yet to realize, what name would you choose? Why?

DIG: 1. What words of Christ are repeated three times in this closing (vv.7, 12, 20)? How do these words sum up the theme of Revelation? **2.** What significance do you attribute to Jesus' claims and names in verses 12-17? Regarding these claims, how is the final state of humanity determined: By some arbitrary reward system, fixed from eternity? By what we have done in this present life? Or by our response to his *universal* ("whoever thirsts") and *undeserved* ("free gift") invitation to simply "come"? **3.** What then do you make of God's summary of human destiny? Is it ever too late for people to change their ways and come to Christ? Why or why not? **4.** In the contrast between those "inside" the city and those "outside" (vv.14-15), what is implied about the basis for our salvation and judgment? What does it mean to "wash" one's "robe"? **5.** What is the meaning of God's final curse in verses 18-19? Knowing what you now do about the seven plagues, the tree of life, and the Holy City, how seriously do you take this warning?

REFLECT: 1. How have you prepared yourself for Christ's second coming? Do you feel more (or less) ready for it, after reading the Book of Revelation than you did beforehand? **2.** How have your perceptions of Jesus, Satan, heaven, and hell changed? Why? **3.** How will these new perceptions affect your worship? Your life-style? **4.** How would you sum up the central truth of this book?

---

*a*16 The Greek is plural.

SUBJECT INDEX

This index can be considered a combination of a regular book index and a Bible concordance. It is obviously not intended to be comprehensive, but it will help the reader locate significant persons, places, events, and concepts of the New Testament.

Entries and subentries appear in **boldface type.**

Scripture reference follow in lightface type.

Beelzebub, Matthew 10:25; 12:24,27; Mark 3:22; Luke 11:14-19

Berea, Acts 17:10,13; 20:4

Bernice, Acts 25:13,23; 26:30

Bethany, Matthew 21:17; 26: 6; Mark 11:1,11,12; 14:3; Luke 19:29; 24:50; John 11: 1,18; 12:1

Bethesda, John 5:2

Bethlehem, Matthew 2:1-8, 16; Luke 2:4,15; John 7:42

Bethphage, Matthew 21:1; Mark 11:1; Luke 19:29

Bethsaida, Matthew 11:21; Mark 6:45; 8:22; Luke 9:10; 10:13; John 1:44; 12:21

Blindness, spiritual, Matthew 15:14; 23: 16-19,24,26; Luke 6:39; Romans 2:19; 2 Corinthians 4:4; 2 Peter 1: 9; 1 John 2:11

Bread, figurative, John 6: 32-58; 1 Corinthians 10:17; 11:23,24

Burial, figurative, Romans 6: 4; Colossians 2:12
of Jesus. *See* **Jesus, events in life of.**

Caesar, Matthew 22:17-21; Mark 12:14-17; Luke 2:1; 3: 1; 20:22-25; 23:2; John 19: 12,15; Acts 11:28; 17:7; 25: 8-12,21; 26:32; 27:24; 28: 19; Philippians 4:22

Caesarea, Acts 8:40; 9:30; 10:1,24; 11:11; 12:19; 21: 8,16; 23:23,33; 25:1-6,13

Caesarea Philippi, Matthew 16:13; Mark 8:27

Caiaphas, Matthew 26:3,57; Luke 3:2; John 11:49; 18: 13,14,24,28; Acts 4:6

Calling, Christian, Romans 8:28; 1 Corinthians 1:9,26; 7: 15-24; Galatians 5:13; Ephesians 1:18; 4:1,4; Philippians 3:14; Colossians 3:15; 1 Thessalonians 2:12; 2 Thessalonians 2:14; 2 Timothy 1:9; Hebrews 3:1; 1 Peter 2:9,21; 5:10; 2 Peter 1:10

Cana, John 2:1,11; 4:46; 21:2

Capernaum, Matthew 4:13; 8: 5; 9:1; 11:23; 17:24; Mark 1: 21; 2:1; 9:33; Luke 4:31; 7: 1; 10:15; John 2:12; 4:46; 6: 17,24,59

Casting lots, Matthew 27:35; Mark 15:24; Luke 23:34; John 19:24; Acts 1:26

Cenchrea, Acts 18:18; Romans 16:1

Cephas, John 1:42; 1 Corinthians 1:12; 3:22; 9: 5; 15:5; Galatians 2:9

Church, Matthew 16:18; 18: 17; 1 Corinthians 12:24-28; 14:1-40; Ephesians 5:25-32; Colossians 1:18-24

Circumcision, Luke 1:59; 2: 21; John 7:22,23; Acts 7:8; 15:1,5; 16:3; 21:21; Romans 2:25-29; 3:1,30; 4: 9-12; 1 Corinthians 7:18,19; Galatians 2:3,12; 5:2-12; 6: 12,13; Ephesians 2:11; Colossians 2:11

Claudius Lysias, Acts 21: 31-40; 22:23-30; 23:17-30

Cleopas, Luke 24:18

Confession, of Christ, Matthew 7:21-23; 10:32,33; 16:16; Mark 8:38; Luke 12: 8,9; John 11:27; 12:42,43; Acts 18:5; Romans 10:8-13; 14:11; 1 Corinthians 12:3; Philippians 2:11; 1 Timothy 6:12; 2 Timothy 1:18; 2:12; 1 John 2:4,23; 4:2,3,15
of sin, Luke 18:13,14; James 5:16; 1 John 1:8-10

Corinth, Acts 18:1,18; 19:1; 1 Corinthians 1:2; 2 Corinthians 1:1,23; 2 Timothy 4:20

Cornelius, Acts 10:1-33

Covenant, Matthew 26:28; Mark 14:24; Luke 22:20; 1 Corinthians 11:25; 2 Corinthians 3:6-18; Galatians 3:15-17; Ephesians 2:12; Hebrews 7: 22; 8:1-13; 9:15-20; 10:16; 12:18-24; 13:20

Covetousness. *See* **Greed.**

Crete, Acts 27:7,12,13; Titus 1:5

Cross, figurative, Matthew 10:38; 16:24; Mark 8:34; 10:21; Luke 9: 23; 14:27; Romans 6:6; 1 Corinthians 1:17,18; Galatians 2:20; 5:11,24; 6: 14; Philippians 3:18

Crucifixion of Christ, Acts 2: 23,36; 4:10; 1 Corinthians 1: 23; 2:2,8; 2 Corinthians 13: 4; Galatians 3:13; 5:11; Ephesians 2:16; Philippians 2:8;

Colossians 1:20; 2:14; Hebrews 12:2 *See also* **Jesus, events in life of.**

Cyprus, Acts 4:36; 11:19,20; 13:4; 15:39; 21:3,16; 27:4

Damascus, Acts 9:2-27; 22: 5-16; 26:12-20; 2 Corinthians 11:32,33; Galatians 1:17

David, Matthew 1:6; 12:3,4; 22:42-45; Mark 2:25,26; 12: 35-37; Luke 3:31; 6:3,4; 20: 41-44; Acts 13:22,34-36; Romans 1:3; 4:6; 2 Timothy 2:8; Hebrews 4:7; 11:32

Deacon, Acts 6:1-6; 1 Timothy 3:1-13

Death, physical, Romans 14: 7,8; 1 Corinthians 15: 21-26,52-57; 2 Corinthians 5:1-8; Philippians 1:20-24; 1 Thessalonians 4:13-16; 2 Timothy 1:10; 4:6-8; Hebrews 2:14,15; 9:27; James 1:10,11; 4:14,15; Revelation 14:13
spiritual, Matthew 10:28; John 5:24-26; 6:48-53; Romans 5:12-15; 6:16,23; 7:9-11; 8:2,6,13; Ephesians 2:1-5; 4:18; 5:14; Colossians 2:13; 1 Timothy 5:6; James 1:15; Revelation 20:14; 21:8

Decapolis, Matthew 4:25; Mark 5:20; 7:31

Demas, Colossians 4:14; 2 Timothy 4:10; Philemon 24

Derbe, Acts 14:6,20; 16:1; 20: 4

Devil, Matthew 4:1-11; 13:39; 25:41; Luke 4:1-13; 8:12; John 8:44; 13:2; Acts 10:38; 13:10; Ephesians 4:27; 6: 11; 1 Timothy 3:6,7; 2 Timothy 2:26; Hebrews 2: 14; James 3:15; 4:7; 1 Peter 5:8; 1 John 3:8,10; Jude 9; Revelation 2:10; 12: 9,12; 20:2,10

Discipleship, tests of, Matthew 10:32-39; Luke 14: 26-33; John 21:15-19

Divorce, Matthew 5:31,32; 19:3-9; Mark 10:2-12; Luke 16:18; 1 Corinthians 7: 10-17

Dorcas, Acts 9:36-41

Dragon, Revelation 12:1-17; 13:1-4; 16:13; 20:2

FOR ADDITIONAL COPIES

WITH QUANTITY DISCOUNTS

RETURN THIS CARD OR CALL TOLL FREE 800-525-9563

IN COLORADO CALL 303-798-1313

SERENDIPITY NEW TESTAMENT

SOFT COVER PRICES:

1-9 copies .... $7.95 ea.

10 or more .... $5.95 ea

Name _____ Phone _____

Church (if applicable) _____

UPS Street Address _____

City, State, Zip _____

BILLING (Check one)

☐ Check enclosed (Made to "Serendipity")

☐ Bill me (Plus postage and handling)

SHIPPING: (Check one)

☐ UPS (4–5 working days)

☐ Post Office (2–3 weeks)

SERENDIPITY NEW TESTAMENT

SOFT COVER PRICES:

1-9 copies .... $7.95 ea.

10 or more .... $5.95 ea

Name _____ Phone _____

Church (if applicable) _____

UPS Street Address _____

City, State, Zip _____

BILLING (Check one)

☐ Check enclosed (Made to "Serendipity")

☐ Bill me (Plus postage and handling)

SHIPPING: (Check one)

☐ UPS (4–5 working days)

☐ Post Office (2–3 weeks)

SERENDIPITY
BOX 1012
LITTLETON COLORADO
80160

SERENDIPITY
BOX 1012
LITTLETON COLORADO
80160